Praise for *Salesforce AI*

Joyce does it again! *Salesforce AI* is the foundation practitioners build from—timeless principles that stay useful even as the platform keeps shipping new capabilities. This is required reading for anyone implementing Salesforce AI, Agentforce, MCP, RAG, or Data Cloud.

—*Andrew Gambini, CDP data and AI architect and marketing science technology leader in a Big 4 consulting company*

Joyce Kay Avila goes beyond explaining Salesforce AI. She connects Data Cloud, reasoning, agents, orchestration, and governance into a clear foundation for building intelligent systems that are not only capable, but human centered. An essential guide to the agentic enterprise.

—*Scott Stafford, enterprise AI strategist and human-centered AI advocate; CEO at Empowering Our Minds*

Detailed, thorough, and easy to follow, *Salesforce AI* brilliantly demystifies Salesforce's AI technical capabilities, and empowers readers to build and govern AI on the Salesforce platform.

—*Lillie Beiting, Salesforce architect, private consultant*

Whether you're a leader, consultant, or new admin in the Salesforce Ecosystem, this book will elevate your Salesforce AI expertise and practical skills.

—*Michael Hopkins, PMP, P.Geo., senior project manager at NeuraFlash*

Everyone is talking about Agentforce but nowhere have the concepts been so fully brought to life as in Joyce's book. Its depth, relevance, and technical guidance make it an easy recommendation for anyone looking to level up quickly.

—Mary Crozier, CEO at Client Cloudcare

Whether you're a beginner just starting out on your Salesforce journey or a seasoned expert, there is something in here for you. This is an incredible resource to keep at your desk to reference as new projects arise. This is a text you'll keep coming back to.

—Stephanie Parretti, sales operations analyst at Netscout

Salesforce AI

Building, Customizing, and Embedding AI Solutions

Joyce Kay Avila

O'REILLY®

Salesforce AI
by Joyce Kay Avila

Published by O'Reilly Media, Inc., 141 Stony Circle, Suite 195, Santa Rosa, CA 95401.

O'Reilly books may be purchased for educational, business, or sales promotional use. Online editions are also available for most titles (*http://oreilly.com*). For more information, contact our corporate/institutional sales department: 800-998-9938 or *corporate@oreilly.com*.

Acquisitions Editor: Andy Kwan
Development Editor: Michele Cronin
Production Editor: Clare Laylock
Copyeditor: Kim Cofer
Proofreader: Piper Content Partners
Indexer: BIM Creatives, LLC
Cover Designer: Susan Brown
Cover Illustrator: Monica Kamsvaag
Interior Designer: David Futato
Interior Illustrator: Kate Dullea

October 2026: First Edition

Revision History for the First Edition
2026-10-08: First Release

See *http://oreilly.com/catalog/errata.csp?isbn=9798341623101* for release details.

979-8-341-62310-1

[LSI]

Table of Contents

Preface

The term "agentic enterprise" entered our vocabulary in early January 2025, right around the time I began working on this book. At its core, an agentic enterprise is one where humans and AI agents work together side-by-side inside governed business systems. The term matters because it describes a real shift in how work gets done. AI agents handle routine complexity at scale, running continuously, so humans are free to focus on exceptions, judgment calls, and relationships. Building the tools for this shift meant Salesforce had to develop new agentic AI, governance, semantic layer, and data integration capabilities all while teams kept building on the core platform.

Six months later, in June 2025, Salesforce released the third iteration of Agentforce, positioning it as everything a modern enterprise needs to build its own agents. Agentforce's newest capabilities include an improved Atlas reasoning engine along with Agent Script and Agent Graph to provide more deterministic control over individual agents and multi-agent orchestration. Agentforce is a product Salesforce is proud of, but its real value isn't as an exceptional tool working in isolation. Rather, it's a key piece of a cohesive agentic stack, 10 years in the making. Available alongside Agentforce is Data 360, built by Salesforce from the ground up. In addition, Salesforce acquisitions in the last decade include Slack, MuleSoft, Own Company, Tableau, and many more.

A suite of products built to work together gives Salesforce a turnkey path to fast time-to-value. Predictive and generative AI solutions aren't bolted on. Instead, they're built directly into the Salesforce core platform and industry cloud offerings, so end users experience their capabilities right in the natural flow of their work. One of the most important pieces of the agentic stack is Slack, often referred to as the front door to the agentic enterprise. It earns that name because it's the primary place where humans collaborate with and direct AI agents, rather than engaging them separately in Tableau dashboards, CRM workspaces, or other systems of engagement.

One of the most exciting developments is the arrival of shared team agents, like Claude Tag, which don't require each user to connect their own tools individually. Instead, a shared team agent draws from one common toolset as needed, governed at an enterprise level. Claude Tag launched in August 2026, and that same month Salesforce announced Slack Code channels. These special channels are a temporary space created by Slack Code and then archived, but remain accessible, once the work is complete. Slack Code launched alongside Anthropic, Cognition, GitHub, OpenAI, and Vercel. The pace of change across the Salesforce ecosystem, and technology in general, shows no signs of slowing.

My goal in writing this book was to bring the full picture of building an agentic enterprise into one place and to demystify Salesforce AI's complexity in ways that Trailblazers understand. Telling the complete story meant going beyond Agentforce alone. It meant explaining what's needed to provide the data foundation, context, and governance that makes an intelligent agentic enterprise possible.

Regardless of where your organization stands in its AI journey, I wrote this book to be concise, comprehensive, and useful in charting your own path forward. Understanding how Salesforce AI helps organizations build their own agentic enterprise will broaden how you think about succeeding in the age of AI and other emerging cloud technologies. A solid grasp of how each Salesforce product works, and why it matters in the bigger picture, will set you up for long-term success even as the products themselves evolve.

Who Is This Book For?

This book is essential reading for technology and data professionals who are builders of the agentic enterprise, especially those incorporating Salesforce CRM, Agentforce, Slack, Tableau Next, or MuleSoft into their enterprise's tech stack. Whether you're an experienced Salesforce professional or someone just beginning their Salesforce journey, there is plenty of information to provide you with an understanding of the Salesforce suite of products used to build the agentic enterprise.

While it is not necessary to have in-depth knowledge about Salesforce products or artificial intelligence, you should at least be familiar with CRM and AI concepts in general. Those who will get the most from this book will typically find themselves in one of the following roles:

- Salesforce architects
- Tableau developers
- Agentforce developers
- Salesforce developers
- Slack administrators
- Salesforce administrators
- MuleSoft architects
- Salesforce consultants

In addition to Salesforce-specific roles, some more general roles will also find this book to be a valuable resource. In addition to builders, this book is a good resource for specialists, strategists, and decision-makers:

- Enterprise AI / ML solution architects
- Technical architects
- Data and analytics engineers
- Citizen developers
- Technology product managers and product owners
- Governance team
- Business stakeholders and sponsors
- CTOs and VPs of technology

There is also a lot of value in this book for data stakeholders, such as IT team leads, technical managers, directors of technical teams, or those who want to keep current with modern AI technologies and trends.

Goals of the Book

The goal of this book is to provide a structured reference that maps the full Salesforce product suite used to build an intelligent agentic enterprise. This book is written with detailed explanations, instructions, and best practices to help build a solid foundational knowledge of AI vocabulary and processes. In addition, the book provides domain-specific vocabulary and detailed explanations of Salesforce AI products and tools. Screenshots of user interfaces are provided along the way for those with little or no access to certain products or tools.

By the end of the book, you will understand:

- How to unlock the value of enterprise data and knowledge to power the agentic enterprise
- The steps for building an AI model to predict outcomes and how to operationalize the predictive results within the Salesforce environment
- How to build semantic models and bring actionable insights into the flow of work
- The steps for building an orchestrated conversational AI chatbot for customer self-service
- The difference between various agentic reasoning engine strategies and which reasoning engine strategy Salesforce selected for its reasoning engine

- How Agentforce agents work under the hood by utilizing Agent Script, Agent Graph, and the Atlas reasoning engine
- How to build standard Agentforce agents and create custom AI agents using a no-code approach
- The various pro-code developer tools available for building and managing Agentforce agents
- How to leverage Slack and use it as the front door of the agentic enterprise
- The various ways to manage multi-agent orchestration agents including Agentforce orchestrator agents and MuleSoft Agent Fabric agent networks
- The importance of leveraging a cohesive Salesforce agentic stack to accelerate strategies for success in an Agentic Era

And you will be able to:

- Use a proper Salesforce AI vocabulary to engage in meaningful conversations with all stakeholders
- Develop a Salesforce AI strategy that can accelerate the time-to-value by leveraging turnkey solutions
- Select the most relevant tools to implement a variety of Salesforce AI capabilities
- Customize existing out-of-the-box Salesforce AI functionality and embed trusted AI solutions
- Create a personalized plan to pass new Salesforce certifications like the Tableau Next and the Marketing Cloud Next exams announced in August 2026
- Utilize Salesforce platform Builder tools including AI Model Builder, Semantic Model Builder, Tableau Next, Einstein Bot Builder, Prompt Builder, and Agentforce Builder

Navigating the Book

This book describes in detail a robust suite of interoperable products assembled by Salesforce to support the intelligent agentic enterprise. As we'll learn in Chapter 1, the cohesive agentic stack assembled by Salesforce is a strategic blend of acquisitions and products built from the ground up. As such, there are many new AI and Salesforce domain-specific terms you'll be introduced to as you work your way through the chapters. You can feel confident you're expanding your vocabulary and knowledge with each new topic and, when in doubt, there are links to additional resources provided for you at the end of the book.

Data strategy and governance aren't new concepts but they're even more critical for an intelligent agentic enterprise. We discuss those concepts in detail in Chapters 2 and 12. The importance of these two concepts to an AI strategy cannot be overstated. Data strategy includes the topic of knowledge bases, and governance includes the concept of trust. Although data strategy and governance are the focus within two complete chapters, the concepts of data strategy and governance are discussed throughout various chapters.

In Chapter 2, we discuss data, knowledge, context, and intelligence as foundational elements for the intelligent agentic enterprise. There can be no Salesforce AI strategy without Salesforce's Data 360 product and, thus, a great deal of information about Data 360, sometimes referred to as Salesforce's context engine, is included in Chapter 2 and also woven throughout the other chapters. Chapter 2 explores the concept of context and its importance to AI agents and sets the stage for Chapters 3 and 4.

Chapters 3 and 4 detail how users can leverage Salesforce Builder tools like AI Model Builder, Semantic Model Builder, and Tableau Next to create context for both humans and agents. Context is provided in the form of predictions and recommendations from AI Model Builder and semantic models from Semantic Model Builder. In addition, context is provided to humans in the form of visualizations and dashboards created using Tableau Next.

Next, we'll explore orchestrated conversational AI chatbots for customer self-service in Chapter 5. You'll learn how chatbots, built using Einstein Bot Builder, are well suited for low-risk deflection situations. Chatbots built with Einstein Bot Builder have options to leverage agentic features to provide an orchestrated conversation for customers. You'll discover how chatbots, no longer required to traverse rigid dialog trees, leverage Agentforce's agentic features.

Agentforce is the subject of the next two chapters. Chapter 6 begins by providing foundational knowledge about agentic reasoning engines before exploring how Agentforce agents work under the hood using Agent Script, Agent Graph, and the Atlas reasoning engine. You'll learn how to build standard Agentforce agents and create new agents using a no-code approach. Then, in Chapter 7, you'll gain an understanding of the pro-code developer tools for building and managing Agentforce agents because sometimes a more complex business use case exists where a solution can't be implemented using a no-code approach.

By this point in the book, you'll have a good understanding of Salesforce features and tools needed to build an intelligent agentic enterprise and you'll be ready to focus on important domains within the enterprise like Sales, Service, and Marketing, which are the topics covered in Chapters 8, 9, and 10. Next, your learning journey will take you beyond traditional Salesforce CRM use cases. In Chapter 11, you'll dive into learning about Slack workspaces for conversational AI and collaboration. Within that chapter, you'll learn about Slack AI native features. You'll also learn about Slackbot, another native capability, as well as Agentforce agents within Slack workspaces.

There is more information about Slackbot in Chapter 12, where you'll learn about Slackbot skills and memory and how Slack operates as a system of coordination. In addition, you'll learn how Agentforce serves as a system of orchestration for multiple agents. Slack and Agentforce are two important topics we'll explore as part of the main discussions about multi-agent orchestration and unified governance.

In addition to those two important topics, Chapter 12 is largely devoted to discussing MuleSoft Agent Fabric and MuleSoft Anypoint Platform, important topics for multi-agent orchestration and unified governance. The topics of governance, observability, and trust as related to the Salesforce platform and Agentforce agents are discussed throughout the book. Unified governance and multi-agent orchestration at the enterprise level are also covered. We waited to discuss these critical topics until the end so that you'd have a better understanding of agents themselves and, thus, what it takes to orchestrate and control agents at an enterprise level.

After you've finished navigating the last chapter, you'll find the Appendix with additional reading to help you continue your learning journey for topics you'd like to explore in more detail.

Coding Examples

Salesforce is a pioneer in the data democratization trend and is well-known for empowering business people with their low-code/no-code platform; such platforms reduce the need for manual coding. This book describes in detail several low-code/no-code Salesforce Builder tools. However, this book also provides details about Salesforce pro-code developer tools and programming languages.

Additionally, the book describes different Salesforce domain-specific programming languages like Apex, developed in 2006, and Salesforce Object Query Language (SOQL), released in 2008. The newest Salesforce domain-specific programming language is Agent Script, released in 2025, and is covered in detail. Agent Script is used to express both deterministic logic instructions and prompt instructions in the same agent through the use of subagent blocks, of which there are many types. However, while this book does not contain actual coding examples, when appropriate, screenshots of sample code, CLI commands, or IDE tools are shown to better explain certain products or tools. For example, YAML files and JSON files are included in screenshots to demonstrate the coding structure of the agent network files within MuleSoft Agent Fabric.

Conventions Used in This Book

The following typographical conventions are used in this book:

Italic
: Indicates new terms, URLs, email addresses, filenames, and file extensions

`Constant width`
: Used for program listings, as well as within paragraphs to refer to program elements such as variable or function names, databases, data types, environment variables, statements, and keywords

> This element signifies a tip or suggestion.

> This element signifies a general note.

> This element indicates a warning or caution.

O'Reilly Online Learning

For more than 40 years, O'Reilly Media has provided technology and business training, knowledge, and insight to help companies succeed.

Our unique network of experts and innovators share their knowledge and expertise through books, articles, and our online learning platform. O'Reilly's online learning platform gives you on-demand access to live training courses, in-depth learning paths, interactive coding environments, and a vast collection of text and video from O'Reilly and 200+ other publishers. For more information, visit *https://oreilly.com*.

How to Contact Us

Please address comments and questions concerning this book to the publisher:

O'Reilly Media, Inc.
141 Stony Circle, Suite 195
Santa Rosa, CA 95401
800-889-8969 (in the United States or Canada)
707-827-7019 (international or local)
707-829-0104 (fax)
support@oreilly.com
https://oreilly.com/about/contact.html

We have a web page for this book, where we list errata and any additional information. You can access this page at *https://oreil.ly/salesforce-ai*.

For news and information about our books and courses, visit *https://oreilly.com*.

Find us on LinkedIn: *https://linkedin.com/company/oreilly*.

Watch us on YouTube: *https://youtube.com/oreillymedia*.

Acknowledgments

I've been fortunate to receive extraordinary support from the talented people at O'Reilly Media, the best technical-book publisher in the world. *Salesforce AI* is my third technical book, and the team behind it deserves far more praise and recognition than I could ever adequately express.

Since March 2021, I've met biweekly with Michele Cronin, who served as the development editor for my three O'Reilly books, including this one. Clare Laylock and the entire O'Reilly production team supported me throughout. I've relied on Michele and Clare's encouragement, expertise, and guidance to help make each book progressively better. I'm immensely proud of the work we've done together.

I'm deeply grateful to O'Reilly Media and everyone who contributed to this book: Andy Kwan (acquisitions editor), Michele Cronin (development editor), Clare Laylock (production editor), Kim Cofer (copyeditor), Susan Brown (cover designer), Monica Kamsvaag (cover illustrator), David Futato (interior designer), Kate Dullea (interior illustrator), Tonya Trybula from Piper Content Partners (proofreader), and Kevin Broccoli from BIM Creatives, LLC and his team Jose Contreras and Christopher Degnan (indexers).

My books include many diagrams and screenshots, and Salesforce has its own unique vocabulary that often requires additional explanation. These make the book more useful and complete, but including them requires an extra level of care and effort from O'Reilly and everyone there involved. Thank you to the entire O'Reilly team for consistently going above and beyond.

A technical book needs to be accurate and complete while remaining within its page limit, and achieving that balance requires thoughtful input and feedback from knowledgeable experts. Thank you to the many Salesforce employees who supported me throughout my journey writing this book including Andrea (Hertzog) Gossett, Bobby Brill, Brad Brechbuhl, Christopher Long, Jackie Moldawer, Josh Vermeulen, Kristen Piña Flores, Martin Kihn, Matthew Miller, Max Comparetto, Mia Moore, Mike Reynolds, Mohamed Bentriou, Nate Nichols, Rahul Auradkar, Richie Ellis, Rob Cowell, and Ryan Batty. I also want to thank the Salesforce community members who served as technical reviewers and supporters, including Alan Luo, Andrew Gambini, Anh Phuong Ta, Chris McClellan, Joy Shutters-Helbing, Lillie Beiting, Mary Crozier, Michael Hopkins, Nicole Pomponio, Sal Gamez, Sarah Thanawalla, Scott Stafford, Stephanie Parretti, and Timo Kovala.

A special thank you goes to Michael Hopkins, who was an exceptional technical reviewer for both of my O'Reilly Salesforce books, and to Martin Kihn, also known as "Agent Marty," who continues to offer encouragement. I'm especially grateful to Bobby Brill and Mike Reynolds who each devoted a significant amount of time reviewing and providing feedback on the AI Model Builder and Slack chapters. Oftentimes, I felt as though my technical questions for them would never end, but Bobby and Mike always took time to respond.

My mother repeatedly asked me when the book would be finished because AI fascinates her and she's been eager to get her hands on the final product. Throughout, I've enjoyed watching her become even more excited about technology as she began using her Apple watch and Alexa-enabled devices for practical tasks and everyday enjoyment. It continues to remind me how much technology can be a positive force in our lives.

One of the sweetest events in my life happened early in the first few months of writing this book. I fell in love with an abandoned Anatolian Shepherd (Cowboy), who we rescued to be our own. He's the first large dog we've owned, and the experience brought plenty of unanticipated challenges, but he's also brought much joy to our lives. He's been my companion through the many late nights I've spent writing to meet deadlines.

As I write this, I realize a pattern emerged. Three books and three animals. I've rescued a new animal with every book I've written. I mentioned Zelda, our beaglier, in my first book. Just as I finished the second book, we rescued Boots, a kitten. Now, with this third book, Cowboy, our Anatolian Shepherd, has joined the family. All 100 pounds of him. Thankfully, all three get along.

A few months into writing, I paused for the first time in quite a while and spent a month in the beautiful country of Georgia with my daughter, Alanna, while she served there as a Peace Corps volunteer. Now, as I'm finishing the book, Alanna has returned to Texas and started a new job nearby as a platform engineer.

The one constant throughout all of my O'Reilly book journeys is the unwavering support and patience from my husband, Robert, and my daughter, Alanna. Thank you for being the best family ever.

CHAPTER 1

Salesforce AI Solutions for Building the Intelligent Agentic Enterprise

Salesforce launched in 1999 by making business software accessible over the internet instead of installed on company servers, a novel idea at the time. Salesforce was also one of the first enterprise vendors to give system access through APIs, which made the Salesforce platform open and extensible. This extensibility allowed developers to connect Salesforce to other systems and also to build custom applications around CRM data, making the Salesforce platform a scalable enterprise solution. Salesforce is also known for creating one of the first enterprise app marketplaces, AppExchange, released in 2005, which allowed third parties to publish add-ons and industry apps that work with Salesforce core functionality.

Since its inception in 1999, Salesforce has also innovated by purchasing capabilities to expand the platform faster than building everything in-house. Salesforce made notable acquisitions of Informatica, Metamind, MuleSoft, Own Company, Slack Technologies, and Tableau during the decade between 2015 and 2025. During that time, Salesforce also built Data 360 from the ground up and created powerful Agentforce capabilities including the Atlas reasoning engine and Agent Script to provide more deterministic control for individual agents and multi-agent orchestration.

Data 360, Agentforce, and the addition of several notable acquisitions to the Salesforce portfolio all served to fill in the missing layers of an agentic enterprise stack. Data integration and unification, context, search capabilities, analytics and visualization, collaboration tools, and native AI agents built with no code were just some capabilities resulting from those acquisitions and the new products built in-house in that decade.

The year 2026 brought more acquisitions by Salesforce including Fin, Simulate, Contentful, m3ter, and Momentum. Salesforce purchased these startups to refine and deepen the existing stack of Salesforce-owned products used to build, customize, and embed AI solutions into an intelligent agentic enterprise.

Salesforce AI is not a single product or a suite of products. Rather, it's an umbrella term for the artificial intelligence (AI) capabilities built into the Salesforce core platform and Salesforce-owned products like Slack and MuleSoft. The concept of Salesforce AI encompasses predictive AI, generative AI (GenAI), agentic AI, data, and trust.

Examples of predictive AI include forecasting outcomes and scoring leads. GenAI capabilities include drafting emails and summaries. Agentic AI consists of autonomous and semi-autonomous agents that complete work-related actions. The data layer includes unified data and its associated context. The trust layer relates to keeping the data private and enhancing AI security.

Salesforce AI is crucial for the intelligent agentic enterprise, allowing agents to reason across connected systems and take governed action. This matters because work today is done by both humans and agents, not just humans. Traditional enterprise systems were designed for humans to click, view, decide, and take action by manually moving work through processes. Modern enterprise systems are built for agents to take action autonomously or semi-autonomously, transferring work back to employees when appropriate. Thus, today's tech stack in an intelligent agentic enterprise must serve two users: humans and agents.

Building and maintaining an intelligent agentic enterprise requires many layers. Multiple layers are needed because intelligent agentic enterprises aren't just doing the same work faster. They're actually changing how work gets done.

For example, multiple agents, like those built with Agentforce Builder, operate in an ecosystem together and need to be orchestrated. Multiple ecosystems like Salesforce, SAP, Oracle, and Workday require coordination of an enterprise's integration and agentic assets, as well as coordination of all ecosystem agents. An enterprise agent network also needs coordination with human workers.

Intelligent agentic enterprises need multiple layers to provide systems where data, business processes, agent execution, and control are separate but connected. I've identified 12 distinct layers of an intelligent agentic enterprise (Table 1-1).

Table 1-1. Distinct layers of an intelligent agentic enterprise

Layer	Purpose
System of record	Stores what is true
System of reference	Trusted cross-system view
System of context	Explains what it means

Layer	Purpose
System of insight	Tells you what it implies
System of work	Executes the business processes
System of engagement	How humans interact with it
System of collaboration	How humans collectively work together
System of agency	How individual agents act
System of orchestration	How agents collectively work together
System of integration	Connects everything
System of control	Keeps interactions safe and compliant
System of coordination	Makes different ecosystem actors behave like one system

An agentic enterprise can be assembled from multiple building blocks, or a layered platform approach, like Salesforce, can be used to build an intelligent agentic enterprise. A layered platform is one that offers a variety of solutions in a governed stack rather than a set of loosely connected tools. A layered platform compounds the value of each individual solution because solutions reinforce each other for governance, integration, and reusability purposes. The same underlying data model, application programming interfaces (APIs), and metadata can support the entire enterprise without rebuilding anything from scratch or cobbling together disparate solutions.

Salesforce offers a variety of solutions with capabilities for addressing all layers. In fact, many Salesforce solutions address the requirements of more than one layer (Table 1-2). However, Salesforce's advantage is not feature count. It is the fact that Salesforce offers a composable, governed operating fabric for building and maintaining an intelligent agentic enterprise.

Table 1-2. Salesforce solutions supporting the layers needed for an intelligent agentic enterprise

Chapter(s)	Salesforce solutions	Layer
2	Data 360	System of reference System of context
3	AI Models (for predictions)	System of context System of insight
4	Tableau Semantics	System of context System of insight
4	Tableau Next	System of insight System of engagement
5	Einstein Bots	System of engagement
6, 7	Agentforce	System of agency System of orchestration

Chapter(s)	Salesforce solutions	Layer
8, 9, 10	Customer 360	System of record System of work System of engagement
11, 12	Slack	System of engagement System of collaboration System of coordination
12	MuleSoft	System of integration System of orchestration System of coordination System of control
	Built into the platform	Einstein Trust Layer

A *system of record*, also referred to as the system of truth, is where records are updated and maintained. It's frequently the location where records are initially created by a user or a system. It's possible for record updates to occur outside of the system of record prior to ultimately updating the system of truth. The system of record is considered the authoritative source within an enterprise for a particular data entity. For example, the underlying customer relationship management (CRM) data store is the system of record for customer relationship data.

A *system of reference* aggregates and harmonizes data from multiple systems of record to provide a complete view of the data. Importantly, a system of reference isn't used to create original data. Examples of systems of reference include some, but not all, master data management platforms (MDMs) like Informatica and customer data platforms (CDPs) like Salesforce Data 360 (D360). D360 is unique, though, because it's also where context is created for enterprise data and content knowledge bases.

A *system of context* offers a better understanding of the data by layering semantic meaning and relationships on top of the system of record or system of reference data. A system of context is even more critical for AI-driven solutions designed to deliver personalization for customers and contextual intelligence for enterprise analytics. The D360 platform serves as a system of context as well as a system of reference because it's where Salesforce users leverage structured and unstructured data to create semantic models, vector embeddings and indexes, and data graphs.

A *system of insight* is the analysis built on top of data and its context. In this system, analysis is undertaken to find patterns, predict outcomes, and recommend next-best actions. Tableau Semantics, Tableau Next, and AI Models used for predictions are all built on top of D360 and provide valuable insights for an intelligent agentic enterprise. AI predictive model outputs provide context, via predictions, as well as insights from the model's top predictors and prescriptions. Similarly, semantic models provide context while the metrics built on top of the semantic model offer insights.

The *system of agency* is a layer where autonomous and semi-autonomous agents reason, choose actions, and invoke tools. Agentforce is Salesforce's system of agency.

A *system of orchestration* is how agents collectively work together. Agentforce achieves a system of orchestration using an Agentforce orchestrator agent whereas MuleSoft uses an agent broker. Both approaches centrally route and govern agent actions across systems.

The *system of work* is an operational layer where work gets done. It's where tasks and workflows occur and where actions, including semi-autonomous and autonomous actions, are taken. For example, it's where data can be input, edited, or queried by both humans and agents. Often, a system of work exists on top of a system of record, as is the case for Customer 360, Salesforce's CRM software. Within Customer 360, humans access different applications depending on whether they need to perform work related to sales, service, or marketing functions. Workflows and customer processes supporting Customer 360 are included in the system of work.

A *system of engagement* is an interface layer where humans interact with business processes through engagement surfaces such as chat and messaging apps, chatbots, portals, mobile, or web. Tableau Next, Einstein Bots, Customer 360 apps, and Slack are conversational interfaces where humans interact with business processes and agents. In addition to being a system of engagement, Slack is also a system of collaboration.

A *system of collaboration* offers a place for human interactions where people, projects, shared context, and culture are brought together in one environment. A system of collaboration emphasizes alignment on work across teams rather than simply a one-way broadcasting of information.

A *system of coordination* is required for structured alignment across many actors. It's the layer that supports multiple agents, services, workflows, and humans synchronizing tasks, handing off context, managing dependencies, and resolving exceptions. Slackbot, a personal agent for work available in Slack, was recently given the ability to support a system of coordination from the frontend. With the release of the Slackbot MCP client in June 2026, Slackbot was given the ability to serve as an orchestration interface. MuleSoft coordinates on the backend. MuleSoft is also the Salesforce solution for the system of integration and the system of control.

The *system of integration* connects data sources, applications, services, and APIs to enable information and work to flow across systems. MuleSoft connects Salesforce solutions to external systems and helps expose governed assets across the enterprise.

The *system of control* is the layer that enforces policy, unified governance and compliance, operational guardrails, and auditability across the entire enterprise. MuleSoft is the Salesforce AI solution that ensures an enterprise can trust automations and agentic actions.

The Einstein Trust Layer is a secure AI architecture designed to safeguard data privacy and enhance AI accuracy. It's designed to safeguard data privacy and enhance AI accuracy. In addition, the Einstein Trust Layer promotes responsible use of AI. The Einstein Trust Layer capabilities apply to GenAI and Agentforce features. You can find more information about the Einstein Trust Layer in the Salesforce documentation (*https://oreil.ly/9O_BO*).

The Einstein Trust Layer is built into the Salesforce platform. Tableau Semantics, Tableau Next, and AI Models are accessible in D360. Einstein Bots leverage Agentforce technology. Therefore, the operating fabric of the intelligent agent enterprise is found in five main Salesforce solutions: C360 + D360 + Agentforce + MuleSoft + Slack.

How is the operating fabric applied in practice? Let's consider an intelligent agentic enterprise supported by Salesforce solutions available using C360, D360, Agentforce, MuleSoft, and Slack (Figure 1-1).

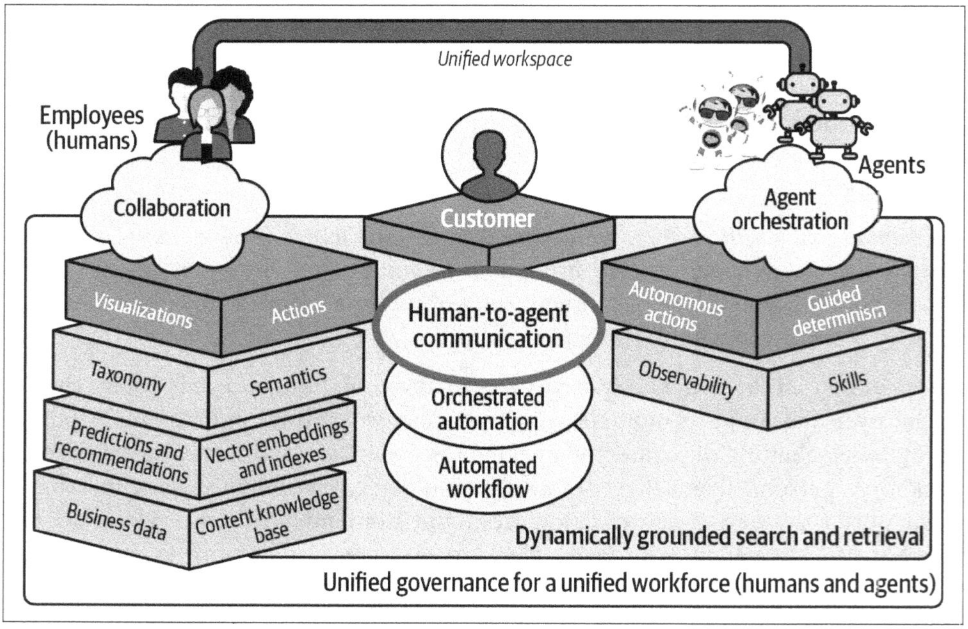

Figure 1-1. Intelligent agentic enterprise supported by Salesforce AI solutions

An intelligent agentic enterprise includes human employees and agents, both completing work-related actions often with the assistance of automated workflows. All actions, including automated actions as well as actions taken by humans and agents, need to be coordinated. Humans collaborate with each other, agents require orchestration, and the communication between humans and agents can be accomplished via text, voice, multimodal, or biometric. Humans and agents both need a way to locate relevant information within a knowledge base. Context—in the form of semantics, vector embeddings and indexes, and taxonomy—is important for both humans and agents. Humans prefer visualizations, which agents don't need.

An intelligent agentic enterprise supported by Salesforce solutions is purpose-built. Therefore, it's important to consider the implications of removing a Salesforce solution from the equation. If you elect not to include Einstein Bots in your enterprise, it may not be an issue because there are other Salesforce solutions that offer an alternative system of engagement layer. However, some Salesforce solutions address a specific layer that no other solution provides.

One important note is that Data 360 (D360), Tableau Semantics, Tableau Next, AI Models, Agentforce, Einstein Bots, and Customer 360 are all associated with the Salesforce core platform. Slack and MuleSoft work better in conjunction with Salesforce core solutions but they're not required. Thus, Slack and MuleSoft can be valuable solutions for enterprises who don't yet use Salesforce core solutions.

Now that we understand what it takes to build an intelligent agentic enterprise, let's look at a roadmap (Figure 1-2) for how we're going to become knowledgeable about all of these Salesforce solutions.

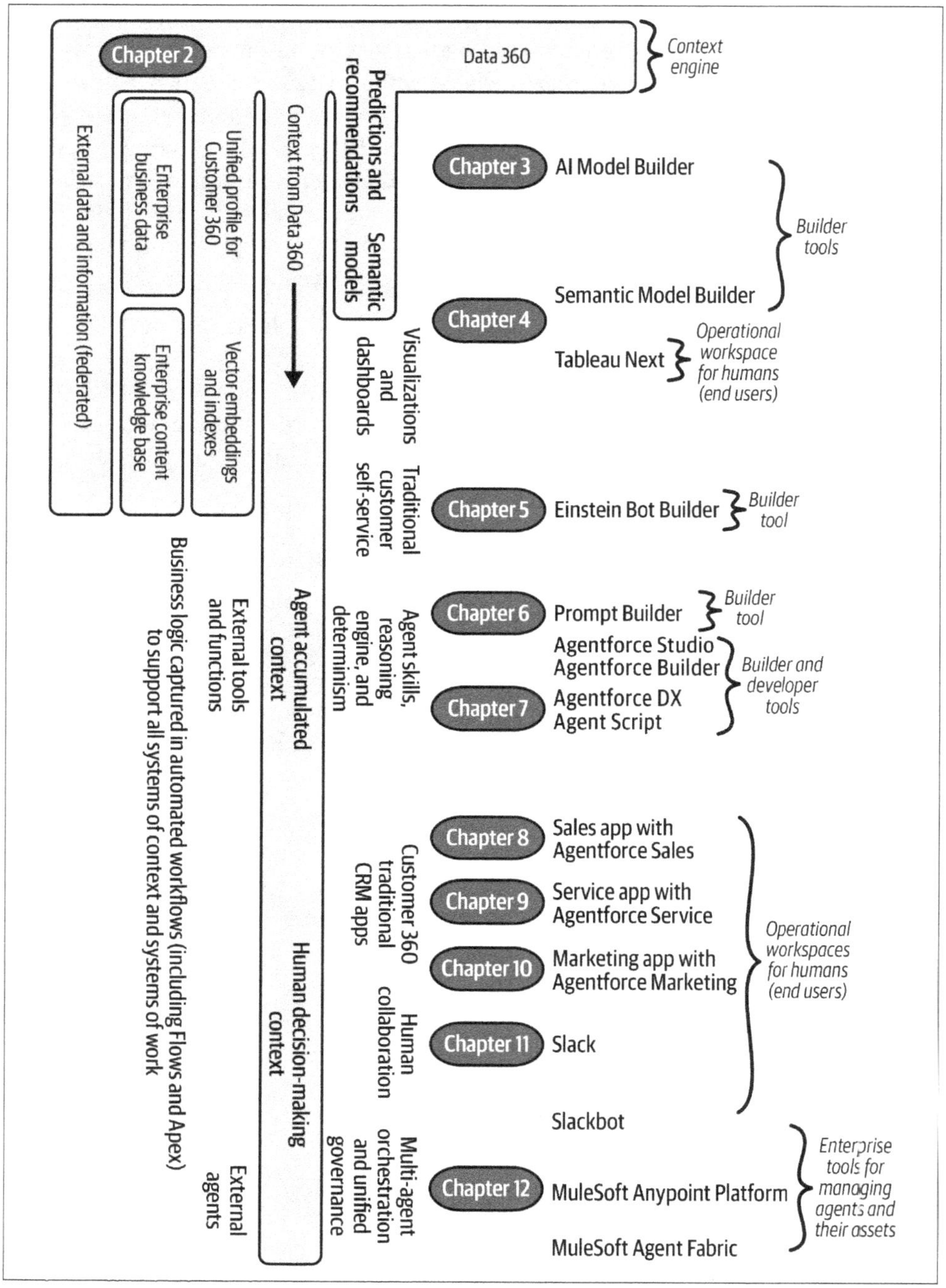

Figure 1-2. Salesforce AI solutions for building the intelligent agentic enterprise

We'll begin with D360 and the foundational elements for the intelligent agentic enterprise. We'll learn about data, knowledge bases, and the D360 context engine. We'll explore AI Model Builder, Semantic Model Builder, and Tableau Next products and features followed by an exploration of Einstein Bot Builder.

We'll learn how to create and manage Agentforce agents built on D360 data and context, using both no-code and pro-code approaches. We'll discuss C360 apps where the business logic is captured and automated with workflows using Salesforce Flows and Apex code. We'll learn about Slack, a unified workspace where humans collaborate and agents and humans work together. We'll then explore MuleSoft, including the MuleSoft Anypoint Platform and MuleSoft Agent Fabric.

During our learning journey together throughout the next 11 chapters, we'll discover a great deal about predictive AI, GenAI, and agentic AI. We'll also learn how Salesforce leverages those technologies to offer a full suite of solutions for building and maintaining an intelligent agentic enterprise.

CHAPTER 2

Foundational Elements for the Intelligent Agentic Enterprise

As we learned in Chapter 1, a robust suite of interoperable products assembled by Salesforce supports the intelligent agentic enterprise (Figure 2-1) and includes the security offerings and scalability expected from an enterprise-ready solution. AI agents (agents) doing the work are a central part of the solution, but each part of the agentic system is integral to the success of the agentic enterprise and shouldn't be overlooked. We'll focus on agents in later chapters but before we get there, let's build a foundational knowledge of the underpinning elements needed to support agents and humans in the intelligent agentic enterprise. Data 360 (D360) is the gateway to building the foundation for the agents needed in an intelligent agentic enterprise. It's where all customer data is harmonized using information accessible from external sources as well as from data within Salesforce core and near-core platforms.

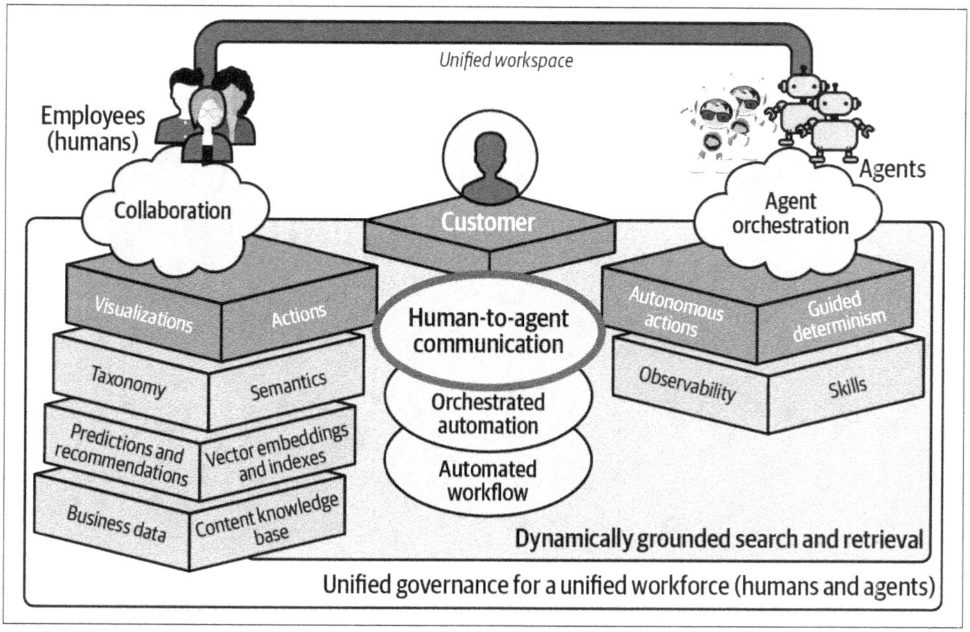

Figure 2-1. Intelligent agentic enterprise supported by Salesforce AI solutions

The D360 application (app) is also where context preparation and insight generation is undertaken (Figure 2-2) using Salesforce Builder tools like AI Model Builder and Semantic Model Builder. Context preparation is necessary so that relevant information can be found more quickly from among the vast amounts of available information. Vector embeddings and indexes are one example of context preparation. Contextualizing the data for use also means that it's easier to generate insights and understand the rationale. For example, building semantic models and creating metrics is needed by agents for engaging in conversational analytics with humans and also supports creating more insightful visualizations.

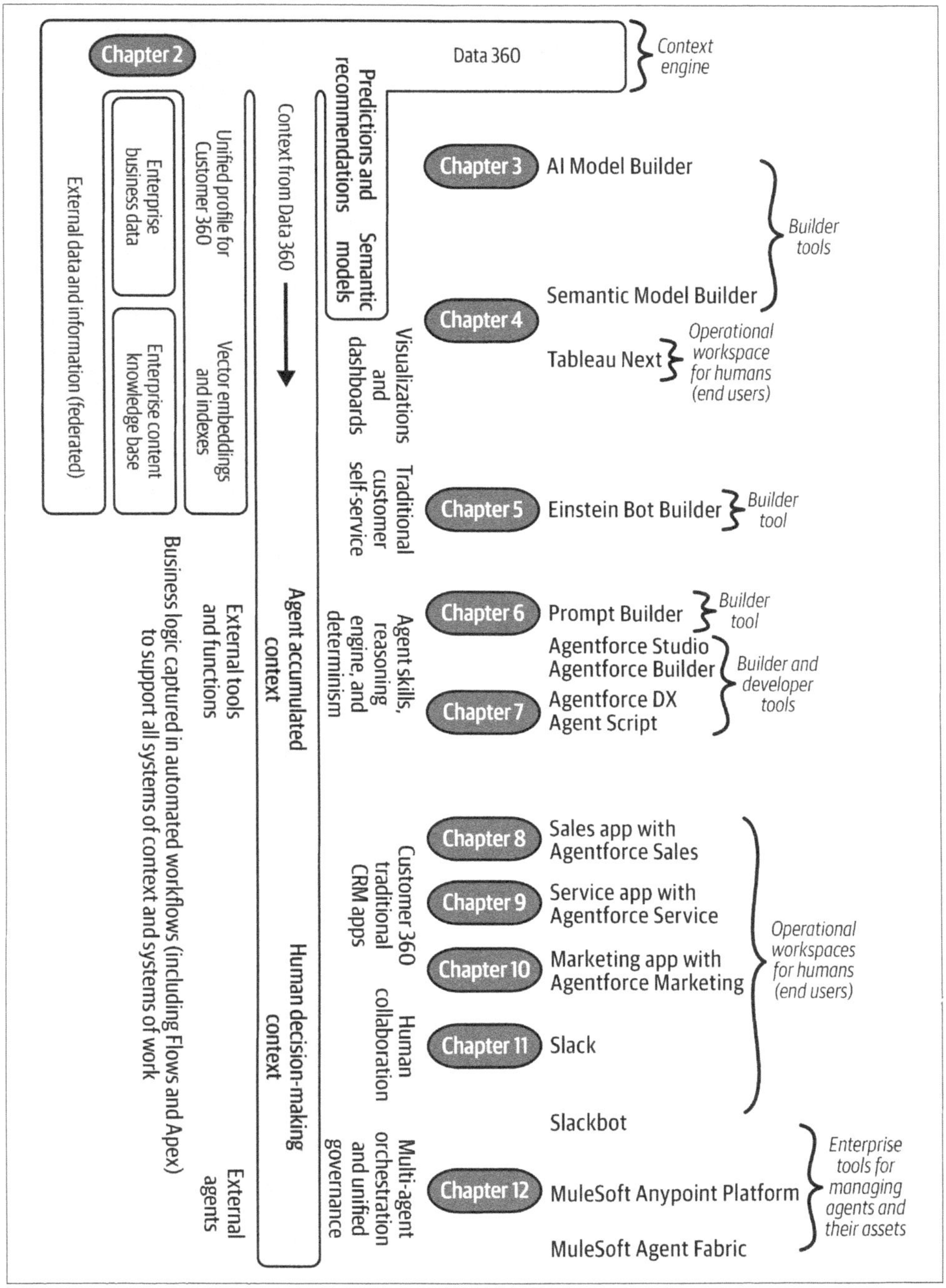

Figure 2-2. Salesforce AI solutions for building the intelligent agentic enterprise

In this chapter, we'll explore four main topics to build our foundational knowledge to better prepare us for future learnings:

- Information preparation for agents and humans
- Business information including customer information
- Enterprise content information
- Enterprise intelligence of agents and employees

First, we'll discover how AI powers the intelligent agentic enterprise by defining an agent's elements and explaining dynamic grounding. In that section, we'll learn what it means to create AI-ready information for humans and agents. Of course, the process of creating AI-ready information relies on customer information and enterprise content information, the next two topics. As part of the discussion about the customer, we'll explore what it means for a customer data platform (CDP) to provide a unified Customer 360 (C360) view and how D360 offers capabilities for ingestion and zero copy interoperability of external data. Next, we'll learn about enterprise content information curated for customers, employees, and agents and the best practices for creating multimodal knowledge content for humans and AI. In the final section, we'll consider the enterprise intelligence of employees and agents.

Getting Started

Let's discuss background knowledge and things you should know to help you get the most out of this chapter.

Background Knowledge

You should have a basic knowledge of the Salesforce platform. Some recommended resources include Packt Publishing's *Salesforce for Beginners*, 2nd edition, by Sharif Shaalan and Timothy Royer and O'Reilly's *Salesforce Certified Platform Administrator Study Guide* by Mike Wheeler.

It's helpful to understand the following terms, which were described in Chapter 1: system of record, system of reference, system of context, system of insight, system of work, system of engagement, system of collaboration, system of agency, system of orchestration, system of control, and system of coordination. An understanding of these system concepts is important because we'll revisit them throughout the book.

What You Should Know

Throughout the book, we'll use the term *agent* exclusively for referring to an AI agent, and we'll make use of different terms, like *sales rep* and *service rep*, to indicate when the work is performed by a human. The terms *bot* and *chatbot* are not used interchangeably because there is a difference. A bot is a broad term that refers to any automated program that performs a specific task. Examples of bots include web scraping, data processing, and chatbots. A chatbot is a specific type of bot designed for conversational interactions. It's important to realize Einstein Bot Builder is used to build only chatbots, not any other type of bot.

We'll briefly discuss some important AI terms and concepts in this chapter that will be covered in more depth in future chapters:

- Machine learning (ML)
- Semantic models
- Natural language processing (NLP)
- Large language model (LLM)

We dive into ML in Chapter 3 when we explore building prediction models for greater intelligent foresight. Chapter 4 focuses on data analytics built for conversations and actionability in the flow of work. There we'll also learn about semantic models. Semantic models provide context for agents as well as help users build better visualizations.

NLP is explained in Chapter 5 when we cover orchestrated conversational AI for customer self-service. LLMs and reasoning engines are discussed in Chapter 6 when we focus on building and managing agents. Resources are listed in the Appendix for readers who desire to dive deeper into certain technical topics including the AI topics mentioned.

Throughout this chapter and beyond, there is much discussion about the D360 platform. D360, previously known as *Data Cloud*, refers to the Salesforce app that serves as the system of reference for customer-related data and content knowledge bases and also serves as a system of context. D360 is sometimes referred to as a *context engine* especially as it relates to providing context for the Atlas reasoning engine. As both a system of reference and a system of context, D360 is a critical component of any Salesforce AI strategy.

D360 architecture and functionality will be explained as needed to provide an understanding for Salesforce AI. However, you can find more detailed coverage of the D360 platform in my book *Hands-On Salesforce Data Cloud* (O'Reilly, 2024).

Within the chapter, most notably in "Agentforce Data Library" on page 54, explanations are provided about functionality that incorporates knowledge articles and Knowledge articles. We'll use the term *knowledge articles* when referring to content knowledge articles that can exist in any platform, including external knowledge management platforms or the Salesforce platform. The term *Knowledge articles*, with a capital "K," refers specifically to those content knowledge articles that exist in standard Knowledge objects within the Salesforce core platform.

This chapter mentions several different Salesforce products and features. We don't discuss which specific licenses or packages must be acquired or which permission sets are required to achieve the functionality described. You'll want to discuss those topics with your Salesforce Account Executive (AE) and your Salesforce implementation partner.

How AI Uses Data and Knowledge to Power the Intelligent Agentic Enterprise

There's been a great deal of focus in the media about how AI technology continues to offer increasingly more capabilities for enterprises, especially because of advancements of LLMs, which play an important role in agents. This is certainly true. However, there's two very important points to remember when making strategic decisions about how to use AI to power an intelligent agentic enterprise.

First, there are other AI capabilities besides LLMs that bring value to enterprises that should not be overlooked. Specifically, ML and NLP have been providing business value for a while and continue to provide significant value, especially when combined with the dynamic abilities of LLMs.

Second, the real value of AI comes from its integration into enterprise business processes, one of which is supporting humans in their normal flow of work. To further make that point, let's review some examples of how AI powers customer service and sales use cases.

Examples of How AI Powers Sales and Customer Service Use Cases

AI powers the intelligent agentic enterprise where humans and agents work together. LLMs are at the heart of an agentic enterprise with ML and NLP sharing the workload. There are also other AI elements, such as search and retrieval needed to turn understanding and language generation into actionable insights. As a reminder, these three essential elements each perform important functions:

- NLP is used, in part, to understand the user's intent and to identify the associated entities.
- LLMs handle reasoning and rich language generation with the ability to adapt to an individual user's style and preferences.
- ML powers predictions, rankings, and personalization.

There are plenty of examples where individuals leverage AI technology for personal purposes like planning a vacation. Since we're focused on customer data and content knowledge bases herein, let's focus on two enterprise work-related examples.

First, let's consider an internal sales rep who wants help with today's meeting with Company X, a fictional company. Specifically, the sales rep wants a summary of the last three calls with the company along with suggestions on what to emphasize in the meeting. AI capabilities can certainly help fulfill that request.

NLP uses speech-to-text on the call recordings then completes a topic and sentiment analysis. Also, the company's past interactions with the enterprise are found by AI retrieving the company's data from the CRM. Some of those artifacts include previous emails and closed won/closed lost opportunities. This information is needed for grounding the LLM's responses.

The LLM uses the information to produce a concise recap of the calls and generates some tailored opening lines from which the sales rep can select along with some talking points. The opening line and talking points style include the appropriate tone and are personalized to correspond to the concerns of Company X. The specific products or offers the AI suggests should be emphasized are based on the recommendations produced by an ML model (Figure 2-3).

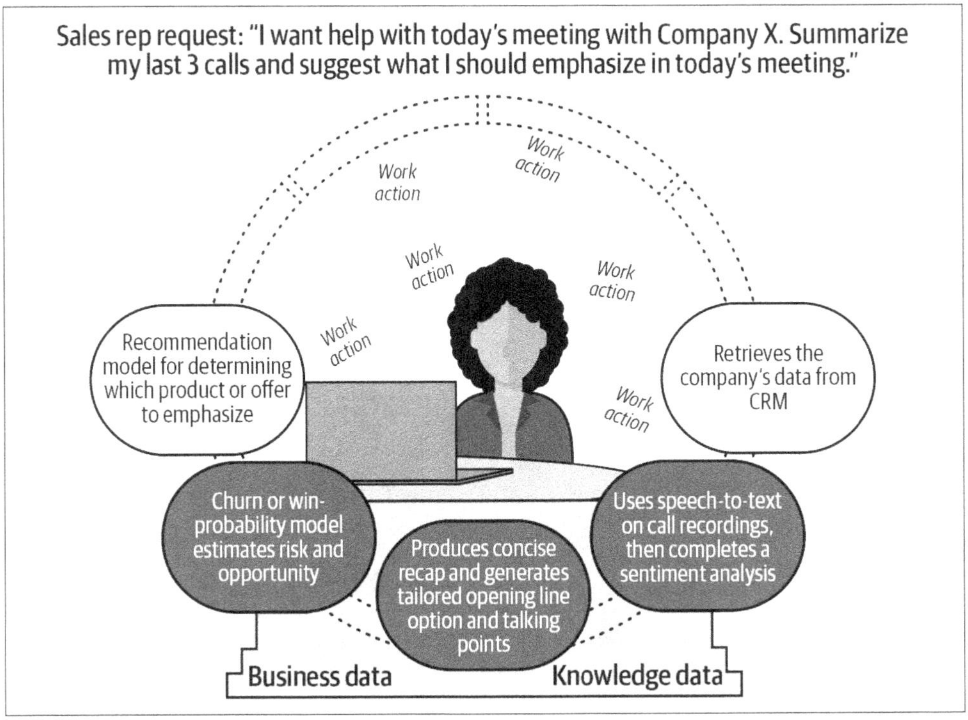

Figure 2-3. Sales rep request

Now, think about a customer who reaches out to a telecommunications carrier with a question about a potential error on their cell phone bill. There are many different channels the customer could use to reach out to the enterprise. For example, the customer could use a self-service chatbot that's either text-based or voice-based, or perhaps the customer uses live messaging to communicate with an enterprise employee who works in the customer service department. In each of those scenarios, AI can help. NLP detects the intent, a potential billing issue, and identifies the invoice as an entity. As a result, it's determined that the customer's account needs to be reviewed for the past few months and those monthly invoices should be compared.

The LLM creates a plan that involves fetching the current and previous months' invoices, comparing line items, checking the knowledge base for any potential discounts and different cell phone plans, and drafting explanations in natural language. ML runs an anomaly-detection or regression model to determine whether the current bill actually deviates from expected usage or pricing and, based on the results, the recommendation model could suggest offering the customer a discount or proposing a new cell phone plan, assuming there was not actually a billing error (Figure 2-4).

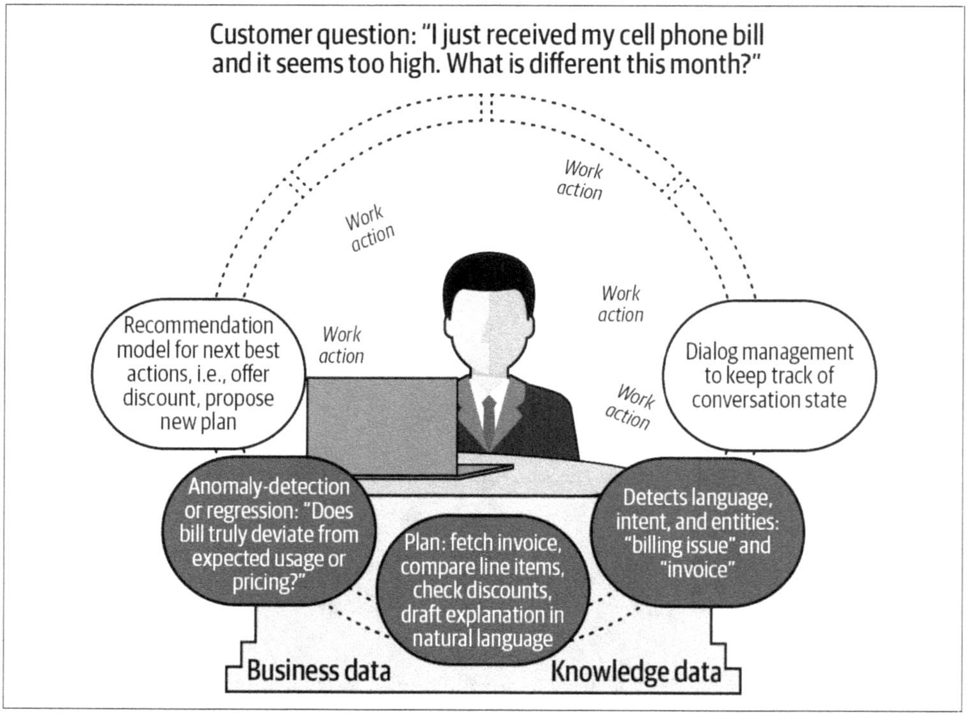

Figure 2-4. Customer service request

We've considered two examples of how AI powers an enterprise with NLP, ML, and LLMs. So, then, what is the relationship between these and an agent? Let's explore that concept now to better understand what an agent is.

What Is an Agent?

Agents are capable of more than what's possible by using an LLM alone. Agents simulate human-like work for tasks like generating summaries or reports, analyzing sales data, and scheduling meetings. They need autonomous task execution capabilities, reasoning strategies, and the ability to interact with external systems to complete goals and achieve results. There are some general elements an agent needs to mimic human workers' ability:

- LLM brain (reasoning)
- Knowledge base (knowing)
- Memory system (remembering)
- Tools and functions (doing)
- Human-to-agent interfaces (communicating)

Powered by generative AI (GenAI) models, an LLM is able to function as an important module of the agent's brain to assist with handling NLP, reasoning, and planning sequences of actions. GenAI is used for natural language understanding and to create new content, whereas reasoning involves breaking down the request or problem into smaller units. There is more to the agent's brain than just the LLM, and we'll discuss this further in Chapter 6 when we explore the concept of agents in much more detail.

The agent interprets input using existing memory and knowledge, and then reasons and plans iteratively if needed. It selects and calls the necessary tools and functions along the way. The agent integrates results from the function calls and updates existing memory before responding or taking more action.

Tools and functions are those that extend beyond the language generation capabilities of an LLM. They include internal and external application programming interfaces (APIs) or functions such as querying databases or sending emails. Memory systems are required for agents to recall past interactions and data. Memory systems include session context and structured short-term memory variables created to provide persistent storage and enable more deterministic agent actions by controlling the execution conditions.

A *knowledge base* is a collection of facts and information about a specific domain. Salesforce users sometimes equate a knowledge base with the content knowledge available in the Knowledge object. However, content knowledge is only a portion of an enterprise knowledge base used by an agent. An enterprise knowledge base includes business data and content knowledge bases, both of which we'll describe later in more detail. For now, it's enough to know that an enterprise knowledge base includes structured, unstructured, and multimedia data encompassing a wide variety of information:

- Customer records
- Product information
- Dynamically generated data
- Approved policies and procedures
- Employee-specific documentation
- External references

Dynamically generated data includes chat logs, usage logs, and user feedback. Policies and procedures describe details found in return policies and service-level agreements (SLAs), whereas employee-specific documentation includes information such as employee training manuals. An enterprise knowledge base contains a wide variety of information and is usually spread between several different platforms used by the enterprise. As a matter of fact, knowledge bases can also include external references to partner resources or third-party information such as industry regulations.

For a knowledge base to really be useful, though, it needs context, which are details about the knowledge base that make it more understandable and usable for agents and humans. Knowledge base context includes artifacts such as prediction models, semantic models, taxonomy, vector embeddings and indexes, and data graphs. This is a critical element of an enterprise knowledge base because, similar to humans, agents don't produce relevant responses if they aren't given enough understandable information, they don't have access to the necessary tools or systems, and they're not informed about the intended audience.

When agents perform poorly, the most likely cause is a lack of curated, contextualized information. Salesforce has several ways to help users ensure their agents have sufficient curated, contextualized information. In this chapter, we'll focus on common approaches used to achieve that objective.

Salesforce provides managed LLMs, prompt templates, and guardrails that make it easy to get started building an intelligent agentic enterprise. In addition, the Salesforce platform offers powerful builder and automation tools that also provide access to external platforms and tools. Importantly, Salesforce provides all the necessary functionality for users to dynamically ground AI with their enterprise knowledge base to provide a curated, contextualized knowledge base. That's what we'll focus on here. We'll first review what we mean by the term *grounding* and how it compares to the *dynamic grounding* approach. We'll then focus our attention on the enterprise knowledge base, which is the business information and enterprise content information used for dynamic grounding.

Dynamic Grounding

Grounding is a process of informing a GenAI model of certain information to help produce intended results and relevant, factual outputs. It's one of the most important ways to customize an LLM's behavior to achieve the best outcomes. One grounding approach is to fine-tune a model by providing more training.

All LLMs are trained with general knowledge. A fine-tuned model is further trained with more knowledge, usually domain specific, that could include proprietary information. Grounding an LLM using fine-tuning actually changes the model and also constrains it because the fine-tuned model possesses knowledge as of a fixed point in time and could require retraining later.

In contrast, *dynamic grounding* is where the LLM is provided with up-to-date information as needed. When AI models are dynamically ground in verified sources of information like Salesforce CRM data and content knowledge bases, the LLM provides more accurate responses to inquiries.

The information used for dynamic grounding can be internal data and knowledge but can also include information external to the enterprise. That way, as internal or external information changes, the LLM continues to be grounded in the most current information. Of course, the accuracy of the grounded responses depends largely on the quality of the sources and the effectiveness of the retrieval mechanisms.

Both approaches, LLM fine-tuning and dynamic grounding, support the goal of enhancing AI capabilities and accuracy. However, the methods are two fundamentally different ways an LLM acquires and utilizes knowledge. Which one is the most appropriate approach is an enterprise architecture decision.

Of the two grounding approaches, dynamic grounding is the more common approach. Retrieval augmented generation (RAG) is a dynamic grounding technique used to connect an LLM to an enterprise knowledge base so that the most relevant information can be retrieved and used. There are different RAG approaches used to organize, connect, and retrieve data:

- Vector-based RAG
- Knowledge-based RAG
- Ensemble RAG

Vector-based RAG relies on a vector database that uses vector embeddings and search indexes. Salesforce uses vector-based RAG. Knowledge-based RAG uses knowledge graphs where data is organized around nodes and relationships so that connections between data are more easily understood. Ensemble RAG combines the results of vector-based and knowledge-based RAG to cross-check the results. Cross-checking results is an effective method for ensuring better results.

When used as a dynamic grounding technique, RAG searches the information first and then generates a response based only on the information returned. Thus, RAG utilizes both retrieval-based models and generative models. That's because retrieval-based models are ML models designed to locate specific information, but those models lack the ability to generate new content from the information. There are different retrieval models, and most modern platforms like Salesforce use a hybrid search retrieval model. It's important to reiterate that AI doesn't provide meaningful business value without access to the enterprise knowledge base.

Understanding enterprise data and knowledge doesn't just require access to the underlying information. Rather, AI needs to understand the context of that data and knowledge. Let's briefly discuss what we mean by the terms *business data* and *content knowledge bases*, which comprise an enterprise's knowledge base. Then we'll discover what it means to create context in Salesforce for the enterprise knowledge base.

Business Data and Content Knowledge Base Overview

Business data encompasses any structured, semistructured, or unstructured data collected or generated by the enterprise to support business operations, decision-making processes, and overall goals. Generally, there are five common business data types:

- Customer data
- Employee data
- Operational data
- Marketing data
- Financial data

Financial data includes financial details like income and expenses as well as assets and liabilities. Marketing data often includes details about marketing campaigns, such as email open rates and website traffic. Operational data differs by industry and may include details such as retailer product inventory. Employee data includes information like employee name, salary, and job title.

Customer data is the focus of our attention, especially since the book is about Salesforce, well-known for its CRM product. Customer data includes demographic data like location, income, age, and preferred method of communication. It also includes transactional data such as purchase history and payment methods. Certain behavioral data, like engagement or search history, can be captured with permission. Customers often provide feedback, a type of attitudinal data.

Business data includes structured data like transactional details, customer demographics, and product inventory descriptions and quantities. Some unstructured data, such as customer survey responses to open-ended questions and purchase terms and PDFs of contract details, is also included as part of an enterprise's business data. It's only recently that enterprises are able to extract more value from unstructured data.

For our purposes, we'll differentiate between business data and business information. Business information is defined as *usable business data with context*. The definition of business information includes two important concepts. First, the data must be usable. Sometimes raw business data needs to be transformed, unified, enriched, aggregated, translated, summarized, or visualized before business value can be extracted. Usable business data includes enough understandable context for humans to make decisions and take actions for which the underlying reasons can be explained or justified.

Second, the data must include context so that the information is usable by AI to produce reliable outputs that support effective decision making. This means the business data may need to be classified, categorized, modeled, or vectorized depending on whether it's structured or unstructured data. While the explanation of context is slightly more nuanced and there is some overlap, the overall concepts are accurately described within this chapter.

In the next section, we'll discuss how Salesforce provides the tools that make it easier to supply context important for improving business outcomes. The tools also help define business terms and data relationships, classify and organize data, as well as create context needed for searching and retrieving information. The context for searching and retrieving information isn't just important for business information. It's a critical element needed for an enterprise's content knowledge base.

A content knowledge base holds an enterprise's information about its products and services as well as answers to commonly asked questions by customers and employees. It's mostly unstructured data comprised of assets like files, images, videos, documents, company policies, and sales playbooks.

Now that we have a basic understanding of business data and content knowledge bases, let's consider some ways we can create context in Salesforce so the data and information becomes more understandable for AI and humans.

Creating AI-Ready Information for Humans and Agents

Humans need high-quality, contextualized information to understand and make sense of data. Yet, humans don't need flawless data or perfect context because they can detect subtle but important inconsistencies in data models and instinctively infer missing context. Humans also easily navigate between inconsistent formats such as when structured data is included within the contents of an unstructured document.

An example is a PDF report with an executive summary in paragraph form followed by embedded charts and diagrams.

AI lacks the human experience and common sense and, thus, more work often needs to be done in an enterprise to make the data and information ready for agents to consume. This is true even when the existing data and information includes clear context, trustworthy data, and well-structured data models. Agents require a more formalized version of enterprise data and information. In essence, they need to have the context gaps filled in for them.

AI is also limited by the amount of text it can process at a time, so we need to prepare the information in advance to make it easier for AI to locate relevant details quickly. We'll use chunking, vector embeddings, and indexing in Salesforce to achieve efficient structuring of the data for AI.

Salesforce Builders have many tools available for designing context-aware architecture for agents that ultimately benefit humans, too:

- Context for improving business outcomes (prediction models)
- Context for defining business terms and data relationships (semantic models + metrics)
- Context for classifying and organizing data (tags and tag taxonomies)
- Context for real-time personalization (data graphs)
- Context for searching and retrieving information (vector embeddings and indexes)

Before diving into each of these tools, though, we'll want to clarify that context preparation isn't the same as data preparation, although both are critical for creating AI-ready information. The goal of data preparation is to achieve quality data that is accurate, complete, and consistent. Achieving the goal often requires removing duplicate records, standardizing data formats, or resolving how to handle missing data. Data preparation and data quality are beyond the scope of this book.

There's something interesting about all the Salesforce context preparation tools we've listed—prediction models, semantic models and metrics, tags and tag taxonomies, data graphs, and vector embeddings and indexes. They're all accessible from within the D360 app, which is the reason we refer to D360 as Salesforce's system of context.

Remember that D360 is also the system of reference used to provide a complete view of the customer. Thus, *the importance of D360 needs to be emphasized here again because there is no Salesforce AI strategy without D360.* Now, let's explore five important context preparation tools available in D360.

Context for improving business outcomes (prediction models)

Business outcomes are the results of actions and decisions made by individuals working for an enterprise. For example, the type of product to manufacture and how much inventory to maintain are decisions made far in advance of when the product is sold. Factoring into the decision are a variety of inputs including how many items an enterprise sold last year. That information is known, but how much inventory will be sold this year is uncertain.

For situations like this, enterprises use ML models to help reduce the risk of uncertainty. ML models use algorithms that handle complexity and are able to provide an understanding of the factors that most influence the prediction. This information can then be used to make recommendations that will likely improve outcomes.

Making informed decisions generally leads to better outcomes, but there's still uncertainty in future outcomes and there are actions that need to be taken in advance of an outcome. Not all decisions and actions are taken far in advance and have major implications, though. Some decisions and actions can even be personalized for individual customers.

For example, a customer browsing an online store could receive a notification that they're eligible for a 20% discount if they purchase $100 or more of items. That discount could have been offered to the customer based on a prediction model providing real-time insights where certain actions to entice the customer to buy now are taken automatically without human approval or intervention needed.

In addition to setting up automations that leverage ML prediction outputs, humans can use agents to assist them with decision making and actions. Agents perform certain tasks exceptionally well, depending on their assigned skills, and they often provide excellent suggestions on what steps to undertake next. LLMs excel at predicting the next word in the sentence, but an agent's LLM brain isn't good at predicting an uncertain future. That's were prediction models powered by ML are required. Thus, an agent needs the additional context provided by an ML model just like a human does.

Creating good ML prediction models that provide accurate predictions and recommendations requires humans, at least for the foreseeable future. Humans who understand the business domain and the unique underlying data are needed to help train the ML model on the enterprise's data. We'll see how this is done when we learn how to build an ML prediction model from scratch in AI Model Builder in Chapter 3. In addition, we'll learn more about the differences between predictions and forecasts in Chapter 4 when we explore Tableau Next.

For now, it's enough to just understand that ML prediction models produce outputs that turn historical data into foresight. Predictions help us estimate future demand, identify which customers are likely to churn, or which transactions seem suspicious.

Recommendations, based on knowing what's influencing the outcome the most, help inform what actions could possibly change the outcome. LLMs rely on ML prediction models to provide that context for improving business outcomes.

Context for defining business terms and data relationships (semantic models + metrics)

We know LLMs are excellent for summarizing existing content or creating new content. They're trained to understand the meaning of words and the relationships between them, especially when words are used to form sentences. LLMs are not so good at understanding words where the meaning depends on how they're used in a specific business domain.

For example, an LLM generally understands a major donor as a supporter whose contribution exceeds the nonprofit's average amount. But does the contribution need to be given in cash only or do property donations count? What if that contribution amount was only exceeded once, 10 years ago? Is it possible for a supporter to no longer be a *major donor* if they haven't donated in many years, or is that designation one that never changes? An LLM needs clearly defined metrics, business terms, and acronyms.

LLMs also struggle to understand relational data models where a large number of columns are present in tables, multihop jobs are needed, the grain isn't the same, or many-to-many relationships exist. Solving these problems requires the relationships and hierarchies be explicitly stated, the grain clearly explained, and any business preferences shared. Business preferences define ascending or descending sorting preferences, for example, and can be included in a semantic data model.

All these contextual issues can be resolved by creating D360 semantic models and metrics. The Semantic Layer menu tab in D360 gives users the ability to create and manage semantic models and metrics. D360 semantic models include standard C360 semantic models and any custom semantic models created with the Semantic Layer menu tab.

Just like Salesforce provides a standard C360 data model, it also provides a standard C360 semantic model. The C360 semantic model provided by Salesforce out-of-the-box offers a unified view of the Salesforce standard CRM data model including the Sales, Service, Marketing, and Commerce objects. The C360 semantic model leverages the C360 data model and includes common tables and dimensions shared across the objects. It also includes metrics. Importantly, the C360 semantic model can be extended to meet specific industry or domain needs.

> The C360 data model focuses on the underlying data structure and relationship between Salesforce objects. It's used in Salesforce core to store and manage raw data. In contrast, the C360 semantic model is used in the D360 app. The native C360 semantic model provides a unified semantic layer to define and manage metrics derived from standard Salesforce objects.

D360 semantic models, including custom semantic models as well as the standard C360 semantic model, are useful for building visualizations and dashboards using Tableau Next. They're also needed for conversational analytics where humans ask questions about the data using natural language while engaging with an Agentforce analytics and visualization agent.

Semantic models can include D360 tags to help classify and manage data objects within the semantic model more effectively. Let's consider tags and tag taxonomies now.

Context for classifying and organizing data (tags and tag taxonomies)

Tags are used in D360 primarily for data governance purposes to help classify data and information based on its type, sensitivity, usage, or domain to align with privacy and compliance requirements.

Each tag is assigned to a taxonomy, which helps support consistent tagging and improves data discoverability. Tag taxonomies also provide more accuracy in the application of policies such as data masking or access control.

D360 comes preconfigured with taxonomies for personal data, healthcare data, financial data, external data, and ethical AI standards (Figure 2-5), visible from the Data Governance tab. That tab is where all tags are created and managed, and it's only accessible to users assigned the Data Cloud Architect or similar permission set. Users can also create a custom tag taxonomy. Tags can be applied manually by the user or automatically when search indexes are created.

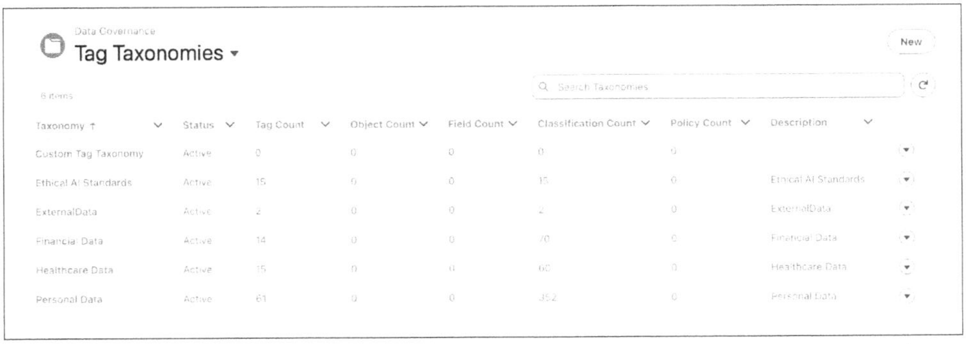

Figure 2-5. Preconfigured tag taxonomies accessible within the Data Governance tab

Within D360, automatic content tagging is turned off by default but can be enabled to occur during search index creation based on the confidence threshold selected. The confidence threshold determines how strictly tags are auto-approved. When the confidence threshold is set to low, all tags are approved. The default setting is medium where only moderately to highly accurate tags are approved. The confidence level can be set to high so that only highly accurate tags are approved, minimizing errors but reducing auto-applied tags.

Tags can be applied at the D360 object-level or field-level. For example, the tags Confidential or Customer Data can be applied to a specific object. Further, tags like Email or SSN identify specific sensitive fields within the object.

Context for real-time personalization (data graphs)

Let's establish some understanding about D360 data graphs so that we have clarity on what those are and, more importantly, what they are not. A D360 data graph combines DMO data you select and transforms it from normalized table data into materialized views. That way, the specific subset of data needed can be precalculated and optimized for frequent queries. This offers lower latency and consumes fewer credits than real-time D360 data graphs.

Real-time D360 data graphs consume more credits than standard D360 data graphs, but the real-time data is needed for live queries associated with real-time personalization. In both cases, D360 provides a dynamic view of the data so changes in the source data are reflected in the data graph. D360 data graphs, which aggregate preselected D360 objects, should not be confused with knowledge graphs or traditional data graphs used in AI.

Traditional data graphs represent data as nodes and edges, otherwise known as entities and relationships, and they're commonly used in AI for knowledge graphs, social networks, recommendation systems, and semantic search. Knowledge graphs leverage a graph-structured data model in support of a RAG approach to organizing, connecting, and retrieving data. Salesforce uses a vector-based RAG approach, rather than a knowledge-based RAG approach, which relies on a vector database and vector embeddings. Let's explore the concept of a vector database and its associated vector embeddings and indexes.

Context for searching and retrieving information (vector embeddings and indexes)

Earlier, we learned about the concept of dynamic grounding where domain-specific knowledge or customer information is provided to an LLM so that it has the necessary context to accurately respond to a question or task. RAG is an example of a dynamic grounding technique and there are several different RAG approaches—Salesforce uses a vector-based RAG approach. This vector embeddings approach relies on a vector database that supports a natural language search across documents to retrieve relevant context for generating a response based only on the information retrieved.

Dynamic grounding sources often include unstructured data like knowledge articles, uploaded files, transcripts, websites, and more. Many unstructured data sources include large quantities of information, making it time-consuming to search through. It's also resource-intensive for LLMs, which have a maximum token or word limit for the amount of information they can process at one time. Chunking and indexing is an effective way to address these limitations.

Breaking text into chunks, such as paragraphs or sections, makes it easier to retrieve only the relevant passages from a document for the LLM to process. Using ML techniques, chunked data is organized and categorized by search indexes via a process known as vectorization. Vectorization converts chunked data into numeric representations known as vector embeddings so that relevant information is easier to find using a retrieval method based on relationships and semantic relevance rather than exact keyword matches.

The retrieval-based model, known as the retriever, is created after the chunking is completed and the search index is ready. Each Agentforce Data Library of chunked and indexed data has its own unique retriever. In addition to using a data library to automatically create indexes, the Search Indexes tab can be accessed by D360 users to create and manage indexes. When creating a new search index, D360 users first need to select the index type.

D360 supports both Vector Search indexes and Hybrid Search indexes. Vector searches leverage the vector database embeddings to retrieve the information with the highest vector search score, indicating the retrieved data closely matches the semantic meaning. This type of search works well for general information searches. In contrast, hybrid search works well when specific or domain-specific search terms are used because hybrid search merges results from the vector search index and the keyword search index to surface the most relevant information.

In addition to standard capabilities, Salesforce offers two unique vector-based RAG approaches: Intelligent Context vector-based RAG and Document AI vector-based RAG. Intelligent Context creates search index configurations supported by multiple file types such as *.docx*, *.pdf*, *.png*, and more. Use cases include testing and validating search configurations on sample documents and creating lenses for specific teams to extract relevant information. In contrast, Document AI is used for automating data extraction from documents for record updates and enhancing RAG responses with detailed table information. Document AI handles complex tables and multipage layouts as it programmatically extracts data from Word, PowerPoint, and Excel files.

In addition to powerful capabilities out-of-the-box, Salesforce gives users options for customization. For example, Salesforce offers a variety of retriever models and tools including the ability to create custom retrievers and to use a retriever playground for fine-tuning, testing, and optimizing retrievers. Users are able to experiment with different chunking strategies as well as build different vector and hybrid indexes to compare results.

Customer Information

In the preceding section, we discussed how to contextualize business data using prediction models, semantic models and metrics, data graphs, tags and tag taxonomies, and vector embeddings and indexes. Contextualized data doesn't provide much value, though, unless the underlying data is usable (Figure 2-6), which means data may need to first undergo transformations, aggregations, unification, or more before humans or agents can understand the customer information.

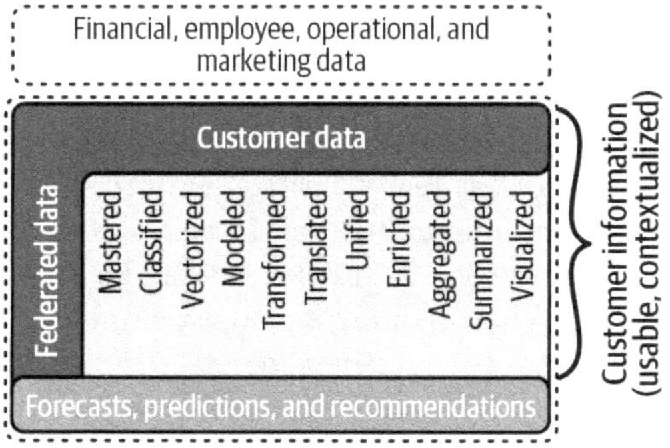

Figure 2-6. Customer data provides value when it's usable and contextualized

For customer data, it's especially important that data be unified to provide a complete view of the customer. Unified customer data doesn't necessarily have to be data that's ingested into a single platform. The data can exist on an external platform as long as it's accessible through a federated approach such as query federation or file federation. Before exploring unified profiles and federated data, let's first discuss how we're using the term *customer* in the book.

Customers and Customer Relationship Management

CRM includes the process of managing interactions with existing and potential customers. An organization's desired goal for managing interactions in the customer lifecycle is to attract potential new customers, convert them into customers, and ultimately turn customers into loyalists and brand evangelists. The customer lifecycle is typically managed by three functional groups: sales, service, and marketing teams. In general, marketers undertake activities to attract new prospects, sales teams work to convert prospects to customers, and service representatives strive to retain customers.

A potential customer is commonly referred to as a *prospect* or *lead*. However, different industries and enterprises use various terms for customer. For example, a customer might be known as a *buyer*, *client*, *shopper*, *consumer*, or *subscriber*. Certain industries use very specific labels to describe their customers. Healthcare companies frequently describe their customers as *patients*, educational institutions refer to their customers as *students*, and nonprofit organizations have *donors*.

There's also a distinction made between whether a customer is an individual person or another company. B2B sales represent transactions occurring between two businesses. B2C sales are those where an individual, rather than a company, is the customer. B2B and B2C customer lifecycle processes are often very different and these differences are reflected in the terminology used and how the various CRM processes and workflows are built.

Another important consideration is the sales lifecycle duration, the time it takes to convert a prospect to a customer. Perhaps an organization is selling expensive equipment to hospitals purchased only through a lengthy Request for Proposal (RFP) process. In those circumstances, the sales cycle is expected to take longer to complete. Salesforce CRM core platform excels at handling longer sales cycles like this example.

Today, Salesforce offers many solutions for sales use cases but, initially, Salesforce was created to solve B2B use cases with a longer sales cycle. This means Salesforce tables, also known as objects, come standard out-of-the-box for Leads, Contacts, Accounts, and Opportunities. In addition, processes such as the lead conversion process also come already built into the Salesforce org. Salesforce added Person Accounts in Salesforce core later to accommodate B2C use cases with a longer sales cycle.

> ### The B2C Term Includes D2C Transactions
>
> The term *direct-to-consumer* (D2C) is often used interchangeably with the term *business-to-consumer* (B2C), although there are differences between them. A B2C company could be a reseller such as a retailer or marketplace operator who purchased the goods at wholesale prices from the manufacturer. Alternatively, it could be a manufacturer directly selling at retail pricing to the consumer. When the company is a manufacturer selling directly to the consumer, it's known specifically as a D2C transaction.
>
> Because Salesforce Commerce Cloud is a scalable solution used mostly by large enterprise customers, it's more likely the organization using Commerce Cloud is a manufacturer conducting D2C transactions. Throughout the book, we'll use the more generic B2C term, which encompasses all types of businesses, but you may sometimes see Salesforce's B2C Commerce Cloud offering referred to as the D2C Commerce Cloud in the documentation.

Salesforce also created specialized solutions for certain industries, such as financial services and health clouds, built into Salesforce core as Industry cloud solutions. In addition, an external B2C Commerce Cloud now exists for use cases where the sales cycle is much shorter so processes like the lead conversion process are unnecessary.

Salesforce's rising popularity with business users 25 years ago was the result of offering a browser-based application layer where sales, service, and marketing teams could perform their work within an easy-to-navigate user interface. The Salesforce platform empowered users to customize their own apps with the availability of no-code builder tools. It was a novel approach in 1999. That system of work and engagement, built on top of a cloud database by Salesforce, served as the cloud frontend powered by built-in workflows and automated syncing on the backend.

The Salesforce CRM underlying storage system was and still is the *system of record* for a metadata-driven, multitenant transactional database optimized for online CRM transactions. However, that core system wasn't built to store or process the petabyte-scale analytical data needed to support a modern system of engagement in an AI era. Salesforce thus evolved by creating D360, a separate app where a system of context could be built upon a connected data layer. That unified data layer, connected to Salesforce core, is a tiered data lakehouse referred to as Hyperforce.

D360 is one of the apps available to users who are logged in to Salesforce, assuming they've been assigned permissions to access that app. Salesforce users navigate to *https://login.salesforce.com* or their enterprise's customer URL to log in to Salesforce. After logging in, users are presented with a home screen personalized for their role (Figure 2-7).

Figure 2-7. Personalized user home screen in Salesforce for a sales rep persona

Salesforce users navigate to the App Launcher in the top left of their home screen to gain access to all Salesforce apps for which they have been granted permissions (Figure 2-8).

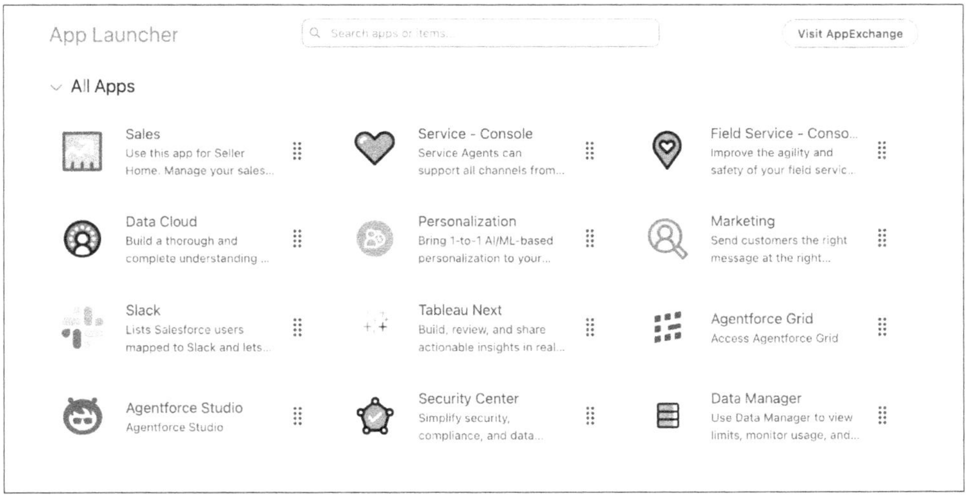

Figure 2-8. App Launcher includes all Salesforce apps for which a user has been granted access

Salesforce CRM apps include Sales, Service, and Marketing-specific apps, among others. Within these apps are Salesforce objects. For example, Contacts are included in both the Sales and Service apps whereas the Lead object is included in the Sales but not Service app. Likewise, the Case object is only included in the Service app.

Those CRM app objects are in a layer known as the *system of engagement* because that's where Salesforce users take action about customers to convert leads, update opportunities, close cases, or send emails. The CRM apps could be slightly different for users working within a Salesforce industry cloud, but it's still the same place where the work gets done.

We'll discuss AI solutions for sales, service, and marketing use cases each in their own chapter. However, many AI solutions extend beyond a single functional department's use case because efficient and effective cross-team collaboration is no longer optional for today's organizations. That's where Slack can really unlock value for organizations of all sizes. With its productivity hacks and new AI capabilities, Slack can be a gamechanger for organizations able to make the most of leveraging Slack's powerful features. That's why we've devoted an entire chapter to Slack and AI capabilities within Slack workspaces.

One critical thing all AI solutions have in common is the need for data, no matter the use case(s) for which they provide solutions. The importance of data to all AI models and use cases can't be overstated. In particular, customer data is critical for the enterprise, but it's not always easy to get a complete view of the customer. The D360 system of reference in Salesforce provides the tools necessary to build a C360 view.

Customer Data Platform for a Customer 360 Unified View

Customer profile and engagement data are stored within an enterprise's various systems of record. Profile data provides information about individuals and includes identifiers, demographic and profile-related attributes, and contact points like email and phone number. Engagement data is for time-series data points like customer transactions and web browsing histories.

It's difficult, perhaps impossible, to get a complete view of the customer when data is spread across different siloed systems. Thus, an enterprise needs to gather all available first-party customer data from CRM software, websites, automation platforms, email marketing software, and point-of-sale (POS) systems into a single repository known as a *customer data platform* (CDP).

Within the CDP, a unified customer profile is created and then third-party data about a customer often augments the customer profile. Third-party data providers often compile information about an individual's interests based on their social media activity or their browsing history. Third-party data isn't as reliable as first-party data, but it can help build out a more complete unified customer profile that can be used to create more business value across the entire organization.

For example, financial services companies endeavoring to grow deposits and generate more revenue from existing customers can use a CDP to activate segments based on major life events like graduation, marriage, childbirth, retirement, and inheritance. Healthcare and life sciences companies can combine data from multiple health telematics systems to calculate a Unified Health Score or identify critical points for intervention in care.

A CDP will likely not solve all issues for customer-related use cases, but it can serve as a centralized source of unified customer data to inform the rest of the technology stack. Salesforce customers use D360 for their CDP needs, which provides input to the context layer needed for the agentic enterprise.

D360 is designed to create a unified profile for an account or a Unified Individual profile (Figure 2-9), which is not the same process as what occurs in an MDM platform. An MDM typically produces a golden record. The two platforms are not mutually exclusive, however. D360 is not an MDM platform, although it can work alongside one.

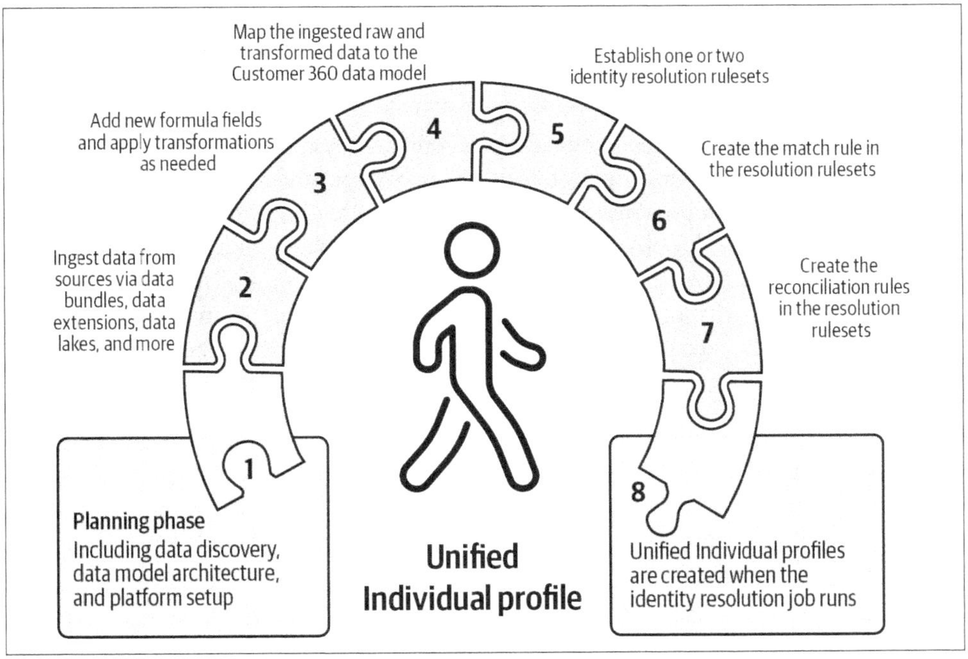

Figure 2-9. Unified Individual profile created within Salesforce Data 360

The distinction between a unified profile created within D360 and a golden record created within an MDM like Informatica is an important one. Even though a unified profile and a golden record are both known to represent the source of truth for a customer, they are very different things. However, golden records and unified profiles are not competing versions of the same customer view. A golden record supports governed operational truth by providing a persistent identity with survivorship, lineage, consent, and stewardship. In contrast, a unified profile supports transactional, behavioral, and engagement context. Understanding the difference between the two helps explain why the underlying D360 data layer is referred to as a *system of reference* and how this makes D360 well-suited to serve as a system of context.

Unified Profile in the Salesforce System of Reference

Many people are familiar with the term *golden record*, which refers to a complete and reliable view of the customer found within an MDM system. In most MDM systems, a golden record is a single data point intended to provide the most accurate and relevant information about a customer. It is the result of an enterprise's continual validation of records that underwent data cleansing and data deduplication processes.

For example, a golden record would likely contain a customer's correct mailing address, phone number, email address, and more. The MDM golden record concept was created out of a need for simplicity and a strong desire to have a single ID for the customer with only the single *best* email and the single *best* phone number.

For most people, this simplistic view doesn't represent reality. For example, it's common for people to have multiple emails: one for work and one or more personal accounts. Sometimes, a person might have a specific email address set up to capture confirmation of tax-deductible donations that can then be given to their accountant, or an email address might be set up for the entire family to use. There could be any number of reasons why multiple valid email addresses exist for an individual. This makes it difficult to determine which specific email address is the best overall email address, so a single complete view of the customer may not realistically be achievable.

Sometimes, multiple golden records are created based on a single contact point such as email or phone so as not to lose the richness of a person having multiple email addresses, phone numbers, or mailing addresses. In most of those situations, an excessive number of golden records would exist, making it unlikely you'd ever see the complete view of the customer.

Even if a single best email and best phone number could be determined, it isn't easy to combine all the individual records into one record because each record could have different attributes. When the attribute labels are the same, it's possible there could be a difference in data type formats that would result in a mismatch between records.

There is one additional consideration. In most MDM systems, it is possible to directly update a golden record, although not recommended. Updating a golden record directly in an MDM system, rather than updating the source system, would result in the creation of yet another source system. You'd end up with the original record in the source system and the updated record in the MDM system, so anyone with access to only the source system would never have the most current information for every individual. Those who have access to both systems would need to first evaluate which system was most recently updated, the source system or the MDM. Giving the user this type of functionality to update a CDP record goes against the very purpose of combining source data to create a single view of the customer.

Salesforce purposely designed D360 to prevent creating another source system. D360 avoids letting a user create a new source record by enforcing a system of reference approach to the data within the platform. While it is possible to perform data transformations on columns of ingested source data, such as changing the data format type of a particular field, it is impossible to directly edit or delete any individual row of a record within the D360 user interface.

The many different Salesforce core objects, external cloud storage locations, and external data platforms where source data is gathered are considered to be the systems of record. These locations are where a user or automated process would enter new data or edit existing data.

Salesforce D360 is a system of reference: the Unified Individual profile record will always refer back to the original data sources. A D360 Unified Individual profile is not a golden record, and the unified profile will only be changed if data in one of the source systems is updated. Let's recap (Table 2-1).

Table 2-1. D360 unified profile versus MDM golden record

	Unified profile	Golden record
Purpose	Create one view of a person that is linked to the source data	Create one authoritative row as the source of truth
Use case	Segmentation and real-time activation (marketing), providing context for AI	Enterprise data quality and governance
Lineage visible	Yes	Abstracted
Mutable values	Yes—changes as the data or the identify resolution rules change	No—intended to be permanent
Conflict handling	Maintain multiple values so the "best" value can be selected at the right time	Forces a "best" value via survivorship rules

Now that we understand more about a D360 unified profile and its purpose, let's dive a bit deeper into the D360 platform.

Data 360 Built on Hyperforce

D360 is an app in Salesforce and it's accessible from the App Launcher like any other app. Salesforce users are familiar with the steps needed to access CRM apps such as Sales, Service, and Marketing. Within each of the Sales, Service, and Marketing CRM apps, there are tabs across the top of the app that provide access to CRM objects like Accounts, Contacts, Cases, Leads, Campaigns, and more. The same is true of the D360 app except that D360 includes many more tabs, and accessing objects in D360 requires more hops to get to the object details. Here is a list of the D360 tabs:

- Activations
- Activation Targets
- Calculated Insights
- Clean Rooms
- Communication Cappings
- Dashboards
- Data Action Targets
- Data Governance
- Data Graphs
- Data Explorer
- Data Lake Objects
- Data Model
- Data Spaces
- Data Shares
- Data Share Targets
- Data Streams
- Data Transforms
- Einstein Studio
- Home
- Identity Resolution
- Process Content
- Query Editor
- Profile Explorer
- Reports
- Search Indexes
- Secondary Indexes
- Segments
- Semantic Layer

It is sometimes confusing to experienced Salesforce users at first because most of the tabs within D360 are also their own separate apps. For example, the Semantic Layer is an app directly accessible from the App Launcher but it can also be accessed via a tab in D360 and also via Tableau Next. It might be helpful to think of the D360 app as a container for several different apps that support building the system of context and the system of reference as well as supporting the unified data layer of the Salesforce system.

Hyperforce, the underlying architecture for D360, doesn't replace the CRM system of record. They're complementary components in the Salesforce system. Hyperforce architecture is explained in detail in my book *Hands-On Salesforce Data Cloud* (O'Reilly, 2024). Let's take a minute to compare the CRM system of record with Hyperforce so that we can better understand the importance of D360.

Salesforce Core CRM System of Record and Hyperforce

Salesforce core is the term often used to refer to the CRM database that serves as the system of record for CRM operations. Different CRM apps are built upon the CRM database to support a system of work. A system of work is the operational layer where work gets done by humans engaging with the UI, automated workflows are completed, and agents take action on the underlying CRM database.

In contrast, Hyperforce is a unified data layer optimized for ingesting and unifying multisource data to support the creation of context usable by humans and AI. Given their different purposes, it's not surprising that they'd have different data models and data types.

Salesforce core uses a relational model with external IDs and hierarchy relationships including lookup and master-detail relationships. Referential behavior is enforced at the application layer, and certain columns like *modification date* are included in every core object. The core data model isn't an ANSI-compliant relational database model. Thus, Salesforce created its own query language in support of the simplified architecture built for less technical users and for making things work in a multitenant shared environment. Salesforce core is optimized for interactive queries rather than scans of large data volumes and, thus, there are limits on the number of objects, fields, relationships, and records for each Salesforce org.

In addition, Salesforce core offers business data types as well as primitive data types like text, number, date, datetime, time, currency, and percent. Business data types are intended to capture and validate business facts within a single record where strong field-level security (FLS) also enables strict governance. Salesforce business data types in Salesforce core include checkbox, picklist, multi-select picklist, email, URL, phone, geolocation, formula, auto-number, and encrypted fields.

Business and primitive data types available in D360 for objects include Boolean, currency, date, datetime, email, number, percent, phone, text, and URL. Similar to formula fields in Salesforce core, Calculated Insights (CI) exist in D360. However, CIs can incorporate more complex calculations and the results are stored in a dedicated D360 object.

Under the hood, Hyperforce is built on Apache Iceberg tables in a lakehouse tier that can provide low-latency storage for customer profiles and events. Whereas the Salesforce core workload is transactional in nature, Hyperforce supports large-scale datasets needed for analytical and AI workloads that include ML, vector searches, and robust segmentation.

Earlier, we discussed a variety of ways to provide context for agent actions and automation tools that included prediction models, taxonomy, semantic models, vector embeddings and indexes, and data graphs. D360 offers menu options (Figure 2-10) where each of those can be created, which is why D360 is known as the *system of context*. Alternatively, these features for creating context are accessible directly from the App Launcher.

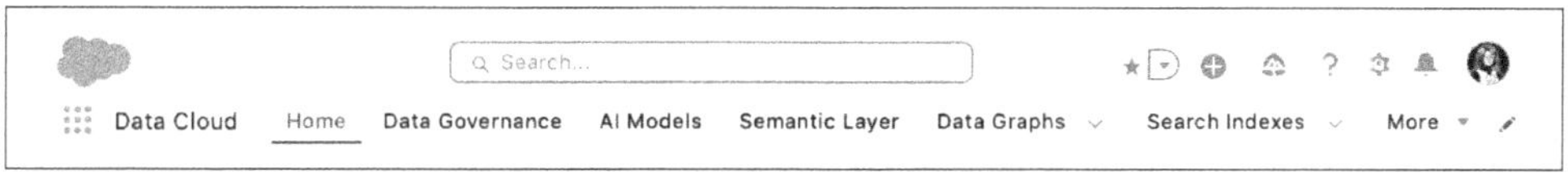

Figure 2-10. Data 360 menu options

The D360 app is where engineers and administrators manage the data objects of the unified data layer (Figure 2-11). Data Lake Objects (DLOs) are the persistent storage layer objects whereas Data Model Objects (DMOs) are logical views. DLOs and DMOs refer to structured objects while Unstructured Data Lake Objects (UDLOs) and Unstructured Data Model Objects (UDMOs) describe objects designated specifically for unstructured data. Unified profiles, a special kind of DMO, are created in D360 as part of the last step in the identity resolution process.

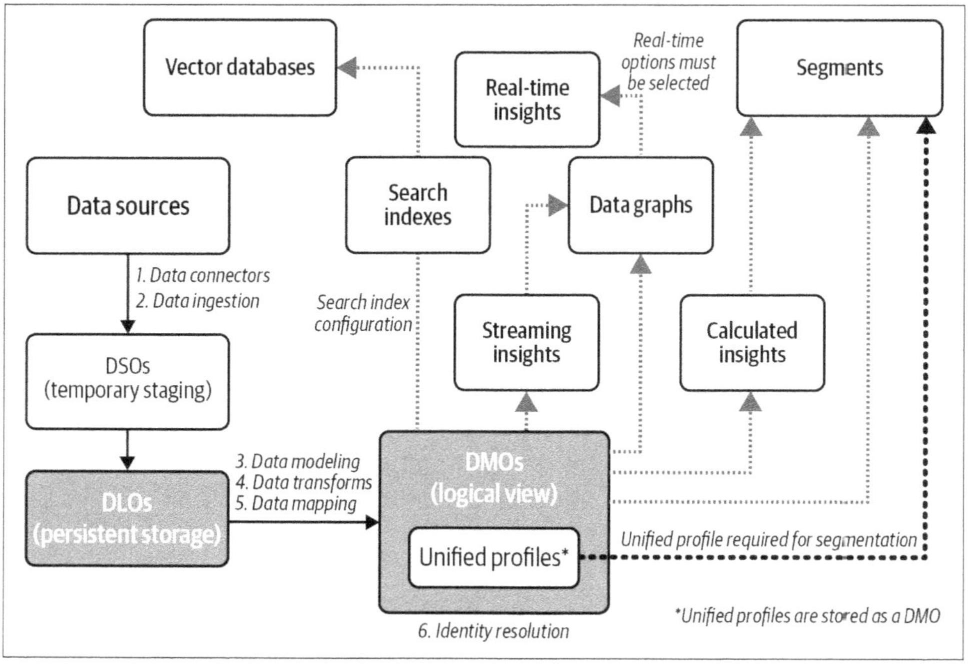

Figure 2-11. Data 360 objects

Unified profiles link information from multiple data sources to provide a comprehensive 360-degree view of the customer. They're mutable, changing to improve the accuracy of the profile when new or updated information is received in D360.

It's important to know that DLOs and DMOs aren't just limited to customer data. The Salesforce system creates new data objects as needed. For example, new DLOs and DMOs (Figure 2-12) are created by the system to track agent interactions and moments when the Agent Optimization feature is enabled.

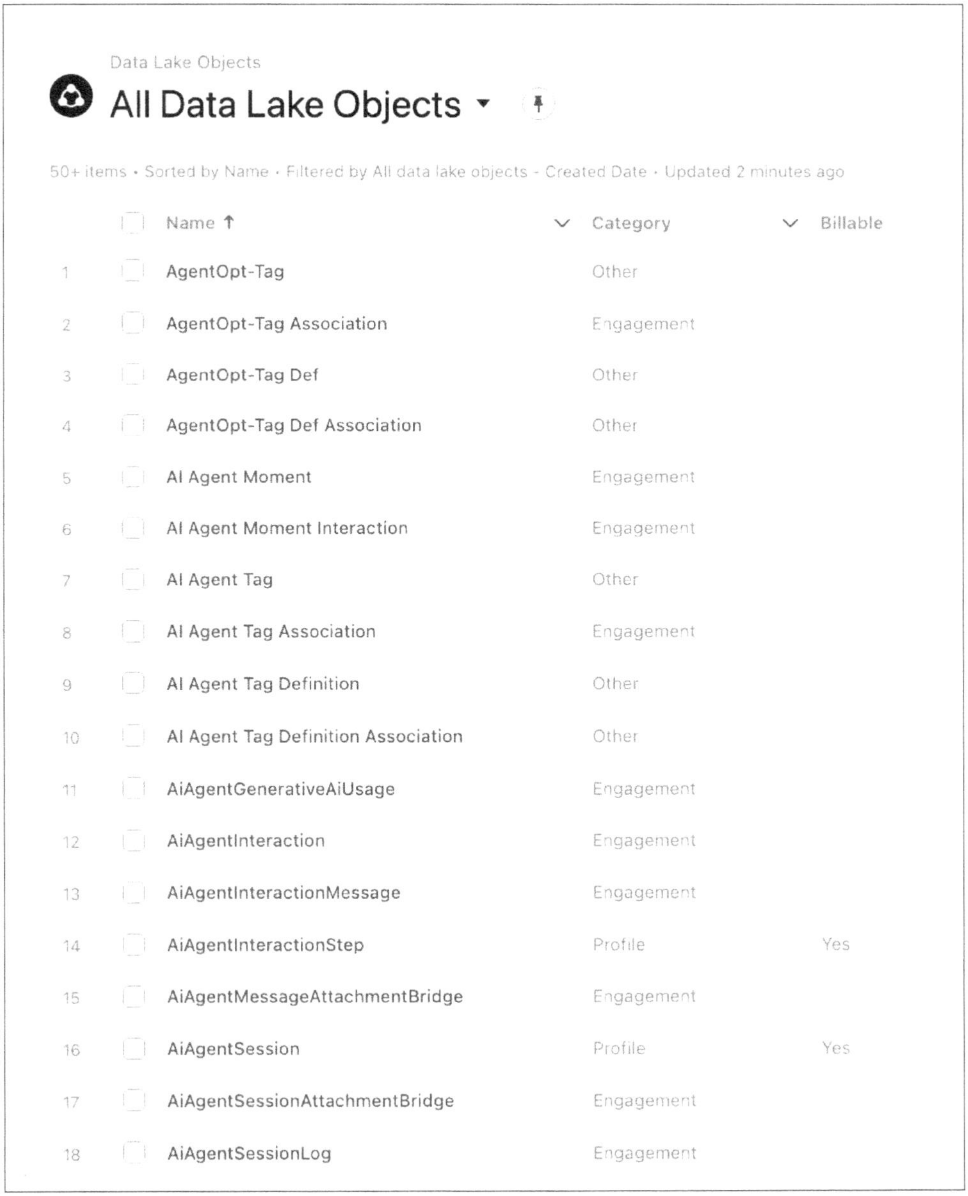

Figure 2-12. New Data 360 objects created when the Agent Optimization feature is enabled

In addition, Salesforce began offering a new D360 DMO in May 2026 called `AiAgentGenerativeAiUsage` to provide information about usage and consumption. Each record in the DMO represents a single interaction event representing details such as whether the interaction was billable, usage quantity, token counts, and identifiers for traceability and audit. You can visit the Salesforce documentation (*https://oreil.ly/vQWMq*) for three use case examples of ad hoc queries: billable usage by agent, token consumption by model, and usage by channel.

Similar to Salesforce core, D360 includes both standard and custom objects. However, a few things are different in D360, most notably Salesforce introduced the concept of Unstructured Data Model Objects (UDMOs) to extend the DMO framework for handling data from external blob stores like Amazon S3 or Azure Blob. Unstructured data includes information from PDFs, images, audio, video, emails, chat transcripts, and more.

Creating UDMOs starts with creating an Unstructured Data Lake Object (UDLO) that points to the files in the blob storage. When the UDLO is mapped to the newly created UDMO, D360 automatically generates the field mappings, chunks, and vector objects. Then the search index is configured on the UDMO for vector search queries. This is possible because of the Hyperforce architecture.

One other important feature of Hyperforce is zero copy interoperability with external warehouses and lakehouses. Because Hyperforce is built on the Apache Iceberg table format, file federation is possible between Salesforce and data lake platforms.

We know that D360 is both a system of reference and a system of context. CRM data is used in creating unified profiles for the D360 system of reference commonly referred to as the CDP. That's only a part of what D360 is built for, though. Earlier, we talked about D360 serving as a system of context for all data types. One of those data types is unstructured data commonly used for content knowledge bases. Therefore, we'd expect to find both Salesforce CRM and content knowledge information in D360 objects.

D360 for Salesforce CRM + Content Knowledge Base

CRM objects hold information about customers and customer-related events like opportunities or cases. CRM data answers many *who*, *what*, or *when* type questions about a specific customer or their deals or support cases. For example, "When was my last touchpoint with Customer X?" or "What products have been returned by our customers the most in the last 90 days?" or "Who is our customer with the highest lifetime value in each region?" Answers to these questions are found in business data.

Enterprises need information to support customers before and after their purchases, though. The information needed for that purpose is commonly referred to as a content knowledge base. A content knowledge base includes information like troubleshooting FAQs, product details, implementation runbooks, or standard operating procedure (SOP) and policy guides.

A content knowledge base commonly answers *how* type questions about how to take a certain action, i.e., what are the specific steps to take, which form is the right one to use, or what department is responsible. A specific question might be "How can I request a change be made to my health insurance policy?" Another example is "What's the next possible action I should take in a situation like this?" These answers can be found in a content knowledge base.

In addition to CRM objects, Salesforce core includes Knowledge objects that can support a content knowledge base for a variety of channels including internal channels for employees, community portals for partners or customers, and public-facing channels. D360 supports ingesting content knowledge from an enterprise's external content knowledge bases, too.

Agents often need to be dynamically grounded in content knowledge bases as well as customer data. This allows the agent to review the facts about the customer then apply procedural guidance from the content knowledge base before responding or taking action. Let's turn our attention now to the enterprise's content knowledge base and its context, which, together, comprise enterprise content information.

Enterprise Content Information

Enterprise content information includes all content knowledge base assets, comprised mostly of unstructured data, and its associated context. Frequently, there is at least one section of an enterprise content knowledge base that is accessible only to employees and enterprise agents. This section may contain intellectual property or other information that an enterprise doesn't want to be made publicly available.

An enterprise's unstructured data documenting an enterprise content knowledge base is usually in PDF files, written articles, images, and videos. These content knowledge base assets hold great value for an enterprise but are infinitely more valuable when there's context associated. Some of the most effective ways context for unstructured data is provided to humans and AI is via taxonomy and search indexes.

Taxonomy management allows grouping of content based on tags associated with categories and/or topics or classifications. This cataloging system of tagging content knowledge base assets helps provide context to human and AI users of the content knowledge base as well as offers one way to restrict access to specific categories or topics. Content tagging can be a manual process or an automated process that occurs during search index creation.

Vector and hybrid search indexes provide valuable context to AI users and are an important component of enterprise knowledge. We've discussed vector and hybrid search indexes earlier. Let's now learn more about what it means to have an enterprise content knowledge base built for customers, employees, and agents. Afterward, we'll explore the Salesforce solution for enterprise knowledge management.

Enterprise Content Knowledge Base for Customers, Employees, and Agents

A content knowledge base stores vast amounts of information for providing answers to questions. The ultimate goal is to quickly retrieve the most relevant information presented the best way possible for the intended audience. Content knowledge bases should be optimized for all audience types including customers who may prefer self-service options. A self-service content knowledge base offers customers access to resources anytime. The added benefit of providing personalized self-service options is that it helps prevent the need to create new support cases, giving service reps more time to handle complex issues.

The intended audience for content knowledge bases includes human users, both internal and external to the enterprise. External users include customers, prospective customers, partners, and others who desire to know more about an enterprise's products or services. This content includes support articles and FAQs designed for public-facing access. Interestingly, an agent can provide personalized content for different personas using the same content knowledge base.

Internal consumers of an enterprise content knowledge base access information about organizational processes and best practices, technical documentation, HR policies, and other repositories helpful for onboarding new employees or maintaining consistency in the enterprise.

Of course, a content knowledge base needs to make it easy for users to find the information quickly. That's where search indexes play a critical role. Thus, it's more important than ever to design content knowledge bases with context. It's also important to create multimodal knowledge content that can be accessed and used by both AI and humans.

Creating Multimodal Knowledge Content for Humans and AI

Multimodal content knowledge bases include images like screenshots and animated GIFs, video, and text. Building a scalable content knowledge base for all audience types and for several modalities isn't a complicated process but does require forethought. Preparing a content knowledge base for humans and AI begins with three best practices:

1. Annotate your media.
2. Create focused, thoroughly explained content that answers common questions, is well-structured, and includes sources.
3. Audit your content knowledge base regularly.

AI grounding requires textual descriptions of visual content for optimal understanding. It's best practice to use alt text as well as image descriptions to explain what's shown in the media content. Image descriptions are often more lengthy than alt text, but it's possible to use the same text for both purposes. If you can only include one of the two but not both, then choose alt text rather than the more lengthy description. Alt text makes knowledge content more accessible for those who use screen readers and can also be effective for AI grounding.

The textual content should be thoroughly explained but focused. Focused content articles cover a single topic or issue, which has several advantages. For one, it's easier to control access. Users are more easily prevented from accessing certain information that's irrelevant to them or inappropriate for them to access for security reasons. It's also easier to know which specific topics are most frequently accessed, which provides valuable information about which content to update and where there might be opportunities to create new content.

When building your content knowledge base from scratch, it's best to begin creating content for the questions most frequently asked by customers and then expand your content knowledge base over time. Creating content that provides value is key, so address topics about the most pressing concerns first and include diverse content formats, if possible and appropriate.

For example, include detailed written step-by-step instructions for specific tasks where the order is important and provide video tutorials when visual guidance is needed. A video demonstrating how to assemble furniture, for example, FAQs that describe how to track an order, and case studies are other popular content formats. Case studies include customer success stories and product use cases. Glossaries are helpful to provide definitions of key terms and industry-specific concepts.

Customer interactions generally come in the form of questions, so it's good practice to identify the question first and then create a detailed response with plenty of specific examples. Err on the side of providing too much information and include technical details if appropriate. AI works best with more complete information so that it can synthesize but then respond to each human differently, depending on the audience.

Like humans, AI prefers well-structured content that includes citations and links to sources. At a high level, the AI needs to know the intended audience and purpose. Specifically, consider whether the article or video is meant for internal employees only or if the content is allowed as public-facing information for generating customer responses. Written content should include grammatically correct sentences and structured paragraphs. It's acceptable to incorporate lists and bullet points when appropriate. Using heading tags like H1 to H6 also helps demonstrate how content is hierarchically related.

Creating an excellent content knowledge base requires more than creating good content because conditions change, making existing articles and media outdated and sometimes incorrect. Superior content knowledge management systems provide options for regularly auditing and updating content knowledge base content.

Humans and AI access an enterprise content knowledge base. Automation features and agents usually access the content knowledge base information directly. Employees responsible for creating and managing content knowledge base content have direct access. However, most human end users connect to the content knowledge base via a user interface with various levels of determinism (Figure 2-13). Human end users include employees needing information for themselves, service rep employees gathering information to support customers, or customers accessing the content knowledge base for self-service.

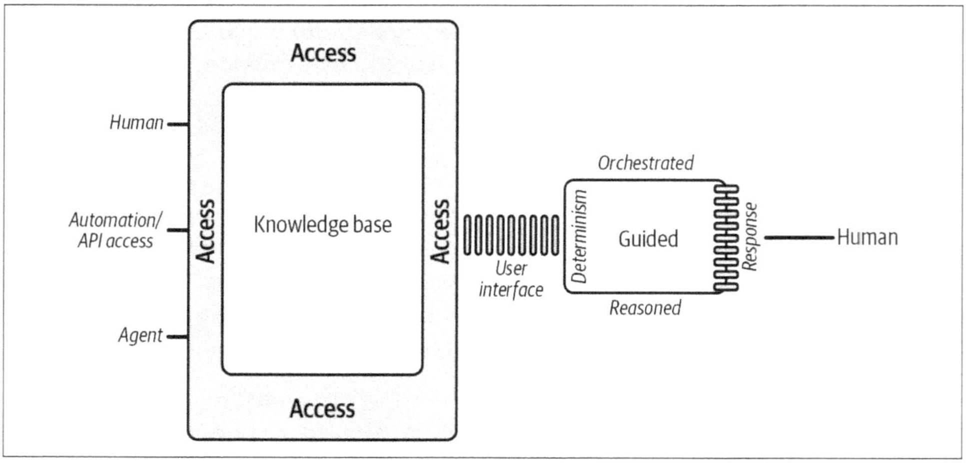

Figure 2-13. Content knowledge base access and use in theory

Now that we have a general understanding about content knowledge bases, let's turn our attention to an example of a content knowledge management system in practice where content knowledge is consumed by users in a variety of different ways.

Salesforce Content Knowledge Base Solutions

Salesforce provides robust content knowledge management capabilities to support several kinds of service use cases. Salesforce's content knowledge base solution is a centralized digital information hub designed to provide answers to questions, help solve issues, and give links to helpful resources. Lightning Knowledge and Enterprise Knowledge products in Salesforce are content knowledge base solutions built for service reps to assist customers. The Agentforce Data Library, built on indexed D360 objects, power the agent actions assigned to agents and chatbots (Figure 2-14).

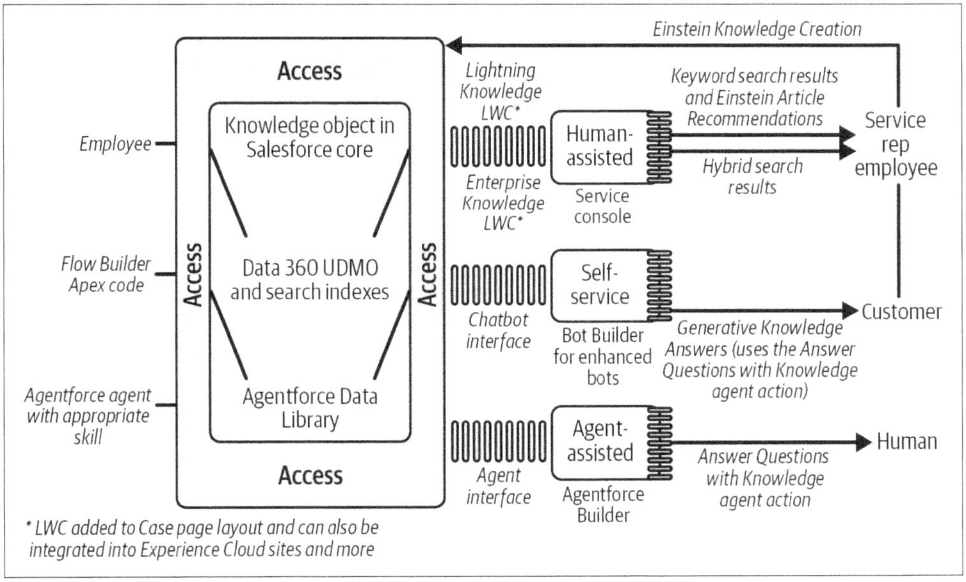

Figure 2-14. Content knowledge base access and use in practice

Content knowledge is delivered to Salesforce employees and customers in many different ways including via interfaces such as Lightning Web Components (LWCs), chatbots, and agents. There are also different options for Knowledge information retrieval and responses. For example, the Lightning Knowledge LWC uses keyword search and the ML predictive capabilities of Einstein Article Recommendations to surface recommended articles in the console. Hybrid search results are used to return articles for Enterprise Knowledge LWC and for Search Answers.

GenAI goes beyond finding *which article is best for answering the question* as is the case with LWC. Instead, Einstein Service Replies and agent actions use GenAI to decide *how to best phrase the answer*, with the response often grounded in multiple articles recommended by the ML predictive model. Chatbots and agents use agent actions leveraging a data library (Figure 2-15).

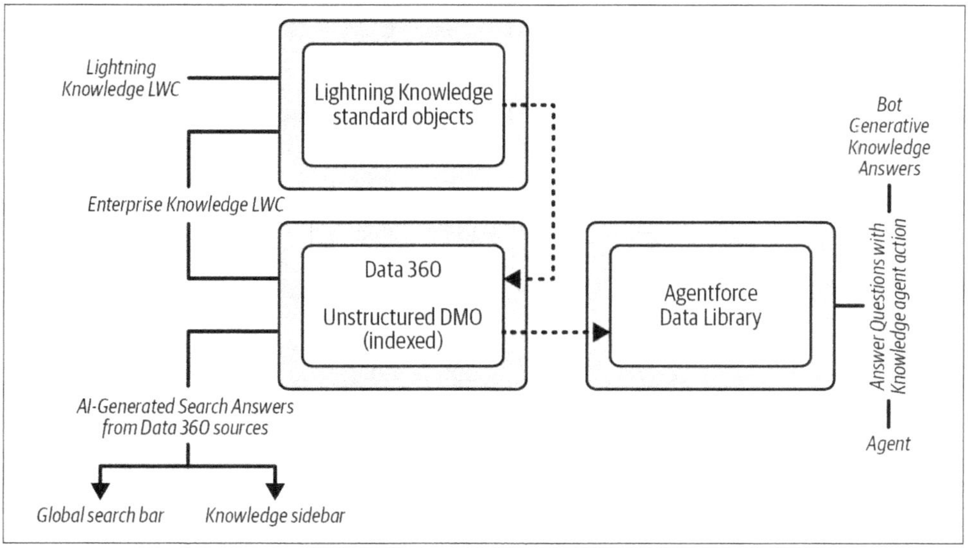

Figure 2-15. Agentforce Data Library used by agent actions

As you're building your content knowledge management strategy, it's important to understand which Salesforce options are available for customer service reps and what opportunities exist to develop self-service chatbots and agents that leverage a content knowledge base. Further, knowing which specific underlying content knowledge data store powers each option helps in deciding which use cases to pursue first as well as for deciding on the most scalable approach.

In the next two sections, there is additional detail about the available options and content knowledge base data stores in Salesforce. The information is broken out between Salesforce Knowledge solutions for customer service reps and for chatbots and agents.

In addition, information about recently retired Salesforce products is included because information about these products and features remains in Salesforce documentation and training materials, and not all enterprises have transitioned to the newer products or features. By including the information in this section and clearly labeling the features as retired, more clarity is provided about what available options can be considered today. However, it's always recommended to speak with your Salesforce AE, who can provide information about the most up-to-date product offerings.

Salesforce Knowledge Elements for Customer Service Reps

Customer service reps using Salesforce have several tools available from which to choose. Lightning Knowledge and Enterprise Knowledge have replaced earlier knowledge bases known as Salesforce Classic Knowledge and Unified Knowledge.

In addition, several new features were introduced to help service reps leverage AI capabilities even more. We'll discuss Einstein Article Recommendations and Einstein Service Replies for Chat and Email, which replaces the Reply Recommendations feature. We'll also learn about AI Grounding and AI-Generated Search Answers from D360, which replaces the Search Answers and AI-Generated Search Answers features from Service Cloud.

Lightning Knowledge and the Lightning Knowledge LWC

Customer service reps access the Lightning Knowledge LWC from the Lightning Service Console. Salesforce users with appropriate access can access the Lightning Knowledge app directly.

Lightning Knowledge is a robust content knowledge management tool accessible by navigating to the Salesforce Knowledge app from the App Launcher. Creating a new knowledge article within the Lightning Knowledge app requires the selection of a record type, such as "How-To," along with filling in information for the title and summary fields.

Properties selected determine whether the article is meant to be visible internally, publicly, or both. The article also needs to be assigned to a category. Another feature, Knowledge Maps, gives users the ability to organize knowledge articles in a hierarchical structure. Although conceptually the same, this approach for creating Lightning Knowledge articles includes more functionality than Salesforce Classic Knowledge, which was retired in March 2026.

> Today's Lightning Knowledge object model (*https://oreil.ly/DIQyU*) is similar to the previous data model. Yet, both function differently from Salesforce standard objects of other features. The Knowledge object model for both Classic and Lightning includes abstract objects not directly used when knowledge articles are created. Instead, records in concrete derivations of the abstract Knowledge objects are created whenever new knowledge articles are created. In Salesforce Classic, the article type determined the article structure, whereas record types are now used to associate articles in Lightning Knowledge.
>
> Being aware of the unique Lightning Knowledge object model is important because these standard objects will be ingested into D360 with the same unique object naming conventions. Thus, it will be easier to understand what's happening with the D360 objects if you're already familiar with the Knowledge standard object data model.

Record types, article properties, categories, and map hierarchy used for Lightning Knowledge are some ways to provide context for humans, especially when they need to filter the list of articles. However, there's a Salesforce feature known as Einstein Article Recommendations that uses a prediction model to suggest the best article to the service rep.

Einstein Article Recommendations

When the Einstein Article Recommendations feature is enabled, a customer service rep sees up to five relevant Lightning Knowledge articles at a time on a case record in the Lightning Service Console. Using the drop-down menu next to each article title, the service rep can elect to attach the article to the case, edit the article, or indicate that the article is not helpful for the case.

An attached knowledge article can then be used to generate a response to the customer using Einstein Service Replies. In that way, Einstein Article Recommendations serves as an input for Einstein Service Replies, a feature powered by GenAI capabilities. Einstein's recommendations refresh within the Lightning Service Console whenever a new case is created or when a field included in the Recommendations model on a case is updated.

In addition to surfacing the Einstein Article Recommendations in the Lightning Service Console, automation features can leverage Einstein Article Recommendations for Flows when sending articles via email to customers. Using this approach is one way to resolve issues proactively.

The Article Recommendations action accepts the Case ID field as input and returns a JSON list of recommendation articles. From there, the flow assigns the output of the action to a collection variable and loops through the collection variables to access the recommended articles and their fields.

Einstein Article Recommendations is powered by a prediction model trained on Knowledge input fields such as subject or description. The model uses supervised learning as it analyzes which Lightning Knowledge articles were attached to a case. The model is then able to score and rank available articles for new cases. The prediction model improves when obsolete articles are updated or removed and if input fields are standardized. For example, using macros or quick texts for input fields helps the prediction model.

Using the curated content of articles attached to the case, GenAI tools in Salesforce can be used to draft an email or chat reply the customer service rep approves as a response to customers. The service rep can approve the response as is or edit the draft before sending it to the customer.

Einstein Service Replies for Chat and Email

Einstein for Replies features help service reps respond quicker and with more personalized content. Einstein Article Recommendations serves as the input for Einstein Service Replies. The Einstein Service Replies feature leverages GenAI to assist service reps as they reply in real time to customers during chats. Einstein Service Replies can also be used by service reps to quickly generate email responses based on an existing Lightning Knowledge article.

Although Einstein Service Replies works out-of-the-box, a Salesforce admin can customize the Service Replies prompt templates in Agentforce Prompt Builder (Prompt Builder) to specify what information Einstein includes or adjust the voice and tone so that responses better fit an enterprise's needs.

> The Service Replies feature and the Reply Recommendations feature can't be used simultaneously. Enabling Service Replies, the newer feature, replaces an existing Reply Recommendations setup if it exists.

Einstein Generative AI needs to be enabled for Einstein Service Replies. In addition, Service Replies for Email requires Lightning Knowledge be enabled and the Knowledge LWC be added to the Case page layout. Lightning Knowledge is recommended but not required for Service Replies for Chat.

The Service Replies for Chat feature can be used by a service rep from within the Lightning Service Console where they can review, edit, and then post replies generated by Einstein. Or, a service rep could reject Einstein's reply and provide feedback.

Einstein analyzes a chat as it unfolds in the Live Chat or Enhanced Messaging session and drafts suggested replies based on the chat context. Einstein can also obtain more context from an assigned data library.

To check whether replies come from conversation context or whether they're grounded in a data library, the service rep can look below each reply for more information. Chat replies grounded in Lightning Knowledge base are shown first. The service rep can click Knowledge to see the Einstein article used as a source for the reply. They can also edit the article and publish updates to the article.

The Service Replies for Email feature can also be used by a service rep from within the Lightning Service Console. While in the console, the service rep reviews the recommended knowledge article shown on the case record and confirms the article selection or chooses a different knowledge article. Einstein then drafts an email response based on the chosen knowledge article.

The service rep reviews and edits the Einstein-generated email response. The final draft is then sent out by the service rep from Salesforce using the Lightning email composer. Alternatively, the user can copy and paste the final email draft into an outside email provider.

Unified Knowledge (retired June 2026)

Unified Knowledge was a Service Cloud product that allowed users to ingest documents from third-party systems into the Salesforce Knowledge object as knowledge articles. External source connectors included SharePoint, Confluence, Google Drive, and more. Currently, Salesforce users should now utilize D360 connectors to ingest and store content knowledge assets in indexed UDMOs.

Enterprise Knowledge and the Enterprise LWC

Enterprise Knowledge previously included access to Unified Knowledge but that feature retired in June 2026. Today, Enterprise Knowledge provides a comprehensive content knowledge base to Salesforce users by accessing both the Lightning Knowledge assets in Salesforce core and the indexed UDMO objects from D360.

The Enterprise Knowledge LWC can be added to the Lightning Service Console where it displays two separate related lists: Salesforce Standard and Enterprise Knowledge. The Enterprise Knowledge LWC uses hybrid search to return results. Service reps using the Enterprise Knowledge LWC can also use Einstein Knowledge Creation.

Einstein Knowledge Creation

A content knowledge base is built by creating individual documents known as knowledge articles. Of course, knowledge articles can be written by experienced service reps and internal human writers. However, there's a real advantage to also using Einstein to help grow a content knowledge base because knowledge articles authored by Einstein are generated quickly and written concisely.

It's possible to grow your content knowledge base efficiently with AI-generated article drafts by allowing Einstein to check existing articles first, then draft relevant articles based on a conversation between a service rep and a customer. After Einstein drafts the article, a service rep can review, edit, and save the article before submitting it for approval. In addition, service reps can leverage the Einstein Knowledge edits feature to revise fields on existing articles based on predefined styles meant to improve the grammar, conciseness, or readability of Knowledge articles.

The Einstein Knowledge Creation feature can be used from the Messaging or Live Chat page. It's also accessible from the quick action menu or from the Knowledge component on the Case record page. Once the service rep selects Draft Knowledge Article, the option appears for the user to draft manually or draft with Einstein. Einstein Knowledge Creation considers different information depending on the location where the draft request was made and whether the Salesforce org has Service AI Grounding set up.

If a service rep makes the request from the Case page and Service AI Grounding is set up, Einstein drafts an article based on case emails, case comments, and case fields in addition to the conversation data. If a Salesforce org doesn't have Service AI Grounding set up, Einstein considers only the conversation data from Live Chat transcripts and Messaging sessions. If a service rep initiates the request from the Message page or Live Chat page using the Knowledge component, Einstein considers only the current completed conversation. Thus, it's important to consider what context to provide Einstein for the desired article.

Service AI Grounding

Salesforce Service AI Grounding informs Einstein for Service which case data and content knowledge information to use when generating summaries or replies for email and chat. After enabling Service AI Grounding, a user selects Knowledge and Case fields for Einstein to use. Title, summary, and key custom fields are most often selected for the Knowledge object articles, whereas subject, description, and comments are frequently selected for Case object records. Selected fields are then indexed.

The Salesforce Case object is used to ground responses for Case Summaries, Knowledge Creation, Service Planner, and Service Replies for Email. The Knowledge object is used to ground responses for Service Replies for Email.

At this time, Service AI Grounding uses Case and Knowledge objects in Salesforce core where the Agentforce Data Library uses D360 indexed UDMOs. However, it's recommended you check Salesforce documentation for the most current information about Service AI Grounding data and information sources.

AI-Generated Search Answers from Data 360 sources

The AI-Generated Search Answers from D360 feature replaces the Search Answers and the AI-Generated Search Answers features from Service Cloud, both of which used the standard Knowledge object as the data source. The AI-Generated Search Answers from D360 feature uses up to five specified D360 DMOs to answer questions. The feature is accessible from the global search bar in Salesforce and via the Knowledge app sidebar. Note that the D360 AI-Generated Search Answers feature impacts credit consumption, unlike the Search Answers and AI-Generated Search Answers features it replaces.

Salesforce Knowledge Elements for Agents and Chatbots

Salesforce chatbots and agents access knowledge base information through an Agentforce agent action that provides access to a data library built from D360 objects. Let's learn more about the Agentforce Data Library as well as the specific agent action built for answering content knowledge–related questions in agents and chatbots.

Agentforce Data Library

Agentforce's Data Library makes curated collections of data available to agent actions assigned to the library. Flows, Apex, and other automation tools can't reference a data library directly but can call an agent action to search for information using the library. The Agentforce Data Library leverages D360's vector embeddings and indexing to provide trusted data sources to agent actions.

The Agentforce Data Library makes it easy to create curated collections because it automates the configuration steps needed to create and map D360 objects as well as to chunk the information and create search indexes for Knowledge articles, fields, file uploads, or web sources. After the search index is ready, a unique retriever is created for each data library. A search index can be referenced by one or more different retrievers. When reviewing retrievers in D360, you'll notice retriever names include prefixes automatically generated by the system to indicate the data source is either a file, Knowledge article, or website.

Custom retrievers can also be used as an Agentforce Data Library source in addition to knowledge articles, files, and web sources. This allows for more data source types, including connecting to companion D360 orgs' data libraries. Data libraries can be created or managed within the Agentforce Data Library section accessible to Salesforce users with access to Setup. Afterward, the specific data library can be selected for use with an agent action that can be assigned to an agent or used in an enhanced chatbot created with Einstein Bot Builder (Bot Builder). Creating a custom agent action isn't necessary because the Answer Questions with Knowledge action is available out-of-the-box as a prompt template.

Answer Questions with Knowledge agent action

The Answer Questions with Knowledge agent action uses hybrid search to locate relevant knowledge articles from the assigned data library and then drafts a conversational answer to the question. This is in contrast to simply returning article links, article summaries, or selected sections of one or more articles. This agent action is assigned to a subagent, which is then assigned to an agent.

> If the Answer Questions with Knowledge agent action doesn't appear when trying to assign the action to a subagent, check to make sure the action isn't already assigned to another subagent in the same agent. Only one subagent per agent can use the Answer Questions with Knowledge action.

This agent action doesn't necessarily have to be assigned to a subagent. It can be called from a chatbot step action known as Generative Knowledge Answers, which is available for use with enhanced chatbots. The standard Answer Questions with Knowledge prompt template can be customized if more personalization is desired.

For example, it's possible to change the data library details or the tone and response length. You can even decide which metadata to include in the response. Examples of metadata that can be included in the response are article titles and links or disclaimers.

This is key functionality for any agent or chatbot. Later, we'll see an example of how this works in practice when we explore how the same Salesforce content knowledge base provides personalized experiences for different users who visit the Salesforce website.

Generative Knowledge Answers for Bot Builder

The Generative Knowledge Answers feature brings GenAI capabilities into an enhanced bot created with Bot Builder by using the Answer Questions with Knowledge agent action. Alternatively, you could instead use a custom agent action with the Generative Knowledge Answers feature, rather than the Answer Questions with Knowledge action. However, whichever agent action is assigned to the Generative Knowledge Answers action step can't be changed later.

The Generative Knowledge Answers action step controls when the chatbot is allowed to use the agent action to generate answers using the Agentforce Data Library. In addition, enhanced chatbots automatically call the Generative Knowledge Answers step when a user asks the chatbot a question that doesn't match any dialog. This results in the agent action searching the assigned data library for information that can be used for a response.

Article Answers for Bots (retired September 2026)

Article Answers was a feature available in Bot Builder and used in Einstein Bots to develop responses from information available in the Lightning Knowledge base. Whenever a chatbot couldn't match a customer input to an intent, Article Answers performed an AI-powered search of Knowledge articles leveraging keyword search and prediction models to select the best article. However, that's not an ideal approach, especially given that knowledge content can be dynamically grounded using vector embeddings and indexes. Thus, the retirement of this feature.

Enterprise Intelligence of Employees and Agents

Enterprises commonly view all files, explanatory articles, how-to videos, and other know-how as intangible assets. Human decision-making context is often missing from these assets despite being strategically valuable. The same is true of agent accumulated context, which is a newer element. Together, human decision-making context and agent accumulated context are the enterprise intelligence (Figure 2-16) portion of the intelligent agentic enterprise powered by AI.

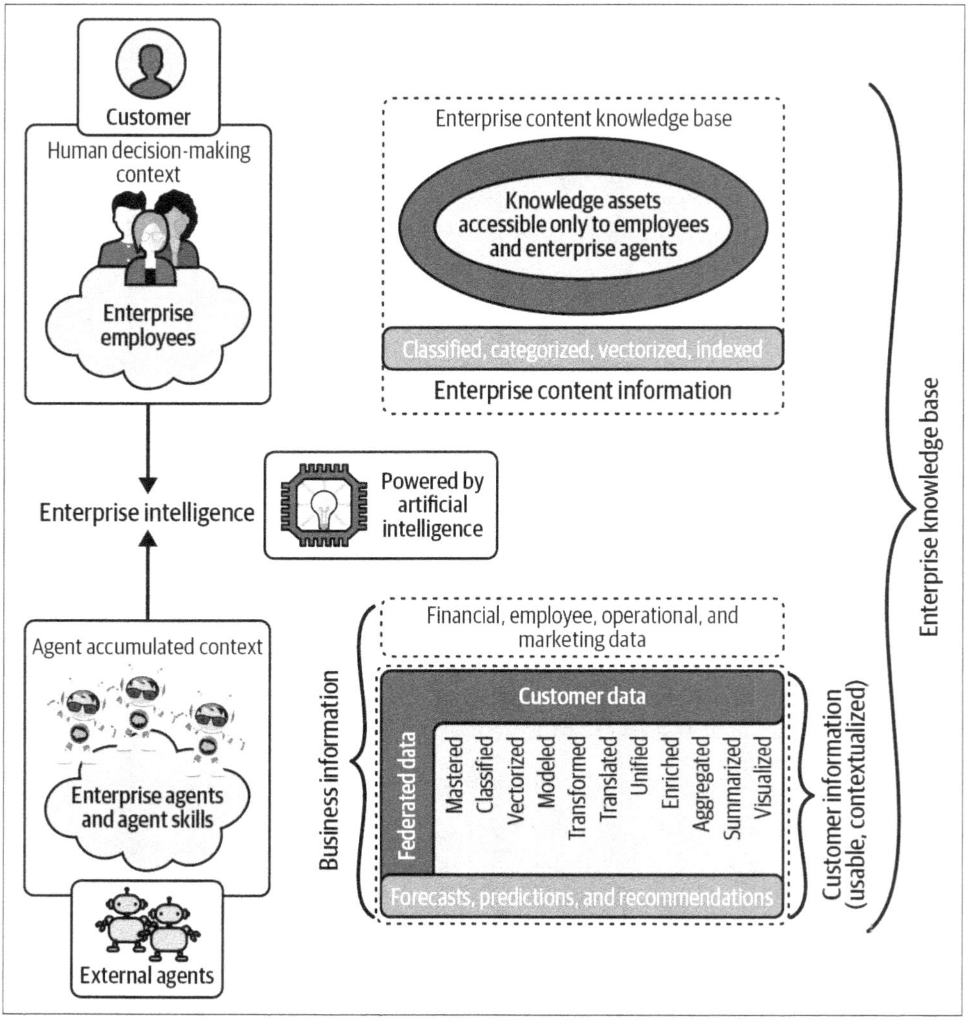

Figure 2-16. Intelligent agentic enterprise powered by AI

It's rare for enterprises to leverage human decision-making context as a strategic asset because decision making is often an unstructured process, which makes it difficult and time-consuming to document. However, recording human decision-making context in the flow of work is an effective way to increase enterprise intelligence. Enterprise intelligence also improves when agents become more intelligent.

We said earlier that five main elements are needed for an agent to mimic how humans perform tasks. An agent needs two more elements to be considered an *intelligent* agent within an agentic enterprise. It's the agent accumulated context and knowledge base context that gives agents increased abilities to perceive or infer information. Those increased abilities make the agent more intelligent and, thus, more likely to provide better responses:

- LLM brain
- *Agent accumulated context*
- *Knowledge base context*
- Knowledge base (business data + content knowledge base)
- Memory system
- Tools and functions
- Human-to-agent interfaces

An intelligent agentic enterprise makes use of intelligent agents and captures human decision-making context to become more intelligent over time. Let's explore agent accumulated context and human decision-making context, otherwise known as enterprise intelligence.

Employees generally come to an organization with experience, training, and acquired skills. Agents come pretrained on massive datasets containing a broad base of general knowledge. Agents become specialized when assigned agent skills by employees. Qualified employees and trained agents are given access to a subset of business information and enterprise content information for better context before generating insights, making decisions, or taking actions.

Improving the quality of insights and decisions first requires an understanding of how they were generated. Recording details about the process provides opportunities to reuse successful processes and improve outcomes. In that way, enterprise intelligence increases incrementally from capturing important details and building on past successes.

Lessons learned help reduce repeated mistakes by employees and agents. It's also easier for employees and agents to offer suggestions or make decisions more consistent with enterprise standards and workplace norms. This leads to more focused training for individual employees and better calibration of internally architected agents. Enterprise intelligence thus increases exponentially as employees and agents become more knowledgeable and more skilled.

Leveling up enterprise intelligence assumes a solid foundation of good business data with valuable insights and a well-documented and easily searchable knowledge base. Even the best skilled employees and agents can't make intelligent decisions without relevant, reliable, accurate, and timely information.

Let's move on to explore agent accumulated context and briefly discuss human decision-making context. We'll consider unified governance for humans and agents at the chapter's end.

Agent Accumulated Context

Agent accumulated context in Agentforce is the set of signals shaping how agents interpret intent, choose features, and determine what actions to take in the correct order. Agents rely on context-rich data and knowledge, as well as assigned skills and calibrated context, to go beyond providing static answers.

For example, a chatbot with access to agent actions can expertly respond to many questions about an enterprise's knowledge base. In contrast, an analytics and visualization agent prepares, models, visualizes, diagnoses root cause, and proposes next best actions in its response to an analytical question. Both solutions leverage data and information context provided within D360. One difference is that an agent may be assigned multiple Agentforce skills and its assigned skill(s) could be robust and include many agent actions. Some agents, like the analytics and visualization agent, can be calibrated by users to receive more intelligence.

Semantic models and search indexes are considered part of an enterprise knowledge base, and they're accessible by Salesforce automation features like flows and chatbots as well as by Agentforce agents. Different from automation features, individual agents can reason and they have unique accumulated context. This is especially true if an agent is calibrated or provided with informed business preferences that include specific details at a business unit level.

In addition, Salesforce users can leverage agent observability and analytics tools to identify business process inefficiencies. Agentforce Observability provides aggregated performance metrics as well as session-level insights, including user feedback. Agentforce session tracing provides granular details about an agent's interactions, which helps users optimize agent configurations to improve performance. Session tracing includes the thumbs-up and thumbs-down information from users who provide feedback about an agent's response.

> Accumulated context matters because it's where the most business value and risk exist in an agent. Thus, it's recommended to treat an agent's accumulated context as a first-class knowledge asset needing to be documented, versioned, and governed.

Consider our analytics and visualization agent we've discussed throughout the chapter. For that agent, let's explore what a lightweight approach to governance might look like if we treated the agent's accumulated context as a first-class knowledge asset (Table 2-2).

Table 2-2. Lightweight approach to governance for analytics and visualization agent

Layer	Ownership	Salesforce tools/features	Artifacts
Semantic	Data and Analytics Governance team	D360 Semantic Model Builder, Tableau Next	Semantic models, metrics, hierarchies, business preferences, Q&A calibration
Agent	Enterprise or IT Operations team	Agentforce Builder, Prompt Builder	Agent subagents and actions, agent guardrails
Observability	AI Platform or AI Enablement team	Agentforce Observability	Session tracing, Agentforce Observability, Tableau Next user feedback (thumbs-up/thumbs-down), cost consumption
Governance	Enterprise Governance team	MuleSoft Agent Fabric	Agent context catalog

A Data and Analytics Governance team assumes responsibility for the semantic layer and thus would be responsible for versioning semantic models and business preferences. They'd communicate major changes to business users, recertify dashboards, and request agent recalibration. The Data and Analytics team would be responsible for periodically performing Q&A calibration on the agent to improve its responses.

The Enterprise IT team is responsible for assigning and limiting skills to an agent and creating new Agentforce subagents and actions. This gives an agent context access and clear goals. Salesforce provides a number of prebuilt agent skills architected around users' workflows. A new analytics and visualization agent has access to three Agentforce skills out-of-the-box, so consider these skills first before building new ones. Those agent skills, discussed in detail in Chapter 4, support conversational and agentic AI for Tableau Next users.

An AI Platform or Enablement team utilizes Agentforce Observability where they monitor agent performance to detect high escalation rates and coverage gaps where the agent frequently provides no response. This team also uses Observability dashboards to identify agents that consume excess credits relative to the business impact.

An Enterprise Governance team reviews all requests for new agents including new analytics and visualization agents. The Governance team considers the risk of proposed agents, especially those that would be assigned skills relating to high-risk areas like pricing or compliance. This team also assumes responsibility for monitoring the agent context catalog used to document which agents are assigned particular skills, what agents have access to certain semantic models, and what business preferences are included.

In essence, the agent context catalog explains in detail the agent accumulated context (Figure 2-17) for each agent. That way, it's easier to understand why a particular agent makes certain decisions or undertakes particular actions.

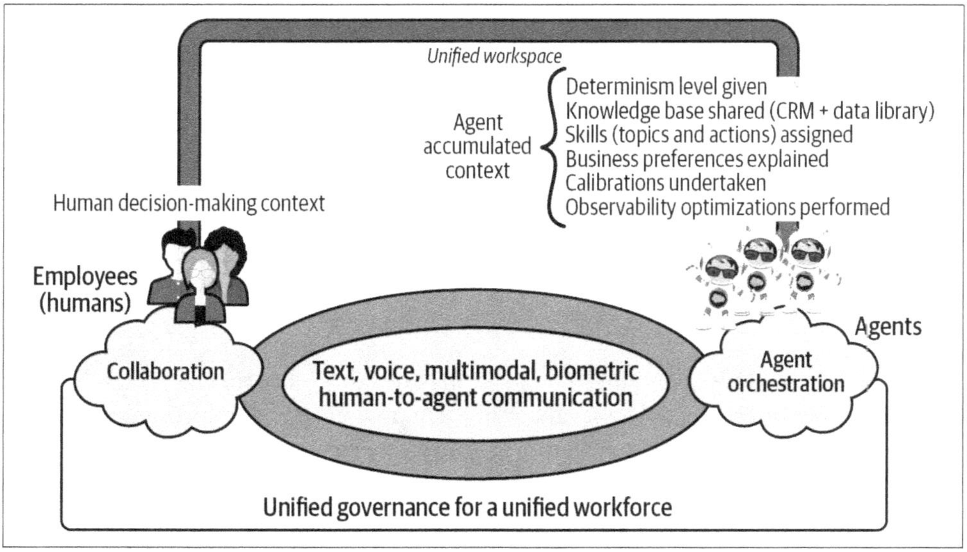

Figure 2-17. Agent accumulated context

Governance discussions about the plan for each agent's accumulated context should be held before agents are built and access to the agent given to human users or other agents. Yet, building governance policies and controls separately for agents and humans isn't necessarily the most effective approach. Rather than a separate AI governance layer created after the fact, it's better to consider a unified governance approach for humans and agents.

Humans are ultimately responsible for agents' actions. Thus, it's important to understand the rationale behind decisions made about an agent. An agent context catalog provides documentation about context given to an agent and it may even include the justification for assigning certain context. Knowing why an agent was not given a particular context is also important.

Human Decision-Making Context

Human decision-making context goes beyond explaining decisions. It includes the rationale and intent behind decisions. This is important especially because some decisions are made about topics where there's not always a consensus due to competing business priorities and ethical considerations.

Capturing human decision-making context as decisions are made creates an easier way for new employees or employees new to a team to get involved in the conversation right away. Slackbot, for example, can provide a summary of Slack threads within a channel when employees just need the highlights to get up to speed quickly. Slackbot, touted by Salesforce as the *personal AI agent for work*, is grounded in Slack channels and threads in a workspace where it accesses messages, user interactions, and conversation history.

In addition, capturing human decision-making context provides an immutable audit trail that justifies decisions. It can also provide information about the circumstances under which human judgment was used to override agent-recommended operational decisions. This audit trail helps satisfy certain regulations like the General Data Protection Regulation (GDPR) *right to explanation* or SOC 2 audit requirements.

Collaboration tools like Slack allow users to document decisions in dedicated channels like `#agent-build-analytics-agent` where humans with authority can approve an agent's access to data libraries or establish guardrails to support engineering service-level agreements (SLAs), for example.

Slack is the system of engagement for human collaboration and, in many cases, is becoming the place where employees actually complete tasks in their normal flow of work. That's because the integration between Slack and Salesforce core makes it possible for users to review customer information, query content knowledge bases, view analytics dashboards, and update Salesforce CRM records all from within a Slack workspace.

Slack users and Agentforce agents can search through knowledge stored in other enterprise sources outside of Slack. This means Slack users have the information needed to discuss options and make decisions quickly within a Slack workspace. For example, enterprise search capabilities support Slack users searching other collaboration tools, file storage systems, code repositories, and more:

- Collaboration tools such as Asana, Confluence Cloud, Jira Cloud, and Microsoft Teams
- File storage systems including Box, Dropbox, Google Drive, OneDrive, and SharePoint
- Code/Dev repositories like GitHub
- Salesforce CRM
- Proprietary knowledge bases and internal wikis accessible via API

Slack provides tools to easily capture rich human decision-making context, and Slack users can be granted access to Slackbot, Agentforce agents, and external agents, all accessible from within the Slack workspace. That's one of the real value propositions of Slack; it can serve as an enterprise's agentic hub.

In March 2026, Salesforce announced a collaboration with NVIDIA to support reference architecture whereby Slack serves as the primary conversational interface and orchestration layer for Agentforce agents. This makes it possible for users in regulated industries, such as financial services and healthcare, to deploy governed

Agentforce agents to be used directly in the flow of work within Slack. Slackbot acts as the coordination layer in an enterprise agentic hub.

Documenting human decision-making context is important when planning for and implementing agents because documentation supports iterative improvements. Humans can better calibrate and refine agents by revisiting the context about the agent. For example, understanding why a specific guardrail was set helps to know whether it's still appropriate when an enterprise's circumstances change. Capturing human decision-making context also makes it easier to confirm decisions are made in accordance with enterprise policies and procedures and that employees are following recommended best practices.

An enterprise's policies and procedures set forth by the governance team need to adequately cover both humans and agents. Given the ever-growing capabilities of agents and how much interaction there is between agents and employees, it's important to approach the topic of enterprise governance holistically using a unified governance approach. We'll discuss governance in more detail in Chapter 12.

Summary

In this chapter, we reviewed some important AI concepts and learned about Data 360, the gateway to building the foundation in an intelligent agentic enterprise powered by Salesforce AI. We also discovered the importance of building context on top of data and knowledge content so that it gives us actionable insights.

Now that we have an understanding of foundational elements, let's turn our attention to exploring some Salesforce tools we'll use to build context and generate insights. In the next chapter, we'll take a deep dive into the AI Model Builder tool and learn how it's used to build and train predictive models from scratch. We'll walk through the steps for creating insights with top predictors and prescriptions after we've produced context with predictions generated from the activated predictive model we've built and trained.

CHAPTER 3

Building Predictive Models for Greater Intelligent Foresight

Salesforce launched AI within its CRM platform in 2016, giving companies the ability to use predictive analytics without the need for the technical expertise and infrastructure typically required to deliver such robust AI solutions. Prebuilt predictive models for lead scoring and opportunity scoring were made available out-of-the-box to Salesforce users. Einstein Prediction Builder (Prediction Builder) and Einstein Next Best Action (Next Best Action) no-code tools also allowed users to quickly create custom prediction models and receive suggested next actions.

However, these powerful machine learning tools for predictive analytics capabilities introduced in 2016 have been retired in 2026 to align with a shift to focus on a Data 360 (D360) strategy. This is because new tools were needed once D360 made data unification possible at an enterprise level. Thus, Salesforce introduced AI Model Builder in 2023 so that users could continue building predictive models from scratch.

> AI Models offers other features that we won't focus on in this chapter. For example, it's possible for users to connect to machine learning models they've already built on external platforms like Amazon SageMaker or Vertex AI. Within AI Models, users can also connect to large language models (LLMs) from providers like OpenAI.

AI Model Builder looks and feels somewhat familiar to users with experience using Prediction Builder for building a prediction model from scratch. The training metrics provided for both are comparable although AI Model Builder is clearly a more advanced tool. The data source used to train the predictive model is different, however. Prediction Builder used CRM records whereas AI Model Builder uses D360 objects. The most important differences between AI Model Builder and Prediction Builder functionality, though, are how the predictive model results are consumed and operationalized. Later in the chapter we'll explore in detail the many ways AI Model Builder results are used in an intelligent agentic enterprise.

We'll discover how AI Model Builder predictive models built from scratch give us diagnostic, predictive, and prescriptive analytical results such as top predictors, predictions, and prescriptions. These observations aren't just surfaced in CRM records like the Prediction Builder outputs. Instead, the results offer multiple actionability options and make real-time personalization possible for customers. These traditional analytics outputs also support conversational analytics and agentic analytics. AI Model Builder is a critical component of the intelligent agentic enterprise, and it relies on data from D360 to create predictions and recommendations (Figure 3-1).

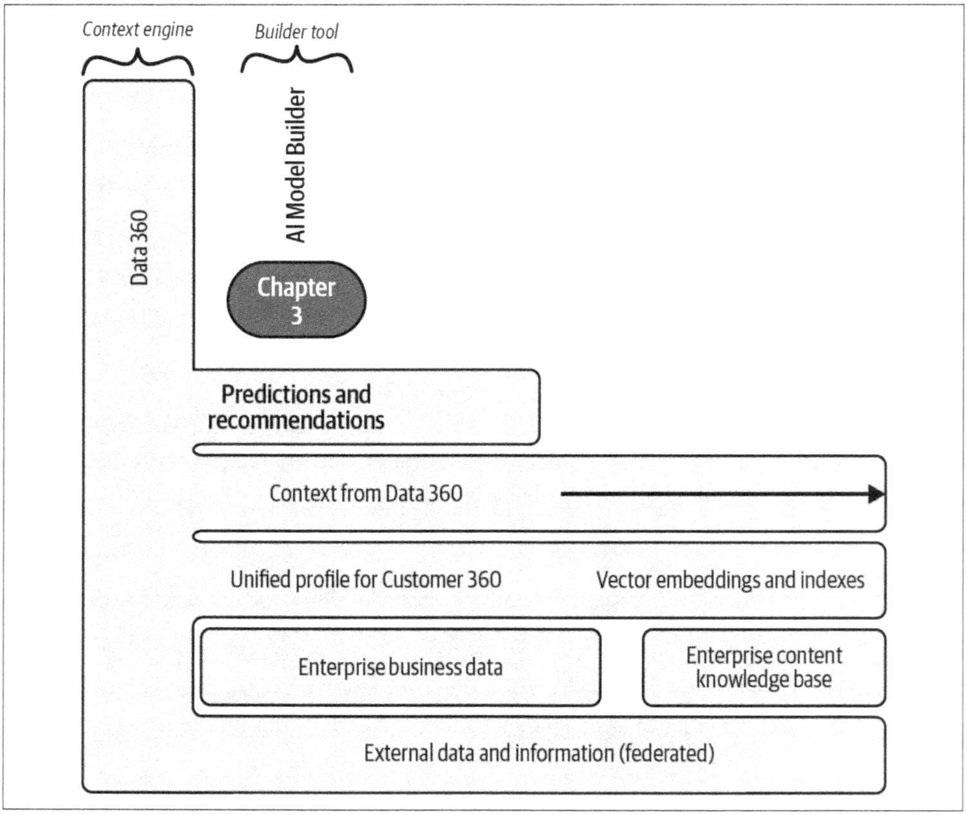

Figure 3-1. AI Model Builder makes use of data from Data 360 to create predictions and recommendations

The predictive AI models built from scratch in AI Model Builder provide actionable results for humans and AI agents (agents). In later chapters, we'll learn more about the ways predictive analytics are used for conversational and agentic analytics. The AI Model Builder predictive model offers a broad scope of available actions because of its ability to be tailored to many different questions relevant for business users.

In this chapter, we'll discuss how the predictive model results can be consumed by automation tools and agents so that humans and agents can use the insights to take action. But first we'll learn how to build the predictive model in AI Model Builder, evaluate the results and improve the model, and then integrate prescriptions into the predictive model.

Getting Started

Let's discuss some background knowledge and some things you should know to help you get the most out of the chapter.

Background Knowledge

Machine learning (ML) is a type of AI that leverages historical data to surface insights, allowing enterprises to make faster, better informed decisions. ML algorithms work on both structured and unstructured data to identify meaningful patterns, detect anomalies, and power predictive models.

There are three ML categories: reinforcement, unsupervised, and supervised learning. In reinforcement learning scenarios, the model attempts to take the best possible action in a given situation through trial and error. The algorithm "learns" by getting feedback on its past outcomes. Training a robot to walk without falling is an example of an application for reinforcement learning.

Unsupervised learning algorithms often use clustering to identify hidden patterns and natural groupings within data. Examples where unsupervised learning techniques excel with business tasks include personalized recommendation systems.

Supervised learning solves linear regression and classification problems. Regression fits a line through continuous data points in an attempt to predict numerical values. It can answer questions that need a numerical response:

- "What is the lifetime value of a customer?"
- "What is the expected revenue for this quarter?"
- "How many days will an opportunity take to close (sales cycle length)?"

In contrast, classification uses a decision boundary to separate data into classes. Multiclass models allow you to classify data into one of three or more classes. Binary classification separates the data into two distinct classes such as "yes" or "no":

- "Is this customer likely to cancel their subscription or renew it?"
- "Is the lead likely to convert?"
- "Will this opportunity result in a 'closed won' or a 'closed lost' status?"

In this chapter, we'll focus on the ML supervised learning category. Specifically, we'll learn how to leverage Salesforce's binary classification and linear regression capabilities to power predictive models built from scratch within AI Model Builder. Here are some additional resources if you'd like to explore the topic of machine learning further:

- *Designing Machine Learning Systems* by Chip Huyen (O'Reilly, 2022)
- *Soccer Analytics with Machine Learning* by Haipeng Gao, Ari Joury, Weining Shen, and Guanyu Hu (O'Reilly, 2026)
- *Machine Learning Design Patterns* by Valliappa Lakshmanan, Sara Robinson, and Michael Munn (O'Reilly, 2020)

> Multiclass models functionality became available in AI Model Builder in May 2026. This functionality allows for classifying data into up to 50 distinct categories. Multiclass models functionality is an excellent option for case classification, often a Service Cloud high-frequency automation requirement.

We'll also discover how to enable the AI Model Builder predictive model to obtain prescriptions, suggested actions identified by the model that could be undertaken to potentially improve the outcome.

What You Should Know

AI Model Builder, the Salesforce tool used to create ML models from scratch, is accessible from the AI Models tab within the D360 application. Alternatively, you can use the App Launcher to select AI Models, which will take you to the tab within D360.

> In April 2026, *Einstein Studio* was renamed to *AI Models* in D360.

The focus in this chapter is on the AI Model Builder capabilities that allow users to build their own predictive AI model using AI Model Builder. In addition to the AI Model Builder capabilities covered in this chapter, Salesforce offers Einstein Discovery for machine learning (ML). Both Einstein Discovery and AI Model Builder use machine learning to analyze data, predict outcomes, and suggest things that can be undertaken to improve the outcome. There are important differences between the two ML offerings, especially relating to model creation and integration, but the most important differences are in how the results are operationalized.

Einstein Discovery is integrated with CRM Analytics (CRMA) and gets its input data from CRM Analytics datasets or templates. AI Model Builder is integrated with D360 and gets its input data from Data Model Objects (DMOs). In addition, AI Model Builder supports third-party model integrations with Amazon SageMaker, Google Vertex AI, and Databricks.

Einstein Discovery ML insights are primarily embedded in CRMA dashboards, whereas predictive results from models built from scratch in AI Model Builder are consumed in a variety of ways so that they can be operationalized and used in the normal flow of work. For example, the predictions can even be retrieved directly from within an Agentforce agent action using a new reference action type. Later, in "Consuming Prediction Results from the Activated Model" on page 97, we'll describe in detail how the predictive results from models built from scratch in AI Model Builder are operationalized.

ML tools give better operational results when they're given better data on which to train. AI Model Builder is no exception. Building a predictive model from scratch in AI Model Builder requires choosing the right variables and giving the model accurate and complete data representative of your organization's business operations. This is where business domain specialists have an advantage because they can help determine whether data points deviating significantly from other observations in the dataset are outliers that indicate faulty data or whether they're indicative of something else to be investigated further. In general, linear regression models used to predict numerical values are more sensitive to outliers than binary classification models.

For the predictive model built within AI Model Builder, one D360 DMO that stores the outcome variable is selected as the root DMO. Data from the root DMO, along with data from any related DMO, can be used to train the model. Note that the model only supports DMOs or Calculated Insights objects that have a one-to-one rather than a one-to-many relationship.

It's important to ensure the root and related DMOs used for the predictive model are optimized for model training. Many tools and capabilities within the D360 platform allow users to prepare and model data to form a single, denormalized DMO. Once the model is trained, it can accept input from many other different data sources to provide predictive outcomes.

> Your enterprise's data governance and privacy standards should be followed when selecting data used in a predictive model, whether for training the model or for predicting observation outcomes.

Throughout Salesforce tools and within the Salesforce documentation, there is some terminology that is not congruent. For example, AI Model Builder uses the term "prescriptions" whereas Flow Builder uses the term "recommendations." Thus, some screenshots included in this chapter still have legacy terms that Salesforce is in the process of updating. Those will be called out when appropriate.

There are other terms in the chapter used interchangeably because they refer to the same thing. For example, Salesforce objects and fields are the equivalent of a database table and table column. Thus, a DMO is synonymous with a database table. When we discuss machine learning "variables," we're referring to Salesforce fields. Each individual Salesforce record is a row that is the equivalent of a machine learning observation in a training set or a prediction. The next section includes a brief terminology explanation list to which you can refer, as needed.

There is one final important note. This chapter describes the AI Model Builder predictive AI capabilities for building and managing predictive AI models from scratch. The chapter doesn't discuss which specific licenses or packages must be purchased or which permission sets are required. You'll want to discuss those topics with your Salesforce Account Executive (AE). In addition, billing considerations for predictive models in AI Models are not discussed in this chapter. Data services usage for predictive models are calculated based on a number of factors including the usage type. Refer to Salesforce documentation (*https://oreil.ly/816mP*) for billing considerations for using predictive AI models in AI Model Builder.

AI Model Builder and Predictive AI Overview

Organizations use predictive AI to drive positive business outcomes. More informed decisions provide opportunities for organizations to act on the information to improve business outcomes. Better outcomes could include enhancing customer experience, increasing operational efficiency, increasing revenue or reducing costs, and proactively managing risk. Acting on predictive AI results comes after the model is built, activated, and consumed (Figure 3-2), but it's important to think through why you're building the model before getting hands-on.

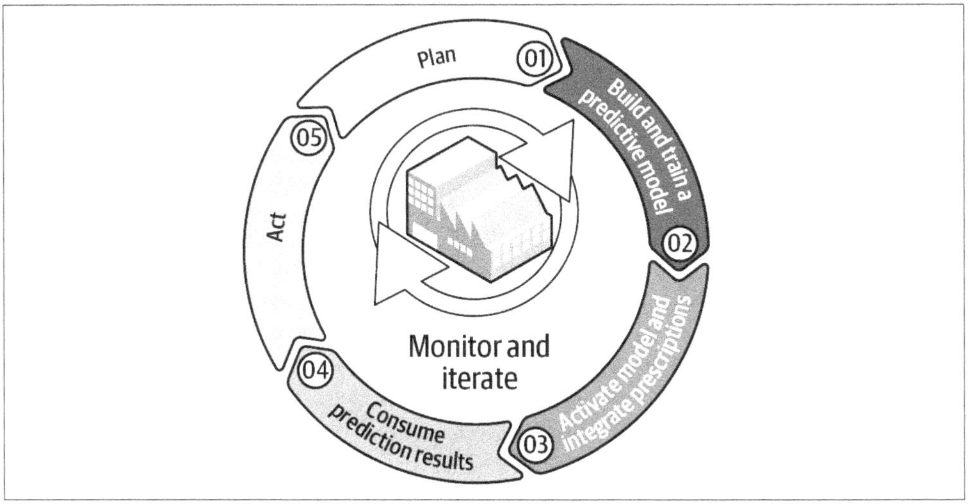

Figure 3-2. Predictive AI lifecycle stages

Planning is the first step in building and managing a predictive model, and it involves knowing whether the data exists to support the model or if data preparation needs to be undertaken before the model is built. Another decision made early on is what kind of consumption pattern is required. For example, one needs to consider whether the prediction results are needed on demand or if they can be consumed in batch. Thus, it's important to understand what occurs at each stage of the lifecycle between planning for and acting on predictive AI results. That's why we'll learn about the predictive AI lifecycle in this section before diving into the hands-on details.

We'll first cover some machine learning and AI Model Builder terms so that it's less confusing when we dive into detailed explanations using this specialized terminology. Then, we'll discuss the lifecycle in three separate sections. Those sections include diagrams explaining how you'll navigate the predictive AI lifecycle stages:

- Building the model
- Evaluating the model outputs and activating the model
- Consuming prediction results from the activated model

Afterward, we'll explore each of these three topics more in depth in their own separate sections. In those sections, we'll learn what specific steps are required in Salesforce to achieve the results to build the model, evaluate its outputs, and consume the prediction results. You can expect to see screenshots in those in-depth sections from D360, AI Model Builder, Flow Builder, and Agentforce actions.

Machine Learning and AI Model Builder Terms

Here are some ML and AI Model Builder terms that you can review now or refer back to later as you navigate the chapter:

- *Actionable variables*, sometimes referred to as *prescription variables*, are the controllable predictor variables in a model created from scratch in AI Model Builder. Actionable variables are important because they're ones where the values can potentially be changed to influence the predictive outcome. For example, a user building a prediction model might select the discount percentage as an actionable variable but not the customer's location. The discount percentage is a predictor variable that likely affects whether the prospect makes a purchase and it's possible to change that percentage. Thus, increasing the discount percentage for a prospect not likely to make a purchase could positively affect the outcome so that a greater percentage discount results in a sale.
- *Binary classification* models predict an outcome that is in one of two groups such as true or false, yes or no, and won or lost. Some examples for binary classification include account churned or not churned, opportunity won or lost, and case escalated or not escalated.
- *Consumer*, also referred to as the *model consumer*, is the application or tool that is the recipient of the predictive model results. A primary consumer interacts directly with the predictive model to supply the inputs and receive the outputs. A secondary consumer is the application or tool that makes use of the prediction results but does not interact directly with the predictive model. For example, a Salesforce Flow is a primary consumer of a predictive model built from scratch. Tableau Next is a secondary consumer of the predictive model because it gets the results from a D360 DMO from which a Predict Job or Batch Data Transform interacted with the predictive model and saved the results in a DMO.
- *Dataset* is the record-level data observations used as the input for the predictive model. The dataset used for model training is historical data with known outcomes stored in a D360 DMO. However, the prediction dataset comes from sources that include CRM Salesforce objects, a screen flow user input, or D360 objects. Unlike training data, input data for an activated predictive model doesn't include a known outcome, yet.
- *Goal*, also referred to as the *model goal*, includes the outcome and whether it's better to minimize or maximize the outcome. For example, minimizing customer churn or maximizing opportunities won are common goals.
- *Inferences* are the prediction results generated from an active prediction model. The inferences from an AI Model Builder prediction model built from scratch include predictions and top predictors. Prescriptions, if enabled, are also an inference from the prediction model.

- *Model capability* is a list view column in the model section of AI Models indicating whether the model built from scratch is a binary or regression predictive model.
- *Model outputs* depend on the model inputs. AI Model Builder outputs include complete training metrics whenever a training dataset is used as input. Those training metrics include the top predictor variables, model accuracy and metrics, and alerts for model improvement. When the prediction dataset is used as input, the model outputs are the prediction results, which include the predictions, top predictors, and prescriptions, if the prescriptions are enabled.
- *Observations* are row-level or record-level sets of data. An active predictive model generates a prediction outcome for each observation based on the input predictor variables for that observation.
- *Outcome* is the business result you want to understand and improve. It's most often a key performance indicator (KPI) such as opportunity win or number of days for case resolution.
- *Outcome variable* in an AI Model Builder model built from scratch is the one field identified in the root DMO that represents the desired outcome.
- *Prediction value* is a prediction result. It's a derived numerical value in AI Model Builder representing a possible future business outcome. The prediction value generated is based on the input provided to the prediction model as well as the algorithm used in the prediction model.
- *Prediction score* is a prediction result. It's a derived value between 0 and 100 representing the likelihood score of a specific binary outcome in AI Model Builder. The prediction score generated is based on the input provided to the prediction model.

> Prediction values and prediction scores are results that can be generated using a predictive model. A value and a score are distinctly different but, for simplicity, we'll frequently refer to prediction values and prediction scores more generically as *predictions, prediction outcomes*, or *prediction results* throughout the book.

- *Predictor variables* are those variables in the dataset that predict or explain changes in the outcome variable.
- *Predictive model*, also known as the *prediction model*, is often referred to simply as a *model* and uses historical data and ML algorithms to discover patterns useful in predicting future outcomes for datasets where the outcome has not yet occurred.

- *Prescription* is a suggested action identified by the predictive model that could be undertaken to potentially improve the outcome. Prescriptions need to be enabled as an integration before they're produced by the AI Model Builder prediction model built from scratch.
- *Regression* techniques include linear regression and logistic regression. AI Model Builder uses linear regression, simply referred to as regression, to produce numerical predictions like the amount for an opportunity or time-to-close a case.
- *Status*, either active or inactive, indicates whether the model is ready for consumption. Inactive models are those that haven't yet been activated. Only active models can be operationalized and used in Flows, Batch Data Transforms, or consumed in other ways.
- *Threshold* in ML is a boundary or cut-off point. The threshold value informs the model how to classify a binary outcome by converting the probabilistic output into a class label. Whether the calculated probability for an observation is above or below the threshold value determines how the model classifies that outcome.
- *Top predictors* are the most influential variables that impact a predictive outcome for a training dataset or a prediction dataset. Top predictors are an output of a trained model that identify the most important variables the predictive model uses to make predictions. Top predictors are also record-specific prediction results from an active model used to explain what influenced the outcome for that particular observation.
- *Training metrics* are the results produced when the training for an AI Model Builder predictive model built from scratch is complete. Training metrics can be accessed by clicking the option in the drop-down menu to the right of the model name in the Predictive Models tab. The metrics provide information about how the predictive model was trained as well as details about the quality of the model.
- *Variable* is a category of data and is how models organize data. A field in the Salesforce DMO column can be an outcome or predictor model variable in an AI Model Builder model built from scratch.

Once a predictive model has been trained using the selected ML algorithm and historical data, it can be activated and used in production to predict outcomes (Figure 3-3). The trained predictive model can also produce more outputs including top predictors and prescriptions.

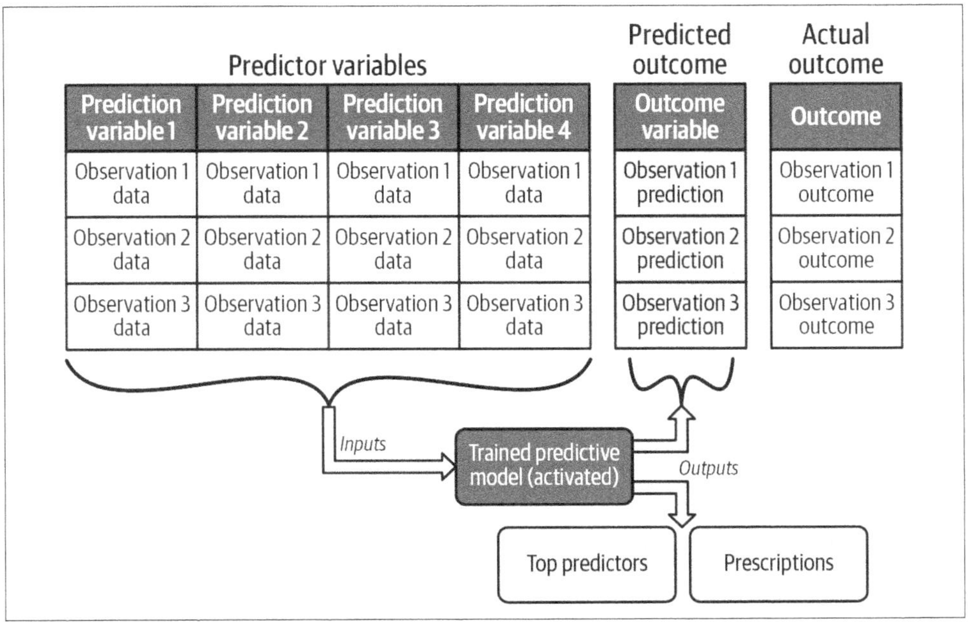

Figure 3-3. Inputs for and outputs of a trained predictive model

Now that we've reviewed some important terms, let's explore how to build a prediction model from scratch in AI Model Builder.

Building the Model to Predict Outcomes

Building a predictive model using AI Model Builder is accomplished without any coding and only requires three inputs:

- Desired goal
- Training dataset
- Algorithm

The desired goal and the training data need to be included in the data source. In general, a predictive model data source might include several datasets. However, a single D360 DMO, known as the *root DMO*, is selected as the data source for AI Model Builder. Additional data from DMOs with a one-to-one relationship with the root DMO can also be used for training purposes. Ensuring the data is optimized for model training is the reason for using only one root DMO as the data source.

The root DMO chosen needs to include the outcome variable and at least a few predictor variables. More predictor variables from DMOs related to the root DMO can also be selected. Along with the outcome variable from the root DMO, the goal of minimizing or maximizing the outcome variable is selected (Figure 3-4).

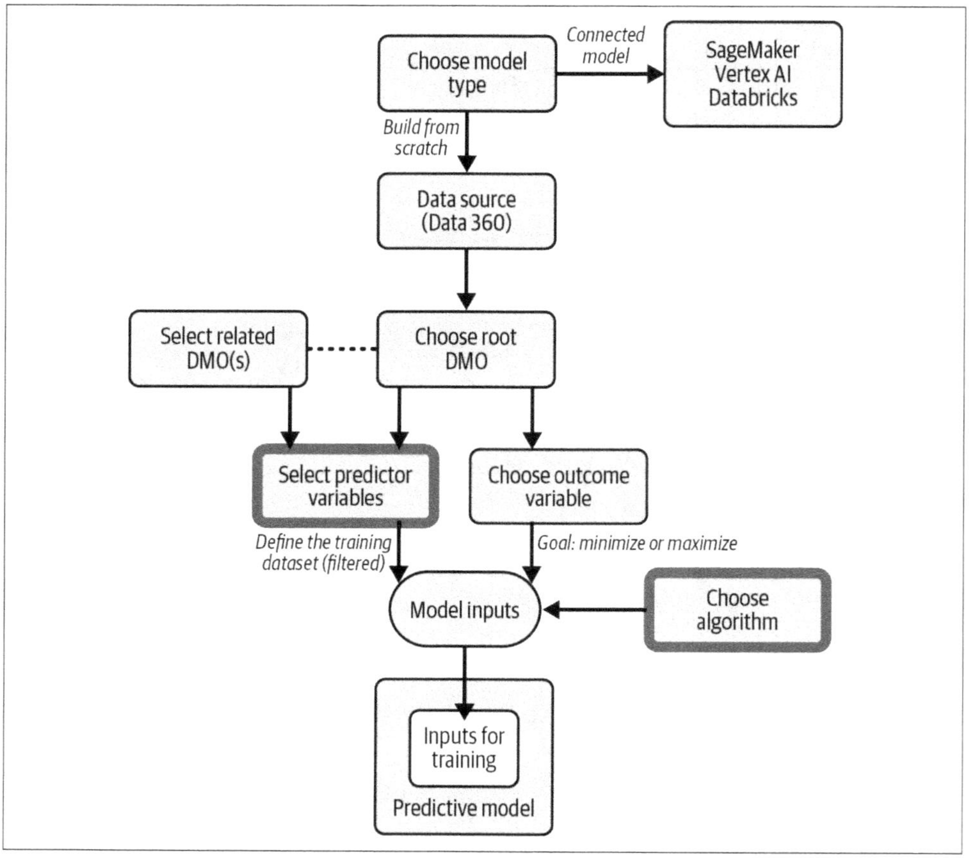

Figure 3-4. Building the model to predict outcomes

The predictive model needs to know which columns and rows will be used for the training dataset. The rows, or individual records, that comprise the training dataset are also known as observations. All observations can be used to train the model. However, you'll most likely want to filter the training dataset to include only a subset of records to focus on relevant data and optimize data volume.

The columns, also known as predictor variables, can be selected manually by the user. Alternatively, you can opt to have the predictor variables selected automatically if you're not sure which predictor variables to use for the model. You'll have a chance later to change the predictor variables, if needed, during the model evaluation phase.

In addition, an algorithm must be chosen from among the three options available. It's best practice to have the algorithm picked automatically unless you're sure which algorithm is the best choice.

There are seven steps in AI Model Builder for the user to complete when building a training model to predict outcomes:

1. Choose model type
2. Select data source (root DMO)
3. Select training data
4. Set goal (after identifying the outcome variable)
5. Prepare variables (identify up to 50 predictor variables)
6. Select algorithm
7. Train the model

Building and training the predictive model is an iterative process. Changes can be made to the inputs of the predictive model while it is inactive. Thus, you'll want to evaluate the outputs of the training model to determine if any changes should be made to the model before activating it.

Evaluating the Model Outputs and Activating the Model

The predictive model is trained on historical observations where the outcome is known. For example, historical observations include both positive and negative outcomes for opportunities that closed successfully with a new deal as well as those that ended without a sale. That training data, along with the desired goal and selected algorithm, are used as model inputs.

Model outputs include the top predictors of the model, those conditions that most significantly influence the predicted outcome. In addition, the predicted outcome for each observation is compared to the actual (known) outcome to produce the model accuracy and metrics information. Alerts for model improvement, if any, are also included as a model output. These three model outputs (Figure 3-5) are used to evaluate the model performance for the purpose of making changes that improve the quality of the predictive model.

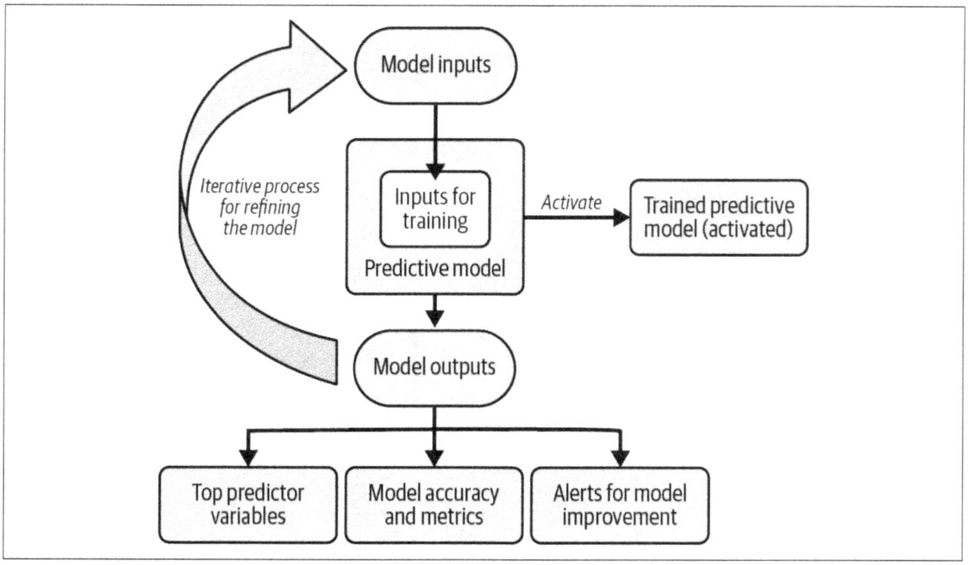

Figure 3-5. Evaluating the model outputs and activating the model

The predictive model quality is critically important because you want accurate predictions from your model. Just as important, though, is that the predictions from AI Model Builder aren't just the results you're focused on obtaining. The predictions are explainable and actionable, too, once the predictive model is activated and consumed. In the next section we'll discuss how to set up predictions so that they can be consumed and made ready for action.

Consuming Prediction Results from the Activated Model

A predictive AI model is built from scratch in AI Model Builder, a feature accessible within the D360 platform. Thus, it's possible to consume the results of an activated predictive model created within D360. An Integrations tab makes it easy for users to set up some consumers. Within that Integration tab, users can create Predict Jobs, Batch Data Transforms, Flows, and Personalization Maps. There are eight ways to directly consume predictive model outputs (Figure 3-6). Note that a Predict Job is counted twice because it's possible to consume prediction results with a batch or streaming Predict Job.

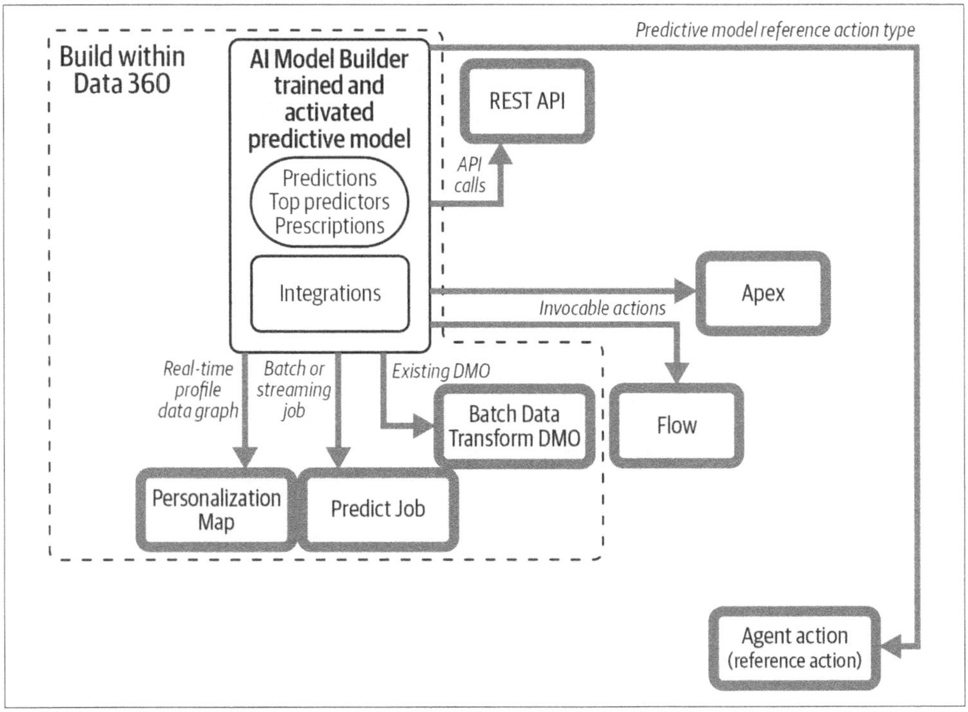

Figure 3-6. Predictive model outputs are consumed directly from the activated model

The input data sources for the eight primary consumers are vast. Many of the consumers map the model's input variables to the data source (Table 3-1). In some cases, the output is saved to a D360 DMO, but in other situations the output is presented to the user who can take immediate action on the results.

Table 3-1. Direct consumers of predictive model outputs

Primary consumer	Input data source	Input variable handling	Output
Personalization Map	Integration	Map input variables to data source at time of setup as a model integration	Model is linked to a real-time data graph
Agent reference action (Predictive Model type)	User conversation or some other data source	Obtain value at runtime	Show in conversation
Flow	CRM data, user input, Data 360, and more	Map input variables to data source at time of setup using an invocable action in Flow Builder	Configured in Flow Builder
Apex	CRM data, user input, Data 360, and more	Programmatically supply input data in the request to the model using an Invocable Namespace	Specified programmatically within Apex

Primary consumer	Input data source	Input variable handling	Output
REST API	CRM data, user input, Data 360, and more	Programmatically supply input data in the request to the model using the public REST API	Specified programmatically; output can be used in a Lightning Web Component (LWC) or an external system
Batch Data Transform	Data 360 DMO	Map input variables to data source at time of setup in Batch Data Transform node	Output updates existing DMO (enhancement)
Predict Job (batch)	Integration	Map input variables to data source at time of setup as a model integration	Output saved to new DMO created for the Predict Job
Predict Job (streaming)	Integration	Map input variables to data source at time of setup as a model integration	Output saved to a new DMO created for the Predict Job

There are also downstream secondary consumers of the predictive model outputs. Also, you'll notice the predictive model results are often consumed outside D360 via REST APIs, Apex code, Flows, and even within Agentforce actions (Figure 3-7).

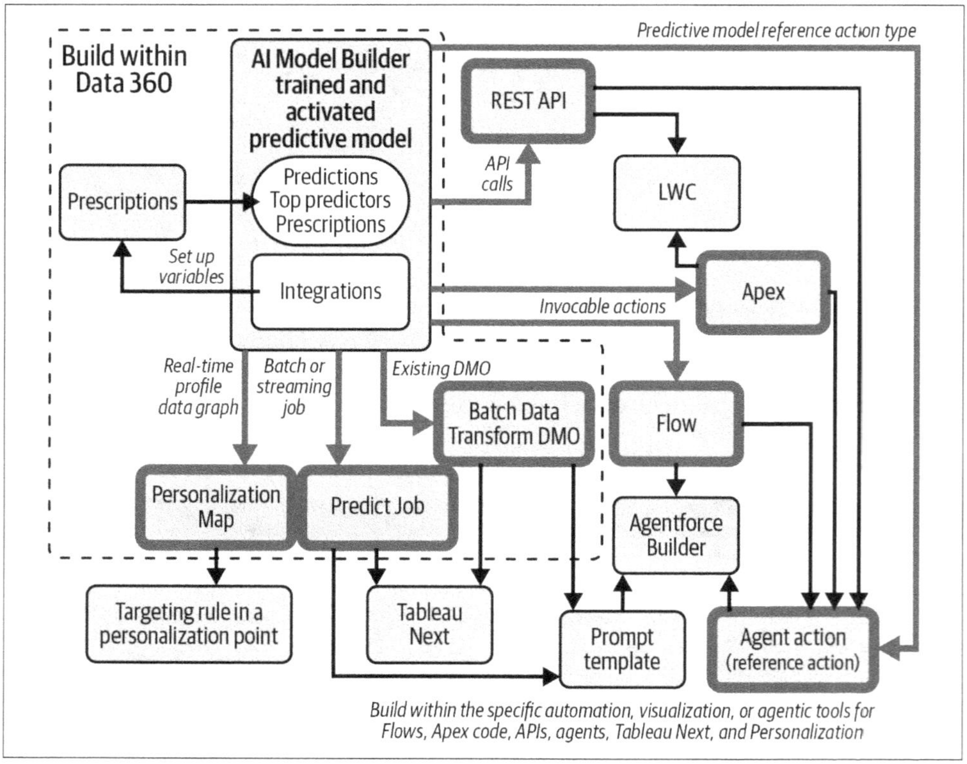

Figure 3-7. Consuming prediction results from the activated model

Agentforce agents created with Agentforce Builder can directly interact with the predictive model via the Predictive Model reference action type to consume the model results directly. In addition, Batch Data Transform DMO information can be accepted as input to an Agentforce agent via the prompt template.

In "Enable Prescriptions" on page 99, we'll learn how to enable predictive model prescriptions. Prescriptions are suggested actions to be undertaken in an effort to affect the outcome. Prescriptions originate from predictor variables that the user identifies as actionable variables, ones over which there is discretionary control. An example of an actionable variable is shipping method if the shipping options could be changed from ground shipping to express shipping for a potential customer. Once prescriptions are enabled for a predictive model, they can be consumed along with the top predictors and the predicted outcome.

> A predictive model produces predictions based on values from input variables supplied at runtime. The training data is not the source for generating predictions for an activated predictive model. Instead, that input data comes from sources that include CRM Salesforce object records, a screen flow user input, or D360 objects. Unlike training data, input data for an activated predictive model doesn't include a known outcome, yet.

In "Consuming Prediction Results from the Activated Model" on page 97, we'll discuss each of these different ways that a predictive model built from scratch can be consumed. But, first, we'll need to learn how to build the predictive model from scratch in AI Model Builder.

Building the Model to Predict Outcomes

Within AI Model Builder, you'll notice a menu on the left where Predict is the default menu (Figure 3-8). From there, you can click the Add Predictive Model button to begin building a predictive model or connecting to an external model.

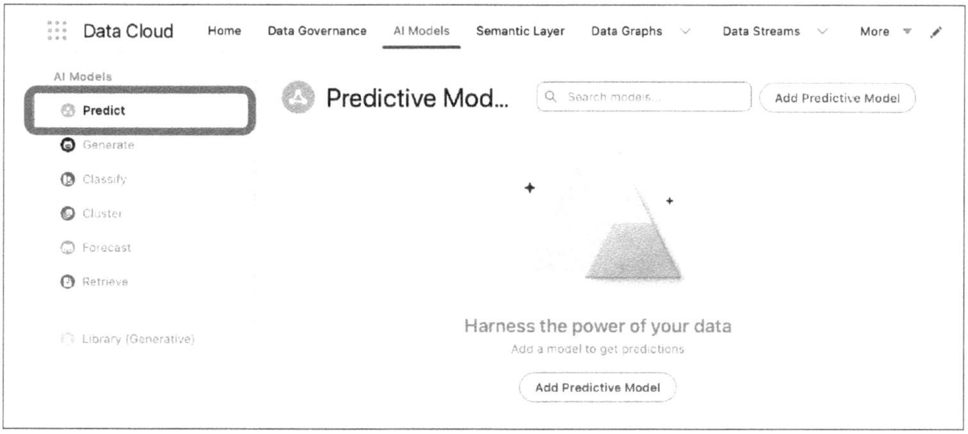

Figure 3-8. Predict menu from the AI Models menu tab in Data 360

In this section, we'll describe the seven steps needed to create a predictive model from scratch. Those steps include choosing the model type, deciding on the algorithm, and selecting and structuring the training data. As part of the process, there is a step for selecting predictor variables for which the user can opt to use Autopilot rather than selecting variables manually. After the evaluation phase, the user can return to these steps again to filter the data or refine variables for better predictive accuracy if the evaluation phase indicates changes are necessary.

Step 1: Choose the Model Type

Creating a model from scratch (Figure 3-9) is an option after a user clicks Add Predictive Model within the AI Models tab. Alternatively, the user could connect to an external model such as Amazon SageMaker, Google Cloud Vertex AI, or Databricks. External models are often built by data scientists and used for complex or unique use cases. The authentication and formats required for connecting an external model depend on which external model is selected.

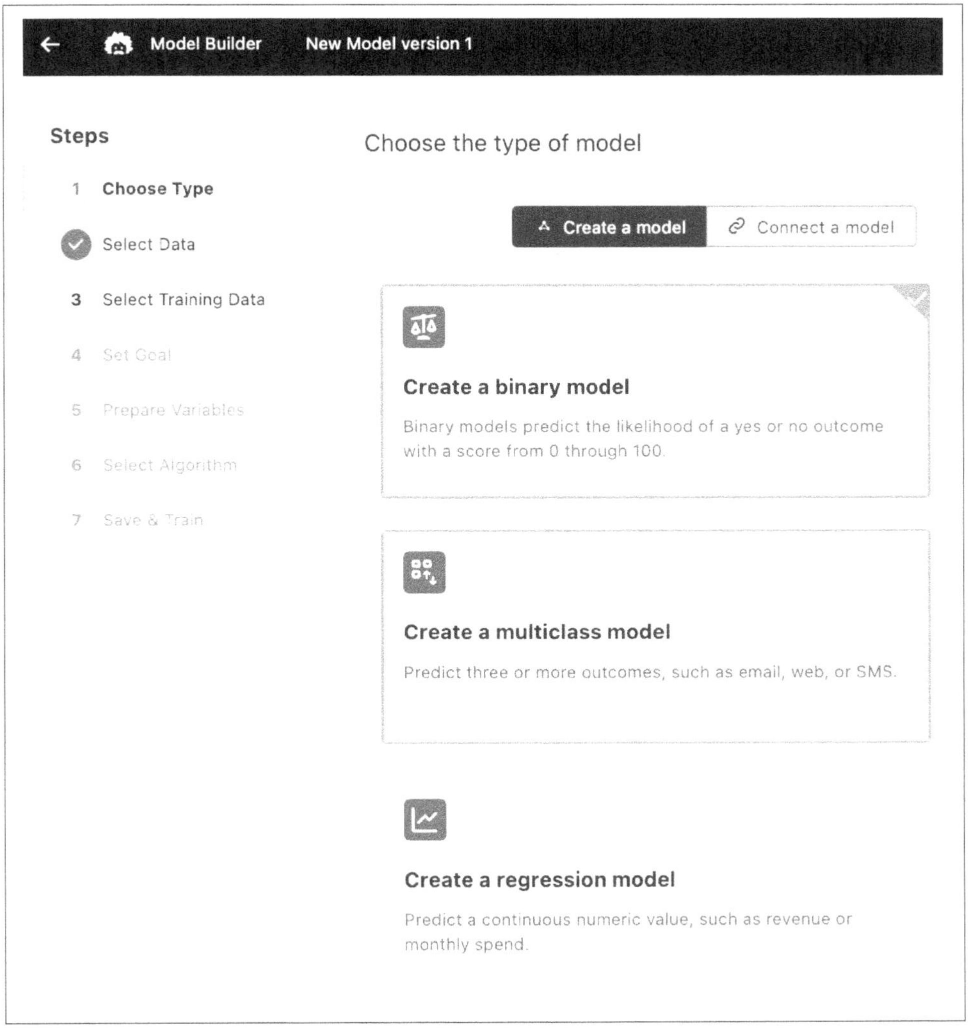

Figure 3-9. Choosing model type is the first step to add a predictive model

It's important to know that connecting any of these external models doesn't change where the model is hosted. The models remain hosted externally, on the third-party platforms, and the model's insights are integrated into Salesforce via application programming interfaces (APIs). However, the focus of this chapter is to learn about creating an ML model from scratch using AI Model Builder.

In previous versions of AI Model Builder, it wasn't necessary to choose in advance the type of model you wanted to create from scratch because there were only two types: a binary model and a regression model. Salesforce would choose from the two model types once the user selected the outcome variable. However, Salesforce has added a new option for creating a multiclass model, and additional models are planned. Therefore, you'll need to select which specific model type you want to build from scratch from the options available to you.

AI Model Builder is powerful and can guide users as they build a model from scratch, assuming the user understands the data and the desired business outcomes the model is being built to optimize. Creating a predictive model from scratch is a good choice for users who want to quickly define a custom machine learning model and who have domain knowledge.

Step 2: Select Data Source

AI Model Builder must know the location of the data upon which it needs to build the training model and make predictions. The user specifies the data space (Figure 3-10) and selects the DMO where the data is located.

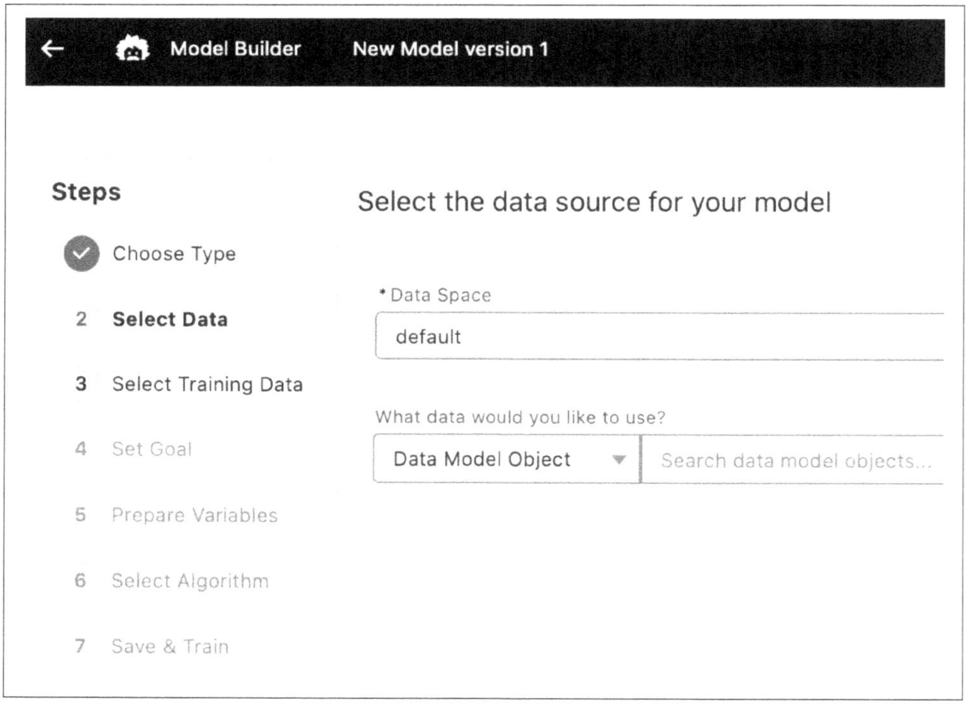

Figure 3-10. Selecting the data space and Data 360 DMO as data source is step 2

Only one DMO can be selected as a data source, so you'll need to confirm all relevant information is included. Once the DMO is selected there is an option to add additional related fields to your data. However, those fields must be within a related DMO that has a one-to-one relationship with the root DMO. For example, if the Opportunity DMO is selected as the root DMO, any fields from the following related DMOs can be included: Account, Account Contact, Contact Point Address, Contact Point Email, Contact Point Phone, Individual, and User.

The DMO selected needs at least three fields, one of which must be the outcome field. The maximum number of fields in the DMO can't be greater than 50. It's possible to select a DMO with up to 350 fields as long as you narrow the selection. Later, in step 5, the specific variables will be selected manually or automatically by using Autopilot.

Step 3: Select Training Data

ML uses historical data to generate predictive outcomes. The training data includes historical data where the outcomes are already known. The model uses the factors present in the past outcomes to know what is most important in influencing the outcome. That knowledge helps the model predict the future outcome of data in the prediction set where the outcome isn't yet known. For binary classification, the model needs both positive and negative examples.

For example, opportunity records with a status of closed won or closed lost are used to train a model that will predict whether an opportunity in the pipeline will result in a closed won or closed lost opportunity. Closed won opportunities are positive training data examples whereas the closed lost opportunities are the negative examples.

In this step of building the training model, you'll select the training set data. An option exists to select all records or a filtered set of records (Figure 3-11).

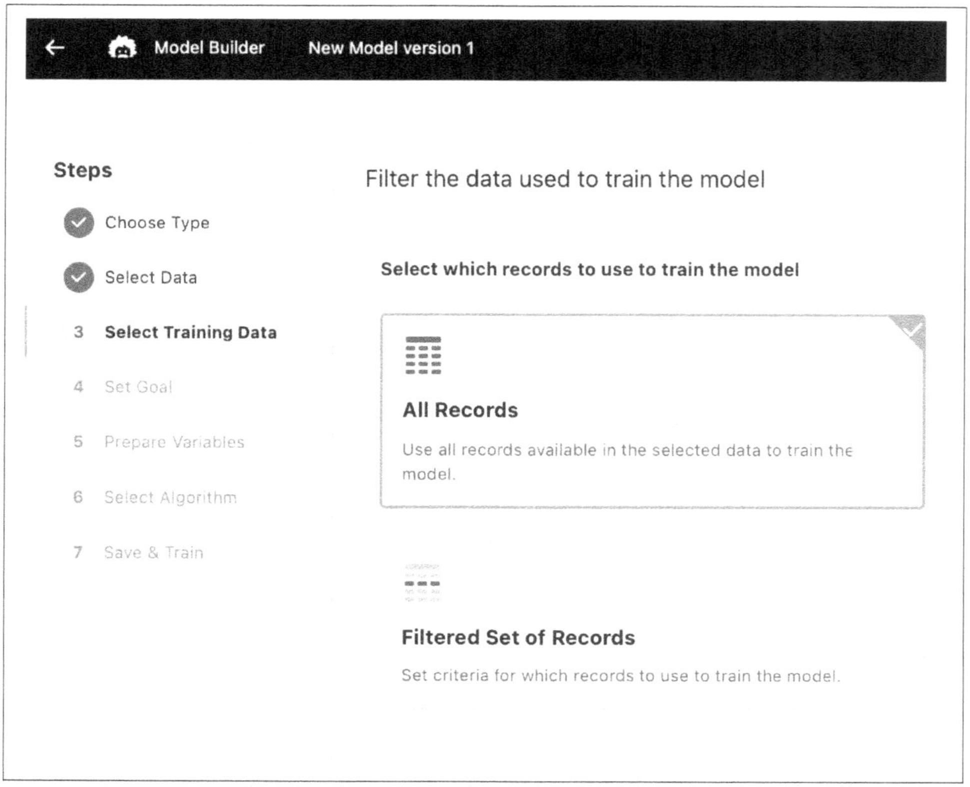

Figure 3-11. All records or only a subset of records can be selected as training data

Filtering the records can result in a dataset that's better suited for building the predictive model. For example, you could limit the training data to only include those observations with a transaction date from the last two years. Remember that you're filtering observation records in this step to obtain a subset of the historical records. You're not limiting variables. That will be done in a later step.

Filtering may also be necessary so that you don't exceed the maximum number of observation rows. The model needs to be trained on at least 400 records but not more than 20 million rows.

Step 4: Set Goal

The reason for building a predictive model is to obtain predictions and insights that, hopefully, give you what you need to influence the outcome. That's the goal. Setting the goal begins with selecting the field from the DMO that is the outcome variable (Figure 3-12).

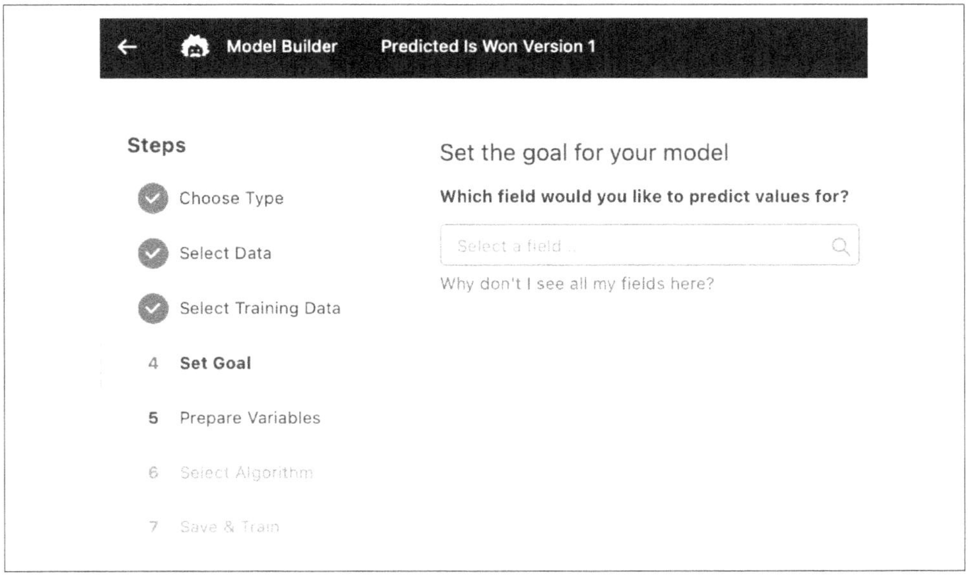

Figure 3-12. Selecting the outcome variable from the DMO is needed to set the goal

Defining the model's goal should align with a business goal such as increasing revenue or decreasing customer churn. Increasing revenue involves maximizing the Total Amount field value from the Opportunity object, also known as the outcome variable. Decreasing customer churn could translate into maximizing the number of opportunities closed with an Is Won = True status. In that case, the Is Won field is the outcome variable.

Setting the model's goal involves choosing the outcome variable and then selecting whether it's desirable to maximize or minimize the goal. In the example just mentioned, you'll notice the business goal minimizes customer churn whereas the model goal maximizes the number of records with an Is Won status. Alternatively, minimizing customer churn could be translated to the model goal of minimizing the Is Won = False status.

Translating business goals into predictive model goals requires some knowledge of the business domain as well as some understanding of the data and how it is captured within Salesforce. In addition, there are some practical considerations that should be top of the mind before even translating the business goal to the predictive goal. The business goal needs to be one that:

- Is measurable and reportable
- Can be supported by a regression or binary classification model
- Has actionable predictors that don't violate ethics or privacy laws
- Is achievable within the constraints of you organization's resources

If the outcome of the business goal isn't measured and reported on today, it's unlikely your organization will have the data to build a predictive model. In addition, there needs to be actionable predictors that don't violate ethics or privacy laws. In essence, if you don't have any levers to pull that can affect the outcome then there's not a lot of value in predicting the outcome.

In earlier steps, we chose our data source and identified our training data. In this step, we'll select the field to predict. We'll only be shown those fields from the DMO that are possible for the model to use. For example, if we select the Opportunity DMO as our data source, we'll have the following choices:

- Expected Revenue Amount
- Total Amount
- Probability
- Is Won
- Opportunity Forecast Category
- Is Closed

If we select a text field as the outcome variable, the model knows to expect a binary classification output (Figure 3-13). We then need to choose which value, either "true" or "false" in this case. We must also select whether we want to minimize or maximize the outcome variable. In the example where we select the Is Won as the outcome variable (Figure 3-13), we'll want to select the option "Maximize (Increase is Favorable)" because our goal is to achieve more Is Won opportunities.

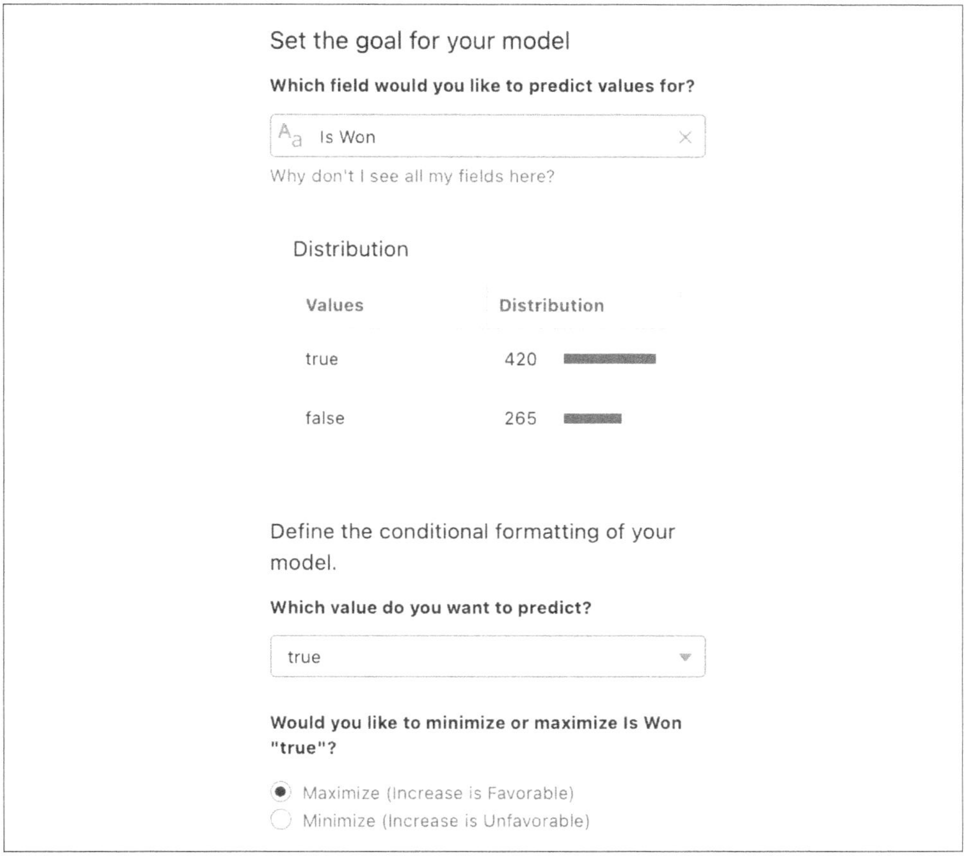

Figure 3-13. Minimizing or maximizing the goal is selected after choosing the field

If we select a numerical field as the outcome variable, the model knows to expect a regression analysis output (Figure 3-14). In this example where we select Total Amount as the outcome variable, we'll want to select the option "Maximize (Increase is Favorable)" because our goal is to increase the opportunity amount as much as possible.

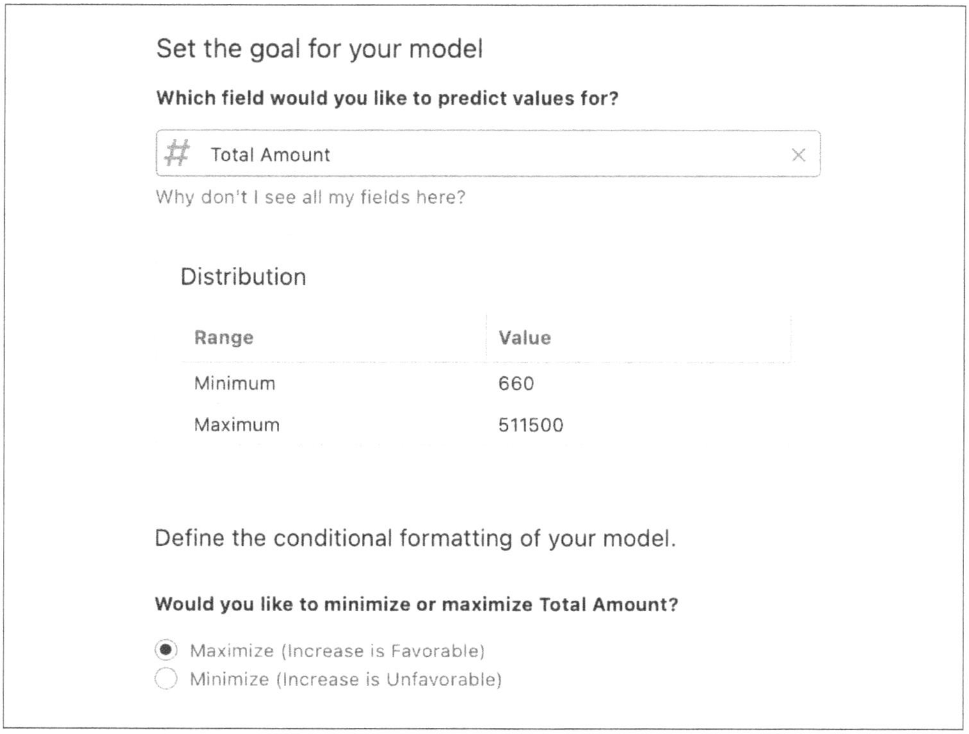

Figure 3-14. Regression models also require selecting whether to minimize or maximize the field for the desired goal

After we set the goal by choosing the outcome variable and selecting whether to minimize or maximize the variable, we'll need to prepare the predictor variables. There is only one outcome variable, but multiple predictor variables are expected.

Step 5: Prepare Variables

When navigating to this step, you'll notice the Autopilot is enabled by default (Figure 3-15). The Autopilot will automatically find the most relevant variables for your predictive outcome. Using Autopilot is especially useful if you're unsure which variables are the most relevant.

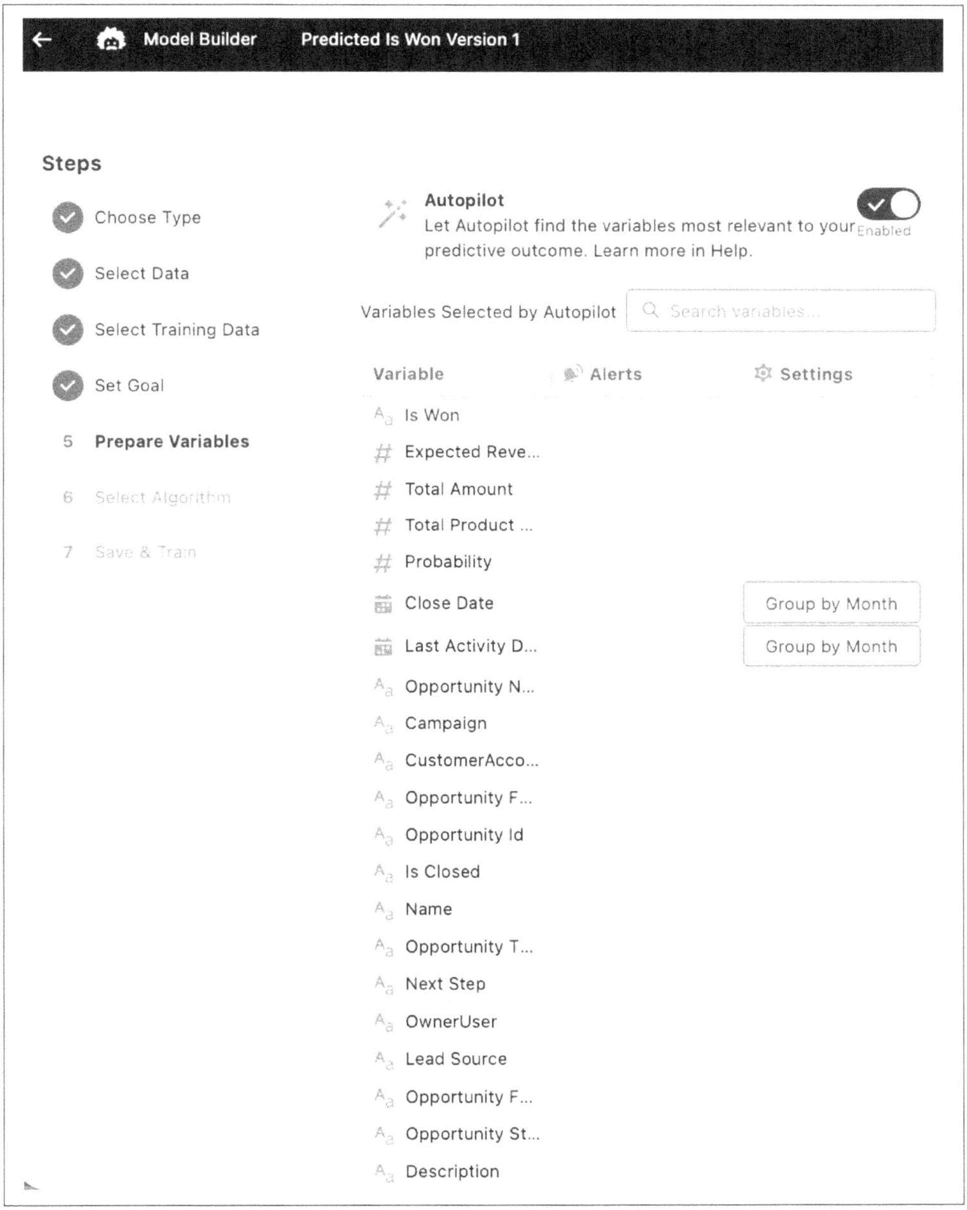

Figure 3-15. Autopilot automatically selects the most relevant variables for your model

If you toggle Autopilot off, you'll need to manually select the variables. Make sure you don't choose irrelevant fields or fields that might contain sensitive or private data such as personal identification numbers, medical information, or financial data. Also, avoid selecting fields that can be used to discriminate against people based on protected statuses like gender, race, or religion.

You'll notice the option to "Group by" in the settings for some variables. A user can group by the month of the year or by the day of the week in those situations. For example, date fields settings offer you the option to group by month, which has the effect of making it easier for the predictive model. However, you wouldn't want to group by month if you need a daily forecast. Instead, change the grouping to the day of week in that scenario.

Step 6: Select Algorithm

Selecting the ML algorithm for the predictive model is very important because the algorithm is what assesses the data. There are three predictive models available in AI Model Builder:

- Generalized Linear Model (GLM)
- Gradient Boosting Machine (GBM)
- Extreme Gradient Boosting (XGBoost)

AI Model Builder users don't need to be data scientists, though, to select the most appropriate algorithm for the data. Just let Einstein pick the best algorithm for your use case. Automatic selection is the default for this step (Figure 3-16).

If you toggle off the Automatic Selection option, you'll be presented with other algorithms. The recommended algorithm will be clearly labeled and is the default selection, but you could choose a different algorithm from among the choices provided.

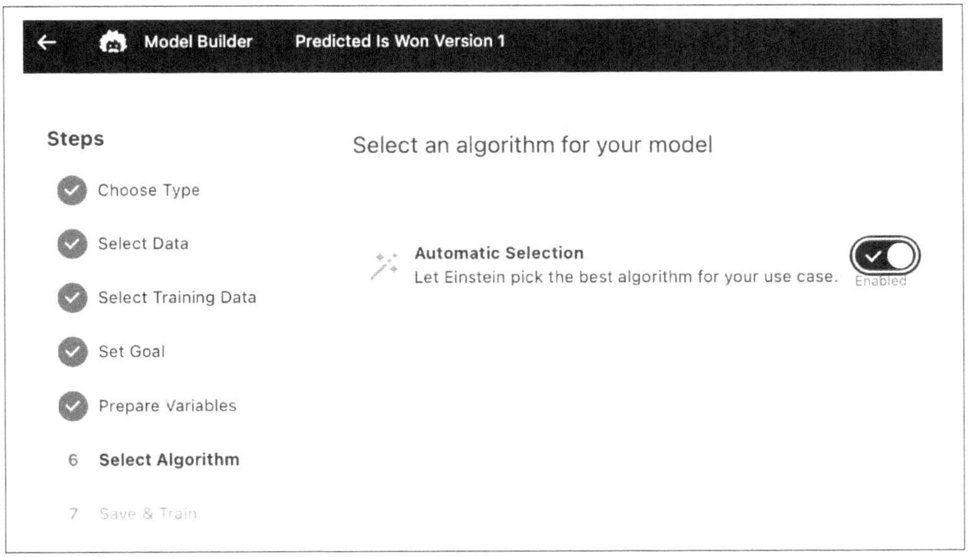

Figure 3-16. AI Model Builder can select the most appropriate algorithm for your model

We're nearing the end of the steps needed to build a predictive model from scratch in AI Model Builder. At this point, you can still return back to previous steps at any time. Just click the back arrow in the top right corner of the screen. However, your selections will not be saved if you exit out of the screen. Be sure to save your model choices in the next step because your selections will not be saved if you exit out of the screen before completing the last step.

Step 7: Save & Train

In this final step, you'll review the choices you've made. You can't save and train the model if any of the selections don't meet the requirements. The version number is not editable, but you can include version description information. To the right of each choice is a clickable pencil (Figure 3-17) that allows you to edit your selections for any of the previous steps.

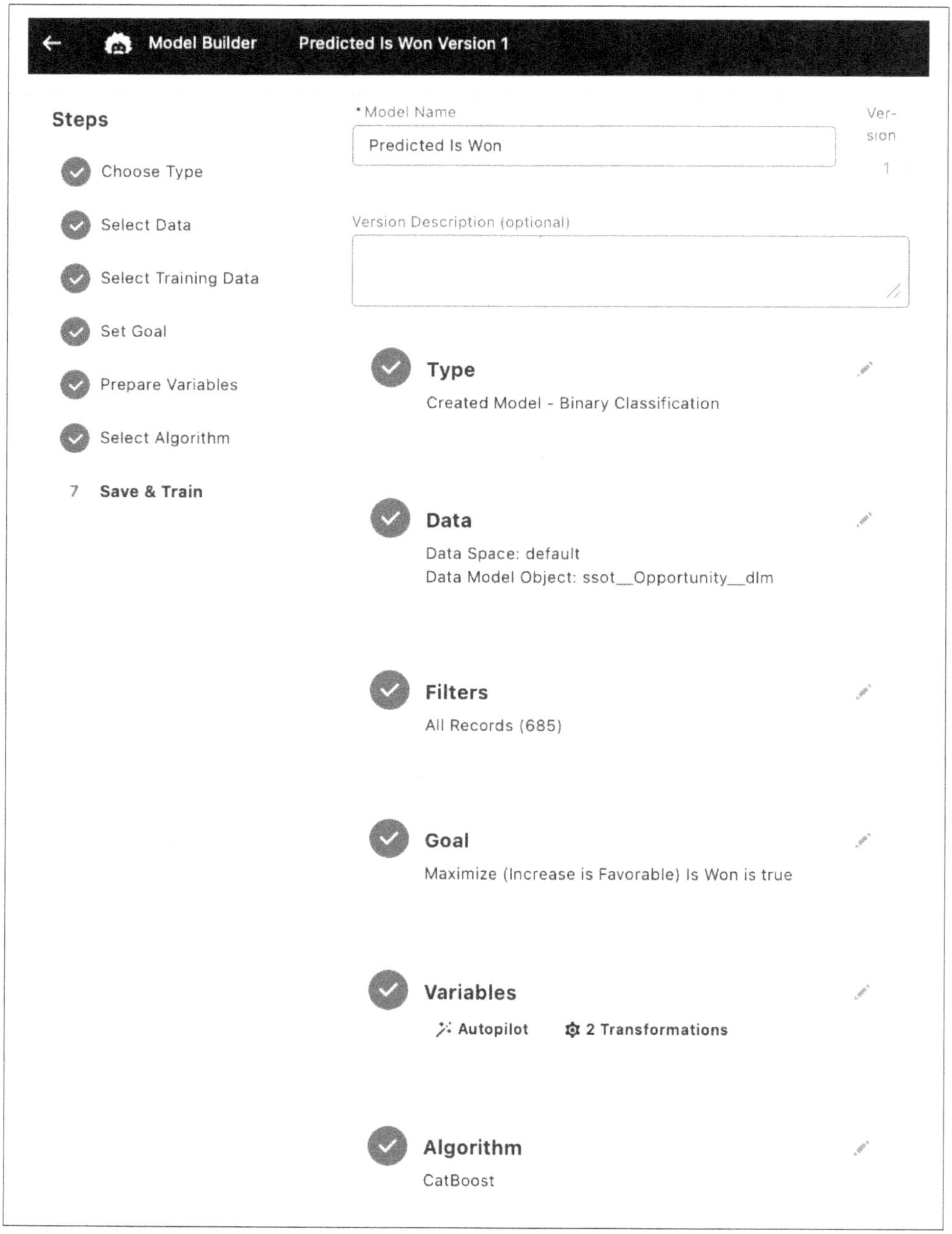

Figure 3-17. Use the pencil icon to edit any solutions made in previous steps

You can save your model to begin the training process once all requirements are satisfactorily met. It can take up to 24 hours for the model to be trained, during which time changes can't be made to the model. You'll want to evaluate the model outputs once training is complete. It's possible you'll need to return back to one or more of these steps to make changes later, after reviewing the model metrics. It's especially important to resolve any alerts that appear as output after model training.

Evaluating the Model Outputs and Activating the Model

Any predictive model created from scratch in AI Model Builder should at least predict outcomes better than if you hadn't used a model at all. The first inputs selected to build the model are rarely the best, though. However, you're able to improve that model by evaluating the model outputs and making changes until you're satisfied. Training metrics, available for all models created from scratch in AI Model Builder, give you clues as to what changes you can make to improve your model.

Training metrics provide information about how the predictive AI model was trained as well as details about the quality of the model. You can view the training metrics by clicking that option in the drop-down menu to the right of the model name in the Predictive Models tab (Figure 3-18) once you've completed the steps to build your predictive model and the model has been trained.

Figure 3-18. The View Training Metrics option is available as a selection in the drop-down menu

The model training quality information includes details about model accuracy (Figure 3-19) and other key metrics. You'll notice the information circles with the "i" in the middle. Clicking any of these info link bubbles provides details about the metric. Try adjusting the threshold for a binary classification model and you'll notice the model accuracy and other metrics will change. Adjusting the threshold higher will result in fewer false positive or negative predictions but also in fewer true positive or negative predictions. That's because the threshold informs the model how to classify a binary outcome. Depending on whether the calculated probability is above or below the threshold value determines how the model classifies the outcome.

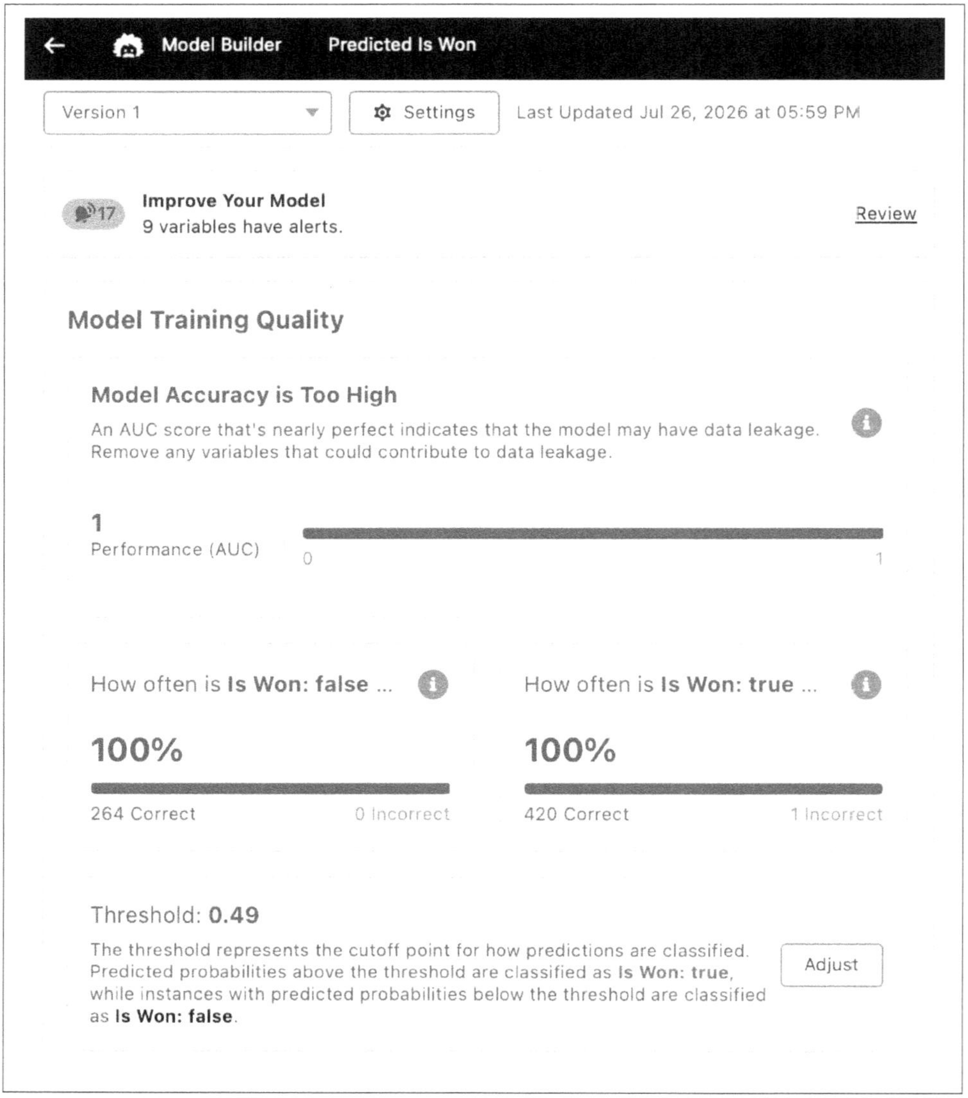

Figure 3-19. Model training quality information includes model accuracy details

Training metrics are based on the predictor variables selected and calculated from the data used to train your predictive model. Once the model is successfully saved in the final step of building the model, it undergoes training and then a prediction is generated for each observation with a known outcome. The prediction is then compared to the known outcome to determine the model accuracy. Random guessing for a binary classification would yield about 50% accuracy, so you'd expect a model accuracy above 50% but lower than 100%.

A model with a very high accuracy could indicate problems such as data leakage. Data leakage occurs when data from a predictor variable that wouldn't otherwise be available at the time of prediction is used to train the model. A highly accurate predictive model with data leakage yields inaccurate results when deployed into production.

AI Model Builder provides tools to help non–data scientists monitor and refine model performance. For example, users are provided alerts with detailed explanations when there are problems with the predictive model (Figure 3-20). Alerts should be reviewed and addressed before activating the model. When changes are made to the model's inputs, the model is retrained with the new information and the training metrics are updated. Machine learning is an iterative process and it could take several tries before you achieve a model that is performant. Even a performant model isn't perfect, which means models still exist with limitations and predictions still come with some uncertainty.

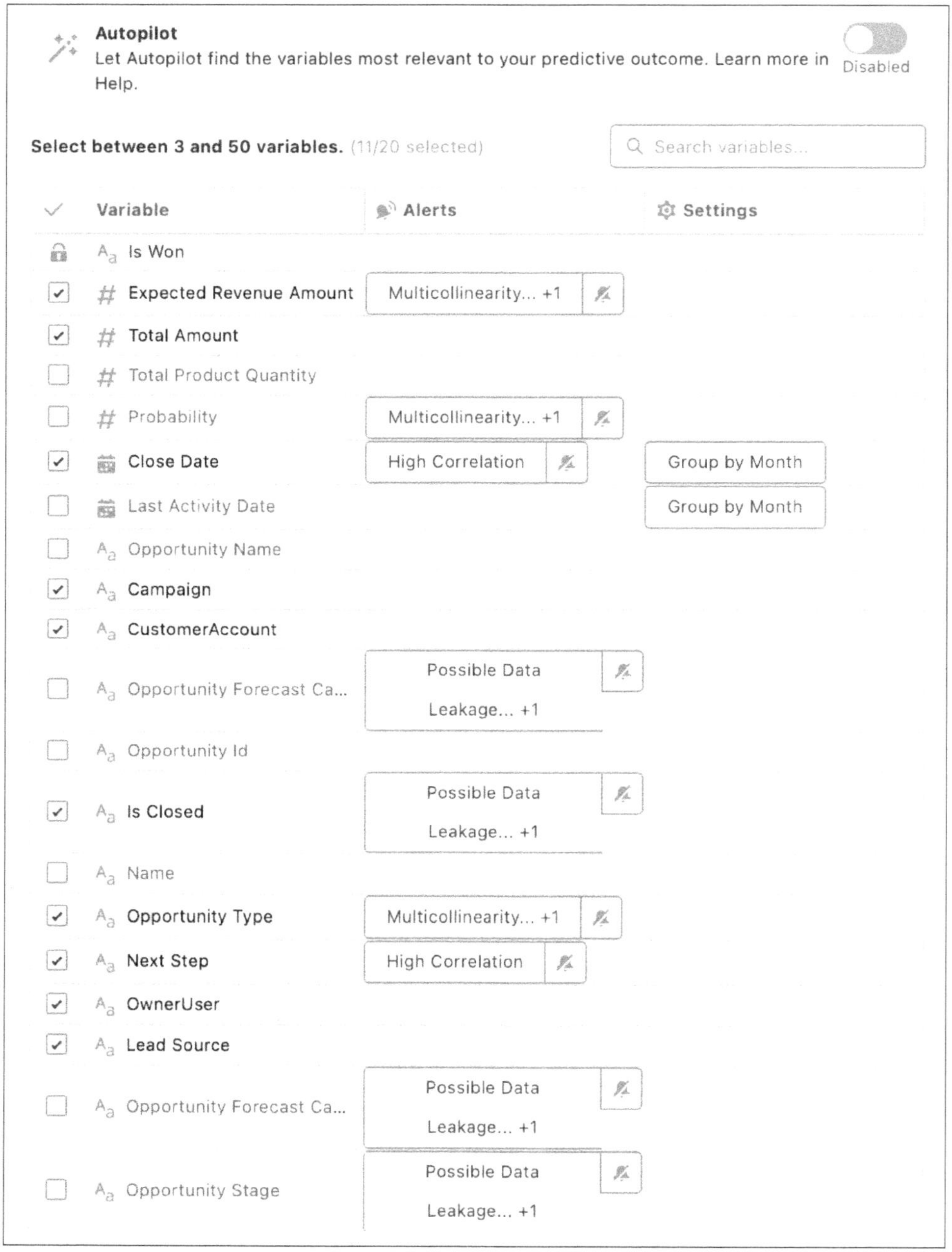

Figure 3-20. Alerts provide details and suggestions on how to improve model quality

In addition to model accuracy, the top predictors are included in the training metrics. Top predictors are those variables that have the greatest impact on predicting the outcome. It's critical to review the top predictors as they relate to model accuracy, of course. It's also important to consider if any of the top predictors are actionable variables. This determines what levers the team can use to potentially change the outcome. It will be much more difficult to influence an observation outcome if none of the top predictors are actionable variables.

Many factors can influence model accuracy and other training metrics. Data quality, data volume, variables used for training, and model complexity are a few examples. For all use cases, it's best practice to ensure your dataset includes actionable variables, that the majority of observations have complete information with high-quality data, and that you're using the right observations to train the model. For users without data science experience, you'll want to use the algorithm selected by AI Model Builder, let Autopilot choose the predictor variables, and rely on training metrics information to help iterate building the training model.

It's time to activate the model after iterating through until you're comfortable with the model quality. The Activate button appears at the top-right corner of the Overview tab for the model. Consuming the predicted outcomes from the model is only possible once the predictive model is activated.

Consuming Prediction Results from the Activated Model

We're ready to discover how to put predictive AI models into action now that we've learned how to build a predictive model from scratch, evaluate it, and activate the model. An activated predictive model can be operationalized to provide inferences in real time, on demand, in batches, and in streams (Table 3-2). Inferences include predictions, prescriptions, and top predictors. Those inferences are obtained and consumed in several different ways in Salesforce.

Table 3-2. Consumption patterns for primary consumers of predictive model results

Primary consumer	Consumption pattern
Personalization Map	Real-time
Agent reference action (Predictive Model type)	On-demand
Flow	On-demand
Apex code	On-demand
REST API	On-demand
Batch Data Transform	Batch
Predict Job (batch)	Batch
Predict Job (streaming)	Streaming

Prediction results are consumed in real time, on-demand, batch, and streaming. Real-time predictions are generated sub-second utilizing real-time D360 data graphs to provide the model inputs via the Personalization Map that controls personalization targeting rules.

On-demand predictions are generated dynamically within the flow of work in only seconds, as opposed to sub-seconds. On-demand prediction results are generated using decision workflows via Flow, Apex, or APIs. On-demand predictions are often viewable in an LWC or within an Agentforce conversation and most often are used for real-time decision making. However, on-demand prediction values can also be stored in an object if appropriate.

Batch predictions are typically stored in DMOs for further use in creating segments or performing predictive analytics. Streaming predictions are generated and updated in near real-time when one of the predictor variable values changes for an observation. Streaming predictions support processes requiring immediate action based on changing data.

Model inferences can be operationalized within the D360 platform using real-time, batch, and streaming predictions. On-demand model inferences can be used programmatically in applications via Apex code and REST APIs and they can be incorporated in flows. In addition, on-demand model inferences can be operationalized within an Agentforce agent action.

In this section, we'll first explore how to build AI Model Builder integrations from the predictive model. Specifically, we'll learn how to achieve five integrations within the D360 platform:

- Identify prescriptions (recommendations) from actionable variables
- Build a personalization map for real-time personalized recommendations
- Create a new DMO with results of a batch or streaming Predict Job
- Enhance an existing DMO with predictions and prescriptions using Batch Data Transform
- Leverage predictions in Flow Builder

Any of the integrations can be built by selecting the Integrations tab after clicking on the model name from the Predictive tab in the Models section. In upcoming sections, we'll discover how to enable prescriptions as well as learn about the predictive model integrations for Personalization Map, Predict Jobs, and Flow Builder that consume the predictive model outcomes. Those features are accessible from the Integrations tab of the predictive model (Figure 3-21), assuming you've activated the model. Otherwise, select the version number, then click the Activate button.

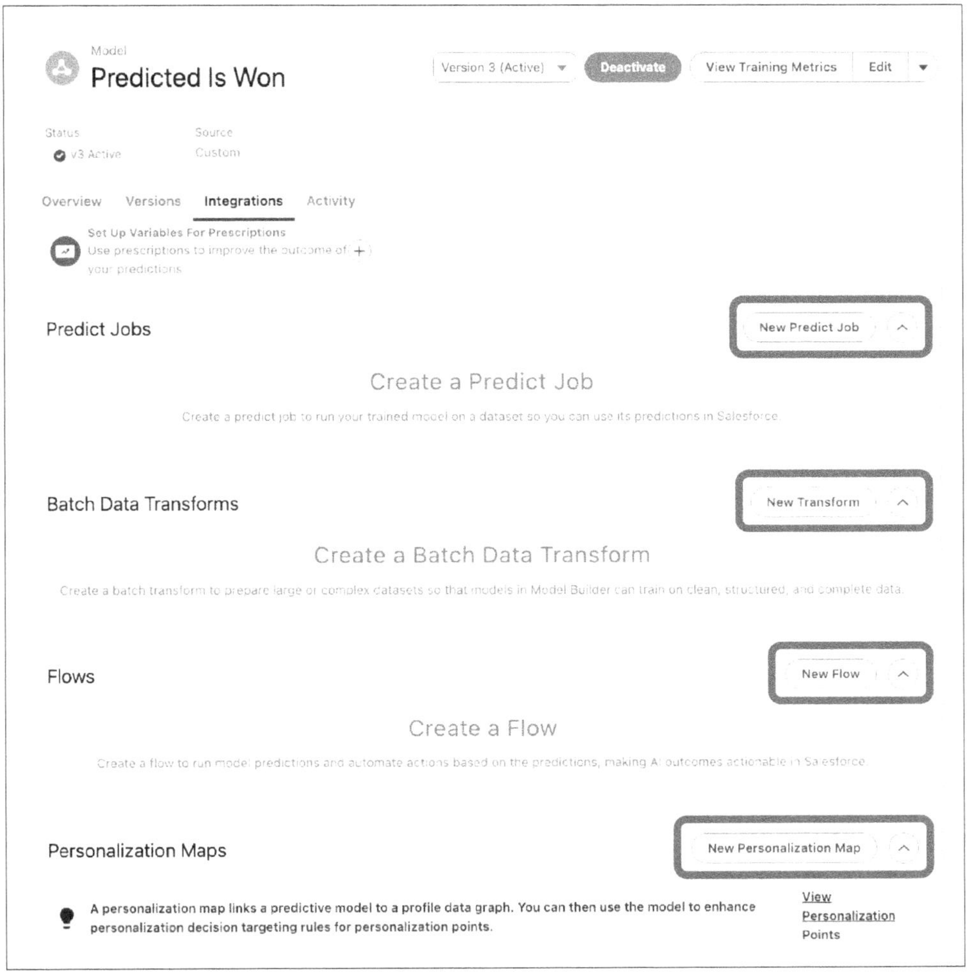

Figure 3-21. Integrations tab of a model built from scratch in AI Model Builder

In addition, we'll explore Data Transforms created inside the D360 platform where an existing DMO can be enhanced with predictions. We'll also learn about four important possibilities for setting up ways to consume model predictions outside D360 using flows, Apex code, REST APIs, and Predictive Model reference action types for Agentforce agents.

Enable Prescriptions

One of the first things you'll likely want to do after activating a predictive model built from scratch is to enable prescriptions. Navigate to the predictive model's Integrations tab and click the + sign (Figure 3-22) to configure the variables for prescriptions.

Figure 3-22. Click the plus sign to configure variables for prescriptions

Next, select all the actionable variables from the list (Figure 3-23) that are relevant. Click Apply.

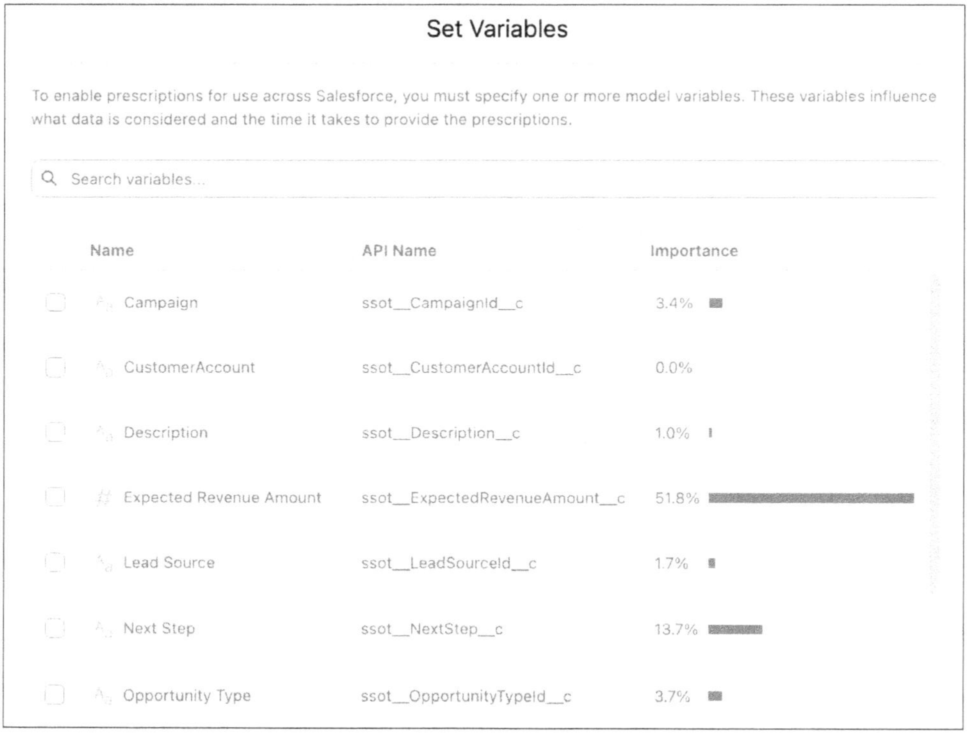

Figure 3-23. Select relevant actionable variables

The prescriptions can now be used across Salesforce in a variety of different ways. You can access and use prescriptions in any way that you can access and use predictions. Let's now explore the various ways predictions, top predictors, and prescriptions can be consumed within Salesforce. We'll start by looking at a real-time approach for using prediction outcomes.

Build Personalization Maps

A personalization map is an integration created to link a predictive model to a profile data graph. A profile data graph is a unified representation of a customer's profile and it's used to dynamically aggregate and update data across various sources in real time.

A personalization map integration informs the decision targeting rules used in a personalization point, which is a key element in Salesforce Personalization. Targeting rules, used to define eligibility, can be based on predictive outcomes or other attributes, Calculated Insights, and segment memberships.

A personalization point represents a very specific point in a customer's experience where a personalization decision is possible. Multiple personalization decisions for different sets of individuals can be included in a personalization point. The personalization decision, affected by the targeting rules, determines which individuals receive which personalization response. For example, a model that accurately predicts a customer's annual spend and their likelihood to purchase could be used to help determine whether the content shown to the individual in real time includes more product recommendations or a discount. Using a well-trained predictive AI model improves personalized recommendations.

The predictive model is linked to a profile data graph by first accessing the model's Integrations tab and clicking the New button to the right of the Personalization Maps section. The profile data graph is selected and its fields are mapped to the model's predictor variables. Afterward, the model's predictions are used for defining targeting rules in personalization points. We'll explore Salesforce Personalization in more detail in Chapter 10.

Create Predict Jobs to Save Predictions in a New DMO

AI Model Builder's Predict Jobs feature allows you to save the predictions, top predictors, or prescriptions of an active predictive model to a new DMO. The prediction results stored in the new DMO can then be used anywhere in Salesforce including within Agentforce Builder and Tableau Next.

There are two types of Predict Jobs available. A streaming Predict Job automatically updates prediction values in the DMO whenever any data on an input variable changes, whereas a batch Predict Job requires a manual data refresh. The results of streaming and batch Predict Jobs are stored in an ML Prediction type DMO that is not mapped to a DLO.

A batch or streaming Predict Job is created by first accessing the model's Integration tab and clicking the New button to the right of the Predict Jobs section. Just four quick steps are all that's needed to create a new Predict Job.

Step 1 is for setting the model inputs. Select the DMO where the inputs exist and then map the fields to the model variables. Step 2 is where you'll give the new DMO an object name. That new DMO will be created to store model outputs once the Predict Job is activated the first time. Model outputs can include prescriptions as well as predictions, assuming the prescriptions were previously enabled. Step 3 is for scheduling updates. This is the step where you'll select whether the Predict Job is streaming or batch.

> Streaming jobs don't support externally stored data sources where the data isn't actually stored in the DMO. Examples include zero copy or Bring Your Own Lake (BYOL). You'll need to use batch jobs for these data source types.

The last step is for reviewing the information you submitted in the previous three steps. After clicking the Save button, you'll be asked to provide a Predict Job name. It's important to remember that you'll need to activate your Predict Job in the Integrations tab before the DMO will have values that can be used to create segments, include in reports and dashboards, use in Flow Builder workflows, or other downstream activities.

If the Predict Job is a batch job rather than a streaming job, you'll need to run the job manually whenever predictions need to be updated in the DMO. That can be accomplished by selecting Run from the drop-down menu to the right of the Predict Job name in the Integrations tab.

Enhance an Existing DMO with Predictions and Prescriptions

Sometimes it's preferable to enhance an existing DMO rather than store predictive model outputs in a separate DMO using a Predict Job. In those cases, a Batch Data Transform can be used to add predictions and prescriptions to the DMO. The Batch Data Transform can be accessed from within the AI Model Builder Integrations tab or directly within D360.

Within D360, click the Data Transforms menu tab and then click the New button in the top-right corner. Select the Batch Data Transform option and click the Next button. Click Data Model Objects and then click the button to Add Input Data. Select the DMO where you want to store the predictive model output. It's important to select a DMO that includes the predictor fields needed for the model.

Changing the DMO resets the data used in the transformation. Thus, you'll need to start over to create the data transformation if you change the DMO in the transform editor at any time.

Click the plus sign to the right of the DMO and then select the AI Functions option to add a new node (Figure 3-24). Select the predictive function to be used in the transformation followed by the Next button. You'll notice only active models appear in the list from which you can select.

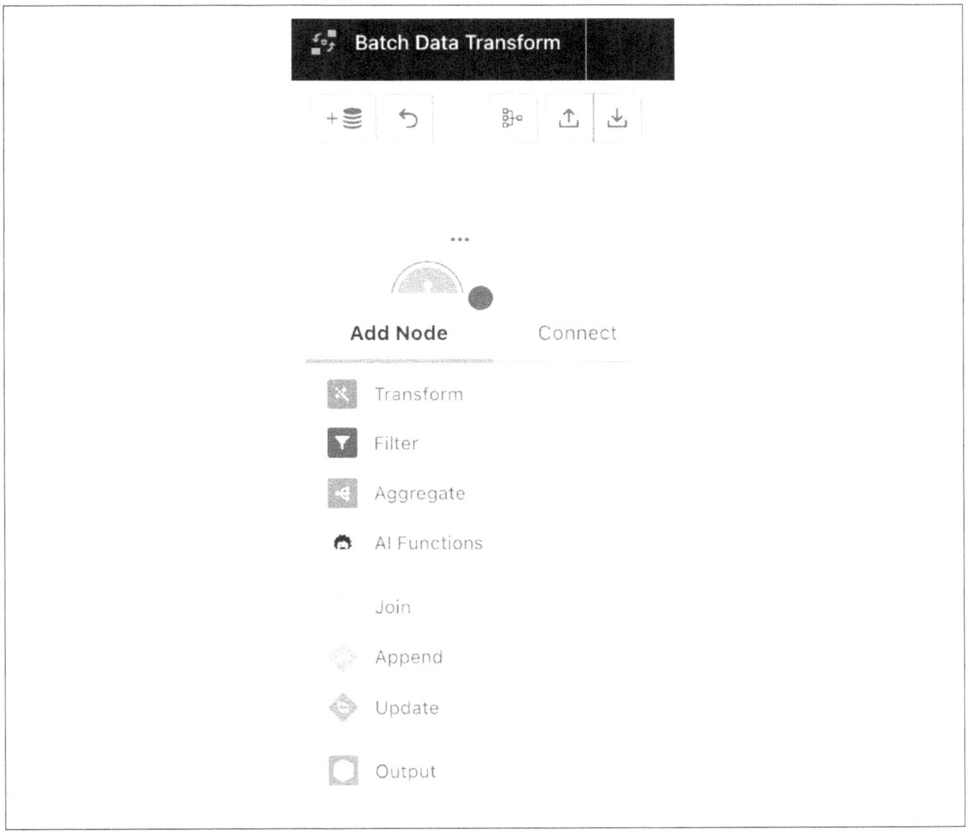

Figure 3-24. AI Functions node is available as an option in Batch Data Transform

Next you'll see two tabs, a Map Fields tab and a Modify Output tab. Review the mappings on the Map Fields tab and make changes, if needed. Under the Modify Output tab, select up to three top predictors and three prescriptions by clicking the plus sign to increase the number from the default of zero (Figure 3-25). If you don't include any top predictors and prescriptions, only the prediction value will be added to the DMO. Click the Apply button once you've made any changes.

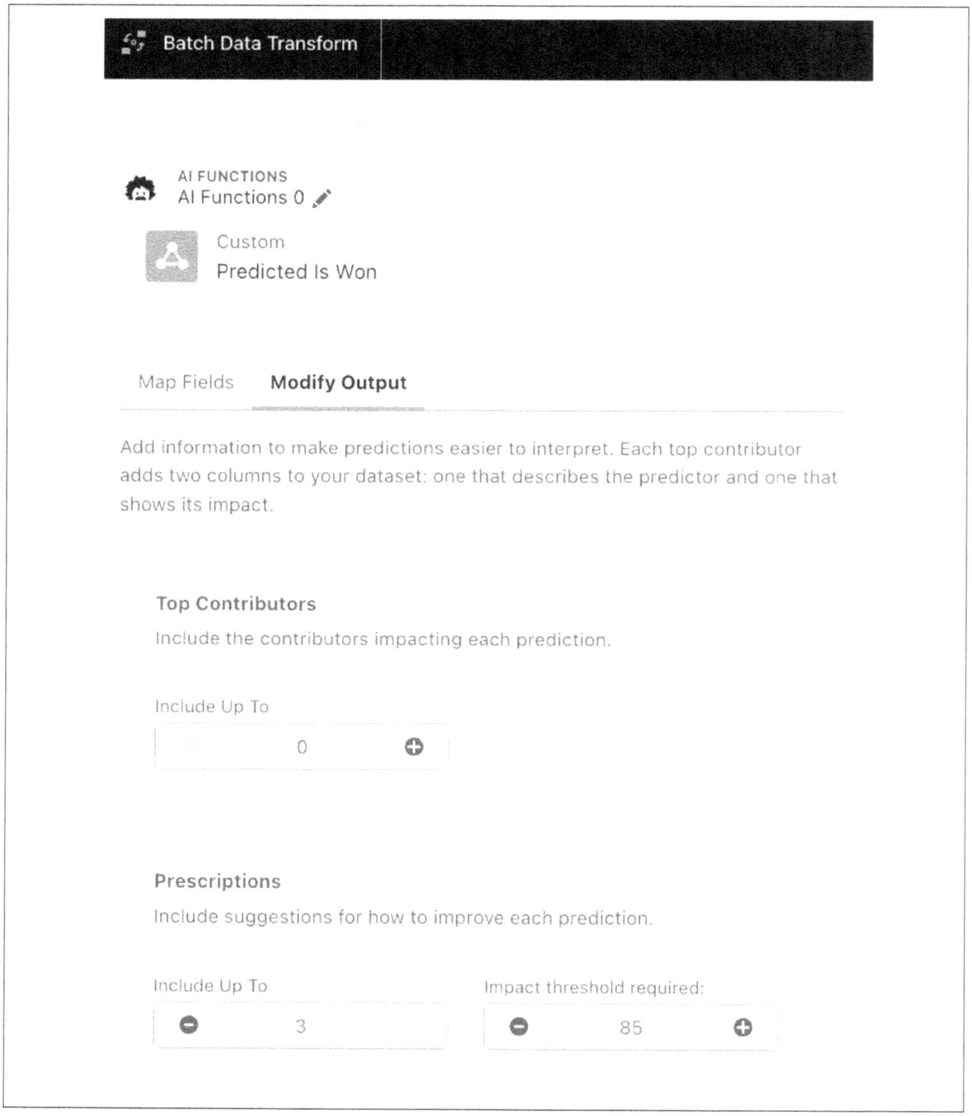

Figure 3-25. Up to three top predictors and three prescriptions can be included as outputs

You're able to preview your new data and check the columns before clicking the Save button in the top-right corner. If you included top predictors and prescriptions, your DMO will include the top factors that contributed to the predicted outcome for each observation along with suggested actions to improve the outcome. The predictive outcomes for each observation saved in the DMO can be used to create derived columns and run calculations, and the results as well as all the data included in the DMO can be used in other Salesforce applications including Agentforce Builder and Tableau Next.

Leverage Predictions in Flow Builder

Flow Builder can be used to generate predictions on demand within the flow of work. All predictive models built from scratch in AI Models and activated are surfaced as actions in flows of all types in Flow Builder. You'll need to choose the type of flow based on how you ultimately want to use the prediction.

For example, create a record-triggered flow if you want to add a prediction to a record or you want to automate certain actions whenever a prediction score exceeds a threshold. Alternatively, create a Screen flow if the purpose is to display predictions on a Lightning page for user interaction.

The Get Records element is used to retrieve data required for the predictive model, and the Action element is where you'll choose the prediction model as well as make the selection whether to include prescriptions and/or top predictors.

Enable Recommendations (Prescriptions) and Top Predictors in the Flow Builder Action Element

If you want to use recommendations and top predictors in the flow, you'll need to enable them (Figure 3-26) in the Action element and select a number between one and three. In Flow Builder, the term "recommendations" is currently used instead of the term "prescriptions" that appears in AI Model Builder. However, Flow Builder will use the updated "prescriptions" term at some point in the future.

The default is three for recommendations and top predictors if they're enabled and no value is specified.

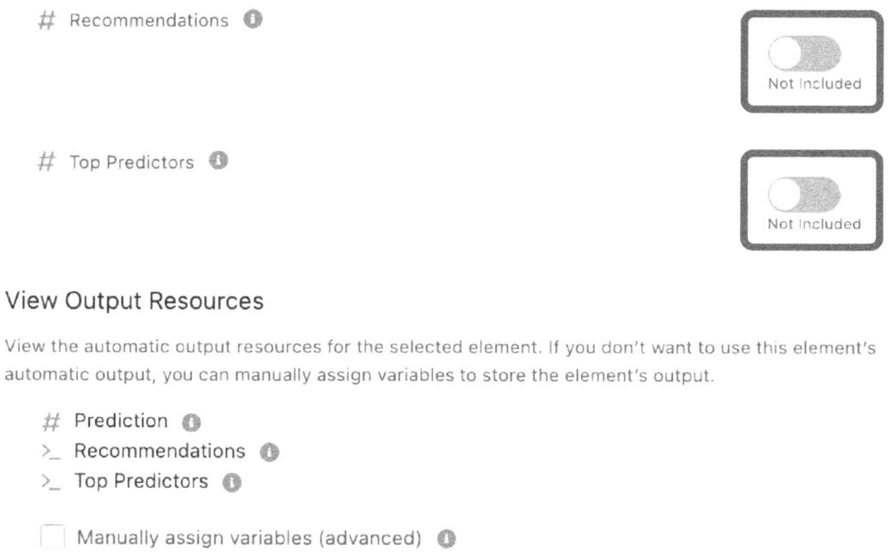

Figure 3-26. Recommendations (prescriptions) and top predictors are not automatically enabled in the flow

You'll want to make note of the prediction threshold set for the model if you elect to use a Decision element for specifying possible outcomes based on the score. The threshold represents the cutoff point for how predictions are classified, and that information can be found in the training metrics section of any classification predictive model built from scratch in AI Model Builder.

Flows are one of the primary consumers of predictive models built from scratch in AI Model Builder. The outputs from the flow can be saved to a record, displayed on the screen, used to send notifications using the Notify flow element, or used in Agentforce reference actions and prompt templates. A little later in the chapter we'll discover how Agentforce makes use of a predictive model built from scratch as both a primary and secondary consumer of the model.

Get Predictions Programmatically with Apex Code or REST APIs

Agentforce also consumes output from Apex code and REST APIs via agent actions. Apex is similar to Flows in how it interacts with the predictive model. When a predictive model is activated, a custom invocable action is automatically created and that invocable action can be used in a flow or executed within Apex using the Invocable namespace.

Apex code can be created to retrieve predictions, top predictors, and prescriptions programmatically from the model. Those predictions are then used in business logic to automate decision-making processes and trigger specific actions based on prediction outcomes. In addition, those predictions obtained with Apex code can be used in Salesforce UI components like LWCs. Alternatively, LWCs can display predictive outcomes shared with REST applications.

REST APIs are another primary consumer of predictive models built from scratch. Predictions, top factors, and prescriptions are obtained by using the predict endpoint. In addition to providing prediction results to an LWC and embedding prediction results into external systems, the public REST API can integrate with other internal Salesforce components including Agentforce.

Use Predictive Intelligence in Agentforce

Agentforce prompt templates and agent actions can incorporate predictive intelligence from models built from scratch in AI Model Builder. The blend of predictive AI and generative AI (GenAI) makes for a powerful combination that helps improve the flow of work and results in more informed decisions with better business outcomes.

Prompt templates are customizable, reusable, detailed prompts designed to safely connect with LLMs for the purpose of producing contextually relevant responses. An important way that prompt templates provide context is that they are grounded in Salesforce data such as CRM records. They can also be grounded by predictions generated from AI Model Builder.

Prompt templates are not a primary consumer of a predictive model, meaning that they don't interact directly with the predictive model. However, it's possible to augment LLM prompts with predictions, top predictors, and prescriptions generated from many of the primary consumers of predictive models:

- Flow
- Apex code
- REST API
- Batch Data Transform
- Batch Predict Job
- Streaming Predict Job

The flow merge fields or Apex merge fields are used to embed predictive outcomes in the prompt. DMO merge fields from the Batch Data Transform, batch Predict Jobs, and streaming Predict Jobs can also embed predictive outcomes in a prompt. REST `inputParams` contain the predictions generated from the predictive model and used to embed the outcomes in a prompt.

Prompt templates leverage predictive intelligence from many sources and can even share that knowledge when used as a reference action for an agent (Figure 3-27). There are a few different ways to create a new agent action. One way is by navigating to Agentforce Assets, accessible from the Setup menu, and clicking the New Agent Action button from the Actions menu tab.

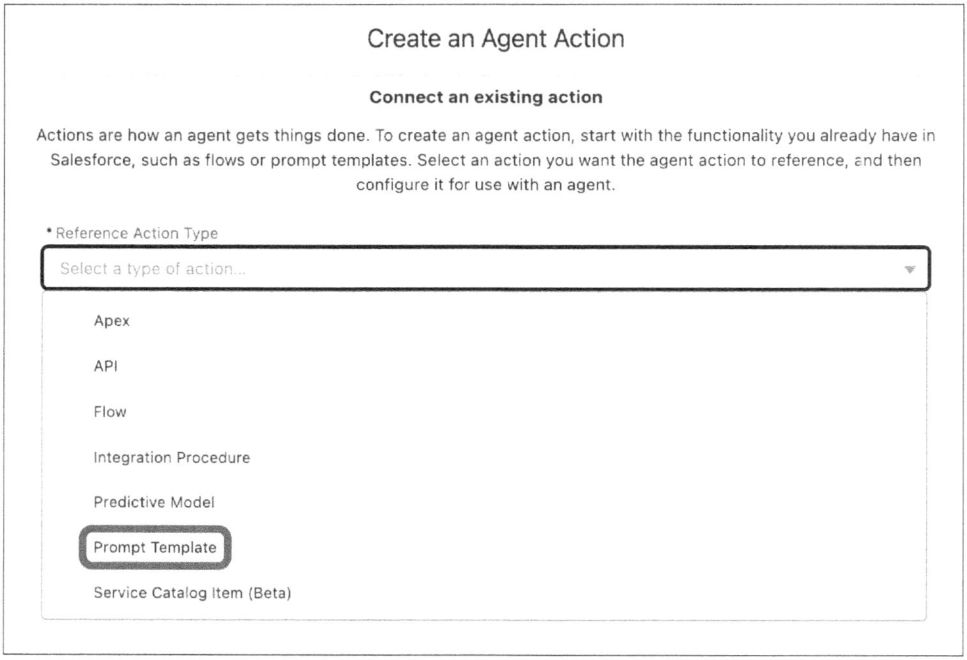

Figure 3-27. Reference action types for agent actions include Prompt Template as well as Predictive Model

Agent actions help agents perform specific tasks. Retrieving data, updating records, and generating responses are examples of agent actions. The underlying Salesforce functionality that powers the agent action is known as a reference action. Here are some examples for the reference action types of Apex, API, Flow, and Prompt Template:

- Execute Apex code for custom complex business logic
- Call an API to retrieve data
- Run a flow to update a record
- Use a prompt template to generate a response

Until recently, one of those four reference action types were used whenever predictive model outcomes were needed in an agent action. However, with the introduction of the Predictive Model reference action type, an agent can interact directly with a predictive model built from scratch in AI Model Builder.

Whenever the agent action with the Predictive Model reference action type is used, the action becomes a primary consumer of the model. The agent action sends relevant data to the predictive model and the results are returned to the agent. If a human is the intended recipient of the prediction outcomes, the agent provides those outcomes to the user in a clear and understandable format using natural language.

Predictive AI Model Lifecycle

Throughout the chapter we've described the predictive AI model lifecycle in mostly a linear way, but that's not how the lifecycle occurs. Continuous and iterative progression is undertaken for several reasons. Training a model takes time, and it's especially important to review the model's outputs before putting the model to use in a production environment.

In addition, predictive models become less accurate over time. This phenomenon, known as model drift, occurs mostly because real-world data often diverges significantly from the training data used to build the model. Many factors contribute to this divergence including changes in trends, seasonal fluctuations, operational changes, as well as new or discontinued categories of products or services.

Model quality decreases as predictive models experience model drift. Thus, even though some steps are performed in a linear fashion, predictive models need continuous monitoring and iterative improvement capabilities as part of the predictive model lifecycle. It's important to check results, review assumptions, and make adjustments to try new things and fine-tune your approach as you learn what is successful in improving model quality.

AI Models supports the ability to monitor and iterate by enabling users to select actionable variables, refine thresholds, and filter data. Another way users identify and address areas for model improvement is with AI Model Builder's versioning capabilities. Experimenting with new versions gives users the opportunity to improve model quality, which ultimately results in better business outcomes.

All binary classification, multiclass, and regression predictive models built from scratch, as well as third-party predictive models, are listed under the Predictive tab in the Models section of AI Models. The listing includes both active and inactive models. There's also a column indicating when the model was last modified.

You can click on a model and navigate to the Versions tab to view information about the model versions (Figure 3-28). It's normal to have several versions of the model because it's sometimes necessary to make changes to the model and/or to retrain the predictive model built from scratch.

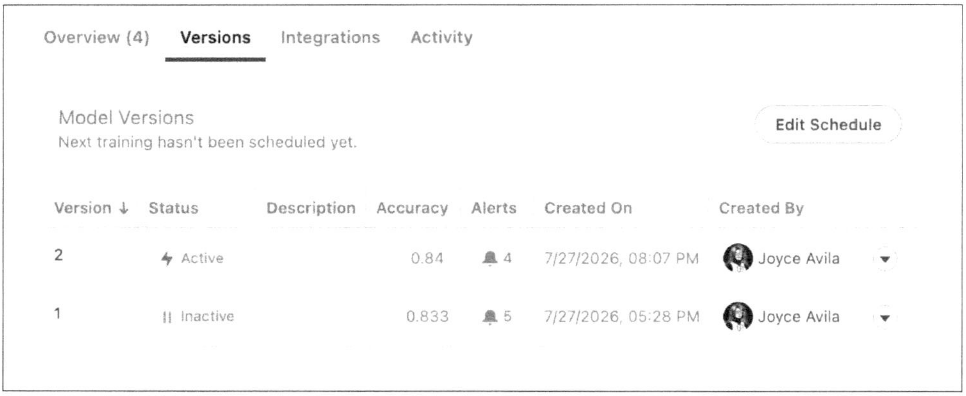

Figure 3-28. Model versions and their respective status are included in the Versions tab

You don't need to deactivate a model to make changes because making changes to an active model is possible. The current version of the model is active while the new version is undergoing training (Figure 3-29). After making changes and retraining the model, you'll need to activate the new version and select the new prescription variables again before using the new version in production.

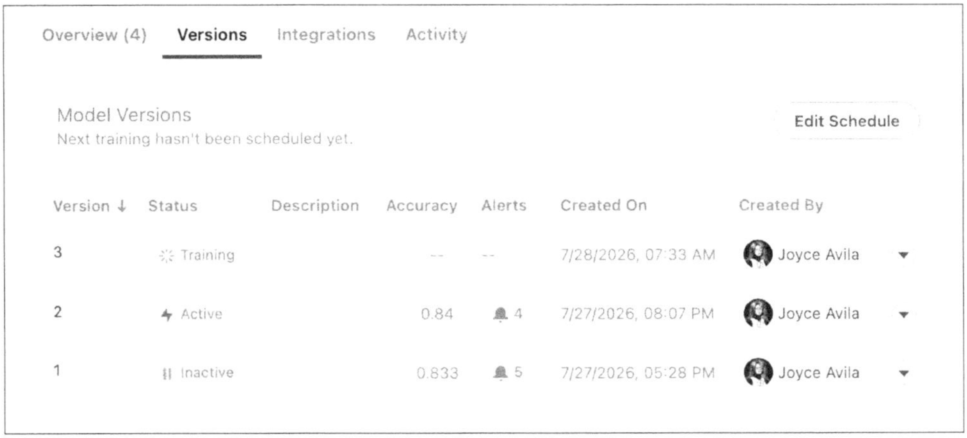

Figure 3-29. Predictive model version 3 has been saved and is undergoing training

In addition to manually managing model refreshes, it's possible to automate the process. There's a feature in AI Models known as automatic model refresh, a retraining feature for deployed models that can be set up on a recurring weekly or monthly schedule. There's also an option to rescore records after the prediction model is retrained and then have an email notification sent to users listed on the recipients list. Set up an automatic model refresh by navigating to the prediction definition in the Model Manager tab. Within the settings panel, click the Schedule button from the Model Refresh subtab.

> Using automatic model refresh is not a "set it and forget it" solution. Evaluating AI Models' prediction model health and data quality should still be undertaken on a regular basis. In addition, you'll need to periodically review the cadence of the refresh schedule to make sure it is still relevant anytime the rate of change in your source data is modified.

Thus far, we've discussed how to build and manage predictive models in a home org. However, Data Cloud One supports multi-org access, enabling you to scale predictive AI across companion orgs. Within a companion org, a predictive model is read-only, but predictions from an activated model stored in a DMO in the home org can be used in a companion org. In addition, companion orgs can use Flow, Apex, or agents to invoke a model in the home org and get predictions on demand.

Summary

In this chapter, we explored the AI Model Builder tool and learned how to build predictive models from scratch. We also discovered how to enable and leverage top predictors and prescriptions for greater intelligent foresight. In addition, we learned ways to operationalize predictive model results so that actionable insights are available to both humans and agents.

In the next chapter, we'll continue learning about context and insights with agentic analytics built for conversation and actionability in the flow of work. We'll take a deep dive into Semantic Model Builder, which leverages Data 360 to provide context for a conversational agent and Tableau Next visualizations. Tableau Next displays visualizations and dashboards and it also serves as an operational workspace for humans. We'll explore Tableau Next in detail and learn about the Agentforce analytics and visualization agent.

CHAPTER 4

Agentic Analytics Built for Conversation and Actionability in the Flow of Work

Employees in an intelligent agentic enterprise rely on data visualizations to highlight patterns, trends, and relationships. This is especially true in the era of big data where data analytics plays a crucial role in helping individuals discover insights that lead to actions likely to improve outcomes.

For example, users monitoring patient outcomes for a chain of hospitals benefit from trend charts and heatmaps showing hospital readmission rates, length of stay, and complications by hospital, diagnosis, and treatment pathways. Based on the insights, next steps could include actions to alter treatment pathways, revise discharge protocols, or introduce support for high-risk therapies.

An important agentic enterprise goal is bringing the action layer closer to the visualization layer to eliminate the need for switching between screens or platforms. Powered by Salesforce AI capabilities, Tableau Next offers new options for achieving this goal of creating agentic analytics for the intelligent agentic enterprise. We'll highlight several examples in this chapter.

Building relevant visualizations requires context provided by a semantic layer, an intermediary between the unified data layer and user applications like dashboards. The semantic layer, sometimes referred to as the knowledge layer, is important when building shared meaning that can be leveraged across the entire enterprise. In addition, the semantic layer grounds agents in ways that allow them to provide the most relevant and complete information to users through a conversation layer using natural language.

This chapter's objective is to learn how to leverage Tableau Next and Agentforce to support data analytics built for conversation and actionability in the flow of work for an intelligent agentic enterprise supported by Salesforce AI productions (Figure 4-1). As part of that journey, we'll explore the Data 360 (D360) application (app) where we'll navigate the Semantic Layer feature for building semantic models. We'll spend time in the Tableau Next app and we'll also become well-informed about the skills assigned to an analytics and visualization agent for supporting analytical conversations between the agent and an individual.

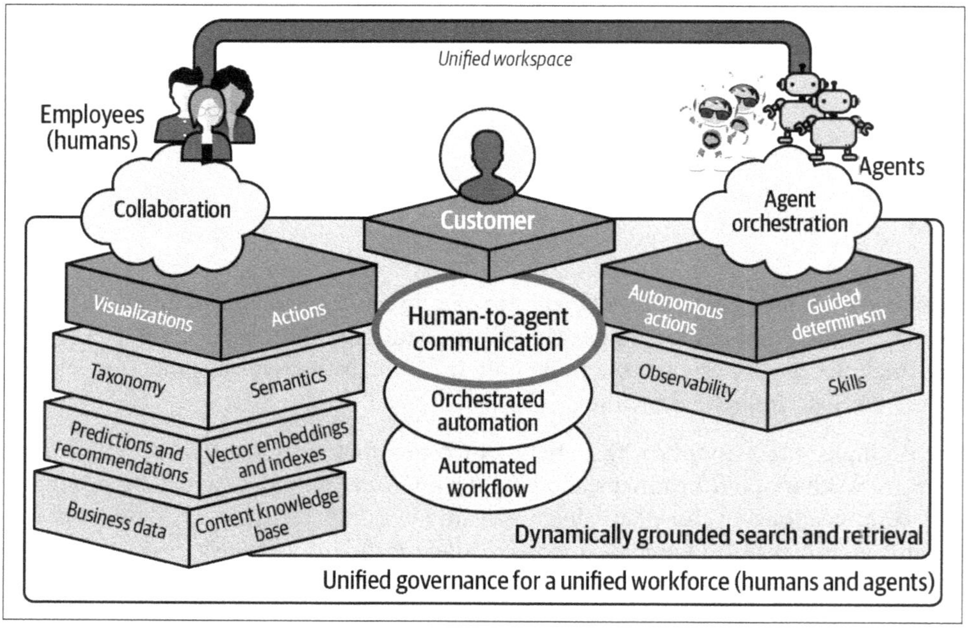

Figure 4-1. Intelligent agentic enterprise supported by Salesforce AI solutions

Specifically, we'll experience creating semantic knowledge using the Semantic Model Builder functionality accessible within the Salesforce D360 app (Figure 4-2). Afterward, we'll dive into the Tableau Next app and workspaces where we'll learn about visualization builders and dashboard builders available to users.

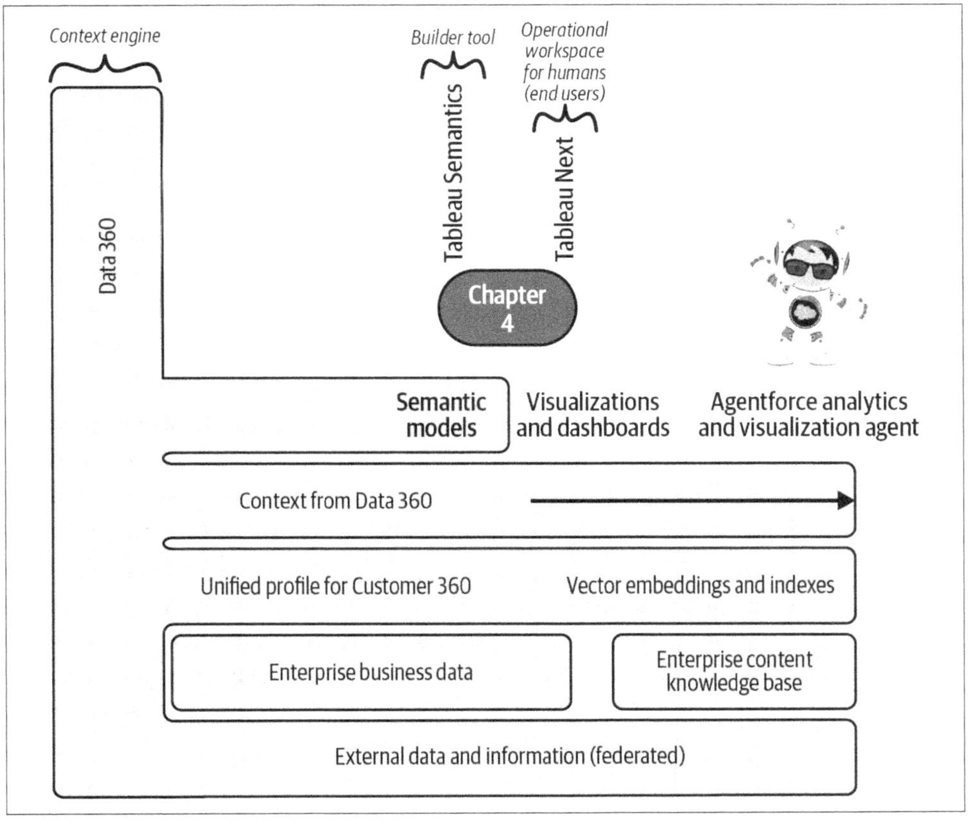

Figure 4-2. Tableau Semantics leverages Data 360 to provide context for a conversational agent and Tableau Next visualizations

We'll close out the chapter learning about three agent skills assigned to a visualization and analytics agent: Data Pro, Concierge, and Inspector skills. An analytics and visualization agent with these out-of-the-box skills unlocks conversational analytics by translating users' natural language questions into semantic queries. The actionable insights returned by the agent's queries to the user include visualizations, explanations, and recommendations.

Bringing insights and actionability into the flow of work is truly a paradigm shift with the ability to transform the way humans collaborate with each other and work with agents in a seamless conversational way. This chapter describes in detail how Salesforce gives intelligent agentic enterprises the ability to achieve this paradigm shift with Tableau Next and Agentforce.

Getting Started

Let's discuss some background knowledge and some things you should know to help you get the most out of this chapter.

Background Knowledge

You should have a basic knowledge of what agents are and how they fit into an enterprise's overall AI strategy. We learned about agents and Agentforce previously in Chapters 1 and 2. In later chapters, we'll discover in more detail how to build an agent within Salesforce. If you want to deepen your understanding, *AI Agents: The Definitive Guide* by Nicole Koenigstein (O'Reilly, 2026) is an excellent resource.

We'll come to understand how analytics and visualization agents built with predictive and autonomous monitoring capabilities go beyond just proactively alerting individuals or teams. The agent autonomously acts to gather the details needed for explaining the reasons and also for offering recommendations to potentially improve the outcome. Agentic analytics brings the conversation to the user proactively.

Those recommendations presented to users by an analytics and visualization agent come from prescriptions generated from a prediction model built from scratch in AI Model Builder, which was discussed in detail in Chapter 3. Armed with that knowledge about prediction model outputs, we are now better prepared to understand how predictions and recommendations generated from AI Model Builder are different from forecasts generated within Tableau Next.

Let's clarify some terminology to help in our understanding of predictions and forecasts. Forecasting techniques predict future values with different time horizons or levels of granularity. Forecast horizons can be short-, medium-, or long-term. For example, revenue aggregated by region is often forecast months or years in advance. Whether a specific customer will churn is a more short-term and more granular prediction, however.

Statistical and mathematical forecasting methods are often used by finance, operations, or planning teams for revenue and demand purposes. When used in classical statistics and time-series approaches, the term "prediction" generally means that the future forecasted value is made under explicit conditions.

In contrast, machine learning (ML) forecasting methods use the term "prediction" as a generic term for machine learning model outputs based on a trained model that uses an algorithm and optimizes results for accuracy. Machine learning model outputs include predictions, top predictors, and prescriptions. Prescriptions form the basis of recommendations that often result in actions taken to improve the predicted outcome.

Statisticians, mathematicians, and computer scientists use precise terminology. In practice, however, most data analysts and business users understand that "forecasts" generally refer to predicted future values generated from statistical models. Forecasts are typically less granular and have a medium- or long-term horizon. In practice, "predictions" refer to the output of a machine learning model built for more granular use cases and also includes "prescriptions," commonly referred to as "recommendations."

> Predictions, top predictors, and prescriptions need to be materialized (saved to a data storage location) before they can be used by Tableau Next. Thus, the results from the machine learning model must be saved in a D360 DMO if they are to be used in Tableau Next. Materializing prediction values only happens after the prediction model has been built and trained. In contrast, a forecast can be created by Tableau Next users themselves in very limited circumstances without using a model that needs to be trained. A forecast value created in Tableau Next is not materialized.

Experienced Tableau users already know how to add forecasts to a visualization because Tableau products such as Tableau Desktop and Tableau Public have forecasting capabilities built-in. Thus, many Tableau users are familiar with forecasting features. If you're early in your Tableau learning journey, *Tableau Strategies* (O'Reilly, 2021) by Ann Jackson and Luke Stanke can help fill in your knowledge gaps.

There are many features and functionalities of Tableau Next, including forecasting, that Tableau builders and users will find similar to what they've worked with before. However, one of the main differentiators of Tableau Next is that it's built on top of D360 so that there are consumption-based costs associated with querying the data layer. In addition, the conversational and agentic analytics made possible by Agentforce for Tableau Next are also consumption based.

Consumption-based pricing might be a new concept for Tableau builders and those who've built and used Salesforce CRM Analytics dashboards. The queries powering CRM Analytics dashboards don't incur separate consumption charges when they query Salesforce CRM data stored in Salesforce core. In contrast, Tableau Next queries the D360 data layer, which results in consumption charges assessed for each query.

Aligning fees charged with consumption charges, rather than a specific fixed fee, means that enterprises only pay for what they use. Enterprises are rewarded for building assets optimally and accessing resources only as needed. Thus, visualization and dashboard designers need to build solutions with consumption costs in mind to take advantage of savings possible with optimal design.

Billing considerations, in general, are discussed in this chapter, but data services usage for Tableau Next is calculated based on a number of factors including the usage type. Tableau Next is built on D360 and uses generative AI (GenAI) services. Both Tableau Next and D360 are consumption-based products.

Visit the Salesforce Help pages (*https://oreil.ly/jKJce*) for more information about billing considerations for Tableau Next. You also can find more information about Tableau Next best-practice recommendations, limits, and guidelines on the help pages (*https://oreil.ly/AswE4*).

What You Should Know

Users of other Tableau products like Tableau Cloud and Tableau Desktop understand the concept of assets. Tableau Next assets include familiar content such as metrics, visualizations, and dashboards as well as workspaces.

Unlike other Tableau products, however, Tableau Next is one of many apps (Figure 4-3) accessible via the App Launcher on the Salesforce platform. Other apps available on the platform include Sales, Service, and Marketing, which are all included as part of a traditional customer relationship management (CRM) software suite. D360 and Agentforce Studio apps are also accessed via the App Launcher. We learned about D360 in Chapter 2 and we'll explore Agentforce Studio in Chapter 6.

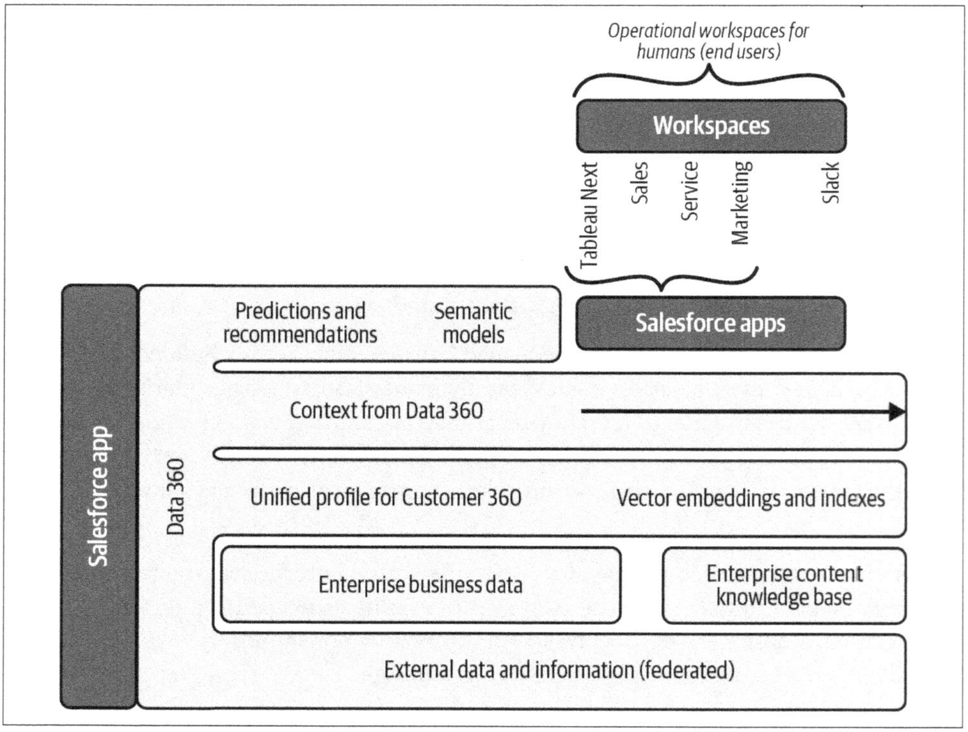

Figure 4-3. Tableau Next workspaces are accessible after users log on to the Tableau Next app available on the Salesforce platform

We'll learn about Sales, Service, and Marketing apps in later chapters. Those apps are excellent systems of work but, as we'll discover, Slack workspaces offer collaborative conversational CRM where employees from different functions can work alongside each other while also effectively leveraging an abundance of specialized agents. The same concept of a collaborative workspace in Slack applies to a workspace in Tableau Next.

In the Tableau Next app, workspaces give users the ability to create, add, and reuse analytic assets. Tableau Next workspaces were built for collaborative and flexible data analysis. Just as with Slack workspaces, the emphasis in Tableau Next workspaces is collaboration. In addition to visualization sharing, Tableau Next users can leverage a variety of different workspace assets created by others.

Workspace assets include semantic models built using D360 objects. In addition, data objects such as the Data Lake Object (DLO), Data Model Object (DMO), and Calculated Insights (CI) object are assets available for use in Tableau Next workspaces. For many reasons, using D360 objects for visualizations and dashboards is a new concept even for experienced Tableau users. For one, D360 objects can leverage external federated data without needing to copy and ingest data into Salesforce D360.

> It's important to realize both the semantic and visualization layers associated with Tableau Next connect only to the D360 platform unified data layer. Thus, building semantic models and Tableau Next visualizations requires an understanding of D360 objects.

We'll briefly discuss data governance for Salesforce users who are responsible for building semantic models. The information is relevant for human users who need access to the semantic models and underlying data. Building the semantic models is a necessary step before conversational analytics are enabled. When users interact with agents in a conversational manner, the agent first reviews the data it's been given access to via the assigned data library that we learned about in Chapter 2. The agent then considers the data governance applied to the human user before responding. In later chapters we'll learn more about how agents interact conversationally with Salesforce users.

> Some agent terminology changed in April 2026. For example, agent *topics* were renamed to *subagents*. Within this chapter, the updated subagents term is used instead of agent topics. However, the previous terminology is viewable in some screenshots because the Salesforce app has not been completely updated to reflect the change.

This chapter describes Tableau Next and the semantic layer in detail along with specifying Agentforce capabilities needed for achieving conversational and agentic analytics. The chapter contents are not intended to be comprehensive enough for scoping or detailed planning for deployment integration, or enablement. Instead, the intent is to provide sufficient information for readers to become informed about Tableau Next and Agentforce capabilities and to better understand how these features are important to an overall agentic enterprise's strategy.

We also won't discuss which specific licenses or packages must be acquired, details of consumption costs, or which permission sets are required to achieve the functionality described. For one thing, the exact licenses required change over time and consumption costs and licensing fees are negotiated. Thus, your Salesforce Account Executive (AE) and implementation partner can best answer those questions.

Building Blocks for Conversational and Agentic Data Analytics

Data is the foundational building block for any analytics solution built for an agentic enterprise. Data sources make their way into the unified data layer and that data is modeled, transformed, and mapped. It's possible to expand data access to create a more complete understanding of an enterprise by leveraging data stored outside of Salesforce through bidirectional data-sharing capabilities.

Data about past events tells a story about what happened and why certain things transpired. Historical data alone doesn't lead to making better decisions about what should be done today, however. That's why business users need more information, such as predictions and prescriptions, to help them know what actions will most likely lead to better outcomes. Predictive models are powerful, and the predictions, top predictors, and prescriptions output from the model are useful for a number of different purposes including for analytics.

Before analytical tools like Tableau were available, data analysts and other business users reviewed static reports that limited who could truly engage with and understand an enterprise's data. Tableau democratized traditional analytics by offering a drag-and-drop interface where users could create charts, graphs, and dashboards to visually explore the data.

Tableau was founded in 2003 with the goal of improving data analysis and making data more accessible to people through visualization. It was later acquired by Salesforce in 2019. Tableau offers many powerful products for querying data and generating data visualizations. Paid products include Tableau Desktop, Tableau Server, Tableau Prep Builder, Tableau Vizable, Tableau Mobile, Tableau Cloud, Tableau Prep, Tableau CRM, Tableau Bridge, and Tableau Pulse. Free products currently include Tableau Public and Tableau Reader.

Tableau's newest product innovation is Tableau Next. It offers the same powerful functionalities for agentic enterprises with which Tableau users have become accustomed. In addition, Tableau Next has the advantage of being built on top of the Salesforce platform, which means actionability can be integrated directly in Tableau Next. A little later in the chapter we'll explore the various actions Tableau Next users can take without navigating away from their current screen.

Actionability in the normal flow of work is also possible because of the conversational and agentic analytic capabilities available with analytics and visualization agents. Conversational and agentic analytics require specific agent skills and business context. That context provided to analytics and visualization agents comes from the semantic layer.

The semantic layer is a critical building block built on top of the data layer using the Semantic Model Builder accessible from within Salesforce D360. The Semantic Model Builder can also be accessed via the Tableau Next workspace, which is why it's part of the Tableau grouping (Figure 4-4).

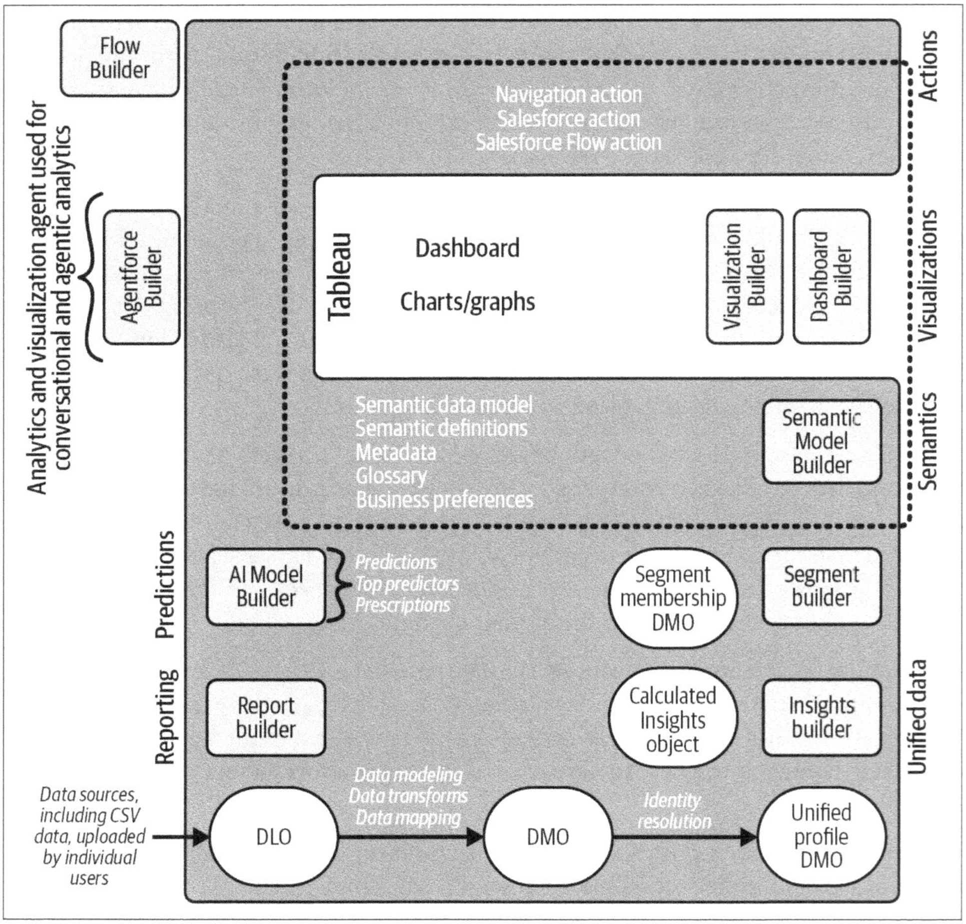

Figure 4-4. Semantics and visualizations built on top of a unified, contextualized data layer

Our focus here is on three specific building blocks. We'll explore the Semantic Model Builder and learn how to create semantic knowledge that can be used for analytics and visualization agents as well as for Tableau Next visualizations created for humans. Next, we'll discover the Tableau Next app and workspaces that include access to the Visualization Builder and Dashboard Builder. Finally, we'll learn about the three agent skills available out-of-the-box for building an analytics and visualization agent for conversational and agentic analytics.

Before we consider each of those three building blocks, though, it's important to explain a few concepts. We want to explain what it means to bring actionable insights into the flow of work. In addition, we'll want to understand the importance of embedding actionability into visualizations and dashboards.

Bringing Actionable Insights into the Flow of Work

Actionable insights are what we strive for when we report on and analyze data. Accurate reporting provides a summary of what occurred at the data layer along with some basic explanations of why something happened. Understanding trends over time is easier for humans when the information is presented visually, which is why it's important to prepare visualizations and dashboards for employees who rely on insights for decision making.

It's easier to distribute charts and graphs in the flow of work versus sharing many tables of information. Visualizations also improve storytelling. People more readily understand complex information when it's presented visually rather than when it's offered as raw data and numbers.

Reporting provides some insights, but the use of data analysis techniques like statistics and ML, grounded in more context, yields better results with richer explanations. The best insights reveal the most details about why something happened and go a step further to offer recommendations on how best to improve outcomes. That's where machine learning (ML) plays a vital role.

Surfacing actionable insights within the flow of work for an organization's human users is an experience Salesforce continues to iterate on in a number of ways:

- Modes for delivering insights to users for questions prepared in advance
  - Dedicated Salesforce app for reports and dashboards
  - Selected visualizations and metrics on a Salesforce console home page
  - Prediction fields and visualizations surfaced on Salesforce record pages
  - Visualizations and other insights embedded externally
- Frequency of insight delivery
  - Regular intervals
  - Near real time
  - On demand
- Modes for delivering insights to users supported by agents
  - Conversational analytics
  - Agentic analytics
- Variety of audience types for insight delivery
  - Individual
  - Team

It's most common for users to access Salesforce functionality directly in app pages within the platform on a desktop or using the Salesforce mobile app. Salesforce users log in to the desktop or their mobile phone and then access apps via the Salesforce App Launcher. Tableau Next is one of those apps and it's where users can access all their visualizations and dashboards built on top of the D360 unified data layer.

Tableau Next visualizations and dashboards present information on demand. Queries of the data are executed every time a dashboard is opened by a user. If a user refreshes the screen, the queries are executed again. Thus, insights surfaced in Tableau Next are provided on demand rather than real time, which is the optimal choice for delivering insights to users via visualizations.

In certain scenarios, especially for those situations where decisions and actions can be defined in advance, the near real-time delivery of actionable insights is more appropriate. Fortunately, the Salesforce platform supports the delivery of insights into the flow of work for those situations.

As an example, real-time information is available in the D360 layer when needed for use cases like personalization for real-time marketing. Further, machine learning predictions support a D360 real-time profile data graph used for real-time personalization by providing information relevant for a targeting rule in a personalization point.

For situations where humans need to review the insights before action is taken, AI can provide access to certain types of insights much more quickly. Conversational and agentic analytics capabilities allow users to ask ad hoc questions about the data and also to request alerts be delivered in the flow of work whenever there is something of which the user should be aware.

Sometimes, a user's flow of work is outside the Salesforce core platform. In those situations, metrics and dashboards can be embedded externally. Salesforce users whose flow of work is primarily within collaboration tools like Slack and Teams can leverage Tableau Next visualizations and functionality including the conversational and agentic capabilities.

For example, an individual can be notified via a private direct message (DM) anytime one of their assigned accounts with an opportunity greater than one million dollars is likely to churn. Other times, a team working together within Slack might be informed about a significant change in a shared metric. As a result, they could communicate via the channel to determine the best course of action. Or it could be a cross-team collaboration group pulled together in a huddle to provide input and make real-time decisions based on an unexpected alert.

Surfacing insights to users within their normal flow of work is transformational. The real magic, though, is going beyond surfacing actionable insights and recommendations in the flow of work. Embedding actionability alongside the insights makes it possible for users to continue their flow of work without any friction. Tableau Next visualizations and dashboards offer that functionality today whereby users can take action on the same screen where those actionable insights are surfaced.

Embedding Actionability Within Visualizations and Dashboards

Tableau Next users rely on charts, graphs, metrics, and agents to surface trends and insights as well as to explain the reasons behind the results. Targets, thresholds, predictions, and prescriptions provide the basis for understanding what actions are available and should be taken so that the path forward will likely improve.

For example, a marketer may desire to pause underperforming ads and further promote well-performing ads based on trends in a campaign's impressions, clicks, or sign-ups over time without having to leave a dashboard built for the marketing team. An individual member of the sales team could elect to reprioritize a sales outreach strategy when their pipeline dashboard highlights a currently stalled deal of high value. A sales leader might want to change pricing discounts based on pipeline and revenue details presented in a dashboard.

In many traditional situations, a user leaves the dashboard and navigates to one or more different screens or systems to implement those desired changes. However, Tableau Next offers a frictionless approach for users who want to take action right in the flow of work, without ever leaving the visualization or dashboard. Importantly, Tableau Next is built on top of the Salesforce platform, which means it's possible to build out flows that can be leveraged within Tableau Next dashboards. This creates many different opportunities for actionability.

A user can access a simple URL navigation or they can be given the ability to post to an open Salesforce case without leaving the visualization. In addition, a flow built to leverage other tools such as MuleSoft connectors makes it possible for a user to write data back to an original data source that exists outside of Salesforce.

All of these actions and more can be taken by a user from a Tableau Next dashboard once the action has been set up and added to the dashboard. Of course, the flows need to be built in advance and the user needs to have the appropriate access and permissions to view the dashboard as well as to execute flows that power the actions.

Now that we better understand what it means to bring actionable insights and actionability into the flow of work, we're ready to focus on the three main Salesforce building blocks for creating conversational and agentic analytics. The first of those is semantic models.

Semantic Models

Semantic models can be built and managed within the D360 app by accessing the Semantic Layer tab. Alternatively, users with access to the Tableau Next app can create and manage models there. In addition, the Tableau Semantics connector for Tableau Desktop and Tableau Cloud allows access from D360 or Tableau Next.

In “Tableau Next Workspaces” on page 146, we’ll navigate semantic models in the Tableau Next app. Here, let’s see what the experience is like in the D360 app.

Navigating Semantic Models in D360

The listing of all semantic models accessible by a user can be viewed from the Semantic Layer tab within the D360 app. Notice the default page (Figure 4-5) is the Models tab. There is also a Metrics page tab that provides a list view of all semantic model metrics.

Figure 4-5. Default page of the Models tab within the Semantic Layer menu tab of the D360 app

Each existing semantic model name in the list view is presented as a clickable link that opens up the Semantic Model Builder when clicked. Alternatively, there is a way to open up the Semantic Model Builder from within a Tableau Next workspace. Clicking the button to create a new semantic model while in Tableau Next gives users the option to add an existing semantic model or create a new model (Figure 4-6). It’s possible to create a new semantic model from scratch, create from an existing model, or create from a Data 360 data kit. New semantic models can also be created from Tableau-published data sources.

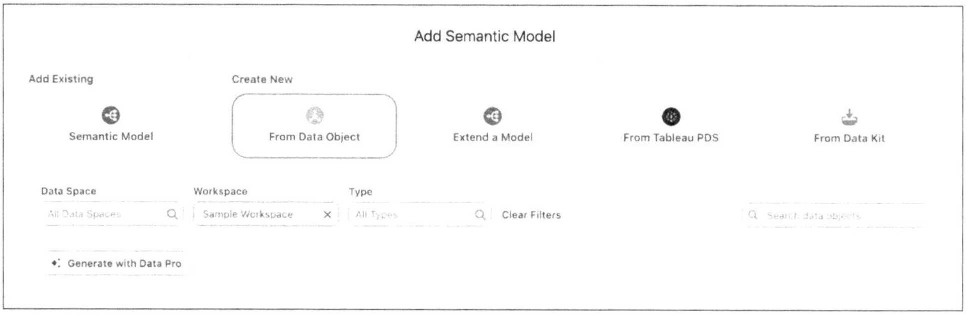

Figure 4-6. Initial screen for creating a new semantic model

New semantic models can be created from a data kit or from scratch. They can also be created from an existing model or retrieved from a Tableau-published data source. If you elect to start with a new model, you'll need to select the data space and then choose your D360 objects (Figure 4-7) from among the DMO, DLO, and CI object choices available to you.

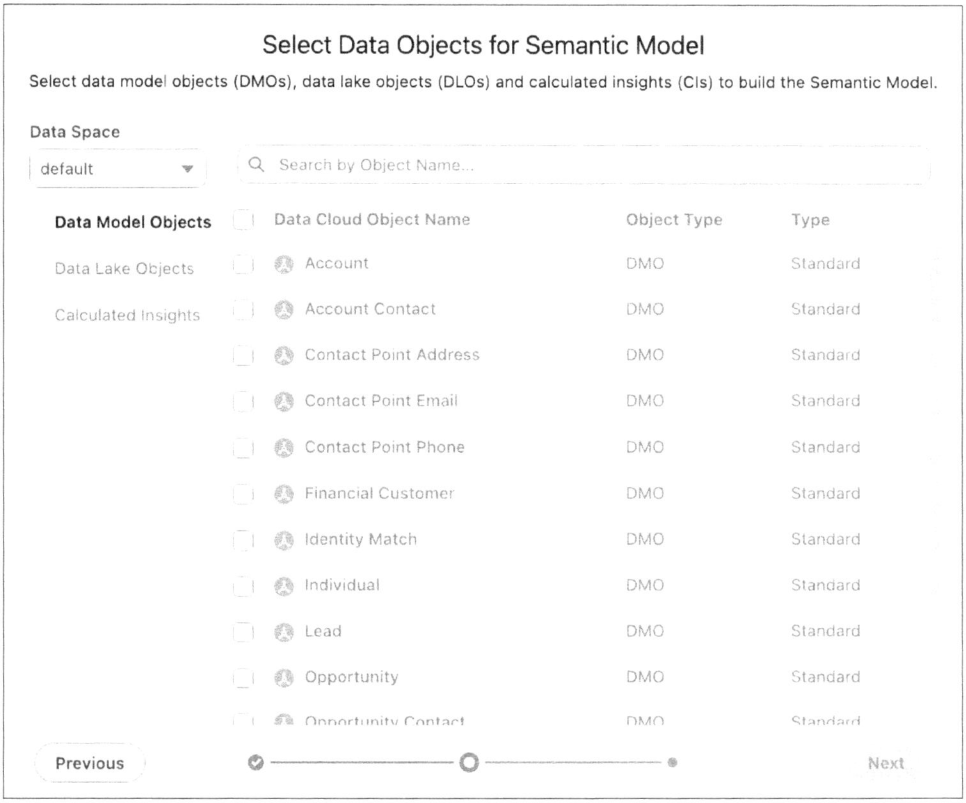

Figure 4-7. Selecting the data objects from the data space for the new semantic model

Give your semantic model a name, include a description, and then click the Create button. Whenever you create a new semantic model or edit an existing model, you enter the Semantic Model Builder.

Semantic Model Builder

The Semantic Model Builder is the tool users leverage when adding or editing definitions for the semantic model. Data objects are listed in the model definitions and appear on the canvas. Relationships can be created between data objects manually or by using the Semantic AI relationship suggestions at the top of the canvas (Figure 4-8). A semantic model relationship connects different object tables based on common fields. It's recommended that users try using relationships to combine data before considering other options because relationships in the semantic model are established between data objects to enrich the data model without the need to define a join type.

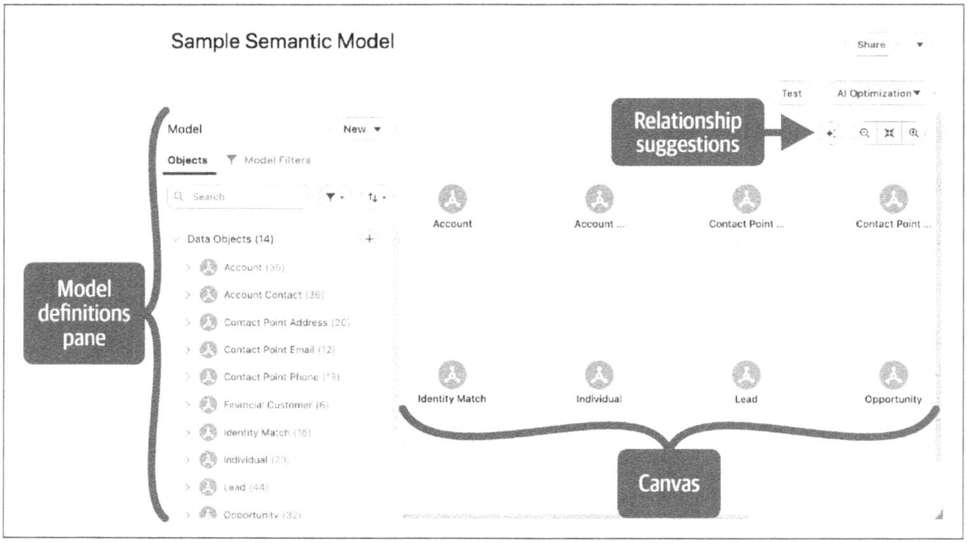

Figure 4-8. Semantic Model Builder pane and canvas

Data object field attributes can be changed in the Semantic Model Builder and those changes only apply to the fields in the specific semantics model. Modifications made to Data Object field properties don't change anything in the D360 object. For example, the field type property determines if the field is used as a dimension or measure in the semantic model. The field visibility property is such that all fields are visible by default, but you could change the visibility of an individual field so that it's not visible to end users who access this semantic model.

Related data objects can be grouped in Semantic Model Builder to segment customers based on demographics, behavior, or purchasing patterns. In addition, data objects can be grouped to correct data errors or to answer "what if" questions. Use the Create Group option appearing next to the dimension or measure name to create groups. In addition to the option to create a group, the ability to create a numeric bin exists for data object measures.

If needed, additional data objects can be added to the canvas by clicking the New button at the top of the screen and selecting the Add Data Objects option (Figure 4-9). In addition to adding new data objects, users can add new metrics, calculated fields, parameters, dimension hierarchies, and logical views.

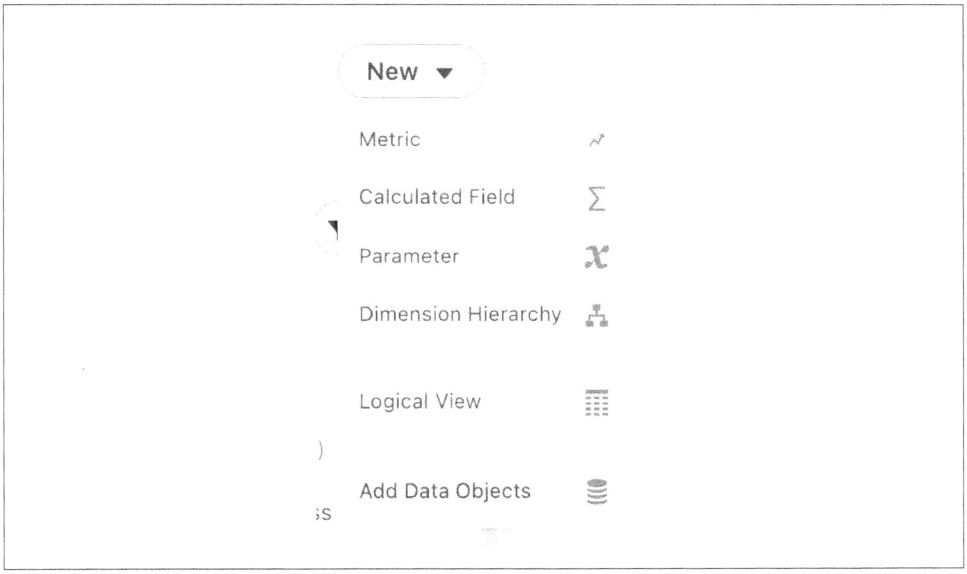

Figure 4-9. Adding new data objects or other items to the Semantic Model Builder canvas

Semantic model metrics are key performance indicators (KPIs) tracked over time. Revenue over the past quarter or conversion rates over the past year are examples of metrics. A metric needs a time dimension as well as a measure or calculated field representing the KPI. Metrics created in a semantic model are used in Tableau Next and for analytics and visualization agents. These metrics are similar to Tableau Pulse, another Tableau product used outside the D360 platform.

Users can also create a new logical view directly in Semantic Model Builder. A semantic model logical view is a separate data object composed of two or more tables connected to each other using special join types. Users query logical views without needing an understanding of the underlying data objects. Relationships can be created between logical views. In addition, logical views can be used in calculated fields and metrics.

On the top right side of the Semantic Model Builder is an AI Optimization button where users can manage business preferences (Figure 4-10) among other things. The AI Optimization feature is disabled by default and must be enabled in the Tableau Next settings by an administrator. This feature provides a health score and recommendations for model improvement. Specific permissions, such as Tableau Next Admin, are required to access and use this feature.

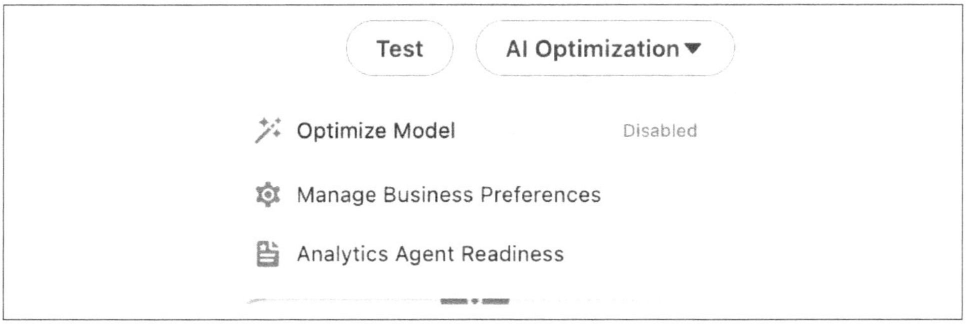

Figure 4-10. Managing business preferences and other features within Semantic Model Builder for AI optimization

Business preferences are important for analytics and visualization agents because they help the agent respond better to users' questions. More specifically, business preferences are used in the Agentforce Data Analysis subagent associated with the Concierge and Inspector skills.

Business preferences (Figure 4-11) are added to provide interpretation or output preferences; for example, explain unique terminology or spell out acronyms. Define sorting preference, either ascending or descending, and specify certain fields always to return when certain questions are asked. For example, include in the business preferences that you want the agent to always return the account name, account ID, and opportunity name whenever a user inquires about an opportunity.

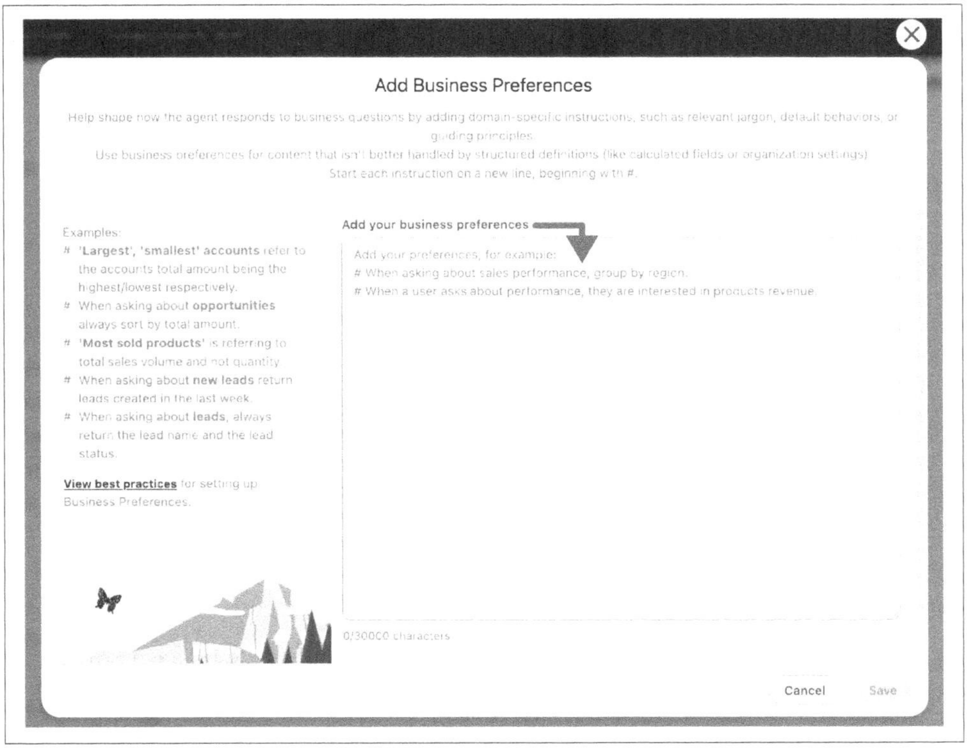

Figure 4-11. Adding business preferences in the Semantic Model Builder

Business preferences descriptions are best kept short to help reduce the risk of confusing the agent. Complex instructions need to be broken down into simpler steps. It's important to be thorough in the number of business preferences entered, but an overly lengthy list could result in conflicts. When that happens, the agent uses the most recently entered business preference above any other conflicting instruction.

Semantic models are extensible, but business preferences are not inherited from a semantic model. Thus, you'll need to copy/paste the business preferences. Alternatively, a data kit can be used to distribute the business preferences with the semantic model.

When we explore Tableau Next later, we'll see that it's possible to create calculated fields while creating visualizations. However, certain things like creating metrics and adding business preferences need to be done within the Semantic Model Builder.

The Tableau Next app makes it a seamless experience to navigate between workspace assets like visualizations, dashboards, semantic models, data objects, and data connections. So it may not seem obvious initially that you're navigating out of Tableau

Next into semantic models. These models are not actually built in Tableau; they're built on top of the D360 platform. The distinction should be more clear once you explore data governance for semantic models and realize that access to the models used in Tableau Next is dependent on the D360 data space selected.

Data Governance for Semantic Models

Data governance for semantic models is unique, much different from what Salesforce or Tableau administrators have used before. As such, we'll include some basic information about semantic model governance features describing two main security access points.

We'll first understand how the system determines who can view semantic models. Next, we'll learn about the policies that determine what data is available to users during model design and when executing queries from Tableau Next or an analytics and visualization agent.

Semantic models data governance is composed of two main types: dataspace permissions and policy layers. Dataspace permissions are foundational permissions. Users without the required dataspace permission won't see that the semantic model exists.

Users who can see semantic models may view or edit all underlying data, a portion of the data, or none at all. Viewing and editing semantic model objects and object fields is based on five factors—four distinct policy layers and deny policies:

- Attribute-based access control (ABAC)
- Object-level security (OLS)
- Field-level security (FLS)
- Record-level security (RLS)
- Deny policies

Deny policies always override the other policies, which helps protect sensitive data at both the design stage and the query stage. This is important because administrators with certain permissions have broader visibility into the models and the data than they would otherwise based on the policies assigned to them. In addition, administrators may share a semantic model even if they aren't the owner. If you're responsible for data governance in your enterprise, you may want to review the full details about data governance in the Salesforce Help documentation (*https://oreil.ly/9yC1i*).

Semantic models are applied to all data sources connected and ingested into the D360 platform. Semantic models are an integral part of the D360 platform and critical components for an agentic enterprise. More specifically, semantic models power data analytics consumption by both humans and agents. Later we'll learn the role of the semantic layer for analytics and visualization agents when we explore the Concierge and Inspector and Agentforce skills. First, let's explore how individuals navigate the Tableau Next app and what part semantic models play in creating visualizations and dashboards for users.

Getting Started with the Tableau Next App

Tableau Next is a composable analytics AI platform built with several features that bring insights and actionability into the flow of work. Before exploring Tableau Next visualizations and dashboards, let's first orient ourselves in Tableau Next. In this section, we'll first learn about navigating Tableau Next. Then we'll learn how to add new data sources in Tableau. Lastly, we'll explore workspaces, which is how project assets are organized in Tableau Next.

Navigating the Tableau Next App

The Tableau Next app is accessed from the App Launcher (Figure 4-12) after logging in to Salesforce.

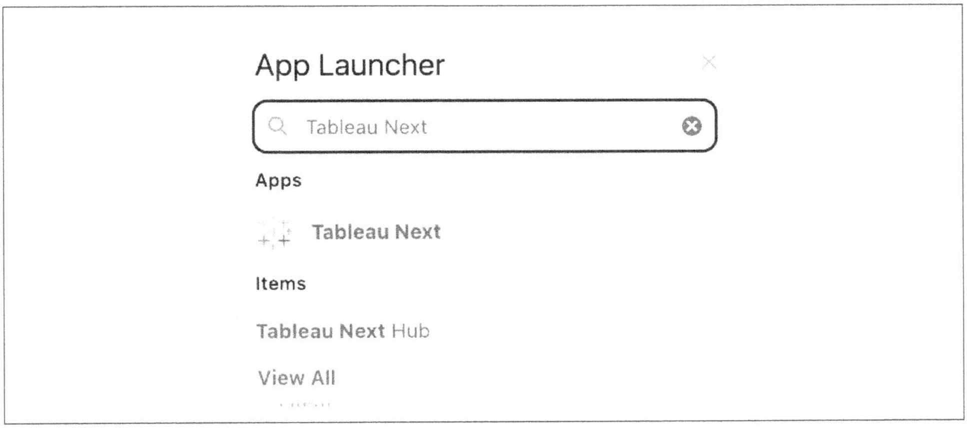

Figure 4-12. Tableau Next is accessible from the Salesforce App Launcher

Within Tableau Next, a user can access seven main menu options. Reach out to your Salesforce administrator if any of these menu options don't appear. Some features need to be enabled first. In other situations, users need to be granted specific permissions before the navigation menu item appears in Tableau Next:

- Home
- Browse
- Following
- Conversations

- Q&A Calibration
- Agent Settings
- Data Monitor
- Task Manager
- Administration

As we review each of the menu options, you'll notice the Add button is accessible no matter which option is selected. We'll discuss the Add button last. The default menu is the Home page, so let's explore that menu option first.

Tableau Next Home

Once you've navigated to the Tableau Next Home page by selecting the Tableau Next app from the App Launcher, you'll notice a greeting along with a considerable amount of information (Figure 4-13). This is where you'll access your enterprise's analytics-related assets.

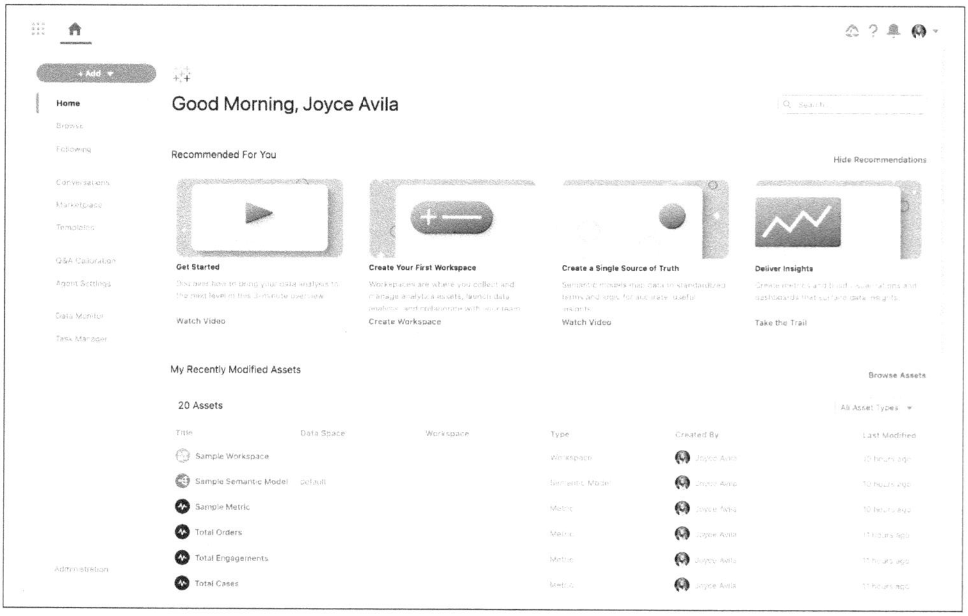

Figure 4-13. Tableau Next app Home page

In the top-right corner is a search bar where users can perform keyword searches for assets. Just below the greeting and the search bar is a list of curated resources including videos and Trailhead modules followed by a section for recently opened assets.

The bottom section of the Home page includes a list of recently modified assets. Initially, up to 20 assets are displayed and there is a Show More button at the bottom of the screen. There's also a drop-down menu to the right of the asset list giving users the option to filter by asset type. Filtering by workspace or user is possible if multiple workspaces or users exist.

If it's your first time logging in to the Tableau Next app, your screen may look different from the one here because you likely won't have any assets created yet. You can still navigate around the menu options, though, to orient yourself before getting started.

Browse and Following

Below the Home menu option in the Tableau Next app is the Following menu item where users can follow one or more metrics or dashboards. There are two menu tabs on the Following page: a Following menu tab and a Browse menu tab (Figure 4-14).

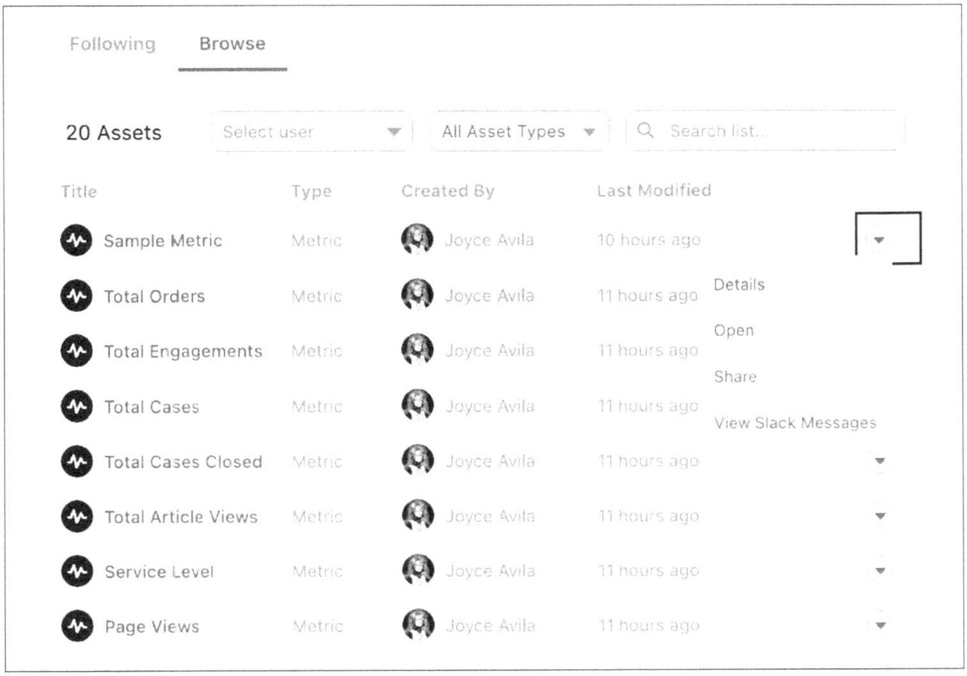

Figure 4-14. Browse the menu tab located on the Following page within the Tableau Next app

The list of assets a user can follow is listed on the Browse page and can be searched via drop-down menus offering searches by user or asset type. There's also a keyword search box available.

To the right of each listing is an arrow for a drop-down menu. The drop-down for a dashboard allows users to click Details or Open. Clicking the Open option from the drop-down achieves the same results as clicking on the asset title from the list.

The drop-down menu for a metrics asset offers more options. In addition to the ability to view the details or open the metric, a user has the option to share the metric or view related Slack messages about it. The metric can be shared in Slack or embedded in a third-party app (Figure 4-15) so that you receive updates wherever you're working without needing to navigate back to the Tableau Next app.

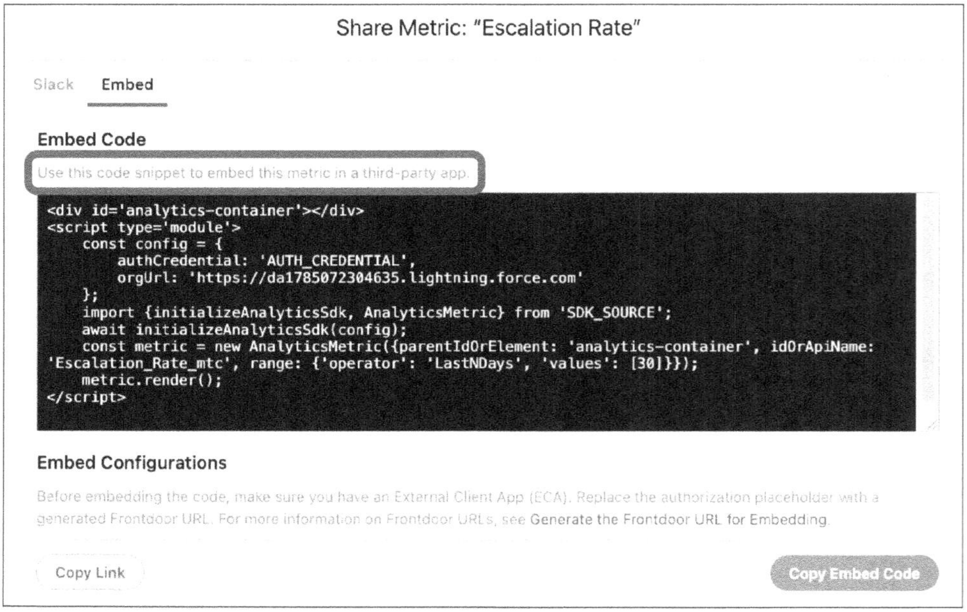

Figure 4-15. Code for embedding a metric outside of Salesforce

The asset listing titles are clickable links that take the user directly to the metric or dashboard selected. Clicking on a metric title or using the drop-down option to open the metric takes the user to that specific metric page so that the user can view details about the metric. The user can also filter the metric, change the time range, or set a new goal.

In the top-right corner of the metrics page, a user can click Follow (Figure 4-16) or use the drop-down menu to manage followers. Notice the Agentforce agent is accessible to the user if needed. Also included is Guidance Center information and the Help option.

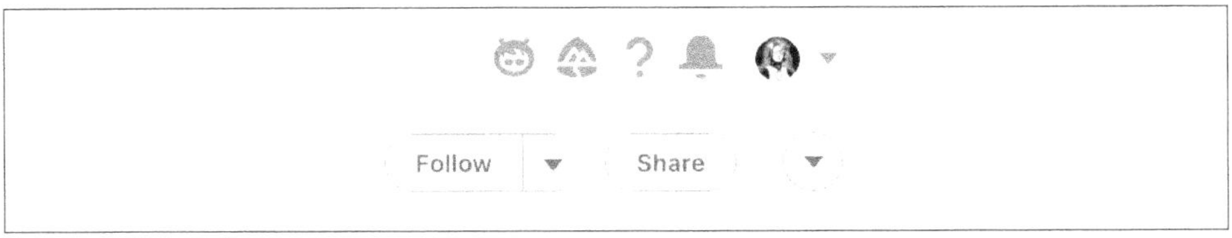

Figure 4-16. Managing followers is achieved by clicking Follow or using the drop-down menu

The Agentforce agent accessible from the metrics page is an analytics and visualization agent that we'll learn more about in "Analytics and Visualization Agent" on page 160. An analytics and visualization agent is built with the Agentforce Builder tool, but it can be refined within the Tableau Next app using the Q&A Calibration feature.

Q&A Calibration

Q&A Calibration is where users create, manage, and test agent questions for validating an agent's understanding of the semantic model. You'll first need to select an agent with Concierge skills from among the analytics and visualization agents created for your enterprise. Your organization may have only one analytics and visualization agent with Concierge skills but there could be more. Request that Tableau Next generate questions (Figure 4-17) after you select the model or manually add questions yourself.

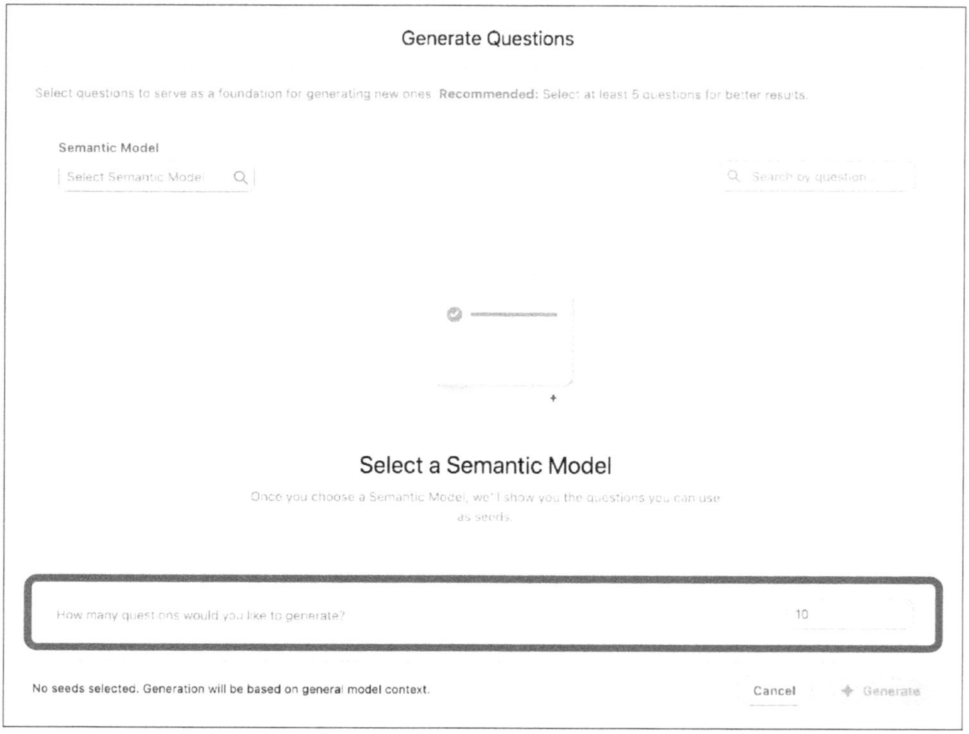

Figure 4-17. Request that questions are generated for you unless you want to manually add questions

Questions are classified as New initially and then a user classifies the agent's response as either Verified or Inaccurate. Verified questions are saved in a repository linked to the semantic model and help guide future agent responses. Questions classified as Needs Validation (Figure 4-18) were previously verified but require revalidation due to changes in the semantic model.

Figure 4-18. Questions classified as Needs Validation require revalidation due to changes in the semantic model

Inaccurate answers can be calibrated by providing more context or modifying the semantic model. The Tableau Next calibration feature is an excellent way for users to fine-tune their semantic model on a regular basis because building and maintaining semantic models should be an iterative process. Periodic reviews of the questions and answers should be undertaken.

That's why the calibration details also include the date and timestamp for when the question was classified. After calibrating an incorrect response or any time a user wants to manually review a response again, the user can retest the agent's response.

Task Manager

The Task Manager navigation option opens to a dashboard that provides a centralized view for administrators to review, update, and complete admin actions for Tableau Next. This Task Manager allows admins to manage and track the status of requests as either Not Started, In Progress, or Complete.

Templates

The next Tableau Next menu option in the navigation pane is Templates, which allows users to create a new template from which new dashboards can be created. When creating a new Tableau Next template, the user gives the template a name, version number, and description, and includes information that highlights the benefits of and use cases for the template. Users should include additional highlights (Figure 4-19) when there is more than one benefit or use case for a given template. In addition, the template can include up to three target audiences and three industries as well as up to five images that best showcase the Tableau Next template.

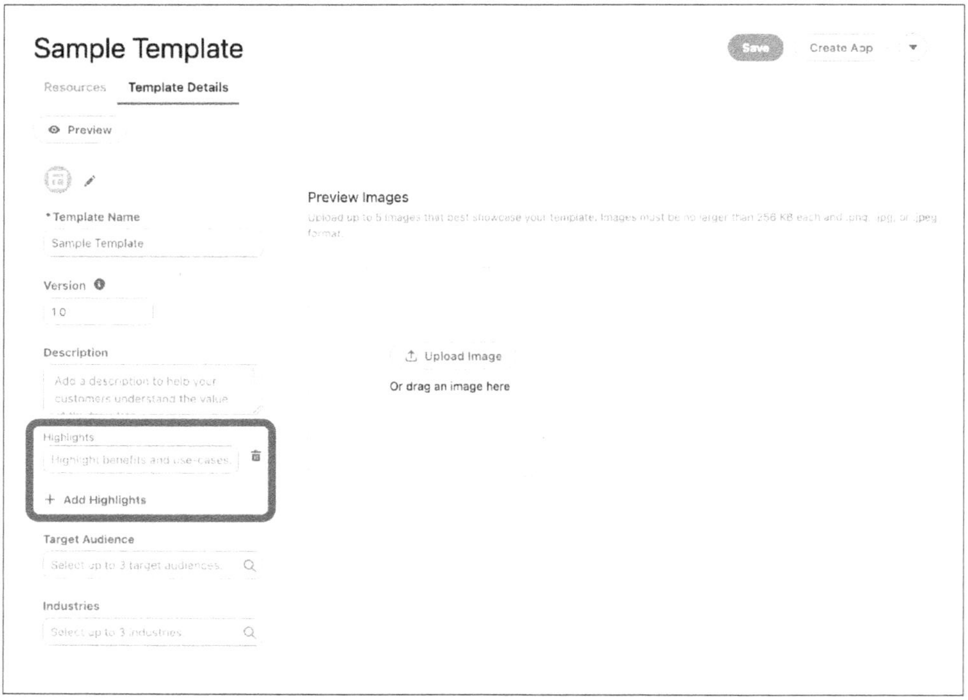

Figure 4-19. Creating a new template with name, version number, description, benefits, and use cases

Creating and using templates helps promote consistency across dashboards. Templates also help establish and enforce best practices and accelerate project delivery. Tableau Next templates can be shared internally with your teammates or publicly listed on the Marketplace.

In addition to creating a template from scratch, users can navigate to a completed dashboard and generate a template from the action menu (Figure 4-20).

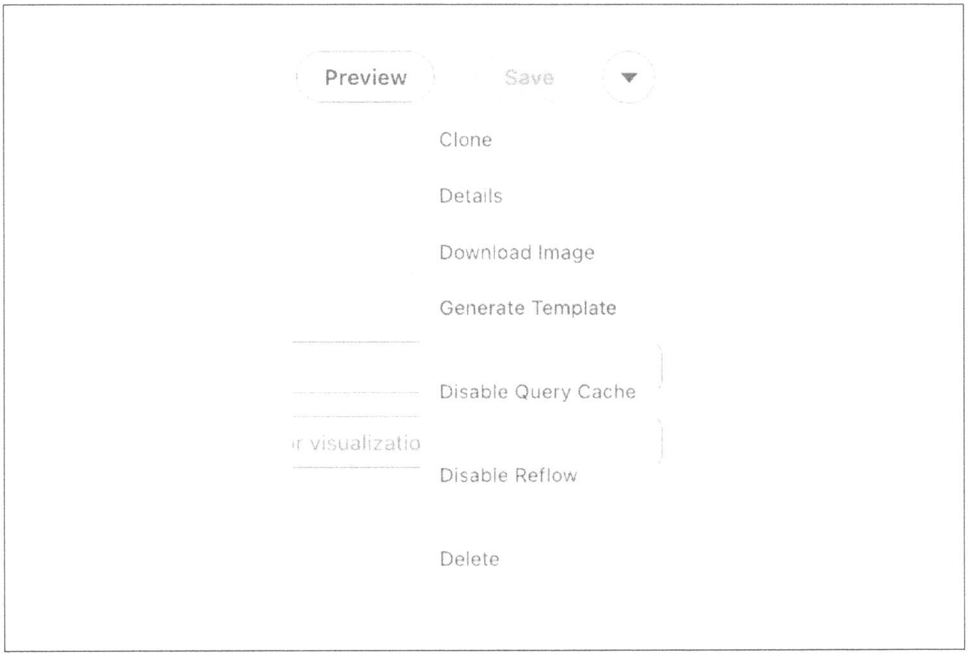

Figure 4-20. Generating a template from the action menu of a completed Tableau Next dashboard

After generating a new template from an existing dashboard, don't forget to upload preview images and add the details to your template to tell users why they should use it.

Data Monitor

The Tableau Next Data Monitor provides users a centralized view for tracking, monitoring, and managing data object refreshes (Figure 4-21).

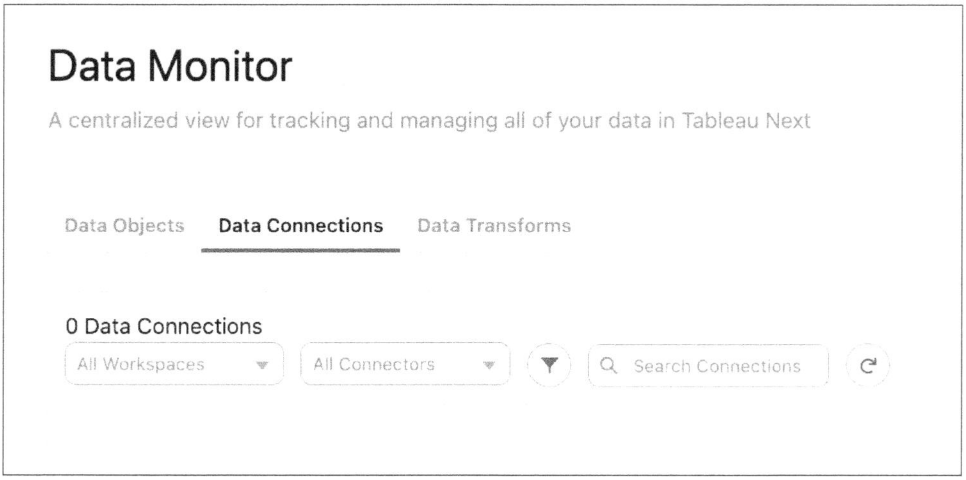

Figure 4-21. Tableau Next Data Monitor

The default list view includes details about the connection method and the last refresh time, among other things. To the right of the object name is a drop-down menu offering users the option to open the object or get more details. Clicking the option to get more details opens up a small window to the right with those details (Figure 4-22).

Tracking, monitoring, and managing data object refreshes in D360 offers several benefits. Saving resources and improving performance can result from ensuring efficient data processing by avoiding unnecessary refreshes. In addition, tracking refreshes helps identify and resolve issues if data ingestion errors occur. Importantly, users can access details about refresh history to gain insights into the number of records processed, added, or removed. This helps provide more trust in data accuracy and reliability.

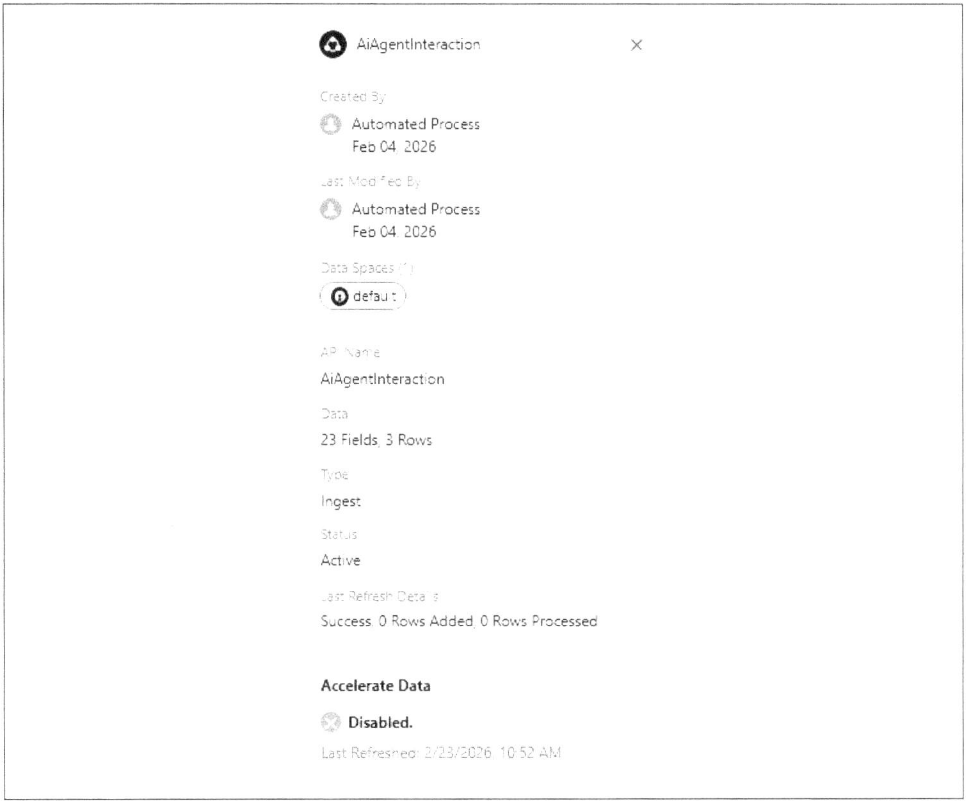

Figure 4-22. Connection details of a data object refresh

Administration

There is one menu option meant for Tableau Next administrators who are given access to perform some administrator tasks. Tableau Next administrators can manage users, permission sets, external client apps, and settings (Figure 4-23).

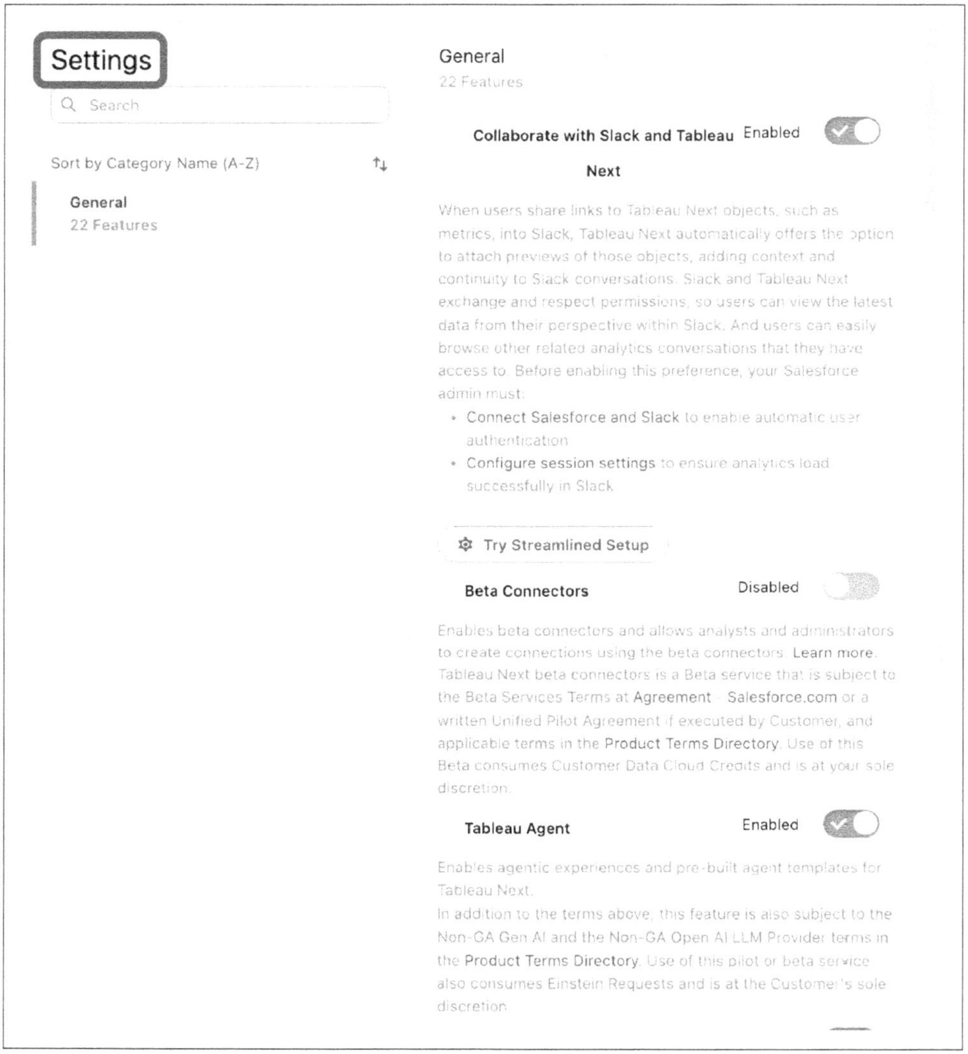

Figure 4-23. Tableau Next settings available to administrators

The settings information is important to review to confirm that necessary features like Agentforce for Analytics, Q&A Calibration, and access to Tableau Next Marketplace have been enabled.

Add button

As we navigated through all the Tableau Next menu options, there was always the Add button at the top of the screen so that users can get immediate access to add a new workspace or data source in addition to adding a new dashboard, visualization, or semantic model (Figure 4-24).

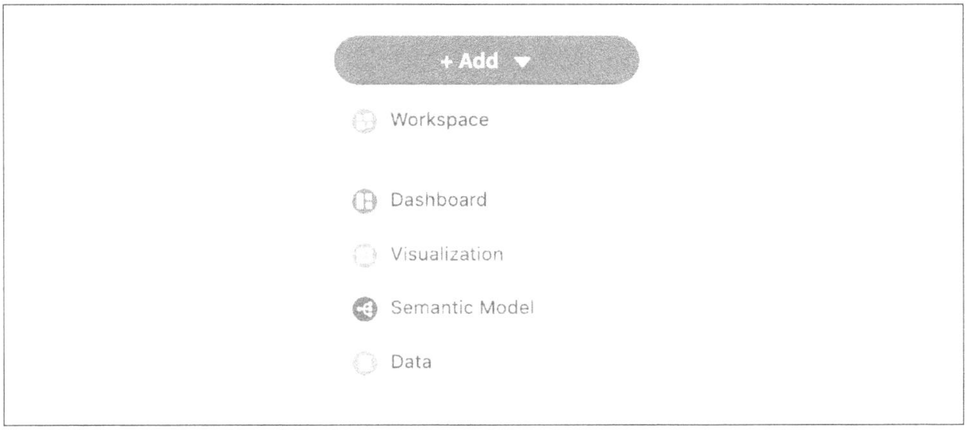

Figure 4-24. The Add button is always accessible from any Tableau Next menu option

We learned about semantic models earlier and we'll cover dashboards and visualizations a little later. In the next section, let's first explore how to add data sources in Tableau Next and then how to create a workspace.

Add Data in Tableau Next

Sometimes Tableau Next users need to add data sources or perform a one-time data upload. Users might want to add data for the purpose of modifying or extending semantic data models without impacting the base model. For example, users might want to add new calculations, add more objects, or adjust relationships between existing objects. This is especially useful for users who want to explore new ideas by combining local datasets with production data without impacting the production environment.

Users first need to select the workspace and then choose whether to add data from an existing source or create a new source (Figure 4-25). Users can upload a file with an *.xlsx* or *.csv* file extension. Uploaded files appear as a new DLO in the workspace.

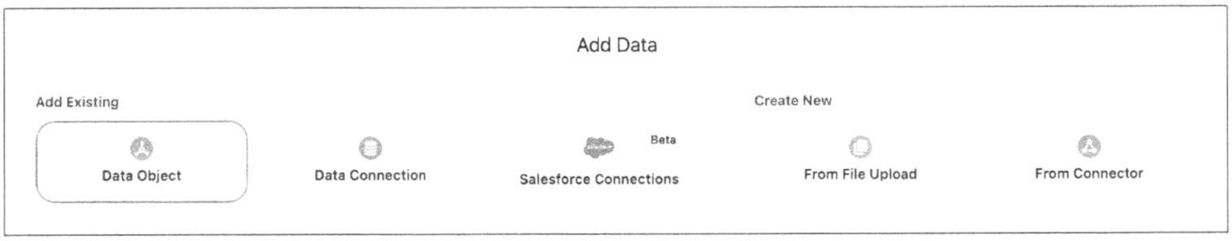

Figure 4-25. Add data from an existing source or create a new data source

Alternatively, users can add data via connectors (Figure 4-26).

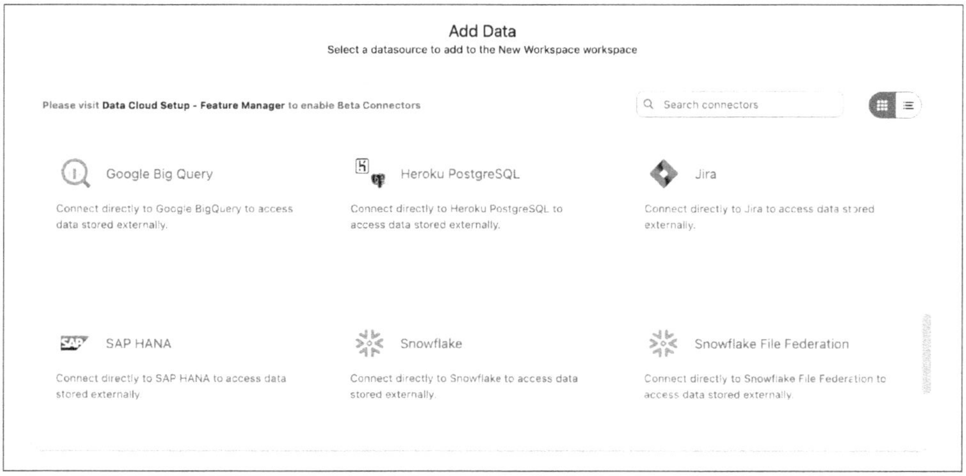

Figure 4-26. Add data in Tableau Next using connectors

Users access new data sources in the workspace once a connection has been established. Several connectors are available, including ActiveCampaign, Airtable, Amazon Redshift, AWS Aurora PostgreSQL, Azure MySQL, CockroachDB, Databricks, Google Big Query, Jira, ServiceNow, Shopify, Snowflake, SurveyMonkey, Trello, and WordPress.

Tableau Next Workspaces

Tableau Next assets, such as Data Connectors and Visualizations, are organized in a workspace. At first glance, a Tableau Next workspace may seem similar to other Tableau workspaces or to a Tableau workbook, but they are, in fact, not the same. Let's consider Tableau Server, Tableau Cloud, and Tableau Desktop workspaces and workbooks so we can better understand how Tableau Next workspaces are different from them.

Tableau Server is a web-based sharing and collaboration analytics platform hosted and maintained within the enterprise firewall. Tableau Cloud (previously Tableau Online) is the SaaS version of Tableau Server. Tableau workspaces used in Tableau Server and Tableau Cloud contain one or more sheets that include views, dashboards, or stories. A story is a sequence of visualizations.

Tableau Desktop is data visualization software available for Mac and PC. Tableau Desktop workbooks are synonymous with Tableau Server and Tableau Cloud workspaces except they often include data sources that include local Excel or Access files. Thus, a Tableau Desktop workbook needs to be "packaged" before sharing. A packaged workbook contains a copy of any referenced local files or Tableau extract files.

In contrast, a Tableau Next workspace uses only D360 objects as data sources. Even files uploaded for use in Tableau Next are stored in a D360 object. In addition, a Tableau Next workspace serves as a much broader environment where analytic assets are created, added, and reused. Within a Tableau Next workspace, capabilities exist for establishing data connections, building semantic models, creating metrics, and sharing visualizations.

Using the Add button from any menu within Tableau Next, a user creates a new workspace that initially has no assets (Figure 4-27).

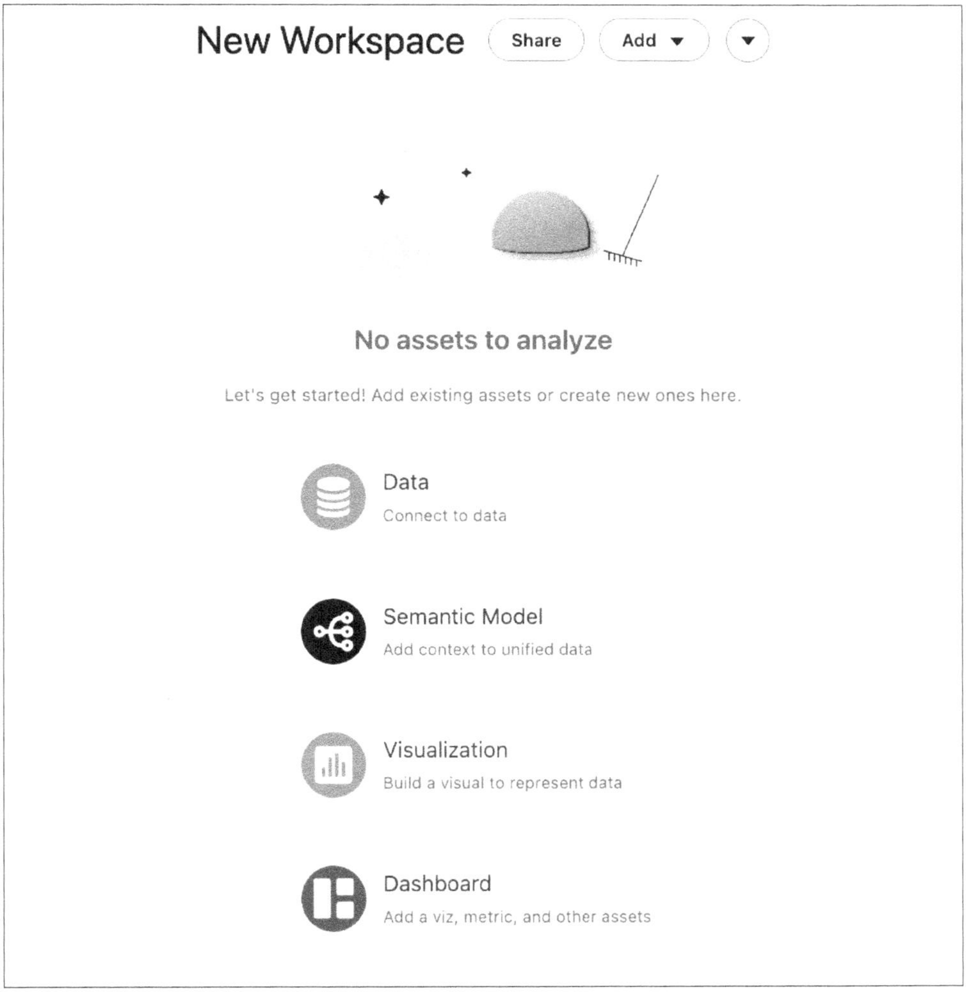

Figure 4-27. New Tableau Next workspace created without any assets

Within this new workspace, a user can connect to new data or add an existing asset that is reused and shared across workspaces in your org. A reused asset has a link to the workspace where it was originally created and it includes an arrow in the bottom-left corner indicating that it is a referenced asset (Figure 4-28).

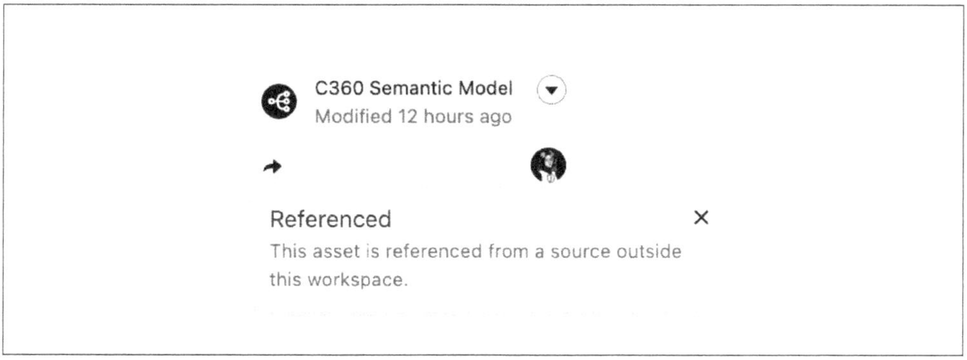

Figure 4-28. Referenced asset label indicates it is a reused asset created in another workspace

Referenced assets can be used in the new workspace and they can even be modified. When updates are made within the current workspace to the referenced asset, the existing asset in the original workspace isn't changed. However, the reverse isn't true. Modifications made to the asset in the original workspace also appear in the referenced asset that exists in your workspace. A single version of the asset is maintained in the original workspace where the asset was created thus ensuring consistency across Tableau Next analyses. This functionality in Tableau Next is similar to the Published Data Sources (PDS) in other Tableau products.

After adding at least one asset, placeholders for all asset types appear (Figure 4-29) in the workspace.

Each Tableau Next workspace includes the following asset types:

- Dashboards
- Visualizations
- Semantic models
- Data transforms
- Data objects—DLO, DMO, CI object
- Data Connections

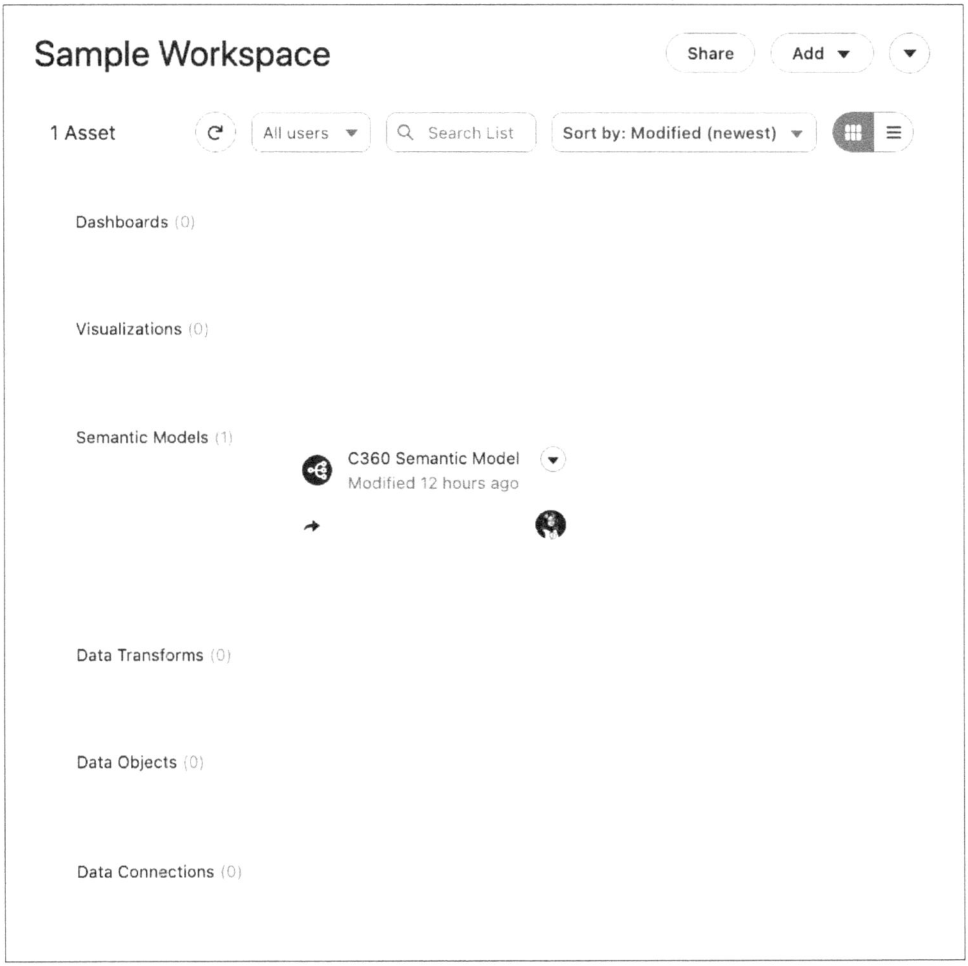

Figure 4-29. Asset type placeholders appear after the first asset is added to a Tableau Next workspace

Workspace assets are used to build more analytical assets within the same workspace, or they can be reused in other workspaces. You'll notice the list of asset types is in a specific order with the most complex asset listed first and the most basic asset listed last. That's because complex assets are built from those assets below them. For example, D360 data objects are used to build a semantic model. Visualizations are built from semantic models and data objects. Dashboards include visualizations and metrics.

Metrics aren't included as an asset in a Tableau Next workspace, however, because they're actually created in Semantic Model Builder as part of the semantic model (Figure 4-30). As we learned earlier, semantic models are used to create calculated fields and metrics. Those metrics can be used to create visualizations, included directly within a dashboard, or embedded externally in places like Slack.

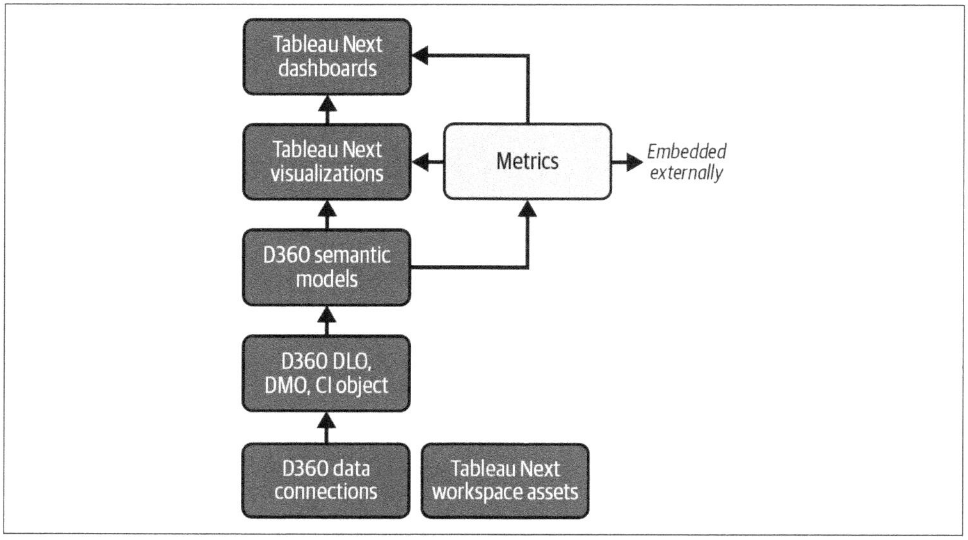

Figure 4-30. Metrics are created in the Semantic Model Builder and can be surfaced in Tableau Next visualizations and dashboards or embedded externally

You can have as many workspaces as needed to organize your projects' analytical assets. Each workspace or asset opened by you appears as a tab, which means you can work in multiple workspaces on different assets at the same time.

We've learned about Tableau Next workspaces and some of the workspace assets like Data Connections and semantic models. Let's now turn our attention to Tableau Next visualizations and dashboards.

Tableau Next Visualizations

Visualizations, like charts or graphs, are powerful ways to present an enterprise's data for analysis and exploration. Tableau Next visualizations are also useful for validating a new semantic model.

Let's explore the Tableau Next builder tool used for creating dynamic, interactive visualizations. Then we'll discover how single-click actions are added to visualizations.

Visualization Builder

Tableau Next Visualization Builder lets users explore data and build charts and tables for sharing insights. Use the Add button from any menu page in the Tableau Next app to create a new visualization. You'll be prompted to select the appropriate workspace or create a new workspace. Alternatively, the builder can be accessed through a Tableau Next workspace by clicking on an existing visualization or by creating a new visualization (Figure 4-31) in a workspace. In either case, you'll need to select the semantic model next.

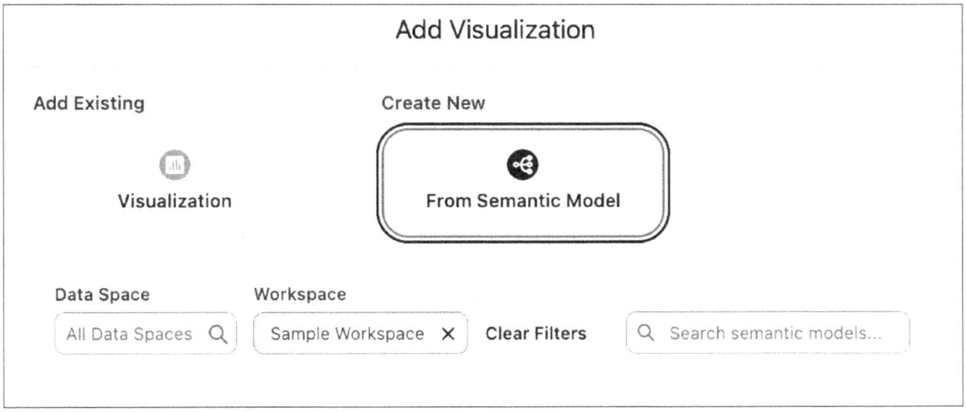

Figure 4-31. A new visualization in a Tableau Next workspace can be created from an existing semantic model after selecting Add Visualization from the drop-down menu

After selecting the semantic model, drag and drop the semantic model fields to the Rows and Columns shelves to give the visualization structure. Select the chart type in the Marks section (Figure 4-32) and use filters as needed. The Tableau Next Visualization Builder should look very familiar to Tableau users.

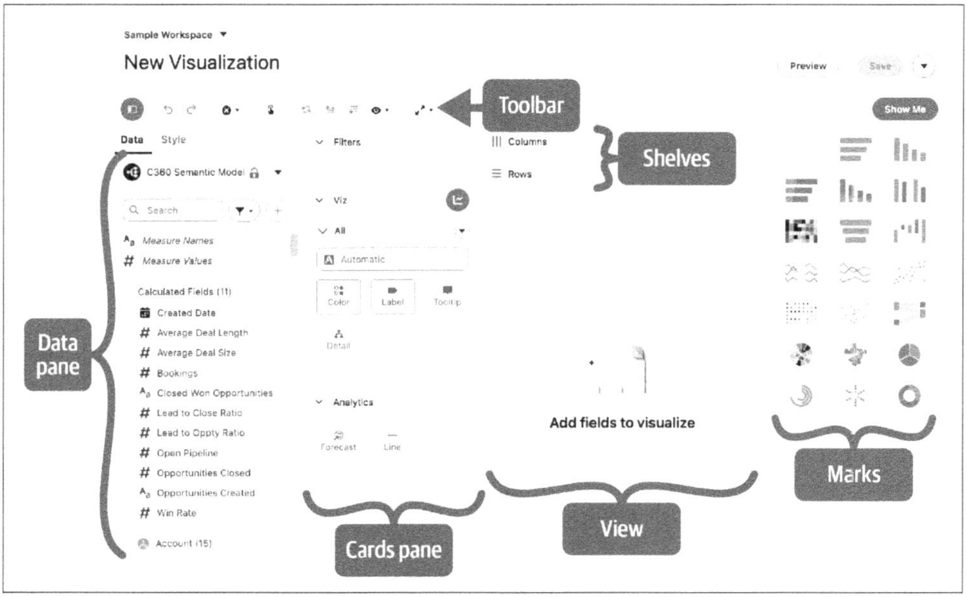

Figure 4-32. Tableau Next Visualization Builder sections including the Marks section

Update the visualization name and save your work. If the available fields in the data pane don't support what you need, you can create a new calculated field in the Data pane manually or by using the "Draft with Einstein" feature. You can also leverage Semantics AI for suggestions.

Parameters, part of the semantic model, can be used within Tableau Next visualizations. CRMA users will recognize parameters as similar to inputs in CRMA visualizations. Parameters allow users to change between fields or field values so that each value's impact can be evaluated separately. An example of a parameter field is country. Parameters for field values can also be used within calculated fields. For example, show me the top 20 where the number itself is a parameter.

It's also possible to create parameters for values outside the dataset. An example is discount percentage, which is a useful parameter for forecasting purposes. Doing so allows users to explore what-if scenarios in dashboards to learn how different inputs might affect the outcome.

In Tableau Next, users add forecasts to line charts containing a data value and at least one measure. Users select the forecast duration based on the chart's time interval of days, weeks, or months while considering forecasting requires three or more data points at the aggregation and group levels selected. For example, monthly forecasting requires at least three months of data and yearly forecasting requires at least three years of data. In addition, the user chooses whether to fill missing data points with zeros in the forecast and specifies how many recent periods to exclude from the forecasting data.

Adding Single-Click Actions to Visualizations

It's possible to add an action to a Tableau Next visualization from within the Visualization Builder by clicking the Toggle Action Panel button in the Toolbar section. There are two types of actions for builders to add to a Tableau Next visualization. The first is a navigation action (Figure 4-33).

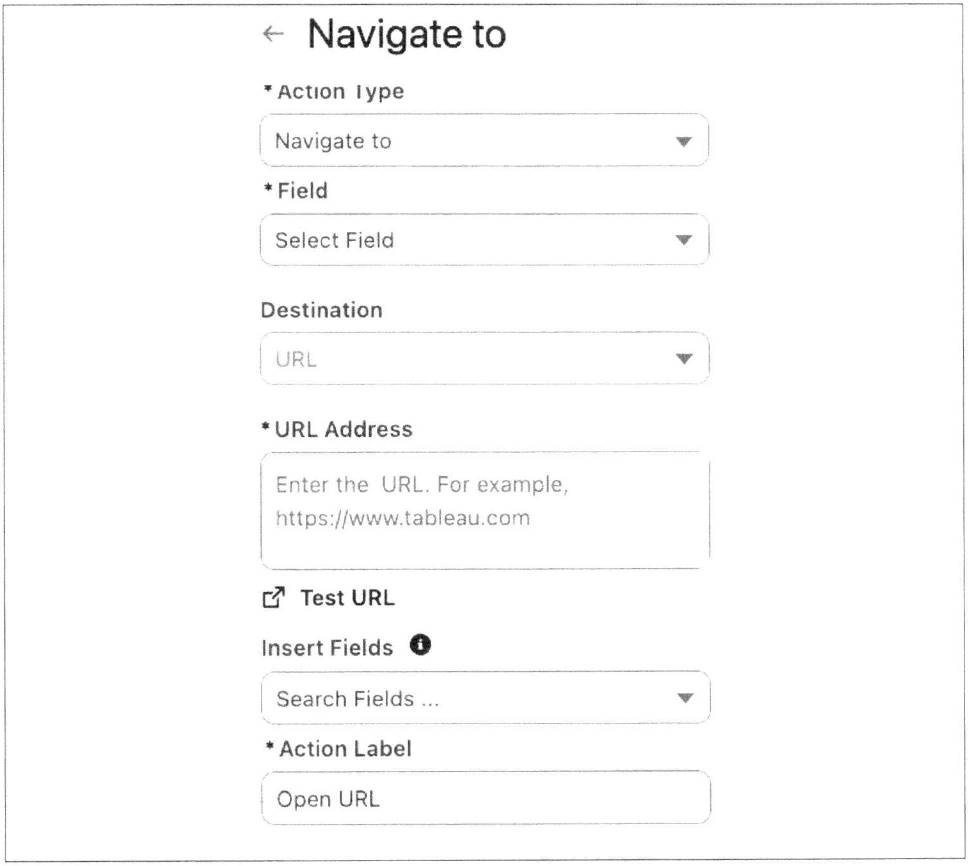

Figure 4-33. Creating a Tableau Next navigation action

Notice the ability to test the URL. You can also insert one or more fields into the URL or appended at the end of the URL but it's not required.

The second option for adding a new action to a Tableau Next visualization is with a Salesforce action (Figure 4-34).

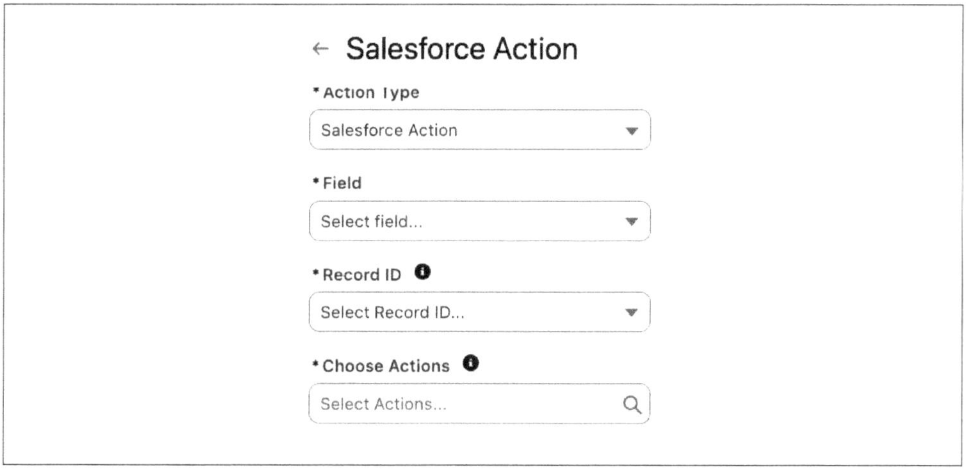

Figure 4-34. Creating a Salesforce action within Tableau Next

You'll select a data field and then the record ID. You'll notice the record ID must be included in the visualization for the record action to work. You can then choose up to five actions from the menu selections offered (Figure 4-35). When implemented, a Tableau Next user can click one button at a time to invoke a different Salesforce action from a visualization.

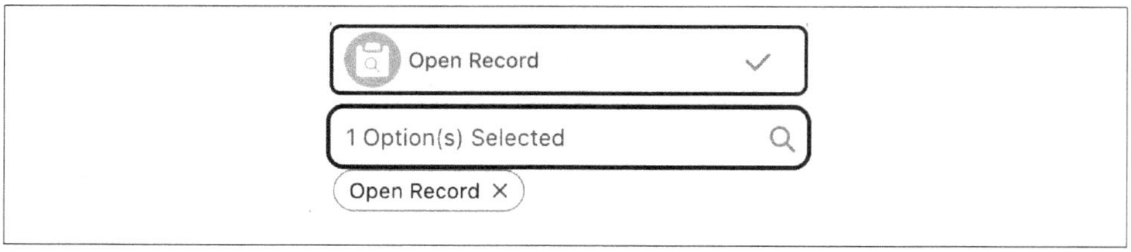

Figure 4-35. Salesforce actions available to the Tableau Next user

Salesforce actions for visualizations can be either object-specific quick actions or global actions. At this time, the Send Email action is only available for records in the Cases object that use Salesforce-native actions.

For a greater variety of options, users can add Salesforce Flow actions to Tableau Next dashboards. Let's explore more about Tableau Next dashboards.

Tableau Next Dashboard

A Tableau Next dashboard (Figure 4-36) isn't a static visualization of data. Instead, it's a dynamic interactive platform offering analytics on demand along with built-in actionability.

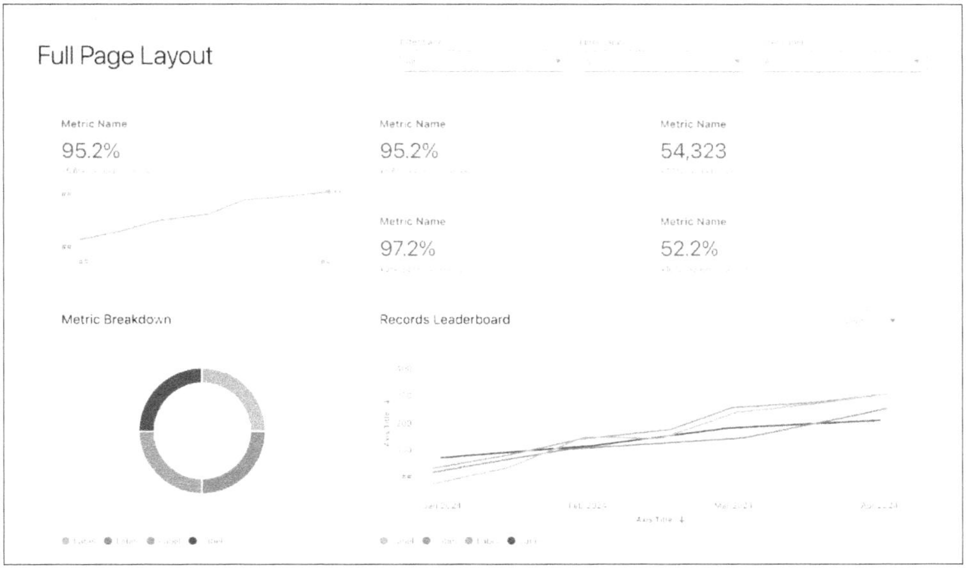

Figure 4-36. Tableau Next dashboard

The underlying queries supporting metrics and visualizations on a Tableau Next dashboard are rerun every time the dashboard page is refreshed. That way, users can make well-informed decisions based on the most current data and then take action right from within the dashboard.

Let's explore the Tableau Next Dashboard Builder to discover how a user builds the dashboard within a canvas. Then we'll learn how single-click actions are added to dashboards.

Tableau Next Dashboard Builder

Use the Create button from any menu page in the Tableau Next app to create a new dashboard. You'll be prompted to select the appropriate workspace or create a new workspace. Alternatively, navigate to an existing workspace and use the drop-down menu at the top right to create a new dashboard in the current workspace.

Tableau Next dashboards can be created by choosing a Marketplace template (Figure 4-37). Alternatively, you can start with a blank dashboard.

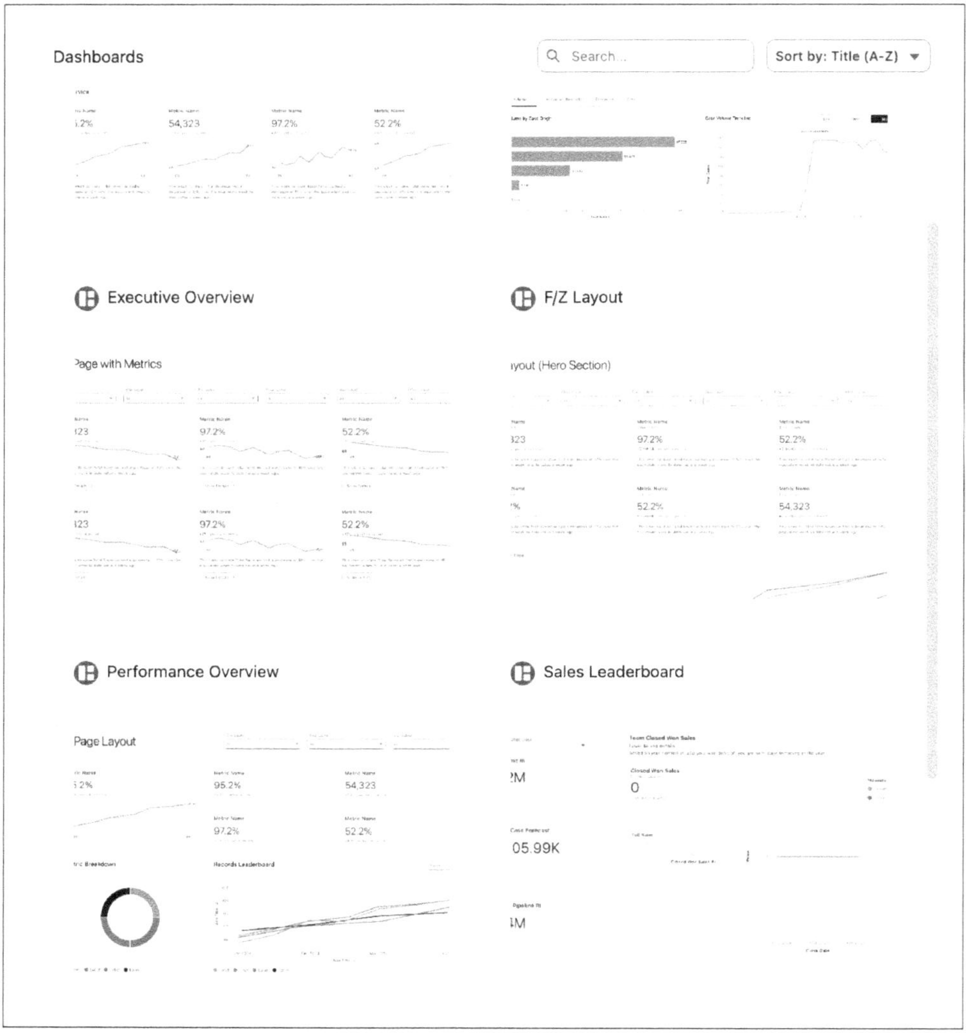

Figure 4-37. Tableau Next Marketplace templates

The Dashboard Builder (Figure 4-38) is where users add widgets onto a canvas and then arrange those charts, filters, metrics, and text within the canvas. Users finish configuring the dashboard using the Design tab on the dashboard panel. Users can then share a completed dashboard with others in the organization.

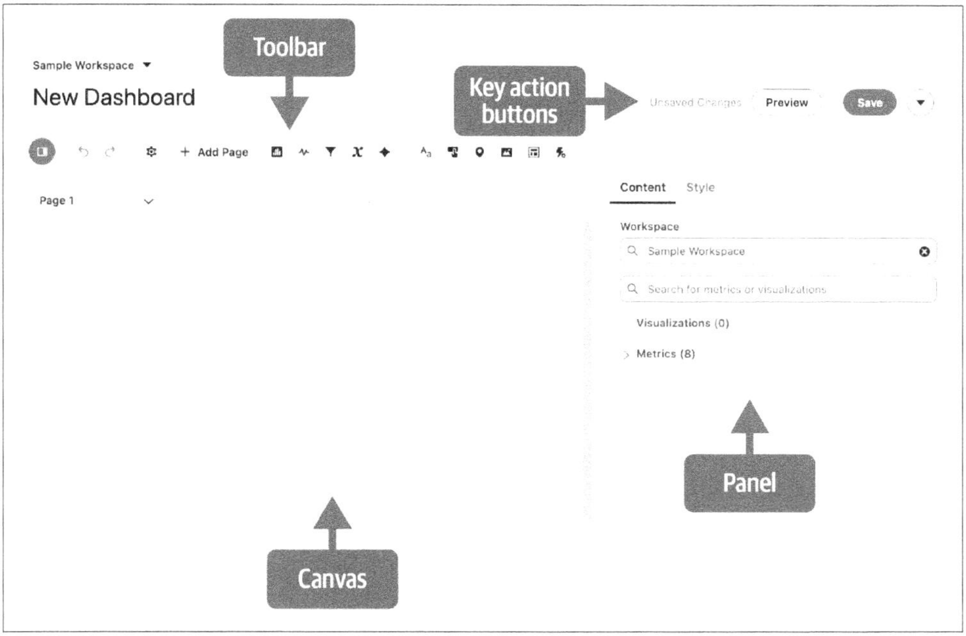

Figure 4-38. Tableau Next Dashboard Builder

The tools located within the Toolbar assist the user with dashboard development including tools for adding visualizations, metrics, lists, texts, images, buttons, and containers. Also included are tools for arranging dashboard content and adjusting the overall layout.

Key action buttons help users finalize and disseminate a dashboard. Buttons are available for previewing and saving a dashboard, cloning or downloading the dashboard, or preparing it to be embedded in another app.

The dashboard panel includes two tabs: Content and Style. The panel provides contextual controls to help users fine-tune the style and content of the dashboard. Controls include options for selecting data sources, configuring visualizations, applying formatting, and setting interactivity.

Previously, we mentioned Tableau Next visualization and dashboard designers should consider consumption costs when making design choices. In addition, designers should provide as much context for users as possible, especially because it may be difficult for users to know what is included in the semantic model that powers the dashboard.

One suggestion is to add a text widget on the dashboard to help users know what's included in the semantic model. That way, they have a better understanding of the type of questions they can ask to get answers. A text widget is an excellent design choice for this situation since no query is needed to power a text widget. Thus, text widgets don't incur consumption costs.

Adding Single-Click Actions to Tableau Next Dashboards

Actions added to Tableau Next dashboard are achieved via the Actions tab (Figure 4-39) on a container widget property panel.

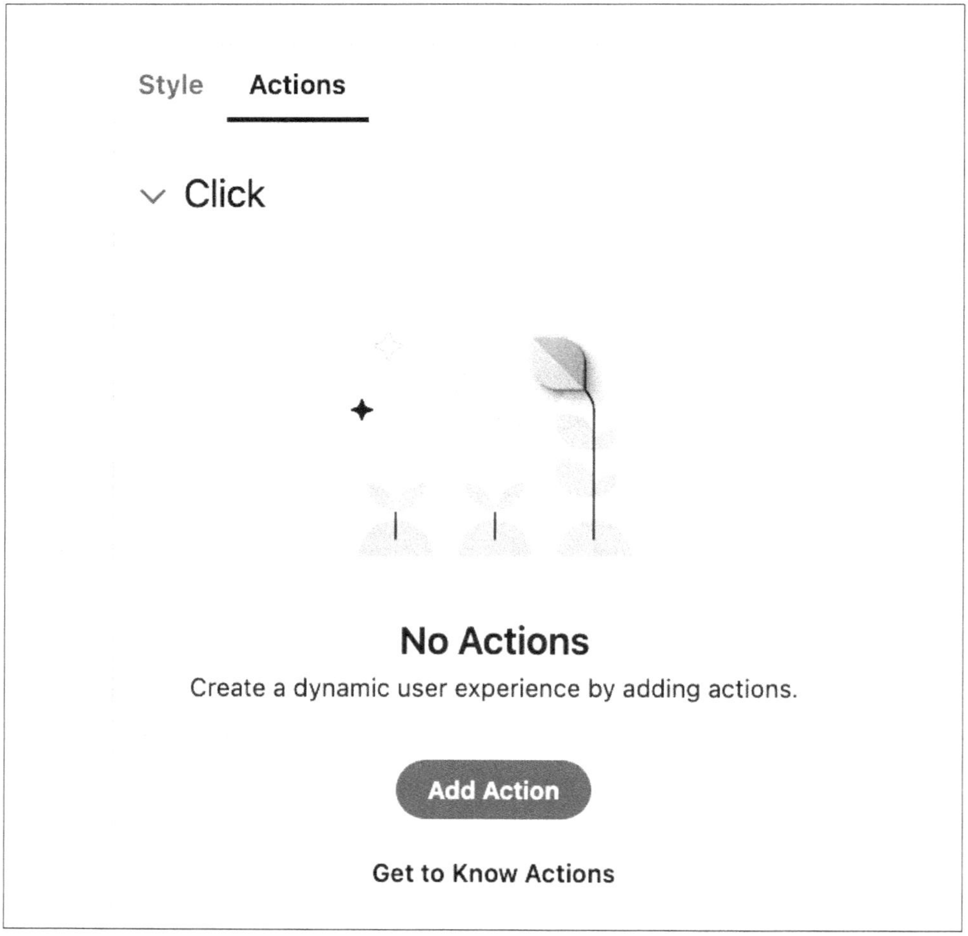

Figure 4-39. Actions tab of a container widget property panel in Tableau Next

A dashboard widget can include multiple navigation items, but there can only be one Salesforce Flow action (Figure 4-40) added per widget.

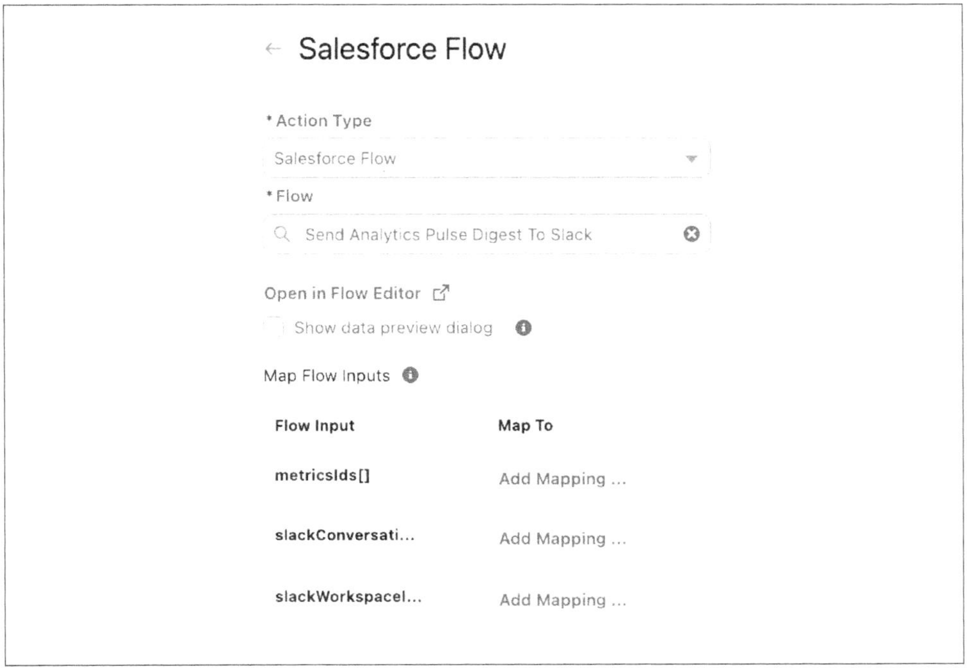

Figure 4-40. Building a Salesforce Flow action for a Tableau Next widget

When setting up the Salesforce Flow action type, an option exists to open the action in the Flow Editor. That way, changes to the flow can be made, if needed, without having to navigate away from the current screen. In addition, it's possible to map the flow edits in the Tableau Next Dashboard Builder without ever leaving the page.

Salesforce Flows are powerful and they give Tableau Next users many options to complete tasks quickly. When combined with Agentforce capabilities, these actions become even more powerful.

For example, a Tableau Next dashboard user might observe three weeks elapsed since their last touchpoint with a contact associated with an open opportunity. The user clicks a Draft Email button, which invokes a scripted flow. The flow reviews details about the most recent interaction, accesses LinkedIn, and obtains current information about the individual. Next, the information is summarized and an email drafted. The user reviews both the summary and the proposed communication before sending the email to the contact.

In upcoming chapters, we'll learn more about Agentforce and how to build agents using building blocks such as subagents and actions. We'll also learn how to invoke subagents and actions in Salesforce Flows. Throughout the book, we'll introduce some prebuilt Agentforce agents like the analytics and visualization agent. This particular agent is provided out-of-the box to Tableau Next users with access to Agentforce.

Analytics and Visualization Agent

Agentforce provides an out-of-the-box template for users to create their own analytics and visualization agents. The name of each analytics and visualization agent depends on the name given to it by the individual who creates the agent. One or more subagents are assigned to an agent by the creator. If the agent needs conversational analytics capabilities, also known as the Concierge skill, the creator would assign that skill and any other necessary subagents to the agent (Figure 4-41). Alternatively, create an orchestrator agent along with three separate specialty agents, rather than adding three separate skills to one agent.

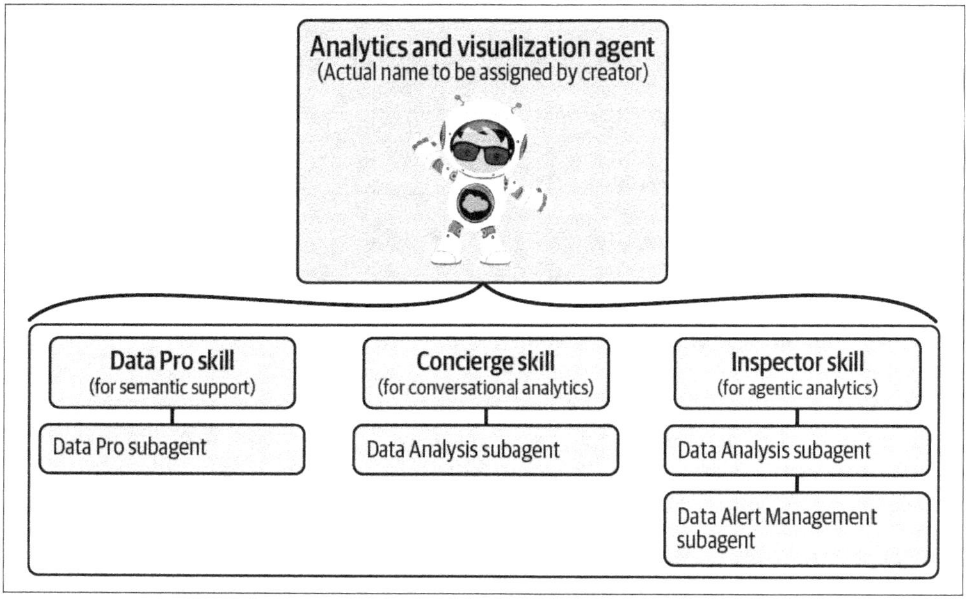

Figure 4-41. Analytics and visualization agent skills

An analytics and visualization agent in Salesforce can be easily created from an Agentforce Builder template. Agentforce Builder is a low-code tool that simplifies the creation and deployment of agents in Salesforce. Select the Analytics and Visualization template (Figure 4-42) from among the template choices when building a new agent in the Agentforce Studio app. Then click the Next button at the top right of the screen.

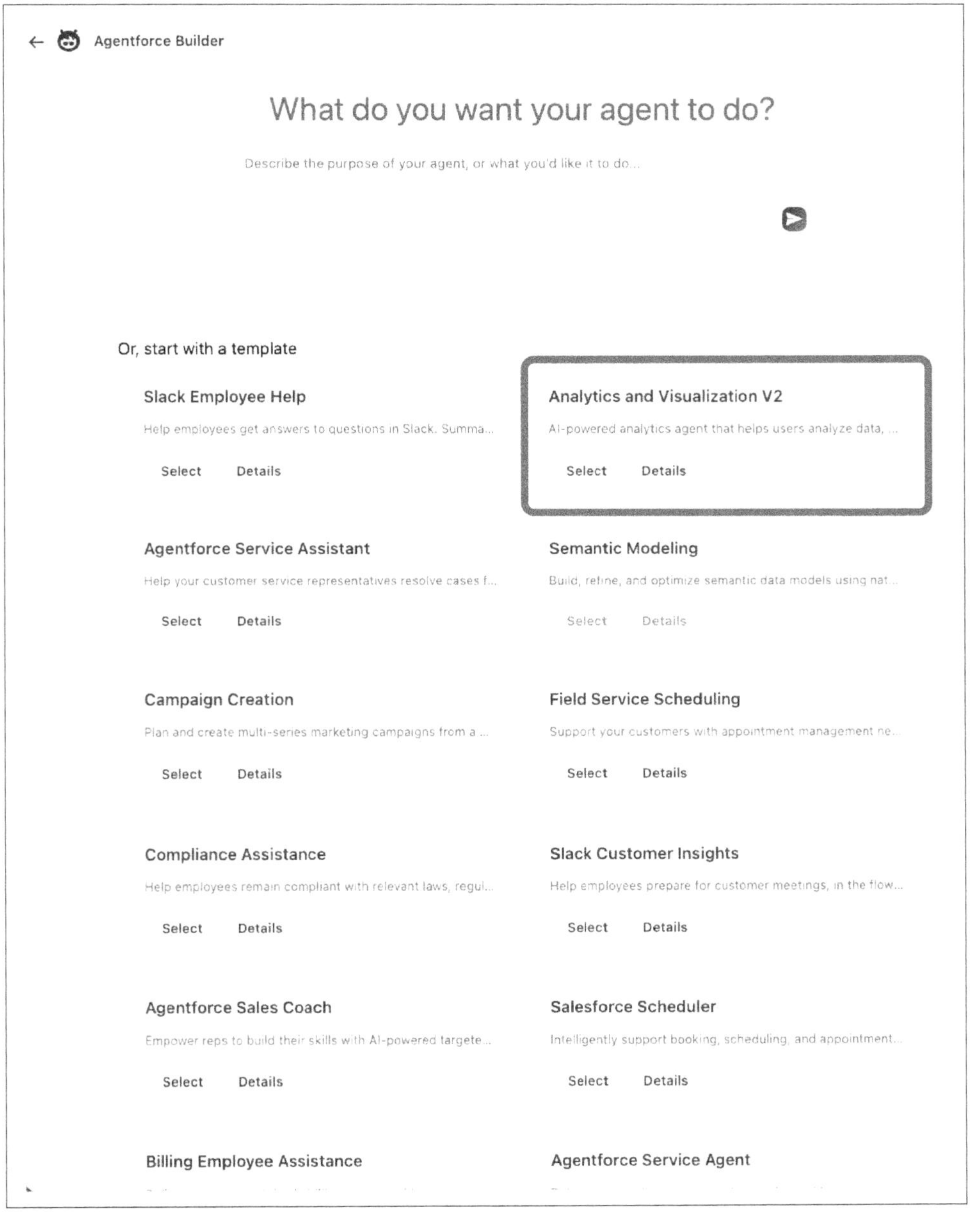

Figure 4-42. Selecting the Analytics and Visualization template for the agent

Although the Analytics and Visualization agent comes with the Data Analysis subagent pre-selected (Figure 4-43), you can always add more subagents in the next step when customizing your agent. Alternatively, you can remove any subagents that you don't want to include.

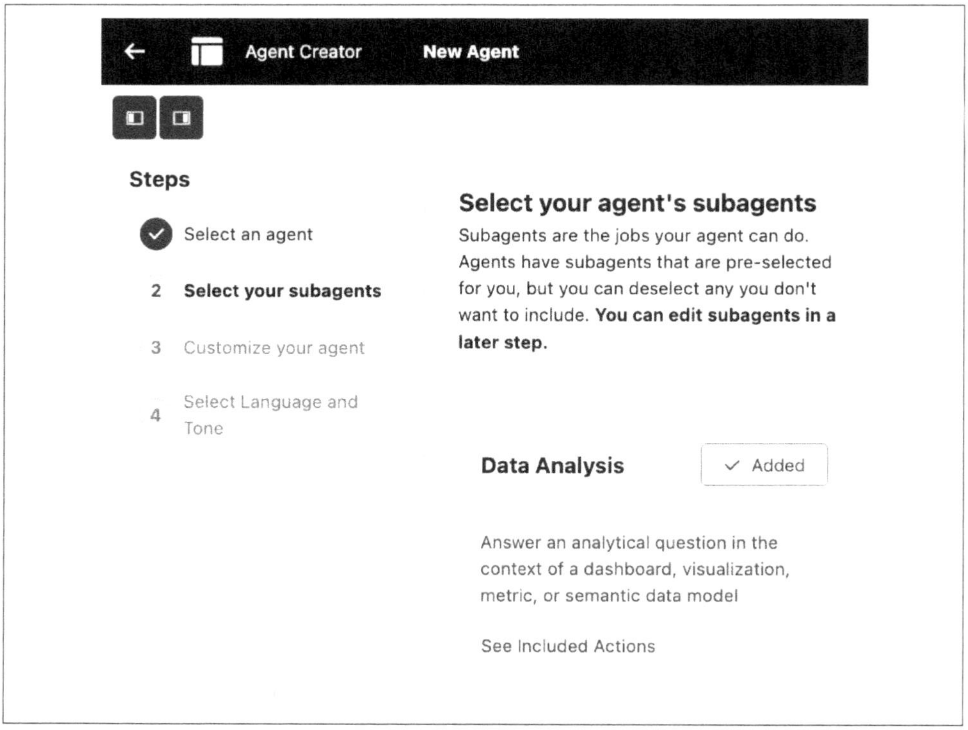

Figure 4-43. Data Analysis subagent preselected in the Analytics and Visualization agent template

Salesforce provides these prebuilt subagents out-of-the-box, but there's more to be done before the agent can actually be deployed for users. An analytics and visualization agent needs information about what data source to use and in which channels the agent will be accessible to users, among other things. Without defining the important configuration details, a warning is displayed when attempting to activate the agent (Figure 4-44).

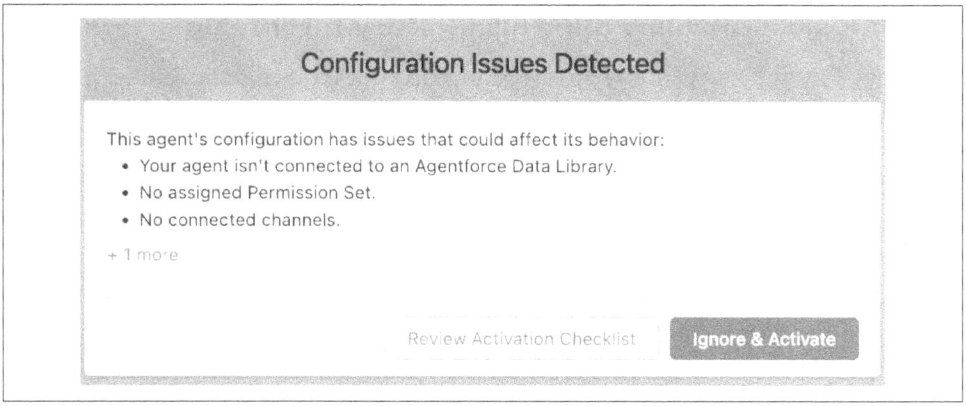

Figure 4-44. Warning details for configuration issues detected

We'll explore more details about agent configurations in subsequent chapters. For now, let's focus on understanding more about what this particular agent can do and what questions it can help answer for users.

> As you're building agents, you may come across access to Agent Analytics, which is not a type of analytics agent. Instead, Agent Analytics is a tool designed to analyze the performance of agents such as Employee agents and Service agents by capturing and monitoring session data. Agent Analytics details provide insights into agent behavior, user interactions, and performance trends. Those insights can be surfaced in Tableau Next.

Analytics and Visualization agent subagents are used for three different agent skills: Data Pro, Concierge, and Inspector. The Data Pro skill is aligned with the Semantic Model Builder to help users build out relationships and calculated fields in semantic models.

The Concierge skill contains a powerful subagent with many actions, including one with the ability to add calculated fields in a semantic model. The Concierge skill is designed to answer business users' questions about visualizations, dashboards, metrics in the semantic model, and more.

The Data Alert Management subagent, combined with the subagent from the Concierge skill, makes up the Inspector skill, which supports autonomous monitoring of metrics. Including the Concierge skill within the Inspector skill makes it possible for users to receive context around the data alert. Let's explore each of the three Tableau Next agent skills in more detail.

Semantic Model Building Using Agentforce Data Pro Skill

The Data Pro skill is available to users working in the Semantic Model Builder. The Data Pro capabilities give users two important features. Users are able to create calculated fields using natural language and they can also create new semantic model relationships.

The Suggest Relationships feature is accessible by clicking the sparkle icon (Figure 4-45) in the top-right corner of the Semantic Model Builder canvas.

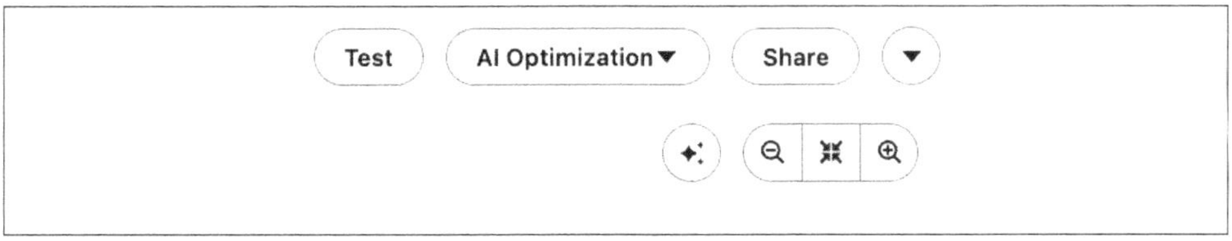

Figure 4-45. Sparkle icon of the Semantic Model Builder canvas reveals suggested relationships

Throughout the canvas, icons appear between objects once the user clicks the sparkle icon. When a user clicks any icon between two objects, a new Recommended Relationship window appears. Within that window, the fields used to establish the relationship are displayed. A user creates a new relationship by clicking Apply or edits an existing relationship by clicking Review. Alternatively, the user clicks Reject, causing the user to no longer see the specific suggestion.

Data Pro's suggestions use the structure, metadata, and relationships already defined in the semantic model at the time of request. Suggestions are provided only for primary and foreign key fields. Composite keys, shared dimension data objects, and logical views are not supported.

The second AI feature available for Semantic Model Builder is the ability to use natural language to create new calculated fields. This Agentforce action is available in both the Data Pro and the Concierge skill. Alternatively, you can use the "Draft with Einstein" feature (Figure 4-46) available in the Semantic Model Builder that provides similar functionality.

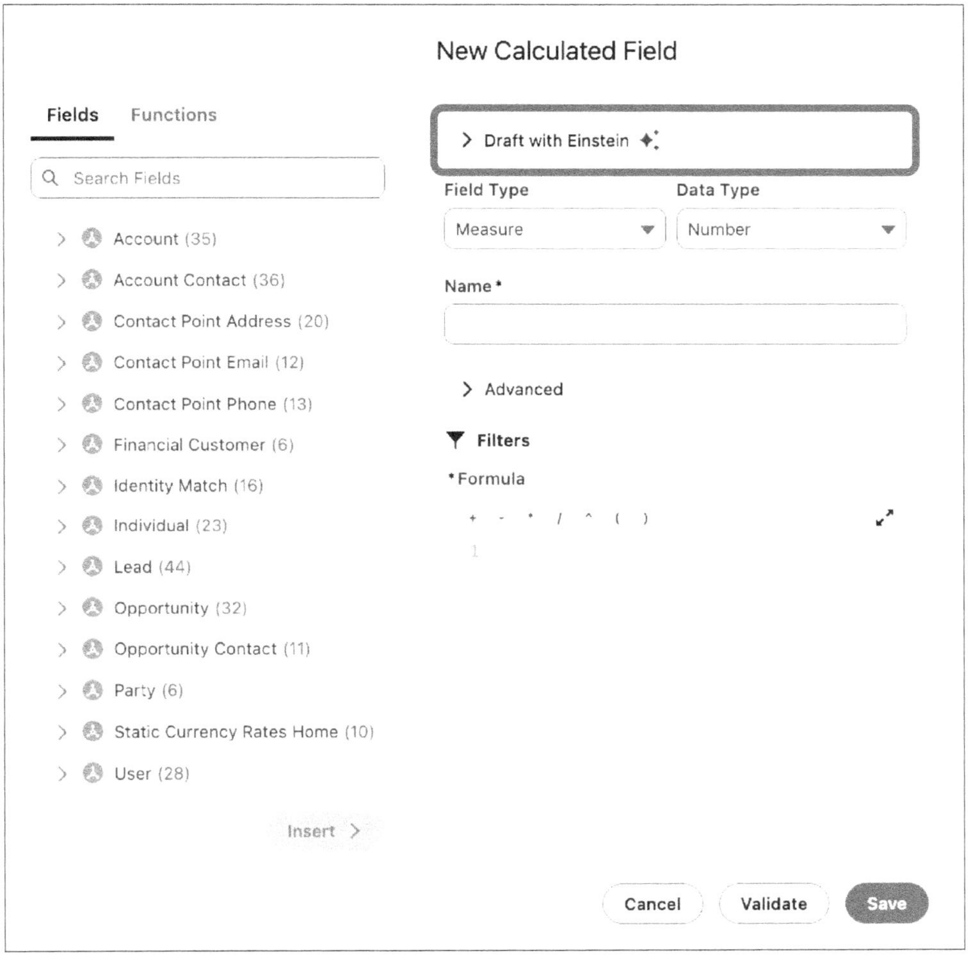

Figure 4-46. "Draft with Einstein" feature uses natural language to create new calculated fields

Both the Data Pro experience and the "Draft with Einstein" feature give users the option to describe the desired field using natural language. This allows users to create the new field without understanding the Tableau Next syntax required to build the formula. Users can only create formulas where predefined relationships exist between DMOs no matter whether they create the calculated field manually or by using the "Draft with Einstein" feature or the Data Pro experience.

Every formula generated using AI still needs to be reviewed for accuracy. In addition, the calculated field results depend on clean, well-labeled data and detailed query requests.

There is one very important difference between the "Draft with Einstein" feature and the Data Pro experience. The Einstein feature is a one-turn experience. You'll need to start over anytime you want to make changes to the formula. In contrast, users engage in a conversation with Data Pro by answering questions posed by the agent before the most suitable calculated field is created.

Conversational Analytics Using Agentforce Concierge Skill

Earlier, we briefly explored the Analytics and Visualization agent template available to quickly build a new Agentforce agent with analytics and visualization capabilities. The actual name of the agent in a production environment varies based the input of the human who creates the agent from the template.

The agent with analytics and visualization capabilities automatically appears for users signed in to Tableau Next whenever the person navigates to a metric details page (Figure 4-47) or a dashboard within Tableau Next. The agent also appears for embedded Tableau Next dashboards. In addition, the agent is available on metrics and dashboards shared in Slack for any user assigned the appropriate license and permissions.

Figure 4-47. Metrics details page where an analytics agent automatically appears for users

Concierge is able to filter individual metrics and can answer questions about metrics using any dimension defined in the semantic model, not just dimensions that exist on a metric. If needed, the agent using Concierge will ask you to clarify the dimension to be used to break things down. Here's an example of a conversation between an Analytics and Visualization agent and a human where the agent needs help from the user to clarify an intent for an ambiguous query:

- *Marketing Manager*: "Rank the best performing campaigns."
- *Agent*: "Do you mean by engagement or revenue impact?"

Sometimes an agent needs more semantic knowledge from the user and, in those situations, the agent then updates the semantic layer with the information by creating a new calculated field:

- *Sales Manager*: "Display quick wins over time for Product X."
- *Agent*: "Could you define Quick Win?"
- *Sales Manager*: "Opportunities created and closed within the same quarter."

The end-to-end flow for an a human user-agent interaction using the Concierge skill always begins with the user initiating the conversation in Tableau Next or Slack from a metrics page or a dashboard. The agent, powered by Agentforce, selects the *Data Analysis* subagent and executes Agentforce actions to provide an analytics content response to the user (Figure 4-48). That response outcome to the user could be in the form of a visualization, dashboard, explanation, or recommendation. The outcome could also include creating a new calculated field.

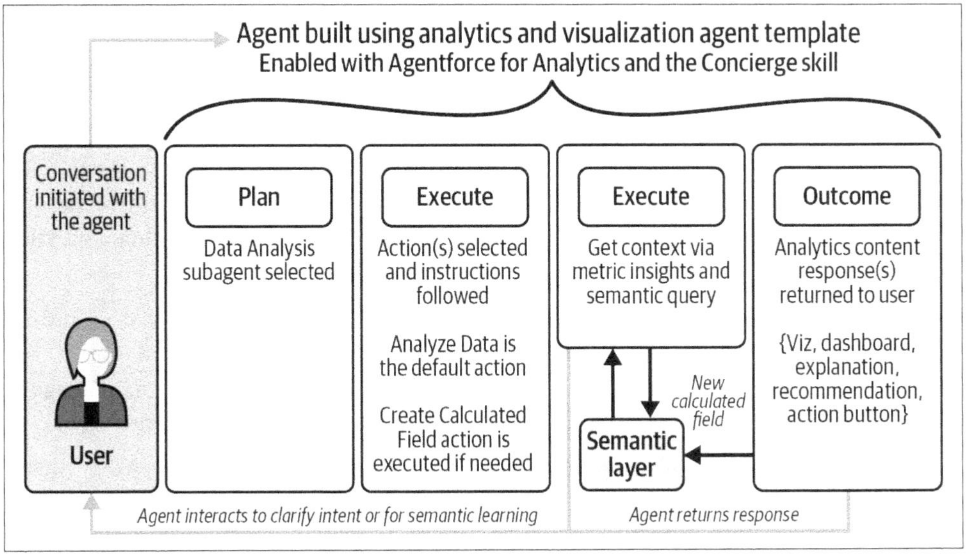

Figure 4-48. Actions undertaken by an Agentforce Analytics agent when providing a response to the user

Concierge can answer questions about and provide visualizations for predictions and forecasting, assuming the prediction information were written into a DMO and then added to a semantic model. AI Model Builder prescriptions are what's needed for Concierge to offer recommendations to users. In Chapter 3, we discovered how to use AI Model Builder to create predictions, top predictive factors, and prescriptions that can be stored in a DMO. Earlier in this chapter, we learned how a DMO can be incorporated in a semantic model that an analytics and visualization agent leverages when interacting with a user in Tableau Next or Slack.

> Don't confuse Tableau Next's Analytics and Visualization agent with Tableau Agent. Both use natural language to accomplish tasks. However, Tableau Agent is part of Tableau Cloud.
>
> The Analytics and Visualization agent's Concierge skill is more powerful than Tableau Agent because it's an Agentforce skill with access to Salesforce platform tools and the D360 data and semantic layers. Thus, Concierge users can obtain better insights and are also able to take infinitely more actions in the flow of work.

The outcome an analytics and visualization agent provides to a user is grounded in much contextual information. The analytics and visualization agent using the Analyze Data default agent action operates on two parallel paths. If the user's question can be answered using metric insights then the outcome is more deterministic.

Thus, it's helpful for users to define and build metrics in the semantic layer even if there isn't a need to create a materialized version of the visualization to share with end users. The agent will search the available metrics when responding conversationally and will provide a visualization, if appropriate, along with any other analytics content responses needed including insights and explanations.

The agent will consider the descriptions, names, fields, and any filters that are available in the defined metric. Rather than a user determining which filter to select, the agent automatically processes the various filters by toggling through them. The agent ultimately selects the most appropriate filter that best matches the user's question.

There is a second path the agent traverses. That path to produce a semantic query answer may necessitate the agent interacting with the user for semantic learning or to clarify user intent (Figure 4-49).

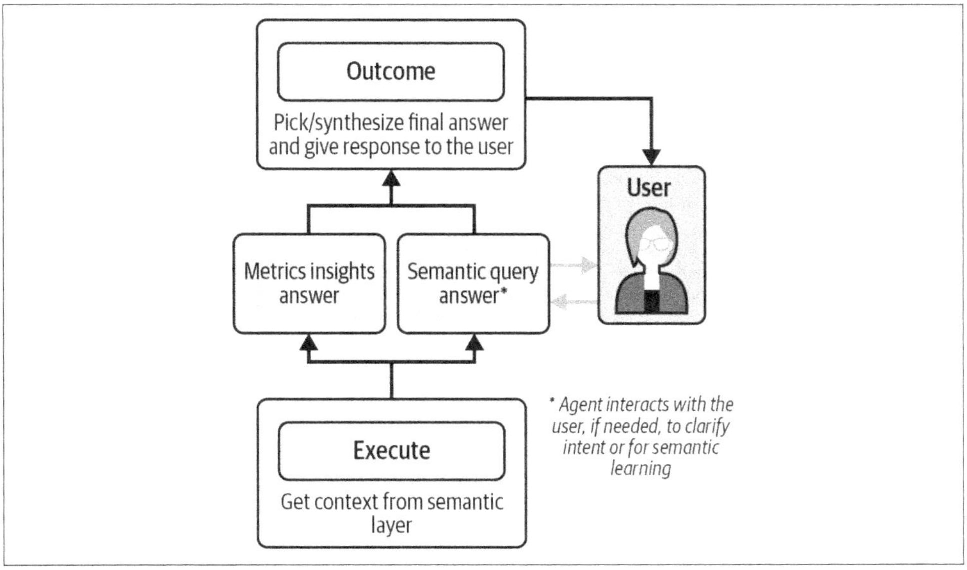

Figure 4-49. Agentforce analytics and visualization agent interacts with the user if needed

The semantic query path starts with the agent searching through the semantic data model. The last step is where the agent provides content responses that are evaluated by the agent first before the final answer is given to the user:

1. Searches the semantic data model including relationships, calculated fields, and metrics
2. Obtains additional semantic knowledge information from semantic definitions, metadata, glossary, and business preferences
3. Interacts with the user, as needed, to clarify intent or for semantic learning
4. Generates a query
5. Provides analytics content responses including visualization, insights, and explanations

Two answers, generated in parallel, are then synthesized by the agent. A confidence score is provided with each answer so that the agent can choose what information to present based on that score. Sometimes the scores vary slightly, which is why the user could receive a slightly different answer today to the exact same question that was asked yesterday.

Agents and large language models (LLMs) are inherently nondeterministic, which is why they need more context, not just more data, to provide the best responses. Leveraging business preferences and other features in D360 Semantic Model Builder to enhance the semantic model helps ensure answers are consistently accurate.

There are certain behavioral norms and limitations for questions that Concierge users should consider. First, questions requiring nonmaterialized predictions are not supported. We've previously mentioned that Concierge can provide predictions and recommendations as long as the information is stored in a DMO and available in the semantic model. You'll want to use AI Model Builder in D360 to build a prediction model for any new predictions or recommendations you want surfaced in semantic layer and available for Concierge.

Also, the agent prioritizes any time range explicitly specified in a question and ignores any other dashboard filters. For example, a user might ask about "closed opportunities for last month" in which case the agent won't consider dashboard filters for any other time range. In addition, there is a limit to the number of records that the agent returns in a response. At this time, that limit is 50 records.

Limitations and behavioral norms for the Concierge skill are likely to change over time, though, as Salesforce continues to invest in improvements. Thus, it's recommended to review Salesforce documentation (*https://oreil.ly/kUjLH*) for the most current limitations as you consider your own use cases for this skill.

Another important thing to keep in mind is that an analytics and visualization agent offers even more functionality for business users because enterprises creating a new agent with Concierge abilities will almost always include the Data Alert Management subagent, too. This gives users the ability to set autonomous monitoring so that they receive data alerts when certain conditions are met.

Agentic Analytics Using Agentforce Inspector Skill

An agent enabled with the Inspector Skill via the Data Alert Management subagent checks once per day, at most, for any conditions specified. The default is set so that checks are performed daily but that can be increased if desired. If a condition is met, a notification is sent to one or more channels selected by the Salesforce administrator. In addition to the alert notification triggered by the Data Alert Management subagent, the agent then utilizes the Data Analysis subagent before sending information to the user. This allows the agent to explore the underlying reasons why the alert was triggered. Thus, the agent provides an explanation and recommendations along with the alert notification.

Here are some examples of different types of alerts that users might set with the Inspector skill for an analytics and visualization agent:

Metric threshold alerts
: Occurs when a metric exceeds a specific value or falls below a certain threshold

Range-based alerts
: Triggered when a metric is outside of an expected range

Time-based alerts
: Triggered on a regular time interval

Proactive data alerts
: Notifications for an event like a significant change in a metric

Custom condition alerts
: User-defined conditions for metrics monitoring

For example, a user accessing the agent on a metric page could type "Alert me when this metric is above 50,000." The agent repeats the conditions for the alert and asks the user to confirm. After setting up an alert, it can be managed by the user on their Tableau Next Following page.

Similar to the Concierge, the Inspector skill is built with business users in mind. This skill uses the Data Alert Management subagent in addition to the Concierge Skill subagents that we explored in "Conversational Analytics Using Agentforce Concierge Skill" on page 166. That's why the agent is able to provide some additional information other than just a notification. The agent provides context around the alert with insights and recommendations.

Inspector delivers the alert notification to users via desktop, email, and mobile. A Salesforce admin edits the delivery settings for notification supported channels by searching for Notification Delivery Settings in the Quick Find box. The "Data alert notification" underneath Tableau Next (Figure 4-50) is the one that determines how users will be notified about any data alerts.

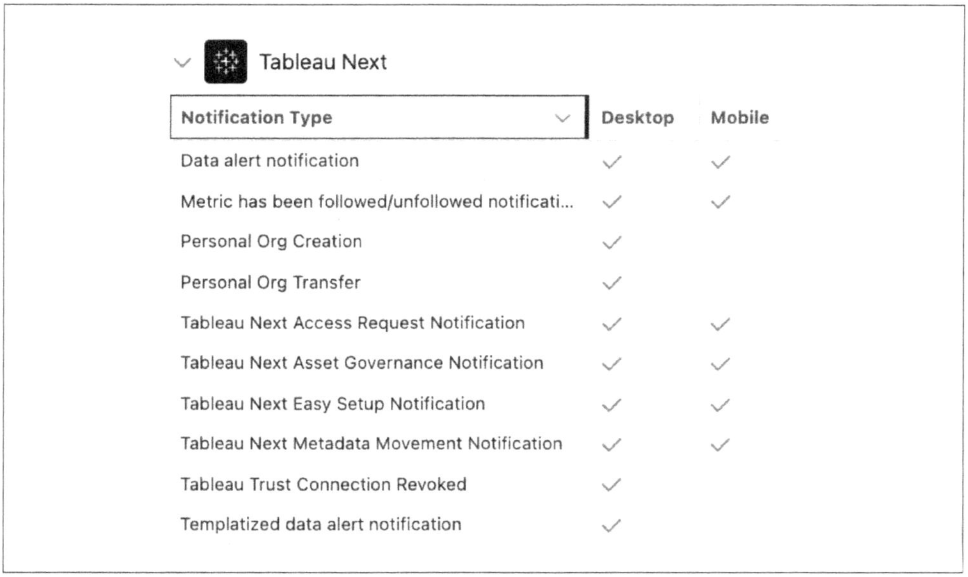
Tableau Next

Notification Type	Desktop	Mobile
Data alert notification	✓	✓
Metric has been followed/unfollowed notificati...	✓	✓
Personal Org Creation	✓	
Personal Org Transfer	✓	
Tableau Next Access Request Notification	✓	✓
Tableau Next Asset Governance Notification	✓	✓
Tableau Next Easy Setup Notification	✓	✓
Tableau Next Metadata Movement Notification	✓	✓
Tableau Trust Connection Revoked	✓	
Templatized data alert notification	✓	

Figure 4-50. Delivery settings for Tableau Next data alert notifications

The Inspector skill, along with the Concierge and Data Pro skills, are all Agentforce skills that incorporate subagents built using Salesforce platform builder tools. These skills can be assigned to one or more Agentforce agents operating within the Einstein Trust Layer. No data or conversations with the agent are saved to the LLM and neither are used to train the model. Instead, trust is built into the analytics and visualization agent experience through thumbs-up or thumbs-down ratings and encouraging feedback from end users. In addition, agents with the Tableau Next Concierge skill can be calibrated to provide better responses over time. Ratings, user feedback, and calibration are used to improve the analytical conversational experience for an intelligent agentic enterprise powered by Salesforce AI.

Summary

In this chapter, we learned about context and insights with agentic analytics built for conversation and actionability in the flow of work. We took a deep dive into Semantic Model Builder, explored Tableau Next in detail, and learned about Agentforce analytics and visualization agents.

In the next chapter, we'll learn about orchestrated conversational AI chatbots used for customer self-service use cases. We'll explore Einstein Bot Builder and discover how it can be used to build chatbots that leverage agentic features when engaging with users in an orchestrated conversation. We'll also compare the self-service characteristics of Einstein Bot Builder with those available in Agentforce agents.

CHAPTER 5

Orchestrated Conversational AI Chatbots for Customer Self-Service

Conversational AI chatbots, built with Einstein Bot Builder (Bot Builder), are very powerful and effective technology tools offered by Salesforce. In this chapter, we'll learn in detail how to leverage Bot Builder to create conversational AI chatbots. As part of that discussion, we'll learn about intents, intent sets, and intent models. We'll even learn how to integrate agentic capabilities into our chatbot using an Agentforce subagent. Salesforce provides all the necessary pieces of the puzzle that allow you to build and maintain conversational AI bots relevant for many different use cases.

Chatbots are especially useful for customer self-service because they're well suited for these low-risk deflection situations. Einstein chatbots are session-bound, channel-native conversational flows that are built for triaging and resolving high-volume, low-complexity inquiries. Typical use cases involve responding to questions that can be answered with FAQs and lightweight flows like password resets or order-status checks.

We'll learn how Einstein chatbots now have options to leverage agentic features to provide an orchestrated conversation for customers. For known scenarios like password resets, Einstein chatbots use a dialog-based flow. However, chatbots no longer have to traverse rigid dialog trees all the time. Leveraging Agentforce's Generative Knowledge Answers, the chatbot triggers the Answer Questions with Knowledge agent action whenever a customer's utterance doesn't match a scripted intent. In those situations, the Einstein chatbot retrieves information from a Data 360 (D360) indexed knowledge base to return a synthesized, conversational response.

Einstein chatbots given Generative Knowledge Answers capability are optimized for situations that only require information or guidance. AI agents (agents) are better suited for scenarios where understanding, decisions, and actions are needed. Each of these technology solutions plays an important role in most intelligence agentic enterprises. As such, we'll close out the chapter with a comparison of the self-service characteristics between Einstein Bots with Generative Knowledge Answers versus an Agentforce agent.

Getting Started

Let's discuss some background knowledge and some things you should know to help you get the most out of this chapter.

Background Knowledge

There is no prerequisite background knowledge for this chapter. Possessing Salesforce knowledge of Salesforce Service functionality, including Omni-Channel routing, is helpful but not required.

What You Should Know

Einstein Bots is a Salesforce product used to build chatbots. However, the terms *bot* and *chatbot* are not used interchangeably in this chapter because there is a difference between the two. A bot is a broad term that refers to any automated program, including chatbots, that performs specific tasks. Web scraping, data processing, and task automation are also automated programs referred to as bots. In comparison, a chatbot is a type of bot specifically designed for conversational interactions. It's important to clarify the terms and note that Bot Builder is only used to build chatbots, not any other type of bot.

This chapter focuses on text-based chatbots for simplicity. However, the same technology is available for voice-based chatbots. Throughout the chapter, we'll be using the term *user* to describe the Salesforce user who builds and maintains the chatbot. We'll use the term *customer* when referring to the human interacting with the chatbot. Thus, the chapter describes customer-facing chatbots, although chatbots can also be created for internal use. Examples include a Human Resources bot or an IT Support chatbot that helps an organization's employees get answers to questions such as "What's our travel reimbursement policy?" or "How do I report a problem with my laptop?"

Conversational AI Chatbots

Before exploring how to use Bot Builder, we'll want to ensure we have a good understanding of conversational AI chatbots. To that end, we'll first review chatbot categories, Salesforce chatbot types, and the anatomy of an Einstein conversational AI chatbot.

Chatbot Categories

A *chatbot* is a conversational tool that streamlines the approach for automated responses to customer queries. Traditional chatbots are powered by structured rules and rely on specificity. These chatbots follow predetermined paths to provide responses and, as you'd expect, they excel at handling straightforward, predictable queries. Traditional chatbots are a great choice for FAQ-style interactions where menu options and if-else statements suffice. However, if you need a chatbot that understands context and can handle multiturn conversations, traditional chatbots are the wrong choice. Instead, you'll need to build a conversational AI chatbot. It's even possible to add GenAI capabilities to a conversational AI chatbot.

AI chatbots represent a fundamental shift in how chatbots interact with customers. They make use of machine learning (ML) algorithms and natural language processing (NLP) so they can understand a customer even when there are grammar or spelling mistakes or when the customer says things differently than expected.

There are four main categories of chatbots. Let's briefly review those now:

- Traditional chatbots (aka *menu-based* or *rule-based* chatbots)
- Conversational AI chatbots (aka *self-learning chatbots*, *contextual chatbots*, or *intelligent chatbots* that include NLP capabilities)
  - Pure AI chatbots without any menus or rules
  - Hybrid AI chatbots with dialog blocks that can include menus and rules
- GenAI integrated conversational chatbots (aka *virtual assistants*)
- GenAI chatbots

Traditional chatbots are also known as *menu-based* or *rule-based* chatbots. These chatbots rely heavily on menus and many rules that direct the chatbot action or messaging. Many traditional chatbots allow customers to input text, and the traditional chatbot will likely be programmed to redirect the customer back to the menu when the chatbot is unable to understand the customer's text.

Self-learning chatbots use NLP to understand a customer's text and ML algorithms to better understand the customer's intent. NLP chatbots appear smarter and more conversational to the customer for many reasons, one of which is that they retain context because they're able to handle multiturn conversations. Self-learning chatbots are impressive, but they're even more powerful when combined with the capabilities of a menu-based chatbot. Hybrid chatbots typically include a menu to help customers who need to know what the chatbot can do. Menu options could include choices such as Main Menu, Transfer to Agent, or End Chat. Most conversational AI chatbots are hybrid chatbots.

A conversational AI chatbot can incorporate GenAI capabilities to provide an enhanced chatbot capable of real-time conversations that offer personalization, summarize large amounts of material, and can even provide customized recommendations. GenAI integrated conversational chatbots leverage GenAI capabilities for a specific purpose, when needed, then the conversation returns back to dialog blocks. GenAI integrated conversational chatbots are sometimes referred to as virtual assistants.

Well-known examples of GenAI integrated chatbots available publicly include Sephora's Virtual Assistant and Salesforce's Agentforce Virtual Assistant. For these vendors, the goal of making information more accessible is to increase product sales and usage. For other vendors building GenAI integrated chatbots, information is the product. A well-known example is O'Reilly Answers, which uses a large language model (LLM) to summarize trusted content of multiple publishers available on the O'Reilly learning platform.

GenAI chatbots are publicly available powerful chatbots that typically offer access through subscription services. Well-known examples of GenAI chatbots include OpenAI ChatGPT, Google Gemini, Perplexity, Microsoft Copilot, and Anthropic Claude. It's important to remember that the chatbot responses for this chatbot type can vary for the same input because GenAI chatbots and GenAI integrated chatbots are powered by LLMs, which are nondeterministic.

Within Salesforce, conversational AI chatbots are powered by the Einstein intent model. The Einstein intent model uses ML algorithms, when necessary, to predict the customer's intent when they make a request of the chatbot. Einstein chatbots are, by default, created as enhanced chatbots, which allows for the chatbot to integrate LLM capabilities or to transfer the conversation to an agent or human representative. Integrating with LLM capabilities requires the user to enable the Generative Knowledge Answers feature on the Overview page in Bot Builder by clicking the checkbox in the Knowledge section to "Use features that intelligently search for knowledge articles with this chatbot."

The Generative Knowledge Answers feature uses the *Answer Questions with Knowledge* agent action to generate chatbot answers. Thus, you'd need to set up Agentforce and D360 in addition to Service Cloud and Salesforce Knowledge if you choose to integrate GenAI features with your Einstein chatbot. D360 is required for all Agentforce implementations. In addition, all data sources and knowledge articles for Generative Knowledge Answers are indexed in D360.

We'll discuss the Einstein model and Knowledge LLM capabilities in later sections. First, we need to review the two Einstein chatbot types available to users because, until recently, that's the first decision to be made when creating a new chatbot in Salesforce.

Salesforce Chatbot Types

There were two chatbot types available to be built within Salesforce, standard or enhanced, up until the Salesforce summer '26 release. The choices between these two depended on which Omni-Channel routing was enabled in your Salesforce org.

Omni-Channel routing is an automation feature used to intelligently route cases or chats received across various channels to the most qualified and available human, chatbot, or agent based on predefined criteria. Salesforce orgs previously using standard Omni-Channel routing were able to create standard chatbots. Orgs using enhanced Omni-Channel routing create enhanced chatbots.

Currently, the default chatbot type is enhanced Omni-Channel routing. This is because as of summer '23 the enhanced Omni-Channel routing is automatically enabled in Salesforce orgs by default. In addition, the standard Omni-Channel routing retired with the summer '26 release when Salesforce automatically upgraded orgs to the enhanced Omni-Channel.

> You'll need to clone any existing standard chatbots as enhanced chatbots if you're planning to transition chatbots built from standard Omni-Channel routing.

Some advanced features are available on both standard and enhanced chatbots. For example, session timeout control and the First Message Intent recognition setting can be enabled for both chatbot types. Session timeout control allows users to specify the number of minutes a chatbot waits for a customer response before ending the message. The First Message Intent recognition setting feature recognizes the intent of the first message a customer sends.

There are, however, many benefits to using an enhanced chatbot rather than a standard chatbot:

- Multilanguage support
- Disambiguation
- Agentforce Service agent creation
- Integrate GenAI

Enhanced chatbots with Messaging components have full multilanguage support, which means the chatbot can now translate a dialog to another language. In addition, disambiguation can be enabled to allow enhanced chatbots to suggest the most probable dialog to the customer when the chatbot can't recognize the customer's intent. Often, the chatbot presents a list of options to the customer, based on the possible intents the chatbot identifies. Although currently in beta, an Einstein enhanced chatbot can be used to quickly build an Agentforce Service agent.

> The main difference in how standard and enhanced chatbots achieve functionality is based on their routing approach. Standard chatbots use *connections* for routing and enhanced chatbots use *flows* for more flexible routing.

One important benefit of using an enhanced chatbot is the ability to integrate GenAI into your enhanced chatbot. The Answer Questions with Knowledge action can be used to search for relevant information within your knowledge base and then generate conversational answers. The Generative Knowledge Answers data sources and knowledge articles are indexed in D360 so that the agent action searches for relevant information using the assigned data library's search index and retriever. The user sets up the chatbot so that the data sources and knowledge articles are accessed whenever a customer asks the chatbot a question that can't be matched to an existing dialog. You can find more information about this feature in "Overview Page" on page 196.

We now know that enhanced chatbots are the default chatbot type in Salesforce. We're also aware that conversational AI chatbots can be built when the Einstein intent model is enabled. So, how exactly does an Einstein AI chatbot work? Let's dive into the anatomy of an Einstein AI chatbot to find out.

Anatomy of an Einstein Conversational AI Chatbot

Before we explore the inner workings of an Einstein AI chatbot, let's first discuss how the Einstein AI chatbot interacts with its environment. In a simplified version of the Einstein AI chatbot's environment, there are two main systems with which the Einstein AI chatbot interacts (Figure 5-1).

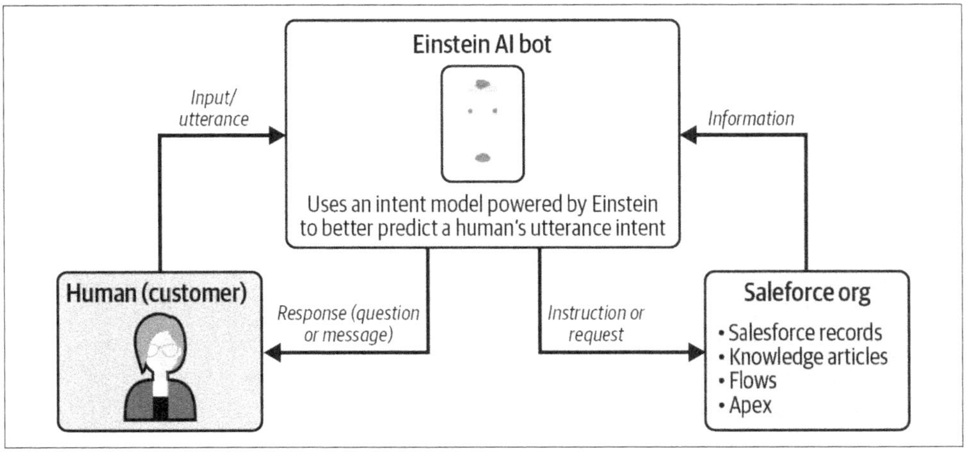

Figure 5-1. Einstein AI bot interaction with a human and the Salesforce org

Initially, a human communicates with the chatbot by providing input in the form of text within a chat or message. The chatbot attempts to match the customer's input, known as an utterance, with an intent. For example, if a customer types "Could you book an Italian restaurant near me," that utterance might be matched with the intent labeled RestaurantBooking. The correct intent is identified with certainty if the utterance is an exact match for the intent based on sample utterances provided in advance by the user.

If not, the intent model uses a combination of named entity recognition (NER) and natural language understanding (NLU) capabilities to better comprehend the customer's utterance (Figure 5-2). This allows the chatbot to better predict the customer's intent using an ML algorithm and deep learning neural networks. When it's time to respond to the customer, the chatbot uses natural language generation (NLG), another form of natural language processing (NLP). Refer to the second edition of the *Natural Language Processing in Action* book by Hobson Lane, Hannes Hapke, and Cole Howard (Manning, 2019) if you're interested in exploring the topic of NLP further.

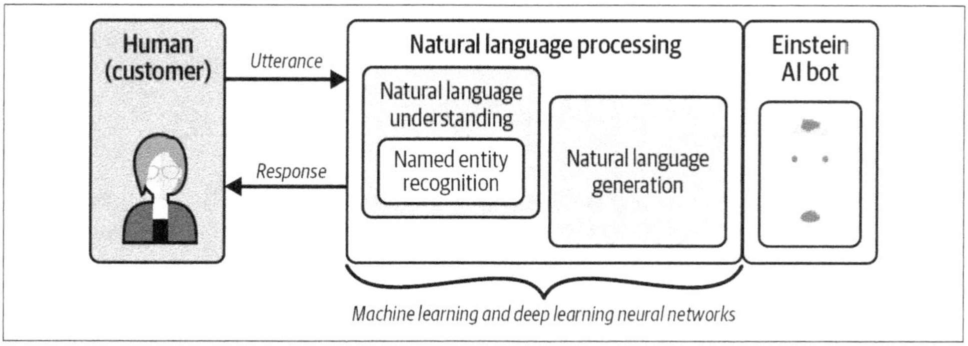

Figure 5-2. AI chatbot conversation powered by Einstein

Once the chatbot knows the customer's intent, it either sends a response back to the customer or sends an instruction to the Salesforce org. The response to the customer could be in the form of a message giving the user an answer, or the response could be in the form of a question asking the customer for more details. Alternatively, the chatbot sends a message to the Salesforce org. That message could ask for Salesforce record details, information from Knowledge articles, or possibly request an action to be undertaken via a Salesforce Flow or Apex code.

The user doesn't have direct access to the Einstein capabilities that power the AI chatbot conversation. So, what exactly can the user access and create within the chatbot? First, it's important to remember that each chatbot is versioned, which means that a chatbot can always be rolled back to a previous version by the user. As such, the custom parts of a chatbot such as custom variables and entities are associated with a particular chatbot version, so we need to consider each chatbot version.

Within each chatbot version, there exists one or more dialogs (Figure 5-3). Within each dialog, one or more steps are created. Within each step is one component from among the following choices: Questions, Messaging components, Actions, and Rules. Each component can include items like dialog intents, variables, entities, and goals.

Dialog intents and utterances are required for chatbots that don't use menus since that's the only way the chatbot can understand what the customer wants. The Einstein intent model, if enabled, gives the chatbot its AI capabilities. The intent model is assisted in its training by the user defining dialog intents and associated utterances in addition to assigning variables and creating entities.

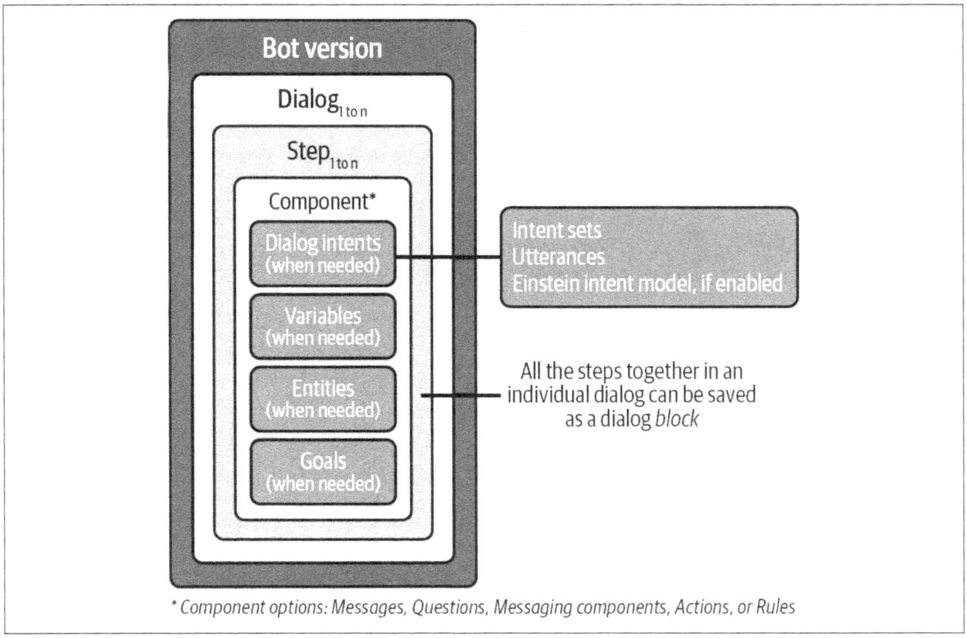

Figure 5-3. Each AI chatbot version includes dialogs, steps, and other components

These dialog intents, variables, and entities are fundamental pieces required for AI chatbots to understand and respond to human language effectively and to carry out the tasks as intended by the customer. We'll explain these terms in much more detail in upcoming sections. In addition, we'll discuss goals that are established by the user to help measure the effectiveness of the chatbot and to identify areas for improvement. Before we explore the fundamental chatbot components, let's first consider conversation design and chatbot design. This will help us build more effective dialog intents, variables, and entities for our chatbots.

Conversation Design and Chatbot Design

Conversation design (CxD) incorporates the concepts, strategies, and processes required to craft conversations that build better relationships with customers. CxD experts help design better conversational approaches for human-to-human interactions as well as for human-to-chatbot conversations.

Improving human-to-human conversations can be achieved by creating frameworks and dialog examples used for training service reps. On the other hand, effective human-to-chatbot conversation design is achieved somewhat differently because the conversational flow with chatbots is built in a very declarative and predefined way. This has its advantages because a chatbot stays on track. However, because the conversations are predefined, it's more likely a chatbot can leave customers feeling annoyed, especially if the chatbot exhibits bias because it wasn't built to be inclusive of variations in language. That's why it's important to engage a conversation design expert when creating chatbots.

> Conversation design requires a human to possess a unique skillset. It's not enough to be trained to create outstanding copy, design superior graphical user experiences, or build excellent conversational user interfaces. Instead, a proficient conversation design expert often has a background in linguistics and a good understanding of AI technology, along with user experience domain knowledge.

Conversation design involves strategic thinking about how and what should be said, and not everyone can create great chatbot scripts. It's not just about using good writing skills. Conversation design experts leverage years of research on linguistic patterns to strategically build conversation dialogs that won't frustrate, alienate, mislead, or overwhelm users. Similar to other design projects, conversation design and chatbot creation is a team effort. Engineering and ops teams are usually responsible for implementing conversation design and deploying chatbots.

A conversation designer creates a vision of the service experience and then outlines what the chatbot is expected to do for each use case. The designer creates a turn-taking structure between the chatbot and the human by writing out actual sample dialogues. Next, the designer will likely use a prototyper like Botmock or Botsociety to output a video for stakeholders to view and then create an annotated transcript to help others understand the design strategy. Importantly, the designer should create an infrastructure architecture flowchart demonstrating how each dialog use case fits together.

In addition to planning chatbot content, designers also design conversation openings and closings. A chatbot opening often includes an introduction and a greeting. For example, "Hi. I'm Barney the Bot. How can I help you?" A simple closing, such as "Thank you," can be used to end a chat once the human utters words that indicate they're ready to end the conversation. A designer decides on the appropriate use of emojis and emoticons and often selects a machine-like font style such as Roboto Mono or Orbitron. A conversation designer may elect to build in response delays for the chatbot, short pauses that make conversation snippets seem less artificial.

After designing chatbot conversations, the team should do a final check to ensure they've created a sufficient number of intents and utterances. Einstein chatbots require at least three intents and a minimum of 20 utterances. More intents and utterances improves accuracy, so it's best to create more than the minimum number. Best practices also recommend intents be balanced in the number of utterances tied to them so they don't skew the model in any particular direction. Additionally, each utterance should be unique and have some variation in word length. Once the conversation design is complete, it's time for the team to begin the chatbot design.

To enable chatbots, search for Einstein Bots in the Quick Find box from the Setup menu. Click the toggle on next to Einstein Bots. Next, accept the terms if you agree. You'll initially be on the My Bots tab by default, but you can switch to the Bot Templates or Bot Blocks tab (Figure 5-4).

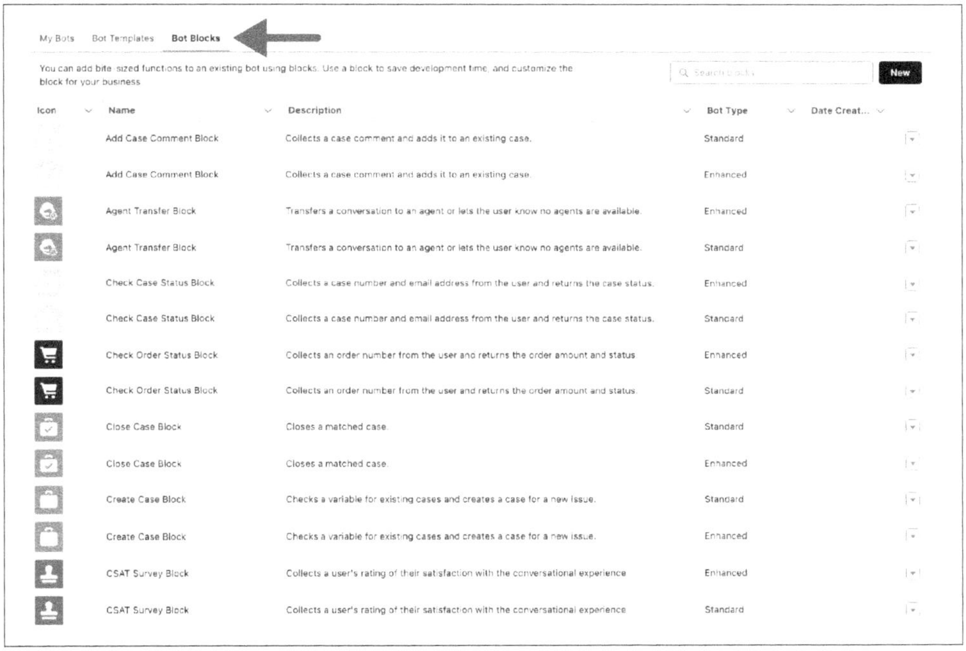

Figure 5-4. Bot Blocks tab for Einstein Bots

These tabs each serve a different purpose:

My Bots
: To see existing chatbots and create new chatbots

Bot Templates
: Offers minimal setup options for creating chatbots from prebuilt skills, store intent data, and more

Bot Blocks
: Provides prebuilt blocks to save development time; it's also possible to add bite-sized functions to an existing bot block

Previously, Smart Features was a tab where users had the ability to configure Article Answers to perform an AI-powered search of Knowledge articles and responses. However, that feature was retired in September 2026 and replaced with an Agentforce action (Figure 5-5). The Einstein Bots Generative Knowledge Answers feature uses the Answer Questions with Knowledge action whenever a chatbot can't match a customer input to an intent.

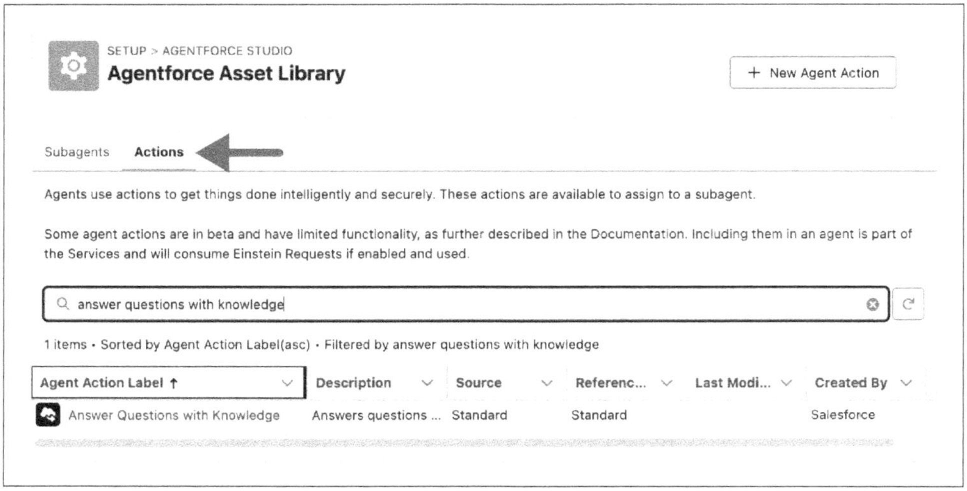

Figure 5-5. Agentforce standard action titled Answer Questions with Knowledge

Now we're ready to discuss intents, intent models, and intent sets first because you'll likely want to create some intent sets early in your chatbot building journey, after reviewing any intent sets that already exist or for which you have access. Next, we'll learn how to create a new chatbot. You'll need to create a chatbot before accessing the Bot Builder. We'll then explore the Bot Builder in detail, reviewing each Bot Builder page.

Intent, Intent Models, and Intent Sets

If we look again at Figure 5-1, we see that the chatbot receives an utterance from the customer. An utterance is the message sent from the customer to the chatbot that informs the chatbot what the customer wants. Once the chatbot knows what the customer wants, it can take action to accomplish the request. *Intent* is the term for what the customer actually wants the chatbot to do.

An utterance consists of meaningful phrases and often is in the form of a question or sentence. Here are some examples of utterances:

- Can I speak with an agent?
- I'd like to talk with a real person.
- Get me to the customer service department.
- Agent.

These utterances are expressions of a few ways a customer can state their desire for the chatbot to transfer the conversation to a non-AI agent, an agent who is a human customer service representative. One intent, like TransferToAgent, will be associated with many utterances. One of the first things you'll need to do before getting hands-on-keyboard to create your new chatbot is to determine what intents you want your chatbot to fulfill. Then make a list of utterances that customers could use to ask for that intent.

As of summer '21, all new utterances require a language to be identified. Utterances that were created prior to summer '21 have an associated language of *unassigned*. You'll want to edit the chatbot to change the language from unassigned to English or whatever language is appropriate.

> One way to identify intents for your chatbot is to review your customer service representative's chat logs. Identify common tasks performed by service reps where a chatbot could handle the request instead. One example might be to create a chatbot that can make new appointments and update existing appointments instead of having this type of task handled by a human.

Once you've identified an intent you want your chatbot to fulfill, you can manually add utterances to the intent within Bot Builder. However, you'll likely want to create an Einstein Intent Set for any intent that might be used for multiple chatbots. This will allow you to reuse your intents when creating a new chatbot or when adding a new intent to an existing chatbot. Intent sets are not created within the Builder. Instead, you'll access intent sets via the Setup menu. Use the Quick Find box to search for and click the Einstein Intent Sets link. From there, you'll see a list of all intent sets already created. You can also click the New button in the top-right corner to create a new intent set. Give the intent set a name and then click the Save button. You'll then be presented with the option to edit the intent name details, add new intents and utterances, or add new entities (Figure 5-6). We'll learn about entities later, in "Entities Page" on page 200.

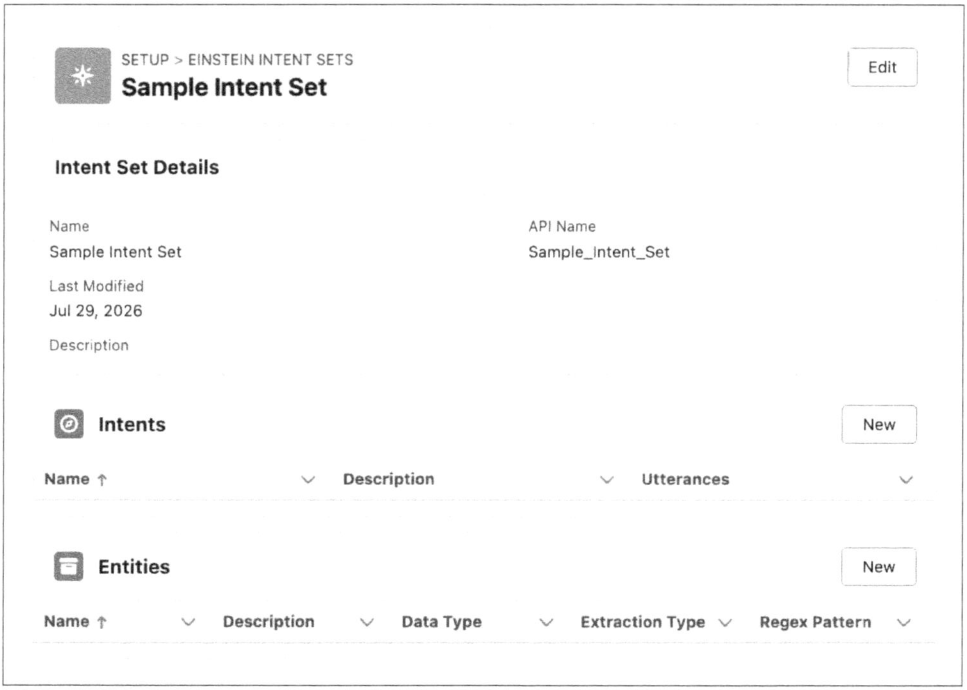

Figure 5-6. Intent Set page where new intents and entities are added

You'll notice that each intent set can include multiple intents. Each intent within the set needs to have utterances added to it.

Later, we'll see how to add intents to dialog components when building a chatbot within Bot Builder. Each dialog intent can have utterances added to it by an intent set as well as manually input by the user. The total number of utterances for the intent is the combined number of utterances from the intent set as well as those manually entered.

Give careful thought to the number of utterances to add to each intent. The intent model is more accurate when it has many utterances as training examples. Thus, in general, more utterances per intent are better, although the quality of the utterances is key. However, each chatbot will need more than one intent, which means you'll need to keep a balance between intents to maintain the model's accuracy. You should strive to include roughly the same number of utterances per intent for each intent in the chatbot.

> When an intent needs text identification but there aren't enough utterances available to keep the intent model balanced, use Exact Matching. Exact Match utterances are case-sensitive. Exact Matching is enabled from the dialog page in Bot Builder. Once the Exact Matching setting has been enabled for an intent, it can't be turned off.

Whether a chatbot uses AI or not, intents are always needed unless customers interact with a chatbot using only menus or buttons, rather than free-form text input. Many utterances are associated with each intent, and each intent is associated with a component inside of a dialog.

A chatbot understands a customer's intent by using an intent model to predict the most likely intent based on the customer's utterance, assuming there isn't a direct match of the utterance to the intent. Once the chatbot understands the customer's intent, it's able to take the necessary action using the instructions provided for it within the chatbot dialog, as long as the permissions assigned to the bot allow it to do so. Thus, it's essential for the chatbot to understand the customer's utterance and choose the right intent.

We've discussed how important it is to provide a sufficient number of relevant utterances for each intent upon which to train the intent model. In addition to providing the utterance dataset for the intent, the user needs to select the intent model. Salesforce offers two intent models for Einstein Bots: the original intent model and a cross-lingual model. The default intent model is the cross-lingual model, although the model can be changed in the Overview page of the Bot Builder.

The original intent model requires at least three to five intents with 20 utterances per language per intent. In contrast, the cross-lingual model requires only two or more intents with at least one utterance per intent per language. The main differences between the models are the following:

- Input requirements
- Model training
- Model performance

The original model requires 20 utterances, uses 80% of the supplied utterances for training the model, and uses the remaining 20% of utterances to calculate the model's F1 score. In contrast, the cross-lingual model allows utterance testing using the Input Tester on the Model Management page with any supported language, before or after adding training data. In addition, the cross-lingual model uses all utterances for model training and for calculating model performance.

It's possible to switch between the two models, but you must meet the prerequisites for the model you want to enable. You're unable to change a cross-lingual model to an original model if the chatbot uses a language that's only supported for the cross-lingual intent model. After changing the model, if allowed, you'll need to rebuild the model via the Model Management page in the Bot Builder.

Although both models can be used for single- or multilanguage chatbots, they have different minimum requirements and are meant for different use cases. For one thing, the cross-lingual model can be trained on as little as one utterance per language. The cross-lingual model is useful when you want to test utterances in any supported language, before or after adding the supported language to your model. It also gives you a unified view of intent performance for all the languages defined for the chatbot using the cross-lingual model.

It's necessary to think about ways to create the best intent model in advance. It's also important to monitor your intent model frequently because your model changes as your chatbot interacts with customers and as you add new capabilities. You can find more information about how your intent model is performing by visiting the Model Management page in Bot Builder.

> Provide a better customer experience by planning for and then creating your chatbot with a simple and clearly defined use case before adding more complexity to the chatbot. It's recommended to focus on the most common customer inquiries first. Create two to five intents, then gradually expand chatbot functionality. Limit intents to no more than 100 for accuracy and group similar intents to improve classification.

Monitoring your model should be part of your overall strategy for intent data management. Be sure to test any new additions to the intent model in a sandbox because adding more utterances and intents to a live chatbot impacts the customer experience. You can import intent data to any chatbot dialog where you've turned on the Intent Enabled option. Chatbot intent data can be exported using Data Loader to access the Intent Utterance object. In addition, Einstein Intent Sets can be used to move utterances and entities between Salesforce orgs via change sets.

We've explored intents, intent sets, and the intent model and learned how to create a new intent set by navigating to the setup menu. We also discovered that you'll learn more about the intent model management when we review the Model Management page within Bot Builder. Now, we're ready to learn how to create a chatbot. We'll need to create a chatbot first and then access the Bot Builder from a specific chatbot we've created.

Creating Einstein Chatbots

Before gaining access to the Bot Builder to customize your chatbot, you'll need to create the chatbot first. There are three ways to create a new chatbot:

- Creating an Einstein chatbot from scratch
- Creating an Einstein chatbot from a template
- Cloning an existing Einstein chatbot

In addition, a user can make use of prebuilt bot blocks to develop chatbots faster. Let's briefly discuss these ways of creating Einstein chatbots and accelerating chatbot development.

Creating an Einstein Chatbot from Scratch

To create a new Einstein chatbot from scratch, search for the Einstein Bots page in the Quick Find box of the Setup menu. Once on the Einstein Bots main page, you'll see a list of all existing chatbots. There's a blue New button to the right of the screen that can be used to create a new chatbot. Click that button and then select whether you want to create a standard or enhanced chatbot. In "Salesforce Chatbot Types" on page 177, we described standard and enhanced chatbots. Currently, enhanced chatbots are the default.

Once you select enhanced chatbot or standard chatbot, you'll be asked whether you want to start from scratch or use one of the existing prebuilt templates. If you select the option to start from scratch, you'll be asked to personalize your chatbot (Figure 5-7). Give your chatbot a name and then select the primary language.

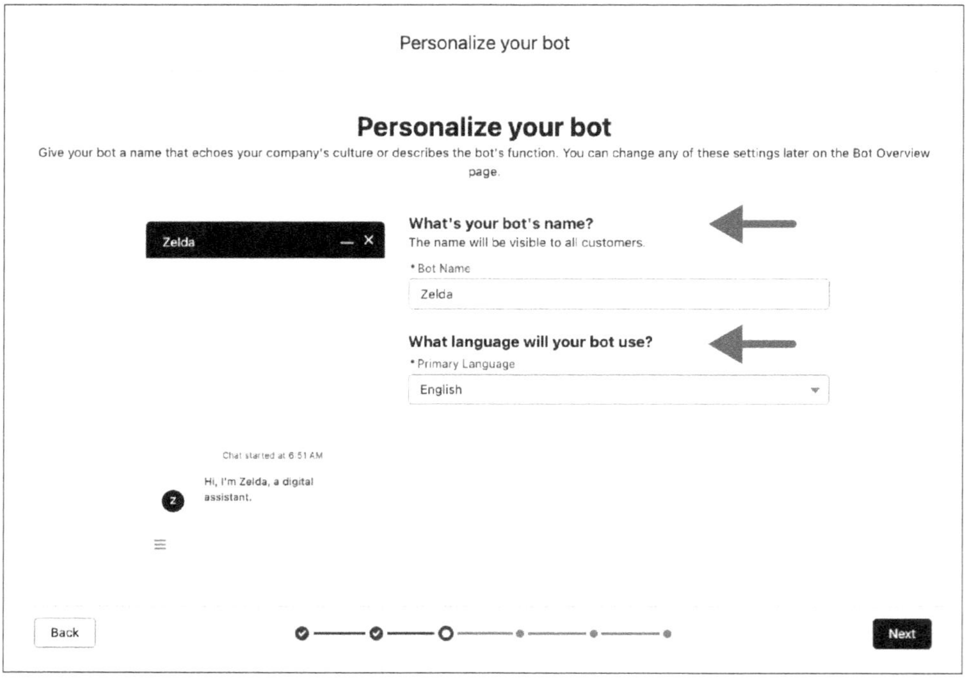

Figure 5-7. Personalize a chatbot with a unique name and the selection of the primary language

After clicking Next, you'll be given more options to personalize your chatbot (Figure 5-8). You can accept the default greeting message provided or provide your own greeting. Then you can add up to three menu items, which equate to dialog actions. Some suggestions for these actions include Check My Order, Report a Problem, and Find a Product. Notice that all these actions begin with an action verb, which is a best practice.

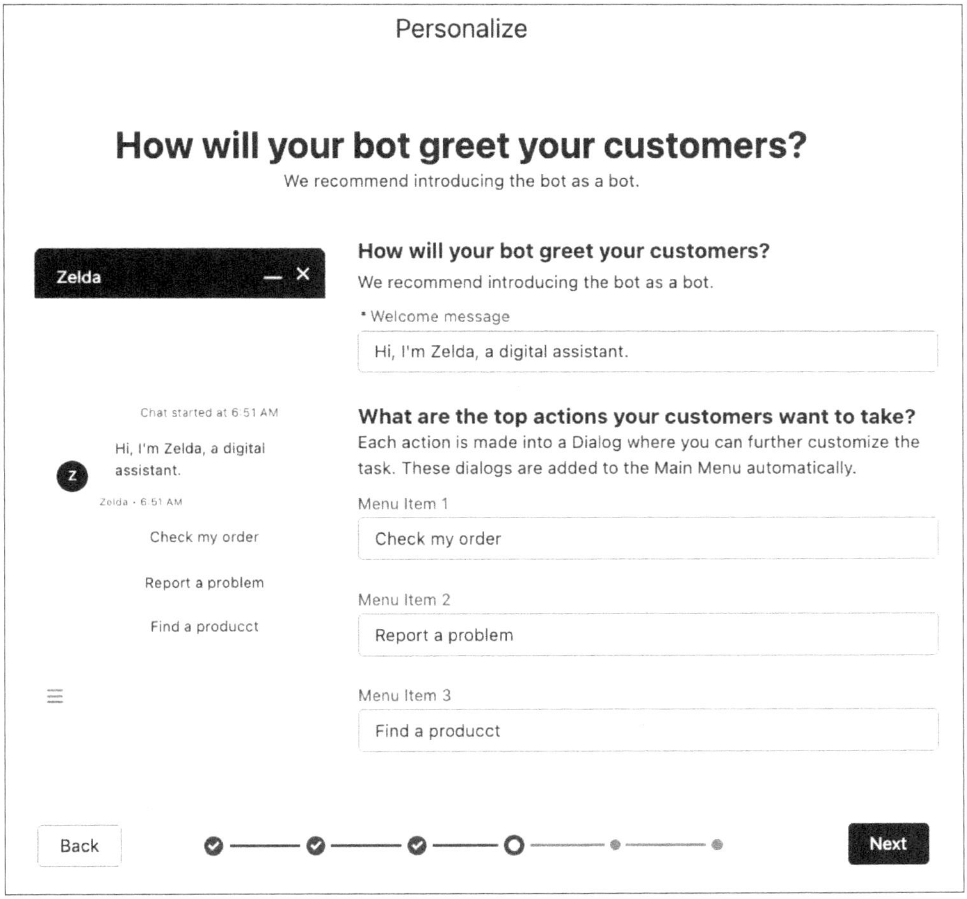

Figure 5-8. More options to personalize your chatbot

On the next screen, the box for creating an inbound Omni-Channel flow will be checked by default (Figure 5-9). If you've already created an outbound Omni-Channel flow, you can select it now. Otherwise, you can create the flow and add it to the chatbot later.

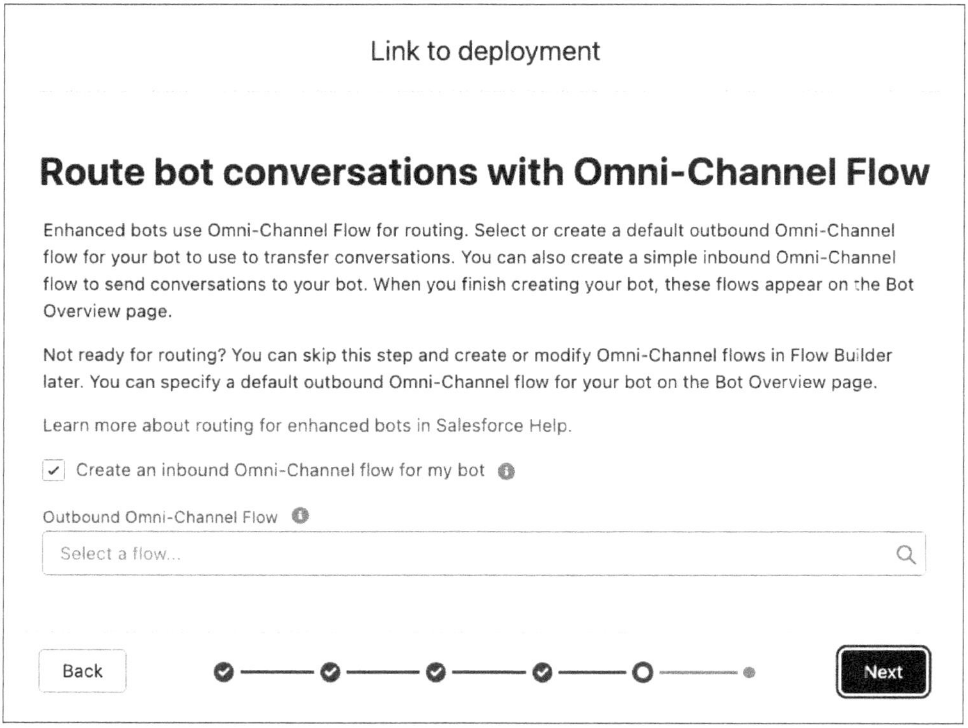

Figure 5-9. Linking the chatbot to an outbound Omni-Channel flow while also creating an inbound flow

Next, you'll see a summary screen informing you of the various things that will be created once you click the Proceed button (Figure 5-10). Salesforce will automatically create custom dialogs for the Welcome message and for the Main Menu actions you indicated. System dialogs and chatbot analytics will be created. If you kept the default box checked for the inbound Omni-Channel flow, it will also be created.

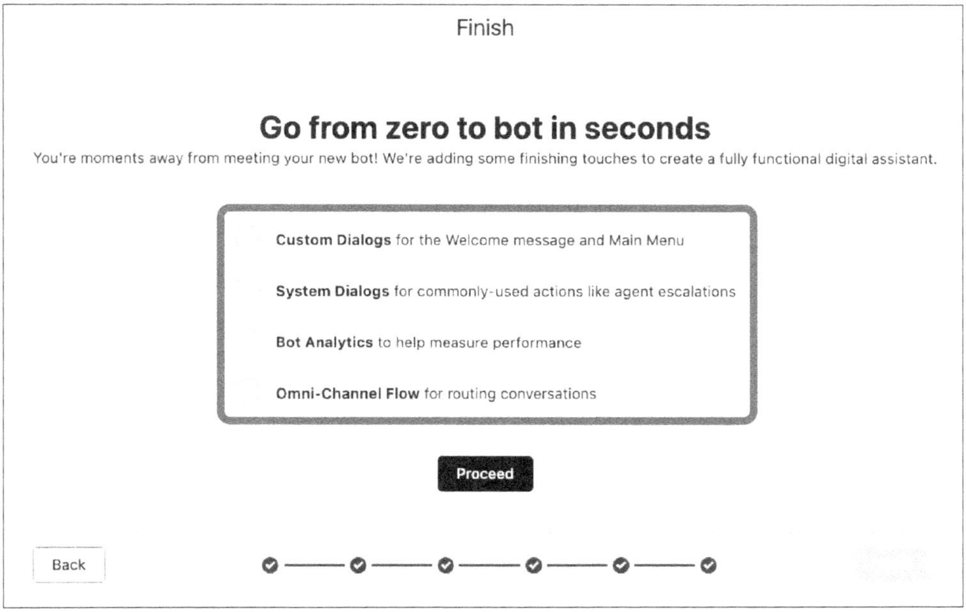

Figure 5-10. Summary screen indicating the items Salesforce will create for the chatbot

After clicking Proceed, the chatbot will be created and the Bot Builder will open up for you. When the Bot Builder first opens up, it's on the Dialogs menu page (Figure 5-11).

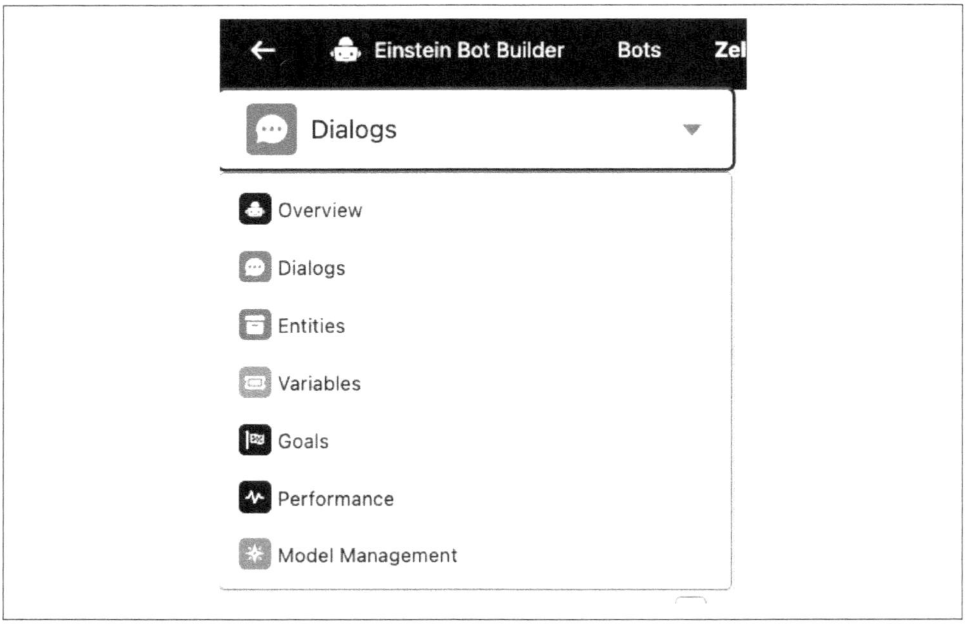

Figure 5-11. Dialogs menu page of the Bot Builder tool

You're now ready to build out your new chatbot using the Bot Builder. We'll explore the Bot Builder in detail a little later in the chapter.

Creating an Einstein Chatbot from a Template

Instead of selecting the option to Start from Scratch when creating a new chatbot, you'll instead select the template you want to use from among the existing prebuilt templates. If the template doesn't yet exist, you may want to build the template first. You can package chatbot templates and share them between orgs or on the Salesforce AppExchange.

Once you select the desired template, you'll be asked to personalize your chatbot with a name. You won't need to specify how the chatbot will greet users as you did when you created a chatbot from scratch. You will, however, need to select whether you want to create an inbound Omni-Channel flow and/or use an outbound flow. You'll be presented with the screen asking you to click the Proceed and Finish buttons. When the Bot Builder screen opens up, you'll see the chatbot already built out to the template's specifications. From there, you can edit the existing chatbot as desired.

Cloning an Existing Einstein Chatbot

Cloning an existing chatbot gives users the ability to quickly create a similar chatbot. Cloned chatbots inherit intent and utterance data from the original chatbot. They also inherit settings from the Bot Overview page such as chatbot type, primary language, connections, intent enhancement choices, and Knowledge features if enabled. After cloning a chatbot, the user can add channels, create more dialogs, add more dialog intents, and build an intent model.

Standard chatbots can be cloned as a standard or enhanced chatbot. However, an enhanced chatbot can only be cloned as an enhanced chatbot. Cloning a standard-to-standard or enhanced-to-enhanced chatbot is straightforward. Just click on the drop-down to the right of the chatbot name and select the Clone option. Enter a unique chatbot display name, hit the Tab key, and then click the Save button.

Cloning a standard chatbot as an enhanced chatbot isn't quite as easy and requires some features to be reconfigured. The following will be accomplished through a guided cloning experience:

- Context variables are mapped to their corresponding messaging objects.
- Conversation routing is automatically created for inbound and outbound conversations.
- Custom dialogs need to be created by the user to replace some system-created dialogs such as "Transfer to Agent Next Step" and "Transfer to Agent."

Further action is required. Although conversation routing is automatically created, you'll still need to customize and activate the routing in Flow Builder. In addition, any custom dialog that uses the Set Routing Rule Type rule step to transfer conversations to a queue or chatbot is cloned as an empty placeholder dialog. You'll need to re-create the steps within the dialog.

Using Einstein Bot Blocks to Accelerate Chatbot Development

In addition to cloning an existing chatbot and using a template to help you accelerate your chatbot development, you can also use Einstein bot blocks. Bot blocks are prebuilt dialogs that can be added to a chatbot. You can create your own bot blocks or use one of the many standard bot blocks provided for you. For example, there are bot blocks available as standard or enhanced chatbot types for the following: Add Case Comment, Agent Transfer, Check Case Status, Close Case, Data Disclosure Block, and more.

Bot blocks can be created from the main Einstein Bots page within Setup. A bot block is added to a chatbot from the Dialog page within the Bot Builder. Click the plus sign (+) on the Dialog page to import an existing bot block into the chatbot.

Einstein Bot Builder

Creating a new chatbot takes the user directly to the Dialogs page in Bot Builder. When you want to access the Bot Builder later, you'll just need to access the main Einstein Bots page from the Setup menu and click on the name of the bot you want to access and work on within Bot Builder. The Dialogs page is the default page in Bot Builder but you can easily navigate to any of the other pages in Bot Builder by clicking the arrow to the right of the page name. From there, you can access any one of these pages:

- Overview
- Entities
- Variables
- Dialogs
- Goals
- Performance
- Model Management

The Bot Builder offers an intuitive interface and robust set of tools, allowing users to create and manage AI-powered conversational chatbots. Let's explore each of the Bot Builder pages in detail beginning with the Overview page.

Overview Page

The Einstein Bots Overview page summarizes your chat project information including the chatbot name, application programming interface (API) name, description, chatbot type, primary language, last modified date, and last modified by details (Figure 5-12).

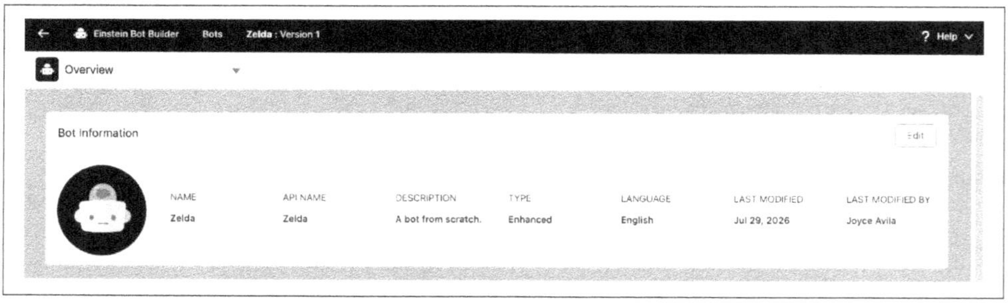

Figure 5-12. Einstein Bot information Overview page

Each chatbot has a primary language, and languages can be added (Figure 5-13) by clicking the Add button in the Conversation Languages section on the Overview page.

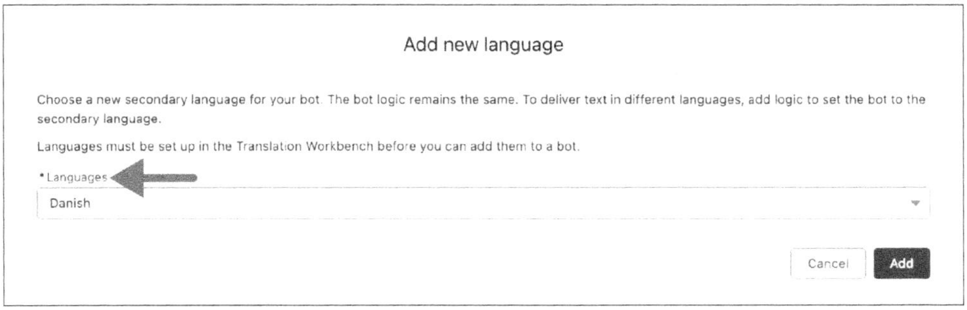

Figure 5-13. Adding secondary languages for the chatbot

Einstein Bots can connect to different endpoints. For example, chatbots support channels for in-app and web chats as well as messaging channels like SMS, Facebook Messenger, and WhatsApp. Within the Connections section on the Overview page, an API or Slack connection can be added. The Slack app name is required when adding a Slack connection. When adding a connection to an API, you'll need to supply the integration name and select the connected app (Figure 5-14).

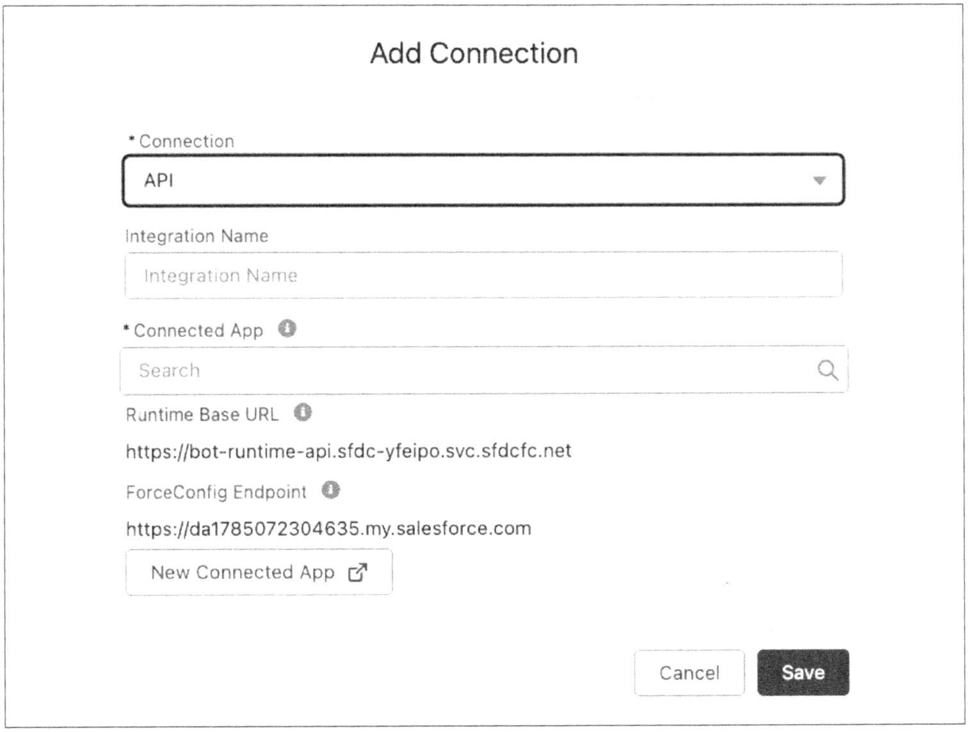

Figure 5-14. Add the integration name and select the connected app to add a new chatbot connection

The next section in the Overview page is for Inbound Omni-Channel Flows, which routes conversations to your chatbot based on the rules defined in the flow. You'll want to build out the Omni-Channel flow in Flow Builder. In addition, you can click the drop-down arrow to the right of the flow name if you want to add the route to the routing settings for an enhanced channel.

You can add the same flow to multiple channels, but a channel can have only one inbound flow. To add a flow to a channel, your channel must be active. It's possible to manage channels on the Messaging Settings page in Setup. Some possible channel types include Custom, Embedded Messages, and Text, along with Apple Messages for Business, Facebook, and WhatsApp.

> You'll need to enable the Messaging Settings from Setup before establishing connections with channels like WhatsApp, Facebook, and Text (SMS).

The last section in the Overview page is the Settings section (Figure 5-15). This section allows for setting customizations for chatbot response delay, log conversations, chatbot user, outbound Omni-Channel flow, third-party NLP provider, intent enhancements, and Knowledge features.

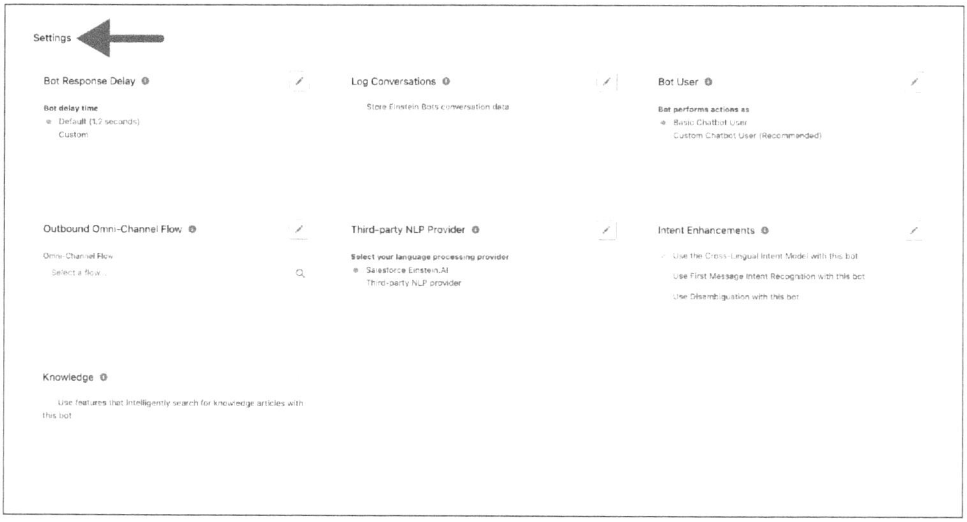

Figure 5-15. Updating chatbot customizations within the Settings section

The default bot response delay time is 1.2 seconds, but it can be customized to allow for a custom delay ranging from 0 to 3 seconds. Delaying your bot responses provides the human more time to read messages and also gives the bot a more human-like tendency. Use the pencil icon to make changes to this or any other setting.

Conversation data from bot sessions is stored based on the default settings for each channel your bot is connected to, and storing chat transcripts, including customer data, is disabled by default. If you want to make chat transcripts accessible in the Events log, you can update that setting in this Overview section. Enabling the Log Conversations setting in the Overview section makes transcripts available in Einstein event logs. The event logs can be accessed from a tab within the Performance section of the Overview page.

Each Einstein bot has a bot user whose profile and settings determine what the bot can access or what actions it can take. The default setting is for a basic chatbot user. However, it's recommended to create a custom chatbot user, especially if your bot's actions require additional access for features from Salesforce Field Service.

The next section, Outbound Omni-Channel Flow, specifies the default flow the bot uses to route conversations to a human. The routing destination is determined by the rules defined in the flow. For example, the conversation could be transferred to the record owner or to a queue.

It's also possible to establish an API connection to a third-party NLP provider. The default for each chatbot is Salesforce Einstein.AI, but Salesforce gives users the bring-your-own language processing provider option.

Within the Overview page, an Intent Enhancements section allows users to select the option to allow bots to recognize the intent of the first message a customer sends. This is now possible even with cross-lingual intent models, which give a unified view of intent performance for all the languages defined for a bot. A bot can recognize intents with minimal training when using the cross-lingual intent model. However, the bot needs at least two intents and one utterance per intent per language, and you'll need to rebuild the bot's intent model every time you turn on switch between intent models.

> Beginning October 2023, newly created or cloned bots and bot versions default to the cross-lingual intent model, including single- and multilanguage bots. If desired, the cross-lingual intent model can be disabled in the Intent Enhancements section of the Overview page within Bot Builder.

Another option for intent enhancements is turning on Disambiguation for your bot. Bots are better able to understand customer intents when Einstein Bot Disambiguation is enabled. A bot with Disambiguation enabled can suggest the most probable dialogs when a user's intent can't be recognized. If the user selects a suggested dialog, that information is used to improve the bot's cross-lingual intent model. Without using Disambiguation, the bot immediately moves to the Confused dialog if it can't confidently determine an intent.

One other bot setting available in the Overview section is the option to use features that intelligently search for knowledge articles with the bot. Enabling the Knowledge option allows the bot to be trained to respond conversationally to customer requests using Knowledge articles in the Knowledge base. After selecting the option to use the feature for intelligent search, you'll need to select the "Answer Questions with Knowledge" dialog action from the Dialog page.

Make sure you've met the prerequisites to use the Knowledge option before enabling this feature. Lightning Knowledge, D360, and Agentforce Data Library must all be enabled. You'll also want to create at least 10 knowledge articles. By default, Generative Knowledge Answers grounds its response on all knowledge records and fields. To limit the amount of information used for grounding, you can select "Custom Knowledge records and fields" and then select a data library.

If you don't have a data library already set up, you can do so from the Agentforce Data Library setup page. Alternatively, you can use your knowledge domain URL if you have one. Once you've saved your changes, you'll have the "Answer Questions with Knowledge" dialog available on the bot's Dialog page.

One optional, but important, capability of this feature is that you can let the bot show its sources to the customer. When a bot delivers the response, it can also deliver the knowledge article sources. To enable this feature, select Show Sources and enter your knowledge domain URL in the dialog step details.

Entities Page

AI Bots with NLP capabilities leverage entities to better understand user queries by extracting and analyzing the meaning of an utterance from intents. As a result, the bot can provide the most relevant and personalized response. That's because entities provide the bot with essential context about certain details such as dates, times, locations, quantities, and more.

For example, a customer's utterance stating, "Tell me what restaurants are near me" would need two entities. The first entity is the *restaurant* and the second entity is the *user's location*. The entities might relate to an intent labeled *RestaurantsCloseby* or something similar. In another example, a customer might ask, "What is the weather today in Dallas?" which would result in three entities: *temperature*, *today*, and *Dallas*, which would be associated with a *WeatherInquiry* intent. Most of the time, the *nouns* in an utterance equate to entities.

Remember that an utterance is the entire input received from the customer, and the intent is the shortened version of what the customer actually wants. Entities help bridge the gap of understanding between the utterance and the intent. Bots know more about the customer's utterance because users inform the bot about an entity, including the type of data input expected from the customer. This allows a bot to recognize an entity in customer input and then save that information to a variable. We'll discuss variables in the next section.

There are two entity types within Bot Builder: system and custom. System-defined entities are prebuilt and intentionally generic so they can be reused frequently across a bot. For example, a Text system entity accepts any text input by a user. The following system entities are provided within Bot Builder:

- Boolean
- Date
- Datetime
- Email address
- Location
- Money
- Number
- Object
- Organization
- Percent
- Person
- Phone Number
- Text

The other type of bot entities are custom entities, which are more narrow in focus to specifically match customers' needs and preferences. An example of a custom entity could be a customer's order number of their transaction history. The page to create a custom bot entity (Figure 5-16) is accessible after clicking the New button on the Entities page within Bot Builder.

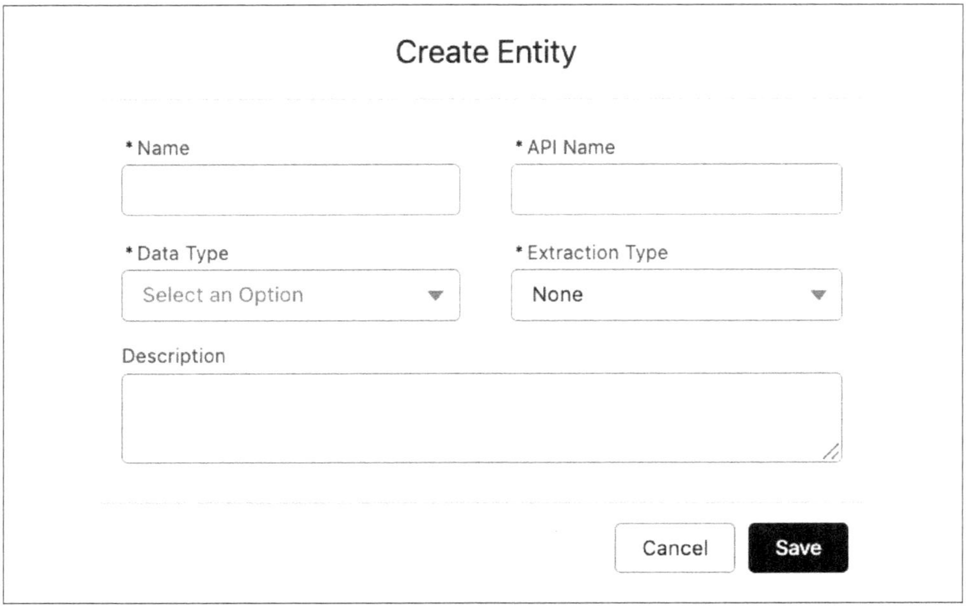

Figure 5-16. Page to create a new custom chatbot entity

Enter the entity name, then hit the Tab key to have Salesforce automatically populate the API name. Select a data type: text, number, Boolean, date, datetime, or currency. It's optional, but recommended, to provide a description before saving the entity.

If the data type selected is Text, an option will appear allowing you to select an extraction type: none, pattern, or value. Enter the regex pattern if the entity type selected is Pattern. If the entity type selected is Value, you'll need to click on the saved entity name to add new values.

Custom entities can be shared across versions of the same chatbot. Note that it's possible to edit or delete a custom chatbot entity but not system chatbot entities.

Chatbot entities are especially useful when combined with *Conversation Repair*, which provides extra messages to help the user correct the input formatting if the user's response doesn't match the entity format.

Variables Page

Chatbot variables are dynamic placeholders used to store input data from the user. Variables can also be used to display certain data as output to the user. Thus, variables can be used within dialog actions as inputs and outputs and can be inserted as a portion of the text in questions and messages using merge syntax. It's important to know that variables are specific to the version of the bot in which they're created.

Chatbot variables are of three types: system, context, and custom. Context variables can be either standard out-of-the-box variables or custom-created context variables.

System variables are provided to access backend information of conversations. They can't be edited or deleted. Examples of system variables include Answer Input, Answer Results, Current Conversation Language, Knowledge Action Citations, Knowledge Action Result, Last Customer Input, and Referrer Bot ID.

Later, in "Dialogs Page" on page 206, we'll observe how system variables and standard context variables are identified with a tag before the variable name. For example, [System] Last Customer Input (Text) and [Context] Contact ID (Text) are variable names that can be selected by the user when creating a dialog action.

Context variables let your chatbot gather customer information regardless of channel. Standard context variables come out-of-the-box with your chatbot and include the following: Contact ID, End User ID, Routable ID, and Chat Key. These prebuilt context variables allow a chatbot to look up contacts regardless of channel and then access any related object. For example, if the chatbot conversation uses Chat, the Contact ID is read from the LiveChatTranscript object. However, if the conversation uses Messaging, the Contact ID is read from the MessagingEndUser object tied to the MessagingSession object.

> Context variables are read-only variables.

You're able to add additional context variables if desired. Custom context variables help the chatbot use information it learns throughout a conversation with the customer. Custom context variables can be linked to multiple channels and objects. As such, they'll need to be mapped to the various connections and field name for each connection.

Custom variables allow your chatbot to save information gathered from your customers or store output from Salesforce. For example, consider the unique identifiers assigned to each airport worldwide. The Airport Code entity used for booking a flight would need two variables: Departure Airport Code and Arrival Airport Code.

Clicking the New button gives you the option to create a custom chatbot variable or a new context variable (Figure 5-17).

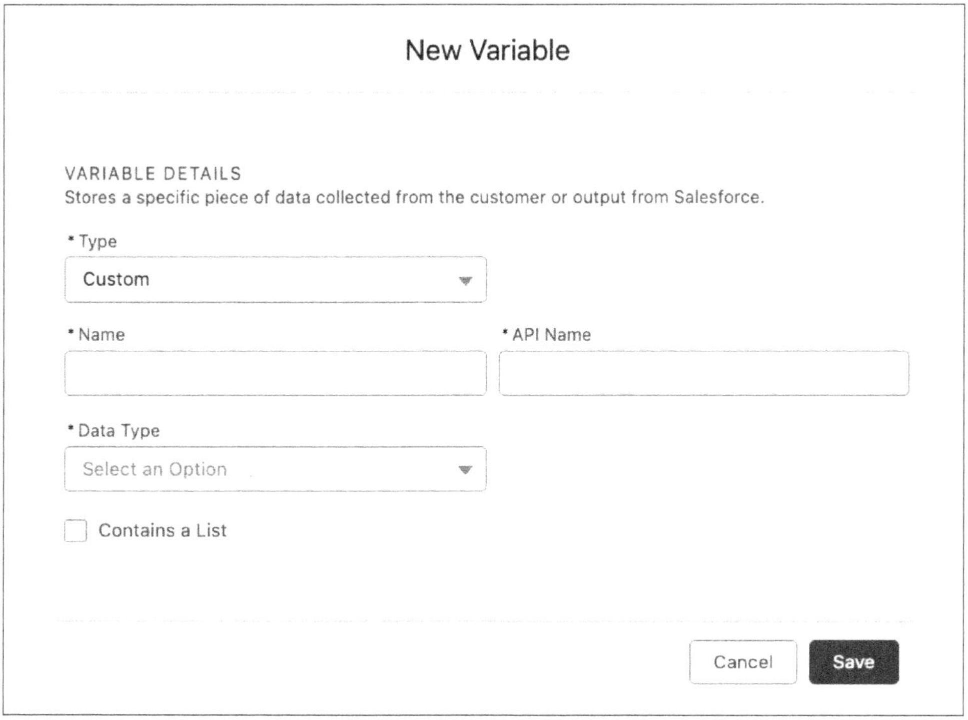

Figure 5-17. Select the type of new variable, either a custom or context variable

Creating a custom or context variable requires you to input a name and API name. You'll also need to select the data type. The following data types are available: Text, Number, Boolean, Date, Datetime, Currency, ID, and Object. An ID data type variable is a text variable with a restricted character count. Object data type variables store full records with fields. For example, you can retrieve a contact record using a flow and then store that record in an object variable. Afterward, you can access a contact record field within that object variable.

For custom variables, you can indicate whether the variable contains a list. That option is not available for context variables. In addition, when creating a custom variable with an ID data type, there is an option to associate the variable with a specific sObject type. The default sObject type is Any, but that can be changed to Bot, Content Version, Omni-Channel Flow, Queue, or Skill.

After the user inputs the details for a new variable, the next step is to click the Save button. There is an additional step required when creating a context variable. After saving the new variable, you'll click on the name of the context variable to be taken to the screen where you can map it to a connection type and a field (Figure 5-18). You can add multiple connections for each context variable.

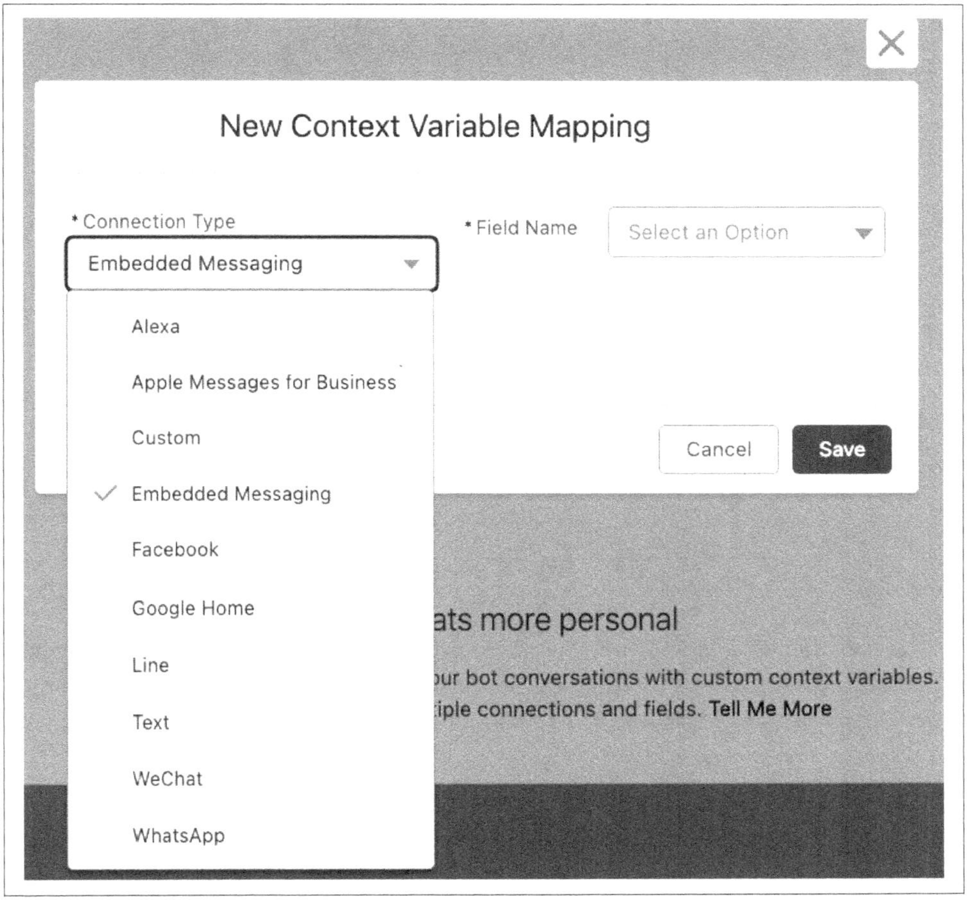

Figure 5-18. Select the connection type for mapping a new context variable

Well-defined variables are a prerequisite for chatbot actions requiring Flow or Apex, such as updating a user record or creating a case. As such, you'll likely need to create variables in an Einstein Bots Flow (Figure 5-19) as well as Bot Builder to unlock the full functionality of Einstein Bots.

Flow Definitions

All Flows ▾

350+ items • Sorted by Flow Label • Filtered by All flow definitions • Updated 3 minutes ago

Flow Label ↑	Flow API Name	Process Type	Trigger	Active	Template	Package State
Einstein Bots - Find Cases	SDO_Service_SunnyBot...	Autolaunched Flow		✓		Unmanaged
Einstein Bots - Find Locations Near Contact	SDO_Service_LunaBot_...	Autolaunched Flow		✓		Unmanaged
Einstein Bots - Find Order Product Summa...	SDO_OMS_Einstein_Bot...	Autolaunched Flow		✓		Unmanaged
Einstein Bots - Find Order Summaries	SDO_OMS_Einstein_Bot...	Autolaunched Flow		✓		Unmanaged
Einstein Bots - Find Orders	SDO_Service_SunnyBot...	Autolaunched Flow		✓		Unmanaged
Einstein Bots - Find Session Init Records	SDO_Service_SunnyBot...	Autolaunched Flow		✓		Unmanaged
Einstein Bots - Get Address Record	SDO_Service_LunaBot_...	Autolaunched Flow		✓		Unmanaged
Einstein Bots - Get Case Summaries for C...	SDO_Service_LunaBot_...	Autolaunched Flow		✓		Unmanaged
Einstein Bots - Get Contact Id	SDO_Service_SunnyBot...	Autolaunched Flow		✓		Unmanaged
Einstein Bots - Get Customer Context	IntroBotPreChatContext	Autolaunched Flow		✓	✓	Managed-Installed
Einstein Bots - Get Order Product Summa...	SDO_OMS_Einstein_Bot...	Autolaunched Flow		✓		Unmanaged
Einstein Bots - Get Order Summaries	SDO_OMS_OMSBots_G...	Autolaunched Flow		✓		Unmanaged
Einstein Bots - Loopback Current Dialog N...	SDO_Service_SunnyBot...	Autolaunched Flow		✓		Unmanaged
Einstein Bots - Make User Input Available t...	EchoValue	Autolaunched Flow		✓	✓	Managed-Installed
Einstein Bots - Return Case by CaseNumber	SDO_Service_LunaBot_...	Autolaunched Flow		✓		Unmanaged
Einstein Bots - Transfer to Queue	SDO_Service_LunaBot_...	Omni-Channel Flow		✓		Unmanaged
Einstein Bots - Update Case Order Summ...	SDO_OMS_Einstein_Bot...	Autolaunched Flow		✓		Unmanaged
Einstein Bots - Update Case Subject	SDO_Service_SunnyBot...	Autolaunched Flow		✓		Unmanaged

Figure 5-19. Chatbot Flows

Similar to other Builder tools, it's possible to create new versions as you continue updating and refining a chatbot. Now that we've considered how to create chatbot variables and entities, we're ready to explore the Bot Builder Dialogs page.

Dialogs Page

Bot Builder defaults to the Dialogs page because that is where you'll spend most of your time building the chatbot. Dialogs are the heart and soul of a chatbot. Within each chatbot are several dialogs. Each dialog includes the instructions needed for the chatbot to complete a specific task, such as answering FAQs, collecting user information, or providing recommendations.

On the Bot Builder Dialogs page, you'll find some dialogs already created (Figure 5-20). Some dialogs are included automatically: Welcome, Main Menu, Confused, End Chat, Transfer to Agent, No Agent, and Error Handler. The other dialogs are ones that you created when you first created the chatbot from scratch. If you used a template or cloned a chatbot instead, the dialogs of the template or original chatbot would show up in the new chatbot. You'll notice to the right of the Search box is a drop-down menu where you can click to add a new dialog or dialog group. You can also import a block.

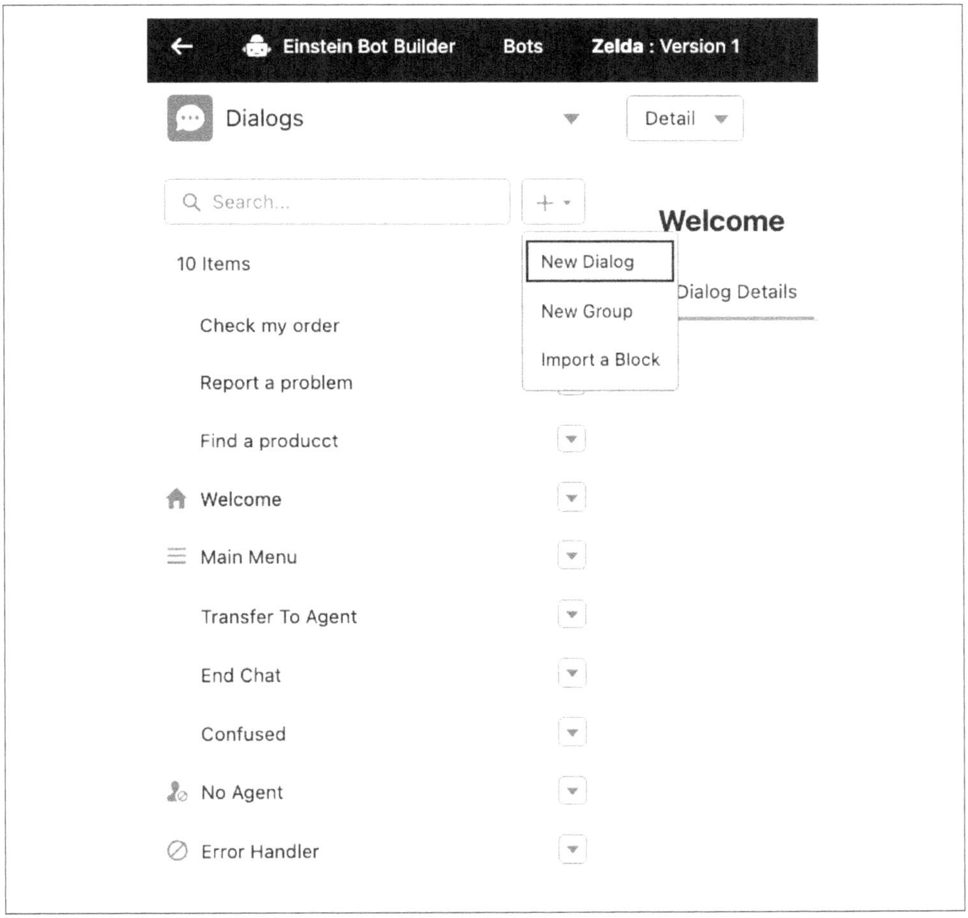

Figure 5-20. Dialogs page includes a list of dialogs along with ability to create new dialogs

The Welcome dialog is the first component called when the chatbot is needed in action. That Welcome dialog should contain a welcome message used to greet the customer. Generally, the main menu appears after the welcome. Dialogs can be created and grouped under Error Handler to process various types of errors that could occur during a conversation. The Confused and No Agent dialogs are automatically called if the chatbot doesn't understand the user input and no human representative is available.

Dialogs consist of one or more steps. Steps are created by selecting a component from the Dialog Component Library. The following components are available from the library:

- Messages
- Questions
- Messaging components
- Actions
- Rules

The Dialog Component Library appears on the left side of the screen, just below the list of dialogs. You can see the list of components in a list view or a tile view (Figure 5-21).

After the last component is created, there is always a Next Step component included in the dialog that informs the chatbot what to do next. Some examples of the Next Step component including the following:

- Wait for customer input
- Start another dialog: Main Menu
- Transfer to an agent

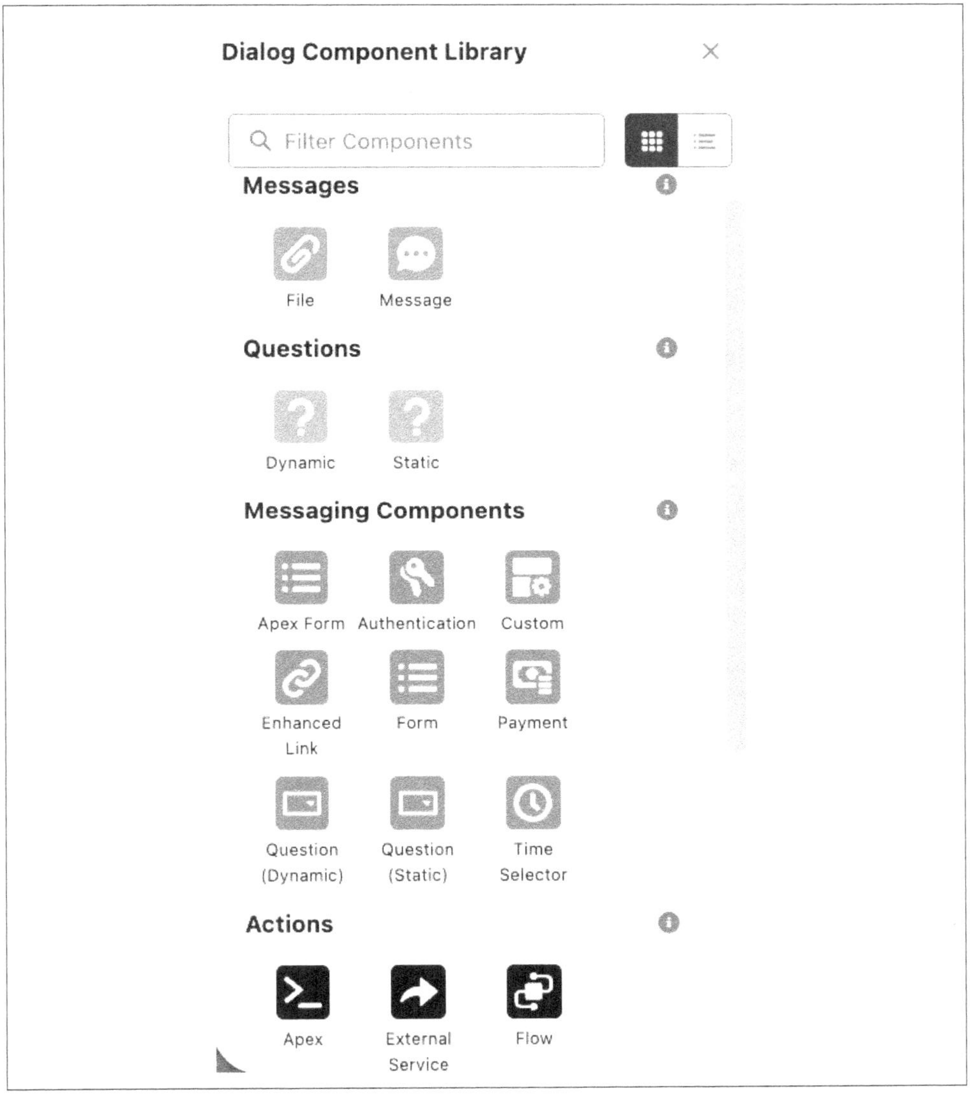

Figure 5-21. Tile view of dialog components that are part of the Dialog Component Library

To the right of each dialog name is a drop-down arrow. Clicking the arrow reveals several options available (Figure 5-22).

Figure 5-22. Drop-down arrow to the right of each dialog name includes several options

When you click on a specific dialog name, you'll see the dialog description in the middle of the screen. The dialog description (Figure 5-23) includes a tab for the Dialog Details, Dialog Translations, and Dialog Intent if the component uses an intent.

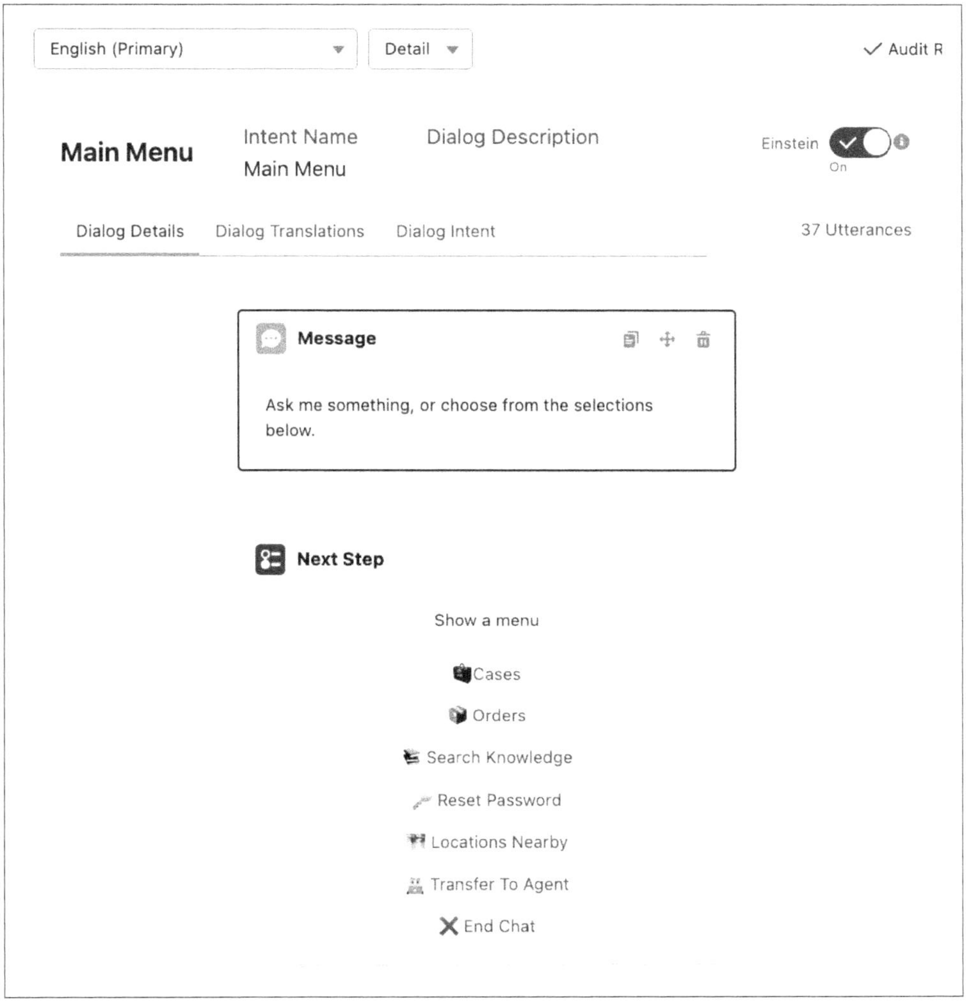

Figure 5-23. Dialog Details menu tab for the chatbot's dialog description

Notice above the dialog description that you're viewing the chatbot in detail view. The detail view shows the specifics of one dialog at a time. Clicking the drop-down menu gives you the option to look at the entire chatbot in map view (Figure 5-24). The map view helps you better understand the relationship between dialogs and also the order of operations for nested dialogs. The order of operations is based on the Next Step at the end of each dialog.

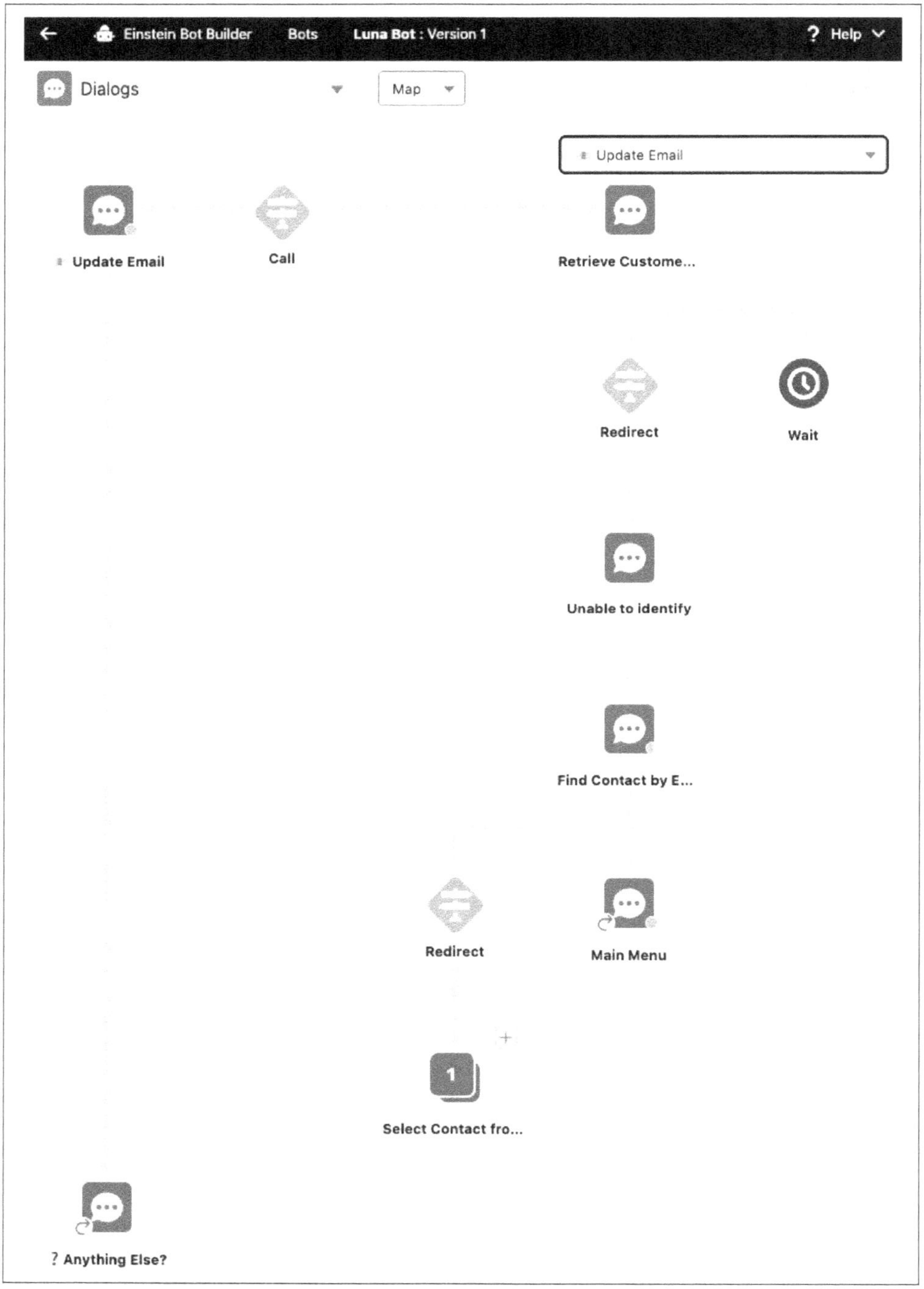

Figure 5-24. Map view shows the entire chatbot details

The Dialog Intent tab is where you're able to add intent sets, discussed in "Intent, Intent Models, and Intent Sets" on page 184, or manually add utterances to your intent. You'll have the option to enable Einstein (Figure 5-25) for each dialog in which you use intents. You'll want to turn on Einstein to build an intent model that helps your chatbot understand your customers. Then the chatbot can identify intents based on similar words. You'll build your model on the Model Management page. When Einstein is off, or you don't meet the minimum requirements to build an intent model, your chatbot exactly matches customer inputs with an utterance on this page. When the chatbot finds a match, it routes the chat to this dialog.

Figure 5-25. Enable Einstein by toggling the button in the top-right corner of screen

There's an important consideration for deleting a dialog with intents. You must first remove any intent sets from the dialog before deleting the dialog. It's not necessary to remove any utterances you've added manually.

There could be an impact if you fail to remove intent sets from a dialog before deleting the dialog. The intent set could become attached to the deleted dialog such that the intent is no longer visible on the intents setup page and, thus, can't be used in a different dialog.

Now that we have an idea of what features are available on the Dialogs page, let's review each of the different components in detail and then close out the section with a discussion of some important considerations for creating chatbots on the Dialogs page.

Dialog components

New dialog components can be added as an additional step within a dialog (Figure 5-26). To add a new component step, navigate to the component preceding the new component. Hover your mouse over that existing component, then move your cursor down the page slowly until a plus sign appears. Click the plus sign. You can then select any of the components within the Dialog Component Library. Once you select a new component you'll notice the step properties appear to the right. The step properties are specific for the component you've selected.

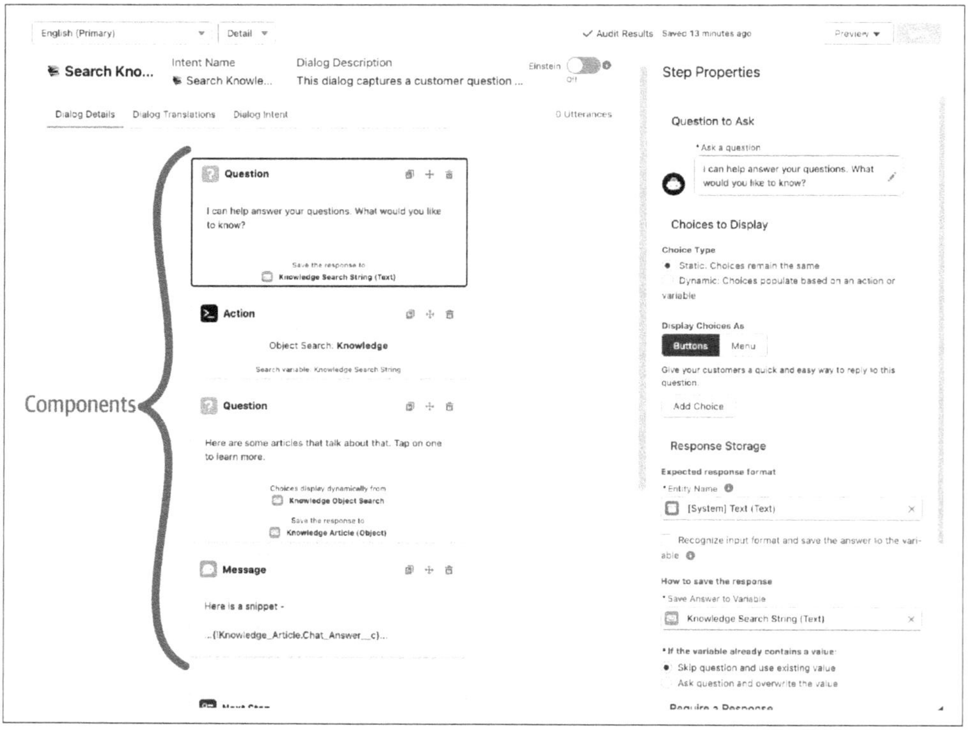

Figure 5-26. Adding new dialog components as an additional dialog step

Using the Messages component from the Dialog Component Library, your chatbot can send or receive a file in addition to displaying a message to the customer. The Messages component is different from the Messaging components in the Dialog Component Library. The Message component includes two selections: File and Message. Messaging components is a grouping of components that offers many choices including Question (Enhanced), Payment, Authentication, and the ability to create a custom component.

When selecting the File option from the Messages component, you'll need to select the file interaction as either Receive File or Send File. When displaying a message to your customer, you can use merge syntax to display collected information. For example, the message could be *Your order number is `{variableName}`*.

Using the Question component, you can ask your customer a question and save the answer to a variable. Questions can be created based on the following component options:

Static
: Static question choice options remain the same. The user types in the question and then provides the static choice options to be displayed as either buttons or menu items. Next, the user provides an entity name associated with the expected response format. A variable is also selected and the user needs to choose what action the chatbot should take if the variable already contains a value.

Dynamic
: Dynamic choices are populated based on an action or a variable. Action types include Apex, External Service, Flow, From List Variable, or Standard. In addition, the user defines a backup rule that informs the chatbot what to do if the action doesn't result in any choices to display. The user then needs to provide an entity name, select a variable, and choose what action the chatbot should take if the variable already contains a value.

There is something unique about using Messaging components. You'll need to create a component from the Messaging components in Setup before you can use it with your chatbot. Messaging component types that can be created include the following:

- Question
- Time Selector appointment
- Enhanced Link
- Auto-Response
- Notification
- Payment
- Form
- Authentication
- Custom

The Question component is used to post a question with set choices to guide the customer's response. The Question with Options component can be created using a static or dynamic option. The static option provides a list of options that don't change, such as a list of store locations. The dynamic option connects to a Salesforce object for the purpose of showing customer-specific options. A list of recent orders is an example of a dynamic option for the Question with Options component.

The Time Selector component is used to convey available time slots for the customer to book an appointment. The Enhanced Link component is used to send a link that doesn't require a response. The Auto-Response component sends automated messages at certain times, such as a link at the end of a messaging session.

Notification components send an informational message. A delivery update is an example of a common notification component. Payment components can request and process payments. A Form component prompts customers to complete a series of fields. The Authentication component uses single sign-on to access data from other systems. The Custom component embeds an external app in messaging sessions.

The Actions component offers components that perform an action on your data, such as update a record or get data and store it in a variable. The Dialog Component Library for the Actions component includes the following options:

- Apex
- External Service
- Flow
- Goal
- Disambiguation Feedback
- Knowledge Feedback
- Object Search
- Send Email
- Standard

You're able to invoke Apex methods, integrate your chatbot with a registered external service, or call a flow using an action component in Bot Builder. Of course, you'll need to build the actions in advance by creating the Apex code, external service, or flow. Likewise, a goal, object, or email will need to be created before you can use the action component for these items.

The Rules component gives your chatbot the ability to perform specific actions like calling a dialog from within the current dialog, redirecting to a different dialog, clearing a variable value, or transferring the conversation to a human. Here are the options available from the Dialog Component Library for Rules:

- Call Dialog
- Clear Variable
- End Chat
- Redirect to Dialog
- Send a Message
- Set Language
- Set Routing Type
- Set Variable
- Transfer

You can add multiple rule actions in a component step by using the Add Rule Action in the Step Properties panel. In addition to using any of the Rules component options, you can create a condition sentence using a variable, an operator, and a value. In the Step Properties panel, click Add Condition, and then specify any required parameters. You'll need to add AND/OR functionality in the Condition Requirements field if you create multiple conditions.

Important considerations

As you're creating your new chatbot using component steps in each dialog, there are some important considerations to keep in mind. First, you should save often and make sure to save the work that is completed in one dialog before moving on to another dialog. You can always use the Revert button to return to a previous saved version if you add functionality that doesn't work as intended.

To the left of the Save button is a Preview button you can use to test your chatbot. The Text Preview option is available for both standard and enhanced chatbots. Only standard chatbots have the option for a Rich Content Preview.

Once you're done building your chatbot, you'll need to activate it. Before you can make any changes or additions to the chatbot, however, you'll need to deactivate it. Chat buttons on your sites connect to human representatives instead of the chatbot when you deactivate the chatbot. Those buttons are disabled, however, if there are no customer service representatives available.

You'll want to monitor standard reports about dialogs to help you better understand how customers are interacting with your chatbot's dialogs. Here are some standard reports about dialogs available in the Reports tab:

- Dialog entry points today and last 30 days
- Dialog frequency today and last 30 days
- Dialogs cancelled today and last 30 days
- Dialogs used per session last 7 days
- Transfer to bots by dialog today and last 30 days
- Sessions ended by dialog today and last 30 days

While these standard reports provide a lot of valuable information, there are chatbot goals you can establish and monitor that will better inform you about your chatbot's effectiveness. Goals can be established on the Goals page within Bot Builder.

Goals Page

After planning for and building a chatbot, you'll need a way to measure whether the chatbot is performing optimally. One way to optimize chatbot performance is to define specific objectives or outcomes you want the chatbot to achieve during user interactions. This is accomplished within the Goals section where you can define and track these objectives to measure the chatbot's effectiveness. Setting goals early allows you to define your chatbot conversations with that goal in mind and then fine-tune your conversation design based on goal performance. Clicking the New Goal button gives you the option to create a new goal (Figure 5-27).

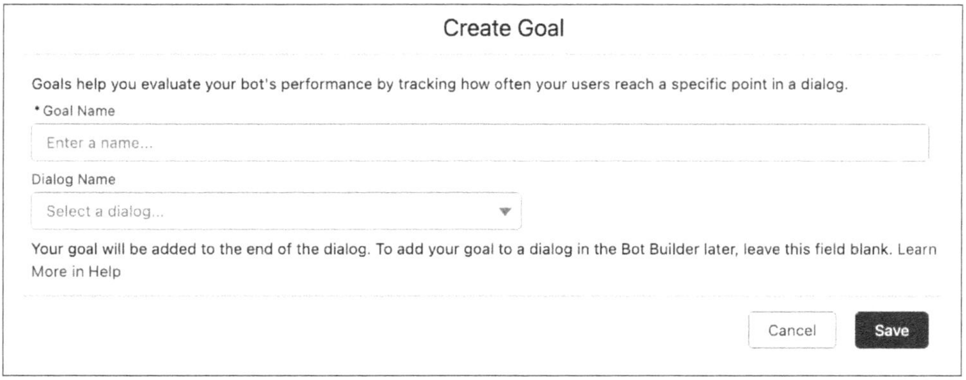

Figure 5-27. Page to create a new chatbot goal

In addition to providing a goal name, you'll want to select the dialog with which to associate the goal. A new goal can be created without specifying a particular dialog if you intend on adding the goal to a dialog in the Bot Builder later.

You can establish a goal based on how often users reach a specific point in a dialog. For example, goals could be established to track how often a chatbot returns a knowledge article, schedules an appointment, resolves a support issue, or generates an order number. High-performing chatbots reach these established goals more frequently. Thus, monitoring goal performance allows you to determine where the chatbot is successful and where improvements are needed.

> Support for special characters in goal display and API names was removed from Einstein Bots in spring '23. Chatbots that contain goals with special characters can't be saved or cloned. It's recommended you review any goals created before spring '23 and delete any affected goals. Re-create the goals with names that contain letters, numbers, and underscores only.

The Goals page shows a list of a chatbot's goals. The performance data showing completed goal counts for each goal is available for the last 180 days. Renaming a goal resets the completed goal count to zero for that goal. However, moving an existing goal to another dialog doesn't reset the count. Deactivating and then reactivating a chatbot doesn't reset the goal count. The count just resumes when the chatbot is reactivated.

The completed goal count is the only performance measure available on the Goals page. There are, however, myriad standard chatbot reports that can give you a broader view of chatbot performance. For example, there are reports for goals completed by dialog today and goals completed by dialog in the last 30 days. There are also reports for sessions with completed goals today and sessions with completed goals in the last 30 days. These standard reports are accessible in the Reports tab within Salesforce. In addition, the Performance page provides an option to view chatbot performance using CRM Analytics. Let's learn more about the Performance page now.

Performance Page

Monitoring and analyzing chatbot activity is a necessary precursor to refining chatbot activity. The Performance page offers two tabs that provide insights into your chatbot's activities:

- Dashboard
- Event Logs

The Dashboard section on the Performance page doesn't include any prebuilt dashboards (Figure 5-28). However, you can visit Salesforce AppExchange to install the latest Einstein Bots Value managed package, which includes a dashboard powered by Einstein CRM Analytics in Analytics Studio. The dashboard reveals important metrics such as the last hour's performance in terms of the total number of sessions, duration of sessions, the number of escalations, and more. In addition to using your existing chat data and chatbot performance metrics, the dashboard also includes cost information specific to your organization like cost per service rep per hour. The purpose of the Einstein Bots Value dashboard is to let your organization measure the chatbot's value against business objectives.

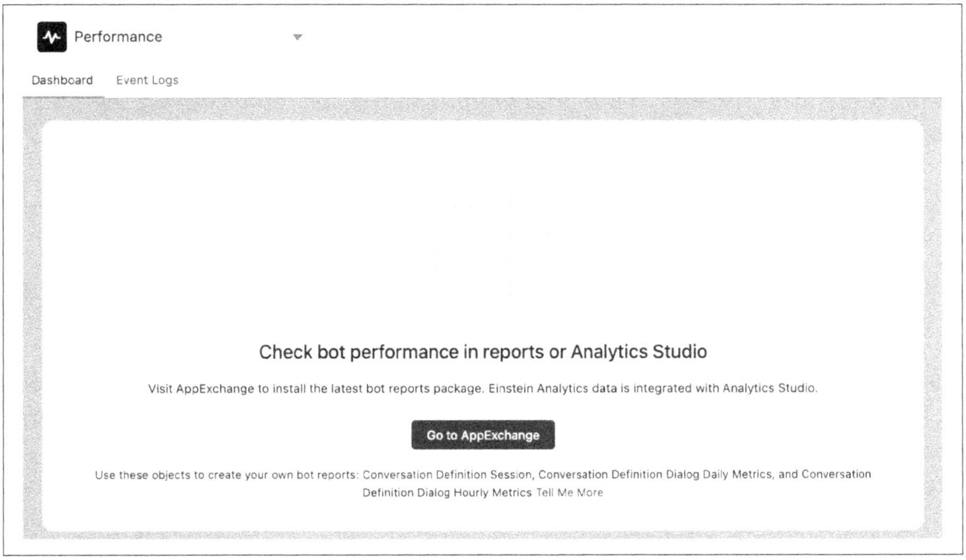

Figure 5-28. Performance page doesn't include any prebuilt dashboards

Alternatively, you can access native chatbot reports from the Reports tab in Salesforce core, or you can build your own chatbot performance reports and dashboards. Using standard reports, you can create reports on all chatbots or a specific chatbot across data ranges to identify your customers' most used dialogs and to identify areas for improvement.

When creating those standard reports, you'll have access to key metrics such as Conversation Definition Sessions, Conversation Definition Dialog Daily Metrics, and Conversation Definition Hourly Dialog Metrics objects. You also have access to some out-of-the-box digital engagement reports that provide chat and message usage reports, average messages per session per day, and average chat messages. Using reports and dashboards to provide feedback about a chatbot's activities is crucial to evaluating and improving the chatbot's performance.

In addition to creating reports and dashboards, it's recommended that you periodically review the chatbot's event logs from the Event Logs tab within the Performance page of the Bot Builder. Event logs are helpful to identify key trends and to discover possible new intent additions to the chatbot.

> Chat data and event logs are only available for the previous seven days. Thus, you'll need to download the data or migrate it to a separate Salesforce object if you want to extend monitoring capabilities longer than a weekly cadence.

The Event Logs session provides details about all the sessions for a particular chatbot. You can navigate to a particular session to debut that specific chatbot journey. It's important to know that chatbot activity is automatically logged without sensitive information. The Message, Input, and Output values are replaced with the phrase "Sensitive Data not available."

> You'll need to enable the Log Conversation checkbox in the Overview menu page within Bot Builder if you want to access the actual message, input, and output data within the event logs.

The Event Logs tab is a great place to troubleshoot your chatbot, especially for powerful and complex chatbots that accept input from multiple channels and utilize several Apex and Flow actions. Chatbot improvements can be as simple as adding new utterances or adding new balanced intents. You might also consider more bot training to improve your chatbot intent model performance. Bot Training is accessible as a tab within the Model Management page.

Model Management Page

Bot Training and Model are the two tabs available on the Model Management page. There's also a Model Sharing tab for organizations approved for this beta feature.

Chatbot training is crucial no matter the chatbot type. Rule-based chatbots need extensive planning to incorporate all the necessary menus along with utterances and intent mapping if text input is allowed. AI-powered chatbots need sufficient training data and require ongoing model refinement. It will likely take several months of training and optimization before a new chatbot accurately understands and responds to user inputs.

Chatbot training shows you the intent the chatbot identified from the utterance. You have the option to inform the chatbot of the correct intent if the chatbot chose wrong. These corrections help improve the chatbot's conversation quality because the chatbot is much more likely to make the right choice in the future.

> If it's the first time you're building an intent model for the chatbot, make sure you've turned on Einstein for at least two dialogs before clicking the Build Model button.

After building the intent model for the chatbot, you'll be shown a model summary that includes a model F1 score. The F1 score is a statistical measure ranging from zero to one, with one being the highest possible score. The closer your F1 score is to one, the more likely the chatbot correctly predicts the intent every time it has a conversation with the customer. When appropriate, recommendations are provided for each intent and these recommendations are viewable after clicking on the intent name. Be sure to click the Build Model button again to rebuild your model after making changes to intent or utterances based on the recommendations.

The Model Management page is also the location where you can share your intent model with other external Einstein.AI orgs, which allows you to use shared models to classify intent on other external datasets. This model sharing feature is currently in beta.

Einstein Chatbots and Agents

When appropriate, an Einstein enhanced chatbot can transfer conversations to an Agentforce Service agent (ASA) as well as to a human. If preferred, a chatbot can be used to create an agent instead. Let's look at both of these options.

Transfer Conversations from an Enhanced Chatbot to an Agentforce Service Agent

Omni-Channel flows are used to route customers to the point of contact that fits their use case best. Enhanced chatbots can work well as a starting point to greet customers, resolve common inquiries, verify customer information, and filter spam messages. When it's appropriate, transferring the conversation to an agent is as simple as transferring the conversation to a human agent.

Transferring conversations from an enhanced chatbot to an AI Service agent requires two steps. You'll first need to create an Omni-Channel flow that transfers a messaging session to an agent with the following steps:

1. Create an Omni-Channel flow from scratch.
2. Add a Route Work action immediately before the end of the flow.
3. Include the following required fields under Set Input Values:
   - Service Channel: New Resource
   - New variable with Text data type: RecordId
   - Service Channel: Messaging
   - Route To: Agentforce Service Agent and the agent's name
4. Save and activate the Flow so that the Route Work flow action appears in the Inbound Omni-Channel Flows section of the agent's details page.

Next, you'll need to create a new chatbot dialog that transfers the messaging session using the newly created Omni-Channel flow. Complete the following steps:

1. Open your chatbot in Bot Builder. Deactivate your chatbot if it's currently active.
2. Select the Dialog page from the menu if it's not the default page.
3. Add a dialog and provide a descriptive label such as "Transfer to agent."
4. From the Dialog Component Library, drag the Set Routing Type action onto the canvas. In the Step Properties panel, complete the required fields:
   - Route Type: Omni-Channel
   - Route Source: newly created Omni-Channel flow
   - Destination Variable: New ID Variable
   - Create new ID variable: "Agent" or similar descriptive name
5. Click Add Rule Action. For the Rule Action field, select Transfer. For the Destination Variable, select the newly created ID variable.
6. Save the dialog and activate your chatbot.

Transferring to an agent is often necessary when the conversation can't be resolved with a simple self-service chatbot. When conversations are more complex, sensitive, or require more personalization, the conversation might need to be transferred to an AI Service agent or to a human.

Create Agents from Einstein Bots (Beta)

Salesforce now provides a way to create a new agent from an enhanced chatbot using a new Salesforce tool. The Create Agent from Bot tool makes it easy to move the chatbot to Agentforce, and the chatbot stays active so that the transition can occur in the timeline you choose. The Create Agent from Bot tool creates a new agent from an enhanced chatbot in three steps:

1. The tool gathers details about your chatbot's elements, including dialogs, action steps, and intents.
2. The tool then generates subagents and actions based on the chatbot's details.
3. The tool then defines settings that determine how the agent behaves and presents itself in conversations.

Afterward, there's work to be done to finish creating the agent because not all chatbot elements are moved by the tool. You'll need to consider the following:

- The chatbot user isn't transferred, so you'll need to assign a user to the new agent from the agent details page.
- The chatbot's connected channels and Omni-Channel flows aren't moved.
- System dialogs, such as the Welcome dialog, aren't moved. If desired, you can add a static welcome and transfer message from the agent details page.
- Dialogs that use data from the knowledge base, including the Generative Knowledge Answers Gen AI functionality, aren't moved.
- Dialogs that transfer conversations aren't moved. You'll need to add the Escalation subagent to your agent to transfer conversations.
- Rich content and Messaging components aren't moved. Set up adaptive response formats for your agent to format agent responses based on Messaging components.
- Action steps using an Apex class or flow are moved, but other action steps, such as those that use object search, aren't moved. You can always add these custom actions after creating the agent.
- The chatbot's primary language is transferred to your agent, but additional languages aren't moved.

In addition, it's important to note that there are some enhanced chatbot elements that aren't moved and can't be re-created in Agentforce. Examples include Bot goals, Knowledge feedback, action steps that don't have an output, action steps that only help the chatbot navigate conversations, and action steps that create feedback logs.

Einstein Bots with Generative Knowledge Answers Versus Agentforce for Self-Service

Generative Knowledge Answers was added to Einstein Bots so that an Agentforce-based subagent could generate a relevant answer to the bot even when no designed dialog matches the intent. Using the information from Generative Knowledge Answers, the bot creates a conversational response that it then surfaces as its own message to the customer. Customers perceive the chatbot as intelligent because it can answer novel questions as long as the content exists in the Agentforce Data Library.

Using Einstein Bots with Generative Knowledge Answers is useful when the underlying information changes frequently because, otherwise, chatbot dialogs would need frequent reconfiguring to match the new information. Adding Generative Knowledge Answers to Einstein chatbots enables more self-service for long-tail queries while still allowing users to create dialog-design solutions for common use cases like password resets where most variants of the question are known and configurable and the underlying policy information rarely changes.

In contrast, Agentforce agents offer a more general-purpose, autonomous, or semi-autonomous execution layer where agents do more than just answer questions. As we'll see in Chapter 6, Agentforce agents reason across different contexts and take actions. The Answer Questions with Knowledge agent action is only one tool among many used by agents as they fulfill actions like updating records or calling external tools. Similar to chatbots, agents can engage in conversation with customers via chat channels. However, agents are also designed to take actions that resolve issues based on established policies and approvals. Let's summarize the self-service characteristics of both and highlight those scenarios where each solution is the best fit (Table 5-1).

Table 5-1. Comparison of self-service solutions

Characteristic	Einstein Bots with agent action	Agentforce agent
Focus	Conversational UI for knowledge-based responses	Embedded in workflows for reasoning and action
Data grounding	Mostly Lightning Knowledge articles plus indexed Agentforce Data Library content	Indexed Agentforce Data Library plus access to enterprise CRM and external data
Orchestration	Scripted dialog plus subagent when dialog doesn't match intent	Orchestrates its own tools for data retrieval, updates, workflows, and handoffs
External use cases	Shipping or return FAQs, product demos and explanations, assistance not requiring complex action	Service issues requiring complex order updates, troubleshooting, multistep case resolution flows
Internal use cases	HR or IT FAQs, policy questions	Internal automations requiring execution like IT provisioning or updating benefits

Einstein Bots with an agent action provided by Generative Knowledge Answers gives enterprises an orchestrated conversational AI within a tightly constrained knowledge-centric boundary. It's best for external and internal customer self-service use cases where the goal is accurate guidance grounded in curated content. Agentforce agents are given access to tools and use reasoning strategies to perform meaningful work on the customer's behalf. In Chapter 6, we'll explore in detail how Agentforce agents are built to reason and take action on behalf of humans.

Summary

In this chapter, we discussed the difference between four main categories of chatbots:

- Traditional chatbots
- Conversational AI chatbots
- GenAI integrated conversational chatbots
- GenAI chatbots

In addition, we learned that Salesforce offers two chatbot types: standard and enhanced. Enhanced chatbots make use of Omni-Channel routing and are the default chatbot type.

We also explored the anatomy of an Einstein conversational AI chatbot, which includes dialogs, steps, and components, with components including items like dialog intents, variables, entities, and goals. The importance of dialog intents and intent models was then reviewed.

Next, we learned how to create an Einstein chatbot from scratch, from a template, or by cloning an existing chatbot. We also learned how Einstein bot blocks can accelerate chatbot development. We were then ready to explore Bot Builders functionality available on each of the following pages:

- Overview
- Dialogs
- Entities
- Variables
- Goals
- Performance
- Model Management

We finished the chapter by exploring Einstein Bots and agents where we learned how to transfer conversations from an enhanced chatbot to an Agentforce Service agent. We then described how to create agents from Einstein Bots, which is currently a feature in beta.

We're now more informed about conversational AI chatbots and much more aware of the powerful capabilities of Bot Builder. But there's more that Salesforce offers users who want to build conversational AI solutions. In the next chapter, we'll explore Agentforce and Salesforce AI Builder tools.

CHAPTER 6

Building Standard Agents and Creating New Agents Using a No-Code Approach

AI agents (agents) differ from other AI tools in that agents can plan, reason, and act. As such, they are capable of simulating human-like work behavior. However, agents can only perform work effectively and efficiently if they're given access to LLMs and other tools as well as the most accurate, precise, and relevant input.

In Chapter 2, we discussed how a single agent can mimic human behavior when granted autonomous task execution capabilities, provided contextualized information, and given access to the right tools and functions. We included a list of some main elements needed for this to occur, and we previously covered in detail several of those elements. We also explored the concepts of context and dynamic grounding, agent accumulated context, and semantic models.

Here, we'll expand our knowledge of how agents execute tasks autonomously using agentic reasoning. We'll discover more about an LLM's role as the brain of a reasoning engine and discuss a reasoning engine's working memory. In addition, we'll explore new additional agent needs required to mimic human work behavior and that also allow us to oversee their work—an inference engine and agent observability. Our focus in this chapter is on those four agent elements that are italicized:

- *LLM guided by a structure* (the brain of the reasoning engine)
- *Inference engine* (the reasoning engine)
- *Memory system* (working memory in the reasoning engine)
- *Observability* (oversight)
- Agent accumulated context (intelligence)
- Knowledge base (knowing)

- Knowledge base context (understanding)
- Tools and functions (doing)
- Human-to-agent interfaces (communicating)

It's important that we learn about reasoning engines to better understand the Salesforce Atlas reasoning engine (Atlas) and what features we, as Salesforce builders, can access and use to create our own intelligent agentic enterprise. Our understanding will also help us make better choices among many alternative ways we can provide input to an agent powered by Atlas.

After exploring new concepts about reasoning engines, we'll turn our attention to understanding Atlas. Then, we'll discover Salesforce standard agents available out-of-the-box. Finally, we'll explore the building blocks needed to create our own individual Agentforce agents using the Agentforce Builder in Agentforce Studio.

As a reminder, we're focused in this chapter on individual Agentforce agents that come out-of-the-box or that we can build using a no-code approach. In Chapter 7, we'll explore pro-code developer tools. In Chapter 12, we'll focus on multi-agent orchestration and unified governance.

Getting Started

Let's discuss some background knowledge and some things you should know to help you get the most out of this chapter.

Background Knowledge

This chapter assumes you have a basic understanding of LLMs, and information about LLMs shared in previous chapters should be sufficient. However, if you're interested in learning more, *An Illustrated Guide to AI Agents* by Maarten Grootendorst and Jay Alammar (O'Reilly, 2026); *Hands-On Large Language Models* by Jay Alammar and Maarten Grootendorst (O'Reilly 2024); and *Prompt Engineering for LLMs* by John Berryman and Albert Ziegler (O'Reilly, 2024) are three excellent books.

This chapter provides descriptions and technical explanations needed to understand and use Agentforce. If you're interested in a behind-the-scenes story of how Salesforce built the Agentforce platform, I'd recommend Martin Kihn's *Agentforce* book, published by Wiley in June 2025.

What You Should Know

The new Agentforce Builder became generally available in February 2026 and offers advanced features like deterministic logic and natural language prompts. It replaced the legacy Agent Builder.

This chapter describes the underlying technology that powers Agentforce and explains the building blocks you'll need when creating new agents. The chapter doesn't discuss which specific Salesforce licenses or packages must be purchased or which permission sets are required. You'll want to discuss those topics with your Salesforce Account Executive (AE).

In addition, billing considerations for Agentforce are not discussed in this chapter. For one thing, Agentforce currently offers several different pricing models including a Flex Credits model where you pay for actions performed and a Conversation model where you pay a flat fee per conversation. One new Agentforce pricing model charges only when the agent resolves the issue. Your Salesforce AE or implementation partner can help you understand your billing options for agentic services.

Agentic Reasoning Engines

AI reasoning engines have been used for more than 50 years. Early reasoning engines modeled human expertise by creating expert systems with explicit rule-based logic. Expert systems produced deterministic, predictable, and explainable results, but these systems aren't equipped to handle interconnected facts and rules. Graph-based approaches like knowledge graphs were created to handle these complexities.

In the early 2000s, reasoning engines moved toward probabilistic strategies including machine learning and neural networks. Although capable of producing results to complex problems, these reasoning engines lacked the explainability of more deterministic approaches. LLMs are another probabilistic approach and they have incredible language abilities capable of producing seemingly intelligent responses and outputs. However, consistency and precision are often lacking.

These two types of reasoning, deterministic and probabilistic, differ in how they handle uncertainty and outcomes. Inputs and rules always determine predictable outputs with deterministic reasoning, which is why they're often used for systems where absolute precision is required. In contrast, probabilistic reasoning deals with likelihood and uncertainty, quantifying the chance of a different outcome rather than there existing one predictable outcome. Probabilistic reasoning is a good choice for use cases with incomplete data or inherent randomness. Modern agentic reasoning engines combine the power of probabilistic reasoning with the precision of deterministic reasoning.

While agentic reasoning engines differ in implementation, most have a standard architecture that includes an LLM guided by a structure, an inference engine, and working memory (Figure 6-1). The architecture supports accepting inputs from a user or system, usually in the form of a prompt. Integrations with tools and external systems are part of the general architecture of a reasoning agent like Atlas. Integrations often include access to a knowledge base and knowledge base context, as well as human interactions via conversational user interfaces. Reasoning engine outputs in the form of newly derived facts or assertions, explanations and recommendations, and plans can be re-input into the reasoning engine or given to the user or system as the final output. In modern architecture, reasoning engine outputs can be observed and explained.

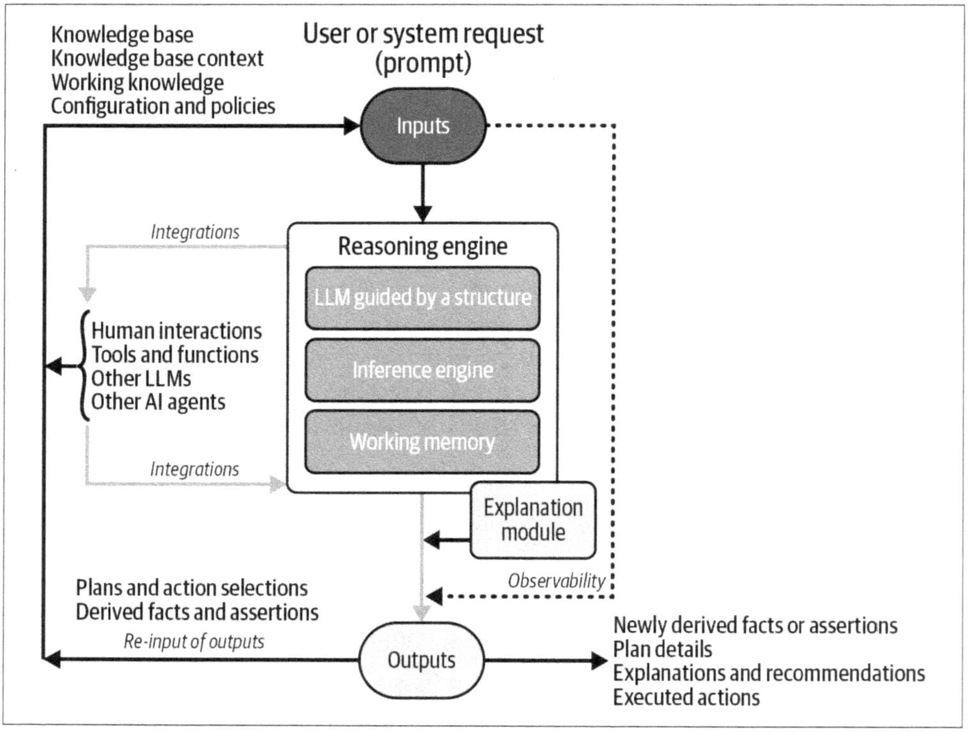

Figure 6-1. Agentic reasoning engine general structure

We'll first discuss inputs, outputs, and integrations to and from a reasoning engine before learning more about each of the three main components of a modern agentic reasoning engine: working memory, inference engine, and the LLM guided by a structure.

Inputs, Outputs, and Integrations

A reasoning engine receives a user or system request, also known as a prompt, along with other inputs that an individual agent or agent orchestrator needs to reason through the request and produce one or more outputs. There is plenty of other input the reasoning engine receives in addition to the original task request:

- Knowledge base
- Knowledge base context
- Working knowledge
- Configuration and policies
- Plans and action selections (from output)
- Newly derived facts and assertions (from output)

Knowledge base and knowledge base context include business information, content knowledge bases, semantic models, prediction outputs, and more items that are useful for dynamically grounding an LLM. Working knowledge is an input not to be confused with working memory, which is required by all knowledge information. Working knowledge informs the reasoning agent about which specific knowledge details are the most relevant, whereas working memory is part of the reasoning engine that includes session context and structured short-term memory variables used to provide persistent storage and enable more deterministic agent actions. For example, let's consider a CRM use case. A knowledge base might include the Account, Opportunity, and Case standard objects, whereas the working knowledge identifies which specific account, opportunity, or case record is the one of interest. If the reasoning engine needs additional information from a human, the human's response is added to the reasoning engine's working knowledge.

Configuration and policies are not part of the knowledge base. Rather, they are inputs that help shape how the reasoning engine plans and control which paths are followed. Included in configuration and policies are security and governance constraints for limiting what information or tools an agent can access and what actions they're allowed to take. For example, can the agent view only some database records or all records? Furthermore, is the agent authorized to make changes to the records? Also included in the configuration and policies are any cost or latency budgets and determinism adjustments.

Using inputs provided, a reasoning engine provides five main outputs. Of those, two are implicit action outputs and four are explicit action outputs:

- Plans and action selections that are re-input (implicit)
- Plan details describing which tools to call or actions to take (explicit)

- Executed actions (explicit)
- Explanations and recommendations (explicit)
- Newly derived facts and assertions (explicit) that are re-input (implicit)

For explicit outputs, the reasoning engine provides human-readable outputs in natural language formats for giving information about derived facts and assertions, plan details, or explanations and recommendations. Executed actions include updating records, sending emails, provisioning resources, creating analytics visualizations, handing off the task to a human, and many other types of actions. The configuration and policy inputs limit the possible action selections and, ultimately, executed actions taken.

In addition, the explanation module that produces the explanation outputs is part of a broader concept about agent observability. Agent observability focuses on the agent's behavior and internal logic. More specifically, observability is concerned with everything the agent thinks and does, including reasoning steps, tool calls, memory operations, and responses. The explanation module uses the agent observability information to formulate human-readable responses that explain what happened and why the agent took the action it did.

Generating outputs often requires access to other capabilities that extend the language generation capabilities of an LLM and that support the reasoning engine's reference engine:

- Human interactions
- Tools and functions
- Other LLMs
- Other agents

Most modern agentic reasoning engines integrate with tools and functions for tasks like searching files, querying and updating databases, and sending emails. These are often implemented as function calling or tool access by the LLM with a guided structure for generating outputs. Not all interactions are with system tools or system functions, however. The reasoning engine can interact with a human through an integration to receive more input. That input might be in the form of new or clarifying information, more instructions, or another request, which then becomes new input to the reasoning agent and is added to the reasoning engine's working knowledge. Alternatively, the AI can execute an action that routes an entire task to a human who then takes responsibility for completing the task. An example is when an agent escalates a service case to a human.

Reasoning engines frequently call multiple LLMs through integrations. Often there's a main reasoning LLM that accesses smaller or specialized models for various purposes like classification or embeddings. Sometimes, an LLM serves as an orchestrator that routes tasks between LLMs. More recently, some reasoning engine architectures treat entire agents as callable components. Each of these agents, when called, comes with their own tools and logic.

Integrations to and from reasoning agents take many forms, although direct integrations are the most common:

- Human-in-the-loop integrations
- Direct integrations using application programming interfaces (APIs), tool and function calls, and Model Context Protocol (MCP) standards
- Message-bus and event-driven integrations
- Shared data and storage interfaces
- Embedded, in-process integrations

Direct integrations are frequently used by the reasoning engine to produce a tool or function call or for using APIs to access external systems. In addition, direct integrations leverage MCP and other protocols that standardize how tools and contexts are exposed and invoked.

For more long-running workflows or multi-agent collaboration within the same platform where decoupling is important, the reasoning agent may need different integration approaches where the reasoning engine publishes the task or event and a downstream service or agent consumes them and responds asynchronously. When orchestrating between platforms, the state and coordination live outside the reasoning engine's LLM, so a workflow engine is needed to manage the interactions. The workflow engine may be triggered through events or APIs.

In the case of an out-of-bound integration, sometimes an explicit API or tool call is not needed because various systems or components share the same state. This way, they don't need to directly call each other. The state may be shared in a database, vector stores or knowledge graphs, and filesystems or object stores. For example, a reasoning engine could write intermediate results or plans into a database to which other systems or components are granted read access to use the information.

When the reasoning engine runs inside of a hosted process, the integration is simply the act of calling local libraries and hosted API or using native plug-in APIs and SDKs to interact with the host app. Integrations make it possible for the reasoning engine to accept inputs and to provide outputs.

We've explored what kind of inputs are accepted into the reasoning engine, what kinds of outputs are produced, and how the reasoning engine uses integrations for inputs and outputs. Let's turn our attention now to the reasoning engine's working memory, inference engine, and the LLM with a guided structure to support a reasoning strategy.

Working Memory, Inference Engine, and LLM

A standalone LLM is capable of interpreting natural language and generating human-readable responses and explanations. However, it isn't meant for complex tasks, especially those involving multiple steps where iterative planning is required and results need to be checked against constraints. An LLM serves as an important reasoning engine component that drafts and refines multistep plans when the LLM is supported with a guided structure and paired with an inference engine and provided with some working memory.

Working memory

A reasoning engine's working memory is a temporary, structured, centralized repository of active facts and intermediate conclusions. It's best described as a "scratch pad": a location used by the reasoning engine for the current task or problem. Working memory is not meant for storing long-term knowledge.

In modern reasoning system architecture, working memory is often implemented as in-memory key-value stores, in-process object graphs, or even temporary tables. If required, working memory can be implemented using an embedded database. Working memory is initialized when there is a task request made or a problem to be solved. The working memory details change as new inference rules are introduced, new outputs are re-input, or new inputs are received from integrations.

Inference engine

An inference engine applies logical rules to the knowledge base and its context to derive new facts or assertions. The inference engine does so by employing both data-driven and goal-driven reasoning paradigms known as forward chaining and backward chaining. A forward chaining approach begins with simple facts and then applies inference rules to extract more data until the stated goal is reached. Backward chaining starts with the end goal and works backward through inference rules to find facts that support the goal.

Reasoning paradigms like forward chaining or backward chaining determine how the inference engine applies the logical rules. The various reasoning paradigms are associated with one of three main inference engine types:

- Classic symbolic inference engine (deterministic)
- ML inference engine (probabilistic)
- LLM inference engine allowing for a hybrid approach

A classic symbolic inference engine is a deterministic one that doesn't use ML or LLMs but uses a forward chaining or backward chaining approach. Using the forward chaining reasoning paradigm, this inference engine starts with known facts and then finds all rules with conditions that match those facts, making sure to repeat the process until there are no more rules to apply or until the goal is reached. Forward chaining is a data-driven approach. In contrast, backward chaining is a goal-driven approach that begins with the end in mind. The goal is known in advance.

ML inference engines are probabilistic rather than deterministic, and it's common for a trained model to be executed at runtime. ML inference engines support goals such as identifying and preventing fraudulent transactions. LLM inference engines, another type of probabilistic inference engine, generate outputs based on patterns and correlations rather than causal understanding, which may sometimes lead to unpredictable outputs. However, LLM inference engines can be used for a hybrid approach that is not entirely probabilistic.

There are different ways to achieve a hybrid approach that leverages deterministic as well as probabilistic approaches when needed. Later in the chapter we'll see how Salesforce created a hybrid reasoning architecture. First, let's briefly review the different ways that guided structures can be used to support a reasoning strategy. This will help us better appreciate why Salesforce transitioned Atlas to reasoning and acting (ReAct) from a chain of thought (CoT) reasoning engine as part of their goal of achieving a hybrid reasoning engine.

LLM with a guided structure to support a reasoning strategy

LLMs originated from simple natural language processing (NLP) tasks. In modern reasoning engine architectures, LLMs can be guided by a structure such as a chain, tree, or graph. This guidance is often necessary to solve complex tasks needing to be split into several intermediate steps before reaching the final solution. Whether a reasoning strategy requires tools or not is another way to differentiate reasoning strategies. Let's consider six different reasoning engine strategies (Table 6-1), how they differ in their characteristics and search style, whether they use tools, and the difference in their topology.

Table 6-1. Reasoning engine strategies

Strategy	Topology	Characteristics	Search style (path)	Tools
Chain of thought (CoT)	Single chain	Linear	Single trajectory	No
Chain of thought self-consistency (CoT-SC)	Multiple independent chains	Self-consistency	Parallel search	Optional
Tree of thoughts (ToT)	Tree	Parent/child relationships	Multipath pruned search	Optional
Graph of thoughts (GoT)	Graph	Nodes are thoughts and edges are dependencies	Graph search	Optional
Reasoning and acting (ReAct)	Single chain	Loop for refinement	Single interaction loop search	Yes
Reasoning and planning (RAP)	Tree or graph for global plan	Planning is explicit and separate from execution	Depends on the execution reasoning engine strategy	Yes

We'll briefly explore each of the multiple reasoning engine strategies, but only two strategies have been used in Atlas. Initially, Salesforce made use of the CoT reasoning strategy. More recently, the reasoning engine strategy was changed to the reasoning and acting (ReAct) strategy in Atlas. This change makes it possible for users to create an Agentforce Orchestrator agent for managing multiple Agentforce agents. We'll discuss the Agentforce Orchestrator agents in Chapter 12 when we explore multi-agent management and orchestration.

A CoT reasoning engine strategy was the one initially chosen by Salesforce for Atlas. A CoT approach involves a single chain structure (Figure 6-2), which works with almost any LLM. This reasoning strategy is used to create a single series of thoughts with each one relying on the previous thought. The CoT reasoning engine strategy is excellent for structured, deterministic problems and is often used for small planning problems, logic puzzles, or math and coding problems. Although CoT can't use tools within a reasoning engine that employs a CoT strategy, it is often a strategy used with an LLM that is called by a reasoning agent employing a more complex reasoning strategy.

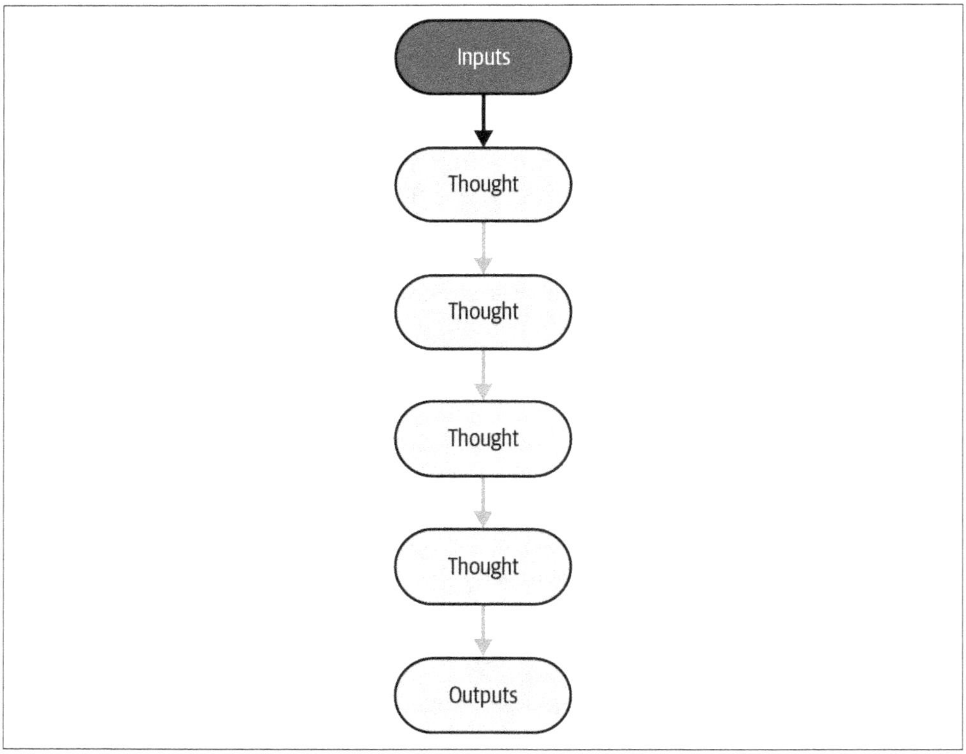

Figure 6-2. Chain of thought (CoT) reasoning strategy

The CoT reasoning strategy is often combined with self-consistency (CoT-SC), which produces multiple independent CoT results in parallel (Figure 6-3). Using this approach, the same question is asked multiple times and, thus, the same answers likely appear multiple times. If there is more than one answer returned, which almost always happens, then the answer that occurs most frequently is chosen as the "correct" one and the others are discarded. It's more expensive to use a CoT-SC approach because of the number of times the same question is asked. This reasoning engine strategy is chosen when the reliability of the answer matters more than cost.

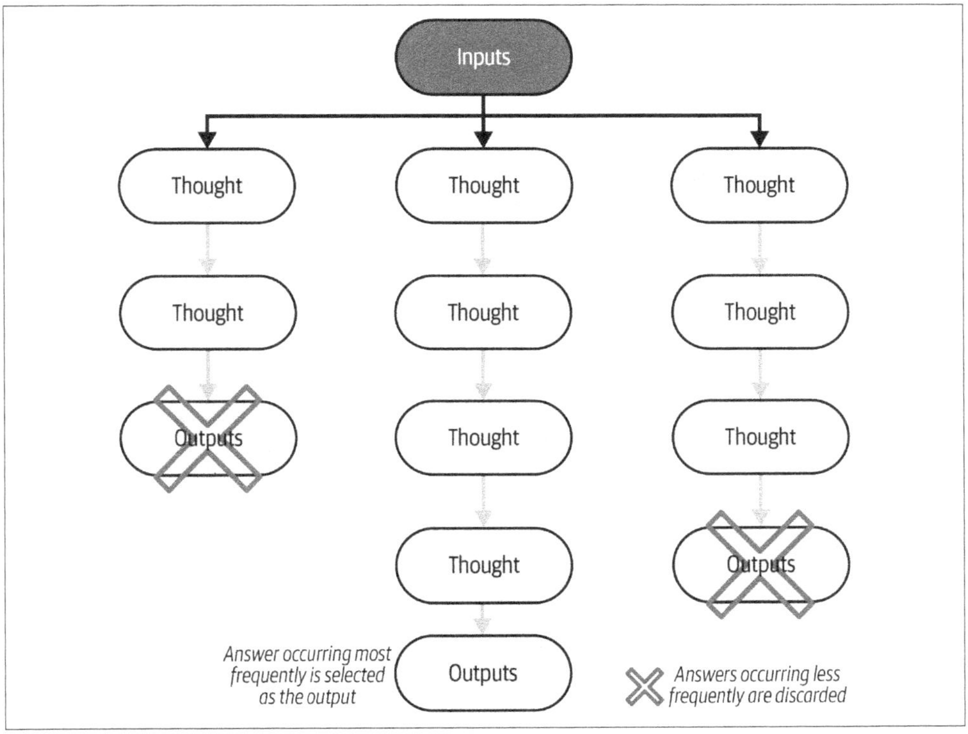

Figure 6-3. CoT-SC reasoning strategy produces multiple CoT results in parallel

The tree of thoughts (ToT) reasoning strategy uses a tree topology to branch out from a chain in a parent/child hierarchical relationship (Figure 6-4). ToT reasoning strategy uses a multipath pruned approach using search algorithms such as breadth-first search (BFS) and depth-first search (DFS). The BFS algorithm explores all branches at each level before proceeding to deeper tree levels, which makes it a good choice for problems where the shortest path or shallowest solution is ideal. The DFS algorithm explores one branch deeply at a time before exploring other branches, which makes it a good choice for problems requiring detailed exploration.

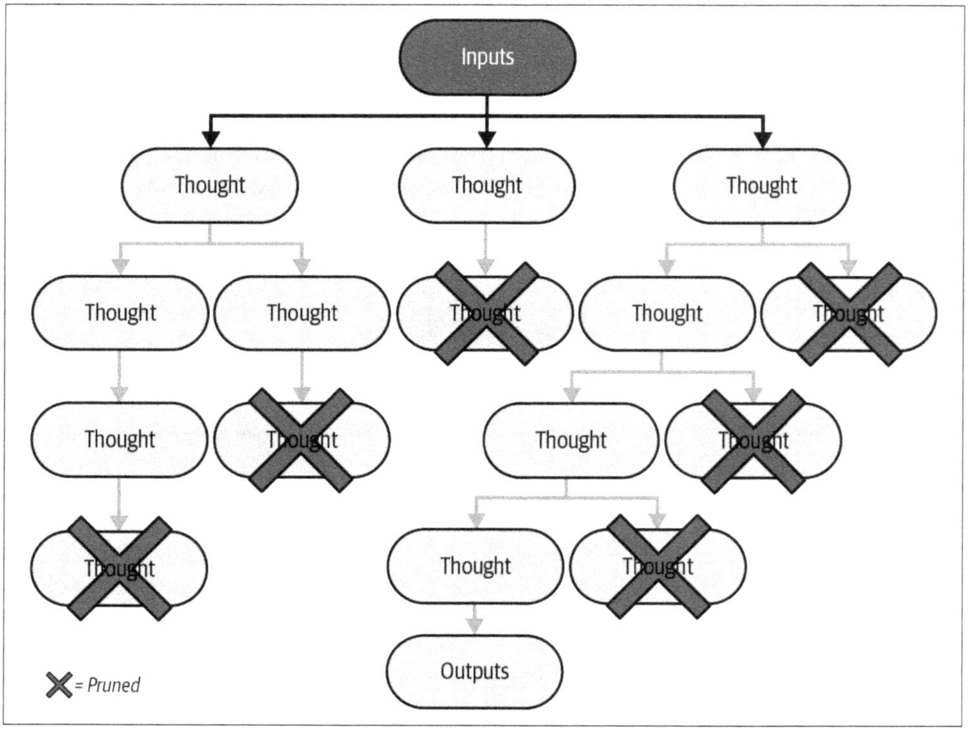

Figure 6-4. Tree of thoughts (ToT) reasoning strategy

The graph of thoughts (GoT) reasoning strategy leverages a graph topology (Figure 6-5) where nodes represent thoughts and edges represent dependencies. Thought refinements are made through looping, and pruning is also undertaken during the reasoning process. The GoT graph topology often uses search algorithms and heuristic solvers. It is best for tasks that include complex constraints and dependencies like scheduling and multidocument reasoning.

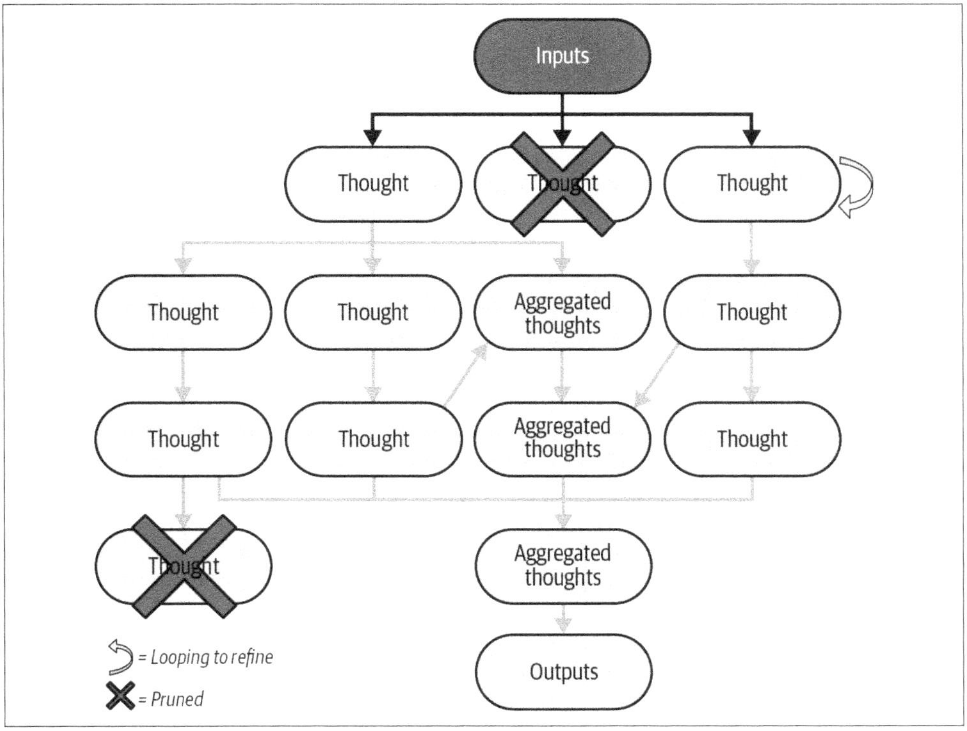

Figure 6-5. Graph of thoughts (GoT) reasoning strategy

The reasoning and acting (ReAct) loop reasoning strategy combines the step-by-step approach found in CoT with tool calls, referred to as actions. The loop is explicit, which gives the LLM some control over the reasoning strategy. The loop starts with the thought, proceeds to an action, followed by an observation (Figure 6-6). The reasoning process loops back to the thought if more information is needed or, when the looping is complete, the reasoning engine produces one or more outputs. The ReAct reasoning strategy integrates with retrieval augmented generation (RAG) and is the current strategy used by Salesforce in Atlas. We'll explore ReAct and RAG further on.

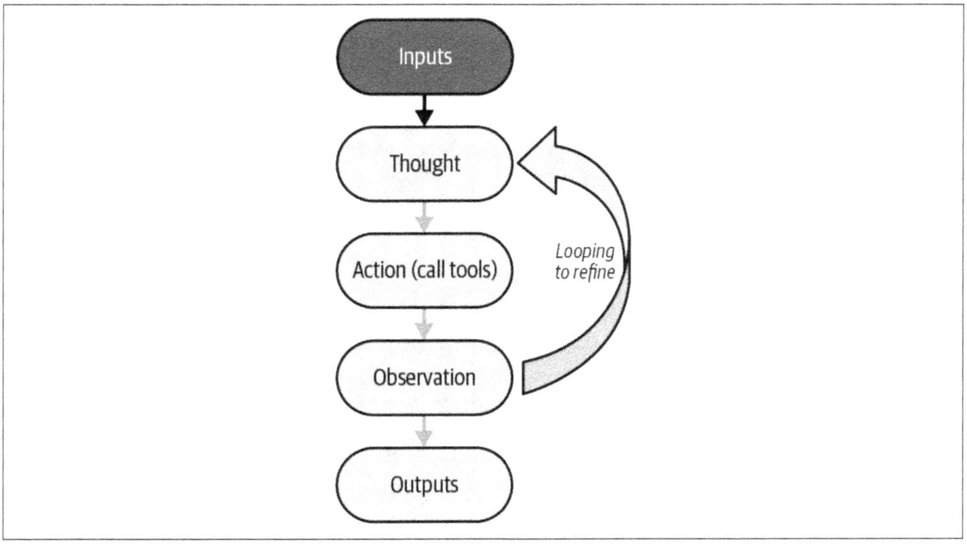

Figure 6-6. ReAct reasoning strategy

The reasoning and planning (RAP) strategy separates planning from execution. RAP global planning uses a tree or graph topology to control a separate execution layer (Figure 6-7) that often uses CoT, ToT, or ReAct reasoning strategies.

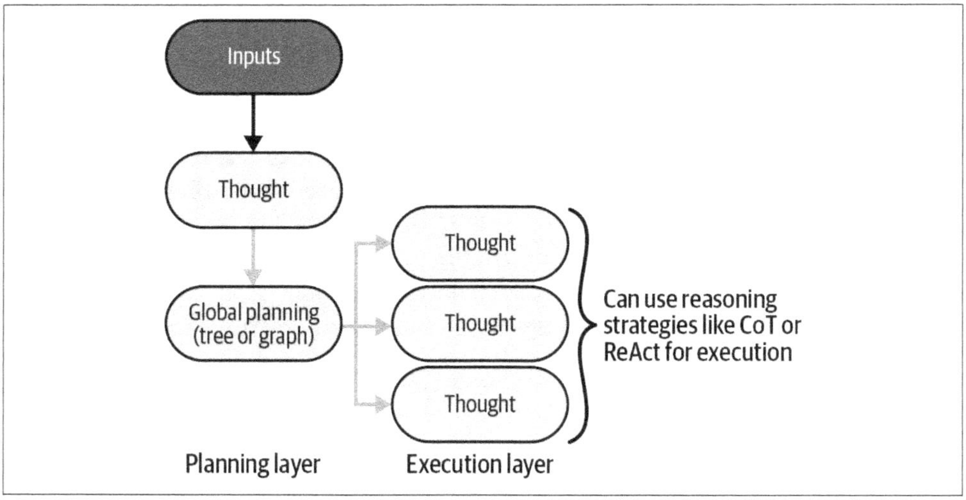

Figure 6-7. Reasoning and planning (RAP) reasoning strategy

In summary, a reasoning engine is the system responsible for an agent's planning and control activities, which includes interpreting the input, deciding which inference to run and in what order, orchestrating tools and knowledge retrieval, and applying configurations and policies. An inference engine is a system component that solves for a single step.

How Salesforce Agents Work

Previously, we learned about reasoning agents and the strategies employed to simulate human behavior in a work environment using thoughts and actions. We'll now apply that foundational knowledge to help us understand Agentforce and how Salesforce-created agents work.

Salesforce first employed a CoT reasoning strategy. Then it switched to a ReAct reasoning strategy around December 2025. In addition to making upgrades to Atlas, Salesforce created a new declarative domain-specific language (DSL) that combines natural language instructions with programmatic expressions, creating more deterministic, context-aware agent workflows. This new declarative DSL language is known as Agent Script.

We'll save the deeper dive into Agent Script syntax for Chapter 7. In this section, we'll focus on understanding Agent Script conceptually and why it's necessary to support guided determinism needed for hybrid reasoning. Later, we'll also explore how the no-code Agentforce Builder Canvas view visualizes and generates the script via natural language.

An Agent Graph exists between the human-readable Agent Script language and Atlas (Figure 6-8) to help unify LLM-based reasoning with structured business logic, effectively resulting in hybrid reasoning. Deterministic execution is separated from probabilistic LLM reasoning based on the details provided in the Agent Script code. Thus, not every thought or action must be routed through the reasoning engine. This solution gives users more fine-grained control and enables more deterministic agentic behaviors, such as task delegation and controlled handoffs, while maintaining governance through native integrations with Data 360 (D360), Salesforce Flows, and the Einstein Trust Layer.

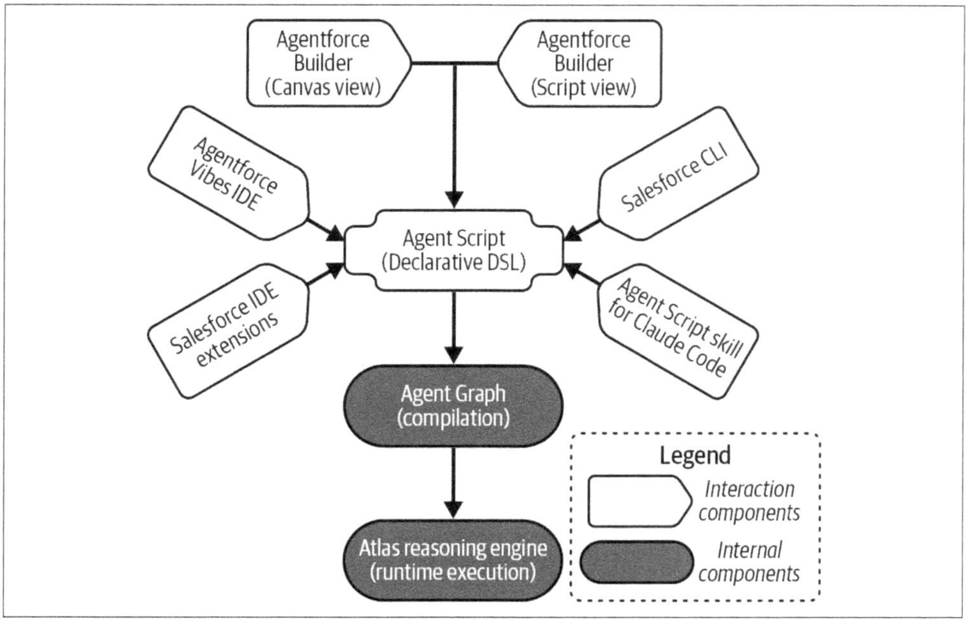

Figure 6-8. Agent Script, Agent Graph, and the Atlas reasoning engine

Salesforce users leverage various interaction components, many of which are programmatic in nature, to create or modify Agent Script. However, Agentforce Builder offers nondevelopers the ability to work with Agent Script using authoring tools within a Canvas view or a Script view. We'll explore Agentforce Builder a little later in this chapter and we'll learn about pro-code solutions for developers in Chapter 7.

Agent Script code is compiled and executed by Salesforce internal components that enforce deterministic behavior. The two Agentforce internal components, Agent Graph and Atlas, are not directly accessible to Salesforce users. Atlas reads the compiled code and traverses the Agent Graph based on the current session state. At each node of the Agent Graph, Atlas decides whether to execute deterministically or to invoke the LLM. Let's further explore Agent Script, Agent Graph, and Atlas.

Agent Script

Agent Script is Salesforce's newest programming language. It is used to define an agent's behavior as well as to provide the agent with necessary business logic. Agent Script, structured as key-value pairs, can include nested subproperties and is used to express both deterministic logic instructions and prompt instructions in the same agent.

Deterministic logic instructions sufficiently define conditions and action sequences that don't require LLM involvement to execute the code. The agent simply follows a predefined execution path no matter how the input is phrased by the user or the system. On the other hand, prompt instructions are intended for anything needing judgment or interpretation as well as for tasks where natural language generation is required. Prompt instructions aren't prescriptive, but rather provide guidance interpreted by the LLM at runtime.

Agent Script was designed to be used by Salesforce admins and others who aren't necessarily experts in graph architecture or graph languages but who need to create deterministic agentic workflows. Agentforce Builder, available within Agentforce Studio, is the recommended environment for developing most new agents and is especially useful for rapid prototyping and simple use cases. Agentforce Builder offers a Canvas view and a Script view for users to build subagents and create agent instructions and executable logic.

Agentforce Builder's Canvas view provides a block-based interface where users build with Agent Script by using natural language with AI assistance. Blocks are expanded for viewing the underlying script. The Script view is a more advanced option allowing users to write and edit scripts directly with features like syntax highlight, autocompletion, and validation. Salesforce users can elect to update Agent Script code in the Canvas view and then easily switch to the Script view and vice versa.

Programmatic options for creating and maintaining Agent Script code include the Agentforce Vibes IDE and Salesforce IDE extensions for integrated development environments (IDEs) like Visual Studio. Salesforce builders can also use the Salesforce command-line interface (CLI) or an Agent Script skill for Claude Code. Agent Script provides agents with the necessary information to prevent confusion or misinterpretation. That allows the agent to traverse the Agent Graph throughout the session based on the context and user intent.

Agent Graph

The Agent Graph is intended for use by the agent's reasoning engine, not the Salesforce user who authored the Agent Script code. Thus, users don't have direct access to the Agent Graph, although an agent's Agent Graph is indirectly controlled through the use of Agent Script code. It's helpful to understand the purpose of the Agent Graph and its importance in creating a hybrid reasoning engine rather than having a purely deterministic or probabilistic reasoning engine for an agent.

The Agent Graph is created when the Agent Script code is compiled. Traversal of the Agent Graph by the agent is not strictly linear or tree-based. As such, it does not follow a rigid, predetermined sequence. Instead, the Agent Graph is a directed graph topology with supporting loops, branching, and conditional logic, which allows for the dynamic traversal of nodes. The way Atlas navigates an Agent Graph closely simulates complex, multistep workflows that represent real-world business processes. The Agent Graph topology includes three important components:

- Nodes
- Edges
- State

The directed graph's nodes represent actions, or reasoning blocks, within an agent's logic. Each node defines either a specific step or process the agent can perform or a possible decision the agent can make. An edge defines the logical flow and relationship between steps, processes, or decisions and determines where agentic control moves next. As the agent progresses toward the goal, the directed graph maintains awareness of its state while also maintaining current information about variables. The Agent Graph runtime explicitly manages persistent states rather than relying only on an agent's conversational memory. That persistent state is passed between nodes enabling purposeful tracking of the primary goal as well as conversation history.

Governance is enforced in both the Agent Graph and Atlas. The Agent Graph encodes business policies, compliance rules, and step-by-step controls within its structure based on the information supplied in the Agent Script code. Thus, the Agent Graph defines the agent's boundaries. Atlas is responsible for ensuring the rules are followed during execution. Of course, all agents are governed by the Einstein Trust Layer, which provides safeguards for data handling, prompt injection defense, and critical actions.

The Agent Graph models the path for a single agent, although communication between agents or external systems can be managed as part of an agent's actions within the reasoning engine. Let's explore how Atlas uses the Agent Graph to implement agentic reasoning.

Atlas Reasoning Engine

Atlas powers Agentforce agents by using advanced reasoning methods with agentic loops. More specifically, Atlas uses a ReAct reasoning strategy (Figure 6-9) to plan actions, evaluate outcomes, and then adapt based on new information. Atlas also supports retrieval augmented generation (RAG) techniques, including semantic search across structured and unstructured data, so that the reasoning engine can locate the most relevant information for the agent.

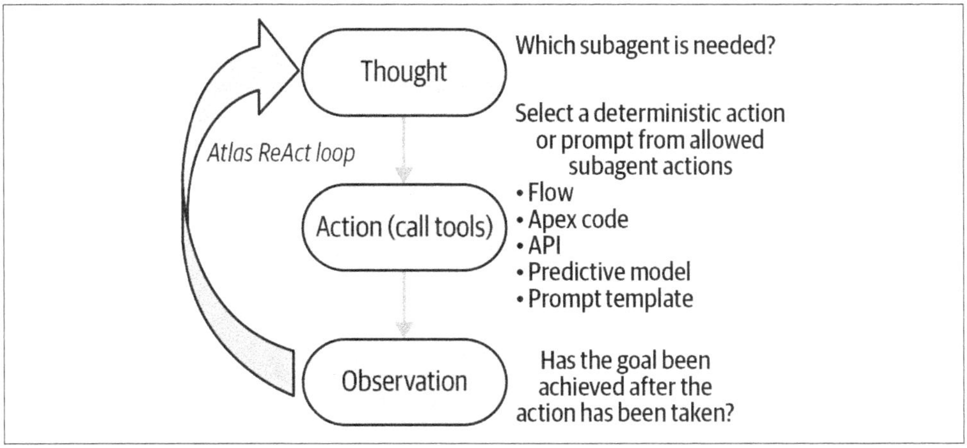

Figure 6-9. Atlas uses a ReAct reasoning strategy

An Agentforce subagent can take action by leveraging standard actions, prompt templates, Flows, Apex code, and REST APIs for which it's been granted permission to use. For example, a subagent action might be used to draft or revise a sales email, query records, or connect to third-party tools, MCP servers, or other agents. Interestingly, a Salesforce agent can function as an orchestrator agent of Agentforce agents where the relevant subagent is called as an invocable action, which has its own ReAct loop (Figure 6-10).

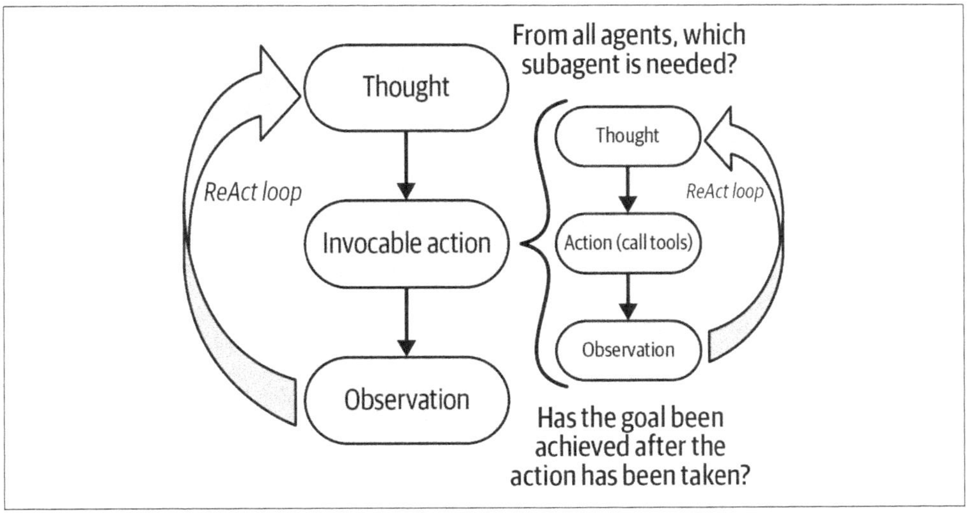

Figure 6-10. Agentforce is able to call another Agentforce agent as an invocable action

Slackbot can be used as an orchestrator agent for Agentforce agents. We'll explore Slackbot in Chapter 12. For a multi-agent architecture that involves agents other than Agentforce agents, you'll need to use MuleSoft Agent Fabric. In Chapter 12, we'll explore MuleSoft Agent Fabric, which can be used for multi-agent orchestration and enterprise governance for multi-agents. For now, we're focused on individual Agentforce agents.

Earlier, we mentioned governance is enforced in both the Agent Graph and Atlas, with Atlas ensuring rules are followed during execution. Previously, we also learned reasoning engines often include modules (Figure 6-11) that explain how conclusions or other outputs were reached. Modern reasoning engines such as Atlas also perform deliberate, system 2 reasoning, which means they observe and review whether the current plan or answer satisfied the goal before iterating.

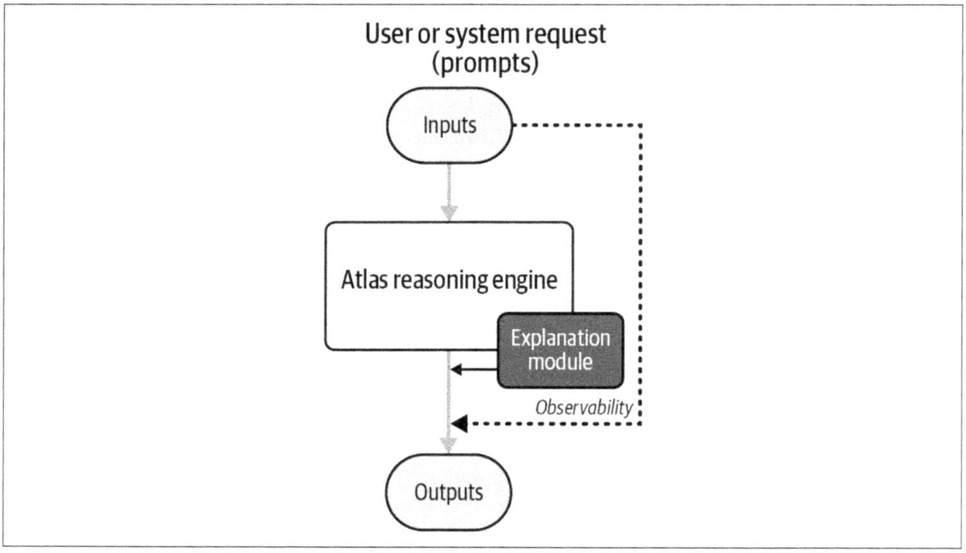

Figure 6-11. Atlas reasoning engine's observability includes explanation module

Atlas explanations for Agentforce agents are accessible to users in one of three scenarios:

- Prompt given to an agent includes instructions to provide explanations to the user
- User requests explanation after response is provided by an agent
- Admins can review users' feedback about explanations within Agentforce Observability

A Salesforce admin can configure the Agentforce agent to share its reasoning or steps for a given action, or a user can request explanations from the agent after it gives a response. In addition, a Salesforce admin can view users' session-level feedback about the agent's explanations within Agentforce Observability. Salesforce admins have a centralized dashboard in Agentforce Observability for monitoring, analyzing, and optimizing Agentforce agent performance in near real time. Features include deep observability, live health monitoring, adoption analytics, and detailed logs to identify and resolve issues. Robust features allow admins to explore individual conversations, inspect agent configurations, and set up real-time alerts on key metrics for optimal agent health and performance.

Configuring the Agentforce agent to provide explanations as output and letting users provide feedback of thumbs-up or thumbs-down provides visibility into the agent's behavior, which ultimately prevents hallucinations. When enabled, session-level tracing allows admins to analyze every user interaction with an Agentforce agent. Each step and action can be reviewed in detail to pinpoint when any issues occur or identify where improvements are needed.

Conversation clustering by intent groups is a feature where similar user goals are grouped together. This makes it easier to identify patterns and optimize Agentforce logic for specific intents. Further, quality scores for each user interaction measure how relevant the agent's responses are. This helps highlight misinterpretations or inefficient flows where agent performance can be improved.

The session-level tracing, conversation clustering by intent, and quality scores for each interaction provided within Agentforce Observability support transparency and trust. They also give users and admins the opportunity to better understand and refine an Agentforce agent's decision making.

We've explored in detail how Agentforce agents work, but how does our newfound knowledge of Agent Script, Agent Graph, and Atlas help us? Let's consider some practical guidelines based on our understanding of how Agentforce agents work.

Agentforce Agents Perform Better with Less Cost and Reduced Risk

Although we haven't yet explored how to build an Agentforce agent, we do now understand how Agentforce agents work. We know Agent Script gives us the power to inject determinism into our Agentforce agents and that we have access to Salesforce observation and monitoring tools to better understand an Agentforce agent's reasoning process. We also know that information can be given to an agent via an input prompt or the agent can use an action to retrieve the information when it's needed. Thus, we can improve an Agentforce agent's performance. We can also build and maintain agents so that they undertake actions with less cost and reduced risk. Let's consider how this can be achieved with a few recommended best practices.

We've identified three specific best practices for making agent design choices as they pertain to agent reasoning:

- Minimize unnecessary LLM calls and inefficient data handling by creating fewer, better aligned subagent actions.
- Supply deterministic business logic in Agent Script and structure workflows to ensure required steps are always followed, thus ensuring predictability and only using Atlas when needed.
- Provide knowledge as an input, when appropriate, rather than have an agent initiate an action to retrieve the information on demand.

In Figure 6-10 describing the reasoning strategy, we see that Atlas first determines which subagent is needed, and an appropriate action is then selected by Atlas from among the options aligned to the subagent. The action, which could involve calling a tool, is initiated and then Atlas determines whether the action achieved the goal.

As you would imagine, Atlas could have difficulty selecting the best action if there is an overabundance of actions associated with a subagent or if there are only a few actions and none of them align well to the subagent's description. In those situations, the Agentforce agent's performance is degraded and the costs are high because of excessive LLM calls undertaken to ultimately achieve the goal.

In addition to creating fewer, better aligned subagent actions, it's recommended that you use Agent Script to supply deterministic business logic when other deterministic methods such as Flows can't handle the complexity needed to achieve a goal. We'll explore Agent Script in detail in Chapter 8. For now, it's enough to know that using Agent Script guided determinism results in agents that are flexible yet more predictable and less costly.

The dollar value cost for an Agentforce agent to complete a deterministic task is generally less costly than when Atlas uses an LLM to complete a probabilistic task. Deterministic tasks often involve rule-based logic, which requires less compute costs. In contrast, probabilistic tasks rely on LLM reasoning, context retrieval, and decision making, which incur higher costs due to increased LLM usage.

There are other design choices that affect overall cost paid for an Agentforce agent's work. One consideration is if the knowledge should be supplied as a prompt input or, alternatively, have Atlas initiate an action to retrieve the information on demand. Let's consider an example that we know well. In Chapter 3, we discovered that there are numerous ways prediction results can be consumed from an activated model created from scratch using AI Model Builder (Figure 6-12).

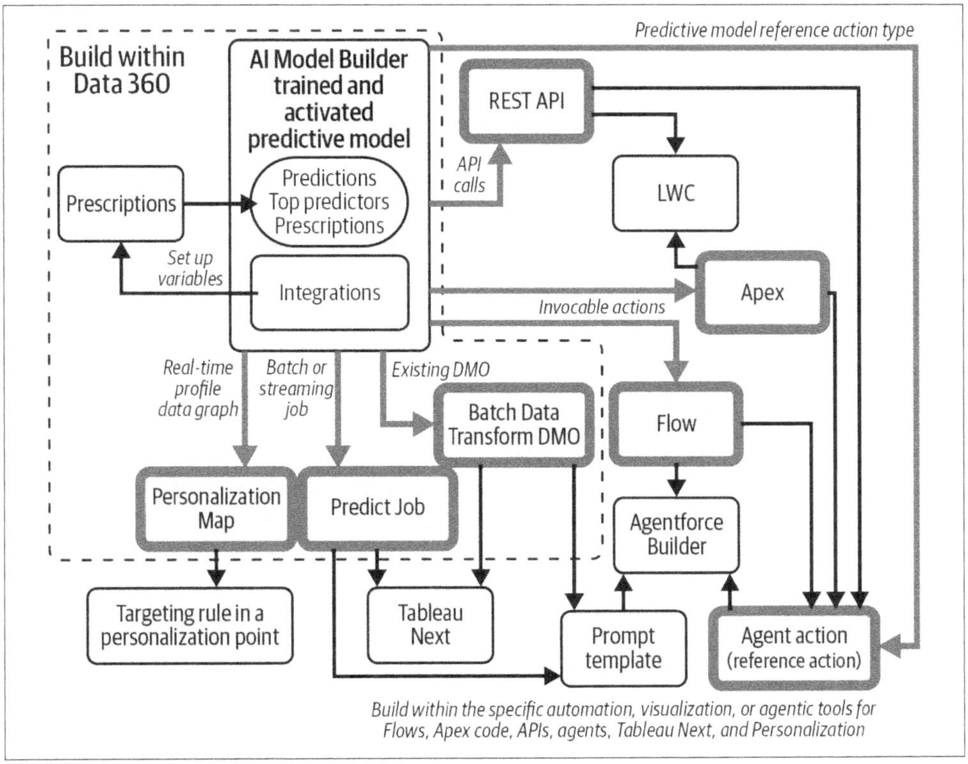

Figure 6-12. Agentforce Builder is a consumer of prediction results from an activated model

Of those, only the prompt template can take advantage of batch processing from a DMO batch transformation or batch Predict Job to pass along the prediction results as a knowledge input. Four other action types provide prediction results on demand (Table 6-2).

Table 6-2. Consumption patterns for primary consumers of predictive model results

Primary consumer	Consumption pattern
Personalization Map	Real-time
Agent reference action (Predictive Model type)	On-demand
Flow	On-demand
Apex code	On-demand
REST API	On-demand
Batch Data Transform	Batch
Predict Job (batch)	Batch
Predict Job (streaming)	Streaming

This is important to know because a batch consumption pattern is generally less expensive than on-demand. Using an agent reference action, Flow, Apex code, or REST API to call the AI Model Builder to produce predictions on demand is typically more expensive than using precomputed prediction values generated via batch and stored in a DMO. On-demand prediction incurs compute costs every time Atlas calls the model, whereas batch predictions leverage preprocessed results, which results in lower runtime expenses. Of course, the exact cost depends on the number of predictions, model complexity, and frequency of calls, but on-demand inference generally costs more.

Understanding how Agentforce agents work empowers you to make more informed decisions about Agentforce agent architecture that ultimately result in more trustworthy, more effective, and less costly Agentforce agents.

Agentforce Agents

Let's now explore what steps occur after the Agentforce agent is invoked (Figure 6-13), and let's see how Atlas orchestrates workflows using the Agent Graph guided determinism. As we review the steps, we'll pay attention to the various building blocks used so we can explore each separately.

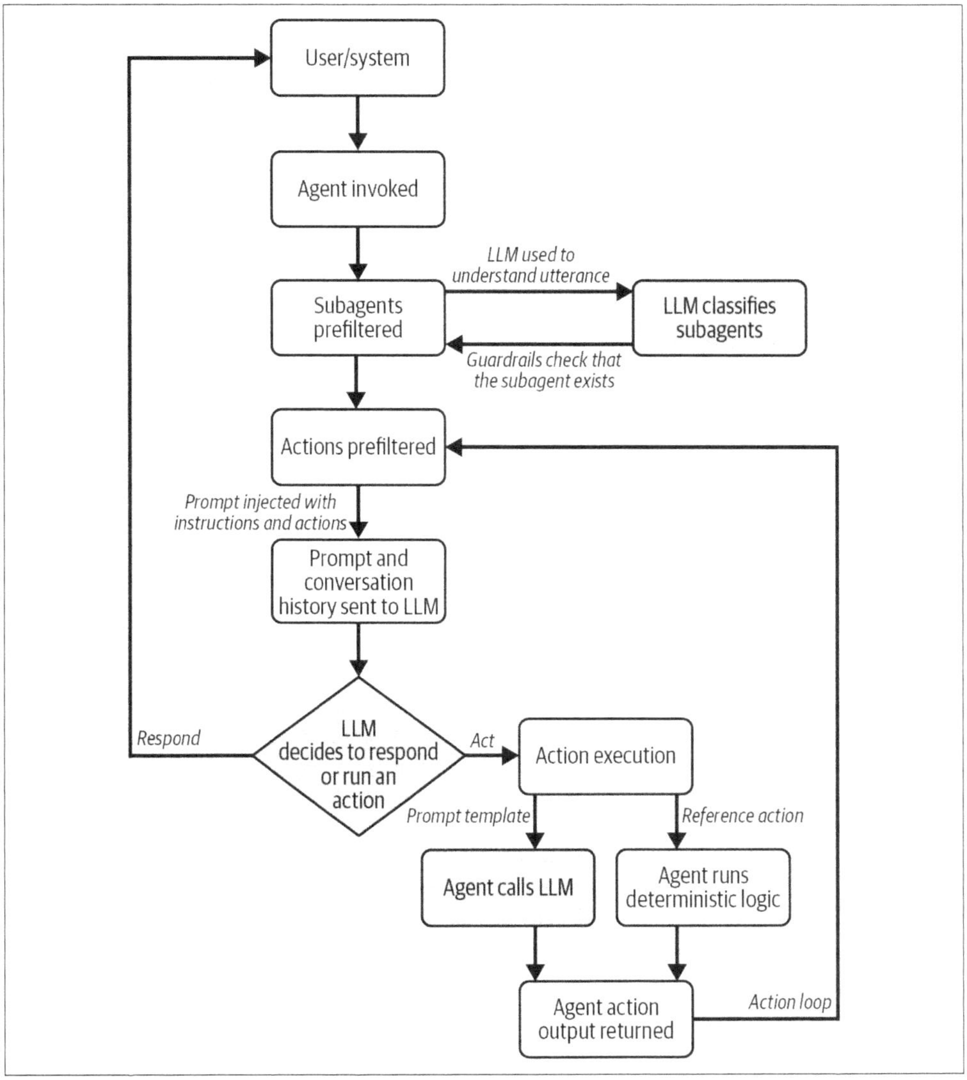

Figure 6-13. Agentforce agent steps after agent is invoked

A user or system provides input by asking a question or giving the Agentforce agent a goal. As we learned earlier, that Agentforce agent can be a single agent with a specific set of subagents or it could be an orchestrator agent, like Slack. In the case of an orchestrator agent, the invoked agent can utilize subagents from all the various Agentforce agents it's orchestrating. However, agent variables created in Agent Script can be used to filter the available list of subagents before it's sent to the LLM. The LLM then selects the subagent most closely matched to the user's intent from the question or desired goal supplied. This now becomes the focus subagent, which guides the rest of the conversation or process.

A subagent includes detailed actions that can be taken and, similar to the previous step, agent variables can be used to filter the available list of actions. The list of available agent actions, along with a set of agent instructions, is sent to the LLM along with any conversation history. The LLM then decides whether to respond or execute an action.

Agentforce actions can be executed using deterministic logic whenever Apex code, a Salesforce Flow, or an Agent Script reference action is executed. Deterministic logic is best used for enforcing critical business logic, authentication, and transaction steps. It's also a good choice when a long list of IDs needs constructing or sensitive sequence-dependent processes should be undertaken.

If the action needed isn't a deterministic one, the Agentforce agent calls an LLM using the information provided in the prompt template. LLMs are excellent for use cases where judgment, natural language understanding, or contextual interpretation is needed. It's possible for actions to combine both deterministic and prompt-based approaches.

Whenever an Agentforce agent action is executed, the agent action output is integrated into the conversation history and the LLM again evaluates whether to respond or take an action. Every action taken results in additional information the LLM needs to move closer toward completing the goal.

In our explanation of the steps taken by an Agentforce agent, we've mentioned four important building block terms to explore further: subagents, actions, instructions, and prompt templates (Figure 6-14). Let's consider them in detail now.

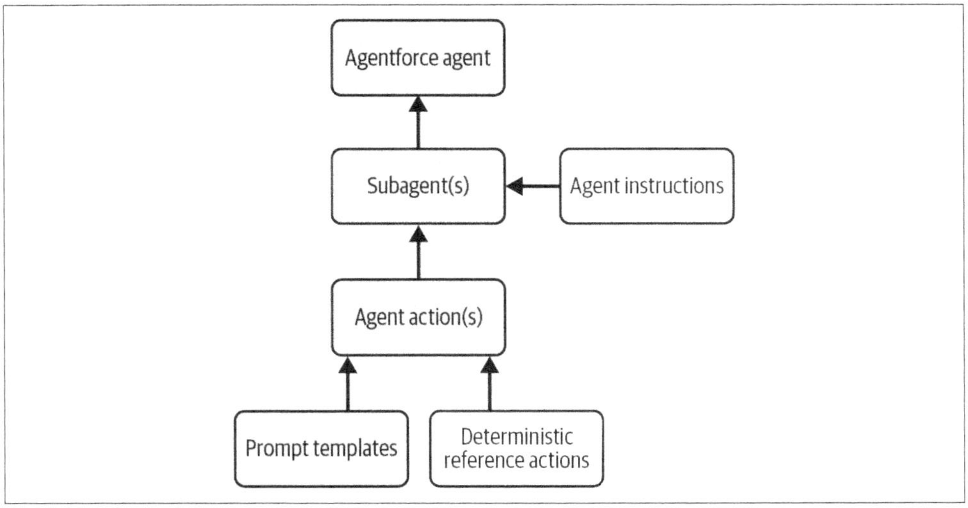

Figure 6-14. Agentforce agent building blocks

Agentforce Basic Building Blocks

Salesforce provides many standard Agentforce agents, subagents, agent actions, and prompt templates, making it easy for enterprises to get Agentforce agents into production quickly for the most common use cases. In addition, it's possible to customize or create your own prompt templates as well as create or customize Agentforce agents, subagents, and agent actions.

Agentforce agents

Salesforce standard agents are available out-of-the-box or as a prebuilt template. For some standard agents, a template exists in Agentforce Builder within Agentforce Studio. Other agents require enabling first and then some setup processes need to be completed before the Agentforce agent is ready for use. For example, there are some Agentforce agents for sales use cases that need to be enabled, including the Account Management agent and the Partner Success agent. Most of the standard Agentforce agents operate semi-autonomously, acting on behalf of users but driven by user prompts rather than running unattended workflows. However, a few standard Agentforce agents are capable of operating autonomously. Examples of autonomous Agentforce agents include the Sales Coach agent and the Lead Nurturing agent, both of which will be discussed in Chapter 9.

Agentforce Studio is a Salesforce application accessible from the App Launcher. From within Agentforce Studio, clicking the New Agent button on the top right gives you access to a number of Agentforce agent templates (Figure 6-15) within Agentforce Builder.

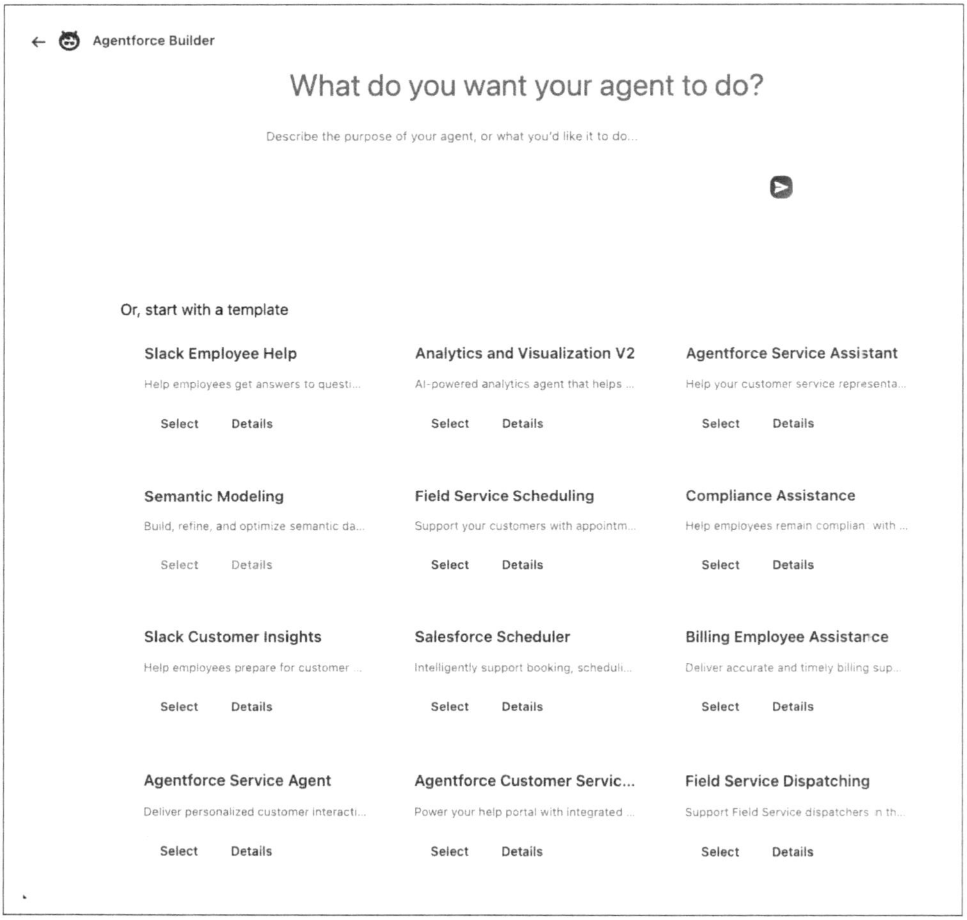

Figure 6-15. Agentforce standard agent templates available in Agentforce Builder

Many Agentforce agents are assigned multiple subagents. It's even possible to connect a complete Agentforce agent as a subagent by creating an Agentforce orchestrator agent. Both the Self-Service and the IT Service Management orchestrator agents, natively available for service-related use cases, require a Customer Profile graph (Figure 6-16). The Greeting Profile Data Graph is selected during the configuration of the orchestrator agent.

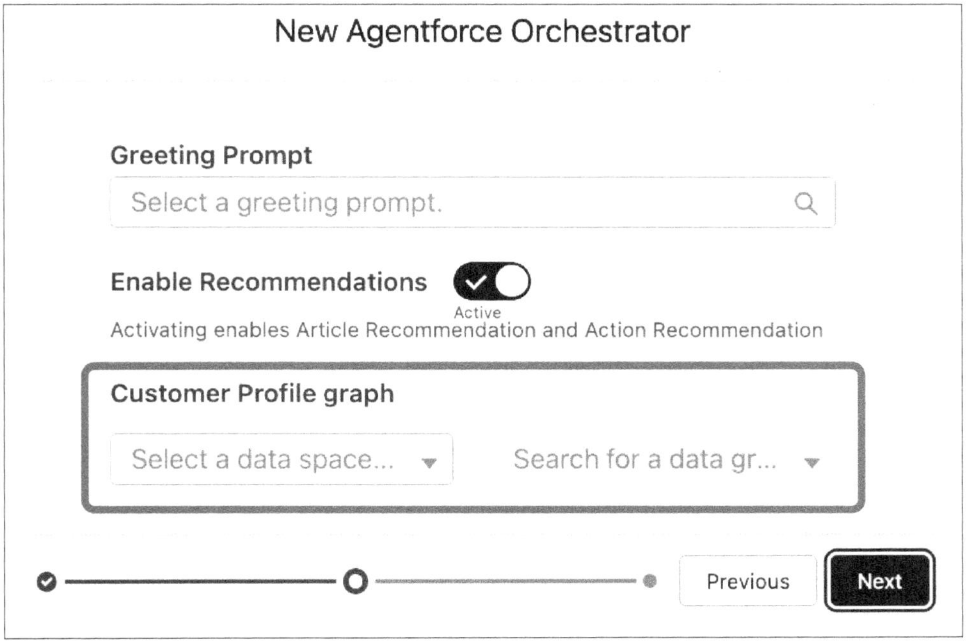

Figure 6-16. Customer Profile graph required for service-related orchestrator agents

In addition to adding or creating subagents for an agent, an agent's settings, variables, connections, and data can also be updated within the Agentforce Builder Explorer pane (Figure 6-17).

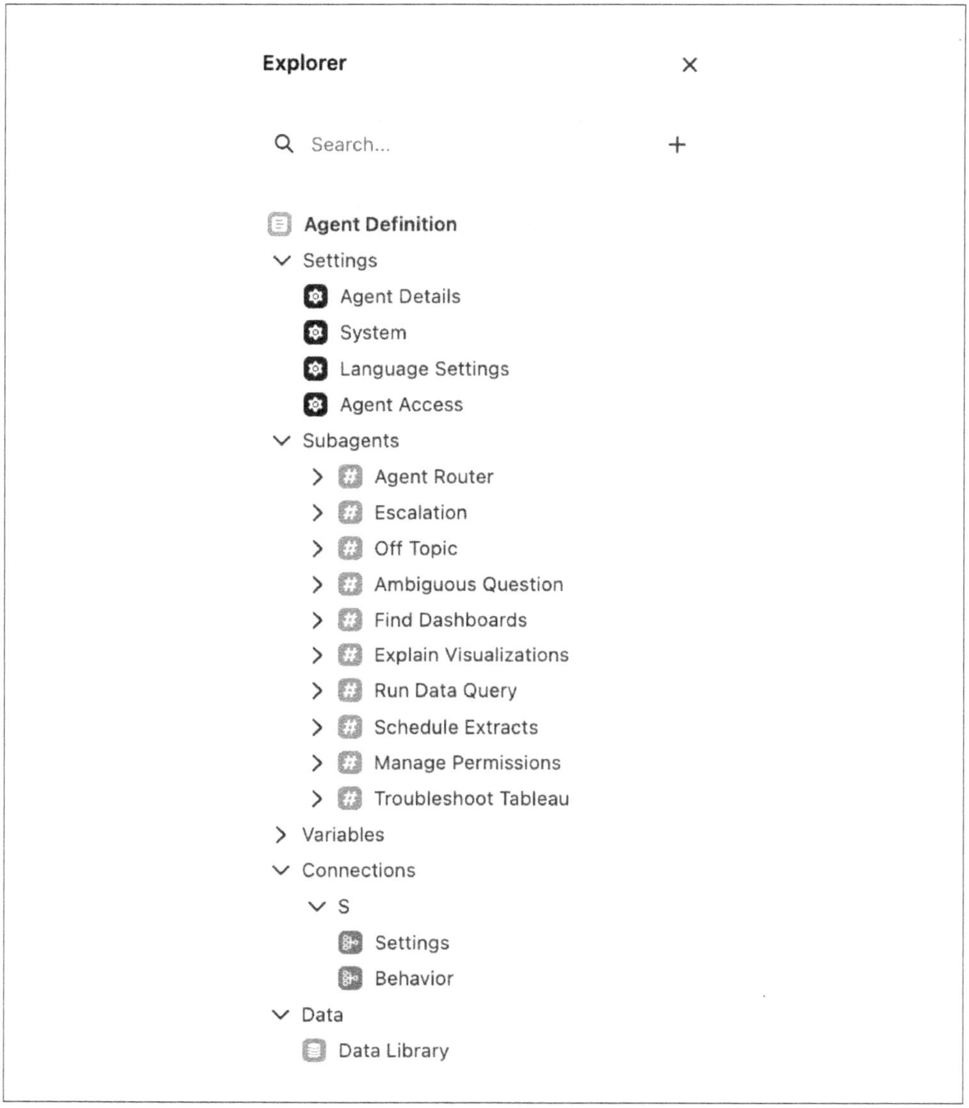

Figure 6-17. Agentforce Builder Explorer pane

The Connections menu option is where new connections can be added to an Agentforce agent so that the agent can be deployed to that channel. You'll notice that Slack is one of the available connections (Figure 6-18), assuming you're building an Agentforce Employee agent or a Slack Employee agent. The Slack connector won't be visible, however, if you're building an agent that can't be natively deployed to Slack.

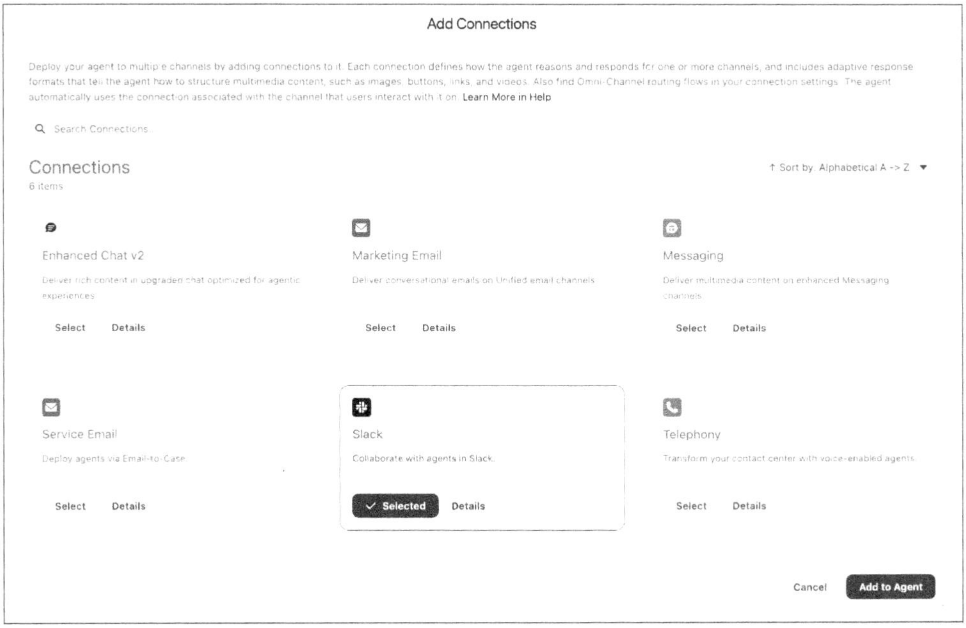

Figure 6-18. Agentforce channel connectors include a native Slack connection

Each connection includes the necessary settings for routing flows, adaptive response formats, and escalation messages. An agent can have more than one connection selected and, if needed, custom connections can be defined for unique cases where native connections don't exist.

> The Agentforce Employee agent is a broad category of agents built in Agentforce Builder that can be customized with subagents and actions. An Agentforce Employee agent supports multiple channels, including Slack. In contrast, a Slack Employee agent is specifically designed for Slack and includes Slack-specific actions like creating canvases, performing searches, and answering frequently asked questions using Slack resources.

While working in Agentforce Builder to create or manage agents, there are three distinct sections: the Explorer pane on the left that we've been discussing, the Canvas in the middle, and Agentforce chat on the right (Figure 6-19).

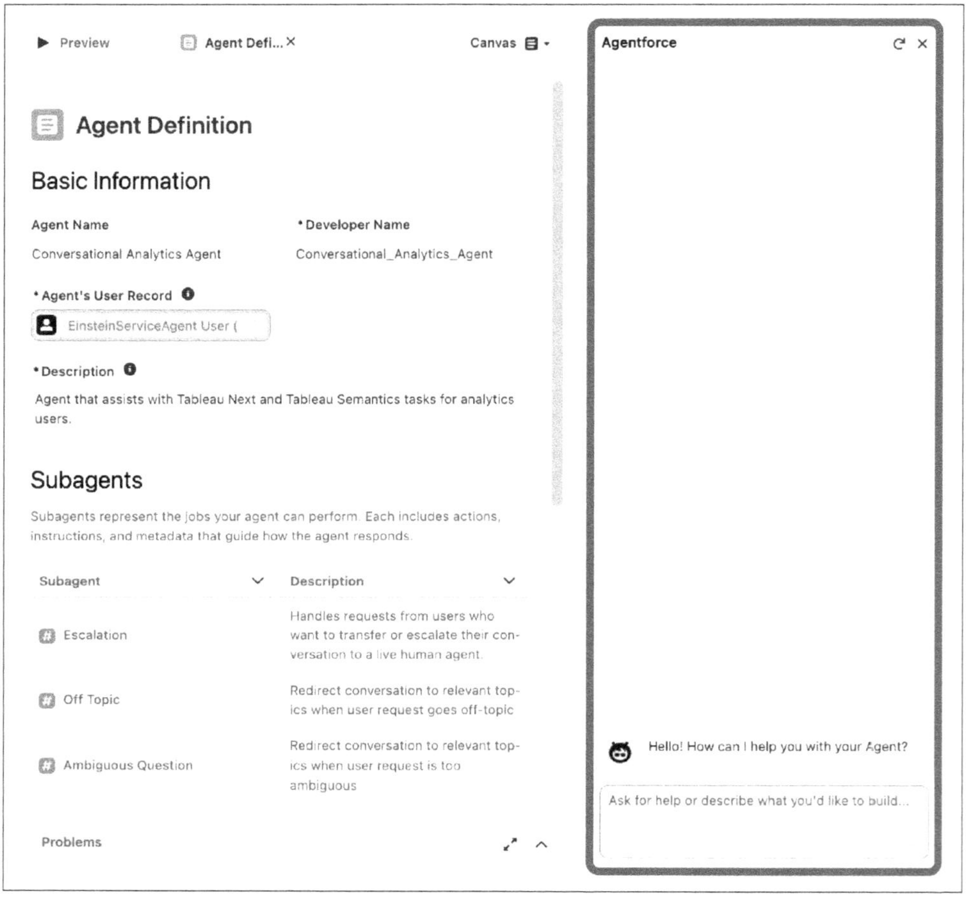

Figure 6-19. Agentforce chat on the right can assist with building an Agentforce agent

The Canvas view displays the agent definition, but if you toggle to the Script view, you'll see the Agent Script code instead of the agent definition. If you click the Preview button, you'll have the option to test your Agentforce agent (Figure 6-20). If you need help at any time, you can leverage the Agentforce chat window on the right to get some help with the Agentforce agent.

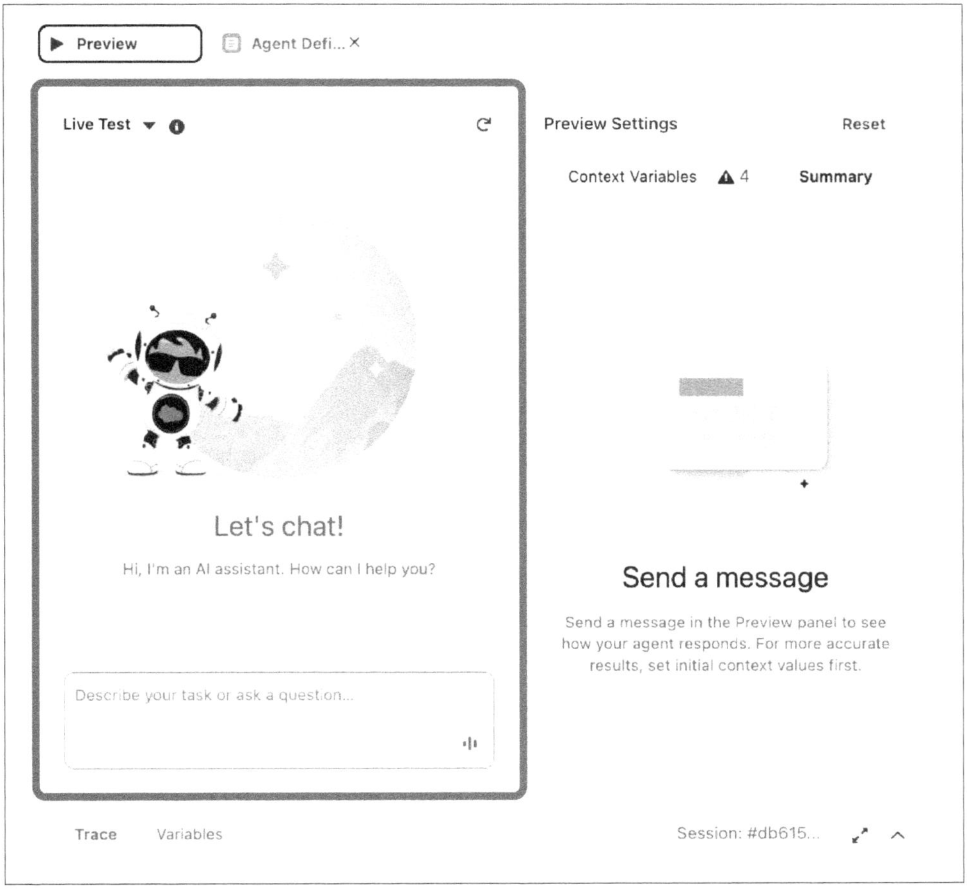

Figure 6-20. Preview your Agentforce agent's performance

The Preview button can be used with mock data or live data to show you how your agent will behave. Both modes can trigger billable events such as agent actions and AI reasoning from Atlas. Utilities like escalations or subagent transitions, however, do not incur billing charges.

Previewing agent behavior is important, especially when making changes to the selected LLM or when changing which decisions are handled by deterministic logic versus those that are delegated to the LLM.

Subagents (formerly called topics)

An Agentforce agent typically has many subagents assigned to it. Agentforce subagents, formerly called topics, are categories of agent actions that define the job or jobs an agent performs. A subagent includes agent instructions (Figure 6-21) and one or more actions. Agent instructions are written in natural language and tell your agent what to do and how to reply. Inline actions, such as conditionals or setting variables, run before any LLM reasoning.

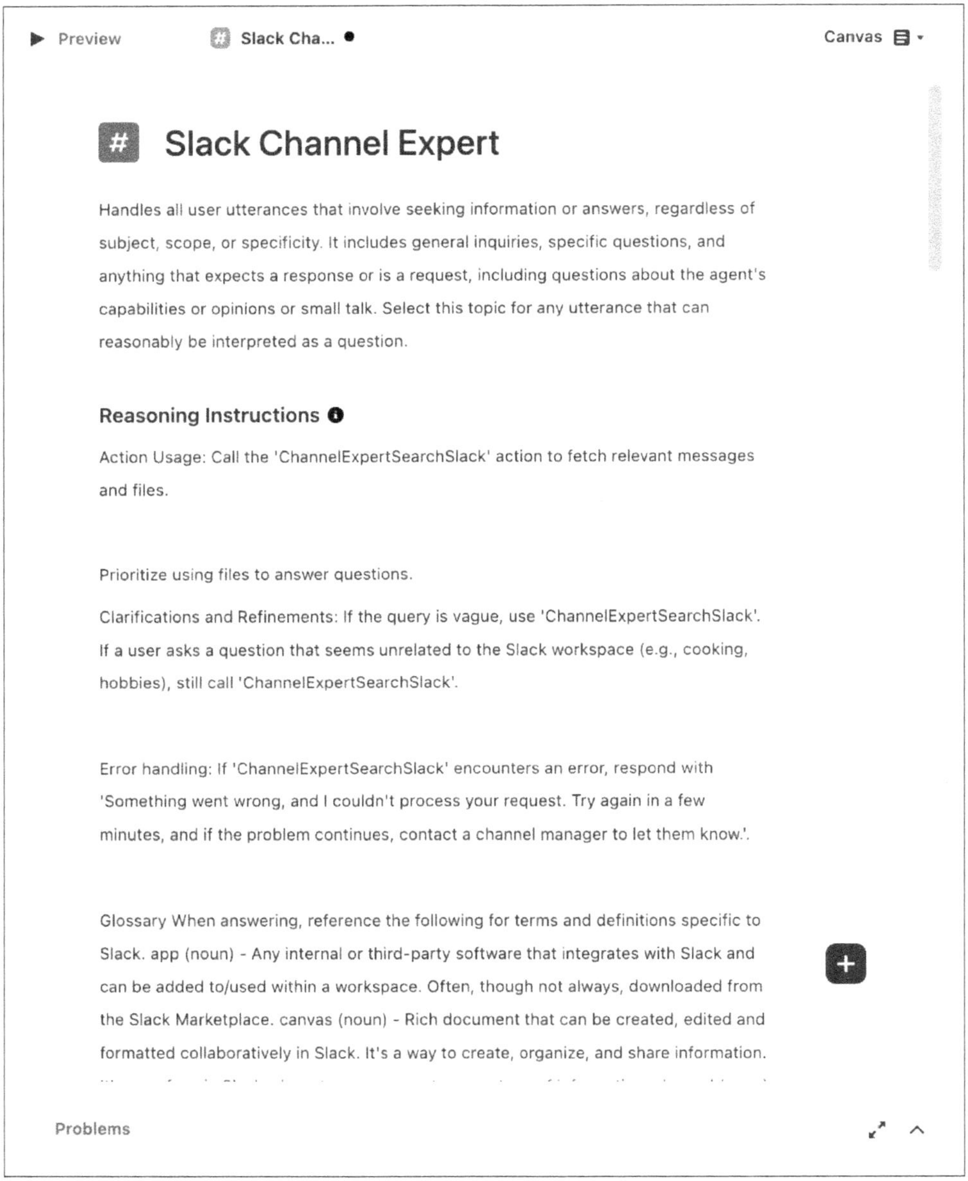

Figure 6-21. Example of a subagent's instructions

Subagents are an important component of an Agentforce agent. As such, Salesforce gives users control over many aspects of building and managing subagents, including the ability to configure an LLM override within the Agentforce Builder Canvas. Agentforce agent outputs can vary in the actual content shared and the way the content is presented. Thus, it's important to test any LLM overrides before migrating to a production environment. As mentioned previously, using the Preview button and evaluating changes in a Salesforce sandbox should be undertaken before deploying any LLM overrides to a Salesforce production environment.

Agent actions

Agentforce agent actions are the individual tasks an agent performs intelligently and securely. Agent actions able to be performed deterministically are created using reference actions that incorporate functionality created using tools like Apex code, Flows, or Agent Script reference actions. Otherwise, prompt templates are used to create agent actions given to the LLM for execution.

The Agentforce Studio Asset Library in Setup displays a list of available agent actions created using Flows or prompt templates (Figure 6-22) available to be assigned to a subagent.

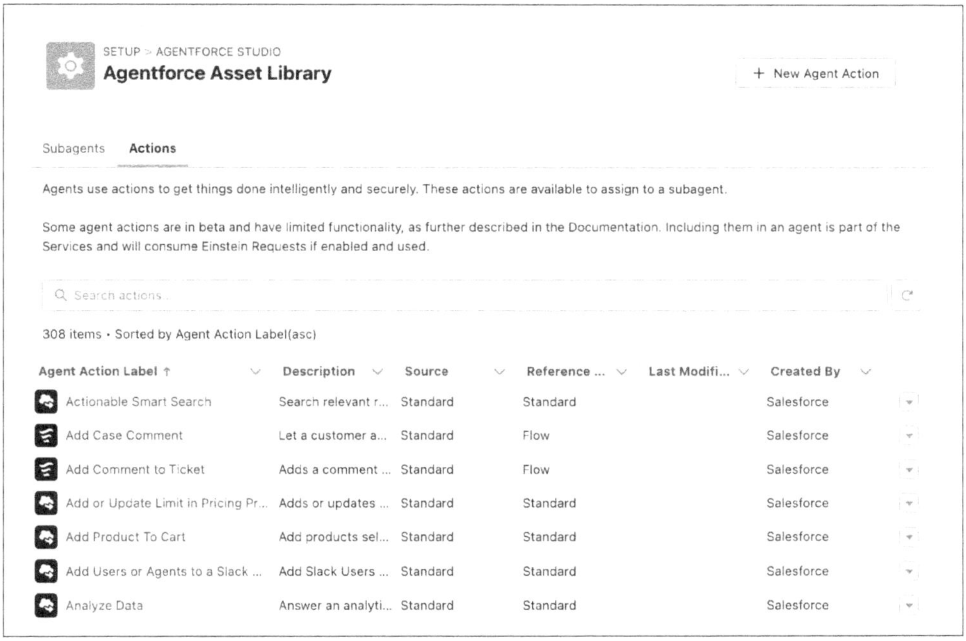

Figure 6-22. List of agent actions available included in the Agentforce Asset Library

It's within the Agentforce Asset Library that you can also create new agent actions. To create an agent action, you'll first need to create functionality in Salesforce using Flows, prompt templates, Apex, AI Model Builder predictive model, or whatever tool is appropriate for creating the functionality in advance. Selecting the action type (Figure 6-23) is the first step in creating a new agent reference action.

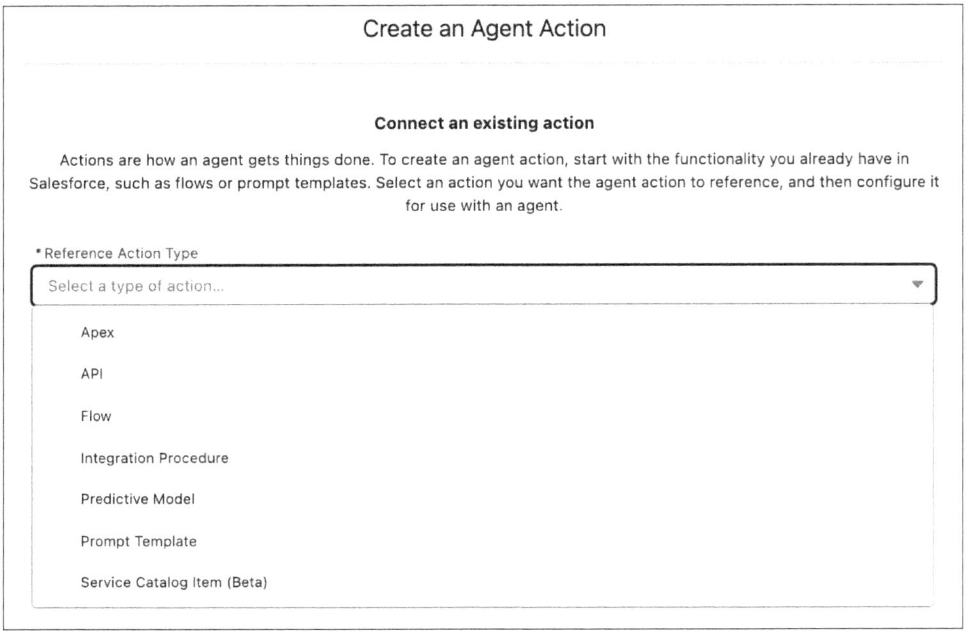

Figure 6-23. Reference action types

Reference actions currently available include Apex, API, Flow, Integration Procedure, Predictive Model, Prompt Template, and Service Catalog Item. Creating new prompt templates is achieved using the Agentforce Prompt Builder (Prompt Builder) tool (Figure 6-24), which is accessed through the Setup menu. Salesforce provides more than 25 prompt template types from which to choose when creating a new prompt template. You can change the default model by selecting a different standard model or you can import your own custom LLM.

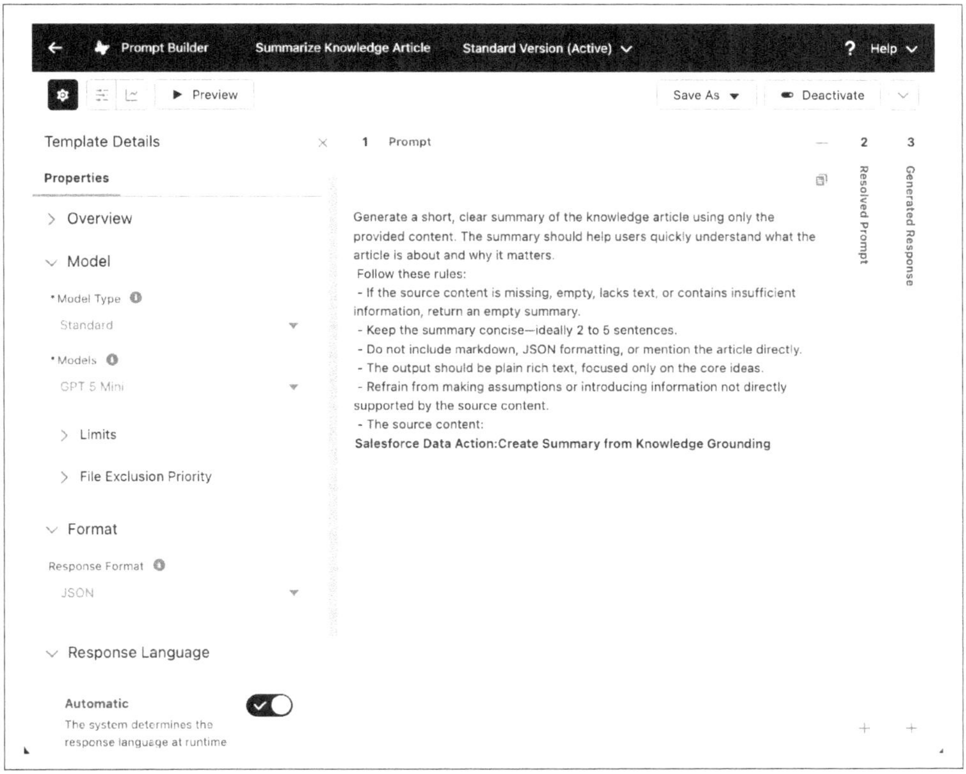

Figure 6-24. Agentforce Prompt Builder template settings

Configuring the action requires an agent action description and loading text as well as the inputs and outputs. Inputs are the data and parameters an agent action needs to run properly. The outputs are results the agent provides after completing an action.

Beyond the Basic Building Blocks

Agentforce is the agentic AI platform used by Salesforce admins, developers, and architects to build and maintain autonomous and semi-autonomous agents that take actions using prompt templates or Flows, Apex code, and Agent Script reference actions. Agentforce agents have defined roles, are given access to tools via actions, and are dynamically grounded with knowledge and context from D360. Agentforce agents are then deployed in a variety of channels such as the Salesforce Lightning console and mobile app, Slack, and other web and messaging platforms.

Agentforce 3, introduced in June 2025, has everything a modern enterprise needs to create its own agents for the intelligent agentic enterprise (Figure 6-25).

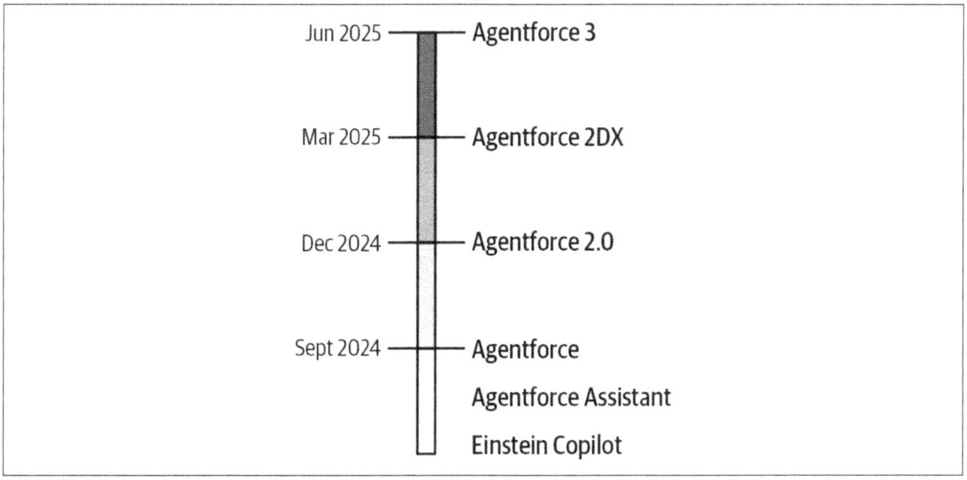

Figure 6-25. Evolution of Einstein Copilot to Agentforce 3

Agentforce 3 includes a larger catalog of prebuilt skills and actions with more than 300 prebuilt agents and actions, including those for industry domains like healthcare, financial services, nonprofit, manufacturing, and automotive. There's also an API catalog with semantic descriptions and detailed information, making it more likely the planner will select the best tool.

Headless agents were introduced along with the ability to invoke agents programmatically. Agent versioning is available, allowing for A/B testing and staged rollout of Agentforce agents. There's also multilingual support. In addition, Agent for Setup helps administrators configure and troubleshoot, and there exists a tighter, bidirectional Slack integration.

Agentforce 3 is powered by a stronger and more capable reasoning engine that easily handles more ambiguous, cross-object, and cross-system work with improved orchestration and lower latency. More Agentforce 3 enhancements include a Command Center that provides a "single pane of glass" to monitor agent health, tool usage, and business key performance indicators (KPIs) per agent or use case. There's also native support for the MCP connectivity, stronger native integration with D360, expanded LLM choice within Salesforce's trust boundary, with dynamic routing and automatic failover across LLM providers.

The menu options within Agentforce Studio (Figure 6-26) is where much of the new Agentforce 3 functionality is available. You'll notice there are agent test suites provided along with access to Agentforce DX. The ability to add AI foundational models is available in Agentforce Studio, too.

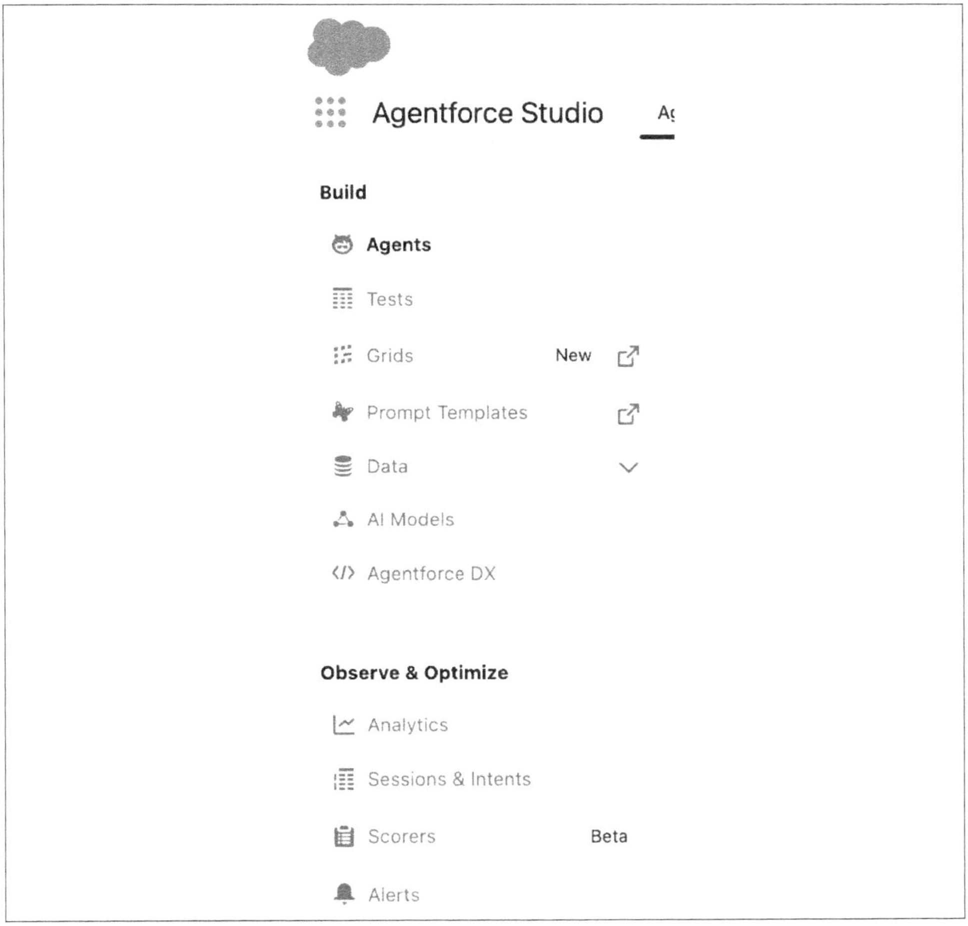

Figure 6-26. Agentforce Studio menu options

In this chapter, we've focused on learning about Agentforce Studio and Agentforce building blocks that can be created or maintained using a no-code approach in Agentforce Builder. In the next chapter, we'll explore pro-code developer tools like Agentforce DX and domain-specific programming languages such as Agent Script. However, no matter whether Agentforce agents are built using no-code or pro-code solutions, there are some best practices that apply to all.

Spend time planning for each Agentforce agent even for what might seem a simple use case. One of the most important design considerations is deciding when to use deterministic logic because excessive determinism reduces conversational flexibility. However, over-reliance on an LLM reduces predictable agent behavior and makes auditability more difficult.

In addition, security and guardrails shouldn't be an afterthought. Clearly define roles and boundaries for the Agentforce agent and think about human interactions to ensure user-input data will not override any prompt instructions.

In summary, decide whether agent actions should be primarily deterministic or prompt-based and identify the person or team ultimately responsible for the Agentforce agent. Make sure there's a plan for continual testing and evaluation of the agent once it's activated and put into a production environment.

Build efficiently and effectively by using standard agents, subagents, and actions when possible. Choose an example prompt template from the Prompt Template Library that's similar to your use case when a custom prompt needs to be created. Then customize that prompt template by replacing placeholder text with real merge fields.

Use an iterative development approach to build, test, and refine subagents in a sandbox environment. Add one subagent at a time to an agent so that you can assess how the agent performs before adding more functionality. Add the fewest number of subagents necessary and avoid overlap of functionality to ensure duplicative work is not created. Consider combining multiple subagents' actions into one subagent if two subagents frequently hand off to each other or share similar actions.

Always write concise, natural language descriptions for each building block. It's important to give Atlas sufficient details so that the most appropriate subagent and corresponding agent action can be selected. Those details are in the form of written descriptions but also include the custom labels and API names for each of the building blocks you create. You'll want to assign label names and API names that are clear, concise, and accurately reflect the building block's purpose.

The goal is to always build trusted, easy, and adaptable solutions for an intelligent agentic enterprise. Salesforce provides many resources to assist architects in their journey. The Salesforce Architecture Center (*https://oreil.ly/Pmn5N*) includes a Well-Architected Framework section, information about patterns and antipatterns, diagrams, and decision guides. The Salesforce Architecture Center provides links to other resources like the Architect Trailblazers group and developer documentation.

Summary

In this chapter, we discovered how to build standard Agentforce agents and create new agents. We took a deep dive into agentic reasoning engines, in general, before exploring the Atlas reasoning engine. We learned how Agentforce agents work and the importance of the Agent Graph and Agent Script for hybrid reasoning.

Agentforce Builder democratizes agent building for most enterprise use cases. However, sometimes complex business use cases require developer tools. In the next chapter, we'll learn about pro-code developer tools for building and managing Agentforce agents.

CHAPTER 7

Pro-Code Developer Tools for Building and Managing Agentforce Agents

We learned a great deal about Agentforce and Salesforce AI Builder tools in Chapter 6. We explored the Agentforce architecture and discovered the importance of Data 360 (D360), Customer 360 (C360), and Slack. In addition, we took a deep dive into Agentforce Builder to experience how Salesforce admins and developers can easily create and maintain AI agents (agents) using a no-code development tool within the Salesforce platform.

However, sometimes a more complex business use case exists where a solution can't be implemented using Agentforce Builder. A pro-code approach can be useful in those instances. In addition, another important benefit of a pro-code development approach is that it allows an agent's source code to be stored in a version control system (VCS) like GitHub. That's where Agentforce DX pro-code development becomes a valuable resource for Salesforce developers.

In this chapter, we'll explain Agentforce DX and describe the many new features available for Salesforce developers including the new Agentforce Vibes integrated development environment (IDE). The Agentforce Vibes IDE, available within the Salesforce platform, supports the Agent Script programming language and provides access to the Salesforce MCP server and the new Agent API. Before diving deeper into these new Agentforce capabilities, we'll learn about the tools, languages, frameworks, and application programming interfaces (APIs) that are already familiar to Salesforce developers.

Getting Started

Let's discuss some background knowledge and some things you should know to help you get the most out of this chapter.

Background Knowledge

It's expected that you have already reviewed the Agentforce architecture from previous chapters. There's also an assumption the reader possesses a basic understanding of Agentforce subagents and actions and how these are created in the Agentforce Builder.

Possessing Salesforce pro-code developer knowledge or experience is helpful but isn't required. The material presented in this chapter will be more high-level to benefit the greatest number of personas.

Democratizing AI development is achieved when nontechnical people, generally those without a computer science degree or a deep understanding of how AI algorithms work, have access to tool types that make it easier for more users to create AI solutions. Salesforce supports AI democratization by providing many out-of-the-box solutions prebuilt for use by business users who may not possess a high degree of technical skill. However, tool options also exist for technical users who need to create Salesforce AI solutions requiring a high degree of customization.

At one extreme, Salesforce provides built-in AI solutions (Figure 7-1) that don't require any technical skill to implement because they're available to use immediately. An example is Einstein Search capabilities, which are built directly into Salesforce and available for all Salesforce users.

At the other extreme are Salesforce Builder tools and developer tools available for Salesforce users to construct their own AI solutions. An example of a Builder tool is the AI Model Builder option for users to create their own predictive AI model from scratch. An example of a developer tool is Agentforce DX, a pro-code collection of tools for Salesforce CLI, VS Code, and Code Builder. Agentforce DX users can create agents with AI assistance using natural language.

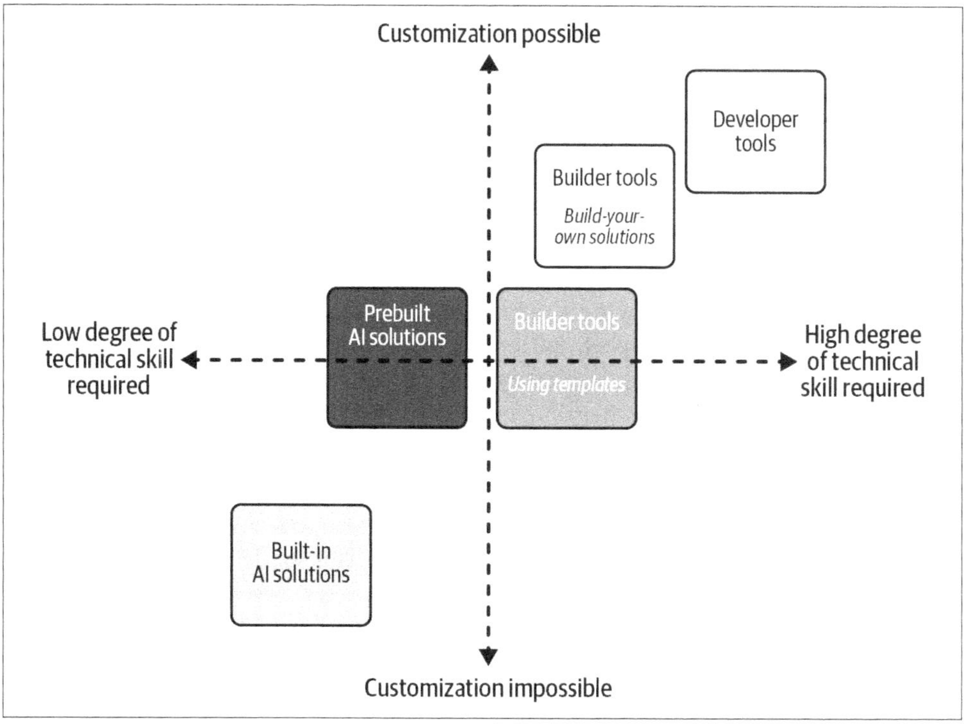

Figure 7-1. Salesforce AI no-code and pro-code tool options and solutions

Most Salesforce Builder tools also come with several prebuilt templates, making it easy for users to get started building their own solutions right away. Customization is still possible, but there is a higher degree of technical skill required for Builder tools than when using prebuilt AI solutions. The majority of Salesforce AI development leverages prebuilt solutions and Builder tools with templates. As such, throughout the book we've focused mostly on describing in detail the tools within these two categories. We will, however, cover Agentforce DX in more detail in this chapter.

What You Should Know

Salesforce IDE extensions, Salesforce DX extensions, and Agentforce extensions are related but distinct tools within the Salesforce ecosystem. Salesforce IDE extensions are general-purpose extensions and include tools for working with Apex, Lightning Web Components (LWC), Visualforce, and SOQL. They're typically used in Visual Studio Code (VS Code) or Agentforce Vibes IDE. Salesforce Developer Experience (DX) extensions are part of the Salesforce DX designed for modern application (app) development. Salesforce DX includes tools like the Salesforce command-line interface (CLI) and extensions for managing scratch orgs, metadata, and continuous integration. Salesforce DX extensions support collaborative and version-controlled development workflows. Agentforce DX extensions extend Salesforce DX capabilities to support agent development and orchestration. Agentforce DX includes tools like Agentforce Vibes, an AI-powered coding assistant, and agent-specific CLI commands.

Historically, Salesforce has been an "API-first" company. Major Salesforce objects and many platform features have REST/SOAP APIs so external apps and integrations can read or write data and trigger some automation. This made Salesforce open and extensible, but the primary user in the "API-first" scenario is still a human in the Salesforce Lightning user interface (UI). Thus, the emphasis in "API-enabled apps" use cases is for developers and integrators to extend Salesforce by calling APIs. Those use cases are ones outside the traditional approach where end users leverage the Salesforce Lightning UI and C360 apps as a system of work for humans.

We briefly explore Salesforce APIs in this chapter and we also explore the concepts of Model Context Protocol (MCP) and CLI commands. This is important because Salesforce has moved beyond "API-enabled apps," where a human is the user, to a Headless 360 architecture.

Headless 360 supports a headless execution layer whose main consumers are agents and external experiences. Every aspect of Salesforce such as the data, workflows, business logic, and controls can now be exposed through APIs, MCP tools, and the CLI rather than only the simple create, read, update, and delete (CRUD) operations and automation features. We explore Headless 360 more in Chapter 12, and you can find additional information about what Salesforce Headless 360 means for developers on the Salesforce Developers blog (*https://oreil.ly/dhLWM*).

Agentforce DX Overview

Agentforce DX extends the Salesforce DX capabilities by allowing developers to work with agents. Salesforce DX is a set of tools created for developers to build, test, and implement solutions on the Salesforce platform that aren't easily solvable with no-code Builder tools and low-code tools like Salesforce Flows. Salesforce DX includes the Salesforce CLI and IDE extensions as well as Salesforce programming languages and development frameworks.

Agentforce DX provides developer access to an Agent API, Agent Script programming language, and a Salesforce MCP server (Figure 7-2). In addition, the new Agentforce Vibes IDE gives Salesforce developers everything they need to interact with agents.

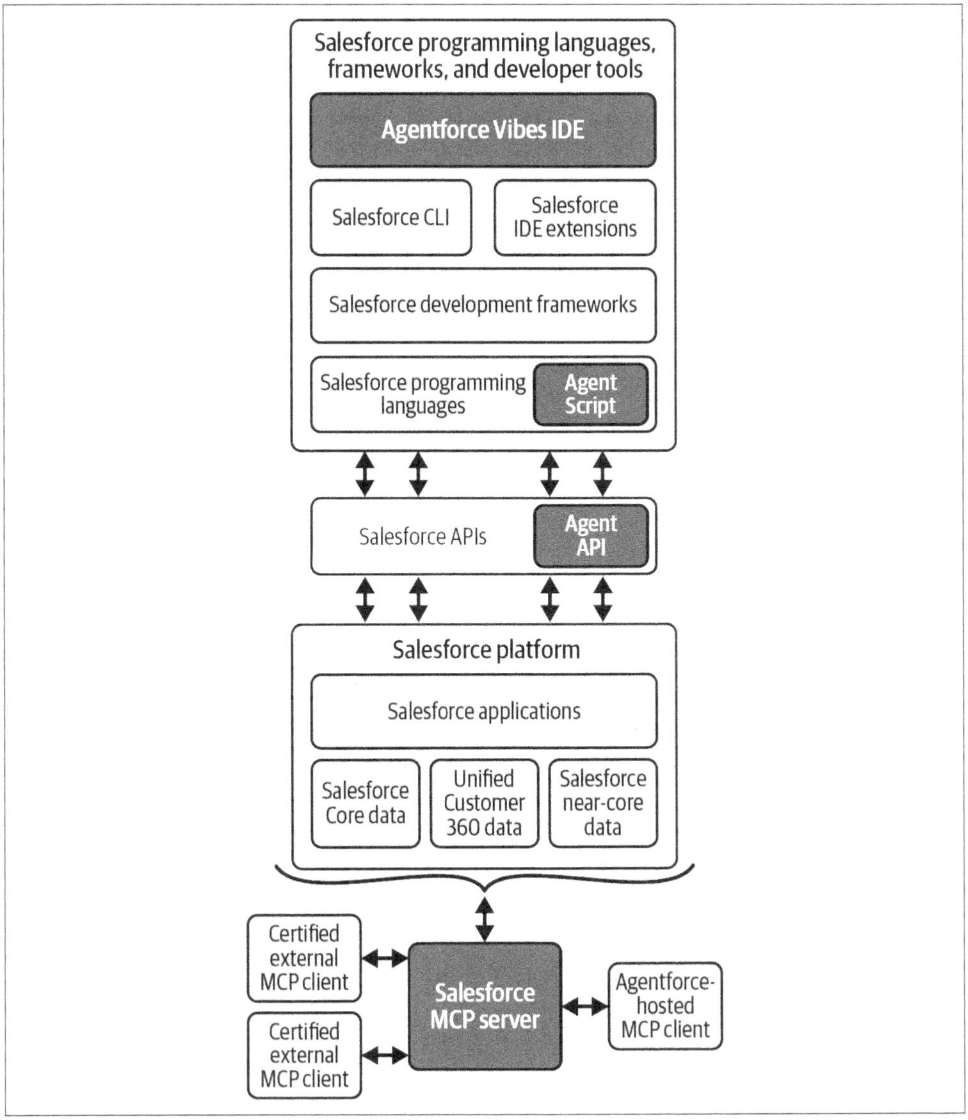

Figure 7-2. Agentforce DX architecture extends Salesforce DX capabilities

Agentforce DX leverages the developer tools, programming languages, frameworks, and APIs already familiar to pro-code developers. To better understand and appreciate Agentforce DX capabilities, we'll first review the important Salesforce DX components. Then we'll dive deeper into the developer features included with the addition of Agentforce DX.

Salesforce Programming Languages and Frameworks

A programming language is a set of instructions developers use to tell a computer what to do and how to do it. Those instructions, written in a specific syntax, provide the machine-readable code a computer needs to create an application, website, or other digital tool. Languages can be of different types, depending on how they're structured. Procedural, object-oriented, and scripting languages are some different language types. Programming languages can be low-level or high-level. High-level languages abstract away hardware details and are easier for humans to read.

Some examples of common programming languages include Python, Java, JavaScript, and SQL. Python is a high-level language often used for machine learning, automation, and web development. Java is an object-oriented programming language used for developing Android mobile applications, web applications, and enterprise software. JavaScript is a scripting language used to add interactivity to web pages. Structured Query Language (SQL) allows users to interact with and retrieve information from relational databases.

New programming languages are sometimes created to address a particular need or to solve domain-specific problems. This is especially true for Salesforce, which has created several languages for Salesforce developers. We'll learn more about Salesforce programming languages in the next section.

In addition to creating domain-specific programming languages, another good option for optimizing software and application development is to create developer frameworks. A framework is a collection of reusable software components offering a more standardized and modular design approach. Frameworks most often result in faster, more consistent, scalable development where code is easier to debug and maintain. There are many Salesforce developer frameworks, including frameworks for custom UI development, often needed to support the different ways users interact with the Salesforce platform and agents. Salesforce custom UI development frameworks will be covered after we explore some important Salesforce programming languages.

Salesforce Programming Languages

The Salesforce core platform is a multitenant, cloud-based environment with a unique data model used for customer relationship management (CRM) purposes. The near-core platforms include specialized solutions for domains such as commerce and marketing.

For these near-core specialized domains, Salesforce created new programming languages. The Internet Store Markup Language (ISML) is used for commerce use cases. There are several marketing-specific Salesforce languages including AMPScript, Server-Side JavaScript (SSJS), and Guide Template Language (GTL).

For the core platform, Salesforce developed the Apex programming language in 2006 and the Salesforce Object Query Language (SOQL) in 2008. Salesforce released its newest programming language, Agent Script, in 2025.

Salesforce developed the Apex programming language to give developers the ability to execute flow and transaction control statements as well as API calls. Apex is used by Salesforce developers to automate processes, add business logic to applications, and integrate with external systems. Specifically, developers use Apex for creating custom web services, building custom controllers for Visualforce pages, writing triggers for performing actions before or after record changes, and implementing complex business logic that can't otherwise be implemented using the Salesforce Flow (Flow) declarative tool. Apex is a strongly-typed, object-oriented programming language similar to Java, and it runs on Salesforce servers to ensure security and scalability.

> Apex doesn't replace Flow, a declarative automation tool used by Salesforce administrators and developers. Apex empowers Salesforce developers to implement very complex business logic that is beyond what Flow can handle.

Apex, a strongly-typed, object-oriented programming language, includes many of the same fundamental building blocks as Java such as classes and methods. An Apex class can be used to create complex custom logic for an Agentforce Apex action. Once the Apex class code is written, the Agentforce Apex action is created by navigating to Agentforce Assets in Setup and then selecting the New Agent Action button.

Choose Apex as the reference action type and Invocable Method as the reference action category (Figure 7-3). Next, select the specific reference action, which is the Apex class written by a Salesforce developer.

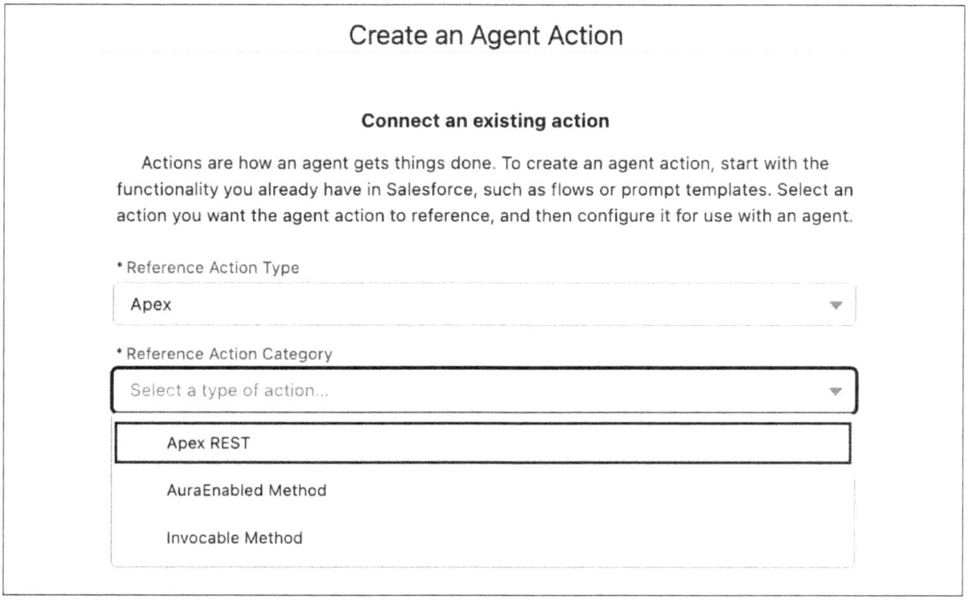

Figure 7-3. Creating an Apex agent action

The agent action label will default to a reference action, although you can change the agent action label if desired. You'll need to finish including the desired details for creating the agent action, making sure to update the input and output sections of the agent action.

> Be sure to include well-written descriptions and labels for Apex classes and agent actions because they will be used to assist the agent and reasoning engine to better understand the action's purpose.

Often found within Apex statements is another Salesforce-specific programming language known as Salesforce Object Query Language (SOQL). SOQL can also be used by developers within the Salesforce CLI and VS Code extensions as well as in Apex code. Built to handle Salesforce's unique data model, SOQL is similar to the `SELECT` statement in Structured Query Language (SQL).

Salesforce's Agent Script is built for controlling agents. The language enables conditional logic and offers guided, deterministic controls for agents. Agent Script allows developers and nondevelopers to define the desired agent behavior with a human-readable expression language. We'll dive into Agent Script in more detail in "Agent Script" on page 290.

Salesforce Developer Frameworks for Custom UI

There are two important frameworks available to developers building a custom UI in Salesforce: the Visualforce framework and the Lightning Component framework. The Lightning Component framework includes both Aura components (Aura) and LWC.

Visualforce uses a tag-based markup language, similar to HTML, along with server-side controllers that make it simple to perform basic database operations such as queries and saves. Visualforce has been used by developers to build custom UIs and is still supported by Salesforce. However, Salesforce recommends Visualforce not be used for any new custom UI development.

Aura components are self-contained and reusable Lightning-based components used to build custom Salesforce apps and interfaces. Salesforce is phasing out support for Aura components and recommends developers migrate from Aura to LWCs. There are many benefits to using LWCs rather than Aura, especially because LWCs leverage modern development practices that are more performant and lightweight.

LWCs are also part of the Lightning Component framework. LWCs are custom elements built with JavaScript that return an HTML rendering, creating Salesforce dynamic and responsive user interfaces. LWCs can retrieve or modify data by calling Lightning Data Service or an Apex method.

In addition, LWCs play an important role in Agentforce. When combined with Flows or custom Lightning types, LWCs can be used in agent actions to accept input data from a user or to display output data from an agent action. LWCs can also allow users to initiate interactions between headless agents and have the results from those interactions displayed to the user. Headless agents are connected via the Salesforce Agent API, one of many Salesforce APIs available to developers.

Salesforce APIs

An API is a software interface that provides a way to connect computers or computer programs. Web APIs, in particular, are created to allow communication and the transfer of data between software applications over the internet. In practice, the term API most often refers to web APIs. Throughout the chapter we'll use the terms interchangeably.

APIs standardize the way applications make requests and provide responses. Thus, applications communicating with each other use an intermediary API so they don't need to know the specific details required to interact directly. For example, ecommerce sites use payment gateway APIs to process transactions rather than creating their own payment processing applications.

The advent of commercial APIs in the late 1990s cemented APIs' critical role in enabling communication and the transfer of data over the internet. Amazon, eBay, and Salesforce were among the first to build commercial APIs offering different types of consumers a program interface they could use to securely access enterprise information and services. Salesforce was an early API pioneer and continues to offer many valuable Salesforce APIs today.

Salesforce offers many different types of APIs including SOAP, REST, and a variety of bulk and streaming APIs. Salesforce makes APIs available for a variety of data from Salesforce platforms. Users can learn more about all Salesforce APIs on the Salesforce developer website (*https://oreil.ly/NTPmf*). Just a few examples of Salesforce APIs are as follows:

- Bulk API 2.0
- Connect REST API
- Data Cloud Connect REST API
- Einstein Bot API and SDK
- GraphQL API
- Messaging for In-App and Web API
- Metadata API
- Pub/Sub API
- Salesforce Reports and Dashboards REST API
- SOAP API
- Streaming API
- Tooling API
- User Interface API

The Models API and the Agent API are two of Salesforce's newest APIs. The Models API supports the Einstein feature for bring your own LLM (BYOLLM) for connecting to a supported provider such as Amazon Bedrock, Azure OpenAI, Google Vertex AI, and OpenAI. The Agent API is a core component for building headless agents. We'll explore the Agent API in "Agent API" on page 283 when we dive into the new Agentforce DX tools and features available to Salesforce developers. Before that, though, let's first review the main tools used by Salesforce developers.

Salesforce Developer Tools

Salesforce provides developers with many different tools, some of which are very specialized tools relevant only when working in the Salesforce environment. However, the tools most often used by Salesforce developers are pro-code development tool types common to a wide variety of development work. Examples include a CLI and IDEs.

You may already be familiar with CLI tools. The macOS, Linux, and Windows operating system (OS) each include a command-line tool. For macOS and Linux users, the primary CLI is the Terminal application that is accessible after opening Finder and entering Terminal in the search field. Clicking the terminal icon opens the CLI tool. In Windows, the primary CLI is the Command Prompt application. Enter "command" or "cmd" in the search field and press the Enter key. Click the Command Prompt shortcut to open the CLI tool. You'll need to know how to open the CLI on your machine if you elect to install the Salesforce CLI and test it with a few commands, as described in the next section.

Within the Salesforce platform, Salesforce builders use buttons and menus when building in a no-code graphical user interface (GUI) like Agentforce Builder. In contrast, the Salesforce CLI tool is a text-based interface where developers can perform more complex development efforts like executing scripts and interacting with other tools such as Git.

We'll explore the Salesforce CLI later in this section so that you're familiar with its functionality, but you won't need to install the Salesforce CLI on your machine if you plan to use the Agentforce Vibes IDE because the Salesforce CLI tool is integrated into Agentforce Vibes IDE. As we'll see later, the Agentforce Vibes IDE is a web-based IDE available to developers only after signing into Salesforce. Alternatively, Salesforce developers can also use third-party IDEs such as Visual Studio, which can be downloaded to a machine. When using third-party IDEs, the Salesforce extensions will need to be added and the Salesforce CLI will also need to be downloaded for use with the desktop IDE.

Salesforce Command-Line Interface

Salesforce CLI installation and configuration is straightforward with only a few steps needed:

1. Read the system requirements (*https://oreil.ly/lOCLi*) prior to installation and configuration.
2. Install Salesforce CLI on your computer using operating system-specific artifacts, TAR files, or with `npm`. Be sure to follow the instructions (*https://oreil.ly/trCEJ*) in the Salesforce Developers doc to install Salesforce CLI correctly.
3. After installation, verify that you've installed Salesforce CLI correctly by executing the `sf commands` command after opening a terminal (macOS, Linux) or command prompt (Windows):

   ```
   sf commands
   ```

   That command will provide you a list of all available CLI commands (Figure 7-4).

joyceavila — -zsh — 120×30

Id	Summary
agent activate	Activate an agent in an org.
agent adl create	Create an Agentforce Data Library.
agent adl delete	Delete an Agentforce Data Library.
agent adl file add	Add files to an existing Agentforce Data Library.
agent adl file delete	Delete a file from an Agentforce Data Library.
agent adl file list	List files in an Agentforce Data Library.
agent adl get	Get details of an Agentforce Data Library.
agent adl list	List Agentforce Data Libraries in an org.
agent adl status	Get indexing status of an Agentforce Data Library.
agent adl update	Update an Agentforce Data Library.
agent adl upload	Upload a file to an SFDRIVE Agentforce Data Library.
agent create	Create an agent in your org using a local agent spec file.
agent deactivate	Deactivate an agent in an org.
agent generate agent-spec	Generate an agent spec, which is a YAML file that captures what an agen…
agent generate authoring-bundle	Generate an authoring bundle from an existing agent spec YAML file.
agent generate template	Generate an agent template from an existing agent in your DX project so…
agent generate test-spec	Generate an agent test spec, which is a YAML file that lists the test c…
agent mcp asset list	List the assets (tools, prompts, and resources) for an MCP server in th…
agent mcp asset replace	Replace the asset set of an MCP server in the API Catalog.
agent mcp create	Create an MCP server in the API Catalog.
agent mcp delete	Delete an MCP server from the API Catalog.
agent mcp fetch	Fetch the live assets (tools, prompts, resources) advertised by an MCP …
agent mcp get	Get a single MCP server registered in the API Catalog.
agent mcp list	List the MCP servers registered in the API Catalog.
agent mcp update	Update an MCP server registered in the API Catalog.
agent preview	Interact with an agent to preview how it responds to your statements, q…
agent preview end	End an existing programmatic agent preview session and get trace locati…

Figure 7-4. List of available Salesforce CLI commands

Next, run this command to see the version of Salesforce CLI you just installed:

```
sf --version
```

4. Optional step: Configure Salesforce CLI with your desired customizations. For example, you can enable autocomplete, set CLI configuration and environment variables, and use Salesforce CLI behind a company firewall.

5. Periodically read the weekly release notes (*https://oreil.ly/TpI1e*) to learn about new features, changes, and bug fixes.

Salesforce developers use the Salesforce CLI to manage Salesforce DX projects, create and install packages, and create and manage sandboxes and scratch orgs. And, now, developers can use agent commands within the Salesforce CLI. Here is a list of the agent commands currently available:

- `agent activate`: activate an agent in an org
- `agent create`: create an agent in your org using a local agent spec file
- `agent deactivate`: deactivate an agent in an org
- `agent generate agent-spec`: generate an agent spec, which is a YAML file that captures what an agent can do
- `agent generate template`: generate an agent template from an existing agent in your DX project so you can then package the template in a managed package

- `agent generate test-spec`: generate an agent test spec, which is a YAML file that lists the test cases for testing a specific agent
- `agent preview`: interactive with an active agent to preview how the agent responds to your statements, questions, and commands (utterances)
- `agent test create`: create an agent test in your org using a local test spec YAML file
- `agent test list`: list the available agent tests in your org
- `agent test results`: get the results of a completed agent test run
- `agent test resume`: resume an agent test that you previously started in your org so you can view the test results
- `agent test run`: start an agent test in your org

All the Salesforce CLI functionality is available whether you use the Salesforce CLI within your machine's terminal or within an IDE's built-in terminal window. Built-in terminal windows are available in third-party IDEs and Agentforce Vibes IDE.

IDEs and Salesforce Extensions

Salesforce developers have the option to use the Agentforce Vibes IDE or a third-party IDE such as Visual Studio. All IDEs, including Agentforce Vibes and Visual Studio, need to have Salesforce extensions installed. Whereas Agentforce Vibes comes with Salesforce extensions preinstalled, developers need to initiate the Salesforce extensions installation if using Visual Studio.

The Agentforce Vibes extension, incorporating the MCP server extension, is included in the Salesforce Extension Pack (Extended). In addition, the Salesforce Extension Pack installs the following extensions:

- Salesforce CLI integration
- Apex Replay Debugger
- Lightning Web Components
- Aura Components
- Visualforce
- SOQL
- Salesforce Lightning Design System (SLDS) Validator
- Agentforce for Developers
- Salesforce Code Analyzer

The Visual Studio IDE can be set up for Salesforce development (Figure 7-5) after installing the application from the Visual Studio site (*https://oreil.ly/MWdjZ*).

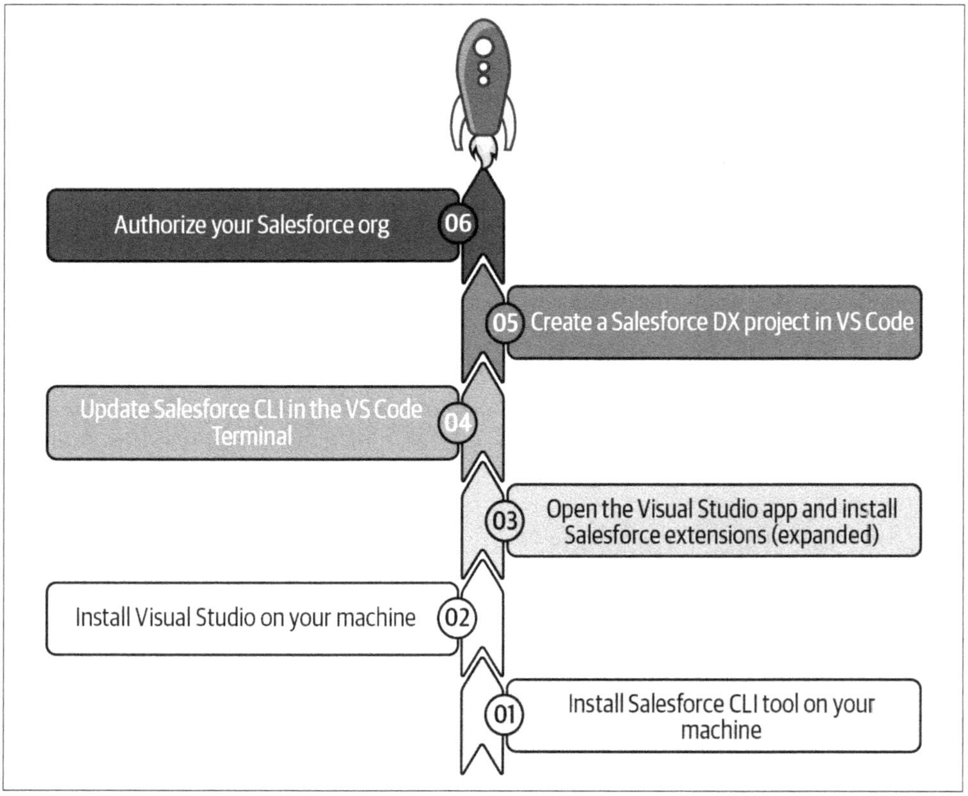

Figure 7-5. Steps to set up Visual Studio Code application for Salesforce development

Be sure to install the Salesforce Extensions Pack (Expanded) and then update the Salesforce CLI in the VS Code Terminal using the `sf update` command. Make sure you've installed the Salesforce CLI before attempting to execute the command.

Next, create a Salesforce DX project. Creating a new project provides structure for the Salesforce org's metadata, data, and other artifacts. These project items can be saved in a version control system like GitHub. However, if you're just wanting to store the project on your computer, you can follow these steps in VS Code:

1. Click View | Command Palette and choose SFDX: Create Project.
2. Click Standard (Standard project template default).
3. Enter the project name.

4. Click Create Project after navigating to the location on your computer where you want to save the new project.

The final requirement to get started is authorizing your Salesforce org so that VS Code and CLI commands can access and work with your org's data and processes:

1. Within VS Code, click View | Command Palette and choose SFDX: Authorize an Org.
2. Click Project Default.
3. Enter an org alias.
4. Sign in to your Salesforce org with your login credentials when the browser window opens the login page.
5. Select the option to allow Salesforce CLI access to your org. A message will appear informing you that the authentication is successful.
6. Close the browser window and continue in the VS Code IDE.

Note that the Salesforce org you've authorized is now set as your default org in your development environment.

Agentforce DX Additions to Salesforce DX

Salesforce has a long history of creating beneficial programming languages, development frameworks, APIs, and developer tools in support of its Salesforce DX program. Agentforce DX extends Salesforce DX with some powerful additions for developers. We previously mentioned the Salesforce Agent API, Salesforce DX MCP server, Agentforce Vibes IDE, and Agent Script programming language as examples of new Agentforce DX features. Let's explore each of those four new features now.

Agent API

The Agent API allows Salesforce developers to programmatically build interactions with agents. Using the Agent API, it's possible to initiate new agent conversations as well as send and receive messages. Developers also use Agent API to integrate agents with third-party platforms and other systems to create autonomous workflows. One of the most powerful benefits of using Agent API is the ability to build headless agent experiences where a UI isn't needed.

Agent API can be used anywhere that a REST API can be called, including incorporating into a website. However, be sure to review these important details before considering implementing a solution using the Agent API:

- Agent API supports both synchronous and streaming message handling. However, there is a 120-second timeout, after which time an HTTP 500 response is received.
- At least one activated Agentforce agent must exist in the Salesforce org before creating an Agent API solution. The Agentforce (Default) agent type is not supported by the Agent API, so the activated agent must of a different type.
- Agent API usage impacts credit consumption as specified in the Generative AI Usage and Billing section (*https://oreil.ly/DVhF_*). Each call to the Agent API consumes Einstein Requests where the number of requests used depends on the API call size and the LLM usage type multiplier.
- Agent API supports only Salesforce connected apps, not external client apps.

Creating a Salesforce connected app and enabling OAuth settings is an important step to create Agent API requests (Figure 7-6). Someone with Salesforce administrator access will need to create the connected app and add the connected app to the activated agent. Be sure to follow the Agentforce Developer Guide (*https://oreil.ly/wRWko*) when creating the connected app as there are several different options that need to be selected and/or deselected.

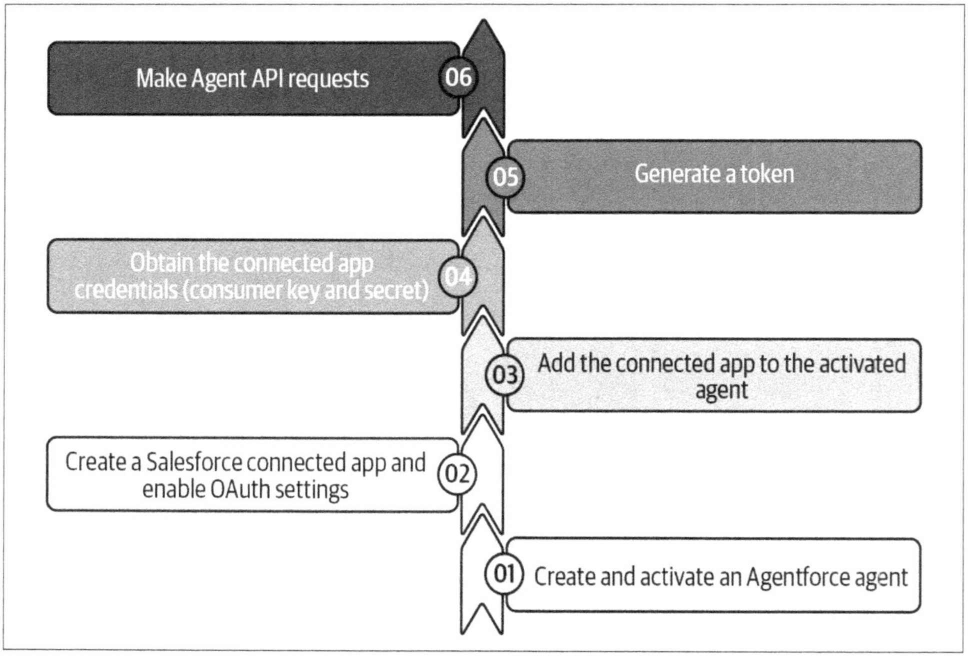

Figure 7-6. Steps needed to create Agent API requests

Creating a session is required to communicate with an agent through the Agent API, and the session ID is used by the agent to keep track of the context throughout the session. Sending and receiving messages using synchronous endpoints is best for simple use cases, especially when the complete response is expected to be returned in its entirety. Streaming endpoints are used when real-time conversations are desired and it's okay for the message content to arrive in chunks.

The Agent API gives Salesforce developers the ability to interact with and control Agentforce agents. Sometimes, though, an Agentforce agent needs secure access to external resources to extend its capabilities. For those use cases, Salesforce DX MCP server is an excellent choice. The Salesforce DX MCP server is a specialized implementation of the MCP designed to facilitate interaction between LLMs and Salesforce orgs.

Salesforce DX MCP Server

LLMs can perform complex tasks using impressive reasoning abilities. However, even the most sophisticated agent has shortcomings because its knowledge is outdated, limited to only the information on which it was trained at a specific point in time. Of course, increasing an agent's knowledge base with current information results in a greater ability to reliably perform an infinite number of more context-aware tasks.

Constant LLM training is infeasible, though. Instead, what if the information could be obtained in real time, as needed, by granting the agent access to external tools and resources where that information resides? Traditionally, developers accomplished these connections by creating custom integration code for each external application, tool, or data source. However, in November 2024, Anthropic released an open source standard for connecting AI applications to external systems.

MCP provides organizations with a "plug-and-play" integration, offering a scalable approach for connecting AI models to real-world data. The ability to dynamically obtain relevant information for an LLM creates more adaptable agents without requiring significant investment and time-consuming development efforts.

MCP is built on a host-client-server architecture (Figure 7-7). MCP hosts are applications that provide an environment for running agents. Within MCP hosts, clients are the components responsible for establishing and maintaining direct connections to MCP servers using the MCP protocol. VS Code, Claude desktop, and agentic frameworks are examples of MCP clients.

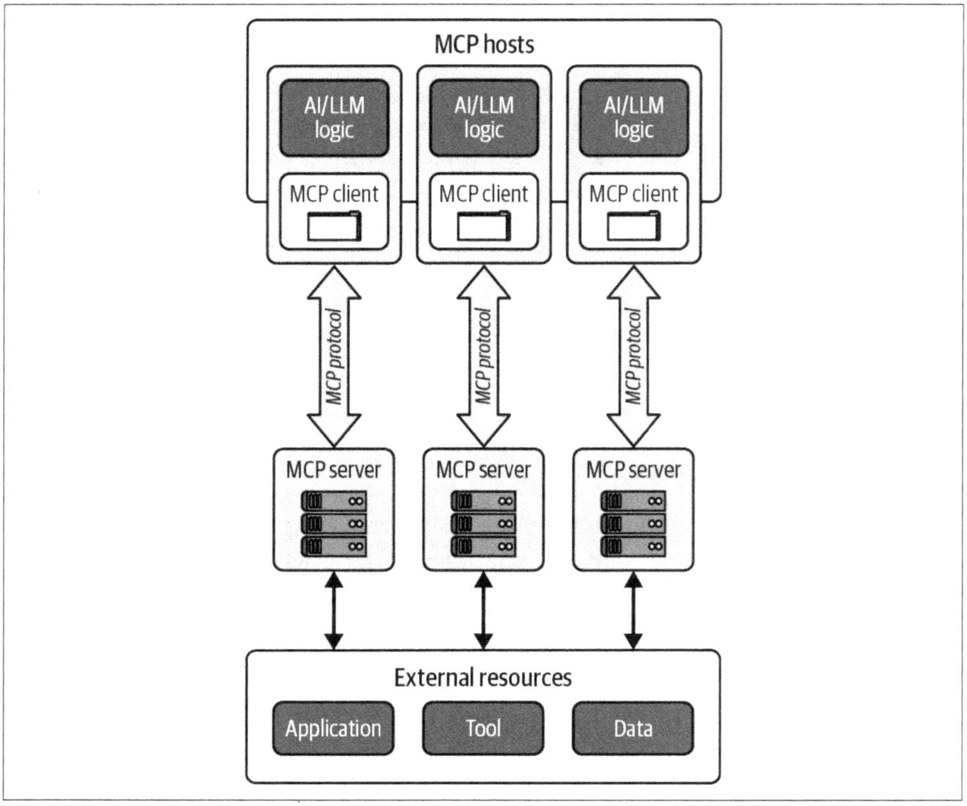

Figure 7-7. MCP host-client-server architecture

MCP servers make resources available for the agent to use. In addition to the MCP server for the Salesforce platform, Salesforce also offers MCP servers for Slack, Heroku, and MuleSoft. Salesforce has even made it possible for Heroku customers to build their own custom MCP server. Even more interesting is that MuleSoft MCP Bridge (MCP Bridge) eliminates the need for building custom MCP connectors and servers. The MCP Bridge is used to handle the mapping of API operations to MCP tools and reduces the need for custom MCP connectors for most use cases. In addition, MCP Bridge converts APIs into MCP servers automatically.

Common external resources available using MCP include applications, tools, and data. Examples of external data resources available from MCP servers include Snowflake, Oracle, and BigQuery. External resource applications with MCP servers include GitHub, Slack, Notion, Google Drive, and Jira. In addition to data and applications, other resources accessible from MCP servers include tools like search engines, calculators, email senders, and workflows such as predefined prompt templates. From within the Agentforce Registry, developers can select an external MCP server from the Salesforce AgentExchange (Figure 7-8) or register an MCP server.

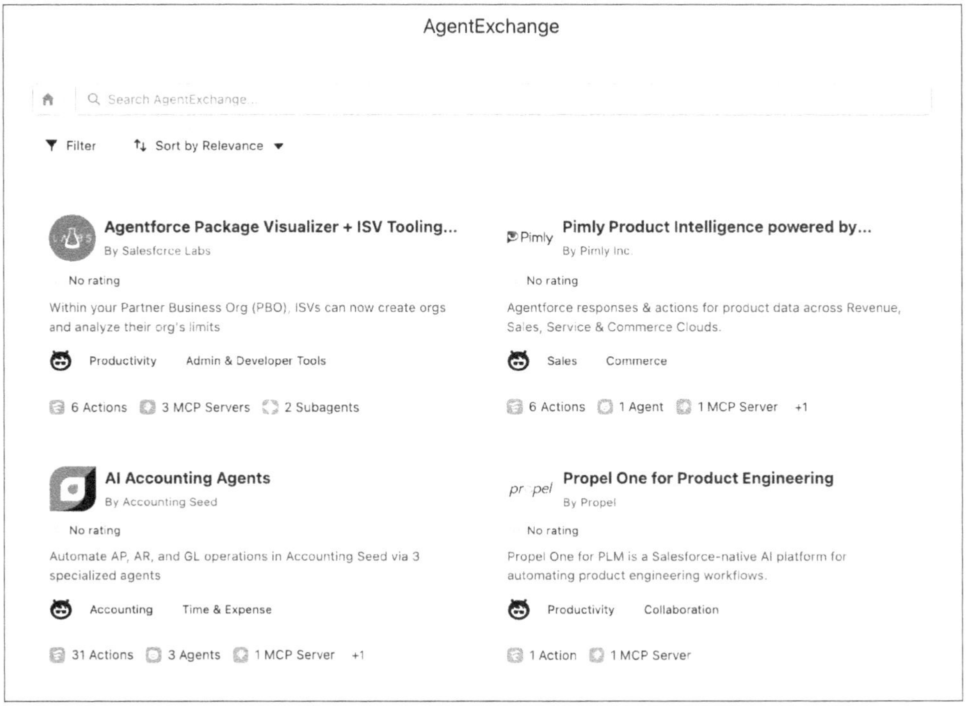

Figure 7-8. Salesforce AgentExchange for MCP servers

MCP is a key component of Agentforce 3. As such, Salesforce announced its local MCP server for developers in May 2025. The open source Salesforce MCP server works with the Salesforce orgs already authenticated in the Salesforce CLI and integrates directly with the DX Foundation libraries used by the CLI.

Salesforce developer's MCP tools are grouped into logical sets so that Agentforce Vibe IDE can dynamically load only the toolsets needed. The following is a list of MCP toolset groups:

- *Core*: set up helpers
- *Metadata*: retrieve and deploy metadata
- *Orgs*: manage and list connected orgs
- *Users*: assign permissions
- *Data*: query org data
- *Logic*: test/run programmatic features

Salesforce expects to release three to five new Salesforce DX MCP tools each month. The following tools will be part of the initial release:

- `sf-list-all-orgs`: lists connected orgs
- `sf-get-username`: identifies the right org username or alias
- `sf-retrieve-metadata`: pulls metadata from a connected org
- `sf-deploy-metadata`: pushes local metadata to a connected org
- `sf-query-org`: runs SOQL queries, returning records as JSON
- `sf-test-apex`: runs Apex tests and test suites

Once they're publicly available, these MCP tools will be accessible within the Agentforce Vibes IDE. Let's explore the Agentforce Vibes IDE and what new functionality is now available for Salesforce developers in that new IDE.

Salesforce-hosted MCP servers are currently in beta with General Availability (GA) targeted for February 2026. This section of the book will be updated as more information about Salesforce MCP servers becomes available.

Agentforce Vibes IDE

Agentforce Vibes IDE is a web-based IDE that recently replaced Salesforce Code Builder. The new IDE comes with Salesforce extensions, the Salesforce CLI, and GitHub integration already installed. Agentforce Vibes IDE is accessible within the Salesforce platform. A user needs only to select Agentforce Vibes from the Setup menu within Salesforce.

However, a Salesforce org admin must accept the terms and conditions for using the IDE before it can be accessed by developers. In addition, the admin needs to grant the View All Data permission to any developer who requires access to the Agentforce Vibes IDE.

Once Agentforce Vibes IDE is open, it's org aware and the metadata from the org is automatically loaded into the Salesforce DX project with automatic authentication. The Agentforce Vibes IDE window includes an activity bar on the left side of the screen (Figure 7-9).

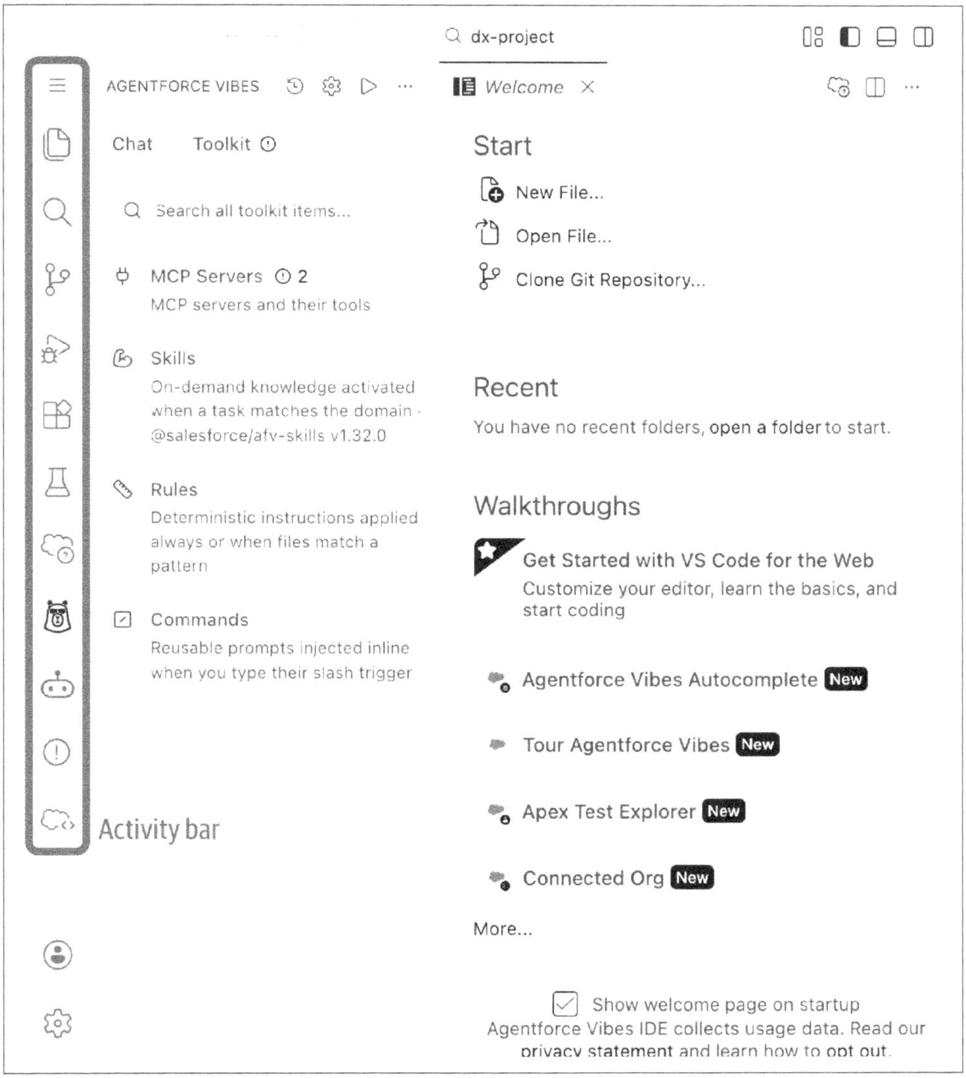

Figure 7-9. Agentforce Vibes IDE window

The activity bar options of the Agentforce Vibes IDE include a new Agentforce Vibes activity option (Figure 7-10).

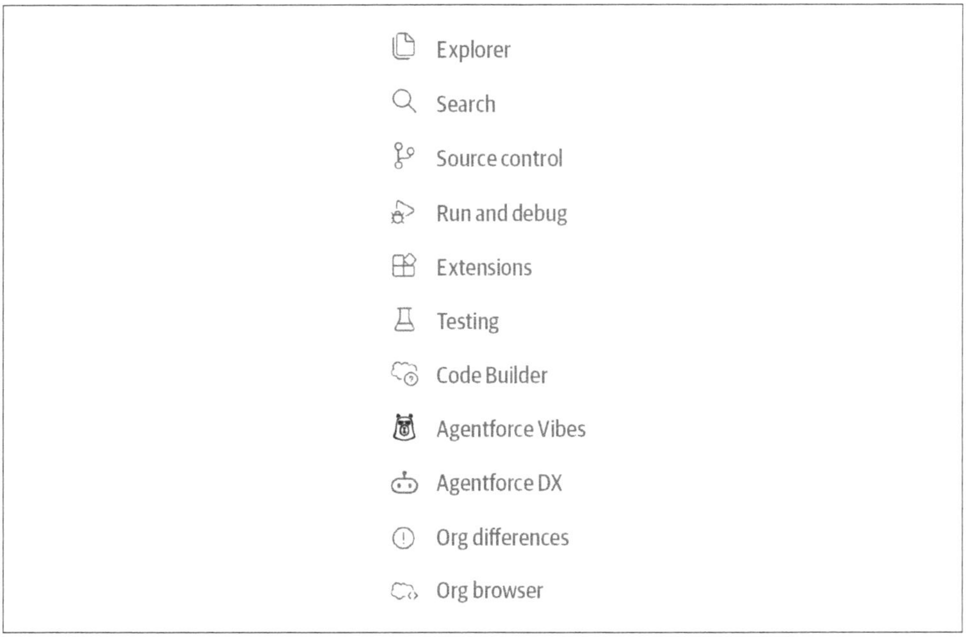

Figure 7-10. Agentforce Vibes IDE activity bar options

The Agentforce Vibes activity option makes possible inline code completion capabilities that suggest code completions to developers when they're creating Apex code or LWC. Agentforce Vibes also gives Salesforce developers the ability to generate Apex code or test cases for Apex methods from natural language prompts.

In addition, the Agentforce Vibes IDE gives developers the ability to preview agent conversations while updating Apex classes and to define complex agent logic using Agent Script. We'll explore the Agent Script programming language in the next section.

Agent Script

Agent Script is a portable JSON expression language used for defining complex agent logic, and much like Python or YAML, Agent Script utilizes indentation to indicate structure. This new scripting language is human-readable, designed for creating easy handoffs, and includes the ability to implement conditional and rule-based business logic for programmatic precision. More predictable and reliable agent behavior is possible with this new programming language because of the ability to incorporate structured business processes into agent reasoning.

Agent Script is a compiled language, which means the code doesn't run directly. Instead, the Agent Script code generates a structured specification known as the Agent Graph, which is consumed by the Atlas reasoning engine (Atlas). The Agent Graph defines reflective loops and multi-subagent or multi-agent coordination, thus ensuring Atlas receives the details needed so that the agent performs as instructed by the Salesforce developer. We explored Atlas and the Agent Graph in detail in Chapter 6.

Previously, we explored the Agentforce Builder Canvas, which is a no-code approach to building agents without the user needing to directly create the underlying Agent Script code. The Canvas view is optimal for simple use cases or for rapid prototyping. However, the Script view gives developers the power to chain actions deterministically, enforce conditional logic, and create precise instructions for when context is passed to the LLM. The Script view is where most development occurs for agents created for an intelligent agentic enterprise.

A Salesforce developer uses a `subagent` block to encapsulate the desired logic. That logic incorporates conditionals, rules, handoffs, and more. Agent Script can be created easily using Agentforce Vibes IDE or within a third-party IDE where the Salesforce extensions have been added. In addition, Agent Script code can be accessed and maintained within Agentforce Builder.

Agent Script is organized into three main categories of blocks: configuration blocks, governance blocks, or execution blocks. Configuration blocks are operational configurations that describe the agent, its defaults, and the languages the agent can access. The `variables` and `connection` blocks are categorized as governance blocks. Execution blocks include the `start_agent` block and `subagent` blocks, reusable components that can exist within several different agents. Let's review the seven different Agent Script blocks now (Table 7-1).

Table 7-1. Agent Script blocks

Block type	Block purpose	Block category
`system`	Defines agent persona, global instructions, and standard messages	Configuration (behavior)
`config`	Core agent metadata and runtime defaults	Configuration (platform/runtime)
`variables`	Declares the global state schema that subagents can read and write	Governance (state schema and data contract)
`language`	Lists which languages the agent supports and how content should be localized	Configuration (capability)
`connection`	Describes how the agent is associated to external channels or entry points	Governance (integration boundary and channel policy)

Block type	Block purpose	Block category
`start_agent`	Special entry-point subagent that executes on every user message and routes to appropriate subagents	Entry/Execution/Flow (global router/dispatcher)
`subagent`	Encapsulates executable logic for a specific capability and includes instructions, deterministic steps, tool calls, and transitions	Execution / Flow (business logic and control flow)

The `system` block is the agent's persona and it's unique to that agent. That block describes how the agent should behave globally and includes any standard welcome or error messages. However, the information in a `subagent` block can override the global system instructions when a different one or constraint is needed. For example, the `system` block might instruct the agent that it's a service agent assistant and that it must always do X and never do Y. A required welcome message is provided along with optional messages for scenarios such as an error message if something goes wrong.

The `config` block provides the agent's identity based on metadata and operational defaults. It's how your agent is recognized by other agents and systems. At a minimum, the agent name and agent type are included. A service agent is somewhat unique because a default agent user is typically set for a service agent.

The `variables` block is used for global state management of the agent and is separate from LLM context memory. Variables can be declared once and reused in Agent Script blocks. They can be set or updated deterministically within the agent logic and can also be used to inject dynamic context within a prompt. For example, the `{!@variables.<variable_name>}` syntax is the way a developer would inject variables dynamically into the LLM prompt instructions. As such, the agent is usually more consistent when relying on deterministic variables rather than LLM conversational memory.

Agent Script supports several variable types:

- Regular variables for a shared state
- Linked variables for binding to external sources, like an action output
- System variables are predefined and prepopulated variables

Regular variables are mutable or immutable variables with types like `string`, `number`, `boolean`, `object`, `date`, `id`, and `list`. A regular variable is one where the variable is initialized with a default value and the agent can change the variable's value. In contrast, a linked variable's value is tied to the source and, thus, the value can't be initialized with a default value and it can't be set by the agent. It also can't be an `object` or `list` variable type. System variables, such as those used to capture a recent utterance, are used in the same places as regular or linked variables in the Agent Script code.

> You don't typically need the @system_variables.user_input variable to capture a recent utterance because the LLM remembers the entire conversation history. However, that particular variable is useful when you need to pass into an action the last thing a user conveyed.

Agent Script variables help you track state that affects agent behavior. They also store data used in conditionals, help pass data among subagents, and are used to show specific information to users. They're required in a reasoning instruction when running an action because you must manually set variables for the inputs and outputs due to the action needing to run before any reasoning takes place. However, you'll want to use variables strategically whenever the agent has access to relevant action inputs. Avoid overusing variables in those situations and, instead, allow the agent to decide the best input rather than being constrained by the variable's data.

The language block declares which language(s) are supported by the agent. Examples include English, French, or Spanish. The language block, combined with the config.default_locale parameter, determines how prompts and the user interface text are selected. The connection block describes how the agent interacts with external channels or systems. This block's information is used in combination with commands like @utils.escalate, which hands off control to a live agent.

The start_agent block is a special subagent that serves as the entry point for subagent classification and routing. From there, developers can use Agent Script to invoke complex transitions using the @utils.transition to command. Agent Script transitions are one-way only. Once the transition is executed, the agent stops working in the current block and discards the existing prompt. Control is immediately passed to the new subagent. Alternatively, the developer can delegate control by referencing a subagent directly inside the reasoning actions. Unlike the declarative transitions, a direct subagent reference works the same way as a standard tool call. Once the directed subagent completes, the flow of control returns to the original subagent.

Subagent blocks encapsulate the agent's executable logic, including agent instructions, deterministic steps, tool calls, and transitions. Subagent actions define capabilities like Flows, Apex code, and APIs, but defining an action doesn't execute it. For that, a reasoning engine is required. We explored the reasoning engine powering Agentforce in detail in Chapter 6.

The Agentforce Builder Canvas groups capabilities together, but Agent Script differentiates between subagent actions and reasoning actions (tools). Subagent actions can be executed every time a subagent is called if a developer uses the @actions.<action_name> command within logic instructions. This works well when data-fetching is required before the LLM begins reasoning. If, instead, the developer wants to let the LLM subjectively decide whether to invoke an action based on context, the action should be exposed as a tool in the `reasoning.actions` portion of the block. Agent Script also introduced the `available when` parameter, making it possible to conditionally show or hide a tool from the reasoning engine based on current variable states.

If you want to explore Agent Script in more detail, there are some excellent resources available from Salesforce including Agent Script Recipes (*https://oreil.ly/TbbeO*), a comprehensive collection ranging from basic concepts to production-ready patterns, and the Agentforce Developer Guide (*https://oreil.ly/3wTpM*) that provides details on how to get started with Agentforce APIs and SDKs.

Summary

In this chapter, we learned about pro-code developer tools for building and managing Agentforce agents. We explored Agentforce DX, Salesforce APIs, Salesforce extensions for IDEs, Salesforce programming languages like Agent Script, and much more. At this point, we have a good understanding of the Salesforce features and tools needed to build an intelligent agentic enterprise. Now, we're ready to focus on important domains within the enterprise like Sales, Service, and Marketing.

In the next chapter, we'll explore agentic sales use cases and workspaces for a unified workforce solution. As part of our discussion, we'll learn about Agentforce out-of-the-box autonomous and semi-autonomous agents. In addition, we'll discover how to enable Salesforce features that are prerequisites for some of the out-of-the-box agents.

CHAPTER 8

Agentic Sales and Workspaces for a Unified Workforce Solution

We learned about individual AI agents (agents) in the previous three chapters and prior to that, we discovered the importance of creating context for chatbots, agents, and humans. We focused our attention on context and agents because they play an important role in the success of an intelligent agentic enterprise. Yet, we know that humans are integral to the agentic enterprise, and the work done by them is essential. Salesforce offers a variety of tool choices for individuals to achieve their work goals.

Earlier, in Chapter 4, we explored Tableau Next, which is an application (app) available directly within the Salesforce platform used by analysts and executives as well as some personas from the sales, service, and marketing teams. Other Salesforce apps available on the platform intended as systems of work for humans include Sales (Figure 8-1), Service, and Marketing, which are all part of a traditional customer relationship management (CRM) software suite.

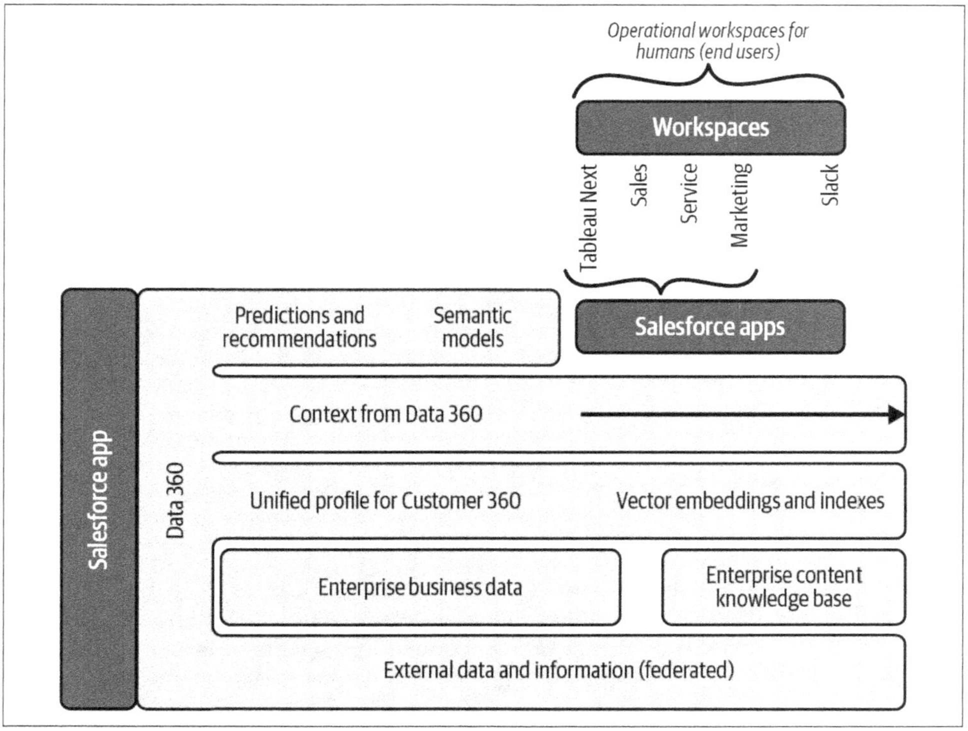

Figure 8-1. Traditional CRM Salesforce apps include the Sales, Service, and Marketing apps

Those apps are excellent systems of work but, as we'll discover in Chapter 11, Slack workspaces are a system of work often preferred by sales, service, and marketing teams. Slack offers collaborative conversational CRM where sales professionals and other employees can work alongside each other while also effectively leveraging an abundance of specialized agents.

Several agents comprise Agentforce Sales and those agents operate within the Salesforce Sales app workspace environment. Agentforce Sales agents can also function within a Slack workspace.

In this chapter, we'll learn about some out-of-the-box Agentforce Sales agents, including two autonomous agents, that operate as part of a unified sales workforce within a Sales workspace. We'll also review examples of agent building blocks specific to sales use cases that are used to support customizing standard agents or creating new agents. But, before we do, we'll need to consider a few things.

Many of the agents available as part of Agentforce Sales require certain prerequisites like Einstein Activity Capture and Einstein Conversation Insights (ECI). Thus, we'll want to explore in detail Einstein Activity Capture, ECI, and ECI-related features.

We'll also learn about Einstein Relationship Insights and Einstein Sales Emails in this chapter. These two features are not agents, but they do provide AI functionality available for sales professionals working in the Sales app on the Salesforce platform.

Getting Started

Let's discuss background knowledge and things you should know to help you get the most out of this chapter.

Background Knowledge

Salesforce offers three distinct Sales and Commerce solution platforms: Commerce Cloud, B2C Commerce Cloud, and Sales Cloud on core (Figure 8-2). Within each of those three sales and commerce platforms, Salesforce offers different levels of capabilities. For example, users can sign up for the Growth and Advanced editions of Commerce Cloud.

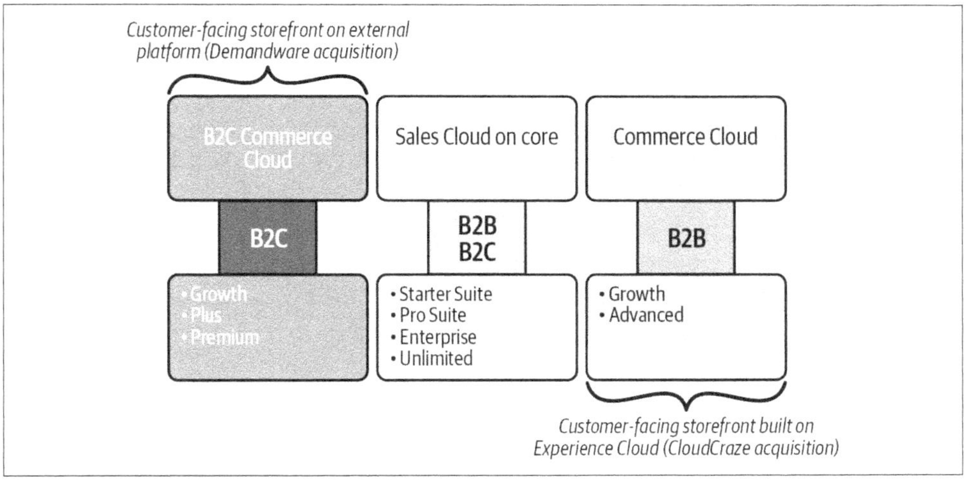

Figure 8-2. Salesforce Sales and Commerce product solution offerings

Commerce Cloud and B2B Commerce Cloud address those sales-specific use cases where the customer sales cycle is shorter, as is common in most ecommerce shopping experiences. As such, they each have a customer-facing storefront.

Previously, Salesforce B2C Commerce Cloud was known as Demandware. B2C Commerce Cloud is an external Salesforce platform considered to be *near-core* rather than *on-core*. Its customer-facing storefront is built on top of the external platform.

The Salesforce Commerce Cloud customer-facing online storefront is built on top of Salesforce Experience Cloud. Commerce Cloud is a B2B solution previously known as CloudCraze. Commerce Cloud began as a native app on the Salesforce core platform.

In contrast, Sales Cloud on core has no online storefront. It's an app used to help internal sales teams close deals on sales that typically have a longer sales cycle. A sales cycle can be defined as the amount of time it takes to close a deal, converting a prospect to a customer. The B2B sales cycle frequently begins with customer research and prospecting, and includes phases for qualification and discovery, presentations, and proposals. Defining the phases makes it easier to identify where deals may be stalled in the sales pipeline so that improvements to the sales processes can be made to shorten the sales cycle.

Salesforce CRM excels at supporting well-defined processes for the sales cycle by providing standardized canonical data models, prebuilt automations, and platform customization options to make a sales force more efficient. Knowing how users typically use Salesforce core features and functionality to manage their sales cycle is key to understanding how AI in the Sales Cloud can be leveraged to help shorten that sales cycle.

In this chapter, we'll focus our attention on AI solutions for sales teams who operate within a longer sales cycle duration. Thus, you'll get the most out of this chapter if you have a basic understanding of Salesforce core sales apps and workflows. Specifically, it's important to be familiar with app objects like Account, Contact, Lead, Campaign, and Opportunity. It's also helpful to understand Salesforce processes such as lead conversion as well as how deals make their way through the various predefined Opportunity stages.

What You Should Know

Salesforce admins have access to new tools that help make it easier for them to discover, set up, and manage Salesforce features like industry cloud setup, workspaces, and Agentforce agents. One of those new features is Salesforce Go, an all-in-one hub designed to simplify the Salesforce admin experience. Salesforce Go, accessible as a menu option after clicking the gear icon, provides more functionality beyond just initial setup of features. Salesforce Go offers visibility into license usage and adoption metrics and it also consolidates product documentation and learning resources.

When admins enable Salesforce AI features, Einstein Generative AI and Agentforce are required. There are also some common prerequisites and steps that admins will need to complete prior to deploying Agentforce Sales agents:

- Einstein Activity Capture
- Einstein Conversation Insights

- Salesforce Inbox
- Salesforce Forecasting
- Salesforce Sales Engagement

Not all agents for Sales requires every prerequisite and not all prerequisites are within the scope of this chapter. We'll cover in detail Einstein Activity Capture and ECI because both of those features are AI-specific, they're required for Sales workspace, and they both have important limitations and considerations.

> Throughout the book, we've described the Einstein Conversation Insights feature, but you may find a different term in the Salesforce documentation. Salesforce announced a name change in July 2026. The new name is Conversation Intelligence.

It's expected that different enterprises are at different stages of their AI maturity and, thus, will focus on those features that are most relevant at that stage. For Enterprise sales teams, the focus occurs in five fundamental levels of maturity:

Level 1
: Data foundation strengthening

Level 2
: Workflow automations for increased efficiency

Level 3
: Predictive AI for a more targeted approach

Level 4
: Generative AI for faster responses

Level 5
: Agents for scaling sales teams

Data foundation strengthening is accomplished using Data 360 (D360) for harmonizing data and preparing a unified customer profile. Automations include creating workflows for quote creation, renewal reminders, contract approvals, and new customer onboarding. Increasing forecast accuracy and prioritizing the best leads and opportunities are examples of using predictive AI for smarter selling. Generative AI features that summarize deals, suggest next steps, draft emails, and provide conversation insights help sellers act faster. Agents are used to manage the sales pipeline autonomously, engage with and nurture leads 24/7, provide conversational deal help, and coach sales reps.

At level 5, humans and agents are working together as a unified workforce for the purposes of growing the sales pipeline, growing deals, and growing revenue. In the chapter, we'll discuss specific agents and standard subagents and actions for sales use cases that are available at the time of publication. Existing agents' names or assigned skills could change. In addition, it's expected new agents, subagents, and actions will be added. Thus, you'll want to review Salesforce documentation for the most up-to-date information.

In addition, we won't discuss in this chapter which specific licenses or packages must be acquired, details of consumption costs, or which permission sets are required to achieve the functionality described. For one thing, the exact licenses required change over time, and consumption costs and licensing fees are negotiated. Thus, your Salesforce Account Executive (AE) and implementation partner can best answer those questions.

Smart Productivity on Core with Einstein Activity Capture

Using Einstein Activity Capture, email and calendar events can be automatically added to the Salesforce activity timeline of related records. In addition, there are related features that can be turned on that will provide email insights, automatically add and update contact records, and offer recommended relationships. Let's explore Einstein Activity Capture and related features now.

Einstein Activity Capture

Einstein Activity Capture is a productivity tool that keeps three types of data synced between Salesforce and a user's email and calendar app: Emails, Events, and Contacts. Emails sent and received by Einstein Activity Capture users are used to create email insights and can be used to generate engagement data. Synced events become Salesforce records and are available in standard reporting. Synced contacts are used to create email insights and recommended connections.

There is quite a bit of flexibility in how Einstein Activity Capture can be set up and used in a Salesforce org. For each Einstein Activity Configuration, it's possible to choose only one, two, or all three data options for including emails, events, and contacts in the configuration. The admin can also choose whether to create the sync only in one direction or bidirectionally. In addition, you can decide which users will be assigned to a particular configuration.

Considerations and limitations of Einstein Activity Capture

There are some very important considerations that should be reviewed before enabling Einstein Activity Capture. These are some of the most important ones. You can review Salesforce documentation (*https://oreil.ly/g25Uv*) for the entire list of considerations for setting up Einstein Activity Capture:

- Einstein Activity Capture users who don't use Inbox must be in an active configuration to connect an account.
- Turning on Einstein Activity Capture in Government Cloud organizations can send data outside the authorization boundary.
- Connected email accounts can only be the email address on the Salesforce user's record and it cannot be an email alias.
- Einstein Activity Capture users can't delete emails that Einstein Activity Capture adds to Salesforce.
- It's not possible to use Einstein Activity Capture and Lightning Sync at the same time.

Einstein Activity Capture is well-suited for testing in a sandbox environment. No data is copied from production to sandbox for Einstein Activity Capture, so you're able to use the sandbox for testing. The Einstein Activity Capture feature needs to be enabled in each new sandbox or whenever a sandbox is refreshed.

How to enable Einstein Activity Capture

Enabling Einstein Activity Capture requires steps to be completed by the Salesforce admin and the end user. The admin needs to choose a connection method and complete the necessary steps. These are the three possible email and calendar services that can be connected to Salesforce: Google G Suite, Microsoft Office 365, and Microsoft Exchange. The steps to enable Einstein Activity Capture are extensive and vary greatly between the three choices. Therefore, it's recommended you review the Salesforce documentation (*https://oreil.ly/dnj18*) for the complete instructions.

After the connection is established, the administrator needs to choose the configuration types. The flow of data is enabled to move in both directions, where applicable, but an admin can change the default settings. The Salesforce admin can exclude emails and events from being added to Salesforce. The admin can also set default activity and enable more features for Einstein Activity Capture.

Salesforce end users also need to complete steps for enabling Einstein Activity Capture after the admin is finished with their part. Users will need to connect their email and calendar to Salesforce, but the specific steps to be taken by end users are dependent on the choices made by the Salesforce admin during setup. It's recommended that the admin review the Salesforce documentation (*https://oreil.ly/1o0Ze*) and provide the relevant instructions to end users. Admins should also notify users that it takes up to 24 hours for emails and events to be added to Salesforce after Einstein Activity Capture has been enabled by users.

Einstein Activity Capture-Related Features

It's possible to enable some additional features, if desired, once Einstein Activity Capture has been set up. You'll just need to search in the Quick Find box for these features and then toggle on the ones to enable.

Einstein Email Insights

The Einstein Email Insights feature picks up signals from an email conversation between a sales rep and a customer or prospect and assigns standard labels such as Pricing Discussed, Scheduling Involved, or Competitor Mentioned. Using these labels gives sales reps a quick way to focus on what's important in their email communications.

When custom Email Insights are used, it's possible for sales reps to edit keywords used in the insights. However, there is a maximum limit of 10 keywords per custom insight label. For greater flexibility, it's even possible to combine insights with each other and with keywords.

Einstein Recommended Connections

When enabled, the Einstein Recommended Connections feature displays details about which of the sales rep's colleagues have the strongest connections to a prospect. The details include the name of the colleague, a brief explanation of the interaction between the colleague and the prospect, and whether the strength of the connection between the colleague and the prospect is low, medium, or high.

The Einstein Recommended Connections component can be added to standard contact and lead page layouts. The component can also be added to Person Accounts page layouts if your organization uses Person Accounts.

Einstein Automatic Contact Creation

The Einstein Automatic Contact Creation feature replaces Einstein Automated Contacts, which was retired. The Automatic Contact Creation feature uses the email and event activity from Einstein Activity Capture to find new contacts and opportunity contact roles to add to Salesforce.

The threshold for event activity and email activity is set in advance, and then a new contact record is created in Salesforce after one of the following situations occurs:

- Event activity shows the Salesforce user met with an external person the number of times specified in the threshold.
- Email activity shows the Salesforce user receives a specified number of emails from the external person.

It's important to note that new contact records created automatically by this Einstein feature will not be updated by the Einstein Automatic Contact Enhancements feature, described in the next section, unless the contact is included in a Buyer Relationship Map.

Einstein Automatic Contact Enhancements

The Einstein Automatic Contact Enhancements feature builds content-rich profiles for Salesforce contacts, thus better enabling buyer relationship maps to also be kept up-to-date. This feature needs the Buyer Relationship Map feature, along with Einstein Activity Capture, to be enabled beforehand.

Einstein Automatic Contact Enhancements use generative AI to identify buyer attributes, department group, and seniority level of a customer or prospect from the Salesforce user's email activity. Those three values are then added to the contact record and appear in the buyer relationship map.

The Seniority Level field reflects the hierarchical position of the contact. The Department Group field represents the business unit, function, or department that contacts belong to in their organization. The Buyer Attributes field, an optional field for the buyer relationship map, reflects the roles that contacts have on a deal or account.

Two groups of fields are updated with the Automatic Contact Enhancements feature: the three fields that update the buyer relationship map and eight additional fields that update various fields on the contact record. If any of those 11 fields are updated manually, the Automatic Contact Enhancements feature will stop updating fields for the group in which that field belongs.

In addition to the three fields used for the buyer relationship map, there is another group of eight additional fields on the contact page that get updated by Einstein Automatic Contact Enhancements. Those fields include: `Fax`, `MailingCity`, `MailingCountry`, `MailingPostalCode`, `MailingState`, `MailingStreet`, `Phone` (business phone), and `Title`.

We've seen many ways Einstein Activity Capture can make sales teams more efficient, but it's not the only way teams can improve efficiency. Salesforce offers another tool out-of-the-box that help sales teams be more productive and, at the same time, gives reps the ability to craft a more personal message. Let's learn more about Salesforce's smart content creation feature known as Einstein Sales Emails.

Smart Content Creation on Core with Einstein Sales Emails

Another generative AI (GenAI) feature that comes out-of-the-box is the Einstein Sales Emails feature, which can be used to generate personalized emails for contacts and leads. Sales Emails uses existing Salesforce data to add context and personalization. For example, when sending an email to a Salesforce contact, the following fields are used for adding context and personalization: Account, Name, and Title. For emails sent to leads, the following fields are used: Company, Industry, Name, and Title.

When the Einstein Sales Emails feature is available, a "Draft with Einstein" button appears on the screen that can be clicked to start the process (Figure 8-3). Sales reps can create new emails by using standard email types available out-of-the-box or custom email types created by a Salesforce admin. Some examples of standard email types include the following: Check In, Introduce Myself, Nudge for Follow-Up, Reconnect, and Send Meeting Invite.

Because Einstein Sales Emails uses GenAI, which is known to include inaccurate or harmful responses, a human review for accuracy and safety of the output is recommended. Of course, a user can generate a new output by starting over if the output fails to meet expectations. Keep in mind, however, that each draft of the email consumes usage against the subscription allowance.

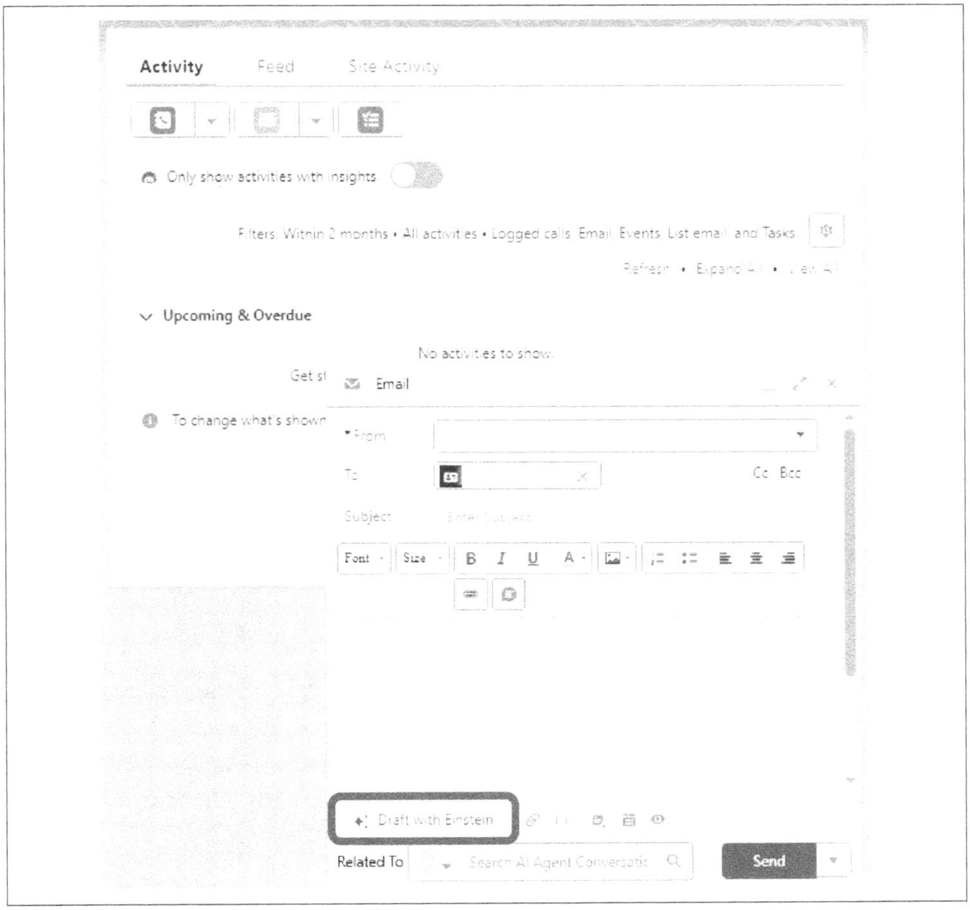

Figure 8-3. Email screen with the option to "Draft with Einstein"

Considerations and Limitations of Einstein Sales Emails

There are some important considerations for enabling Einstein Sales Emails:

- Sales Emails is available in Salesforce Sites but not in Government Cloud orgs.
- Field-level security is enforced, so a sales rep sees a placeholder instead of a value whenever a field is needed for which the user doesn't have access.

There are some important considerations for using Einstein Sales Emails:

- At least one recipient should be listed in the To field and if more than one recipient is listed, Salesforce drafts an email for the first person in the list that matches to a contact or lead record. A recipient must have a lead or contact record in Salesforce.
- Sales Emails supports generating content for new emails but does not draft content for messages where the user replies to an email.
- In addition to the content in the body of the email, Einstein Sales creates content for the subject line.
- Emails can be generated in the following languages: English, French, German, Italian, Japanese, and Spanish. If your desired language isn't listed, be sure to check updates because Salesforce often expands feature support for more languages over time.

How to Enable Einstein Sales Emails

Toggling on this feature gives users the ability to send emails directly from within Salesforce using the Einstein Sales Emails feature to generate the email:

1. Go to Setup > Quick Find Box > Einstein for Sales. Toggle on the Enabled button.
2. Optional step. Emails can be sent directly from Salesforce, but for users who want to send emails from Outlook or Gmail, the admin needs to make sure the Gmail or Outlook integration and sync is enabled and then also edit custom layouts under the Email Application Panes in the Lightning component.

Sales reps' external email accounts will also need to be connected if it's desirable to use Einstein Sales Emails to send emails using Outlook or Gmail.

Using the Einstein Sales Emails capability helps sales teams create more personalized content for emails sent to recipients who have been prioritized based on predictive scoring. For example, personalized emails would be sent to leads with an associated high lead score and to contacts who are key decision makers for prioritized opportunities. For these efforts to be successful, though, it's important that relationship insights be accurate and complete. Salesforce offers the Einstein Relationship Insights feature to assist in that effort.

Einstein Relationship Insights

Just knowing the context around an organization and its contacts is a major challenge many sales reps encounter. It also isn't easy to understand relationships between organizations. Researching to learn more about these relationships and to identify key decision makers in an organization is often a time-consuming manual process.

Instead of manually researching the web and reviewing internal documents, sales reps can use Einstein AI capabilities to scan web content and internal document repositories to discover key relationship networks that were previously unknown. When appropriate, sales reps can use the results to create new Salesforce Account or Contact records to capture the new information.

Sales reps can use Einstein Relationship Insights (ERI) directly within Salesforce while exploring Account and Contact records. Click the Einstein tab to view Einstein Insights within the Salesforce Sales app. Alternatively, sales reps can also access ERI in their browser toolbar while exploring the web.

When accessing ERI within Salesforce, a user can view related person and company records in a graph view. The graph view includes circles representing Account and Contact entities and lines representing the relationship between the entities. A dotted line connection indicates a recommended relationship, and a solid line connection indicates a defined relationship that is either a lookup, master-detail, or many-to-many structured relationship. A user can click the Open icon next to an established Account or Contact record to view the details. Alternatively, the user can click the Add icon to add the recommended Account or Contact entity to Salesforce.

While looking at the graph view, a Salesforce user can explore evidence supporting the recommended relationship between two entities. Selecting two specific entities from the graph allows a user to explore public documents from various sources that support the relationship between the two entities. Next to the supported evidence is the trashcan icon available for the user to access whenever an evidence document should be dismissed.

In addition, a sales rep can use ERI while exploring the web since ERI can be installed as an extension in the Chrome browser. Once the user has navigated to a website and clicks the Explore button on the ERI in the sidebar, the people and organizations with existing Salesforce records will be highlighted in blue on the website. The Open icon appears when hovering over the blue highlighted text.

People and organizations highlighted in red signify that those individuals and companies don't exist in the Salesforce org. The Add icon appears when hovering over the red highlighted text. In addition, the user can also select names not highlighted on the web page and create their corresponding Account or Contact record in Salesforce.

Considerations and Limitations for ERI

There are some important considerations for ERI:

- ERI is supported by a single instance hosted on Salesforce-managed Hyperforce infrastructure in the AWS US East region. Make sure you've considered important implications, including data residency requirements, before enabling ERI for your Salesforce org.
- ERI can be integrated with Actionable Relationship Center (ARC) so that users can create Account and Person records and Account-Contact and Contact-Contact relationships in ARC for the new records. ARC is available in industry clouds such as Education Cloud, Financial Services Cloud, and Nonprofit Cloud.
- ERI can be connected with Salesforce Files, including the files in Chatter feeds and comments, records, and libraries. Exploring documents in Salesforce Files allows for the discovery of more connections.
- Not all editions provide the full functionality described in this section. Be sure to ask your Salesforce AE for additional information about the functionality provided by the licenses available in your org.
- Within ERI, the Contact record is frequently the default Person record object selected, and the Account record is typically the Company record object chosen. However, it's possible to designate different Salesforce objects for those record objects.

How to Enable ERI

Enabling ERI requires steps to be completed by the Salesforce admin in a Salesforce org. To get the most from ERI features, the end user will also need to complete steps for installing the browser extension for ERI.

Before enabling ERI, the admin needs to configure content sources like X/Twitter or Slack so users can explore relationships. Also, ensure custom objects for the Person record object or Company record object field are search-enabled.

The Salesforce admin will complete the following steps to enable ERI:

1. Go to Setup > Quick Find box > Einstein > Einstein Relationship Intelligence. Turn on Einstein Relationship Insights.
2. Configure up to five Person record objects, such as Contact, and up to five Company record objects, like Account (Figure 8-4). Be sure to select the necessary record types, if appropriate. Select the display fields to be used for matching the records.

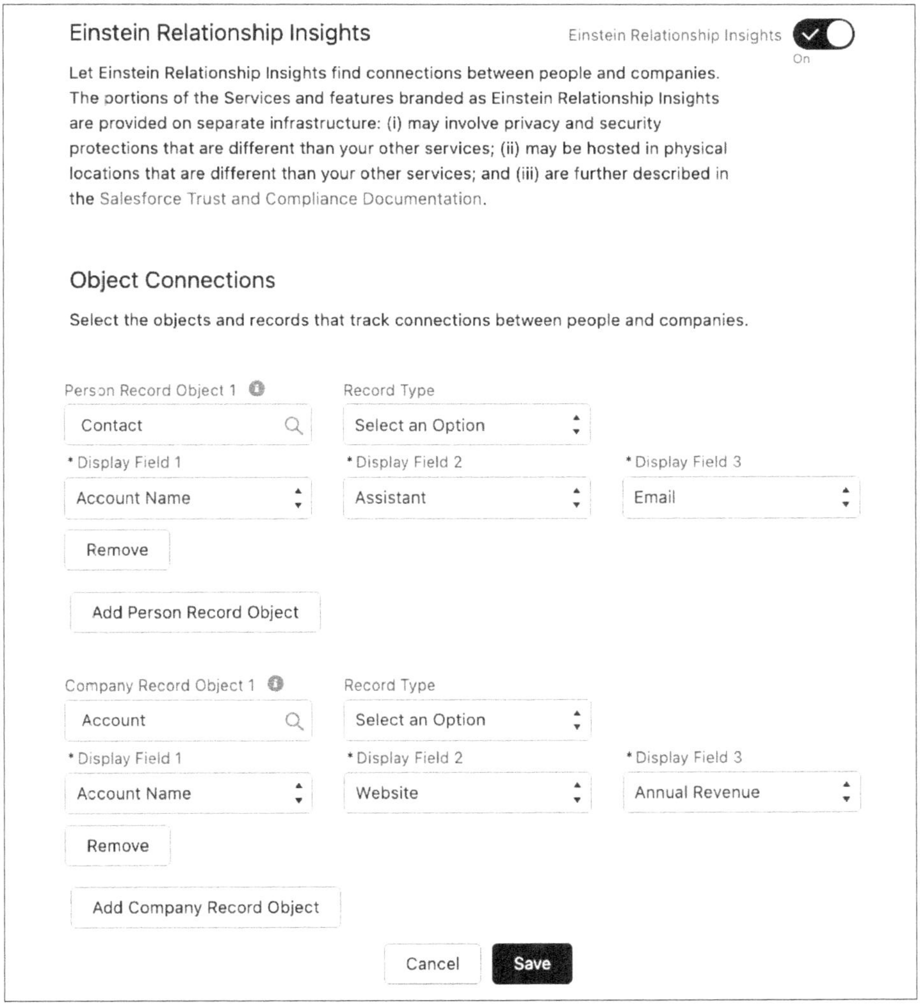

Figure 8-4. Einstein Relationship Insights configuration

3. Under Content Sources, move content sources you've configured to the selected list for all content sources you want enabled for your users (Figure 8-5). Save your work.

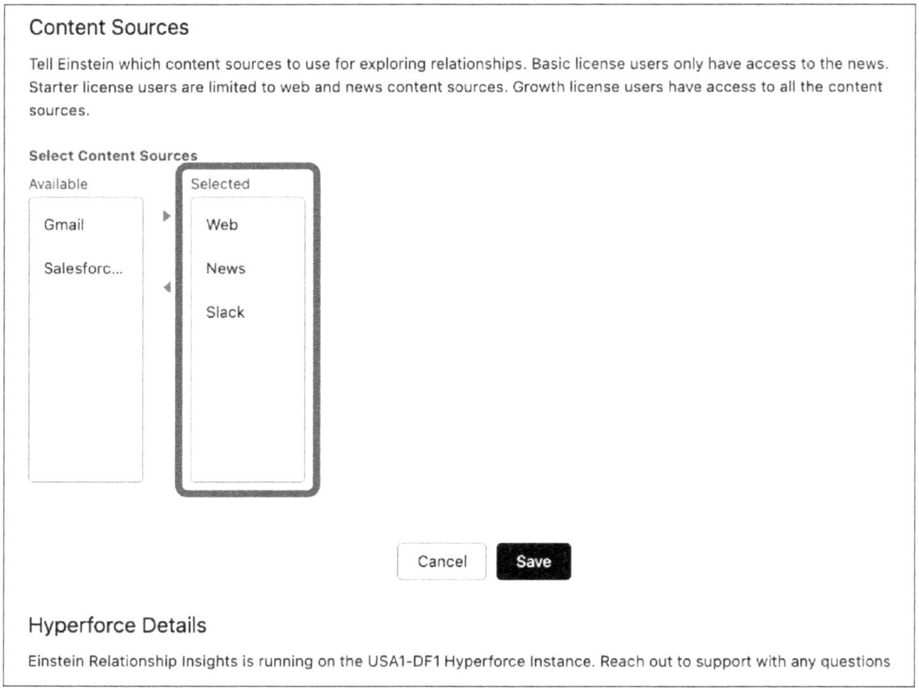

Figure 8-5. Einstein Relationship Insights content sources selection

4. Add the ERI Lightning component to the Account and Contact page layouts.

Salesforce end users need to install the web or browser extension to take advantage of ERI while researching on the web:

1. Navigate to the Salesforce page where the ERI component appears and click the setup icon. The ERI component will most likely be found on the Account and/or Contact record pages.
2. Next, select the browser extension for Chrome under browser extensions. Click Add to Chrome and select Add Extension. Click the toolbar and sign in to Einstein Relationship Insights to begin using ERI.
3. Explore the web using the browser extension by clicking Explore on the sidebar. The user will need to make sure they're signed into ERI.

ERI is able to uncover previously unknown relationships and can be useful for helping sales reps craft the right email message to send to the right person. A sales rep doesn't have to craft that email message alone. In "Smart Content Creation on Core with Einstein Sales Emails" on page 304, we discovered how sales teams can make use of the Einstein Sales Email feature.

Sales teams frequently communicate with leads and contacts by phone, in addition to sending them email messages. Salesforce offers sales teams and their managers a few tools that can assist with these efforts. For example, the Sales Coach agent helps sales reps improve their communications. The agent does so with the assistance of the Einstein Conversation Insights features. To better understand and evaluate these options, let's start by reviewing Einstein Conversation Insights now. We'll explore the Sales Coach agent a little later in this chapter.

Einstein Conversation Insights and Related Features

Einstein Conversation Insights (ECI) is a GenAI tool designed specifically so sales teams can unlock the full potential of sales conversations by automating sales reps' administrative tasks and accelerating time-to-close with actionable insights. These achievements are made possible because ECI provides users with the ability to extract conversation trends and visualize insights.

ECI and ECI-related features are powered by Agentforce, Einstein's GenAI capabilities. ECI is a powerful tool for sales teams that includes built-in capabilities like Call Insights, Call Transcript Snippets, and Call Trend Summary. In addition, it's possible to enable additional ECI functionality such as Call Summaries, Call Explorer, and Sales Signals.

Einstein Conversation Insights Powered by Agentforce

Let's explore how ECI processes actually work (Figure 8-6). First, the Salesforce admin enables ECI, connects it to a recording system, and then informs ECI what keywords are relevant to the sales team. ECI goes to work collecting recorded conversations and processing those recordings for transcription and detection of insights. Once recordings are processed, sales teams can use Conversation Insights to identify key moments, action items, and trends.

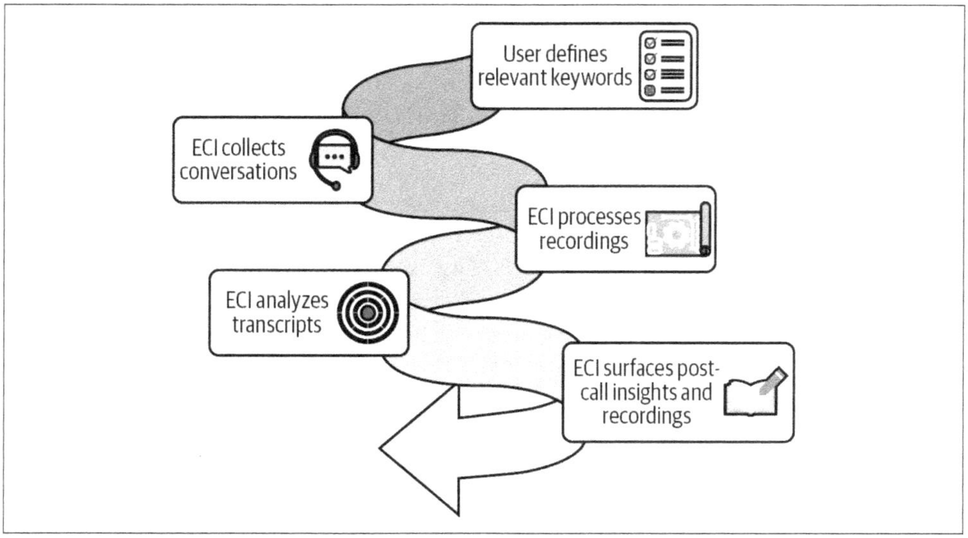

Figure 8-6. How Einstein Conversation Insights works

ECI supports about 40 different languages for analyzing transcripts. However, the automatic insights available from analyzing those transcripts, including Next Steps and objection-related insights, can vary widely by language. Lastly, relevant call records and insights are surfaced in a variety of different dashboard views. For example, sales managers can quickly see talk-to-listen ratios visually because each participant's information is displayed in different colors.

ECI includes built-in functionality including Call Insights, Call Transcript Snippets, and Call Trend Summary. Within Call Insights, Einstein flags key moments across all sales conversations using unique keywords like references to competitor products or features and any mentions of keywords important to closing deals. Automatic Insights for Sales include the following:

Next Steps
: Follow-up, scheduling, and action items mentioned in calls

Pricing Mentioned
: Quotes, cost, payment, and purchase orders mentioned

Challenges
: Issues such as time, additional approval, or other challenge-related phrases

Trending
: Recent words or phrases that appear in a significant pattern across calls

Longest Monologue
: The longest employee talk time relative to the call

Longest Customer Story
: Customer's longest turn speaking in a call

Question
: Questions asked during the call

Objection—Budget
: Objection related to price

Objection—Authority
: Objection calling for input from someone else

Objection—Need
: Objection related to a lack of interest or need

Objection—Timing
: Objection indicating that the timing isn't right

The many out-of-the-box automatic insights can be used for sales and service use cases. However, even though ECI can be used with Service Cloud, it is optimized for sales conversations and, thus, many ECI features for Call Insights, Call Transcript Snippets, and Call Trend Summary are limited to sales use cases.

Call Transcript Snippets lets users drill down when more context is needed for any particular moment. Call Trend Summary provides a visualization of conversation trends across teams, reps, opportunities, or opportunity amounts.

Considerations and limitations for Einstein Conversation Insights

There are many considerations and limitations for ECI. Here are some of the most important considerations:

- To enable ECI, Change Data Capture is required.
- ECI isn't supported in Experience Cloud sites or Salesforce Government Cloud.
- ECI stores some data using a cloud provider in the United States, but data from European orgs is stored in Europe. However, all processing occurs in the United States.
- There are limits to the number of processed hours of calls per year per license. Be sure to discuss these limits with your Salesforce AE.
- Voice and video call record access for Salesforce users is controlled by role hierarchy and sharing rules by default. Thus, managers can review calls made by their entire team.
- Salesforce employees can access and review ECI data, including recorded phone calls or video meetings, for the purposes of improving and training the product.

- ECI is compatible with Sales Dialer out of the box, in addition to Google Meet, Microsoft Teams, and Zoom Meetings for video calls. Dialpad, RingCentral, Aircall, and Amazon Connect are supported but require additional setup.
- Video calls are not processed if they include over 40 participants or if the voice call is shorter than 10 seconds. Video calls over three hours in duration may not process properly.
- ECI features that rely on D360, such as Sales Signals, are not currently testable in a sandbox.
- File types supported include MP3, FLAC, WAV, MP4, and M4A file types, but MP4 files are supported for video only. Each recording is limited to 64 MB.

How to enable Einstein Conversation Insights

Here are the main steps to enable ECI:

1. Go to Setup > Quick Find box > Einstein Conversation Insights.
2. Select General Settings then toggle on the Conversation Insights. It could take several hours for the process to complete, and the Conversations Readiness indicator lets you know when the related dashboards are ready.

> Do not toggle off and on again the button for the Conversation Insights. If you do so, it's likely you'll need to reach out to Salesforce customer support for assistance if you're not able to successfully troubleshoot the issue.

3. Click Connect to connect a voice recording provider. You'll want to connect at least one recording provider.
4. Click Connect to connect video recording providers such as Zoom Meetings, Google Meet, or Microsoft Teams.

> Connecting to voice and video recording providers is your responsibility and, as such, it's also your responsibility to manage consent and comply with local privacy requirements in the way calls are recorded.

5. Optional. Some features aren't required to use ECI but they can be enabled, if appropriate. These features can be turned on: Optimal Speaker Separation, related record matching to automatically match related records to voice and video calls, and insights reports and conversation-related measures for enablement. You can also set the frequency for call highlight emails.
6. Set up Call Insights with the following steps. These steps allow you to configure keyword insights related to mentions of competitors and products that are relevant to your organization. You can also create custom keyword insights for when words or phrases relevant to your teams are mentioned. It's possible to create up to 100 custom insights and each insight can have a maximum of 25 keywords:
    a. Go to Setup > Quick Find box > Call Insights.
    b. Select Configure Insight from the Configurable tab.
    c. Select Keyword Insight or Generative Insight and follow the steps provided.

> Make sure to avoid keywords or phrases that would flag sensitive information that would jeopardize the trust, safety, and privacy of callers and don't include words that would inadvertently or inappropriately affect people based on gender, religion, race, sexual orientation, income level, or any other sensitive category.

    d. Activate and save any relevant keyword insights.

As with all Salesforce AI features, make sure you assign the appropriate permission sets to users so that they have access to any newly enabled features.

Einstein Conversation Insights-Related Features

It's possible to enable some additional features, if desired, once Einstein Conversation Insights has been set up. You'll just need to search in the Quick Find box for these features and then toggle on the ones you want to enable. Alternatively, admins can use Salesforce Go functionality (Figure 8-7) to navigate setting up ECI and ECI-related features.

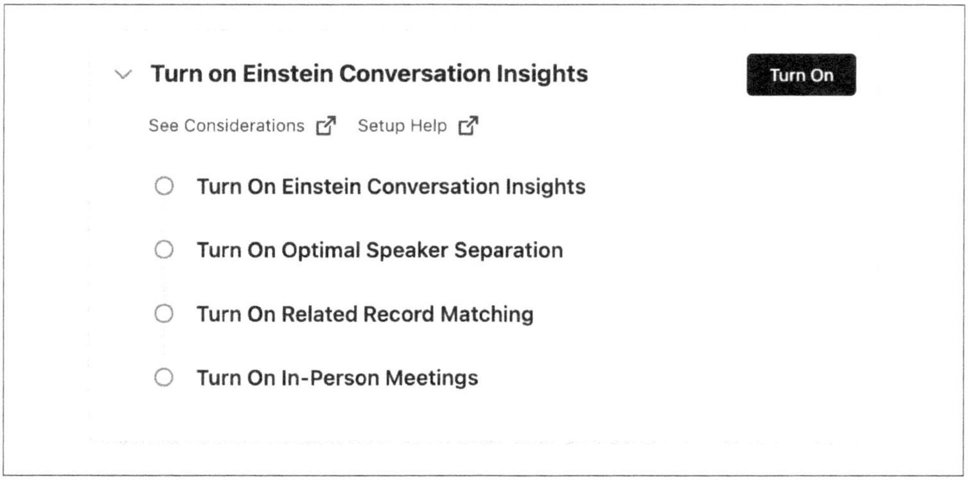

Figure 8-7. Turning on Einstein Conversation Insights within Salesforce Go

Let's explore some of the ECI-related features now. Specifically, we'll learn about Call Summaries, Call Explorer, and Sales Signals.

Call Summaries powered by Einstein Generative AI

Calls and Call Summaries are available in the Call Summaries–related list Lightning Web Component (LWC) on a record page. Use Call Summaries to create a summary for a voice or video call by clicking the Create Call Summary button for the desired call. The Call Summaries feature allows Salesforce users to create editable summaries that can include customer feedback and action items for next steps. Call Summaries can be enabled from Setup after ECI setup is complete.

Call Explorer powered by Einstein Generative AI

While in the meeting playback section, users can click any of the Call Insights tags like Pricing or Challenges to listen to the parts of the conversation that are most relevant. When used as a standard Agentforce action, Call Explorer provides one answer per question, and previous queries and answers are not stored. Call Explorer can be enabled after ECI setup is completed, from Setup or Salesforce Go, and it's also available within Agentforce as a standard action.

Sales Signals powered by Einstein Generative AI

Sales Signals reviews the team's sales calls and highlights important information that sales managers care about most like customer sentiment and what is being said about products and competitors. Einstein provides valuable details like frequency of mentions and deals impacted.

Prior to setting up Sales Signals, both ECI and D360 need to be enabled. D360 needs to be enabled because connecting Sales Signals starts a D360 sync process of historical transcript and insight data up to six months. The connection to D360 also ensures insights data is captured and stored in D360 Cloud going forward. Setting up Sales Signals also requires the configuration of keyword insights within Setup.

After enabling Sales Signals, open the Conversation Insights app and select the Signals tab to access Sales Signals. Next, select either the Product or Competitor category and a keyword to display a dashboard of relevant conversations about the keyword. Conversations are sorted by subagent and display relevant metrics for each subagent on various cards within the dashboard. By default, subagents are sorted based on the highest opportunity values, but users can also sort by sentiment, total signals, and more.

Insights about obstacles or opportunities are easier to see by drilling into each subagent for more details that help uncover trends that are stalling deals. Sales Signals supports up to one refresh every seven days.

Using Sales Signals incurs Einstein usage fees based on application programming interface (API) calls to the LLM gateway and also consumes D360 credits because Sales Signals leverages both Einstein and D360 features. In addition, while ECI supports many languages, Sales Signals is currently only supported in English.

Sales Workspace

Sales workspace is an AI-powered hub in Agentforce Sales that brings together agents, predictive insights, analytics, and humans in one central location. Let's learn more about the Sales workspace including how an admin turns on the workspace in the Salesforce org and how the end user completes the setup.

Enhanced Collaboration for a Unified Workforce

Salesforce pioneered cloud CRM and provided sales reps a centralized space for managing pipeline and customer data with leads, contacts, and opportunities. Workflow automation for tasks such as approval routing and reminders made it so that sales reps spent less time on administrative work. Platform extensibility meant sales objects and workflow could be customized for an enterprise's exact sales motion.

Other innovations came later including mobile app access, Chatter for collaboration, and near-real-time updates, which meant sales reps could work together more easily and also manage deals in the field. Einstein ML predictive capabilities led to better prioritization of leads and opportunities for sales reps and more deal insights. And now, agentic AI with Agentforce and MuleSoft along with enhanced collaboration with Slack and Sales workspace have laid the necessary foundations for a unified workforce.

We've explored Agentforce and MuleSoft in previous chapters, and we'll learn about Slack in Chapter 11. Now, let's focus on exploring the Sales workspace, which allows sales reps to monitor key performance metrics and get AI-driven recommendations for next steps that can be taken directly from the sales rep's home page. Accessing the Sales workspace requires a Salesforce admin to first turn on the workspace and, then, each user needs to complete the workspace setup themselves. Afterward, the agents and Salesforce users work together to achieve sales goals.

Sales Workspace Turned on by the Salesforce Admin

A Salesforce admin navigates to Salesforce Go and selects Sales Workspace (Figure 8-8) to begin the process of turning on the Sales workspace. There are several prerequisites including turning on Einstein Activity Capture and ECI, both of which were described previously.

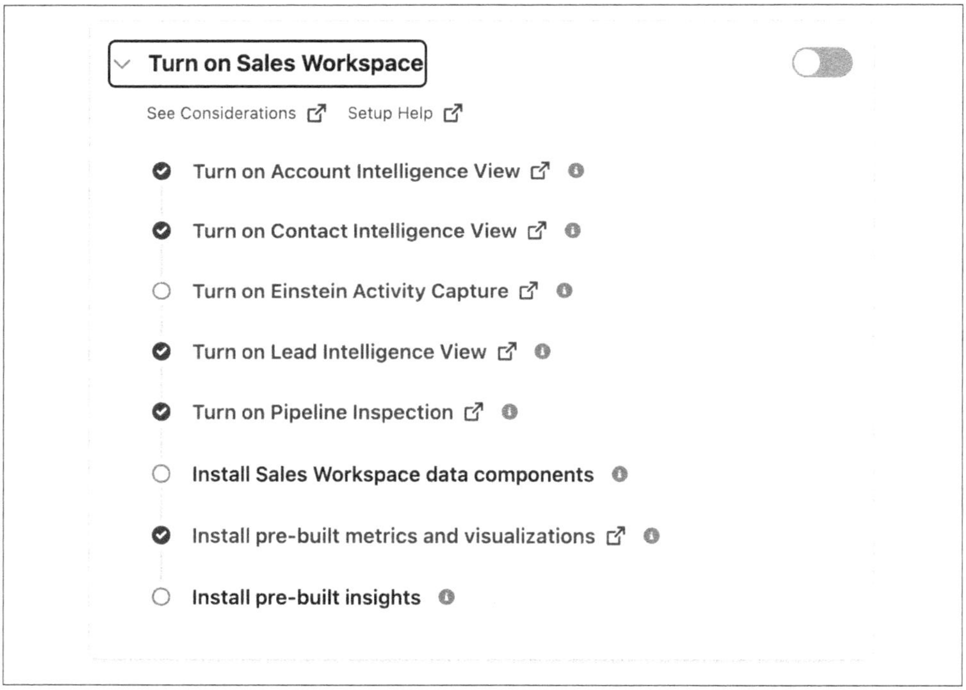

Figure 8-8. Turning on Sales workspace

Once turned on, the Sales workspace pages replace the default home page in Sales and Sales Console apps. Three Sales workspace components must be added to the home page for custom home pages in order for the sales team to access those related insights:

- Agent Completed Tasks component
- Agent Suggestions component
- Workspace Key Metrics component

After turning on Sales workspace and adding components to a custom page, the admin needs to assign individuals a Sales Workspace User permission set, which grants the user access to sales metrics, recommended actions, and agent activity.

Setup Completed by the End User

After a Salesforce admin turns on the Sales workspace feature, individual users need to complete the setup by connecting their email, calendar, and any desired conversation tools. Individuals who've been assigned the necessary permissions for Sales workspace will be guided through a setup process once they've logged in to Salesforce.

A Salesforce end user setting up Sales workspace for the first time is asked to choose their email provider, either Google or Microsoft, and then follow on-screen instructions to sign in to their email provider account and authorize the connection. Afterward, the user's email and calendar information are used to help automate CRM updates and provide a complete view of the customer interactions.

Video conferencing tools such as Google Meet, Microsoft Teams, or Zoom can also be connected so that features like Call Summaries and automated follow-ups can be enabled. Connecting conversational tools is optional.

Once setup is complete, the end user is kept informed of the automated actions taken by agents on their behalf. Tracking the agents' work is done by click on the Agent Completed button near the top right of the screen. The last 14 days of tasks completed by agents are listed and that list refreshes hourly. Three key metrics from D360 are available in the Sales workspace: quota attainment, converted leads, and active accounts.

In addition, Sales workspace displays a prioritized feed of suggested actions. Each suggestion is also accompanied by contextual details such as the related record, and suggested actions to take (Figure 8-9). Sometimes suggested actions include assigning a lead to an agent. Suggested actions could vary per user depending on the features turned on in the Salesforce org and the permissions assigned to the user.

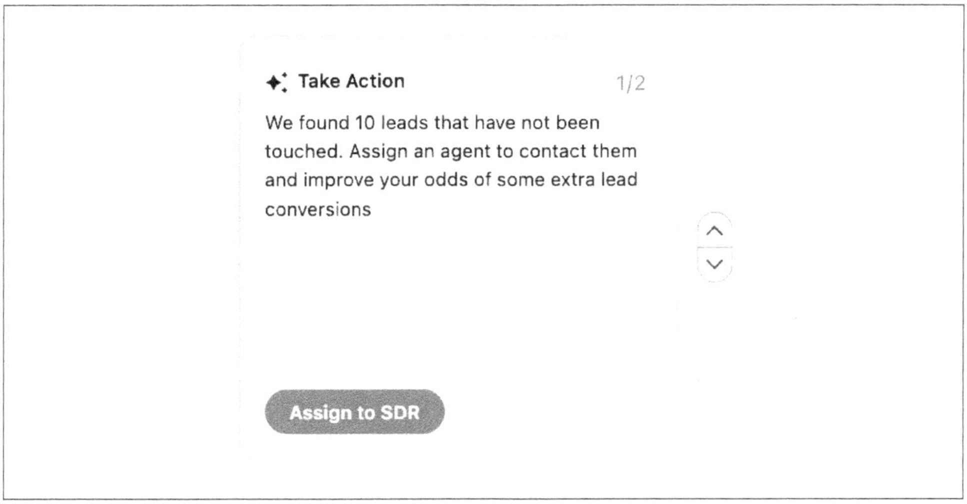

Figure 8-9. Suggested actions to take within the Sales workspace

The Lead Nurturing and Pipeline Management agents are two standard agents that a Salesforce admin enables for the Sales workspace. Let's explore both of those agents and more. We'll explore standard agents, both autonomous and semi-autonomous, and then discuss a few standard subagents and actions.

Agentforce Sales: Standard Autonomous Agents

Salesforce has done a lot of the heavy lifting to create some out-of-the-box agents for sales use cases. Of those standard agents for sales use cases, two are autonomous. The Agentforce Lead Nurturing and Sales Coach agents operate independently, with the overall goal of enhancing sales team efficiency.

The Lead Nurturing agent, previously referred to as the Sales Development Representative (SDR) agent, works around the clock to nurture prospects by automating lead engagement and pipeline growth. The agent takes action autonomously as it sends customized emails, responds to emails, and connects qualified leads with sales reps.

The Sales Coach agent provides personalized coaching to sales reps by analyzing presentations, simulating role-play scenarios, and offering real-time feedback. The Sales Coach agent accesses relevant CRM data as it seeks to help sales reps improve communication and customer engagement.

You'll find both of these agents underneath the "Agentforce for Sales" option in the Quick Find box (Figure 8-10). Once an agent is enabled with the toggle switch, the user will be taken through the guided setup process.

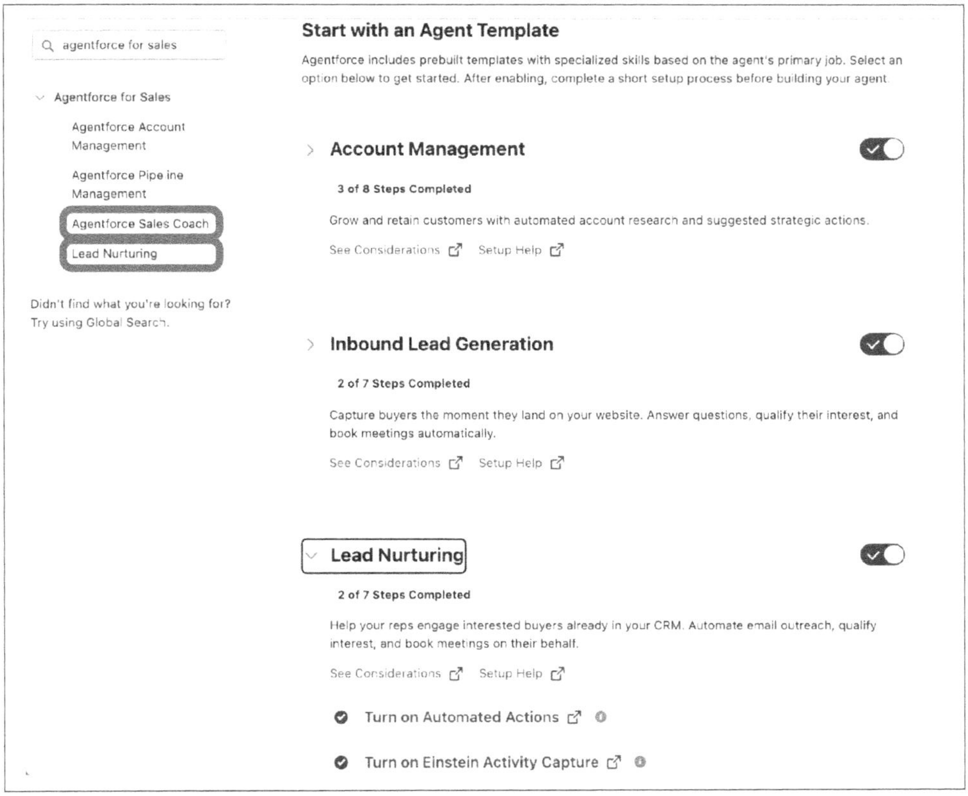

Figure 8-10. Enable Sales agent templates for Lead Nurturing and Sales Coach agents

In the previous section, we learned about ECI and how it surfaces insights and recordings after the call. Setting up ECI is an important step to be completed before enabling the Lead Nurturing agent.

Lead Nurturing Agent

The Lead Nurturing agent powered by Agentforce connects with prospects to address their product inquiries, handle objections, and schedule meetings. The Lead Nurturing agent is customizable so that it can even engage prospects within their preferred channel, such as with SMS text messaging or WhatsApp communications. The Lead Nurturing agent supports operating in many languages.

In addition to D360, which is required for all Agentforce features, the Einstein Activity Capture feature is also required for the Lead Nurturing agent to work.

The Lead Nurturing agent operates like a human user in your Salesforce org, but with special permissions. A Salesforce admin needs to assign permissions to and set up an email account for the agent. Einstein Activity Capture is also required. Human Salesforce users can see the Lead Nurturing agent's emails on the activity timeline of Lead, Contact, and Person Accounts.

Prospects are assigned to a Lead Nurturing agent in one of three ways:

- When the prospect assignment criteria within the Engagement Rules in Agentforce Builder are met
- By an automated action
- When a sales rep sends a prospect to an agent

The Lead Nurturing agent takes the prospect through a flexible set of engagement steps depending on how the prospect responds. Some subagents assigned to the Lead Nurturing agent include Send Outreach, Respond to Prospect, Answer Questions with Knowledge, and Manage Opt-Out. At any time, a Lead Nurturing agent can be stopped from engaging with a specific prospect. The human Salesforce user only needs to go to the activity timeline on the prospect record and choose Cancel Lead Nurturing Agent Outreach.

Sales Coach Agent

The Sales Coach agent powered by Agentforce helps sales teams enhance their skills. The Sales Coach agent delivers tailored role-play session for sales reps to practice their pitches and learn how to better manage objections. The Sales Coach agent focuses on specific deals and offers to offer feedback on strengths and areas for improvement, as well as provides suggestions for actionable steps to help the deal progress.

> In addition to D360, which is required for all Agentforce features, the ECI feature is also required for the Sales Coach agent to give feedback about a sales rep's calls.

Feedback given to sales reps is based on different criteria. The opportunity stage is one of those important criteria. Each opportunity stage has its own prompt template with stage-specific questions the sales rep must answer. The Sales Coach agent analyzes the sales rep's answers to the questions by cross-referencing the answer to the available CRM data.

The Sales Coach agent needs the following features to operate, access CRM data, and generate relevant feedback:

Agentforce
: Used to configure and manage events

Einstein Generative AI
: Powers the prompt templates and guides the LLM to generate feedback for the sales rep

Agent Studio
: Used to configure subagents and actions, power the Sales Coach agent, and ultimately equip the agent with the ability to role-play and generate feedback

D360
: Hosts files and supports retrieval augmented generation (RAG)

The Sales Coach agent can be a valuable tool for managers with large sales teams or for managers who have limited time to coach sales reps. However, there are ethical considerations for using an agent as a coach that shouldn't be overlooked. As with any GenAI product, the Sales Coach agent can experience artificial hallucinations by inventing information to fill missing details or inaccurately assume context for a specific scenario. In addition, different speech variations, homophones, and pronunciations can cause AI transcribers to misinterpret words.

For many reasons, the Sales Coach agent shouldn't be used to score sales pitches. For one thing, LLMs can introduce variability and randomness in rubric-based scoring, and they're simply not designed for consistent scoring of performance. The purpose of the Sales Coach agent is to evaluate content and provide feedback to improve the clarity of messaging and the inclusion of key points.

In addition to the Sales Coach and Lead Nurturing agents, powered by Agentforce, Salesforce offers prebuilt GenAI solutions for sales use cases. Earlier we reviewed the Einstein Relationship Insights, ECI, and Einstein Sales Emails features. In addition to these prebuilt features and out-of-the-box agents, Salesforce provides Agentforce Builder tools so users can create their own customized GenAI solutions for sales-specific use cases.

Agentforce Sales: Standard Semi-Autonomous Agents

In addition to the two autonomous agents, Salesforce offers several semi-autonomous agents for sales use cases. These agents come with the necessary subagents and actions assigned but they each have prerequisites. The Agentforce for Sales section lists the requirements for each agent:

- Account Management
- Inbound Lead Generation
- Inbound Voice Lead Generation

- Guided Shopping—B2B & D2C
- Partner Success
- Pipeline Management
- Prospecting
- Qualification
- Sales
- Sales Management

The Account Management agent automates research and suggests strategic actions that sales reps use to grow and retain customers. The Sales agent provides assistance to individual sales reps by automating time-consuming tasks. The agent can even update Salesforce records.

The Inbound Lead Generation agent engages inbound prospects across chat and messaging platforms, and the Inbound Voice Lead Generation agent engages via voice. The Qualification agent qualifies leads by determining prospect fit quickly, and the Prospecting agent reviews each account's calls, meetings, email history, and then combines it with external information received from third parties to generate a prioritized list of contacts and accounts, which are assigned to sales reps. The Pipeline Management agent uses automated updates and data-driven suggestions to help move deals forward.

> The Agentforce lead generation agents can undertake autonomous actions by creating new Lead, Contact, and Person Account records in Salesforce and scheduling prospect meetings. The lead generation agents are part of Agentforce for Sales, but they're actually designed to expand the scope of an Agentforce Service agent. Thus, these lead generation agents are often found on agents created for service-related use cases.

In addition to the standard Agentforce for Sales agents built for internal sales reps, there are more agents for external use cases. The Partner Success agent supports an enterprise's partners, and the Guided Shopping—B2B & D2C agent answers common product questions or responds with information about a customer's order.

As with other standard agents, these Agentforce Sales agents can be customized. As we learned in Chapter 6, one way to customize agents is by adding new subagents or actions. Agentforce for Sales has many standard subagents and actions already created that are available to add to existing agents or use to create custom agents.

Agentforce Sales: Standard Subagents and Actions

Agentforce is a set of tools used to create and customize agents and includes a suite of assistive and autonomous agents. We learned about Agentforce and the building blocks of Agentforce agents in Chapter 6. For now, let's briefly mention some Agentforce standard subagents that can be used for sales-specific use cases.

Subagents can be added to any pre-existing agent by adding a standard subagent from the Asset Library or creating a new custom subagent. Many sales-specific Agentforce agents are native to the Agentforce platform. Those standard subagents include all the necessary details like classification and scope that come predefined with the subagent. In addition, the relevant actions are already attached to the subagents. Let's look at three subagents and some of their details:

Close Deals

- Classification: Questions related to a user's query to get a detailed deal strategy, comprehensive steps to advance/close opportunities based on past deals won, pricing information for a particular product, conversation signals or customer sentiment related to a specific account or opportunity to strategize next steps or prepare an execution plan
- Scope: Only handles tasks related to providing a tactical guide or detailed deal strategy to close deals
- Actions: Identify Object by Name, Identify Record by Name, Query Records, Summarize Record, and Create Close Plan

Deal Analysis

- Classification: Requests related to a comprehensive strategic brief and analysis for a specific, identified Sales Opportunity, synthesizing recent activities, conversations, and CRM data relevant to that deal
- Scope: Focuses on a single, user-identified Opportunity
- Actions: Identify Key Contacts, Get Conversation Intelligence, Get Account and Account Plan, Get Activities Timeline, Get Conversation Transcript, Get Related Notes, Identify Record by Name, Get Related Emails, Query Records, Get Record Details, Search the Web, Get Activity Details, and Search Conversations

Sales Research

- Classification: Helps sellers learn more about their customers and prospects so they can prepare for meetings, write briefs, and build strategic plans
- Scope: Uses internal CRM data from Account and Leads when the seller needs context, and external web data when they ask for market insights or company updates

- Actions: Get Related Notes, Get Activity Deals, Get Activities Timeline, Get Record Research, Query Records, Search the Web, Answer Questions with Knowledge, Get Record Details, Get Conversation Intelligence, Identify Record by Name, Get Account and Account Plan, and Get Related Emails

In addition to the classification description and scope provided here, each standard subagent also includes a set of instructions. We've discussed three standard Agentforce subagents and their associated actions, but there are many more standard actions and standard subagents that can be selected from the Agentforce Studio Asset Library for use when building new custom subagents or agents. Thus, native building blocks for most use cases already exist. Salesforce makes it easy to build custom subagents and agents; however, it's recommended to first consider standard agents, subagents, and actions that already exist.

Summary

In this chapter, we learned about smart productivity and smart content creation options for Salesforce as well as Agentforce autonomous and semi-autonomous agents natively available for sales use cases. We also discovered how to enable Salesforce features that are prerequisites for some of the out-of-the-box agents.

In the next chapter, we'll explore Salesforce AI features for service-related use cases. We'll learn about case management AI features, field service management AI features, and out-of-the-box Agentforce agents. In addition, we'll touch upon service contract management AI features, which is often an important consideration for field service management.

CHAPTER 9

AI Features for Service Case Management and Field Service Management

In Chapter 8, we discussed how customer engagement works in a CRM solution like Salesforce. Sales staff engage with new and existing customers as they strive to effectively manage leads and increase sales. In contrast, service use cases are managed by customer service staff engaged with customers who use the products and services sold to them by the sales teams.

Communication for service use cases is typically more complicated than for sales use cases. For instance, there are more digital engagement channels available for customer assistance. Further, scaling customer service isn't easy and involves preparing your support systems to handle more customers and increased inquiries. It also means managing higher expectations. Modern customers demand connected experiences, personalized interactions, and proactive service.

Designing a comprehensive approach for customer service management that can be scaled as the organization grows is made somewhat easier, though, with the Salesforce capabilities available for service use cases. There's quite a bit of automation built into Salesforce already. In addition, Salesforce offers a number of AI features for service use cases. The main part of the chapter is devoted to describing those prebuilt AI features for critical service functions:

- Case management AI features for case classification, routing, and wrap-up
- Einstein Reply Recommendations
- Knowledge Management
- Conversational Insights and Conversation Mining
- Agentforce out-of-the-box AI agents (agents) for Service use cases

Case management at scale is needed for service teams to effectively manage and resolve customer inquiries and issues that arise relating to an organization's products and services. Central to case management is knowledge management, which provides the foundation for building an organization's knowledge base so that the necessary content is available to respond to customers.

The Einstein for Replies and Conversations features help customer service teams respond quicker and with more appropriate content. We'll explore Conversation Insights and Conversation Mining features. In addition, there are three out-of-the-box service agents we'll discuss: Service Assistant agent, Agentforce Service agent (ASA), and HR Service agent.

Lastly, we'll explore some Salesforce AI solutions for specialized service use cases:

- Field Service Management (FSM) AI solutions
- Service Contract Management AI solutions often used in Field Service

Which Salesforce licenses or packages must be purchased, the permission sets required for the features, and whether your specific Salesforce org type can support the features are not included. Those are details you'll want to discuss with your Salesforce Account Executive (AE).

Getting Started

Let's discuss some background knowledge and some things you should know to help you get the most out of this chapter.

Background Knowledge

Salesforce offers the Service Cloud on the core platform as the foundation with several additional service add-ons (Figure 9-1). Within the Salesforce Service Cloud, users can sign up for the Starter Suite, Pro Suite, Enterprise, or Unlimited edition. In addition, organizations can add on relevant service features like Service Cloud Voice, Visual Remote Assistant, and Digital Engagement for help with managing multiple channels. A self-service portal can be created on top of Experience Cloud. There's also specialized service offerings for Human Resources, FSM, and Service Contract Management.

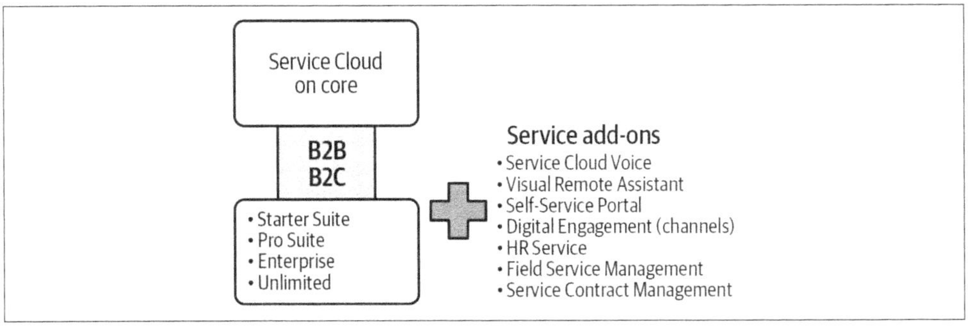

Figure 9-1. Service Cloud on the Salesforce core platform plus Service add-ons

In this chapter, we'll not discuss self-service portal features built on top of the Salesforce Experience Cloud. Instead, we'll focus our attention on AI features for Service Cloud on core. We'll also discuss AI features for FSM and Service Contract Management near the end of the chapter.

Customer lifecycle management

Salesforce's Service Cloud is a platform created to help businesses manage and resolve customer inquiries and issues that arise throughout the customer lifecycle. Customer lifecycle management involves using tools to ensure clients and potential clients receive high-quality, personalized service at all times. You'll get the most from this chapter if you have knowledge about customer lifecycle management, especially the retention step in the lifecycle.

Figure 9-2 shows a simplified version of the retention process, which begins with a case request. A customer's question, feedback, or issue can be documented as a case or work order. Most case requests are initiated by the customer, but cases can be initiated automatically if, for example, a customer logged in to a community portal searches for setup information on a newly purchased product. The search could trigger an automated case request, which could be quickly resolved by sending the customer an email with an attached setup guide.

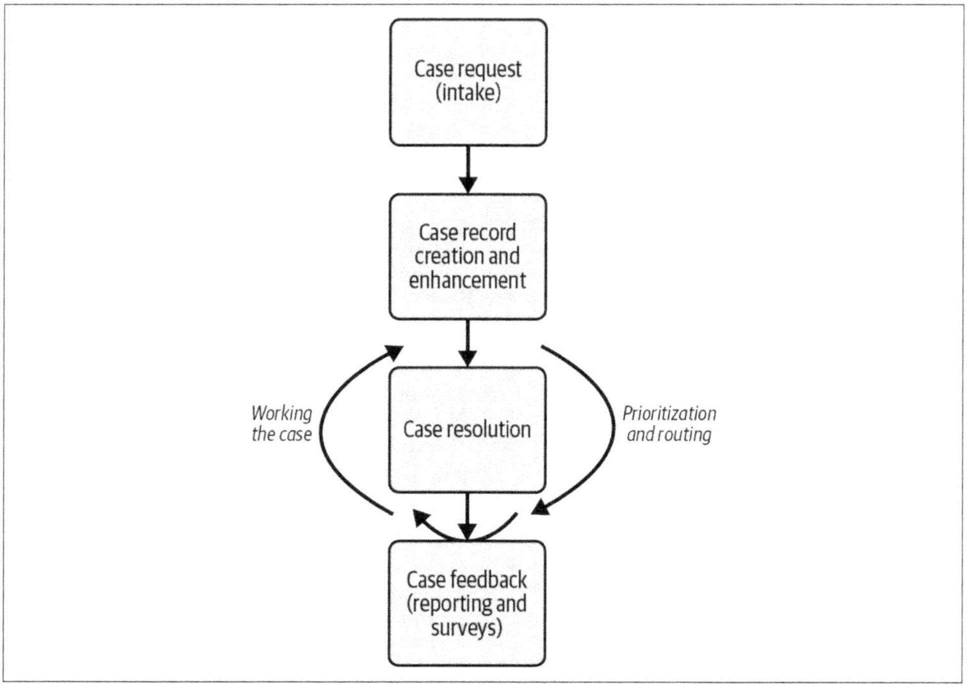

Figure 9-2. Retention process step in the customer lifecycle

When a case record is created from the request, it is often enhanced with additional information. For example, a lookup to the contact records could reveal the case was created for a high-value customer whose recent purchase is still under warranty. Once a case record is enhanced with relevant information, the case resolution process can begin.

Salesforce can dynamically route cases based on service rep availability and skill level. Queues, escalation rules, and entitlement processes and milestones are used to help manage workloads and ensure service-level agreements (SLAs) are met. Customer service agents can use automation features like macros and quick text, access the organization's knowledge base, use service swarming, and leverage AI features to quickly resolve cases.

Service swarming, also known as intelligent swarming, is a collaborative approach to customer service where a team of experts quickly come together to help a customer service rep resolve a case. Depending on the problem, experts can come to the swarm from a variety of departments including finance, legal, operations, sales, engineering, or security.

Salesforce CRM excels at supporting well-defined processes for customer lifecycle management by providing standardized canonical data models, prebuilt automations, and platform customization options to help a customer service team be more efficient. Knowing how users typically use Service Cloud features and functionality to manage their customer lifecycle is key to understanding how AI in the Service Cloud can be leveraged.

Specifically, it's important to be familiar with Salesforce-specific objects like Accounts, Contacts, Case, Case Milestone, Case Article, and Knowledge Article. It's helpful to understand how a Salesforce Knowledge article is created and managed, and how the knowledge base is built. Salesforce Classic Knowledge provides important context for service reps and Agentforce agents as they interact with customers via many different channels.

Creating channels for customer experience interactions

Based on support goals, businesses often maintain many different channels where customers can obtain customer service assistance:

- Email
- Web (website)
- Voice and Video
- Messaging—sometimes referred to as chat:
  - Service Cloud Messaging, which includes messaging apps like Facebook Messenger, SMS text messaging, and WhatsApp
  - Einstein Bots
- Portal and Community

Salesforce email-to-case functionality automatically creates a case record where email exchanges between customers and service reps are tracked. Web-to-case functionality lets customers submit cases themselves through a submission form on an organization's website.

To improve phone support for high-volume call centers, Salesforce offers Service Cloud Voice, which supports multiple telephony systems. Enabling Service Cloud Voice helps provide a consistent customer experience across all digital channels.

Messaging, sometimes referred to as chat, lets customers and service reps communicate using the messaging channel of choice. Although the terms *messaging* and *chat* are often used interchangeably, it's important to note that there are two different Salesforce features incorporating these terms. Salesforce Messaging is the newer feature, while the Salesforce Chat feature was retired in February 2026. With Messaging, the In-App and Web features offer an asynchronous, persistent experience. This allows customers to start, stop, and resume the conversation when it's convenient. In addition, Messaging for In-App and Web supports synchronous conversations.

Messages can originate from customers, or service reps can proactively reach out to customers. Messaging options also include chatbots (also referred to simply as bots). Whether through text or voice, a bot can be set up to answer routine questions, which gives service reps more time to help customers with more complex needs.

Establishing an online community lets service reps share approved content and connect with customers. An online community, built on Salesforce Experience Cloud, can be in the form of a self-service web portal, a help forum, a support site, or something else.

New service channels can be added at any time. However, for a first-time Salesforce Service Cloud setup, the service channels will be created after the case management processes are in place and before the knowledge base is set up (Figure 9-3). AI features and bots are usually added after the case management and knowledge management processes are established.

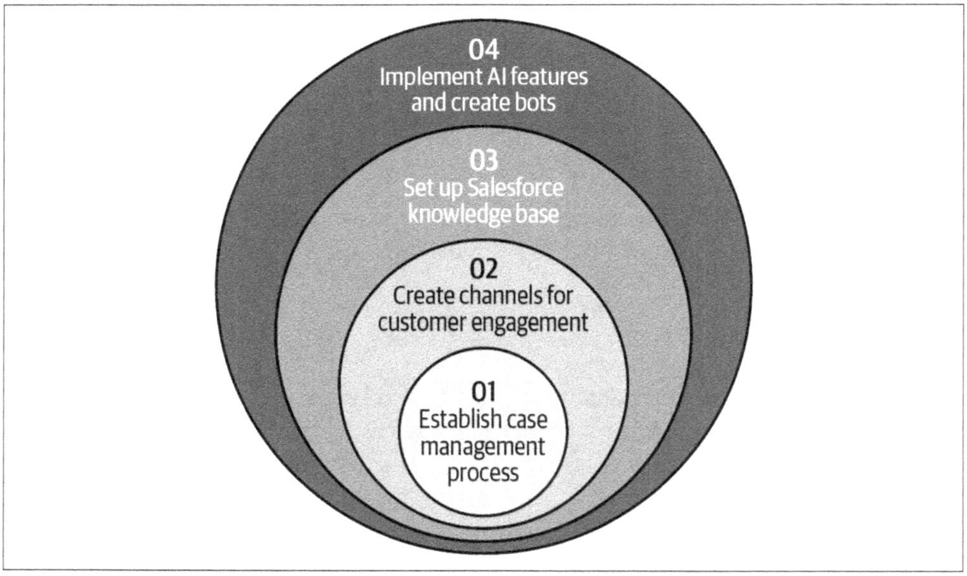

Figure 9-3. Basic steps for a new Service Cloud setup

Managing customer interactions through so many different channels is made easier by Lightning Service Console and Salesforce Mobile app.

Service rep digital engagement with customers

The Lightning Service Console provides a centralized interface that lets service reps view all relevant information about customers and helps them simultaneously respond to cases across multiple channels. The Lightning Service Console integrates with Salesforce Knowledge, surfaces data from other systems, and incorporates predictive and generative intelligence tools. In addition, the unified workspace incorporates AI agents into the Command Center for Service (Figure 9-4).

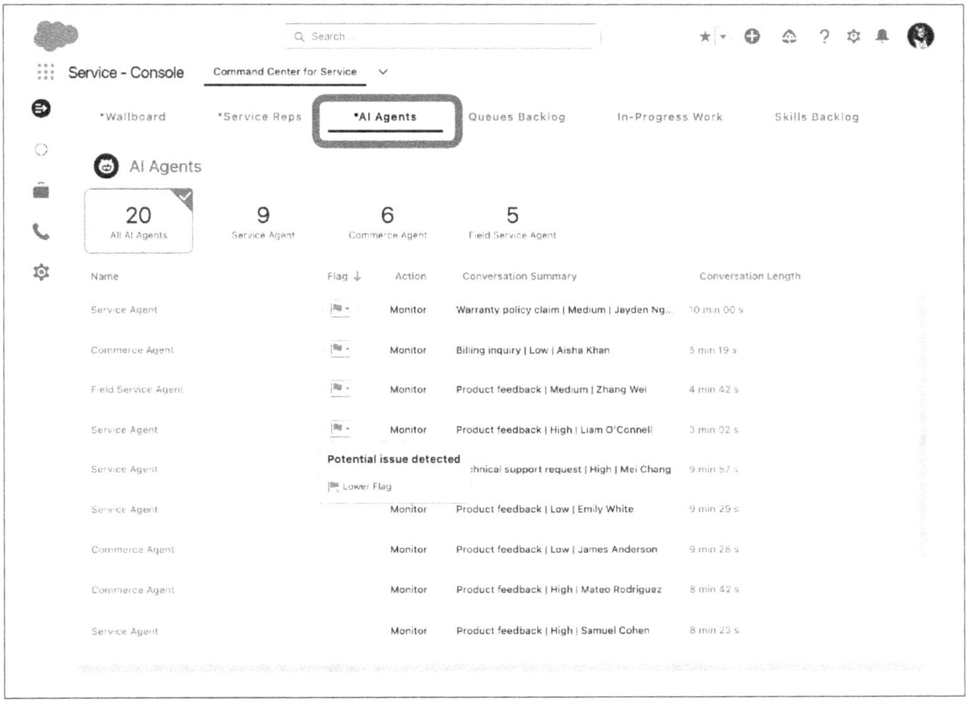

Figure 9-4. AI agents tab in the Lightning Service Console workspace

The Lightning Service Console is a unified workspace giving service reps the ability to support customers who engage on any device, from any location, across any channel. If enabled, the Salesforce Omni-Channel feature routes any type of incoming service work item to the most qualified, available support rep in the Lightning Service Console. Service supervisors monitor service rep workloads and the status of service work items, updating supervisor skill details or changing queues as needed.

For service work items that need to be addressed in the field, the Salesforce Mobile app provides customer service on the go. The app is available on both iOS and Android devices and gives real-time access to the same information available in the Lightning Service Console. However, the interface is optimized for mobile devices. This is especially useful for field service reps. We'll discuss AI features for FSM later in the chapter.

What You Should Know

Throughout the chapter, I'll refer to humans as service reps, customer service reps, field service reps, or service supervisors. I'll reserve the term *agents*, or service agents, for referring to digital labor.

There are many different ways to implement service use case features within Salesforce. Where appropriate to include the information, this chapter specifies how to enable features and also provides details about feature limitations. However, the inherent complexities of service use cases and the many different feature setup options Salesforce makes available for users to create customized solutions means it's infeasible to describe how to enable most service use cases in detail.

Enabling new Einstein AI features requires Salesforce admin privileges. When describing specific instructions or details about Einstein AI features, only information for Salesforce Lightning is included. If your Salesforce org uses the Classic version, you'll need to refer to Salesforce documentation for assistance.

Some functionality, such as Service Intelligence, leverages many different Einstein features to summarize insights in one view. In this chapter, we'll focus on the actual underlying Einstein AI features and functionality, but be aware that there exists some Salesforce-specific features that aggregate insights.

Case Management AI Features

Case management is at the heart of the case resolution process. Salesforce provides important Einstein capabilities for making case management easier and more efficient. Two Einstein apps are available to provide service reps with improved case classification, routing, and wrap-up functionality. In addition, the Einstein Reply Recommendations feature gives service reps suggested responses that can be used in real-time chats.

Einstein Case Classification, Routing, and Wrap-Up

There are two case management apps available within Salesforce: Einstein Case Classification and Einstein Wrap-Up. To set up one or both apps, a Salesforce user first needs to create a model that informs Einstein what closed cases to use for training the model. Then you'll want to enable the Einstein Recommendations component in the Lightning Service Console to leverage one or both of these apps.

After setup, Einstein can automatically classify the case and route it appropriately based on the rules set up in advance. Thanks to the Einstein Case Classification and Wrap-Up apps, the service rep assigned to the case sees the predicted case field values for most checkbox, picklist, and lookup fields on a case when it's viewed in the Lightning Service Console. These values are provided to help the rep wrap up the case more quickly. A service rep can accept the recommendations and click the Save button, or the rep can make changes to the field values.

At this time, Salesforce offers the *Try Einstein* version of the classification apps, which lets a Salesforce admin build one model for each of the two apps. An add-on license is required, however, to obtain full functionality. With full functionality, an admin has the ability to create up to five models per app. The add-on license also allows the admin to set up the app to let Einstein Case Classification automate field classification and route cases automatically without a rep needing to review first.

It's recommended that these Einstein apps be configured directly in a production org rather than a sandbox because you can't copy an Einstein configuration between orgs. Instead, give a small group of service reps access to the Einstein apps in a production org so feedback can be gathered and a productivity comparison can be made between service reps using the apps and those who are not.

> A production org is the Salesforce org used with live customer data and from which companies actively manage their business. A sandbox is a separate environment, most often a copy of the production org, used for a variety of purposes including testing and training. With rare exceptions, it's recommended to build and test in a sandbox before migrating to a production org.

Also, be sure to review the data requirements before setting up either of these apps. Einstein needs a lot of data from closed cases to learn from to predict values on case fields accurately. Also, note that Einstein Case Wrap-Up requires Live Chat to be enabled for cases involving messaging.

Einstein Reply Recommendations

When the Einstein Reply Recommendations feature is enabled, recommended replies appear in a component within the Lightning Service Console Chat and Messaging tab. The reply estimated to work best appears at the top of the list. The service rep can select and send the reply as it appears or the rep can edit the reply before sending. The Einstein Reply Recommendations feature works similarly to the Einstein Service Replies for Chat that we discussed in Chapter 2.

While Einstein Reply Recommendations and Einstein Service Replies offer very similar functionality, there is an important difference. Einstein Service Replies is a Gen AI feature that can incorporate a Salesforce knowledge base in addition to chat history. In contrast, Einstein Reply Recommendations is a predictive AI feature that uses chat transcripts for building a model to identify potential reply types from past chats and service rep utterances. In addition to that model, a second model is used to identify data patterns in live chats to recommend a reply to service reps in real time.

As mentioned earlier in Chapter 2, the Einstein Reply Recommendations feature and Einstein Service Replies feature can't coexist. Reply Recommendations can't be turned on if Service Replies is already enabled.

The Einstein Reply Recommendations feature—in addition to the Case Classification, Routing, and Wrap-Up features—uses traditional AI to provide case management at scale options for service teams. While these are all important features, case management can't be effective without a well-managed knowledge base of articles and other content.

Knowledge Management AI Features

A scalable approach to case management relies on providing customer service representatives and service agents with a knowledge base; a digital library of information about a product, service, or topic. An organization can create a powerful knowledge base to give service reps and service agents the ultimate support tool by using Salesforce Knowledge capabilities.

A knowledge base is built by creating individual documents known as knowledge articles. Of course, knowledge articles can be written by experienced service reps and internal human writers. However, there's a real advantage to also using Einstein to help grow a knowledge base because knowledge articles authored by Einstein are generated quickly and written concisely. In addition to adding to the knowledge base, there's also an advantage to having Einstein recommend relevant knowledge articles to service reps as they work to resolve cases. We discussed content knowledge bases, along with the Einstein Knowledge feature, in detail in Chapter 2.

Conversation Insights and Conversation Mining

Evaluating conversations after the fact and looking for insights into those conversations is something that can be achieved with Einstein Conversation Insights and Einstein Conversation Mining. Let's review both of those features.

Einstein Conversation Insights

While the Service Replies feature can provide assistance to service reps responding via chat or email, the Einstein Conversation Insights feature is a powerful AI feature useful for supervisors to gather insights for completed voice or video calls. Einstein Conversation Insights (ECI) is a Gen AI tool designed specifically for sales teams to unlock the full potential of sales conversations. ECI and ECI-related features are powered by Agentforce, and include built-in capabilities like Call Insights, Call

Transcript Snippets, and Call Trend Summary. In addition, it's possible to enable additional ECI functionality such as Call Summaries and Call Explorer.

ECI was designed for sales use cases and based on the success of the new feature, more Salesforce users are now leveraging the tool for service-related cases. Initially, service and sales calls were combined in one dashboard that appeared in the Sales Console dashboard where supervisors applied service-specific filters or sales-specific filters depending on the need. This approach is still applicable for any Salesforce user assigned both sales and service permissions. However, service supervisors now have access to an ECI dashboard in the Lightning Service Console.

Einstein Conversation Mining

Whereas ECI focuses on extracting insights from call conversations, Einstein Conversation Mining leverages transcripts from written interactions to generate insights from closed cases. From the Conversation Mining report, a Salesforce user can even update an Einstein Bot (Figure 9-5) using the report insights.

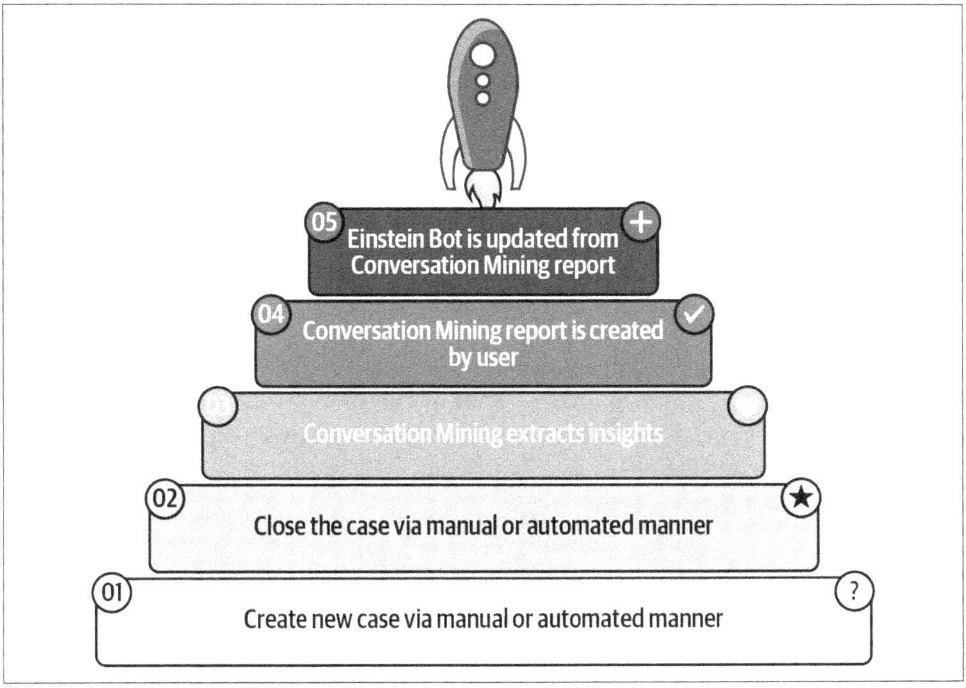

Figure 9-5. Einstein Conversation Mining steps

In the normal flow of work, a new case is created manually by a service rep or through automated methods such as web-to-case or email-to-case. Once the case is closed, Einstein Conversation Mining uses machine learning clustering models to mine the transcript to determine the actual case contact reason. Contact could occur because a person needs to change an appointment, cancel a subscription, get technical support, or any other reason. Einstein Conversation Mining also ascertains the conversation frequency and number of conversation turns to completion for the closed case.

At any time, a Salesforce user can create a Conversation Mining report by selecting a channel, defining a date range, and including any segmentation criteria. The channel selected could be email-to-case, web-to-case, or chat. Segmentation criteria could be based on factors such as average response time or chat duration. From within the Conversation Mining report, a user has the option to send the information needed to update an Einstein Bot. We'll explore Einstein Bots in detail in "Einstein Bots for Service Use Cases" on page 342.

Agentforce for Service: Out-of-the-Box Agents

Einstein Service Replies and Einstein Conversation Mining features are out-of-the-box Salesforce solutions powered by Gen AI. In addition to these prebuilt features, Salesforce offers out-of-the-box agents for service use cases. Two agents now ready for service use cases include the Service Assistant agent and the HR Service agent, both powered by Agentforce. Previously, the Service Assistant agent was known as Service Planner, and you'll still find that older reference in some documentation.

Service Assistant Agent

The Service Assistant agent isn't a fully autonomous or conversational agent. Instead, it's a helpful assistive agent in the form of a Lightning Web Component (LWC) built to suggest service plan steps for service reps to quickly resolve cases. Service Assistant agent is available on a Case record page with real-time case summaries and step-by-step guidance.

Salesforce LWCs are a standardized JavaScript framework that leverages HTML and CSS without needing a third-party framework. Salesforce developers use the framework to create customized pages and functions on the Salesforce platform.

Interestingly, the LWC is only available to a service rep if the case meets eligibility criteria established in advance. This is a great way to prevent excessive costs. For example, the Service Assistant agent could be used only for cases that exist in a certain queue where that queue could be used to funnel complex or high-value cases. Those types of cases probably make the most sense for a service rep to get help from a Service Assistant agent.

Once the service rep clicks the Draft Plan button, a detailed case summary and service plan with actionable steps is presented to the service rep. The Service Assistant agent is grounded in your organization's Salesforce data, including cases and knowledge articles, thus ensuring your service plan is relevant for your specific service policies and standards. A Redraft Plan button appears if the case is updated after the initial service plan is created.

The requirement that new agents can only be created in the new Agentforce Builder, beginning July 2026, doesn't apply to the Service Assistant agent. The Service Assistant agent can't be created in the new Agentforce Builder and, thus, will continue to be supported only in the legacy Agent Builder.

The Service Assistant agent supports customer service teams in their normal flow of work. There's another out-of-the-box Agentforce agent that often handles common use cases without the need for human assistance or intervention.

Agentforce Service Agent

The ASA autonomously handles service tasks and customer interactions. When creating the ASA in Agentforce Builder, you'll notice several subagents are automatically included: Agent Router, Service Customer Verification, General FAQ, Case Management, Account Management, Reservation Management, Delivery Issues, Order Inquiries, Escalation, Off Topic, and Ambiguous Question (Figure 9-6).

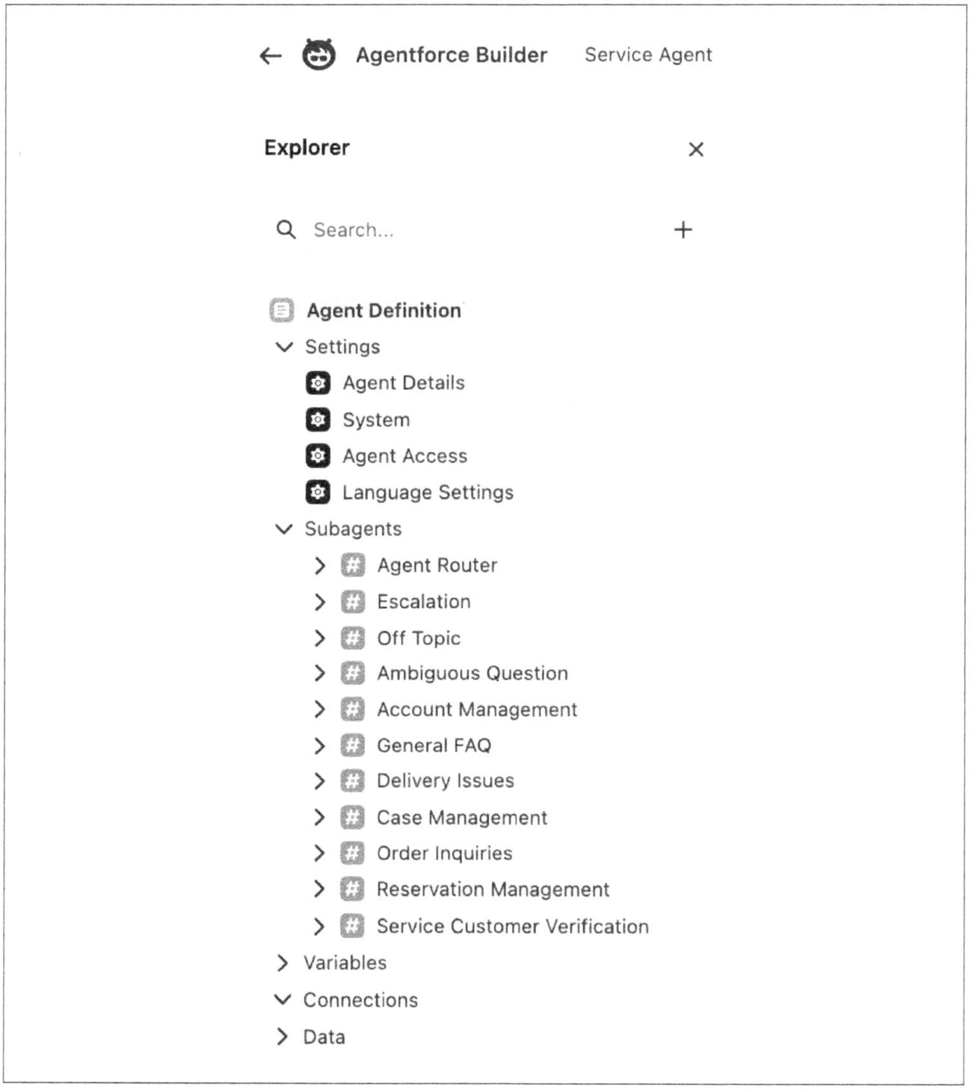

Figure 9-6. Agentforce Service agent definitions

Just as with Einstein Bots, ASA can transfer complex or sensitive conversations to human service representatives. As we learned in Chapter 5, Einstein Bots are built on intent models and use predefined dialogs, steps, and utterances. In contrast, ASA navigates conversations with the help of a reasoning engine and an LLM. Let's compare the building blocks of an Einstein Bot with those of an agent built with Agentforce (Figure 9-7).

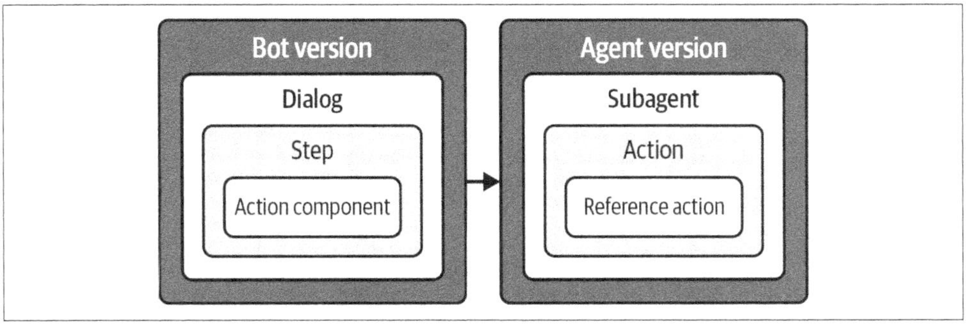

Figure 9-7. Building blocks of Einstein Bot versus Agentforce agent

Agentforce agents like the ASA use a reasoning engine to help interpret users' interactions and utterances, similar to what an Einstein Bot also does. However, the agent's reasoning engine leverages an LLM trained on large amounts of information to help it make decisions about which subagent to choose and which actions to launch. As such, it's important to remember that ASA is a consumption-based product that consumes Einstein Requests and D360 credits based on the usage type, whereas Einstein Bots use a monthly engaged session allowance. However, an Einstein Bot that uses the Answer Questions with Knowledge agent action will also incur consumption-based costs.

One other difference is that Einstein Bots can be built in the Salesforce Classic Experience user interface (UI) as well as the Lightning Experience UI. The ASA requires access to the Lightning Experience UI and cannot be built in Salesforce Classic. Regarding implementation use cases, the enhanced Einstein Bots and the ASA can each be connected to the same customer channels: Enhanced Chat, Enhanced WhatsApp, Enhanced Facebook Messenger, Enhanced Apple Messages for Business, Enhanced SMS, Enhanced LINE, and Bring Your Own Channel.

In addition, Salesforce Voice with Telephony Providers (formerly Service Cloud Voice) is integrated with other channels for a unified experience. Admins use the same routing engine to route voice calls as to route messages, chats, and conversations from other channels. Salesforce Voice, now part of the Partner Contact Center, is built on Salesforce standard objects and is designed for high-volume, high-availability contact centers. It's also relevant for sales use cases. Each sales rep can be assigned a direct inward dialing (DID) phone number for inbound and outbound calls. Salesforce help documentation (*https://oreil.ly/LjBGX*) offers more information on how to use Salesforce Voice to let service reps answer and make calls to resolve customer issues.

Salesforce Voice works with Einstein Conversation Insights, available for both sales and service use cases. We discussed Einstein Conversation Insights in Chapter 8. There are some important steps needed for setting up Salesforce Voice for

Agentforce. Navigate to the Agentforce Voice Setup from the setup menu and complete the setup steps:

1. Create a voice-enabled agent.
2. Configure call routing and call escalation for the agent.
3. Procure a phone number for the channel.
4. Create the messaging channel for Agentforce Voice.
5. Configure telephony vendor settings for call routing and escalation.

The ASA and the Service Assistant agent are both focused on satisfying external constituents, or customers who purchase a company's products or services. There is, however, another out-of-the-box agent available for human resource (HR) teams primarily concerned with supporting internal customers, or employees who work for the company.

HR Service Agent

Salesforce's HR Service Center offering includes an HR Service Console that functions like the Lightning Service Console used by customer service teams. HR Service staff can also leverage a knowledge base created specifically for HR use cases. That same knowledge base can be made accessible directly to employees through a branded self-service portal. Within that self-service portal, employees can engage with the HR Service agent if it's been enabled.

The HR Service agent, powered by Agentforce, assists with many common employee needs: manages employees' PTO requests, provides help changing direct deposit details and enrolling in benefits, and enables employees to update their own employee profile. For complex or highly personal inquiries, the HR Service agent transfers the conversation to a human HR representative who'll assist the employee directly using the HR Service Console tools.

Out-of-the-box agents, including the Service Assistant agent and HR Service agent, can be customized using Salesforce's Agentforce Builder. We explored Agentforce Builder in Chapter 6 and other pro-code Agentforce developer tools in Chapter 7. The ASA is used to solve many service use cases. However, as we learned in Chapter 5, there are some situations where a chatbot is the preferred solution. As such, it's important for us to review Einstein Bots for service use cases.

Einstein Bots for Service Use Cases

Chatbots are often employed for service use cases. Human service reps and AI service agents engage with customers through a variety of channels including phone, web, email, SMS text message, voice-activated devices, and social media. Einstein chatbots provide another channel option through which a company can connect with customers.

Chatbots are also referred to as bots, service bots, and digital assistants and are frequently used for routine service interactions. Bot service use case examples include:

- Answer FAQs such as nearest store location or return policy
- Issue reporting like creating cases on which support reps can follow up
- Information management such as checking order details or updating password
- Scheduling new appointments or updating existing appointments
- Qualification, triage, and routing by gathering information from the customer

Chatbots are based on complex, strictly defined conversational rules that require time and expertise to set up. Salesforce makes it easier, though, by integrating other AI features with Einstein Bots. For example, we learned earlier that conversation mining reports can be used to easily update Einstein Bots.

Chatbots are a reliable, cost-effective solution for use cases needing quick, consistent responses to common questions like handling routine customer service inquiries, collecting basic information, and suggesting relevant resources. However, chatbots struggle with more open-ended conversations because NLP is a less advanced form of AI in comparison to large language models (LLMs), which power agents. Agents understand context and learn from interactions. In Chapter 6 we explored the advanced conversational capabilities of agents, which can easily handle queries outside predefined conversations.

Chatbots need conversation dialogs designed in advance. Dialogs are specific conversation snippets that control the actions a chatbot can take and how the chatbot responds to an utterance. Examples of dialogs include a welcome, main menu, order status, location and hours, transfer to agent, and other recurring dialogs. You can think of each dialog as a subprocess that's either encapsulated, connected, or independent:

- Encapsulated dialog—part of a larger dialog process
- Connected dialog—related to but dependent on each other
- Independent dialog—not related to each other in any way

Designing the conversation flows for each dialog is an important step in the chatbot development process. Refer to Chapter 5 for more detail about conversation design suggestions for improving human-to-chatbot interactions. In that chapter, we also learned how Einstein Bots are capable of leveraging the agentic features of Agentforce's Knowledge Answers, which allows bots to trigger an agent action that provides an orchestrated conversation for customers. You may want to review the comparison of the self-service characteristics between Einstein Bots with Generative Knowledge Answers versus an Agentforce agent in Chapter 5.

Field Service Management AI Features

Thus far, we've discussed many features available to customer service reps using the Lightning Service Console, including Gen AI features and Agentforce agents, along with Einstein Bots for service use cases. Something we haven't yet explored is field service management, the coordination and execution of tasks performed away from the company's offices by mobile workers.

Field service tasks fulfilled by mobile workers include new installation, maintenance, repairs, emergency repairs, insurance claim assessments, and deliveries. Field service tasks also include those required for home healthcare services.

A use case example for heating and air conditioning service could include the following: manage the installation, maintenance, and repair of heating, ventilation, and air conditioning systems; tasks involve scheduling technicians, monitoring inventory levels of parts, and tracking warranties and service history.

It's important to understand the subtle difference between work order management and field service management. They're closely related but each serves different purposes. Work order management involves managing tasks involved in the process of creating, assigning, tracking, and completing field service requests. In contrast, field service management is a broader category. FSM includes work order management as part of the overall management of field operations.

FSM streamlines scheduling and dispatch, enhances communication and collaboration among mobile workers, and helps manage asset inventory. Real-time service metrics from FSM capabilities also help to ensure regulatory compliance and enhance safety standards. Two powerful AI features exist specifically for Salesforce users of Field Service Lighting: Field Service AI features for scheduling and dispatching and AI features for pre-work briefs and post-work summaries.

Field Service AI Features for Scheduling and Dispatching

Routing many field service reps with different skills to geographically dispersed service appointments is a complex problem made even more difficult due to variations caused by a company's unique workflows, metrics, and desired business outcomes. Scheduling automation and route optimization can be solved within Salesforce by installing a Field Service managed package. A Salesforce managed package is a container that includes all the components of a Salesforce application needed to install and run the application. Salesforce makes it easy to get started with Field Service with the new Field Service Guided Setup using Salesforce Go (Figure 9-8).

Figure 9-8. Field Service guided setup in Salesforce Go

A Salesforce admin will need to turn on the basics by clicking the Turn On button in the setup. Next, there are four steps to get ready for scheduling and to unlock Gen AI features: create work types, create service territories, add service resources, and add dispatchers.

Schedule Automation and Optimization managed package for route optimization

Once the setup is complete, the Field Service managed package for Schedule Automation and Optimization uses an optimization engine to find the "best grade" for a complex routing problem. Salesforce uses dynamic algorithms and metaheuristics to break down complexity into smaller solvable problems.

The optimization engine finds the best solution for a complex routing problem by leveraging powerful mapping and real-time traffic data, thus ensuring field service workers arrive at the proper time while providing dispatchers tools to manage in-flight exceptions. Salesforce Field Service also considers details like truck measurements and maximum load capacity. In addition, Einstein Discovery insights can be provided as input and can be especially useful for identifying when certain operational machines should be proactively serviced and maintained.

Salesforce uses HERE.com location and map data, along with Salesforce proprietary scheduling and optimization logic and AI-based algorithms. The map data provides accessible routes for bicycles and pedestrians, in addition to information relevant for automobile transportation and truckload deliveries. HERE's real-time and historic traffic data helps the Field Service optimization engine create schedules and routes that meet specific operational constraints and service-level agreements (SLAs). SLAs are an important part of customer service management and will be discussed in the next section.

Salesforce Field Service offers three optimization types—global, in-day, and immediate:

Global optimization
: Supports long-term optimization for future service by analyzing requirements overnight in batches to update recommended scheduling as service delivery date nears

In-day optimization
: Assists with the current day's active dispatching and near-term optimization, supporting exceptions management and providing scheduling updates for new or changed booking activity

Immediate optimization
: Monitors the current day's schedule for common events like early and late finishes, high-priority appointments, and customer cancellations

The optimization engine is highly configurable and can even re-optimize the day's schedule immediately.

AI-driven optimization based on C360 powered by Agentforce

The Field Service managed package for Schedule Automation and Optimization uses machine learning to provide fully automated scheduling and optimization capabilities. Optimized scheduling is the third stage (Figure 9-9) in Salesforce's "Good to Great Framework" for scheduling field service work.

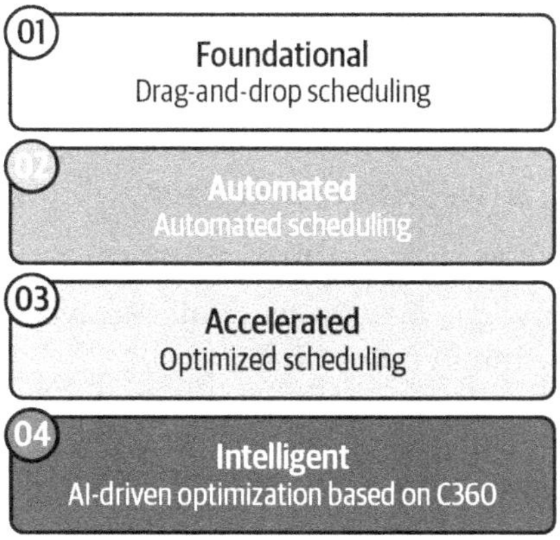

Figure 9-9. Good to Great Framework for scheduling field service work

At the *foundational* level for scheduling, schedulers might use a Gantt chart or some drag-and-drop visual booking tool. Moving up the framework to the *automated* level, schedulers might have access to some automation tools for scoring and scheduling service appointments.

The third stage is supported by traditional AI. This *accelerated* stage is where fully automated scheduling and optimization occurs. This stage is supported by the Salesforce Field Service Lightning Schedule Automation and Optimization managed package.

The highest level in the framework, the *intelligent* stage, uses optimized scheduling from the *accelerated* stage. To provide more personalized outcomes, the intelligent stage incorporates Customer 360 (C360) data unified and harmonized in Salesforce Data 360 (D360).

The powerful schedule automation and route optimization capabilities, powered by traditional AI, are complemented by important Gen AI features available to field service workers.

AI Features for Pre-Work Briefs and Post-Work Summaries

Using Prompt Builder, a Salesforce admin can use the Field Service Pre-Work Brief and the Post-Work Summary templates to customize these Gen AI features and make them available for field service workers.

Pre-work briefs

Once set up, pre-work briefs can be generated right in the mobile app for field service workers. The pre-work brief shows mobile service reps everything they need to know about an upcoming work order. Workers are shown relevant information including asset history, service records, contract terms, and important customer data. For example, the pre-work brief could include the following information:

- Work order reason, e.g., small battery installation
- Work site details, e.g., arrive at the back entrance
- Previous customer interactions, e.g., new customer
- Recommended actions, e.g., offer to do a full site evaluation at no cost to see if there may be other business opportunities

Among other things, pre-work briefs help field service workers grasp the broader context. After the field service worker finishes the work order, a post-work summary needs to be created.

Post-work summaries

Field service reps can ask an agent to generate a post-work summary. The summary can be saved in the post-work summary field on the work order once the field service worker confirms the summary is accurate and clicks the Save button. Using an agent to generate a post-work summary saves time and ensures accurate, comprehensive, less error-prone reports.

It's important to know the post-work summary setup out-of-the-box uses the Summarize Record action, which summarizes only one object by default. However, field service work orders often require information from multiple objects including the work order line item specifics, service appointment details, and assets information. In those cases, a prompt template can be used to add additional objects.

Service Contract Management AI Features

Many service agreements, including field service agreements, require a service contract between the parties. The service contract management lifecycle includes creating, executing, and monitoring legal agreements between service providers and third parties. Third parties can be internal customers, external customers, or both.

Contract management often involves negotiating SLAs that clearly define the service scope and terms. Examples of service contracts include maintenance contracts such as car warranties, IT technical support contracts, and consulting contracts.

Salesforce incorporated Contracts AI capabilities into the Salesforce core platform as an Industries Cloud Einstein feature. I've elected to discuss Contracts AI in detail in this chapter because service contract management is an important service use case.

Contracts AI Capabilities

There are two main key features of Contracts AI, which we'll describe in more detail in the following sections:

- Automated clause generation with advanced clause library management
- Enhanced legacy contract digitization

Defining clauses for contracts is a critical task requiring precision and legal expertise. Salesforce Contracts AI can help. After automatically generating a new clause, based on a natural language description from the user, Salesforce then saves the clause in a clause library for potential repeated use.

Legacy contracts include important information needed for ongoing business operations. However, accessing them is often time-consuming and error-prone because legacy contracts are often filed away in physical cabinets or saved as scanned images or PDF files. Contracts AI can solve this problem by automating the identification and extraction of key data such as contract party names, contract dates, and relevant clauses.

Extract Contract Details and Create Digital Records

With Contracts AI, users can identify and extract contract details and clauses from a PDF file. Before you can use this feature, you'll need to configure a contract extraction template and make sure the context definition is active.

When you're ready to extract contract details using Contracts AI, select Contracts from the App Launcher and then click Extract Contract Details. Select a PDF file to extract contract and clause details, click "Get Started with Extraction," and then click "Extract from File."

Once you've completed all steps, you can view the extracted values and modify any values if required. Select the relevant contract type and make sure all the required fields, such as contract terms, parties involved, and specific clauses, are populated before you create the new contract record.

This powerful Gen AI feature gives users the ability to extract contract details from a file and create a new contract record with the relevant details. This is certainly helpful in situations where a contract is shared in an unstructured data format like a PDF file. In addition to this feature to extract contract details and create digital records, Salesforce offers another powerful Gen AI feature for contract lifecycle management.

Smart Clause Generation

Sometimes an existing contract only needs a new clause rather than a new contract to be created. This is where Salesforce Contracts AI can help. When you're ready to draft a clause with Contracts AI, you'll select Document Clause Sets from the Lightning App Launcher. From there, click the "Draft with Contracts AI" button (Figure 9-10) next to the clause set for which you want to create a clause form.

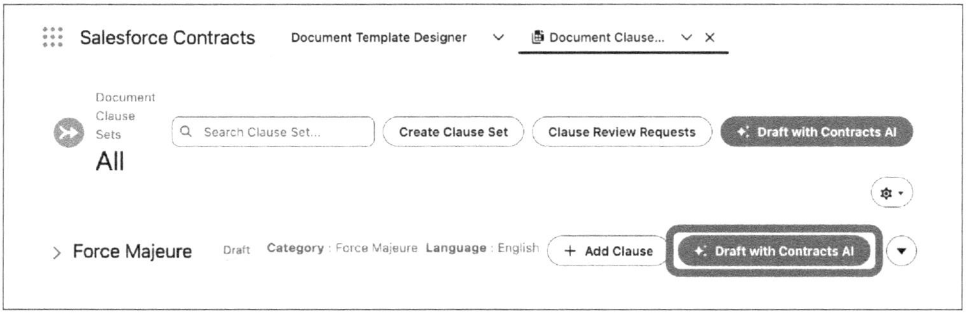

Figure 9-10. Document Clause Sets

You'll have the opportunity to describe your clause in natural language (Figure 9-11) so that Einstein can expertly generate the clause language for you.

After Einstein creates the clause, you'll click "Save to Clause Library" to add the clause to the clause library. You'll need to activate the new clause, initially saved in a draft state, to use the new clause in contracts.

A Salesforce user can even leverage Contracts AI to draft and add clauses to documents and document templates saved in Microsoft Word. A Microsoft 365 Word add-in will need to be set up first.

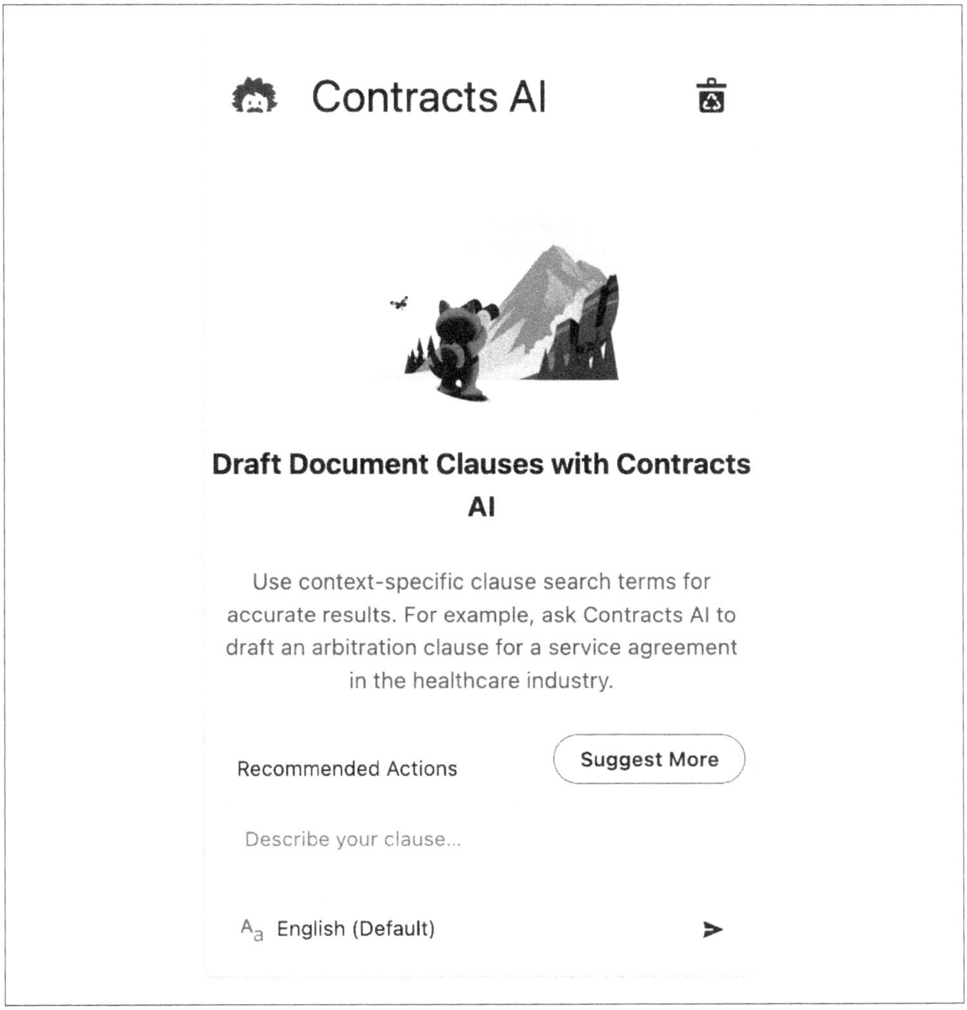

Figure 9-11. Describe your clause in natural language

Summary

In this chapter, we discussed six distinct categories of Salesforce AI features available for service use cases:

- Einstein Case Management
- Einstein Knowledge Management
- Einstein for Replies and Conversations
- Agentforce for Service: Out-of-the-box Agents
- Field Service Management AI Solutions
- Service Contract Management AI Solutions

As you can see from the list of Einstein AI features, there is no shortage of Einstein AI features available specifically for service use cases. In the next chapter, we'll explore Einstein AI features available for marketing-specific use cases.

CHAPTER 10
Predictive and Generative AI Solutions for Marketing Use Cases

In Chapter 2, we discussed the customer lifecycle and how marketers undertake activities to attract new prospects. We also learned that an organization's desired goal for managing interactions in the customer lifecycle is to ultimately turn customers into loyalists and brand evangelists.

In addition, we discussed how some Salesforce functionality requires users to log in to different platforms other than Salesforce core and that Salesforce data can be stored in Salesforce core, near-core, or off-core locations. This is especially relevant for Salesforce marketing use cases. Today and for the foreseeable future, Salesforce has three different marketing-specific tech stacks: Marketing Cloud Engagement, Marketing Cloud Account Engagement, and Marketing Cloud on the Salesforce core platform. The latter is part of the new Marketing Cloud Next suite of applications. Among the three platforms there are different editions available for purchase such as Growth and Advanced editions in Marketing Cloud core and Professional, Corporate, and Enterprise on Marketing Cloud Engagement.

As we'll discuss in detail a little later in the chapter, Salesforce is transitioning to a unified marketing platform with more marketing functionality available on the core platform. In June 2025, Salesforce announced Marketing Cloud Next, which is a series of applications purpose-built for agentic marketing. In this chapter, we'll explore the AI solutions for each of the four Marketing Cloud Next applications on the Salesforce core platform: Marketing Cloud on core, Loyalty Management, Salesforce Personalization, and Marketing Intelligence.

Getting Started

Let's discuss some background knowledge and some things you should know to help you get the most out of this chapter. An overview of all marketing use case features will be provided before we explore the features in more detail.

Background Knowledge

You'll get the most from this chapter if you have knowledge about Salesforce marketing solution options available to digital marketers. We'll discuss an overview of all three platforms, including the newest Salesforce marketing solution known as Marketing Cloud Next.

This chapter includes a great deal of background knowledge information and explanations, much more than any other chapter. This is necessary to build a bridge of understanding needed to help marketers as they transition from Salesforce's legacy platforms to the Marketing Cloud Next suite of apps. Consider, for example, that there is overlap in the labeling of marketing tools:

- Salesforce Personalization is different from Marketing Cloud Personalization.
- Marketing Intelligence is different from Marketing Cloud Intelligence.
- Einstein Engagement Scoring is different from Engagement Scoring.

Salesforce Personalization and Marketing Intelligence are Customer 360 (C360) apps within the Salesforce core platform, which extends the Marketing Cloud Next offering. Marketing Cloud Personalization, formerly known as Interaction Studio, is available on the Marketing Cloud Engagement platform. Marketing Cloud Intelligence, previously known as Datorama, is a standalone cloud-based marketing analytics platform. Einstein Engagement Scoring is an Einstein capability used for smart segmentation in Marketing Cloud Next. It's also available on the Marketing Cloud Engagement platform and is referred to as Behavior Scoring on the Marketing Cloud Account Engagement platform. Engagement Scoring is a rules-based people score that does not use AI capabilities. These various marketing tools are summarized in Table 10-1.

Table 10-1. Selected overlapping marketing tools and capabilities explained

Marketing tool (capability)	Platform	Details
Salesforce Personalization	Salesforce core platform	Customer 360 app; part of Marketing Cloud Next
Marketing Cloud Personalization (Interaction Studio)	Marketing Cloud Engagement	Real-time personalization and interaction management solution
Marketing Intelligence	Salesforce core platform	Customer 360 app; part of Marketing Cloud Next
Marketing Cloud Intelligence (Datorama)	Standalone platform	Cloud-based analytics platform
Einstein Engagement Scoring	Marketing Cloud Engagement, Marketing Cloud Account Engagement, and Salesforce core platform	Einstein AI capability used for smart segmentation
Engagement Scoring	Salesforce core platform	Rules-based people score that does not use AI

The first step for marketers new to the Salesforce platform is to understand the distinct naming conventions of Salesforce's three separate marketing-specific offerings:

- Marketing Cloud Engagement, originally known as ExactTarget
- Marketing Cloud Account Engagement, originally known as Pardot
- Marketing Cloud on core, part of the Marketing Cloud Next app suite

In addition, it isn't always easy to navigate the Salesforce documentation because several AI solutions with the same names, like Einstein Email Guard, exist on all three marketing platforms but with different features, considerations, and limitations. Thus, it's critical to have the necessary background knowledge to ensure you're reviewing the correct Salesforce documentation for your use case.

For these reasons, we'll provide more in-depth background knowledge necessary to better understand the AI for CRM marketing-specific solutions available from Salesforce.

Salesforce marketing solution offerings

Salesforce offers three distinct marketing solution platforms: Marketing Cloud Engagement (MCE), Marketing Cloud Account Engagement (MCAE), and Marketing Cloud on core (Figure 10-1). Within each of those three marketing platforms, Salesforce offers different levels of capabilities. For example, users can sign up for the Growth, Plus, Advanced, or Premium edition of MCAE.

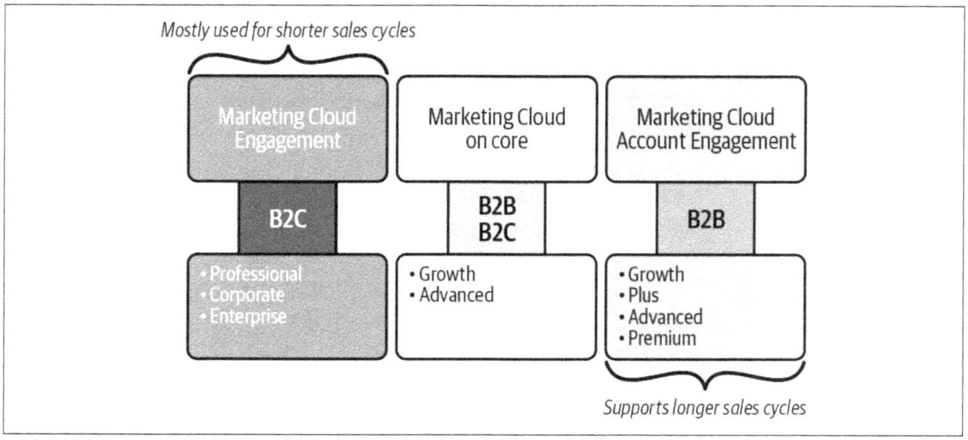

Figure 10-1. Salesforce marketing platforms

The MCE platform is frequently used as a B2C solution supporting digital marketing teams with email marketing, mobile marketing, and digital advertising. It's composed of many Studio and Builder tools, including Journey Builder, to orchestrate multichannel engagement throughout the customer lifecycle.

MCE is used primarily for B2C customers with whom personalized cross-channel customer journeys are created for high-volume, low-consideration transaction purchases. In contrast, MCAE typically operates as a B2B solution working alongside the Sales Cloud.

Market segments using MCE include retail, CPG, communication, and media and entertainment industries. In contrast, MCAE is used primarily for B2B industries with a longer sales cycle where multiple decision makers are involved. Examples include distribution, industrial, professional services, and commercial banking industries.

MCE and MCAE were applications previously acquired by Salesforce. More recently, Salesforce launched Marketing Cloud on core in 2024. Marketing Cloud on core, built on top of Salesforce Core and Data 360 (D360), includes two editions: Marketing Cloud Growth and Marketing Cloud Advanced.

Unlike MCE and MCAE, which rely on external or third-party infrastructure, Marketing Cloud *on core* means no middleware is needed to perform segmentation, create content and reporting, or execute campaigns. No more sync errors or disconnected reporting because everything is done directly inside Salesforce core.

Salesforce Marketing Cloud on the Salesforce core platform, part of Marketing Cloud Next, takes advantage of native CRM objects like Leads, Contacts, and Campaigns. It can also leverage consent management tools. Marketing Cloud Next uses Salesforce Flow for automations. Real-time segmentation is done using Salesforce D360, and content creation and recommendations are powered by Agentforce. Advanced features include A/B testing in flow paths via path Experiment and Einstein Engagement Frequency predictive scoring.

> Many of the AI capabilities within Marketing Cloud Next rely on D360. Because D360 is billed based on consumption pricing, you'll need to factor in this cost when considering the ROI for Marketing Cloud on core AI solution features.

In addition to Marketing Cloud on core, there is now Loyalty Management available on Salesforce core platform. Loyalty Management is technically part of the Salesforce Industry Cloud offerings, but we're including Loyalty Management in this chapter because of its importance to marketing and the customer lifecycle. In addition, it is included as part of the Marketing Cloud Next application suite.

We learned about the customer lifecycle in Chapter 2 when we discussed AI for Salesforce CRM use cases. As part of that lifecycle, a marketer's goal is to expand opportunities by turning customers into loyalists and advocates. Salesforce's Loyalty Management helps marketers foster relationships and create loyalty with personalized rewards powered by behavioral data. Loyalty promotions and segmentation in Loyalty Management leverage unified data found in Salesforce D360.

Marketing Cloud Next

In June 2025, at the Salesforce Connections event in Chicago, Salesforce announced Marketing Cloud Next, a series of applications purpose-built for agentic marketing. Marketing Cloud Next is designed to accomplish its purpose by leveraging actionable data and cross-departmental workflows in addition to autonomous agents embedded across the full customer journey.

In addition to the standard Marketing Cloud on core capabilities, Marketing Cloud Next also includes Loyalty Management, Salesforce Personalization, and Marketing Intelligence capabilities (Figure 10-2). Unlike MCE Personalization and MCE Marketing Intelligence features that exist on an external platform, these Marketing Cloud Next personalization and intelligence capabilities are built on top of Salesforce D360 and accessible as separate apps in the App Launcher.

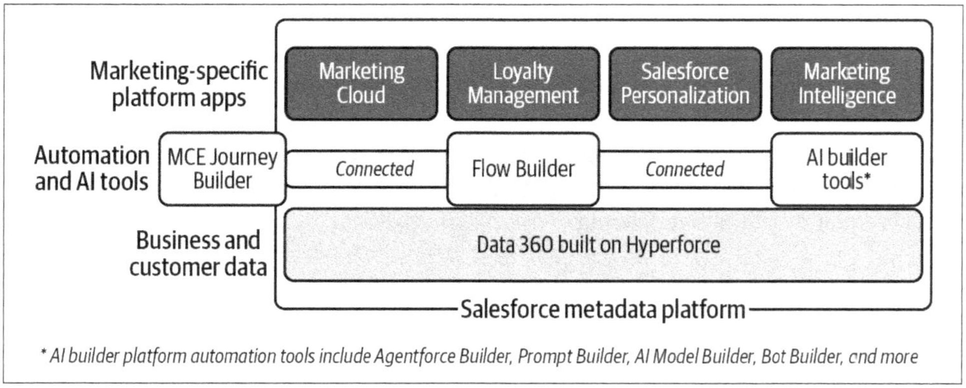

Figure 10-2. Marketing Cloud Next

Marketing Cloud Next is the next evolution for Salesforce as the company continues to build a unified marketing offering on the Salesforce core platform, catering to both B2C and B2B enterprises. Salesforce intends to support their customers who've already made investments on the MCE and MCAE platforms while creating connections that allow a *convergence* toward the Salesforce core platform. For example, it's possible to connect MCE Journey Builder to the Salesforce Flow engine rather than having to re-create MCE journeys in flows on the core platform.

Marketing Cloud Next is built on the Salesforce platform, which means the autonomous AI agents (agents) can fully operate across Sales, Service, and Marketing while orchestrating 1:1 customer engagement across the entire customer lifecycle. Thus, Marketing Cloud Next can put an end to the traditional *do-not-reply* marketing approach often associated with email and messaging campaigns. Using agents, an actual conversation occurs instead of individuals simply receiving a one-way communication via email or text.

This conversational messaging between the customer and the agent blurs the lines between marketing and sales or between marketing and service. For example, a customer can ask an agent for recommendations of what's new from their favorite fashion designer on a retail site while also letting the agent know their clothing size has changed since their last order.

What You Should Know

In Chapter 8, we learned about the Agentforce Lead Nurturing agent when we discussed agentic sales and sales use cases. It's common for the marketing team to take responsibility for the Lead Nurturing agent, so it's recommended you review the details for that agent. In addition, there is a new AI Sales Development Representative (SDR) released in early 2026 that is part of the Agentforce product suite. The AI SDR known as *Piper* is a superagent specifically designed to manage inbound buyer engagement via different modalities including video, voice, and text while switching formats and languages in real time. We won't explore Piper in this chapter, but Salesforce provides a Help article (*https://oreil.ly/TXP0t*) if you're interested in learning more.

This chapter focuses on exploring the AI capabilities for Marketing Cloud Next, including all the AI solutions needed for conversational messaging between humans and agents. However, it's important to understand the differences between the AI solutions available for all three Salesforce marketing platforms. Which specific licenses or packages must be purchased, the permission sets required, and whether your specific Salesforce or Marketing Cloud org type can support the specific features mentioned are not covered in this chapter. These are subjects you'll want to discuss with your Salesforce Account Executive (AE).

Salesforce marketing AI solutions summarized

Some Einstein solutions, like Engagement Scoring, Email Engagement Frequency, Metrics Guard, and Send Time Optimization, are available within all three Salesforce marketing platforms. However, there are many AI features specific to tools within each of the three different marketing platforms. Let's review the AI solutions available across all three Salesforce marketing platforms and then highlight features different across the three platforms.

There are certain Einstein AI features available in all three Salesforce marketing platforms: MCE, MCAE, and Marketing Cloud on core. Those include four predictive AI features:

- Metrics Guard
- Send Time Optimization for Email
- Engagement [Behavior] Scoring for Email and Mobile
- Engagement Frequency

The Agentforce Campaign Creation agent, a generative AI (GenAI) feature, is available for MCAE and Marketing Cloud on core but not MCE. That's logical because MCAE and Marketing Cloud on core use the same standard objects and metadata. MCE is different, though. And even though Agentforce is not available on MCE, there are some GenAI and traditional AI solutions available only on MCE in lieu of the Agentforce Campaign Creation agent. Those include the following features:

- Body Copy Generation
- Subject Line Generation
- Subject Line Tester
- Content Selection

- Content Tagging
- Content Testing
- Messaging Insight
- Copy Insights

In addition, there are some solutions only available on MCE in lieu of the Personalization and Marketing Intelligence capabilities offered on the Salesforce core platform. Those are:

- Recommendations for Audience Builder
- Predictive Intelligence for Audience Builder

The following are available only on MCAE, in lieu of the Marketing Intelligence capabilities offered on the Salesforce core platform:

- Campaign Insights
- Key Accounts Identification
- Attribution, aka Campaign Influence

Marketing Cloud on core has an Opportunity Influence feature similar to the MCAE Campaign Influence feature. In addition, Marketing Cloud on core leverages the powerful segment capabilities available in D360, which includes AI-assisted segment creation.

In addition, AI solution features are available for Marketing Cloud Next applications for Loyalty Management, Salesforce Personalization, and Marketing Intelligence. Builder tools are also available for use on Marketing Cloud on core. Builder tools, in general, were explored in earlier chapters. However, in this chapter, we'll briefly discuss several Agentforce subagents that can be added to any agent. We'll also explore the Agentforce Campaign Creation agent.

One of the important differences between Marketing Cloud on core AI solutions and AI solutions on MCE and MCAE is that D360 is required for Marketing Cloud on core. It's not just required for marketing AI solutions. D360 must be set up before even the most basic Marketing Cloud functionality will work.

D360 is required for Marketing Cloud on core

D360 is required for Marketing Cloud on core to work, and here are required basic steps that need to be completed for Marketing Cloud on core setup. You'll notice that four of the seven required settings relate to D360:

1. Enable D360
2. Create a Salesforce CRM Connector in D360
3. Add a default email channel
4. Add data protection details to records
5. Enable Marketing Cloud
6. Install the following Data Kits for D360: Sales, Marketing Setup Objects, Consent Objects, Flows Integration, Email Channel, SMS Channel, and WhatsApp Channel
7. Set up Identity Resolution in D360

In addition to setting up D360 for basic Marketing Cloud Next functionality, there are certain prerequisites like data graphs that are needed for Einstein capabilities. For example, you'll need to create a D360 data graph if you intend on using Einstein Engagement Scoring, Einstein Engagement Frequency, and Einstein Send Time Optimization features since a data graph is required for these features. If needed, you can get an in-depth coverage of D360 in the O'Reilly *Hands-On Salesforce Data Cloud* book.

How we'll refer to humans in this chapter

As we describe AI for CRM marketing use cases throughout this chapter, we'll be referring often to the impact on the humans receiving the marketing messages. How we actually label humans in the context of Salesforce CRM is influenced by the Salesforce marketing tools used. There are many different labels we can use when referring to a person in the context of Salesforce CRM:

- Lead
- Contact
- Person Account
- Prospect
- Customer
- Subscriber
- Individual
- Unified Individual

Lead and Contact are standard Salesforce objects used in the Sales Cloud as well as in the lead conversion process on the core platform. A *lead* is a person who has expressed an interest in an organization's product or service. *Contacts* are people who've progressed further in the sales cycle and have a relationship with a business account and opportunities, which are deals in progress. A *Person Account* in Salesforce is a person who is both a contact and an account, such as a sole proprietor.

The terms *prospect* and *customer* are frequently used in Salesforce Marketing Cloud Account Engagement. Keep in mind that a customer doesn't necessarily have to be interested in purchasing a product or service. They could, for example, be a donor who contributes to a non-profit.

A *subscriber* is a person who has signed up to receive messages from an organization, such as email messages or SMS messages. In Marketing Cloud Engagement, Subscriber is also an object.

Individual and Unified Individual are Data Model Objects (DMOs) used in Salesforce D360. A Unified Individual record is one that provides a C360 view, known as a unified profile, of a person who could actually have multiple Individual records.

Throughout this chapter, we'll frequently use the term *individual* as a generic term to refer to a person, so an individual isn't necessarily synonymous with a record from the Individual DMO in D360. We'll also use the term *subscriber* to refer to an individual who gave consent to receive marketing messages, so the term subscriber won't refer to an individual record in the MCE platform.

This chapter will focus on describing in detail those marketing-specific use cases for Marketing Cloud Next applications. We'll begin our discussion with the Salesforce AI solutions available on Marketing Cloud on core followed by coverage on AI solutions for Loyalty Management, Salesforce Personalization, and Marketing Intelligence.

Marketing Cloud on Core

Marketing Cloud on core is built on standard Salesforce objects like Account, Contact, Opportunity, and Campaigns. It leverages D360 for basic functionality as well as for all AI solutions. In this section, we'll discuss these seven Marketing Cloud on core Salesforce AI solutions:

- Einstein Engagement Scoring
- Einstein Engagement Frequency
- Einstein Send Time Optimization
- Agentforce agent: Campaign Creation
- Agentforce subagent: Marketing Campaigns
- Einstein Metrics Guard
- Einstein Opportunity Influence

We'll discuss these Marketing Cloud on core AI solutions by dividing them into four main categories: Smart Segmentation, Smart Orchestration, Smart Content Creation, and Smart Measurement.

Smart Segmentation and Smart Orchestration categories include solutions used in Salesforce Flows. The Einstein Engagement Scoring and Einstein Engagement Frequency solutions are used as Einstein Decision element (predictive) models, and the Einstein Send Time Optimization solution is used in a segment-triggered flow. It's easy for some users to confuse the Einstein Engagement Scoring with the Marketing Engagement Scoring, so we'll explore the differences between the two in the sidebar "Einstein Engagement Scoring Versus Einstein Engagement Frequency" on page 370.

For Smart Content Creation, we'll discuss the Campaign Creation agent along with the Marketing Campaigns subagent. Einstein Metrics Guard and Einstein Opportunity Influence are two Smart Measurement features of Marketing Cloud on core that we'll explore.

Smart Segmentation in Flows with Einstein Decision Element Models

Marketers can access either of two Einstein models for smart segmentation purposes: Einstein Engagement Scoring and Einstein Engagement Frequency. Either of these models can be selected using the Einstein Decision element (Figure 10-3). The Einstein Decision element is used within a segment-triggered flow created by marketers from within Marketing Cloud on core. It's important to note that the Einstein Decision Element is supported in automation event-triggered flows, broadcast flows, and segment-triggered flows. It is not supported in record-triggered flows or orchestration flows. Also, the dedicated segment flow capability is now available in the audience flow.

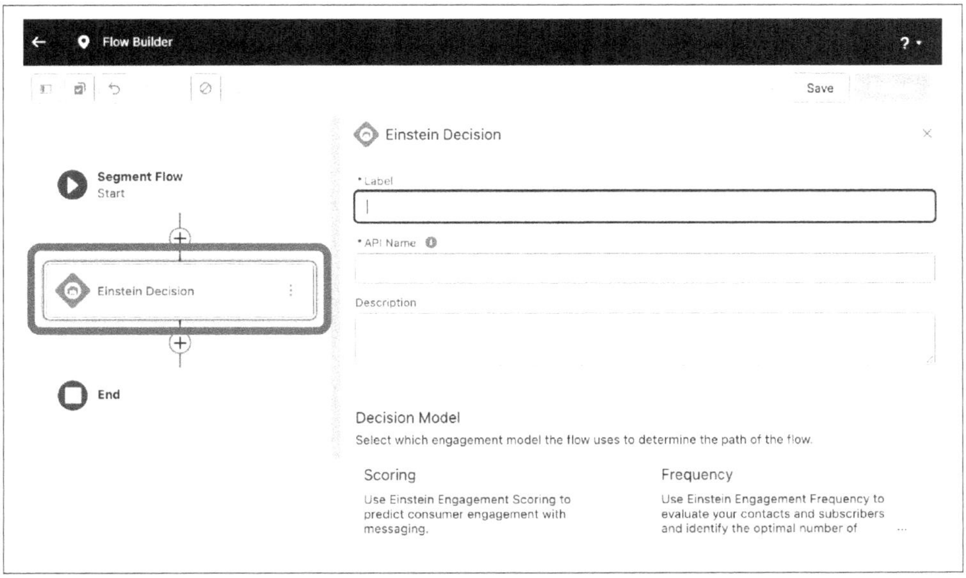

Figure 10-3. Einstein Decision element in a segment-triggered flow

We'll discuss Einstein Engagement Scoring and Einstein Engagement Frequency in detail. However, first we'll want to understand a little about People and Account scoring in Marketing Cloud to help us differentiate between a Marketing Engagement Score and an Einstein Engagement Score. Marketing Engagement Scoring, a type of people score, employs a rules-based approach for scoring whereas Einstein Engagement Scoring uses a predictive AI model.

People and Account scoring

The scoring models feature replaces functionality previously available in the Prospecting Center, which was retired in April 2026. After selecting the scoring models feature from the Setup menu Quick Find box, a new People or Account scoring model can be added. Lead, Contact, and Account records are scored within D360 using a rules-based approach that leverages the Unified Individual or Unified Account object. People scoring can be enabled after the required basic settings have been completed. However, Account scoring cannot be enabled until a data graph has been established in D360. In addition, the selected identity resolution rulesets in the scoring model can't be changed after they're created.

Default or custom rules are used to calculate two scores for people: marketing engagement and marketing fit. Each individual's engagement and fit scores are a simple summation of points. Engagement points can be awarded for various activities such as viewing pages, submitting forms, clicking links, or subscribing to a newsletter (Figure 10-4).

After points are totaled for engagement and fit, an overall marketing score is normalized to provide a number from 0 to 100. The overall marketing score considers a weighted average of marketing engagement and marketing fit scores. Similarly, scores for accounts are rules-based rather than based on a predictive model.

All people scores are stored as Calculated Insights within D360. Engagement Score is stored as an aggregatable measure with a D360 application programming interface (API) name of `Marketing_Engagement_Score__cio`. Fit Score is stored as an aggregatable measure with a D360 API name of `Marketing_Fit_Score__cio`. Overall Marketing Score is stored as a nonaggregatable measure with a D360 API name of `Marketing_Overall_Score__cio`.

Just as with other Calculated Insights, each of the three people scores can be used for segmentation within D360, as previously mentioned. In addition, each of these three scores can be displayed on the lead or contact page within Salesforce core, setting up the D360 Profile Insights component.

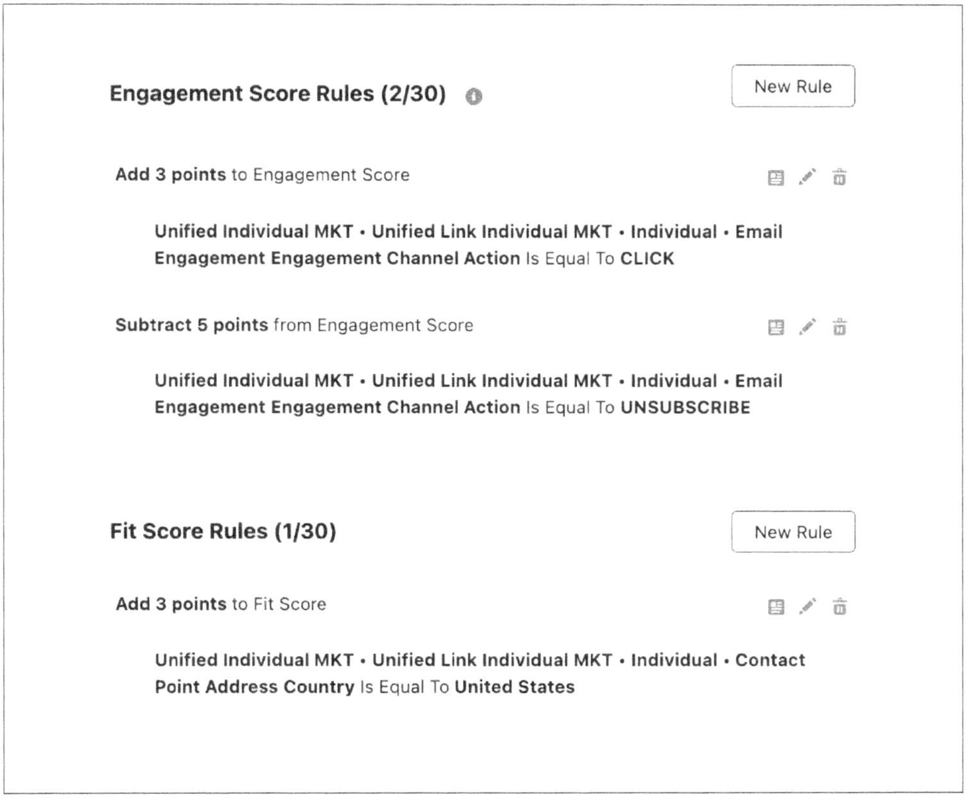

Figure 10-4. Engagement points assigned for rule-based People scoring

The important takeaway is to know that the engagement score that appears on a lead or contact page is not an Einstein Engagement Score derived using a predictive model. Instead, it is just the summation of points assigned through a rule-based model. Now that we better understand the difference between the two types of engagement scores, let's explore Einstein Engagement Scoring.

Einstein Engagement Scoring for email and MobilePush messaging

Einstein Engagement Scoring assigns an engagement score to predict the likelihood a lead or contact will interact with the marketing message, through opens and clicks. It also predicts the likelihood that the lead or contact will stay subscribed. The scoring model uses a predictive AI machine learning model that assigns a score indicating each individual's likelihood to engage with emails or interact with push notifications. An individual can actually be assigned two different Einstein engagement scores, one for email and one for mobile messaging.

The predictive model considers a variety of data. For example, the model could create an engagement score for email based on frequency and recency of email opens and of clicks to view a file, form, video, or other content. Unsubscribes and resubscribes, as well as any spam complaints, are also factors that influence the score. To avoid bias and other ethical risks, the Einstein Engagement Scoring model doesn't include demographic data.

An individual's Einstein engagement score could change for two main reasons:

- Changes in the individual's engagement with the channel messages, either email or mobile
- Changes in the predictive model

As individuals engage with the channel messages, their Einstein engagement score could change. If the person opens an message multiple times and clicks on the links, their Einstein engagement score will likely go up. If the individual deletes several unread messages and then unsubscribes, their Einstein engagement score decreases.

Even if the individual doesn't change their engagement activity, the score could still change because of updates to the predictive model. The Einstein Engagement Scoring model is updated approximately weekly. Thus, an individual's actual engagement score could vary slightly from week to week.

In addition to the actual score generated from the Einstein Engagement Scoring model, the Einstein Engagement Scoring feature also generates specific scores. For example, the following scores are generated for email engagement:

- Email open score
- Email click score
- Email subscribe score

The model also provides the following metrics:

- Email open likelihood
- Email click likelihood
- Email subscribe (retention) likelihood

For each of the three likelihood metrics, there are four possible categories: Most Likely, More Likely, Less Likely, and Least Likely. In addition, the scoring model uses a blended score to bucket subscribers into persona-based groups (Table 10-2). An individual's persona is stored in the Email Engagement DMO Persona field.

Table 10-2. Einstein Engagement persona-based groups

Subscriber persona	Open engagement	Click engagement
Loyalist	High	High
Window Shopper	High	Low
Selective Subscriber	Low	High
Winback/Dormant	Low	Low

For each of these subscriber personas, there are recommended strategies for marketers to consider (Table 10-3).

Table 10-3. Subscriber persona recommendations

Subscriber persona	Recommendation
Loyalist	Increase email frequency, create lookalike audiences, or send exclusive offers
Window Shopper	Include recommendations, test the call-to-actions and incentives
Selective Subscriber	Optimize subject lines, personalize content based on past purchases
Winback/Dormant	User surveys, alternative channels, or win-back campaigns

Individual Einstein engagement scores can be used in a variety of ways. For example, Einstein engagement scores can now be used within a decision element in Flow Builder. The *Einstein Decision* element feature, introduced in the Salesforce summer '25 release, allows users to create branches using Einstein Engagement Scoring and Einstein Engagement Frequency. We'll discuss Einstein Engagement Frequency in "Einstein Engagement Frequency" on page 368.

A decision flow element provides Flow Builder users with the ability to create evaluation criteria for a set of conditions and route people through the flow based on the outcomes of those decisions. This element type functions as an if-then statement for users to easily create branches within a flow based on an individual's Einstein engagement score or engagement frequency. The Einstein Decision element is frequently used in a segment-triggered flow or an automation event-triggered flow.

In the configuration pane of the Einstein Decision element, you'll select any of the available data graph fields as the Resource in a condition. For Einstein Engagement Scoring, the following fields can be selected as a Resource:

- Email Open Likelihood
- Email Click Likelihood
- Email Engagement Persona

There are required steps before the Einstein engagement score can be used in a flow. For one thing, the Einstein Decision element in a flow requires configuration of a D360 data graph. You'll also need to verify that the identity resolution ruleset upon which the data graph is built uses Individual, rather than Account, as the primary DMO. In addition, you must enable the Einstein Engagement Scoring feature from the Setup menu.

It usually takes 24 to 48 hours before the initial scores are generated, but it could take longer if there is insufficient historical data. Once Einstein Engagement Scoring is enabled in an org, you're able to navigate to the D360 app and view the Email Engagement Score DMO.

In addition to using the Einstein Likelihood scores and the Email Engagement Persona in the Einstein Decision element of a Flow, the Engagement Score DMO fields can be used as a criteria when creating segments in D360 (Figure 10-5).

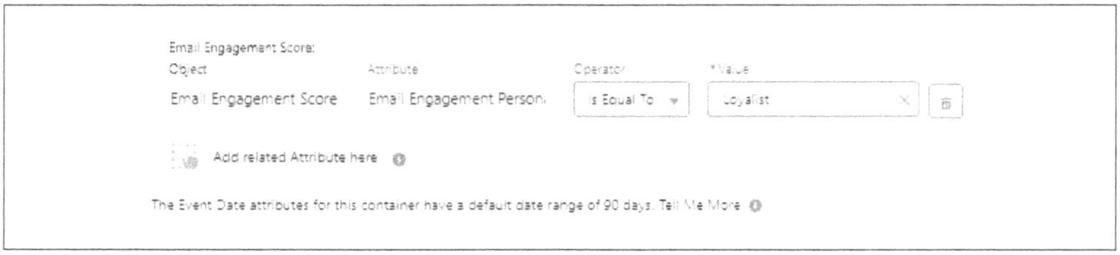

Figure 10-5. Using Einstein Email Engagement Score when creating segments in Data 360

In addition to using Einstein Engagement Scoring for smart segmentation purposes, there's also the Einstein Engagement Frequency feature available to marketers.

Einstein Engagement Frequency

Einstein Engagement Frequency (EEF) assists marketers in determining the right number of emails to send to individuals. Within Salesforce core, EEF can be accessed using Marketing Cloud Advanced edition or with Salesforce Personalization on the core platform.

EEF uses a predictive model to determine how frequently marketing messages should be sent to individuals. The model analyzes up to 90 days of individual subscribers' historical engagement patterns over time. The engagement history considers factors such as email bounces and engagement events including opens, clicks, unsubscribes, and spam complaints. To avoid bias and other ethical risk, the EEF model doesn't consider demographic data. The model also doesn't consider the actual message content, which could vary significantly from message to message.

An individual's EEF score can be used to power the frequency split activity in Expression Builder. The frequency split is an important feature because it considers the optimal number of emails to send to an individual contact across all campaigns. Individuals can be bucketed into one of the categories listed in Table 10-4. Individuals with insufficient data for the EEF model to make a determination will be routed through a default path.

Table 10-4. Einstein Engagement Frequency classifications

Classification	Explanation	Recommendation
Saturated	Receiving too many messages	Reduce frequency to avoid stress
Almost saturated	Close to saturation	Adjustments needed
On target	Ideal frequency	Maintain consistency
Undersaturated	Receiving too few emails	Increase frequency to maximize engagement

Another use for the EEF is as an option within the Einstein Decision flow element. In the configuration pane of the Einstein Decision element, you'll select the Email Engagement Classification field as the metric for Email Engagement Frequency.

There are a few steps needed before EEF can be used in a flow or an expression. As with Einstein Engagement Scoring, you'll also need to ensure that you've created the appropriate D360 data graph and the identity resolution ruleset upon which the data graph is built uses Individual, rather than Account, as the primary DMO. In addition, you must enable Einstein Engagement Frequency from the Setup menu.

When you search in the setup for Einstein Engagement Frequency, be sure to click on the one underneath Einstein for Marketing rather than the one under Einstein Account Engagement (Figure 10-6).

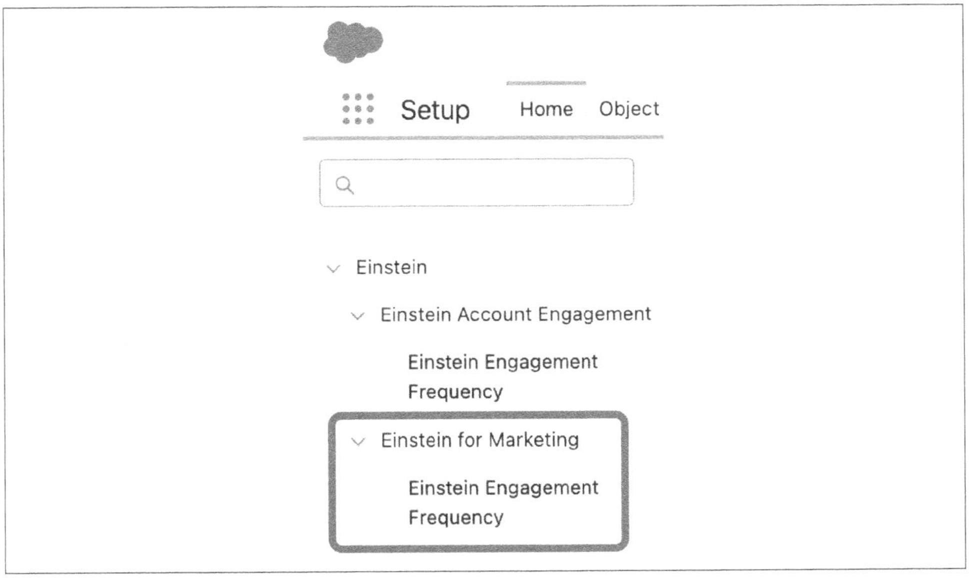

Figure 10-6. Select Einstein for Marketing to enable Einstein Engagement Frequency

The goal of the EEF model is to optimize the frequency with which customers engage with marketing content. Salesforce uses data of other users with similar patterns to adjust the scoring of the messaging frequency for an individual. Salesforce trains each org's model using only that org's user data and, as such, there are requirements that must be met before EEF is available:

- A minimum of 10 subscribers is required for the model to generate an engagement frequency.
- A minimum of five frequencies is required to model for engagement frequency, meaning the audience must receive at least five variants of the sender's promotional messaging over a 28-day period. Transaction emails don't count.

The EEF model and scores are updated approximately once a week.

Einstein Engagement Scoring Versus Einstein Engagement Frequency

Einstein Engagement Scoring, a type of behavior scoring, is a core aspect of marketing automation. Assigning an engagement score to a prospect or customer helps differentiate between prospects who are less engaged as opposed to those who are highly engaged. As a result, it's easier for marketers to send the most appropriate message to the individual. An engagement score is a number from 0–100 assigned to an individual, and an individual can be assigned more than one engagement score because a separate engagement score is assigned for each channel. For example, an individual can have an engagement score for email engagement and mobile SMS engagement.

Whereas Einstein Engagement Scoring influences the actual message to be sent, EEF is a feature that assists marketers in determining the right number of emails to send to individual subscribers. EEF predicts the optimal number of emails to send an individual, which, hopefully, results in maximum engagement. The EEF tool available on the core platform can be accessed with either the Marketing Cloud Advanced edition or separately from Marketing Personalization on the core platform. Both EEF and Einstein Engagement Scoring are AI features available in the Marketing Cloud Next application suite that are most often utilized in flows for segmentation purposes.

Smart Orchestration with Einstein Send Time Optimization

Einstein STO improves customer engagement by personalizing each individual's experience so that subscribers receive a marketing message on the days and times when they're most likely to open and interact with it. Einstein achieves this 1-to-1 customization by evaluating historical email engagement behavior data from which it can then predict an ideal send time.

There are some important considerations for STO:

- Einstein STO is available only for Lightning emails and is not available for Salesforce classic emails.
- Einstein STO requires 90 days of email engagement metrics for each subscriber. Specifically, an individual must have at least one engagement activity in the past 90 days.
- A randomized send time recommendation is selected for new subscribers or individuals who haven't engaged with the organization at least once in the last 90 days.
- Neither demographic data nor actual email content is considered when determining the optimal send time. In addition, data purchased or collected from third parties is not considered.

To enable STO, first verify you've established an identity resolution ruleset that uses Individual as the primary DMO. Next, from Setup, in the Quick Find box, enter Send Time and select Einstein Send Time Optimization (STO) from beneath the Einstein for Marketing listing.

> You must opt in to the global data model to use STO if your Salesforce org uses Marketing Cloud Growth Edition. However, you have the option to use either data model option if your org uses Marketing Cloud Advanced Edition.

You'll select the data option that uses a global model, with pooled data, or the option to enable with your org-specific data (Figure 10-7).

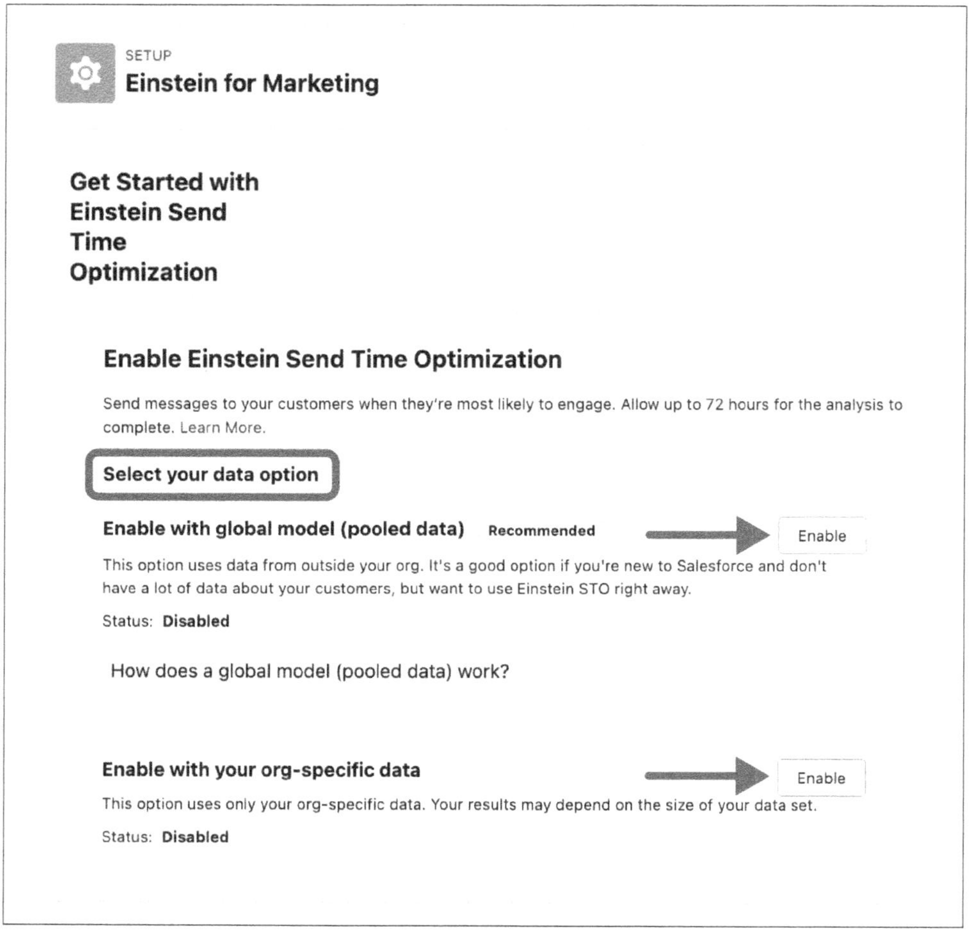

Figure 10-7. Select your data option when enabling Einstein Send Time Optimization

Once STO is enabled, it takes up to 72 hours before results appear. Afterward, the model updates STO details once a week. If the STO feature is later disabled in the Salesforce org, new messages can't use the feature but existing email sends still include optimized send times.

After enabling Einstein STO, a new D360 DMO is automatically created. Make note of the *Hourly Scores By Week* field in the DMO because it will be important when creating a data graph.

Creating a D360 Data Graph

Creating a D360 data graph is required so that STO can be used within Marketing Cloud flows. Users can create a data graph by navigating to the D360 app and following these steps:

1. Navigate to the Data Graphs tab in the D360 app. Click on the New button to start the process of creating a new data graph.
2. Select Start from Scratch and click Next.
3. Select Real-Time Data Graph and click Next.
4. Provide a Data Graph Name. Note that the Data Graph API name will be automatically generated. Select Unified Individual as the primary data model object. Click Next.
5. Accept the real-time consumption limits default settings by clicking Next.
6. Add the Email Send Time Optimization attribute to the data graph hierarchy as shown in Figure 10-8.

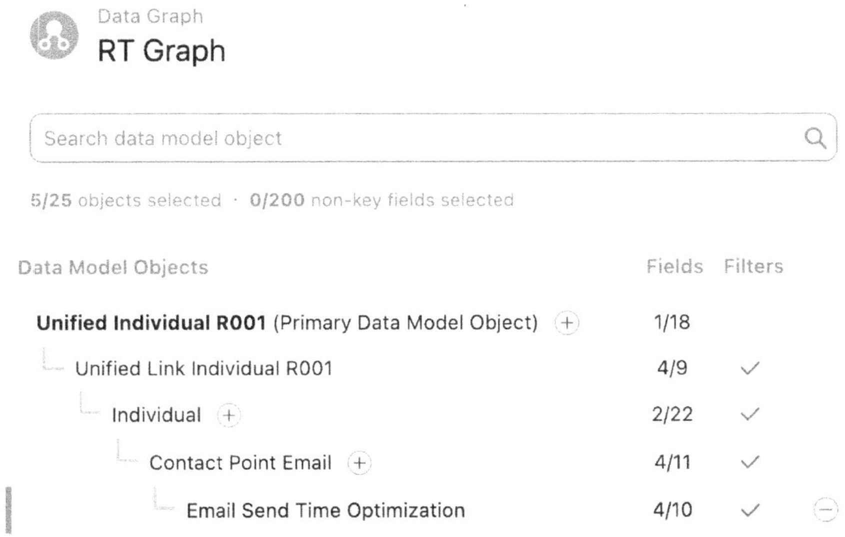

Figure 10-8. Data 360 data graph attributes in a graph hierarchy

7. Select the Hourly Scores by Week field from the Email Send Time Optimization DMO fields, located just to the right of the Data Model Objects hierarchy.
8. Click the "Save and Build" button at the top right of the screen.

With STO enabled and a data graph created, it's possible to use Einstein STO in a segment-triggered flow (Figure 10-9).

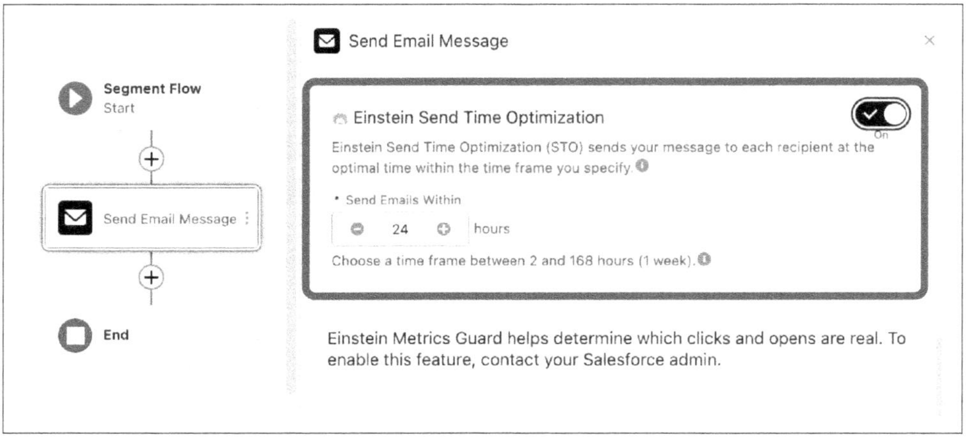

Figure 10-9. Einstein Send Time Optimization used within segment-triggered flow

You'll notice it's possible to toggle on and off the Einstein Send Time Optimization feature for a specific email message. When toggling on the feature for the email message, the time frame interval must be selected. The selected time frame must be at least 2 hours but no longer than 168 hours, the equivalent of one week.

Emails sent based on the STO interval are sent exclusively at the top of the hour. Keep this in mind when determining the time frame value.

For example, you'll want to select a six-hour time frame if you need emails to arrive after 10:20 a.m. and no later than 4:50 p.m. Emails will be sent at the top of the hour to subscribers at 11 a.m., noon, 1 p.m., 2 p.m., 3 p.m., and 4 p.m. based on the individual's send time optimization value. It's pretty straightforward to determine the time frame when sending only one message. It gets more difficult when establishing a waiting period in between two email messages (Figure 10-10).

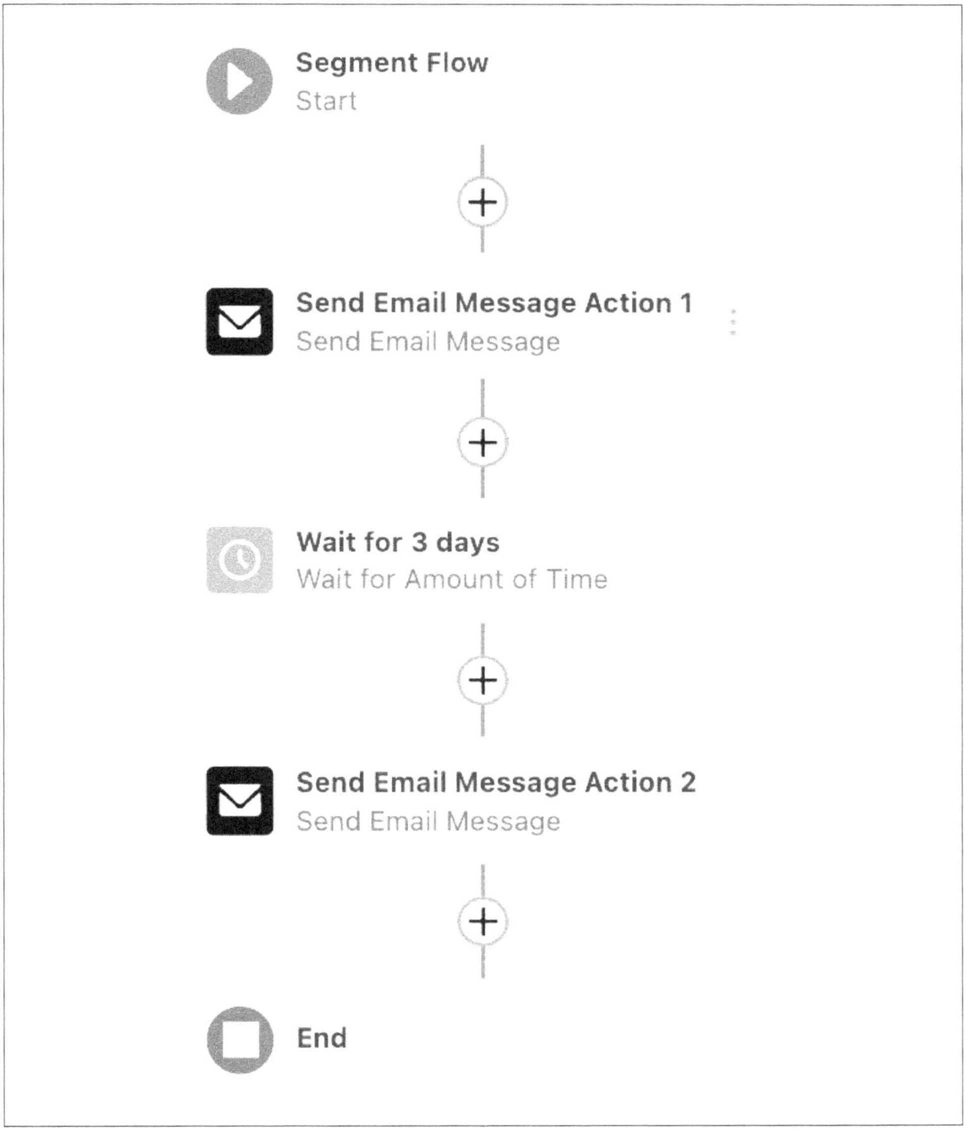

Figure 10-10. Adding a waiting period in between two email messages in a flow

Let's continue with the example of selecting a six-hour time frame for the first email that will be sent sometime between 11 a.m. and 4 p.m. at the top of the hour. We'll assume recipients receive the email one minute after it's sent. Assume you want to wait three days and then send a second email. You again select the six-hour time frame. However, it won't likely achieve the results you desired. People who received an email at 4:01 p.m. will have a time frame of 5 p.m. to 10 p.m. for their second email message (Table 10-5), which won't meet the requirement.

Table 10-5. Email 2 message send times after three-day wait

Email 1 STO send time	Email 1 received	Email 2 send time frame
11:00 a.m.	11:01 a.m.	12 p.m. – 5 p.m.
12:00 p.m.	12:01 p.m.	1 p.m. – 6 p.m.
1:00 p.m.	1:01 p.m.	2 p.m. – 7 p.m.
2:00 p.m.	2:01 p.m.	3 p.m. – 8 p.m.
3:00 p.m.	3:01 p.m.	4 p.m. – 9 p.m.
4:00 p.m.	4:01 p.m.	5 p.m. – 10 p.m.

Fortunately, there's a way to prevent time shifts. Within the Wait for Amount of Time element, use the option to resume at a specific time of day (Figure 10-11). In our example, instead of waiting three days, we'd wait two days and resume specifically at 10:30 a.m. to achieve our desired results.

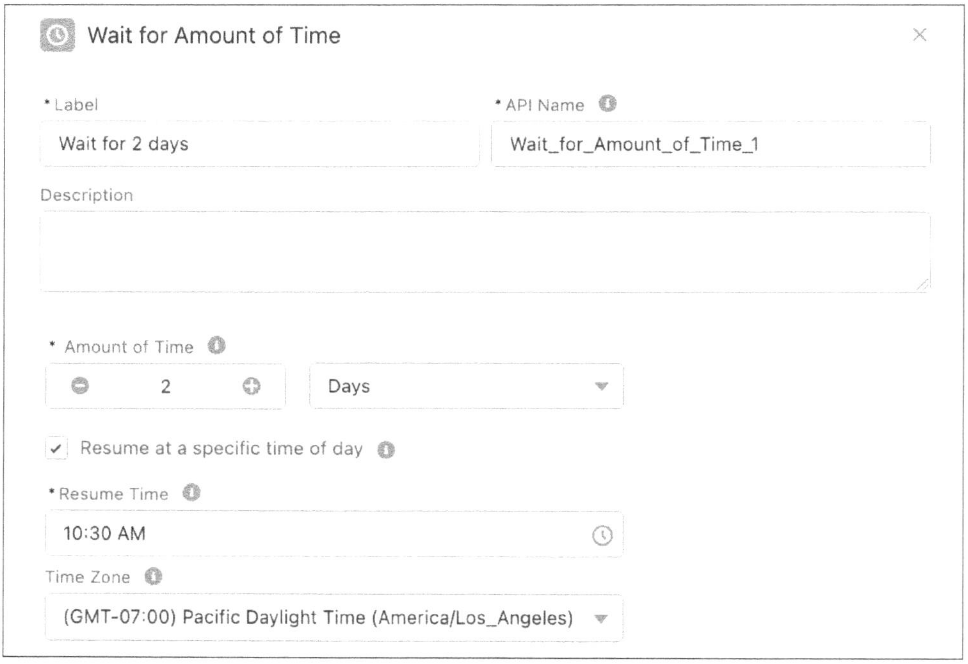

Figure 10-11. Option to resume at a specific time of day

Start time, resume time, and send time windows can be adjusted in your flows. It's helpful to review analytics reports within D360, built on DMO data, that provide a weekly chart showing when your customers typically engage with your messages. In addition to reports and dashboards, Salesforce provides many ways marketers can accurately measure results. We'll see a great example of this in the next section when we learn about Einstein Metrics Guard.

Smart Content Creation

Marketing Cloud on core has the Campaign Creation agent that is used by marketers to co-create marketing campaign content. This Agentforce agent drafts a campaign brief based on the marketer's stated goals and segment target audiences. The agent also drafts content and constructs customer journey flows. In addition, the Campaign Creation agent can generate key performance indicators (KPIs) to track and suggest campaign components to add.

The Campaign Creation agent is a GenAI solution that includes the Marketing Campaigns subagent. Alternatively, the subagent can be added to any other preexisting agent. For Marketing Cloud Growth users, the Marketing Campaigns subagent is available from within the Marketing app by clicking on the Agentforce logo at the top of the page. Marketers describe their campaign and then the marketing agent generates a draft of the campaign brief that includes a preview of the subject line, preheader, and paragraph copy for your email.

> Do not remove the brief from a campaign because a brief is required to use Agentforce agents with campaigns. If you remove a brief from a campaign, the related segments and content remain but the agent can't help you with that campaign.

The output from the Marketing Campaigns subagent can be used in the content builder on the marketing page. When a user clicks the sparkle icon, the agent drafts or revises text for an email, landing page, or SMS message that is grounded in the campaign brief, the assigned brand, and the existing content on the canvas.

The marketing agent can also provide a campaign summary. In addition, the agent tells you the number of opens, the clickthrough rate, and the message delivery stats.

The Marketing Campaigns subagent can also be added to any preexisting agent, such as the default agent, by selecting to add the subagent from the Asset Library. Here are the details for the Marketing Campaigns subagent:

Classification Description
: Users who want to generate, make, create, summarize, or bootstrap their marketing campaigns or briefs should use this subagent.

Scope
: Assists users in generating, making, creating, summarize, or bootstrapping their Salesforce Marketing Campaign and/or Brief objects.

Alternatively, you can create a new Agentforce agent from the Campaign Creation template within Agentforce Builder. The Campaign Creation agent includes the Marketing Campaigns subagent. Agents and subagents were discussed in more detail in Chapter 6.

Smart Measurement

Within Marketing Cloud on core, there are two distinct types of smart measurement AI solutions: Einstein Metrics Guard and Einstein Opportunity Influence. Einstein Metrics Guard is the same functionality for Marketing Cloud on core as MCE and MCAE. However, Metrics Guard needs to be enabled first for Marketing Cloud on core. Einstein Opportunity Influence is similar to Einstein Campaign Influence on the MCAE platform.

Einstein Metrics Guard

Einstein Metrics Guard (Metrics Guard) identifies bursts of open and click activity likely caused by email scanners and bots. Email privacy protection solutions implemented by some client providers have the ability to automatically scan and analyze content for the purpose of identifying potential security threats such as phishing and malware. In doing so, however, these actions can artificially inflate subscriber engagement metrics.

Metrics Guard works behind the scenes as an AI-powered filter to analyze email clicks and opens to determine whether it's likely a human performed those actions. A confidence score, ranging from 0–100%, is assigned and a determination is made based on a specified threshold level.

The goal of Metrics Guard is to help marketers gain insights that provide a more realistic view of subscriber engagement levels, which can be used to create better segmentation on future campaigns. For example, Metrics Guard might predict low engagement for a certain segment. Thus, a marketer could decide not to send the marketing message to that particular segment.

There are a few important things to note. First, Metrics Guard is also available in MCE and MCAE as well as in Marketing Cloud on core. However, Metrics Guard functionality is automatically built into MCE and MCAE but needs to be enabled for Salesforce Marketing Cloud on core. To enable it, complete these steps:

1. From Setup, in the Quick Find box, search for Unified Messaging.
2. Select Email Feature Settings.
3. Enable Einstein Metrics Guard.

Note that if you disable the Metrics Guard feature, your engagement metrics are more likely to include bot activity.

> Metrics Guard can't be disabled in MCE or MCAE. In contrast, Metrics Guard is disabled by default in Marketing Cloud on core and needs to be enabled.

Second, Metrics Guard uses predictive AI capabilities to analyze an individual's historical engagement events and patterns to create a confidence score. Engagement history evaluated includes these values: email sends, bounces, and engagement events including opens, clicks, unsubscribes, spam complaints, and associated timestamps. Importantly, Metrics Guard excludes demographic data in the evaluation, which helps to avoid ethical risks and biased results.

The AI model used for Metrics Guard scoring is discriminative rather than generative in nature. Thus, a customized Metrics Guard model needs to be trained on large amounts of data from a Salesforce org. However, it's unlikely any one Salesforce org has sufficient data for training. Therefore, Salesforce uses a global model of in-house data and outsourced data, with optimized sample weights customized for each Salesforce org. See Chapter 2 for more information about Salesforce global models.

Einstein Opportunity Influence

Understanding which specific campaigns impact opportunities is important. The Einstein Opportunity Influence feature uses marketing engagement data to associate opportunity revenue with a specific marketing campaign effort. An opportunity with a status of Closed/Won is considered, and email and SMS click engagement activity related to a specific campaign is evaluated 30 days prior to status change. No activity data from external sites is considered.

The engagement activity is considered for those people who have engaged with the campaign content and have a contact role on the Closed/Won opportunity. The resulting attribution data allows marketers to accurately report on ROI, adjust strategies for current campaigns, and make informed decisions about future campaigns.

> The standard Opportunity object and the standard Close Data and Amount fields are used for Einstein Opportunity Influence. It's not possible to substitute a custom Opportunity object or custom fields for Close Data and Amount.

There are some important considerations before enabling Opportunity Influence:

- Opportunity Influence can't be enabled in Salesforce orgs where the multiple currencies feature is enabled.
- Opportunity Influence revenue data doesn't reflect campaign hierarchies.
- Unified profile data is *not* used for Opportunity Influence. Instead, revenue is attributed based on engagement data related to Individual DMO records.
- Confirm Campaign Influence hasn't been enabled previously in your Salesforce org before enabling Opportunity Influence. If so, you'll need to disable Campaign Influence or Customizable Campaign Influence from your campaign page layout.

Einstein Opportunity Influence can be enabled by selecting Opportunity Influence in the Quick Find box in Setup. Be sure to review the Readiness Check section and complete any remaining tasks. Afterward, click Enable and then turn on the desired attribution models. First-touch attribution gives credit to the first campaign an opportunity engaged with, whereas a last-touch attribution gives credit to the last campaign a person engaged with prior to the opportunity closing.

Generating attribution data occurs within an hour after Einstein Opportunity Influence is enabled. Afterward, all opportunity records and related engagement data are assessed hourly. Attribution records are generated for opportunities created in the past 30 days based on engagements that happened in the last 60 days. After enabling this Einstein feature, the Opportunity Influence–related list appears on campaign records. The related list, labeled as Performance, displays up to 1,000 opportunity records in order of revenue.

Marketing AI Solutions on Core Using Builder Tools

As mentioned in the introduction, there are many prebuilt AI solutions for marketers. In those rare instances when it's necessary for marketers to build their own Marketing AI solutions within Salesforce core, they can access Builder tools such as Prompt Builder, Agentforce Builder, AI Model Builder, and more. These Builder tools can also be used for the other apps in the Marketing Cloud Next suite, including Loyalty Management.

Loyalty Management

The Loyalty Management app gives marketers the tools to delegate promotion creation and configuration to Agentforce, thereby reducing the time it takes to deliver the right promotion to the right audience at the right time. This is important because one of the most time-consuming tasks for marketers managing customer loyalty programs is developing and optimizing loyalty promotions.

Loyalty Management is built on the Salesforce core platform and leverages D360 data. This makes it easy for marketers to leverage Agentforce capabilities to help with loyalty management tasks and responsibilities. Prebuilt templates and subagents are Agentforce features that can be leveraged by Salesforce Loyalty Management users (Table 10-6).

Table 10-6. Loyalty Management Agentforce features

Agentforce feature	Feature label
Prompt template	Summarize Loyalty Program
Prompt template	Summarize Loyalty Promotion
Subagent	Promotion with Loyalty Accrual Rule
Subagent	Promotion with Spend X Rule

Let's briefly review the prompt templates and subagents available for loyalty management use cases.

Loyalty Management Prompt Templates

Two Agentforce prompt templates are available to marketers who want to use the Einstein Summary component GenAI features to obtain a summary of a loyalty program or loyalty promotions from data that resides across multiple objects. Once Einstein for Loyalty Management is enabled in a Salesforce org, certain changes happen immediately (Table 10-7) to give marketers the tools they need.

Table 10-7. Automatic org changes after enabling Einstein for Loyalty Management

Org change	Purpose
The Einstein Summary component is added to these two record pages: Loyalty Program and Promotion	The component enables users to generate summaries for loyalty programs and promotions
These prompt templates are added: Summarize Loyalty Program and Summarize Loyalty Promotion	The prompt templates work behind the scenes to generate summaries displayed on the Einstein Summary component
These context definitions are added: Loyalty Program Summary and Loyalty Promotion Summary	The context definitions act as a bridge that securely provides the data required by the prompt templates to generate summaries

Using the Summary component, users can securely generate summaries for their loyalty programs and loyalty promotions. Marketers can also take advantage of two Loyalty subagents.

Loyalty Management Subagents

Either, or both, of the Loyalty subagents can be added to any preexisting agent, such as the default agent. Simply select to add the subagent from the Asset Library.

The *Promotion with Loyalty Accrual Rule* subagent gives marketers the ability to create and update promotions that reward loyalty program members for completing eligible accrual activities. The agent can also be used by marketers to draft loyalty promotion emails.

The *Promotion with Spend X Rule* subagent gives marketers the ability to update promotions that reward customers for placing orders worth a specific amount.

The Promotion with Loyalty Accrual Rule and the Promotion with Spend X Rule are two important ways marketers can use Agentforce to efficiently create and update promotions with ease. Agents and subagents were discussed in Chapter 6.

Salesforce Personalization

In addition to the Loyalty Management app, the functionality of Marketing Cloud can be extended with Salesforce Personalization. Personalization is a C360 application powered by D360 to provide personalized experiences across several Salesforce clouds, including the Marketing Cloud. In this section, we'll discuss three Salesforce Personalization AI features:

- Einstein Personalized Recommender
- Agentforce subagent: Personalized Recommendations
- Attribution Intelligence

Personalization uses product recommendations and either goal-based or rule-based content targeting to deliver personalized recommendations to users. In addition, there is an Attribution Intelligence feature available via Salesforce Personalization that addresses an ecommerce use case for tracking key metrics.

> Salesforce Personalization is a C360 app within the Salesforce core platform and is part of the Marketing Next suite of apps. Personalization extends the Marketing Cloud on core offering and is different from Marketing Cloud Personalization. Marketing Cloud Personalization, formerly known as Interaction Studio, is available on the MCE platform.

Personalization on the core platform can be used for creating dynamically varied content for marketing email communications and other marketing channels. In addition, Personalization on the core platform allows path experimentation for segment-triggered flows to help determine the best outcome for a path. Personalization requires an active D360 license to function.

When used alongside Marketing Cloud Next, Personalization is accessible as an application within Salesforce core (Figure 10-12). Alternatively, Personalization features can be accessed via *Personalization as a Service* using D360 to provide real-time personalization functionality across many channels. This means Personalization can be used for many different use cases beyond single-channel marketing.

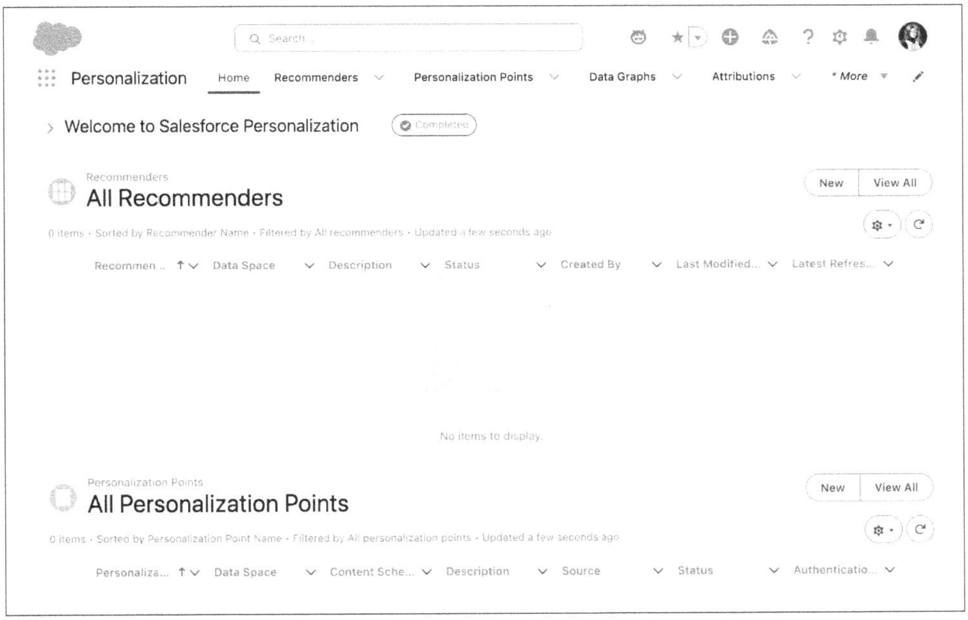

Figure 10-12. Home page for the Salesforce Personalization app on the Salesforce core platform

Personalized recommenders use digital and offline behavior, as well as business context data, to provide multichannel, focused, individualized recommendations. To create these personalized recommendations, a recommender needs to be configured and trained using preselected D360 data graphs. D360 is also where the Salesforce Personalization DMOs are stored. Refer to the Salesforce documentation (*https://oreil.ly/8N6I_*) for more details about the DMOs.

Salesforce Personalization Terminology

Marketing Cloud Personalization is a relatively new Salesforce product, so let's review some terminology that will be helpful as you navigate this chapter:

Personalization point
: Represents a *point* in an experience that's eligible for a personalization decision. This point has a type and response template.

Personalization type
: Identifies the kind of personalized content you want to present. A recommendation is an example of a personalization type.

Personalization response template
: Defines the configuration options available to marketers when building a personalization decision.

Personalization decision
: Determines who's eligible to receive a personalization response using optional targeting rules. Decisions also determine what content to return. A personalization point can contain multiple personalization decisions targeted at different sets of individuals.

Targeting rule
: Determines who's eligible to view personalized content provided by a decision based on specific data points such as attributes, related attributes, Calculated Insights, or segment memberships.

Personalizer
: Calls an additional service at runtime to retrieve the information necessary for a complete decision response.

Recommender
: A type of personalizer that provides targeted product or item recommendations. A recommendation is based on machine learning strategies or Calculated Insights and is usable across channels.

To begin the setup process for Personalization, navigate to the Personalization Setup home page from within the Quick Find menu of Setup. You'll need to deploy foundational data, containing objects and preconfigured insights, by clicking the Deploy button. It will take a few minutes for the Personalization data kit to be deployed and you'll receive a notification message when the process is complete.

Next, set up the Personalization Pipeline Intelligence dashboard, which provides insights into the health and performance of your personalization pipeline. Installing the dashboard requires Daily Personalization Requests and Daily Personalization Unique Calculated Insights be deployed. It's important to note these insights aren't scheduled when installed, so you'll need to configure the scheduling. Selecting a schedule controls when D360 processes Calculated Insights.

Enabling CRM Analytics is required to view the intelligence dashboard. In addition, you'll need to select a data space where the Pipeline Intelligence dashboard will be installed. After selecting the desired data space, click the Install button. There are several considerations and limitations for Salesforce Personalization. Refer to the Salesforce documentation (*https://oreil.ly/OegTN*) for more details.

Einstein Personalized Recommender

Within the Personalization app, it's possible to create a new recommender by selecting the data space and then choosing the profile data graph and the item data graph (Figure 10-13). The recommender needs both data views before making a recommendation to a profile about items. It also needs the signals linking the two model views. The profile data graph has all the people details. The item data graph can be used to recommend any kind of content as long as it's in a DMO with an item data graph built on it. Keep in mind that having those real-time data graphs unlocks many new ways to interact with customers because you can get the right content to them in the moment.

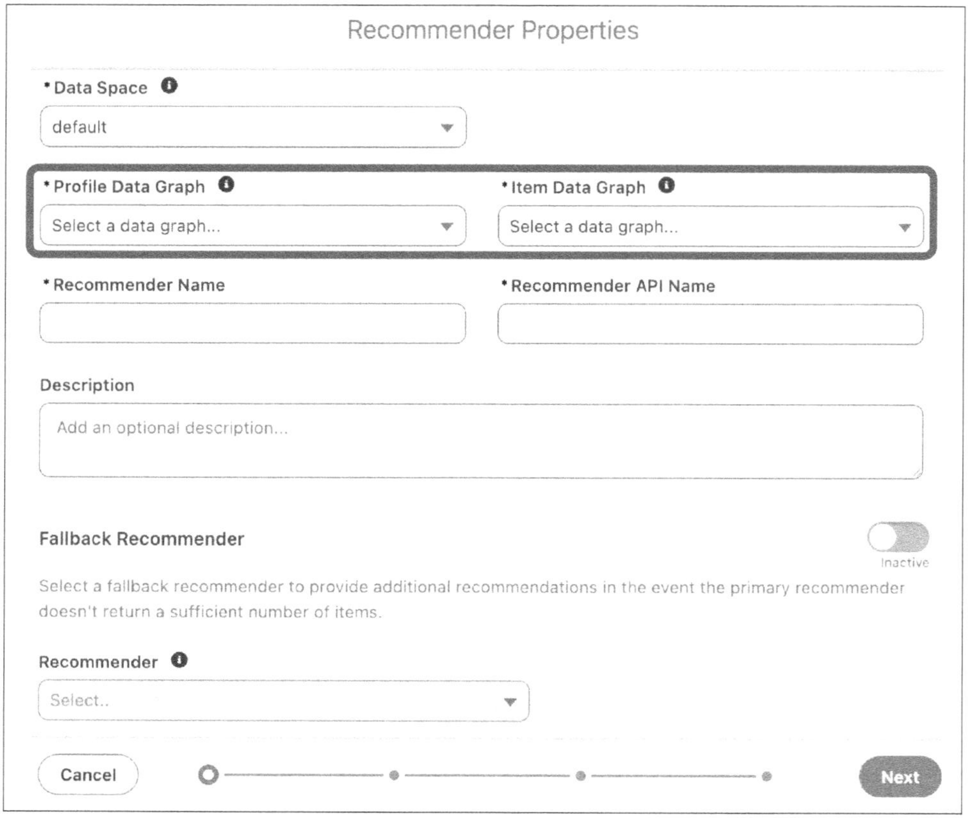

Figure 10-13. Both a profile data graph and an item data graph are required for a recommender

The next choice is to decide between creating an objective-based recommendation or a rule-based recommendation. The objective-based recommendation uses a machine learning model to analyze each user's unique historical behavior in order to make a recommendation that aligns to a specific objective you define. In contrast, rule-based recommendations use business logic to mathematically determine a list of recommendations based on D360 Calculated Insights. We'll focus on objective-based recommendations because they are an AI solution.

When selecting object-based recommendations option, the user is prompted to select an existing objective or create a new objective. *Maximize revenue* or *maximize clicks* are two examples of an object-based objective. Creating new objectives requires the selection of the recommender's purpose, either maximize or minimize, and requires creation of engagement signal metrics, which measure the business outcomes that personalization aims to achieve.

The final step in creating objective-based recommendations is to define the desired filters. This is an additional layer that you can use to either include or exclude items based on specific criteria. For example, you could create a filter to only show articles published within the last 30 days. Perhaps you want to only show articles relevant for the customer's specific industry, or you can match the customer's loyalty tier to only recommend products for which the customer is qualified. Creating filters is a powerful option to employ but it's not required.

> D360 is critical to Personalization functionality. To generate and present unique content experiences, Personalization uses D360 profile and item data graphs, Calculated Insights, segments, and real-time behavioral data.

Some considerations when configuring a recommender include:

- Two D360 data graphs are needed for recommenders: a profile data graph to identify who is eligible to receive personalized content and another item- or catalog-specific data graph to identify which content is available to recommend.
- Calculated Insights must be configured in advance for rule-based recommendations.
- A recommender returns up to 12 recommendations at a time for each personalization point.
- Only one item is selected for display from a list of duplicates if a recommender receives duplicate items for recommendation.

These recommenders will be used within personalization decisions for a variety of purposes because recommenders make it possible to provide individualized, dynamically varied content for many different use cases. For example, an individual will be provided with a very specific personalized credit card offer, rather than an offer for and details about a home loan, if the person is asking credit card–related questions of an agent on a banking website.

Organizations want to excel at anticipating customers' needs and delivering 1:1 experiences, but capturing and keeping an individual's attention often requires a lot of time and money. Further, scaling these 1:1 experiences is impossible with humans alone. Recommenders make many things possible, including seemingly simple but very effective personalized conversations between a human and an agent.

Agentforce Subagent: Personalized Recommendations

The Personalized Recommendations subagent can be added to any preexisting agent, such as the default agent or a Service agent, by selecting to add the subagent from the Asset Library. Here are details for the Personalized Recommendations subagent:

Classification Description
: Handles requests for personalized recommendations or suggestions

Scope
: Triggers the Get Recommendations action and displays personalized recommendations, based on user engagement

Agents and subagents were discussed in Chapter 6.

Attribution Intelligence

In addition to the recommendations provided by Personalization that are applicable across many Salesforce Clouds, there is a unique Personalization AI feature addressing a very specific ecommerce use case. Attribution Intelligence, a Personalization feature, tracks effectiveness against three key metrics: *Add to carts*, *Orders*, and *Revenue*.

It's possible to deploy Attribution Intelligence in any D360 data space running the Personalization app. Begin the deployment process by selecting a data space, an identity resolution ruleset, and then launching the deployment process. When completing the setup steps, the system automatically checks whether you've already deployed attribution data to the selected data space.

Attribution Intelligence requires a specific set of engagement DMOs: Product Browse Equipment, Shopping Cart Engagement, and Product Order Engagement. You'll need to map behavioral event data fields to those DMOs before Attribution Intelligence setup can be completed.

Once attribution objects are installed, you're able to view attribution analysis in Tableau or other business intelligence tools. Tableau is a powerful business intelligence tool owned by Salesforce. Tableau currently extends into several Salesforce products through the Tableau Next offering. One such example is Marketing Intelligence, which leverages Tableau Next prebuilt dashboards for analytics.

Marketing Intelligence

In addition to enabling Tableau Next for Marketing Intelligence, it's also necessary to enable and set up D360. D360 connects and unifies data for analysis in Marketing Intelligence, and Tableau Next powers the visual analytics in Marketing Intelligence, providing access to prebuilt dashboards and insights.

To deploy Marketing Intelligence within Salesforce core, you'll need to install prebuilt dashboards and turn on Marketing Intelligence:

1. Install a Tableau Next workspace
2. Select a data space to deploy
3. Enable Marketing Intelligence

A D360 data space needs to be specified because Tableau Next prebuilt dashboards automatically deploy based on the data space.

> Marketing Intelligence is a C360 app within the Salesforce core platform and is part of the Marketing Cloud Next suite of apps. Marketing Intelligence extends the Marketing Cloud on core offering and is different from Marketing Cloud Intelligence. Marketing Cloud Intelligence, formerly known as Datorama, is a standalone application.

Marketing Intelligence represents a new unified analytics platform for marketers in the agentic age. Vast improvements were made in the past, allowing sales teams to gain better visibility over the sales pipeline but, until now, it's been difficult for markets to get clarity over end-to-end attribution and return-on-marketing investment (ROMI). Marketing Intelligence was built to help marketers achieve those goals. Because Marketing Intelligence is built on the Salesforce core platform, it removes friction and makes cross-functional collaboration much easier. Within Marketing Intelligence, there are three steps marketers take to connect data, enrich data, and then act on data (Figure 10-14).

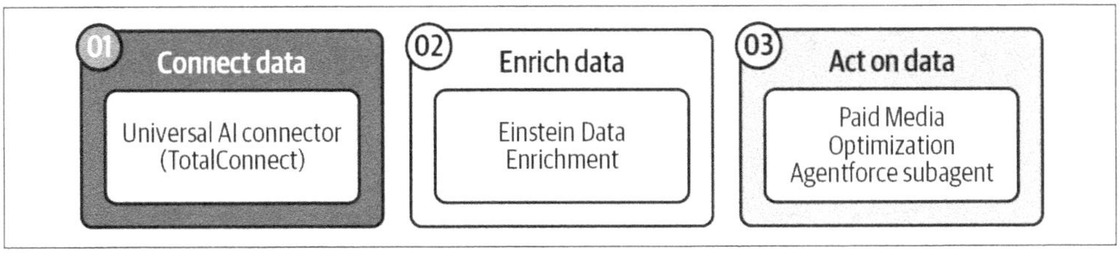

Figure 10-14. Marketing Intelligence AI solutions for connecting, enriching, and acting on data

Each of these steps is associated with a Salesforce AI feature: TotalConnect, a universal AI connector, Einstein Data Enrichment, and a Paid Media Optimization subagent. Let's review each of these now.

Universal AI Connector (TotalConnect)

Marketing Intelligence relies on the functionality of the D360 platform. However, D360 data and Marketing Intelligence data each have a different data viewpoint. D360 focuses on the individual customer whereas Marketing Intelligence centers instead around the campaign. Thus, new types of third-party data need to be ingested into D360 in order for marketers to have a 360-degree view of marketing campaigns.

Fortunately, Marketing Intelligence comes with a streamlined approach, known as Data Pipelines, that makes ingesting third-party marketing campaign data easy. Data Pipelines includes out-of-the-box connectors for major advertising platforms like Google Ads and Meta Ads (Figure 10-15) that not only ingest data into D360 but also automatically map the data to the Marketing Intelligence data model.

For data sources without a native connector, Marketing Intelligence offers a template that can automatically map metrics and dimensions based on data type. Marketers upload data files such as CSV files or Excel files and then TotalConnect, a universal AI connector, maps the source fields to corresponding Marketing Cloud Intelligence fields.

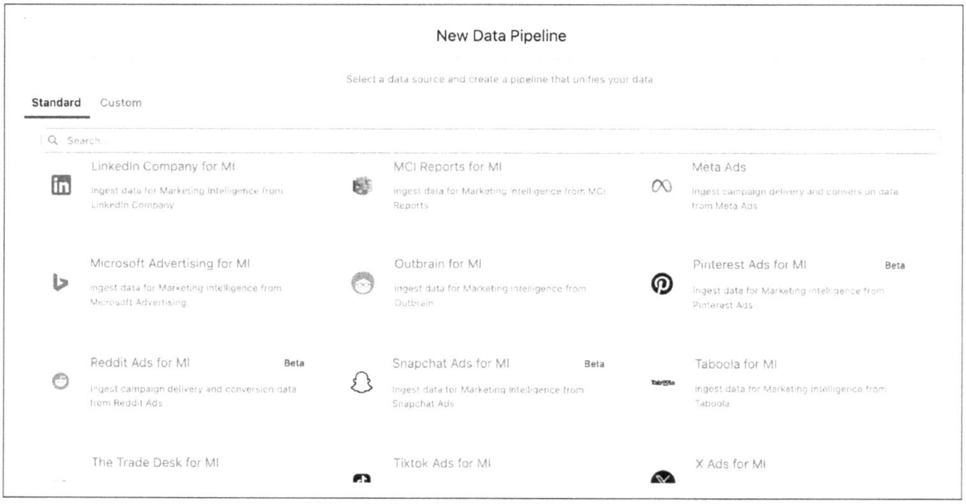

Figure 10-15. Out-of-the-box connectors for creating a new Marketing Intelligence data pipeline

Einstein Data Enrichment

Whether you ingest data using a native connector or TotalConnect, the data sources may not include all the needed attributes. That's where Einstein Data Enrichment becomes important. This Einstein feature, accessible from the Data Management tab in the Marketing Intelligence app, uses GenAI to fill in blanks and add new dimensions to your D360 data streams. To create a new enrichment, here are the steps you'd take within Marketing Intelligence:

1. Under the Data Management tab, click Data Enrichment, New Enrichment, then "Enrich with Einstein."
2. Name your enrichment.
3. Select a dimension to enrich. As an example, you could select Campaign Name. Click Next.
4. Select your enrichment objective. Your options are Data Normalization, Data Extension, or Data Grouping. The Data Extension option extends values with additional attributes and the Data Grouping option groups related values into categories. Make a selection and then click the Next button.
5. Refine using the prompt. In the "Provide instructions to Einstein" box, input the necessary information. For example, "Group by product type."
6. Click the Refine button to view.
7. Verify the results are as expected. Click New Enrichment.

After connecting and enriching your marketing data, marketers will have the necessary data to act on themselves or to leverage an agent to get help optimizing campaigns and managing budgets.

Agentforce Subagent: Paid Media Optimization

The Paid Media Optimization subagent is currently in beta. Paid Media Optimization is designed to help marketers optimize campaigns and manage budgets without manually tracking and switching between reports or dashboards. The subagent will be available to marketers who need to review underperforming ads, receive recommendations on which ads to pause, and pause ads directly from Marketing Intelligence in supported channels.

Summary

In this chapter we focused on marketing-specific AI solutions for Marketing Cloud Next including Marketing Cloud on core, Loyalty Management, Salesforce Personalization, and Marketing Intelligence.

In the next chapter we'll go beyond traditional Salesforce CRM use cases and dive into using Slack workspaces for conversational AI and collaboration. Within that chapter, we'll discuss Slack AI native features. We'll also explore Slackbot, another native capability, as well as Agentforce agents within Slack workspaces.

CHAPTER 11

Using Slack Workspaces for Conversational AI and Collaboration

Slack, the acronym for *Searchable Log of All Conversation and Knowledge*, was launched in 2013 and later acquired by Salesforce in 2020 for $27.7 billion. In comparison, Salesforce paid $15.7 billion for Tableau in 2019 and $8 billion for Informatica in 2025. To date, Slack is Salesforce's most expensive acquisition.

At acquisition time, Salesforce touted (*https://oreil.ly/0VQ91*) Slack as a platform able to "make work life simpler, more pleasant, and more productive." Salesforce's initial plan was to incorporate Slack into its overall vision for Customer 360 (C360) by offering companies a platform that could provide a single source of truth for the business. And, now, with the recent rise of the agentic era, Slack is perfectly positioned to provide the conversational interface supporting humans working with AI agents (agents) as well as with each other. Slack was recently branded as the ultimate Work Operating System (OS), a conversational platform where people, data, apps, and agents come together in a dedicated workspace.

Of course, agents are only as powerful as the context they're given, and Slack is a rich source of contextual information. Within Slack there exists a wealth of knowledge in conversational messages, uploaded files, data from connected apps, and up-to-date information from Salesforce and other external sources. Using this context, AI assistants and agents deliver personalized, accurate, and timely support for Slack users engaging in their normal flow of work.

How Slackbot Describes Slack to Someone Who Has Never Used Slack

I created a prompt asking Slackbot to describe Slack to someone who has never used Slack and this is the response I received:

> Think of Slack as your digital office—it's a messaging platform that brings your team's conversations, files, and work together in one organized space. Just like texting, you can have one-on-one or small group conversations when you need privacy.
>
> It's like texting, but for work. Instead of juggling emails, phone calls, and scattered conversations, everything happens in real-time chat. You can send messages, share files, and get quick responses without the formality of email.
>
> Slack is organized into channels. Rather than one big chat room, you have separate 'channels' for different topics. It's like having different conference rooms for different conversations, so you only see what's relevant to you.
>
> All your conversations are searchable, so that important decision from three months ago? You can find it instantly. Files, links, and discussions all live together where everyone can access them.
>
> Slack connects with the apps you already use—Google Drive, Salesforce, Zoom, and hundreds of others. So updates from your project management tool can automatically appear in the relevant channel.
>
> The magic is that it replaces the chaos of endless email threads and missed messages with organized, searchable conversations that keep everyone in the loop!

Slack is a centralized hub for high-performing workplace collaborations, combining users' collective knowledge and conversations with data sources like Salesforce, Google Drive, GitHub, and SharePoint. On top of that proprietary contextual information, Slack uses intelligent automation workflows, purpose-built generative AI (GenAI) tools, and digital agents to revolutionize the way teams work and collaborate with each other.

In this chapter, we'll explain how Slack AI capabilities assist users in finding and understanding information faster by summarizing, explaining, and translating Slack messages and files on demand. We'll discover how Slack users can effectively use AI Writing Assistant in Canvas. We'll learn how to supercharge productivity by building an AI-powered workflow. Also, we'll explore the difference between AI search and Enterprise Search.

These are Slack AI native features we'll cover:

- Conversation Summaries for threads, channels, and direct messages (DMs)
- File Summaries
- AI Notes in Slack Huddles
- Message Explanations
- Language Translations
- AI Writing Assistant in Canvas
- AI Workflow Generation

These out-of-the-box Slack AI features are easy to use, and don't require implementation setup or user training. Another native offering is Slackbot, the personal agent for work. We'll explore Slackbot and discover how its capabilities compare to the individual Slack AI capabilities available natively.

In addition to Slackbot, we'll learn about agents that can be used within Slack as we explore two different Agentforce agent types. We'll also compare Slackbot to Agentforce agents so that we understand the differences between the two. It's important to be aware of the strengths and limitations of each so we can choose the right AI solution for the intended purpose. This chapter focuses on Slack as a system of engagement and a system of collaboration. Chapter 12 describes Slack as a system of coordination.

Getting Started

Let's discuss some background knowledge and some things you should know to help you get the most out of this chapter.

Background Knowledge

It's recommended that readers have a basic understanding of the Slack platform and Slack terms including the following: sidebar, channels, messages, threads, search bar, canvas, workflow. The Slack Help Center provides a Quick Start Guide (*https://oreil.ly/Nyci9*) for anyone who needs to learn more about Slack before exploring this chapter. There are also more official Salesforce resources to assist in your learning journey:

- Slack Developers website (*https://oreil.ly/ff-ax*)
- Slack School YouTube Playlist (*https://oreil.ly/rvpo5*)
- Slack Community (*https://oreil.ly/MW4r5*)

In addition, readers are expected to have read Chapter 6 about Agentforce. It is recommended, but not required, that readers have a basic understanding of Salesforce Channels, a special type of Slack channel that is tightly coupled with a record in Salesforce. The benefit of using Salesforce Channels is that users can access up-to-date customer information without needing to switch back and forth between Slack and Salesforce. Readers who need more information are encouraged to visit the Slack Help Center (*https://oreil.ly/NvbzQ*) and review an article (*https://oreil.ly/NDG56*) that specifies how to use Salesforce Channels in Slack.

What You Should Know

Slack AI feature availability for each user depends on the Slack workspace plan, whether workspace AI features are enabled, and a user's personal profile preferences.

If a feature isn't available to you, first check your profile preferences to ensure that you haven't disabled a feature yourself. Click your profile picture, choose Preferences, and then choose Slack AI. Then you'll see the Slack AI preferences you can control (Figure 11-1).

Check with your Slack admin to confirm your workspace plan supports the desired functionality and that the functionality hasn't been turned off for the workspace if you don't have access to a specific feature. The Business+ and Enterprise plans are where the majority of Slack AI features are available. At this time, no Slack AI features are available on the Slack free plan. Only a few AI features are included with the Slack Pro plan. Be sure to check the Slack Help Center for the most current information about Slack plans and features (*https://oreil.ly/lhIji*).

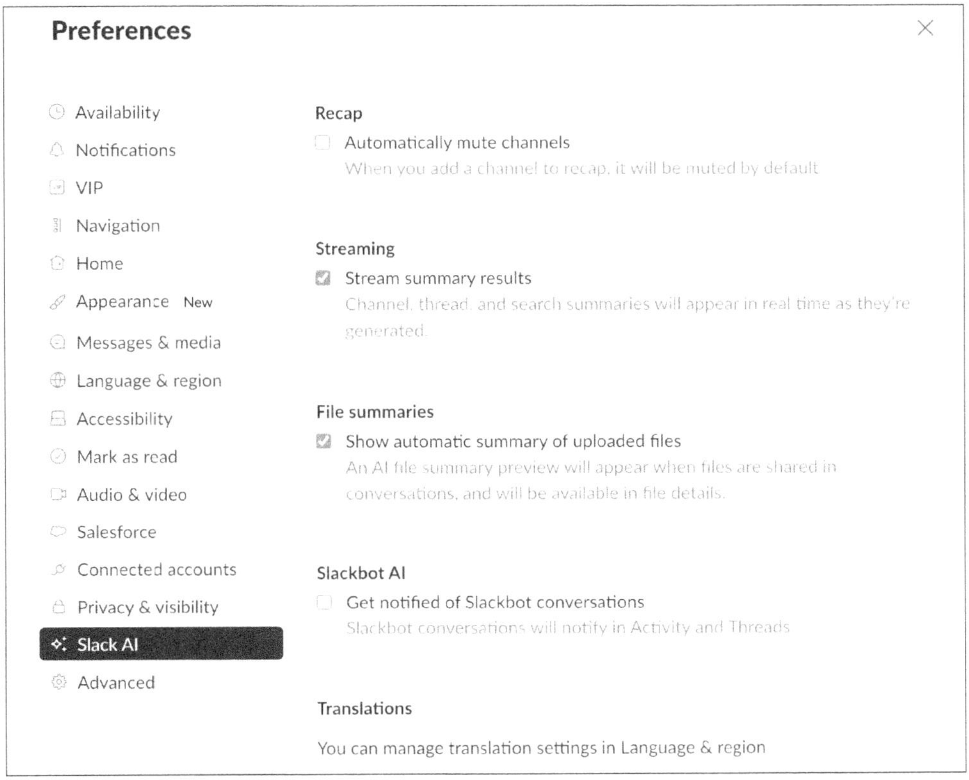

Figure 11-1. Slack AI preferences controllable by the individual Slack user

A Slack admin can view the Slack AI and Agentforce permissions by clicking Admin on the sidebar. Alternatively, the admin can click on the workspace name and then select Tools & Settings > Workspace settings > Permissions.

Next, the admin can select Agentforce or Manage Permissions. If the admin wants to manage Slack AI features, they should click Manage Permissions > Feature Access > AI (Figure 11-2).

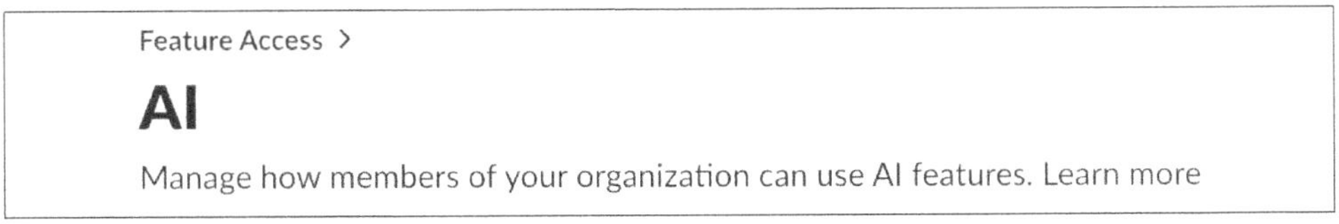

Figure 11-2. Admin steps taken to manage Slack AI and Agentforce features

The Slack AI features (Figure 11-3) can then be managed by the Slack admin.

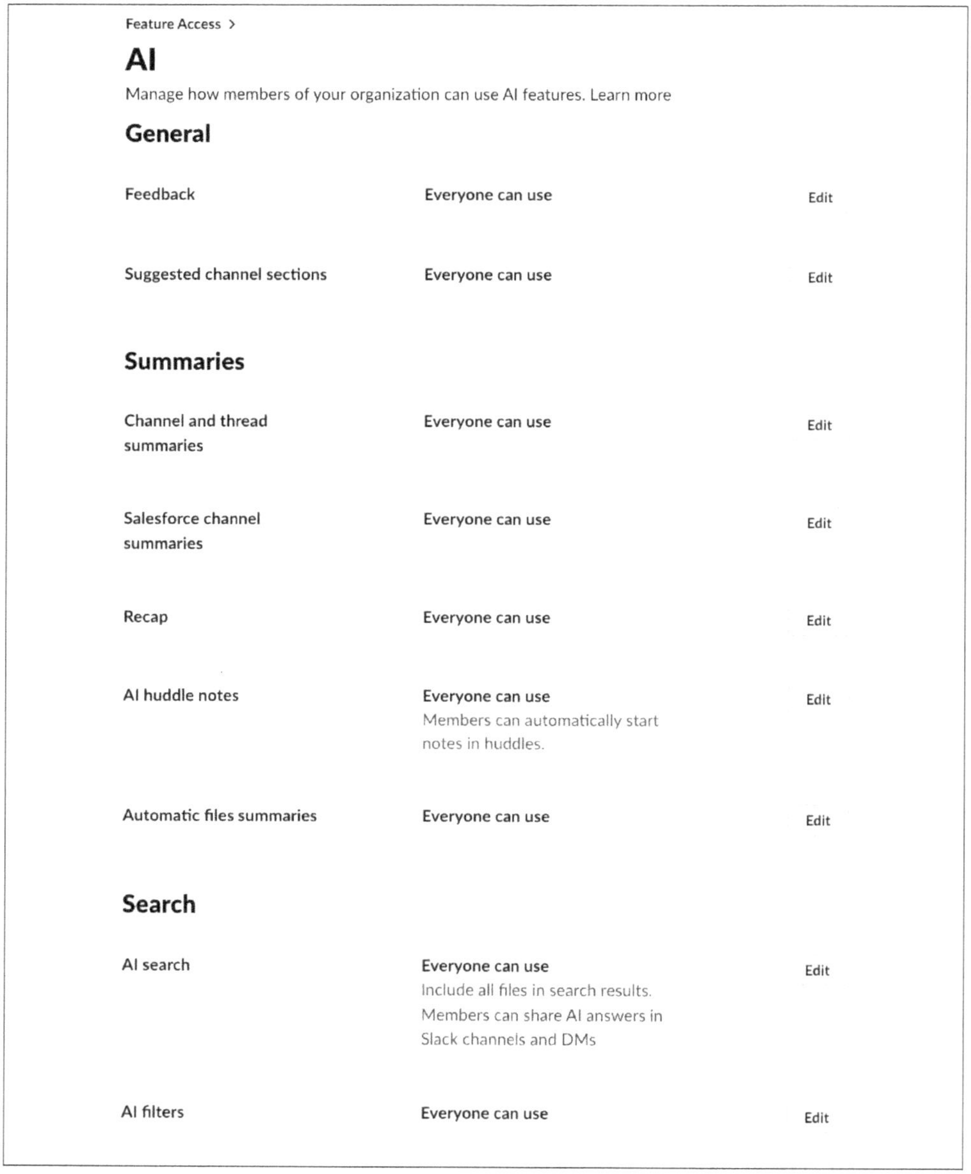

Figure 11-3. Admin view of Slack AI features that can be managed

There are important differences in AI feature administration between Business+ and Enterprise plans. Most notable are the differences around granular user controls. There is limited granular control for most Slack AI features in a Business+ plan. The Slack AI features can be turned on and off only at a workspace-level; either everyone or no one can use a specific AI feature. For example, either everyone in the workspace has access to Conversation Summaries and Recap or no one does.

In contrast, Enterprise plans offer full granular control so that a feature can be turned on for just a select few, if desired. Conversation Summaries and Recap can be turned on for some but not all workspace users, for example. Reach out to your Slack admin with any questions about Slack AI feature availability for your workspace.

There's one more important thing to know for the contents in this chapter: Salesforce announced the retirement of the Slack Channel Expert agent in August 2026. Thus, the Channel Expert agent capabilities described herein won't be available out-of-the-box anymore as a native capability within Agentforce. However, a custom agent with the desired functionality can be created using Agentforce building blocks.

AI for Summarizing, Explaining, and Translating Slack Content on Demand

Collaborative work thrives on clear and concise communication. In such environments, good and effective communication smooths onboarding, improves response times, and allows employees to focus on more strategic and innovative tasks. Setting clear and concise communication guidelines helps prevent costly errors, minimizes conflict, and motivates employees to excel.

The Slack platform enables the practice of clear and concise communication. Common best practices for Slack communication are beneficial for all organizations. For example, Slack users are encouraged to send only one post per message, create well-formatted posts for longer messages, and use threads for message discussions rather than posting every response in the channel.

Best Practices for Clear and Concise Slack Communications

Send one post per message and replace follow-up messages with emojis.

Fewer messages results in more efficient collaboration. Share your complete thought in a single well-formatted message rather than breaking your thought or request into multiple rapid-fire posts. It may be helpful to change your Enter key preferences on your desktop. That way, using the Enter key starts a new line in the message rather than separate messages sent every time you hit the Enter key. Also, it's best practice to replace short follow-up messages with emoji reactions instead. That way, people get fewer notifications, which means fewer distractions.

The value of sending only one post per message extends to agents, too. Agents are more effective at helping users because they can see the entire request or question at once and understand the full context and nuance of what's being asked. Thus, the agent provides a more complete, thoughtful response.

Create well-formatted posts for longer messages.
: Lengthy messages need to be well-formatted with emojis, bulleted lists, and italic and bold text styling so that they can be scanned quickly. This also helps to minimize follow-up questions and messages.

Use threads for message discussions.
: Using threads to respond to messages helps keep discussions organized and keeps the unread indicator from being triggered unnecessarily for others. The *Also send to #channel* checkbox (Figure 11-4) can always be used to send the reply to the channel as its own message in addition to having the response appear in the thread. For example, it would be important to send the reply to the entire channel if a major decision has been made in the discussion.

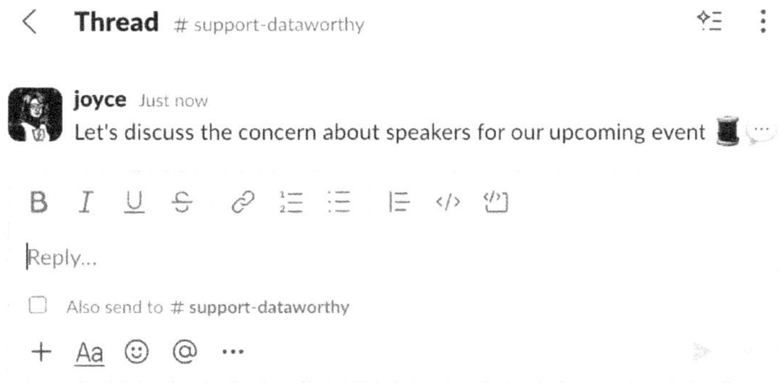

Figure 11-4. "Also send to channel" checkbox is available when responding in a thread

The value of using threads extends to agents, too. Threaded conversations help agents better understand the context of all conversations.

Even if every Slack user in a workspace follows established guidelines and recommendations for clear and concise communications, there can still be an overwhelming number of conversations occurring daily that make it difficult for humans to keep up.

In addition, sometimes an individual doesn't have the expertise or experience to understand every acronym or discussion, or they're new to an existing project and need to get up to speed quickly. Also, enterprise organizations may have multilingual teams who work together. Within the Slack workspace, these challenges are handled by using Slack AI to summarize, explain, and translate content on demand.

Conversation Summaries

The Conversation Summaries feature is helpful for someone who needs to catch up after time away from work or for users who are new to a project and need to get up to speed quickly. Sales leaders can leverage summaries of customer account channels to keep informed at a glance. Summaries are also great for analyzing large volumes of feedback in a dedicated feedback channel.

> It can take longer to generate conversation summaries when a user selects longer time frames or when the message histories in the conversation are extensive.

Conversation summaries can be created for message threads, DMs, and channels. In addition, the Daily Recap feature summarizes multiple channels at once. Sources are cited in each conversation summary, allowing users to review more details as needed.

Summarizing message threads

Slack users can summarize individual threads, if desired. Thread summaries provide quick information about a lengthy conversation, especially one that is time-sensitive or critical. For example, summarizing a message thread is often used to provide the status of an engineering incident to someone who has just been called in to help solve the problem. While viewing the message thread, choose the option to "Summarize thread" (Figure 11-5).

Figure 11-5. Option to summarize a Slack thread within a channel

The summary appears along with the option to show more detail by clicking the down arrow. Details, including clickable sourcing links, then appear after the option to display more detail is selected. In addition, the user can provide feedback about the summary by clicking the thumbs-up or thumbs-down icon. Summarizing threads is a useful feature, but more often, Slack users will opt to summarize DMs or channels.

Summarizing conversations and channels

In channels and DMs, users can summarize unread messages or all messages in the past seven days. When using the summary feature on a desktop, a Slack user can also summarize messages within a custom date range. While in the DM, the user selects "Summarize conversation" (Figure 11-6) and then chooses one of the options. If the user was within a channel instead, the option to select is "Summarize channel."

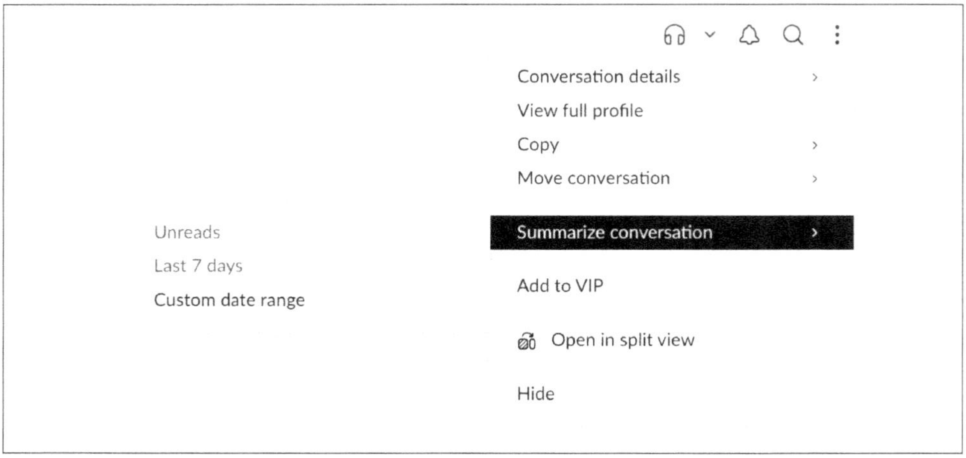

Figure 11-6. Option to summarize conversation within a direct message

The conversation or channel summary appears when it's finished. There's an option to click the down arrow to use more detail and review the summary sources.

Channel summaries highlight key happenings for all unread messages in the channel, messages from the last seven days, or messages from a custom date range. New team members brought into a sales deal, for example, benefit from using a custom date range to catch up on what's happened with the account recently as well as over time.

Daily channel recaps

Daily channel recaps group together recaps from selected channels to help Slack users focus on what's most important to them. Slack users choose the channels to include in their daily channel recap and manage whether to mute or unmute notifications per each of the channels.

When clicking on Recap in the workspace sidebar for the first time, a Slack user will be invited to choose channels (Figure 11-7) to include in their customized daily recap. After choosing the desired channels, click the Add Channels button for any channel that needs to be included in the daily channel recap. If for any reason, Recap doesn't appear in your sidebar menu, just use the Search bar to type Recap.

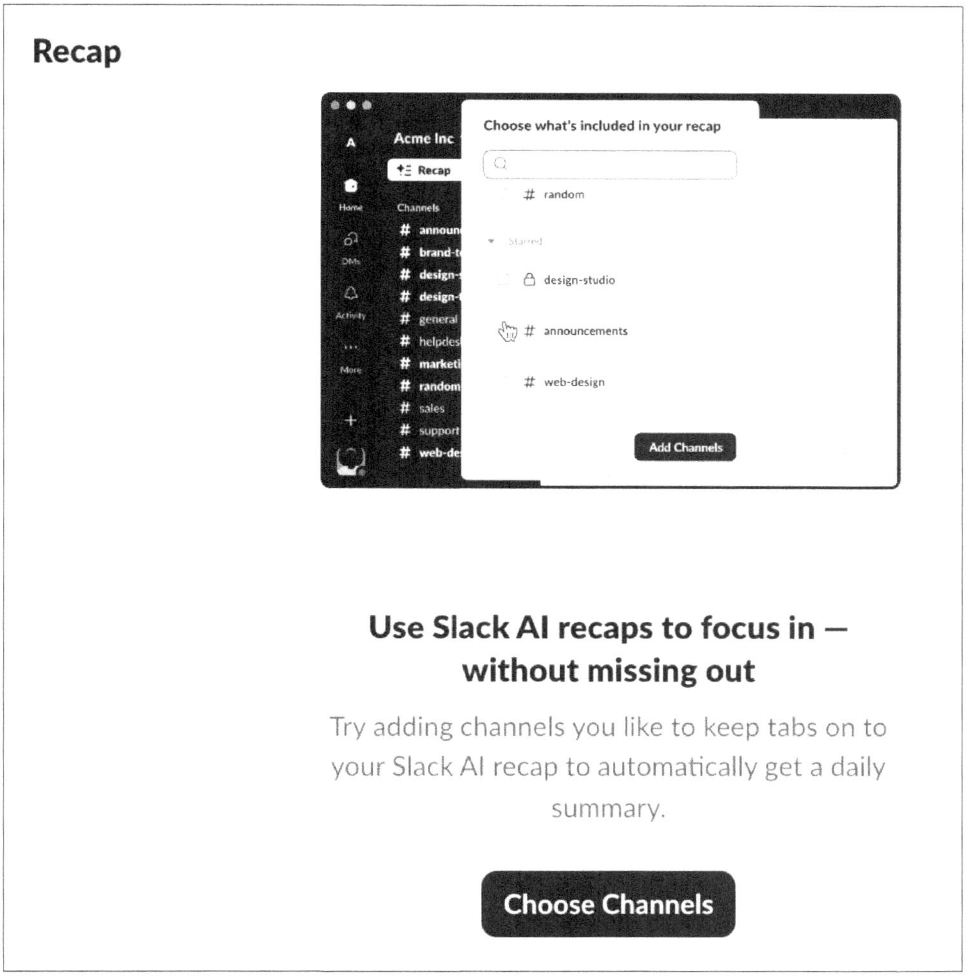

Figure 11-7. Setting up a Slack recap for the first time

From within the Recap menu, users can also click the Settings option to manage their recaps. New channels can be selected by using the search window (Figure 11-8) to find and select the desired channel. Search results return channels the user has joined, not all channels the user can potentially access.

There is no limit to the number of channels each user can add to their daily recap. Deselecting the box to the left of the channel name removes the channel from the recap. In addition, users can elect to mute particular channels while in the Settings option. Muting a channel included in a user's daily recap removes it from their sidebar.

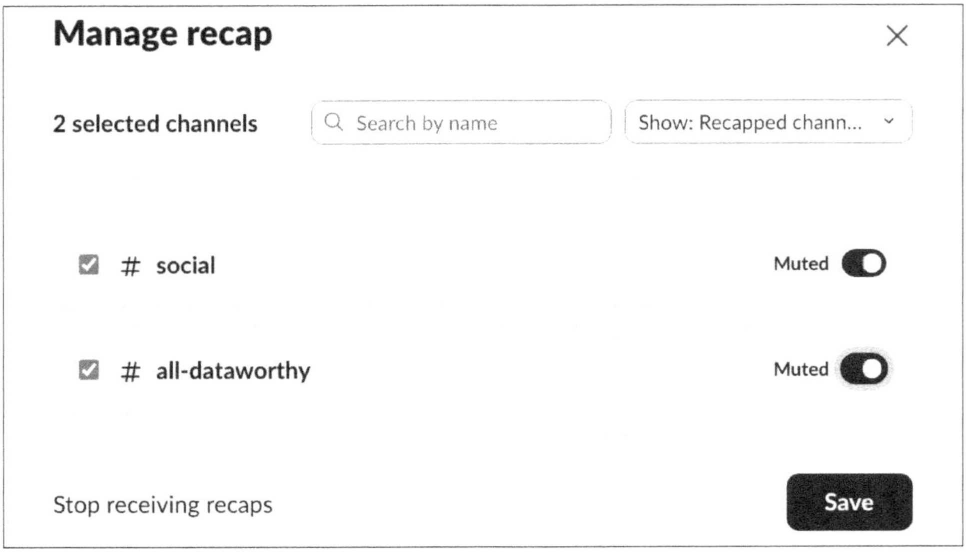

Figure 11-8. Search for channels to add or remove from recap and manage them

Alternatively, users can add new channels to their daily recap from within the desired channel itself or by right-clicking the channel name in the sidebar. Then just select "Add to recap" from the channel menu options (Figure 11-9).

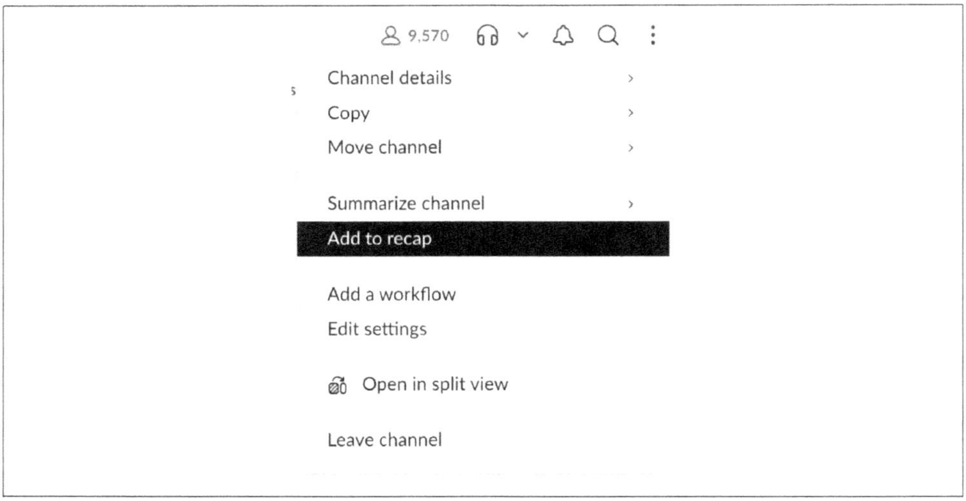

Figure 11-9. Right-clicking the channel name in the sidebar reveals these options

The fast pace of communication makes it difficult for humans to focus on all the conversations. The Slack daily channel recap helps users manage information overload by providing a single view of summarized information, personalized for each individual. Real-time refresh capabilities will be available soon. Those refresh capabilities will include refresh on demand, single-channel recap refresh, sorting, and personalization.

File Summaries

In addition to summarizing conversations, Slack AI can summarize text-based files including *.pdf*, *.docx*, *.pptx*, and *.xlsx* file types. An AI summary is automatically generated and unfurled just below the uploaded file. The File Summaries feature works on mobile as well as desktop. However, the View summary option isn't available for a file unless the file is accessible to everyone in the channel.

Navigate to the Files tab in a channel and click the "View summary" option (Figure 11-10) on the menu to the right of the filename. Note that the file summary is available in the same language as the file, regardless of the language preference for any user. However, it's possible to translate the file summary once it's been generated.

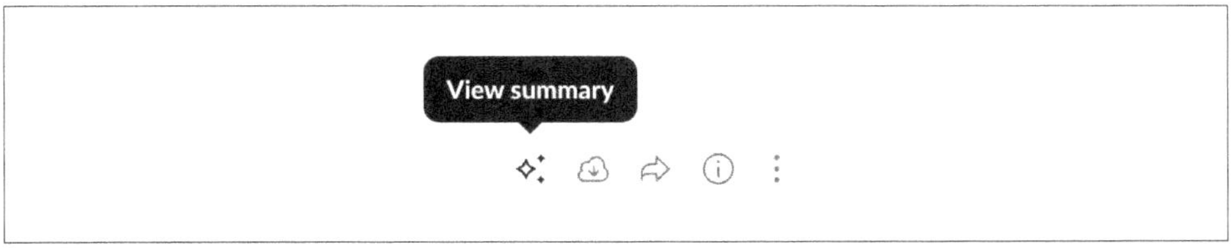

Figure 11-10. "View summary" option available for a file accessible to everyone in the channel

Individuals can control whether files they upload can be summarized. Within the Slack AI preferences section of a user's profile, there is an option to show an automatic summary of uploaded files. When a user uploads a file, it won't be automatically summarized if that option is toggled off, and other users can't summarize the file contents. In addition, security-conscious organizations can request the Slack admin disable the feature for everyone.

AI Notes in a Huddle

Slack's AI Notes functionality can be activated during a Slack huddle. A huddle allows team members to get together virtually for a quick, informal discussion. Huddles can be started in any Slack channel or DM and can include video, multiperson screen-sharing, and note-taking.

Participants in the huddle are notified that AI Notes is turned on and then given an idea of what to expect (Figure 11-11). AI Notes starts a canvas where the real-time conversation and messages are summarized and analyzed. A list of huddle participants and topics discussed are included on the canvas along with comprehensive notes. AI Notes identifies action items and important decisions.

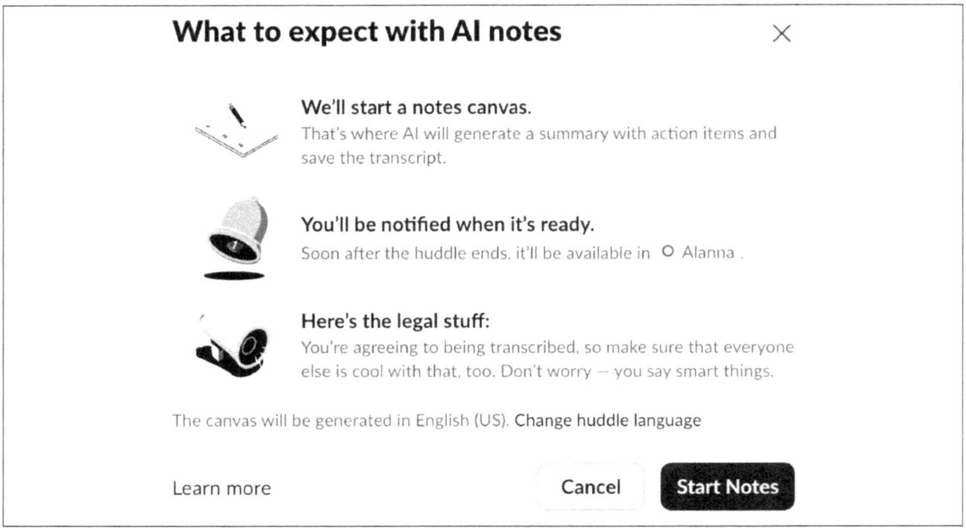

Figure 11-11. Participants are informed of what to expect with AI Notes turned on

Huddle notes appear automatically, and similar to other Slack canvases, these huddle notes can be edited. Anyone in the channel or DM can view, edit, and share the notes. Transcripts are embedded in the canvas but, for privacy reasons, won't show up in search results.

AI Notes can be started manually when a huddle begins. Alternatively, Slack admins can update the settings so that AI Notes starts automatically for each huddle (Figure 11-12). That way, no one forgets to turn on AI Notes. AI Notes can't be used with huddles that include external people or guests.

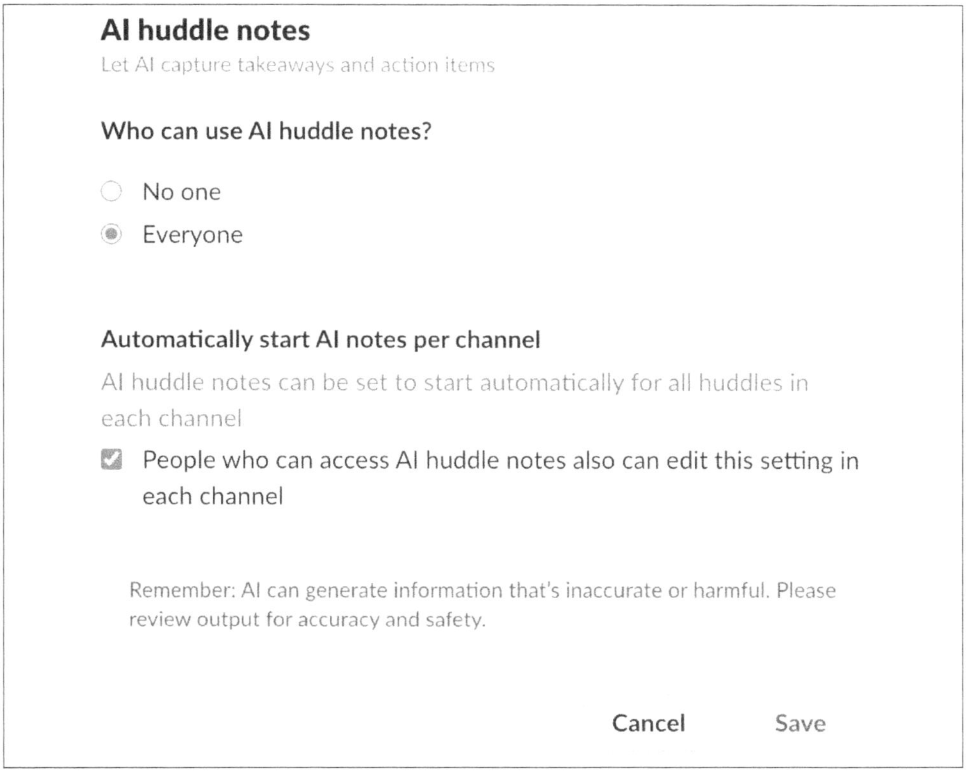

Figure 11-12. Option available to start AI Notes automatically in a Slack huddle

Summarizing information from sources like huddles, messages, channels, and files helps improve productivity because users can get information at a glance quickly while having the option to dive deeper into the details when needed. Sometimes, though, users just need an explanation rather than a summary to better understand the message.

Message Explanations

The *Message Explanations* feature is a great option anytime a Slack user comes across a message containing acronyms or one that includes details unfamiliar to the reader. This is a very useful feature for a user new to the company or to the team.

Message Explanations can explain channel messages, including chats that share images and PDFs. Images up to 4 MB in size can be explained if they are in a JPG, PNG, or GIF format. PDF files up to 10 MB can be explained. Some situations where this feature could be most helpful include the following examples:

- Messages with technical jargon, acronyms, or abbreviations
- References to people or projects not known to the individual
- Unclear cultural context or sarcasm or humor that isn't obvious
- Complex technical discussions outside the individual's area of expertise

In May 2026, the "Explain message" sparkle icon was replaced with Slackbot functionality. Instead of the sparkle icon, you now hover over a message and ask Slackbot (Figure 11-13) to explain something confusing or summarize a long thread.

Figure 11-13. "Ask Slackbot" replaced the previous "Explain message" functionality

The Message Explanation functionality is still available. It's just more flexible and robust because there's not just a single explanation. Instead, you can keep the conversation going with Slackbot by asking follow-up questions.

Language Translations

In addition to getting explanations of messages, users can ask Slack AI to translate messages into a number of supported languages including Chinese, English, French, German, Italian, Japanese, Korean, Portuguese, and Spanish. The languages and region preferences (Figure 11-14) can be selected within a user's profile. From there, the individual chooses their preferred primary language. If no translations are needed, the user chooses a default language that is the same as their preferred language. Alternatively, the user selects a different language for message translations.

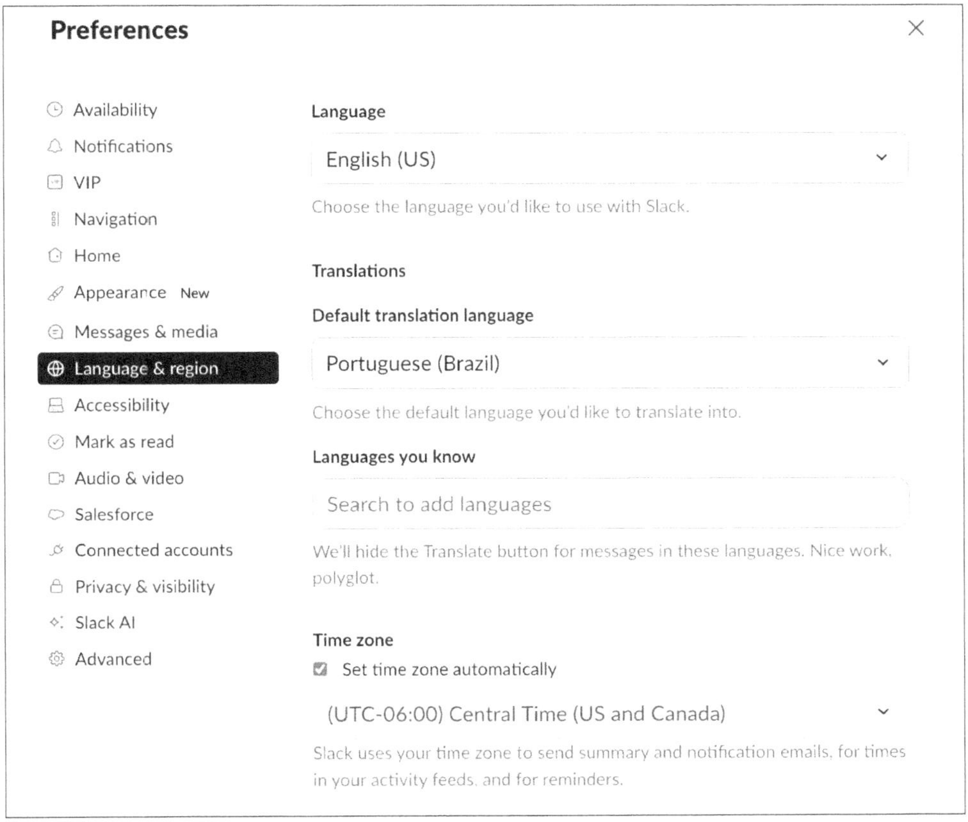

Figure 11-14. Language and region preferences available in each user's profile

AI translations are a good option for multilingual teams because they allow everyone to understand messages no matter the original language in which the message is posted.

Slack messages will generally appear in an individual's preferred language indicated in their profile. However, some messages could still be displayed in the workspace's default language. Thus, the selection of a default language that is not the same as the preferred primary language provides an option to translate the message.

The Translate button automatically appears below messages that are displayed to the individual in a different language than the user's preferred primary language. Clicking the Translate button automatically translates the message. Below the newly translated message, there is an option to revert the translation back to the original language (Figure 11-15). In addition, the individual can provide feedback to let Slack AI know whether the translation was acceptable or not.

Figure 11-15. Clicking "See original" reverts translation to original language

Translations are private. Only the individual who requested the translation sees the translated version of the message. Everyone else sees the original message.

Slack AI features are language-aware. For example, spellcheck in Slack is enabled by default and will automatically detect the language of the message. Misspelled words appear underlined in red, which helps when creating new messages or other content in Slack. Creating new content in Slack is even easier now with the new AI Writing Assistant in Canvas.

AI Writing Assistant in Canvas

The AI Writing Assistant in Canvas, a specific feature within Canvas AI, gives Slack users the ability to leverage AI to draft shareable content. The content created by AI uses the context of all the messages and files accessible to the user, in addition to the general knowledge of the LLM used for writing assistance.

> Content added to the canvas without a source is information that is derived from the general knowledge of the LLM and therefore won't include a reference. Any Slack workspace conversations or files used to create the content, however, will be referenced as a source.

Users need only describe in natural conversational language what they want AI to write, much in the same way they'd communicate with a human assistant. There are example prompts provided to users who need some inspiration and assistance knowing what the AI can do. Here are some examples of prompts shown to Slack users creating a canvas using AI Writing Assistant:

- Recap the past week in the channel.
- Summarize the channel.
- Create FAQs for a channel, a sales training program, or other specific topic.

- Draft a meeting agenda for a 1:1 based on recent conversations, the next quarterly planning review, or any other meeting.
- Brainstorm ideas for improving collaboration in the channel, team-building exercise for an onsite event, or any idea that you want to consider.
- Create a table for comparing the company's paid plans, for a project release schedule, for the roles and responsibilities of people in the channel, and more.

It's better to include as much information as possible when making the request. Otherwise, AI will request additional information, if needed, before creating the content. For example, be sure to include who will attend and where the meeting will take place when asking AI to draft a weekly meeting agenda.

It's important to know that not all canvas format options are supported when asking AI to create content. Profile cards, message cards, and column layout cannot be generated using AI assistance. In those cases, a template is a good option.

Whether using a template or AI to create a canvas, users navigate to the channel where they want to create a canvas and then click the "Add canvas" option at the top left of the screen. Users with the option to write with AI will see it available as a selection (Figure 11-16).

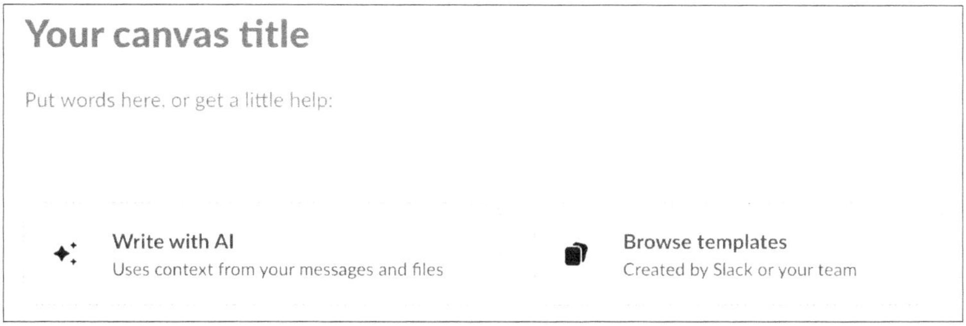

Figure 11-16. "Write with AI" option appears when the "Add canvas" option is selected

After selecting the "Write with AI" option, users input a description of the content or select a prompt from the list (Figure 11-17). Then click the Send button to generate content.

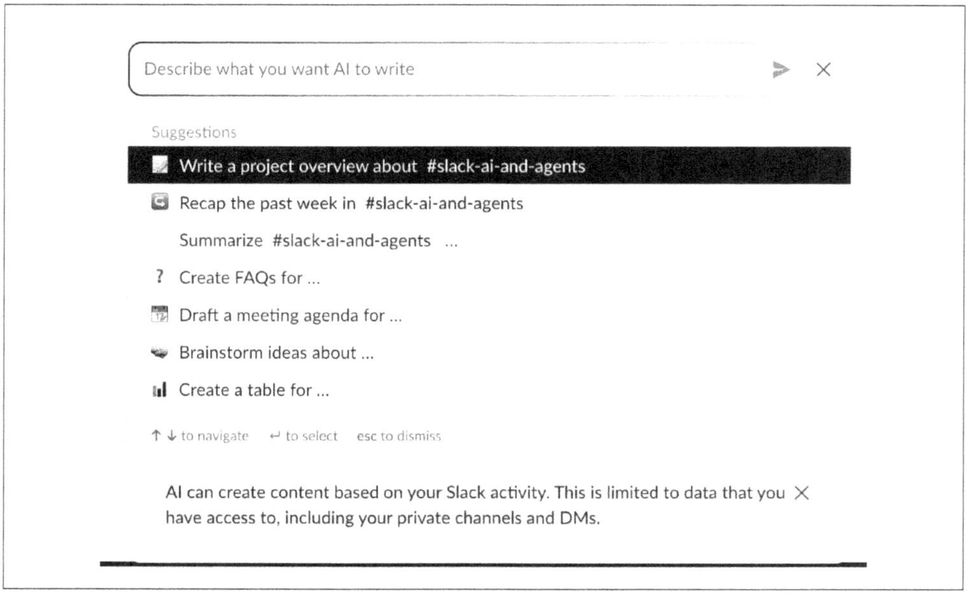

Figure 11-17. Content description needs to be provided for "Write with AI"

Simpler prompts result in quicker responses, whereas complex prompts could take a few minutes to return results. After the content is created, an option appears for the user to keep or discard the content (Figure 11-18). Alternatively, the user can instruct the AI to make changes to the content.

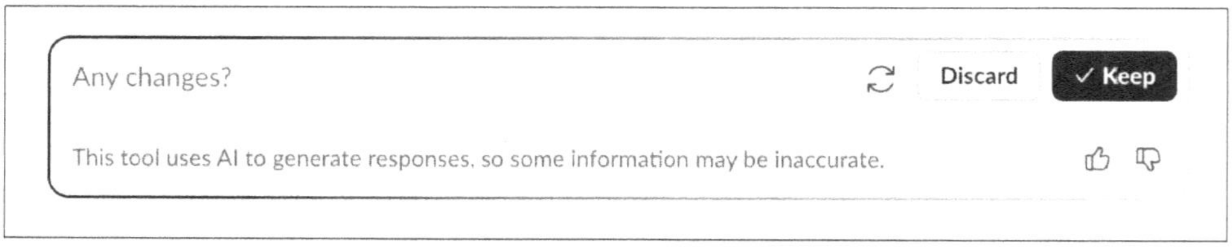

Figure 11-18. User inputs changes, keeps the content, or discards it completely

New content appears highlighted in blue on the canvas. Once the user clicks the Keep button, the blue highlight disappears and the formatting options appear at the bottom of the canvas (Figure 11-19). The "Write with AI" option can be selected to instruct the AI on what should be changed.

Figure 11-19. Canvas formatting options include "Write with AI"

Alternatively, a user can highlight a portion of text and then click "Edit with AI" to make changes. Edits can be described in natural language. A user can even instruct AI to make quick edits such as a request to proofread, make the canvas text longer or shorter, or change the tone. The text can also be translated into another language. In addition, the AI can add a summary or create a checklist of items. Using AI to format content into a table is possible but, as we mentioned earlier, there are some canvas formats like profile cards and column layout that can't be generated using AI.

If, at any time, a user leaves the canvas before clicking the Keep button, all is not lost. The draft canvas is still accessible by navigating to the Files tab in the channel.

AI Workflow Generation and AI Workflow Steps

Slack workflows built to start on a schedule will begin automatically based on that schedule. Other workflows start using a button, webhook, or data change events in Salesforce. Within Slack, workflows can be triggered by events such as joining a channel, creating a channel, or using an emoji reaction. Slack users can leverage Workflow Builder, a no-code solution that helps users automate routine tasks and processes. In addition, AI Workflow Generation and AI Workflow Steps provide assistive building capabilities within Slack.

If your admin gave you privileges to create workflows, you'll see the Workflows option in the Tools section of your sidebar. Alternatively, click your workspace name and select Tools > Workflows. When you click the New button, you'll have the option to create a workflow from a template or build a workflow. Selecting the option to build a workflow opens a window (Figure 11-20) where you can select a prewritten prompt from a list or use natural language to describe the workflow you'd like to build.

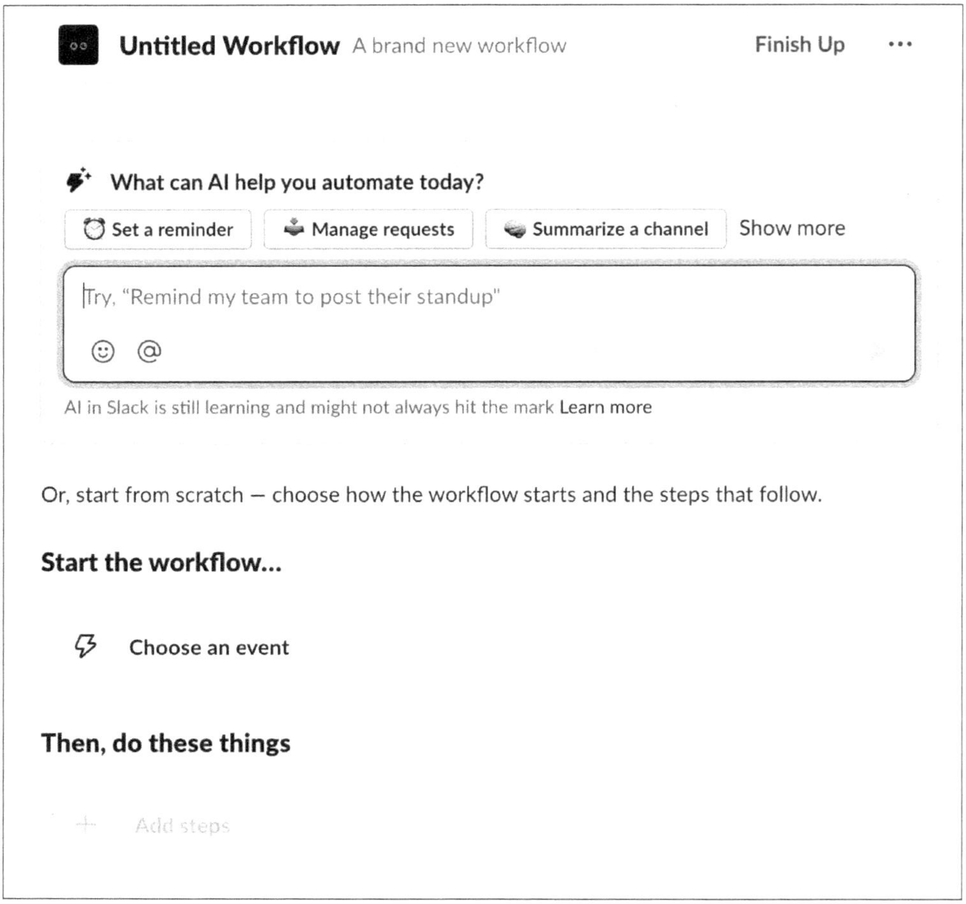

Figure 11-20. Use natural language to describe the workflow or select a prewritten prompt

Or, a user can start building the workflow from scratch, choosing an event to start the workflow then adding steps. Creating a workflow manually may be necessary because there are a few limitations when creating a workflow using Slack AI. For example, it's not possible to use the *When a list item is updated* or *From a webhook* triggers when creating a workflow with Slack AI.

Let's look at an example of how we can use Slack AI to help us build a workflow. Here is the instructions we'll give: "Send me a message when someone reacts with 'SOS' emoji in a channel." After inputting the instruction (Figure 11-21), click the green arrow button.

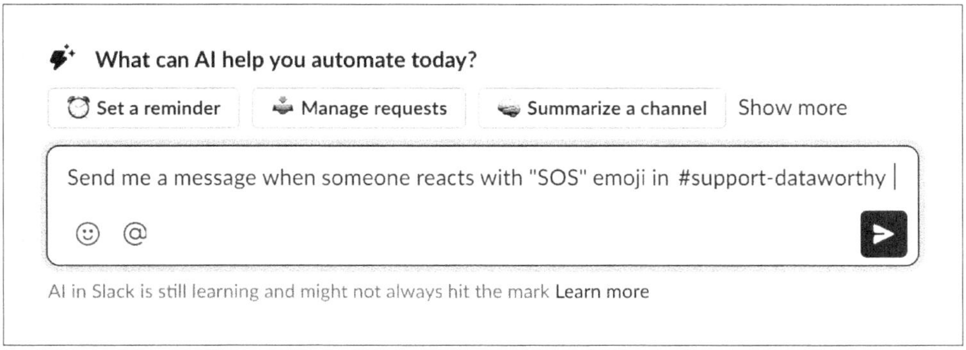

Figure 11-21. Instructions provided to build a workflow that sends a message

Notice that Slack AI gave the workflow a name, determined the trigger and the step, and drafted a message (Figure 11-22). At this point, the user just needs to click the Set Up button.

Figure 11-22. Results of Slack AI fulfilling the user's instructions to build a workflow

Next the user confirms the emoji reaction put forth by Slack AI. More emojis can be added to trigger the workflow, if desired. The channel can also be changed. After confirming the details, the user clicks the Save button (Figure 11-23).

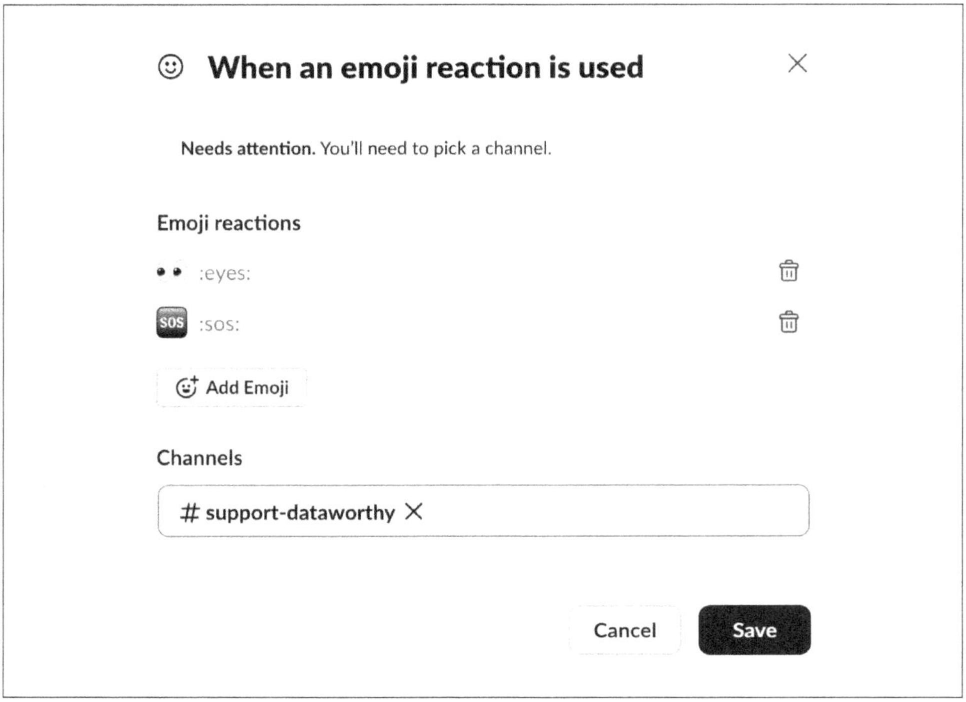

Figure 11-23. User clicks the Save button after any changes are made

Now the user has one final opportunity to confirm the details and then click the Finish Up button (Figure 11-24).

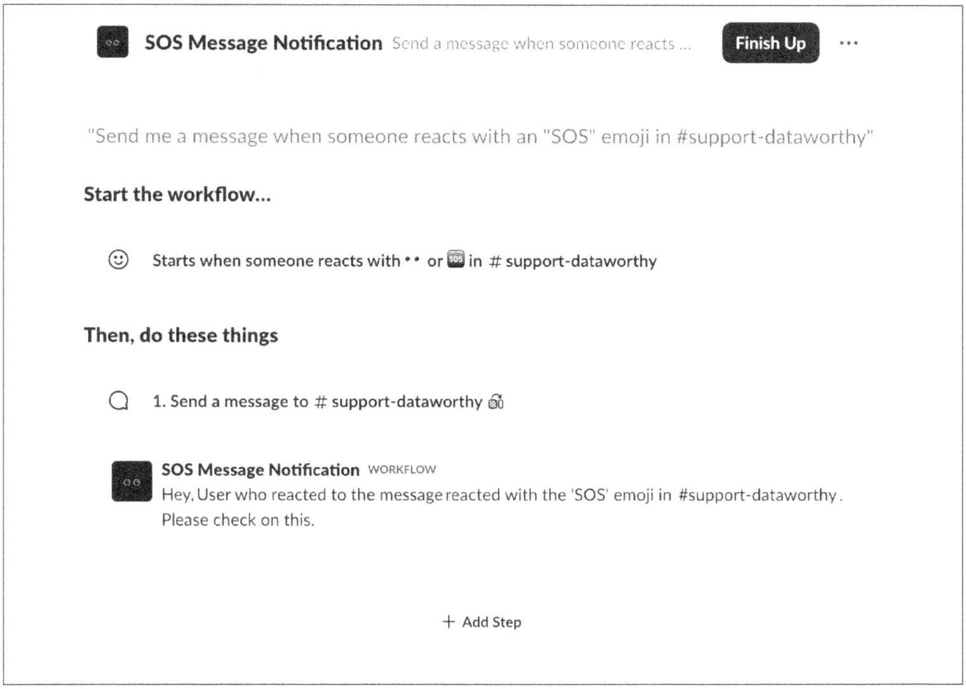

Figure 11-24. User clicks the Finish Up button after the final review

The finalized details are presented to the user, who makes any changes and then clicks the Publish button (Figure 11-25).

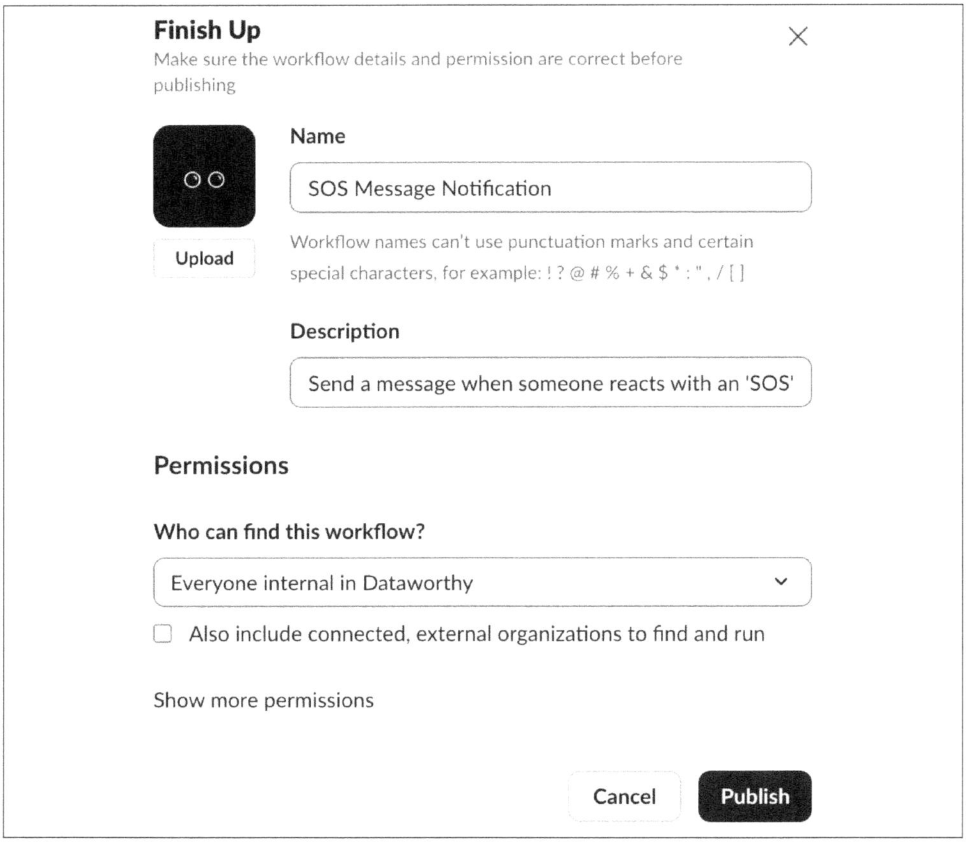

Figure 11-25. Workflow is published once the user clicks the Publish button

Now that the workflow is published, the user can elect to add the workflow to a channel (Figure 11-26).

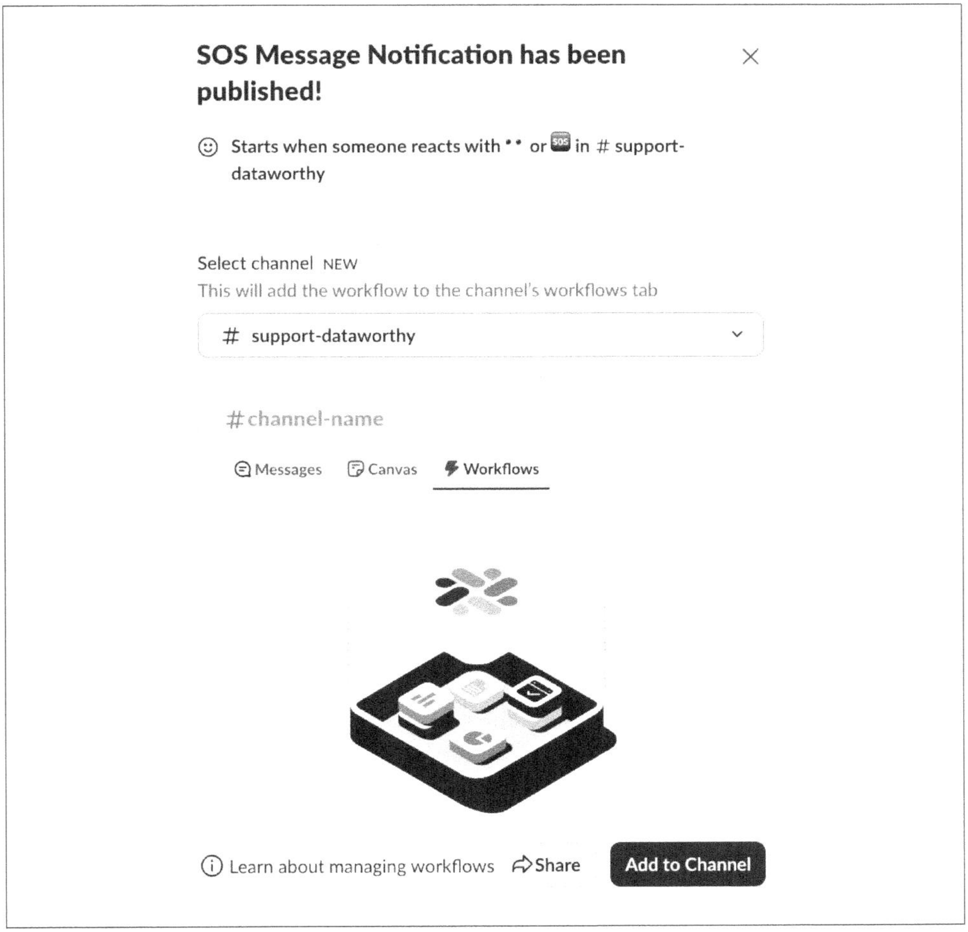

Figure 11-26. Published workflow can be added to one or more channels

In addition to using Slack AI to help build workflows, it's possible to add an AI step in any workflow to generate channel summaries automatically. The generated summary can even appear in a different channel, perhaps one that is devoted to only providing the summary. Using Slack AI to build workflows is very powerful and there are an endless number of possibilities.

Slackbot

Thus far, we've discussed several standalone tools powered by Slack AI. Next, let's explore something more all-encompassing and new. Slackbot is a conversational multiturn agent that was publicly released January 13, 2026. Prior to that, Slackbot primarily functioned as a helper for simple tasks in Slack. Slackbot was rebuilt from scratch to function as the conversational interface to surface business context to users as well as execute tasks across apps and third-party agents.

Slackbot is native to Slack and is inherently granted the same permissions as the running user within the Slack workspace. It's built into Slack, so it understands the content and context of your workspace messages, files, and canvases. It also learns your patterns and adapts to your preferences.

Slackbot is accessible via DM by clicking the Slackbot icon at the top right of the workspace. It's conversational, just like the standalone tools powered by Slack AI. Slackbot and Slack GenAI capabilities are both built around two main use cases: message summarization and natural language search. What then makes Slackbot different?

First, and most importantly, Slackbot incorporates reasoning and handles multistep tasks. Next, Slackbot is seamlessly integrated into Slack so that all the interactions with Slackbot occur within only one DM window. Users don't need to switch tabs or navigate to where the work is done. Slackbot understands the workspace and takes care of finding the information and completing the tasks. In fact, Slackbot's context window is the discussion history of all Slack workspace conversations. For example, Slackbot can do more than just summarize notes from a Slack huddle; it can use information available from the entire Slack workspace to explain *why* decisions were made. Slackbot is also action-oriented, which means it can take action in addition to surfacing information.

When action is required, Slackbot creates canvases and canvas content, documents existing workflows, assists with brainstorming, coordinates meetings, sets reminders, and connects users with the right Agentforce agent for completing more complex tasks. Importantly, every Slackbot interaction respects Slack's enterprise security and access controls. Slackbot only surfaces information to users that they have permission to see, and all actions taken by Slackbot occur within Slack.

Slackbot only shows users information they already have permission to see. For example, Slackbot wouldn't surface content from a private channel where the user doesn't have access. Slackbot isn't a super user who is granted access to everything. Instead, Slackbot works on behalf of the user making requests, using only the user's permissions to fulfill the requests.

All Slackbot actions stay within Slack, ensuring sensitive business data is secure. Conversations, files, and other information related to interactions with Slackbot never leave Slack's infrastructure. Everything Slackbot does is logged and traceable within Slack's system, and Slack admins have full visibility and control over what Slackbot can do. Admins can adjust Slackbot settings as needed.

From Slackbot Prompt to LLM

Within the Slack workspace, a human crafts a message within the Slackbot DM window. In addition to the prompt provided to Slackbot, there is already an awareness by Slackbot of the client context. In other words, Slackbot is aware that a specific user within a particular workspace has input a prompt. The first action Slackbot takes (Figure 11-27) when it receives the prompt is to run preflight checks to ensure the request is appropriate and safe to process. In addition, Slackbot applies permission-aware guardrails as part of the preflight checks. Thus, Slackbot completes tasks and produces outputs using only tools and information for which the user has authorization to access. Afterward, Slackbot gathers context.

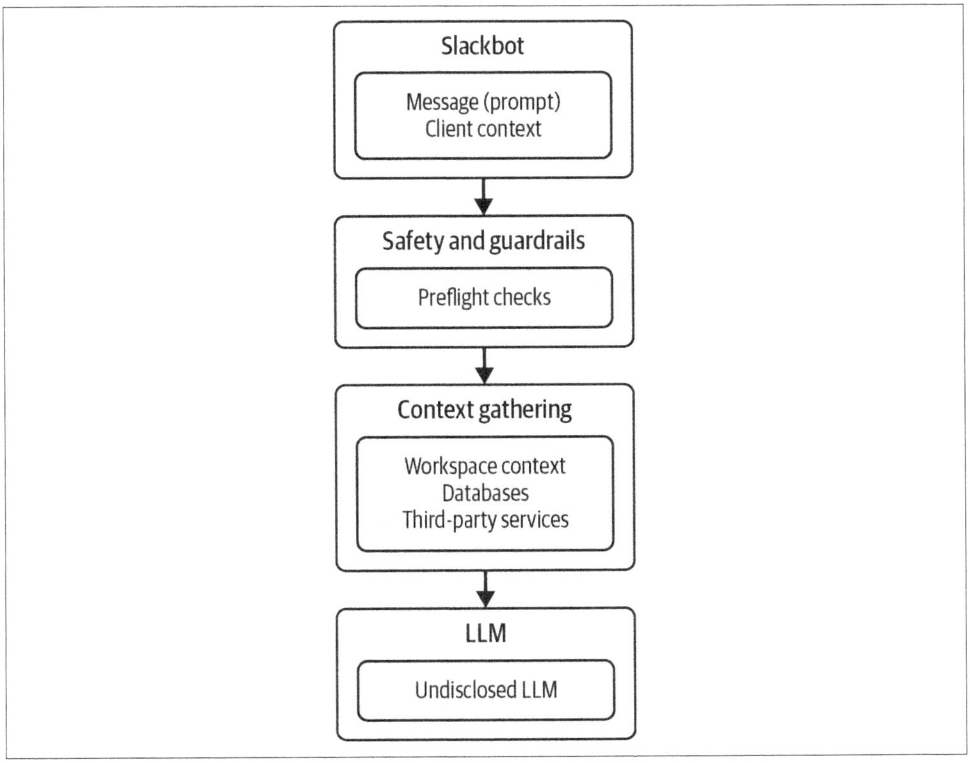

Figure 11-27. Slackbot prompt to LLM

Slackbot gathers multiple types of context including the workspace context, which encompasses messages, files, channels, and connected drives for which the user has access. These sources of information are accessible to Slackbot directly without going through application programming interfaces (APIs). Slackbot can even search Salesforce records, assuming the user has access to those records. In addition to direct database access, Slackbot can use connected apps as context and is able to coordinate some API calls for third-party services such as those using enterprise search capabilities. Enterprise search, synonymous with the term *federated search*, refers to a real-time approach powered by AI using retrieval augmented generation (RAG).

Slack doesn't disclose the LLM supporting Slackbot because Slack is always evaluating model effectiveness and could change the model. Slackbot manages the token budget in a number of different ways including potentially dropping or summarizing files, attachments, and metadata from earlier conversations. In addition, Slackbot continues to experiment with smarter compression, orchestrated subagent retrieval, and better file chunking.

Slackbot and Slack GenAI capabilities are built around two main use cases: message summarization and natural language search. Slackbot is new but the Slack product team is exploring ways for Slackbot to interact with an enterprise's AI ecosystem through protocols like Agent2Agent (A2A) and Model Context Protocol (MCP). In addition, human-in-the-loop approvals is a new feature coming soon. Similar to how Claude Code prompts for approval first, this new Slackbot feature offers users the option to confirm a write action Slackbot may want to take.

Getting Started with Slackbot

Clicking the Slackbot icon in the top-right corner of your workspace will open Slackbot (Figure 11-28). You can enter your prompt directly into the chat window or click one of the buttons if you want help writing a prompt.

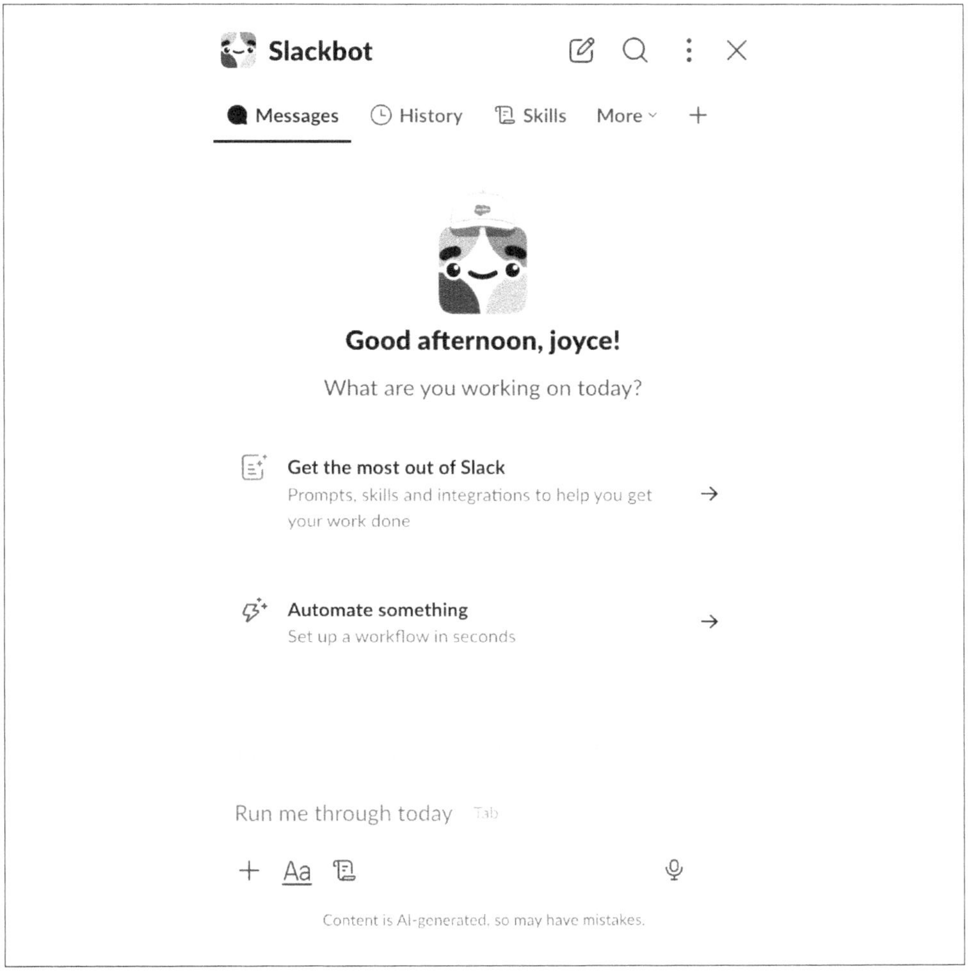

Figure 11-28. Slackbot greeting when opening within Slack workspace

Clicking on "Get the most out of Slack" reveals a suggested list of options (Figure 11-29) for users to engage with Slackbot as they discover, create, find, or brainstorm within the workspace.

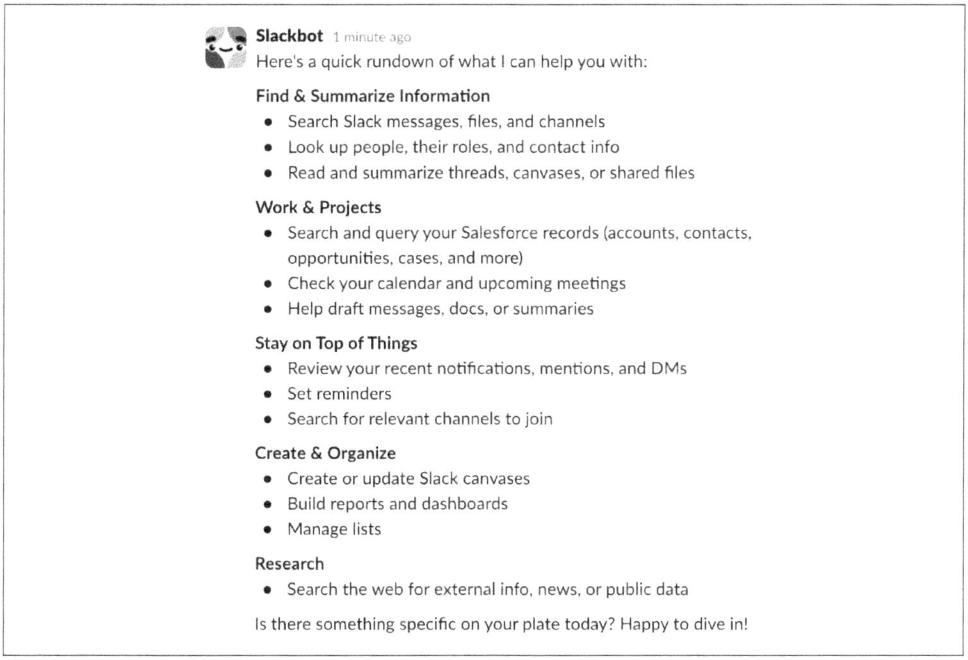

Figure 11-29. A list of commonly used Slackbot capabilities are given to users as a suggestion for next steps

Slackbot can summarize and synthesize information, can create new content, and so much more. Here are a few sample prompts a user can submit to Slackbot:

- "Prepare a one page summary using my writing style that summarizes these uploaded *<document(s)>* combined with Slack conversations from *<channel>* over the last *<timeframe>*."
- "Review *<channel(s)>* and tell me the top 5 most frequently discussed topics. For each topic, tell me who are the top 3 users who have been contributing to the conversation."

It's recommended that users follow common best practices when creating a prompt for Slackbot. Use natural language and avoid industry jargon and technical terms. Be specific and provide the necessary context. For example, you can directly mention users or channels by name. You can also specify that you want Slackbot to only use details from public channels or to include/not include information from your DMs. Build on the conversation and refine as needed.

An important best practice is to specify any time frame you want Slackbot to use when summarizing conversations. Slackbot may decide on the time frame if it isn't specified by the user. For example, Slackbot may choose the time period of seven days if the user doesn't specify the lookback window for a request and has made previous requests with seven days as the period for which to summarize specific channel content.

Slackbot could also shorten the lookback window if the time period requested would return results where the amount of relevant information available far exceeds what is reasonable. Users can ask, but the lookback window may be shortened to reduce the wait time and cost of evaluation.

> Consider requesting information from Slackbot using multiple interactions rather than making one request that would likely return a very large amount of information.

It's also important to instruct Slackbot if it needs to retrieve information outside of Slack. For example, explicitly state if the information you need can be found in a Salesforce org or if you want Slackbot to search Google Drive for a file:

- "Summarize the open opportunities in Salesforce for the <*account name*> account."
- "Locate the <*file description*> from yesterday's presentation within SharePoint."

Slackbot can improve personal productivity. For one thing, it can help users stay organized with reminders and scheduling:

- "Remind me to order swag for my community event."
- "Find a 30-minute slot next week when everyone in this channel is free."

Slackbot can access your calendar events on both Google Calendar and Outlook for specific dates and find upcoming meetings and appointments so that it can provide insights into scheduling. However, it can't see attendee information beyond availability, it can't create or modify calendar events directly, and it isn't able to access private meeting details or content.

Earlier in the chapter, we explored some powerful Slack AI features. Let's now consider those native AI features and how they compare to what is possible to accomplish with Slackbot.

Summarizing Files Using Slackbot Versus Slack AI

We previously learned how to summarize files using the Slack AI File Summaries feature, which we discovered can summarize text-based files including *.pdf*, *.docx*, *.pptx*, and *.xlsx* file types. In addition to those four text-based file types, Slackbot can also summarize canvases within the workspace if the URL is supplied. Slack interprets charts in images and summarizes image files uploaded to the DM. Slackbot asks questions about the image or file if more context is needed.

Using Slack AI to summarize a file requires the user to navigate to the file first. In contrast, Slackbot only needs the user to identify the file to be summarized. Even then, the user doesn't need to know the exact filename or even on which channel the file is located:

- "Summarize today's town hall slide deck."
- "Summarize the file about communication best practices shared by *<user>* this week."

Slackbot can help organize information from files for presentations or reports and can also compare information across multiple files. The user only needs to drag and drop or upload a file into the DM with Slackbot. The user can then ask Slackbot to summarize, analyze, or extract key information from the file in a specific format or style:

- "What are the three key takeaways from this file?"
- "Compare these two presentations and tell me which one has better formatting."

If asked to compare two presentations, Slackbot can analyze items such as visual consistency and layout structure, text formatting, readability, color scheme, design coherence, and the use of headings, bullet points, and whitespace. Slackbot will share what makes one presentation more effective than the other. In addition, Slackbot will suggest improvements. This type of response goes well beyond just providing a summary of the files.

Summarizing Conversations Using Slackbot Versus Slack AI

Previously, we learned how to use the Slack Conversation Summaries and Recap features. We were able to summarize a full thread within a channel. We were also able to summarize unread DM or channel messages, messages from the last seven days, or a customized date range for DMs or channel messages. In addition, we were able to list in one single view any number of channel summaries for a daily recap.

Slackbot can also summarize unread messages, messages from the last seven days, or a customized data range for DMs or channel messages. However, Slackbot can go well beyond these basic use cases. Slackbot can summarize messages by any user, summarize multiple time periods, and compare those summaries in terms of sentiment and user engagement. Slackbot can also compare summaries between channels. Here are examples of two Slackbot prompts:

- "Summarize all messages and comments in this workspace from user <*username*> over the last <*timeframe*>."
- "In separate paragraphs, summarize messages from <*one specific month*> and <*another specific month*> from <*channel*>. Compare the sentiment and engagement level between those two months, indicating the three users who were most engaged in the conversation for each of the two months."

The Slackbot personal agent for work is an intelligent conversational agent that can help answer complex questions involving multiple steps, including summarizing messages and synthesizing information, to provide a response. In addition, Slackbot can create content just as we did earlier by using Write with AI.

Content Creation Using Slackbot Versus Write with AI

Previously, we learned how to create canvas content using AI Writing Assistant. You'll remember that we navigated to the channel and built the canvas for that channel using the "Write with AI" option followed by the Keep button (Figure 11-30).

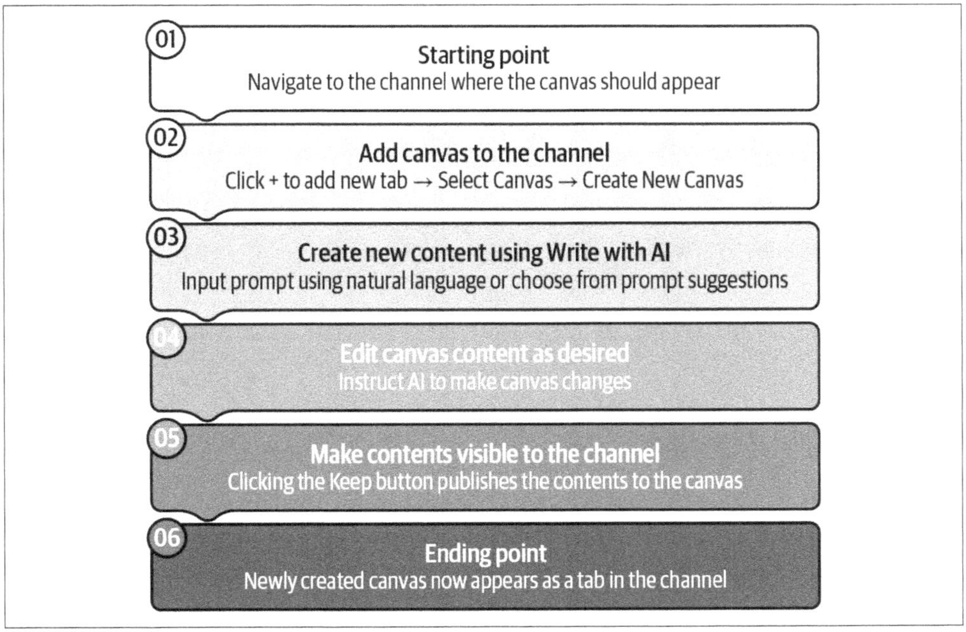

Figure 11-30. Write with AI steps to create a new canvas

Using AI Writing Assistant, we ended up with a newly created canvas appearing as a tab in the channel. We can accomplish the same results using Slackbot even though the process is a bit different. Within a Slackbot DM, users instruct Slackbot to create the canvas, share the canvas contents with the channels, and then make the canvas available as a tab in the channel (Figure 11-31).

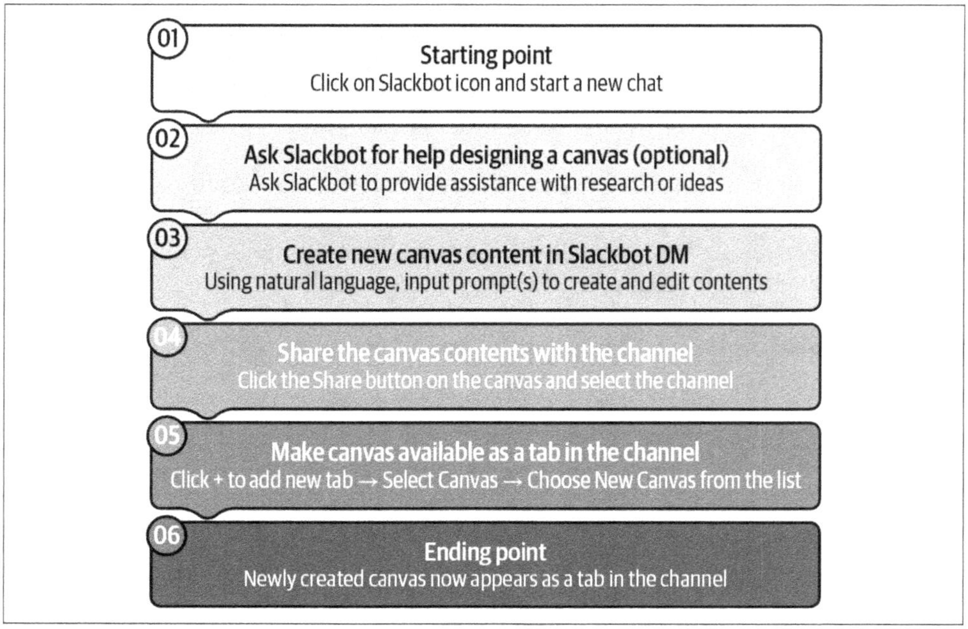

Figure 11-31. Slackbot steps to create a new canvas

When creating content using Slackbot, there are four main pieces of information that need to be supplied by the user:

- Audience
- Purpose
- Content
- Format style or structure

Slackbot needs to know the audience and the reason for the content. Content can be created for a specific channel, as described in Figure 11-31's steps, or for a subset of community members who aren't necessarily members of the same channel.

If specified, Slackbot can create content formatted as a simple list or place the content into details sections. Slackbot can even incorporate interactive elements into the structure. If the user doesn't specify all the necessary information in the prompt, Slackbot will follow up with questions.

Not sure whether to use Slackbot or Write with AI to create content? Table 11-1 lists a few general guidelines and recommendations.

Table 11-1. Creating content with Write with AI versus Slackbot

	Write with AI	Slackbot
Main purpose	Generating text content from scratch or improving existing text	Structured document creation requiring multiple sections and complex formatting.
Recommended use cases	Specific writing tasks of a general nature such as drafting messages, emails, or shorter content pieces	Longer, more detailed content like project documentation or meeting notes needing headers, lists, tables, callouts, and embedded references.
Strengths	Quicker option for users who need AI for simple writing tasks	Accesses relevant information from channels, messages, and files to create contextual content. Multiturn and iterative.

By now, you're starting to see that there are overlapping capabilities between Slack AI and Slackbot, but Slackbot can handle multistep tasks and provide responses to more complex requests for information. However, one of the biggest differences in capabilities between Slack AI and Slackbot is evident when it comes to workflows.

Workflow Building Using Slackbot Versus Slack AI

Slackbot can't directly build workflows but it can analyze existing workflows or processes. Slackbot can provide feedback about workflows and processes because it's trained as a Slack admin. Thus, it knows every workflow feature as well as how and when to use those features. If asked, Slackbot reviews existing workflows to create documentation in a canvas.

Slackbot can also help users brainstorm what kind of workflow might be needed as well as assist with thinking through the logic of the steps. When it's time to create the workflow, though, users will want to leverage the AI feature in Workflow Builder.

Slackbot Chat History

Users can access their complete Slackbot chat history at any time. Messages with Slackbot are stored and searchable just like any other Slack DM conversation. Just click on History to review all previous threads. The "Search in conversation" selection within the Slackbot DM window brings up the Slack search bar with `in:Slackbot` to search through all the DM conversations. It's possible to combine the search with date filters like `after:2025-11-01` to narrow down time frames.

Slackbot chat history is included as Slack data and, thus, the same data retention policies apply. With a few exceptions, the complete Slackbot chat history is accessible. Be sure to consult with your Slack admin if you have any questions about data retention.

How Slackbot Compares to Agentforce

Earlier in the chapter we mentioned that some features, such as Slackbot, require a Business+ or Enterprise Slack plan. However, neither a Salesforce license nor Agentforce credits are required to use Slackbot. This is a very important distinction because not all Slack workspaces are used by enterprises that have their workspace connected to Salesforce.

In the next section we'll explore Agentforce for Slack, which does require Salesforce licenses and Agentforce credits. Specifically, we'll get a detailed understanding of two different Agentforce agent types: Channel Expert and templated Employee Agents, both built for Slack.

Before we dive into Agentforce for Slack, though, it would be helpful to know how Slackbot compares to the two Agentforce agent types we'll be focusing on in the next section. Let's start by considering how users interact with Slackbot versus agents and whether the results of the interaction are public or private (Table 11-2). We'll include in our discussion employee agents that are persona-based agents like human resource (HR), business development representative (BDR), or customer service (CS) agents.

Table 11-2. User interaction with Slackbot versus Agentforce agents

	Slack-native agent	Agentforce custom agent	Agentforce-native agent
	Slackbot	**Channel Expert**	**Employee Agents**
Description	Slack's native personal agent for work	Specialized out-of-the-box agent designed for quick channel deployment	Persona-based agents added to channels as users or accessible to an individual in a DM
Interface for interaction	DM	Channel	DM, channel, or both
Conversation results returned	DM	Thread in a channel	DM or thread in channel
Results accessibility	Private	Viewable by everyone in the channel	Private (if DM) or viewable by everyone in the channel if the question is asked of an agent in the channel

You'll notice that users always interact with Slackbot privately in a DM, and the Channel Expert agent conversations are always publicly available. The user needs to @mention the Agentforce agent in the channel unless a automated workflow was set up. Slackbot is accessed by clicking Slackbot at the top of the screen.

Slack Employee agents available through Agentforce are available for both public and private conversations in Slack. For example, a Slack Employee Help agent for either an Information Technology (IT) or HR channel can provide answers to questions in a channel that can be helpful for everyone to know. At the same time, an HR question of a private nature or concerns about a sensitive IT issue are best discussed privately in a DM with the agent. The user needs to @mention the Employee Agent in the channel, and to access via a DM, the Slack user can select the desired agent from the Agentforce sidebar section in Slack.

Contextual awareness is crucial for AI assistants and agents. Slackbot has access to connected files shared in a channel, any files uploaded in a DM, the history and context of a particular channel, as well as the history and context of the entire workspace (Table 11-3). Of course Slackbot's access to conversations and files is limited to the user's access in the workspace.

Table 11-3. Contextual awareness for Slackbot versus Agentforce agents

	Slackbot	Channel Expert	Employee Agents
Conversation history and context of channel	Yes	Optional (can be deselected)	Yes
Access to connected files shared in a channel	Yes	Optional (can be deselected)	Yes
Access to files uploaded in a DM	Yes	No	Yes
Conversation history and context of the workspace	Yes	No	Possibly

A Channel Expert agent has access to connected files shared in a channel and, by default, can also use the conversation history in a channel as a source when responding to questions. However, a Slack admin can make changes so that a Channel Expert agent only uses uploaded files as data sources when responding to user inquiries in the channel.

The last comparison between the Slackbot personal agent for work and Agentforce agents is around the access to Salesforce records and information (Table 11-4).

Table 11-4. Record access for Slackbot versus Agentforce agents

	Slackbot	Channel Expert	Employee Agents
Salesforce records—read access	Yes	No	Yes
Salesforce records—create and update access	No	No	Yes
Service Cloud knowledge base—read access	Yes	No	Yes
Service Cloud knowledge base—create and edit access	No	No	Yes

Slackbot can query Salesforce records from custom objects and standard objects such as Account, Contact, Opportunities, and Cases using Salesforce Object Query Language (SOQL) and Salesforce Object Search Language (SOSL) programming languages. It can provide direct links to Salesforce records in its responses. Slackbot can query metadata and can also describe Salesforce objects including their structure and fields. There are some limitations. Slackbot can't create, update, or delete Salesforce records. It also can't access Salesforce reports, dashboards, list view, or flows.

Importantly, only Agentforce Employee Agents and custom Agentforce agents can be granted access to create and edit Knowledge articles stored within Salesforce's

Service Cloud knowledge base. However, Slackbot can search for and surface existing Knowledge articles that the user has permissions to review. In addition, Slackbot can provide content for a user to create a Knowledge article themselves.

A robust knowledge base contains glossaries, case studies and articles, troubleshooting tips, how-to guides, and common FAQs. The Salesforce knowledge base was introduced and discussed in Chapter 2. Access to the Service Cloud knowledge base within the Salesforce core platform gives Slackbot and Agentforce Employee Agents much-needed contextual information curated by the enterprise.

Salesforce Channels

Salesforce Channels is one option for Slack users to interact with Salesforce records from within the Slack workspace. It's also one of the many features, including Tableau Next and Agentforce in Slack, that requires a Slack admin and Salesforce admin to work together to create a connection between the two. The instructions on how to create that Slack to Salesforce connection are explained in the next section.

The Salesforce Channels integration between Slack and Salesforce makes it possible for users to avoid context switching and keep customer conversations more organized because much of the work previously done in Salesforce can be accomplished just as easily in Slack.

Salesforce record details are shown in the Slack channel, and alerts can be set up to notify Slack users when record changes happen in Salesforce. In addition, Slack users can update Salesforce fields, add notes, or change record owners within Slack.

Comparing Slackbot to Agentforce agents helps us realize they appear to be complementary rather than competing products. We also noticed from our comparisons that Agentforce has two vastly different kinds of agents. In this next section, we'll explore Agentforce for Slack in much more detail, and we'll learn more about the Channel Expert agent and task-specific Employee agents that leverage Agentforce templates.

Agentforce for Slack

In Chapter 6, we explored Agentforce in detail. We discovered how to build and customize autonomous agents using Agentforce Builder. We also learned how the Atlas reasoning engine functions as the brain behind Agentforce agents, giving them the ability to reason through complex tasks and workflows. These Agentforce agents are accessible in Salesforce, of course, but they can also be deployed to Slack.

There are a few Agentforce agents already built in Salesforce that are ready to be deployed to Slack. The Channel Expert agent and templated Employee agents are ones we've mentioned previously when we compared Agentforce agents to Slackbot. Before attempting to set up and deploy Agentforce agents in Slack, make sure you've first checked to ensure a Salesforce org is connected to your Slack workspace.

Set Up and Deploy an Agentforce Agent in Slack

The assistance of a Salesforce admin is required before any Agentforce agents can be set up in Slack. There is a one-time step required to install a Slack-connected app in Salesforce.

Within the Salesforce environment, a Salesforce admin must complete the following steps:

1. Choose Setup > Quick Find box > Connected Apps OAuth Usage.
2. Scroll down to Slack and select Install.
3. Click Install.

Now it's possible to create an agent connection for any prebuilt Agentforce agent, such as Channel Expert or templated Agentforce agents like the Employee agents. It's also possible for a Salesforce builder to create a custom Agentforce app that can be deployed to Slack.

For each Agentforce agent to be deployed in Slack, the Salesforce admin must complete the following steps in Salesforce to create an agent connection in Slack:

1. Choose Setup > Quick Find box > Agents.
2. Select the agent to be connected to Slack.
3. Click the Connection tab.
4. Click Add.
5. Select API from the drop-down menu below Connection.
6. Select Slack below Connected App.
7. Click Save.

Once the agent connection in Slack is set up by the Salesforce admin, it's time to install the Agentforce agent within Slack. These steps will need to be repeated for each agent to be deployed to Slack.

For each Agentforce agent to be deployed in Slack, the Slack admin must complete the following steps:

1. Click Admin in the sidebar.
2. Select Manage Agentforce from the menu.
3. Click Review Agent next to the agent to be added.
4. Click Install Agent after reviewing the permissions.

Once the Agentforce agent is installed in Slack, the individual Slack users still need to be given access to the agent by the Slack admin:

1. Click Admin in the sidebar.
2. Select Manage Agentforce from the menu.
3. Click "Installed agents."
4. Click Manage Agent next to an agent.
5. Click Edit next to "Who can use this agent?"
6. Choose who can access the agent.
7. Click Save.

The steps describe the actions needed to set up and deploy an Agentforce agent to Slack for workspaces on the Pro and Business+ plans. Instructions for Enterprise plans are similar but may differ a little, mostly because Enterprise plans can have multiple workspaces. Be sure to refer to Salesforce documentation if you're the Slack admin of an Enterprise plan.

All Agentforce agents need to be set up in Salesforce and deployed within Slack before they're accessible via DM for individual Slack users or before they can be added to a Slack channel. The Channel Expert agent will need to be added to a channel by a Slack admin as that agent is not available to users by DM.

Channel Expert for Agentforce Users

Channel Expert is now a custom Agentforce agent designed to offer 24/7 support, offering teams clarity on organizational policies and processes. The Channel Expert agent quickly searches through channel history and connected data sources to find answers. It continually learns and improves and can escalate to a human when needed.

> The Channel Expert agent doesn't work across Slack channels like the Slackbot agent. Instead, the Channel Expert agent is limited to the Slack channel to which it has been added.

The Channel Expert can be added to any Slack channel, but the following are some recommended channels where Channel Expert would be effective:

- Project channel
- Onboarding channel
- IT Help channel

It's common for new people to be added to projects. Having a dedicated project channel with timelines, resources, and FAQs is helpful for everyone but especially useful for teammates newly added to the project. An IT Help channel provides answers to common tech support questions so that tech support personnel can focus on more complex or urgent IT problems.

Setting up a Channel Expert in Slack is a relatively simple process. A Slack admin will need to ensure Slack channel users have a Salesforce license with access to Agentforce before setting up Channel Expert in a Slack channel. The Slack workspace also needs to be connected to that Salesforce org where Agentforce was set up. Beyond that, there are no other requirements.

Channel Expert comes ready to go in Slack; nothing needs to be configured in Agentforce. It's a great choice for Slack teams wanting to add an agent to a channel to help reduce repetitive questions for subject matter experts, especially without going through a complex setup. A Slack admin needs only perform a few quick steps one time after which the Channel Expert agent can be added to one or more Slack channels.

In the Manage Agentforce menu in Slack, the admin simply clicks the Review button next to Channel Expert. The Slack admin will then need to accept permissions.

Now the Slack admin navigates to the Slack channel where Channel Expert is needed. Click on the channel name at the top to open the channel details. In the Agents tab, the Slack admin clicks the Setup button to add Channel Expert to the channel.

The admin makes a choice about the context Channel Expert will use to answer questions. There are two options. Selecting "All channel content" will allow the Channel Expert agent to use past messages in the channel's history as well as shared files including canvas, list, *.pdf*, and *.txt* files. Alternatively, the Slack admin can manually add specific sources of knowledge for the agent's contextual awareness.

The Slack admin has the option to set up a handoff by selecting a channel from the drop-down for "Channel to use when people request help." That way, the user can have their question automatically forwarded to another channel monitored by humans when the agent doesn't provide a sufficient answer to the user's question. The "Ask a Human" button appears with the Channel Expert's response. When the question sent to the help desk channel or a private channel of subject matter experts is responded to by a human, the response gets sent back to the channel thread where the question was initially asked.

> Questions asked of Channel Expert are visible to everyone in the channel, the same as any other message. There's a good reason for this. When the Channel Expert answers, everyone benefits from the answer.

Slack users mention `@ChannelExpert` when asking a question they want the agent to answer. The Channel Expert agent responds in a thread, citing any resources used to answer the question. Anyone in the channel can respond to the thread to ask the agent for more details or clarification. Any information shared in the channel by human users is also available as additional context for the Channel Expert agent to use in its response. Furthermore, if the "Ask a Human" button was set up by the Slack admin, that button can be used by anyone in the channel to escalate the question to a human.

Task-Specific Employee Agents

Within Salesforce, there exists templates for three Agentforce task-specific Employee agents that are purpose-built for Slack:

- Slack Customer Insights agent (Customer Insights agent)
- Slack Employee Help agent (Employee Help agent)
- Slack Onboarding agent (Onboarding agent)

The Customer Insights agent summarizes Salesforce deals and customer information and is used to support sales teams, account managers, and customer success teams. The Employee Help agent can be used to help deflect HR, IT, and legal questions automatically. The Onboarding agent is best for helping new hires ramp up quickly. Once enabled in Slack, these agents come ready to work. However, they can also be customized and enhanced within Salesforce Agentforce Builder.

These task-specific employee agents can be set up as a channel user so that humans can interact with them by mentioning them in the message. Alternatively, a Slack user can start a DM with an Agentforce agent.

> When responding to questions, agents use the appropriate Slack and Salesforce permissions. Therefore, users should be careful when considering whether to share with the rest of the team any agent-generated information provided in a private DM. Instead of sharing the agent's response, users should consider sharing the agent prompt used to generate the answer.

Agent prompts can be shared between users, and because an agent responds based on the permissions of the user, an individual's response from the agent could be different from others. To share an agent prompt, click the three dots icon next to the prompt and click "Copy agent prompt link." The link, rather than the answer, can be pasted into a Slack channel, canvas, or workflow.

Prebuilt Slack Actions for Extending Agentforce

Prebuilt Slack actions have recently been added to Agentforce Builder in Salesforce. Adding these prebuilt Slack actions to an agent offers users the ability to create new channels, create and manage lists to track progress, and to instruct Agentforce to send DMs on their behalf.

The following Slack actions are some of the available actions in Agentforce Builder:

- Slack Enterprise Search action
  - Searches across Slack messages, files, and connected third-party apps such as Google Drive, Asana, and Microsoft OneDrive
- Canvas actions
  - Create a canvas
  - Update a canvas
- Communication actions
  - Send direct messages
  - Send message to channels
  - Create channels
- Channel Management actions
  - Add users to channels
  - Create or look up Salesforce channels
- File Management actions
  - Search across Slack files

Any of these Slack actions can be added to existing or custom Agentforce agents. Using Apex, it's even possible to create custom Slack actions that can be used in Agentforce Builder.

Agentforce Slack actions perform some of the same actions as Slackbot, e.g., search across Slack files and create and update canvases. However, some actions like adding users to channels, sending DMs, and creating channels are reserved for Agentforce agents. Agentforce can make structural changes to a workspace whereas Slackbot cannot. In addition, Slackbot can only read Salesforce records, whereas Agentforce agents can create and update records in Salesforce.

While there are important differences between Agentforce agents and Slackbot, they both can access and understand your Salesforce records and they both understand what's happening in your Slack workspace. Having business context is what sets Agentforce agents and Slackbot apart from external AI tools like Perplexity, Claude, and ChatGPT.

Bring Your Favorite AI Tools into Slack

AI tools like Perplexity, Claude, and ChatGPT are agents with powerful capabilities. They're excellent at research, completing creative tasks, and offering coding assistance as they have an incredible amount of general knowledge.

Even though these tools don't necessarily understand your Slack workspace or have access to your business data, they can be added to a Slack workspace so that you'll have them available in your normal flow of work.

A Slack admin will need to add apps to the company's workspace and then users will connect their personal account (Figure 11-32).

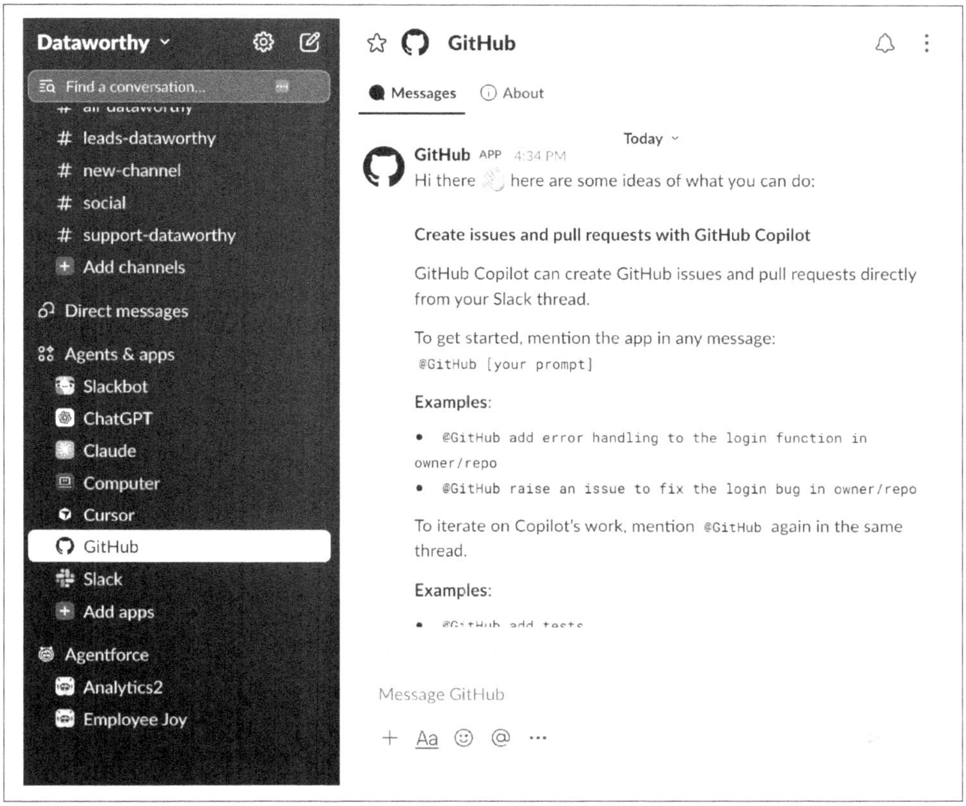

Figure 11-32. Slack users connect their personal account for some apps

A few AI tools like Perplexity allow installation and use without requiring a paid plan. However, most AI tools such as Claude and ChatGPT don't allow the use of their free plan version within Slack.

Users can start a DM with Claude, ChatGPT, Perplexity, and other AI tools. In addition, an AI app can be added to a channel as a user. Before Slack AI and Slackbot, external AI tools such as Claude and ChatGPT were needed if a user wanted to summarize Slack messages. External AI tools still serve many purposes, but Slackbot now provides native built-in AI capabilities within Slack that allow users to connect to Salesforce data, understand Slack workspace context, and abide by the permissions assigned to the user initiating the AI action.

Beginning August 2026, Claude Tag was the new experience in Slack. Claude Tag is the newest way for Slack users to interact with Claude. The new integration offers users three surfaces where Slack users can work with Claude:

- Channel tagging
- DM with Claude
- AI assistant panel

When a user tags Claude in a Slack channel, Claude works through the entire task while the exchange is visible to everyone in the channel. There are some important differences between Claude Tag and Slackbot (Table 11-5).

Table 11-5. Slackbot, Claude Tag, and Agentforce capability comparison

	Slackbot	Claude Tag	Agentforce
Primary use case	Personal agent for one user	Shared team agent in a channel	Enterprise agent
Context scope	User's workspace view and connected apps, personalized context for the user	Channel history and team context shared by everyone	CRM-grounded actions and governed business workflows
Collaboration style	Single-player (individual)	Multiplayer (team)	Orchestrated

Slackbot is optimized for the individual, whereas Claude Tag is optimized for the team. Agentforce is different from Slackbot and Claude Tag in that it exists at the workflow layer and is designed to act on Salesforce-grounded business processes.

Summary

In this chapter, we discovered many Slack AI native features including File Summaries and Conversation Summaries for threads, channels, and DMs. We also learned about AI Notes in huddles, Message Explanations, Language Translations, AI Writing Assistant in Canvas, and AI Workflow Generation capabilities. As we noticed, these Slack AI features are native capabilities that don't require any implementation. We also explored Slackbot, another native capability within Slack. We focused on learning about Slack as a system of collaboration and a system of engagement.

In the next chapter, we'll explore more about Slackbot within Slack and how they operate as a system of coordination. In addition, we'll learn about how Agentforce serves as a system of orchestration for multiple agents. These topics are part of the discussion about multi-agent orchestration and unified governance, which encompasses the system of integration and the system of control in addition to the systems of coordination and orchestration. As such, the majority of the next chapter focuses on MuleSoft Agent Fabric and the MuleSoft Anypoint Platform.

CHAPTER 12

Multi-Agent Orchestration and Unified Governance

An intelligent agentic enterprise needs a unified solution across data, integrations, applications, and engagement so AI agents (agents) can reason, act, work alongside humans, and operate at scale. Salesforce offers a variety of product solutions with which to build an intelligent agentic enterprise. We've explored many of those products already.

Our first chapters were devoted to discussing data, knowledge bases, and context because agents are only as good as the information access. We explored the Data 360 (D360) context engine and Semantic Model Builder. We discovered AI Model Builder and Tableau Next, systems of insight. Salesforce Bot Builder was also explored in detail. We then learned how to create and manage Agentforce agents built on D360 data and context, using both a no-code and pro-code approach.

We discussed Sales, Service, and Marketing applications (apps). Those Customer 360 (C360) apps hold the business logic captured in automated workflows built using Salesforce Flows and Apex code. We then learned about Slack, a unified workspace where humans collaborate and agents and humans work together. In that chapter, we discovered many capabilities of Slackbot.

Now we're ready to discuss in detail the last system layer needed for the intelligent agentic enterprise, the system of integration, orchestration, coordination and control (Table 12-1).

Table 12-1. Salesforce solutions supporting the layers needed for an intelligent agentic enterprise

Chapter(s)	Salesforce solutions	Layer
2	Data 360	System of reference System of context
3	AI Models (for predictions)	System of context System of insight
4	Tableau Semantics	System of context System of insight
4	Tableau Next	System of insight System of engagement
5	Einstein Bots	System of engagement
6,7	Agentforce	System of agency System of orchestration
8, 9, 10	Customer 360	System of record System of work System of engagement
11, 12	Slack	System of engagement System of collaboration System of coordination
12	MuleSoft	System of integration System of orchestration System of coordination System of control
	Built into the platform	Einstein Trust Layer

This chapter focuses on unified governance and multi-agent orchestration at both the platform and enterprise level. We'll begin the chapter by learning more about how to achieve multi-agent orchestration by using Agentforce orchestrator agents. Next, we'll explore multi-agent orchestration, unified governance, and observability of the agent network using MuleSoft. These topics are the main focus of this chapter. Afterward, we'll conclude with a discussion of Headless 360 and Slackbot agentic capabilities.

Getting Started

Let's discuss some background knowledge and some things you should know to help you get the most out of the chapter.

Background Knowledge

MuleSoft, acquired by Salesforce in 2018, is an integration platform used by enterprises to connect agents, applications, data, and devices across cloud and on-premises environments. Integration and connectivity solutions available include:

- MuleSoft Anypoint Platform
- MuleSoft Anypoint Connectors
- MuleSoft Agent Fabric
- MuleSoft Cloud Hub
- MuleSoft Enterprise Service Bus (ESB)
- MuleSoft integration apps

Our discussions in this chapter will focus mostly on the MuleSoft Anypoint Platform features and MuleSoft Agent Fabric. If you're interested in learning more about other MuleSoft products and tools, you may be interested in these three books: *MuleSoft Platform Architect's Guide* by Jitendra Bafna and Jim Andrews (Packt, 2024); *MuleSoft for Salesforce Developers*, 2nd ed., by Akshata Sawant and Arul Christhuraj Alphonse (Packt, 2025); and *Building Integrations with MuleSoft* by Pooja Kamath and Diane Kesler (O'Reilly, 2025).

An intelligent agentic enterprise with multiple agents can benefit greatly from using core MuleSoft functionality, including many features from its Anypoint Platform. In addition, Anypoint Studio and Anypoint Code Builder (ACB) are two MuleSoft tools used for the agent network to create, configure, and manage integration assets, application programming interfaces (APIs), and agentic assets. Anypoint Studio is MuleSoft's desktop IDE, and ACB is a lightweight, cloud-based development environment.

We explored Agentforce agent architecture, the Atlas reasoning engine, and other important concepts in Chapter 6. You'll get more out of this chapter if you're familiar with those Agentforce concepts.

There are two open protocols associated with agents and multi-agent orchestration: Model Context Protocol (MCP) and Agent2Agent (A2A). MCP standardizes the ways agents access tools and external context, whereas the A2A protocol standardizes the way agents discover, communicate, and delegate to each other.

Protocols standardize communication but they don't establish or enforce governance. That's an important distinction. Governance is what makes multi-agent systems secure and enterprise-ready.

What You Should Know

Agentforce encompasses Agentforce Observability, a product that offers tools needed to measure, analyze, and optimize Agentforce agents. It provides session-level details and helps identify trends and areas for improvement in agent interactions. Thus, Agentforce Observability functions as an agent observability plane. An *agent observability plane* focuses on analyzing agent performance and offering insights into unresolved interactions and knowledge gaps.

MuleSoft Agent Fabric, in conjunction with the MuleSoft Anypoint Platform, serves as an agent network control plane. An *agent network control plane* focuses on managing and governing agents across platforms. It provides the necessary infrastructure for discovering, orchestrating, and governing agents. The agent network control pane also includes agent network observability tools for analyzing agent performance across platforms. MuleSoft's agent network observability tools include MuleSoft Anypoint Monitoring (Anypoint Monitoring) and MuleSoft Agent Fabric Agent Visualizer (Agent Visualizer), and Integration Intelligence.

We'll discuss two asset registries: MuleSoft Anypoint Exchange (Anypoint Exchange) for integration assets and MuleSoft Agent Fabric Agent Registry (Agent Registry) for agentic assets. There are other MuleSoft registries that we won't be exploring but it's good to have awareness of their existence. The MuleSoft MCP Registry (MCP Registry) enables discovery, registration, and governance of MCP servers. The MuleSoft Agent Fabric Tools Registry makes it easy to centralize discovery and governance of tools.

The MuleSoft Anypoint Platform includes critical components for managing multiple enterprise agents, and it's important to note that the Anypoint Platform is required for all Agent Fabric capabilities. This is important when considering product and infrastructure design choices.

This chapter describes in detail select MuleSoft products and features, but it doesn't discuss which specific licenses or packages must be purchased to ensure access to those tools. You'll want to discuss those topics with your Salesforce Account Executive.

Managing Multiple Agentforce Agents with an Orchestrator Agent

It's not easy for an enterprise to scale from one agent to many while still maintaining a unified customer experience. Individuals or teams within an enterprise often create agents ad hoc, causing the creation of many different domain agents to perform overlapping and duplicative work. In addition, these unique agents each need their own permissions, data access, and operational oversight, resulting in agent identity sprawl and agent context sprawl. Agent sprawl becomes more pronounced as the number of agents increases over time because it's more likely for teams to lose visibility into all the agents. Agent sprawl results in serious operational and maintenance issues as well as increased security risks due to the inability to adequately govern all these agents.

One approach is to build single agents that can each perform many specialized tasks within a single domain. For example, the analytics and visualization agent we discussed in Chapter 4 was built with three different skills which were each composed of several different subagents. These single agents, sometimes referred to as specialized agents, address many of the problems of agent identity sprawl and agent context sprawl. However, there are still some issues that often arise.

Sometimes enterprises build monolithic agents with a do-it-all solution approach. However, this leads to intent collision, slow responses, and hallucinations whenever a single agent is assigned too many subagents. Even if all specialized agents are created with the optimal number of subagents, it's not always easy for users to know in advance which agent is the right one to engage with for any given situation. Navigating an agent maze is often a confusing experience for the user, and there's no shared context if more than one agent needs to be accessed to solve a problem. The key to solving both of these issues is by designing an end-to-end solution that creates a centralized entry point with access to well-built specialized agents that are invoked as needed, based on the user's intent.

Multi-agent orchestration is built natively into Agentforce to solve the complex problems associated with agent sprawl. Agentforce capabilities give users the ability to create a superagent that orchestrates a team of specialized Agentforce agents each purpose-built to solve a specific domain problem. In addition, the Agentforce MCP client allows an Agentforce agent to connect to external tools and systems such as MuleSoft APIs, Snowflake, Slack, SharePoint, Jira, or other MCP-compliant services.

An Agentforce superagent, also known as an orchestrator agent, manages the orchestration of specialized Agentforce agents focused on their domain solutions as well as the access to external tools and systems. It does all the orchestration behind the scenes for an individual human user within any number of channels, all through a single front door. Of course, Headless 360 capabilities support an Agentforce superagent's ability to effectively orchestrate Agentforce agents and tool access for other agents when human interaction is not needed to accomplish the task. Agentforce orchestrator agents leverage Agent Script, discussed in Chapters 6 and 7, to establish deterministic routing for multi-agent orchestration when precision is needed. An Agentforce orchestrator agent pattern depends on whether access to one or more Salesforce orgs is required. Let's review both multi-agent Agentforce orchestrator patterns.

Agentforce Multi-Agent Orchestration Patterns

Designing and connecting multiple agents requires consideration of agent orchestration and integration patterns. Agent orchestration patterns for multi-agents can be one of two types, depending on whether Agentforce agents need to be orchestrated from more than one Salesforce org:

- Single orchestrator, multiple agents (SOMA)
- Multiple orchestrators, multiple agents (MOMA)

A SOMA agent orchestration pattern is intended for multi-agent collaboration within one Salesforce org. The collaboration across different business units like sales and service is made easier because of shared data and governance.

A MOMA agent orchestration pattern works across multiple Salesforce orgs and requires secure, governed coordination across different data stores and permission boundaries. A standardized A2A handshake is optional but recommended. That way, an Agentforce agent can easily delegate to another Agentforce agent in a different Salesforce org. However, Agent Fabric Agent Broker (Agent Broker) supports both orchestration patterns, SOMA or MOMA, when enterprises prefer to have centralized routing or there's a requirement to apply enterprise-wide policies.

Agentforce Orchestrator Agents

Agentforce orchestrator agents are specialized agents built to delegate tasks to other connected subagents. Connected subagents are independent agents with their own subagents and agent actions. They can be added to an orchestrator agent by clicking on the plus sign next to the Subagents menu in the Explorer panel of the Agentforce Builder. Select the "Connect Agent as Subagent" option (Figure 12-1). Make sure to select only active agents to connect to the orchestrator agent.

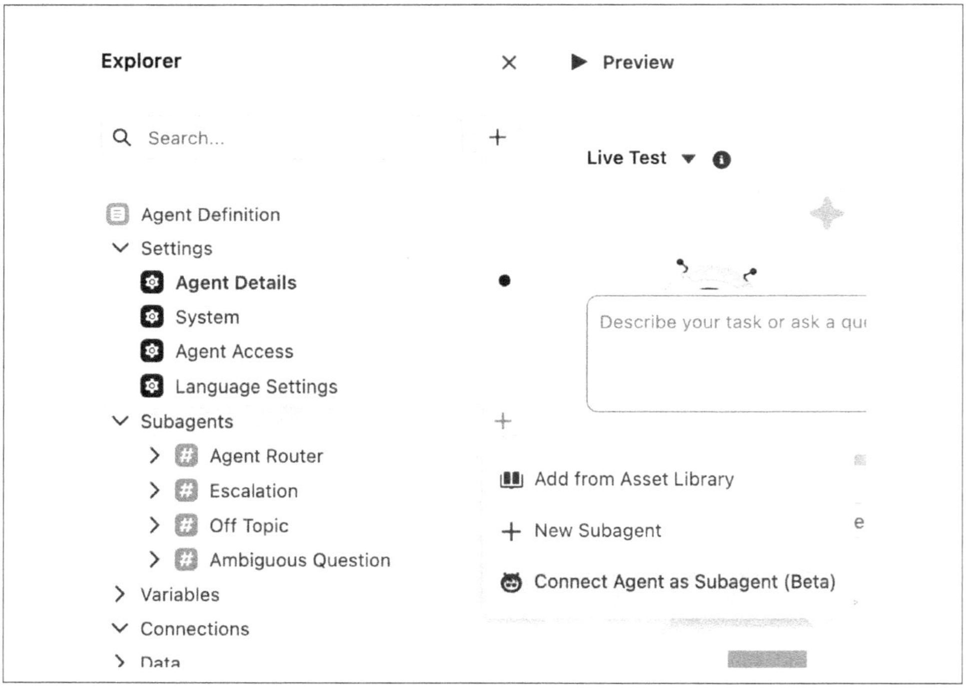

Figure 12-1. Connected subagents can be added to an Agentforce orchestrator agent in Agentforce Builder

There's some considerations of which you should be aware when creating an orchestrator agent. You must add the connected subagent if you use the Agent Router subagent. The Agent Router allows you to specify logic or instructions for routing conversations.

Don't use the Transitions option to add determinism to your Agent Router with connected subagents. Instead, use an option like the If/Else (Conditional). You don't want to use the Transitions option in the Agent Router because it lacks the precision needed for enforcing deterministic behavior.

> Connecting an Agentforce agent as a subagent is generally available as of July 2026.

SOMA operates on Agentforce agents that exist in the same Salesforce org, thus simplifying agent maintenance and governance. In comparison, MOMA extends across multiple Salesforce orgs within the same Data Cloud trust boundary, enabling orchestration without needing to consolidate data models. As such, MOMA requires explicit trust definitions at both the Salesforce org and agent levels to ensure secure interactions. Enterprises using MOMA should consider using MuleSoft tools like Agent Visualizer to monitor Agentforce agent interactions across Salesforce orgs, as well as monitor and govern the interactions of all enterprise agents. In addition, both patterns can also benefit from MuleSoft functionality such as Agent Scanner that automatically discovers and registers new agents.

Federated Orchestration Beyond Agentforce Superagents

Agentforce orchestrator agents are one option for managing multi-agent orchestration of Agentforce agents in Salesforce orgs. Another option is to use an agent broker. Let's briefly compare the MuleSoft solution to the agent options we've already discussed (Table 12-2).

Table 12-2. Comparison of single agent, orchestrator agent, and agent broker

Capability	Agentforce single agent (default)	Agentforce orchestrator agent (SOMA/MOMA)	MuleSoft Agent Fabric agent broker
Best use case	Front door for a domain agent in one Salesforce org	Unify agents in one Salesforce org with one front door or across multiple orgs where there is strict data separation	Federated orchestration across multiple systems
Execution	Completes assigned task using available Agentforce subagents	Chooses which Agentforce agent should act next	Plans, delegates, and applies policy and context as described in the agent network specification
Scope	Single domain within a single Salesforce org	Single or multiple Salesforce orgs	Cross-platform, enterprise-wide
Primary purpose	Performs a single domain task well	Orchestrates the team of Agentforce single agents	Routes and delegates agents across the entire enterprise ecosystem

Scope and control are the two main differences between Agentforce specialist agents, Agentforce orchestrator agents, and Agent Fabric agent brokers. Specialist agents generally handle a narrowly defined task like scheduling or onboarding. They're built to do their one job well. Orchestrator agents route work to the specialist agent that is best suited to complete the task. In addition to routing work, the orchestrator agent is responsible for maintaining shared context between Agentforce agents.

An agent broker coordinates agentic workflows of agents across ecosystems and applies policies for better control and governance. An Agent Fabric agent broker, combined with other tools available from MuleSoft, is the most scalable solution for multi-agent orchestration in an intelligent agentic enterprise.

Managing Multiple Enterprise Agents with MuleSoft Anypoint and Agent Fabric

An enterprise often builds multiple agents in each of its ecosystems, many performing different tasks. Salesforce Agentforce agents, Snowflake Cortex AI agents, AWS Bedrock agents, Google Cloud Vertex AI agents, custom agents, and Slack-integrated agents are some examples of ecosystems where agents are frequently built:

- Salesforce Agentforce agents for automating order management, streamlining claims processes, and executing tasks to enhance customer experience
- Snowflake Cortex AI agents for analytics and data processing
- AWS Bedrock agents for generative AI (GenAI) and workflow automation
- Google Cloud Vertex AI agents for ML and data science tasks
- Custom agents using MCP or A2A standards
- Slack-integrated agents for collaboration and workflow automation

Managing multiple agents across many ecosystems is different than coordinating multiple agents within a single platform. A "multi-agent system" is distributed across platforms, requiring coordination between the various platform agents, keeping track of state, and passing context. It also requires new ways of managing security and governance. An enterprise's multi-agent system and its associated integration and agentic assets is composed of agent networks. MuleSoft's Anypoint Platform and Agent Fabric provide the tools necessary to manage and orchestrate agent networks.

The Anypoint Platform is an integration platform-as-a-service (iPaaS). It's a robust enterprise solution for API design, development, management, and monitoring. Integration projects using the Anypoint Platform leverage reusable connectors, templates, and APIs to accelerate time to value. You're also able to manage, orchestrate, and observe your agent network from within the Anypoint Platform because Agent Fabric features are integrated capabilities within the Anypoint Platform.

Agent Fabric provides the governance backbone for enterprise-wide agentic systems as it helps control security, compliance, and costs across multiple agents, MCP servers, and LLMs. Agent Fabric includes a product offering for an agent registry catalog that serves as a centralized catalog. Using Agent Registry, an enterprise can register, govern, and reuse agents and agentic assets. Traceability and lifecycle control are scalable because of agent registries and agent scanners. Agent scanners automatically discover and register agents across enterprise ecosystems into an agent registry.

Agent Fabric also leverages Flex Gateway to enforce policies on agent-to-application and agent-to-agent interactions. Visit the Agent Fabric documentation (*https://oreil.ly/fi7qq*) for more information about getting started with Agent Fabric.

Anypoint Platform and Agent Fabric don't require Salesforce D360, Tableau Next, or Agentforce for core integration and agent orchestration capabilities. However, those Salesforce products offer features for enhanced analytics, automation, and observability. For example, Agent Fabric's advanced telemetry and agent tracking are features powered by Salesforce D360 and Tableau Next.

It's also important to note that Agentforce is required if your enterprise wants to expose, manage, or automate MuleSoft-powered agent actions directly from Salesforce Agentforce agents. Agentforce actions can be created from API calls using MuleSoft for Agentforce. In addition, the MuleSoft Agentforce connector can be used within Agentforce agents that need to retrieve or take action on third-party applications. Managing and orchestrating agent networks with Agent Fabric capabilities can also be accomplished by incorporating Agent Fabric features within Agentforce agents.

MuleSoft Capabilities for Building and Managing a Trusted Agent Network

Building and managing a trusted agent network requires five key capabilities:

1. Find and publish reusable assets
2. Expose tools and applications
3. Multi-agent orchestration
4. Unified governance
5. Observability

As we'll soon discover, MuleSoft provides all the tools needed to build and manage a trusted agent network. As we discuss the various MuleSoft products and tools, along with their functionality, keep in mind that MuleSoft's greatest value proposition is in regard to asset reusability and control of agent networks. There are 11 different

MuleSoft and MuleSoft Agent Fabric features we'll explore that address the five key capabilities required for building and managing a trusted agent network:

- MuleSoft
  - Anypoint Code Builder for authoring agent network specification (3)
  - Anypoint Exchange (1)
  - Anypoint Flex Gateway and Omni Gateway (4)
  - Anypoint Monitoring (5)
  - MCP connectors (2)
  - MCP Bridge (2)
- MuleSoft Agent Fabric
  - Agent Broker (3)
  - Agent Registry (1)
  - Agent Scanner (1)
  - Agent Visualizer (5)
  - Integration Intelligence (5)

Let's discuss each of the five key capabilities briefly and then dive deeper into how MuleSoft features empower the enterprise to achieve these capabilities.

Finding and publishing reusable assets is an important capability because reusable integration and agentic assets need to be discovered and published in registries. This is achieved using Agent Fabric Agent Scanner (Agent Scanner) and Agent Fabric Agent Registry (Agent Registry) in conjunction with Anypoint Exchange, an integration asset catalog for discoverability and reuse. We'll explore Anypoint Exchange and Agent Registry in "Agents and Other Reusable Assets, Agent Networks, and Asset Catalogs" on page 451. We'll learn more about Agent Scanner in "Unified Governance" on page 464.

Exposing tools and applications through the MCP open protocol allows these resources to be made available for use by agents. MCP connectors are used for invoking Anypoint-managed assets for integration with other MCP systems, and the MCP Bridge makes it possible to expose existing APIs and trusted systems as MCP systems. We'll learn more in "MCP Servers, MCP Connectors and Connections, and MCP Bridge Instances" on page 461.

Orchestration of agents and reusable assets is needed for each agent network. An agent broker routes work across agents, MCP servers, and LLMs in a connected runtime. The agent broker provides an intelligent routing service, whereas the agent network specification, authored using ACB, specifies the runtime topology. We'll learn more about these in "Multi-Agent Orchestration and the Agent Network Specification" on page 462.

Enterprise-wide unified governance of all agents and reusable assets is critical. Governance includes enforcing identity, authorization, and policies. It also includes controlling agent interactions with tools and applications as well as with other agents. The concept of least privilege matters because agents have tool access, data access, and delegation paths. Thus, there is increased risk if agents are given more access than is needed. Anypoint Flex Gateway and Omni Gateway are MuleSoft features we'll discuss in "Unified Governance" on page 464.

Observability of an agent network and reusable assets is achieved with MuleSoft's Anypoint Monitoring, Agent Visualizer, and Agent Fabric Integration Intelligence features. These tools provide users with the ability to monitor agent behavior, map dependencies, and gain insights into how the agent network is actually operating. We'll explore these MuleSoft capabilities in "Agent Network Observability Plane" on page 468.

The following MuleSoft tools and their respective capabilities will be discussed in the next five sections:

1. Agents and Other Reusable Assets, Agent Networks, and Asset Catalogs
2. MCP Servers, MCP Connectors and Connections, and MCP Bridge Instances
3. Multi-Agent Orchestration and the Agent Network Specification
4. Unified Governance
5. Agent Network Observability Plane

Let's get started.

Agents and Other Reusable Assets, Agent Networks, and Asset Catalogs

Agents and other reusable assets are registered in asset catalogs. There are multiple ways for assets to be added to asset catalogs. One of the ways is by using Agent Scanner, something we'll discuss in "Agent Scanner" on page 464. In this section, we'll focus on Anypoint Exchange and Agent Registry, the two asset catalogs used for integration assets and agentic assets. Listing assets in Anypoint Exchange and Agent Registry provides a centralized location for APIs, connectors, templates, agents, and other reusable assets. There are many benefits to making reusable assets discoverable including the ability to promote best practices, ensure better governance, and accelerate project delivery across the enterprise.

We'll learn more about Anypoint Exchange and Agent Registry in a bit, but first we want to define and explain some common terms and concepts:

- Specialized agents, orchestrator agents, and agent brokers
- Agentic and integration assets
- Agent networks, agent network projects, and agent network specifications

We'll close out this section by exploring the ways reusable assets are added to Anypoint Exchange and Agent Registry.

Specialized agents, orchestrator agents, and agent brokers

The main difference between specialized agents, orchestrator agents, and agent brokers is their scope and the types of actions and decisions that can be undertaken. Individual specialist agents are purpose-built for completing a narrowly defined task or for use within a specific domain. Throughout the book, we've discussed many different specialized Agentforce agents available out-of-the-box from Salesforce. We also explored ways to build custom Agentforce agents using no-code/low-code and pro-code development tools.

Orchestrator agents coordinate multiple specialist agents by routing the work to the best individual agent for any given step. Orchestrator agents are also responsible for managing shared context. We briefly mentioned orchestrator agents when discussing Salesforce's choice of reasoning strategies for the Atlas reasoning engine. Agent brokers orchestrate across multiple systems, domains, and platforms. They plan, delegate, and support enterprise policies established to manage and govern a multi-agent network.

Agentic and integration assets

MuleSoft's agentic and integration assets support reusability for an enterprise seeking solutions for integrating systems and automating processes. Agentic assets are used to build, orchestrate, and manage AI-driven experiences. Integration assets simplify an enterprise's integration tasks and can be extended or customized. Some MuleSoft assets such as agent brokers, individualized agents, LLMs, and MCP servers are shared resources (Table 12-3) that support an enterprise's trusted agent network.

Table 12-3. MuleSoft assets supporting the trusted agent network

Asset	Integration asset	Agentic asset
APIs and API groups	✓	
Standard integration connectors	✓	
Gateways	✓	
MuleSoft applications	✓	
Standard integration connectors	✓	
Templates	✓	
Agent brokers	✓	✓
Individual (specialized and orchestrator) agents	✓	✓
Large language models (LLMs)	✓	✓
MCP and AI connectors	✓	✓
MCP servers	✓	✓

Before discussing MuleSoft catalog systems in detail, let's first review the terms *agent networks*, *agent network projects*, and *agent network specifications* so we can better appreciate how each of these terms relates to MuleSoft assets and processes.

Agent networks, agent network projects, and agent network specifications

There are subtle differences in some terminology that we'll want to explore before continuing.

An agent network is an enterprise-wide approach for decoupling agent orchestration from agent deployment to better manage operational risk and eliminate silos. This ensures better security and compliance as agent complexity increases. This is achieved because the agent network integrates with the Flex Gateway to enable policy enforcement and runtime security controls.

An agent network is a central hub for a specific asset group of agent brokers, individual agents, LLMs, MCP servers, APIs, gateways, and more. In addition to coordinating agentic assets, the agent network provides governance, orchestration, and observability for agentic interactions. The network itself is not an integration or agentic asset. Thus, it's not included as an asset in Anypoint Exchange or Agent Registry.

An agent network project includes details about assets such as agent brokers, individual agents, LLMs, and MCP servers. The agent network project includes YAML and JSON files. The agent network YAML file, also known as the agent network specification, provides a human-readable way to describe how multiple agents and agentic assets interact (Figure 12-2).

Figure 12-2. YAML file of an agent network project created in Anypoint Code Builder

A YAML file is how the agent network is built and deployed. It's a critical component needed for defining, orchestrating, and governing multi-agent systems. The YAML file uses a declarative structure to describe agent definitions, configuration details, and orchestration logic, whereas the JSON file (Figure 12-3) is used for storing agent metadata and payload definitions.

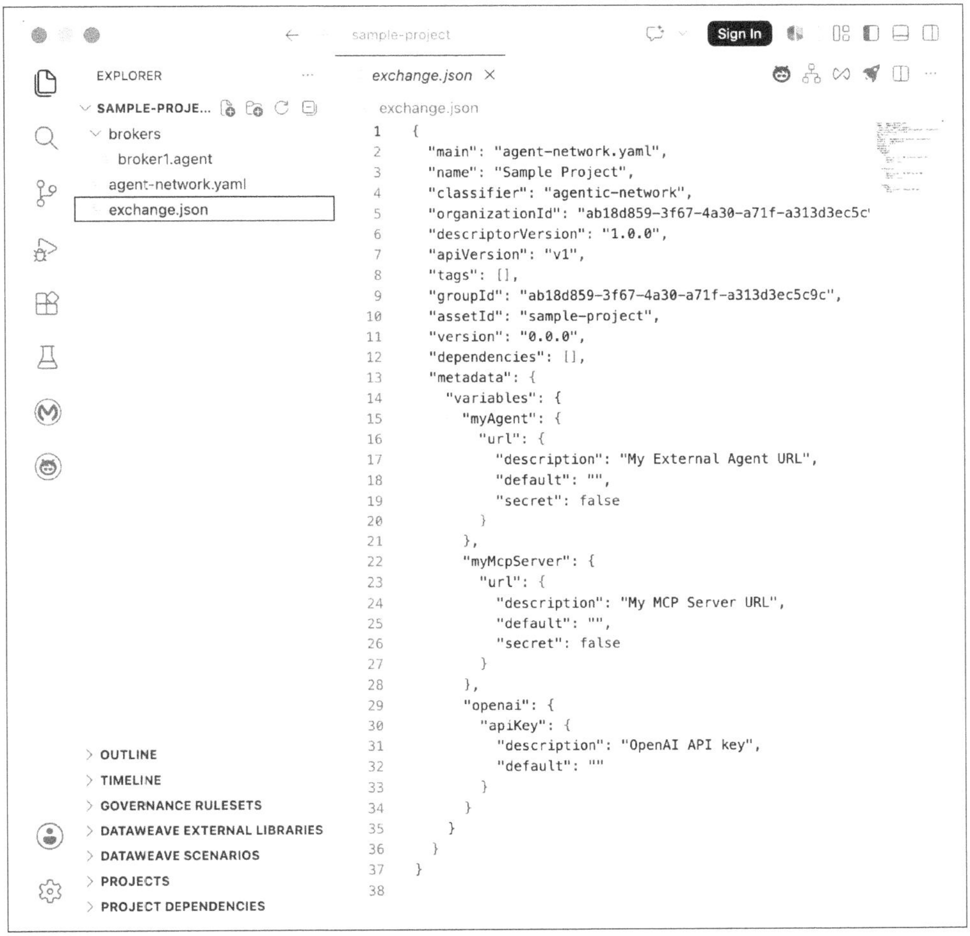

Figure 12-3. JSON file of an agent network project created in Anypoint Code Builder

The agent network project is created and published with ACB. Available as a web-based IDE and Visual Studio Code (VS Code) extension, ACB is where agent network projects are built, deployed, and managed. In addition to the *agent-network.yml* and *exchange.json* files used to configure the agent network, sometimes it's necessary to include additional files for scripts, API specifications, or supporting resources.

Users can build agent network files by leveraging a Plan mode or an Act mode (Figure 12-4) using MuleSoft Vibes within ACB, assuming Agentforce was enabled for the Anypoint Platform. In this way, Agentforce can either gather and share information with users about an architected plan or it can immediately complete the task if the Act mode button was toggled on.

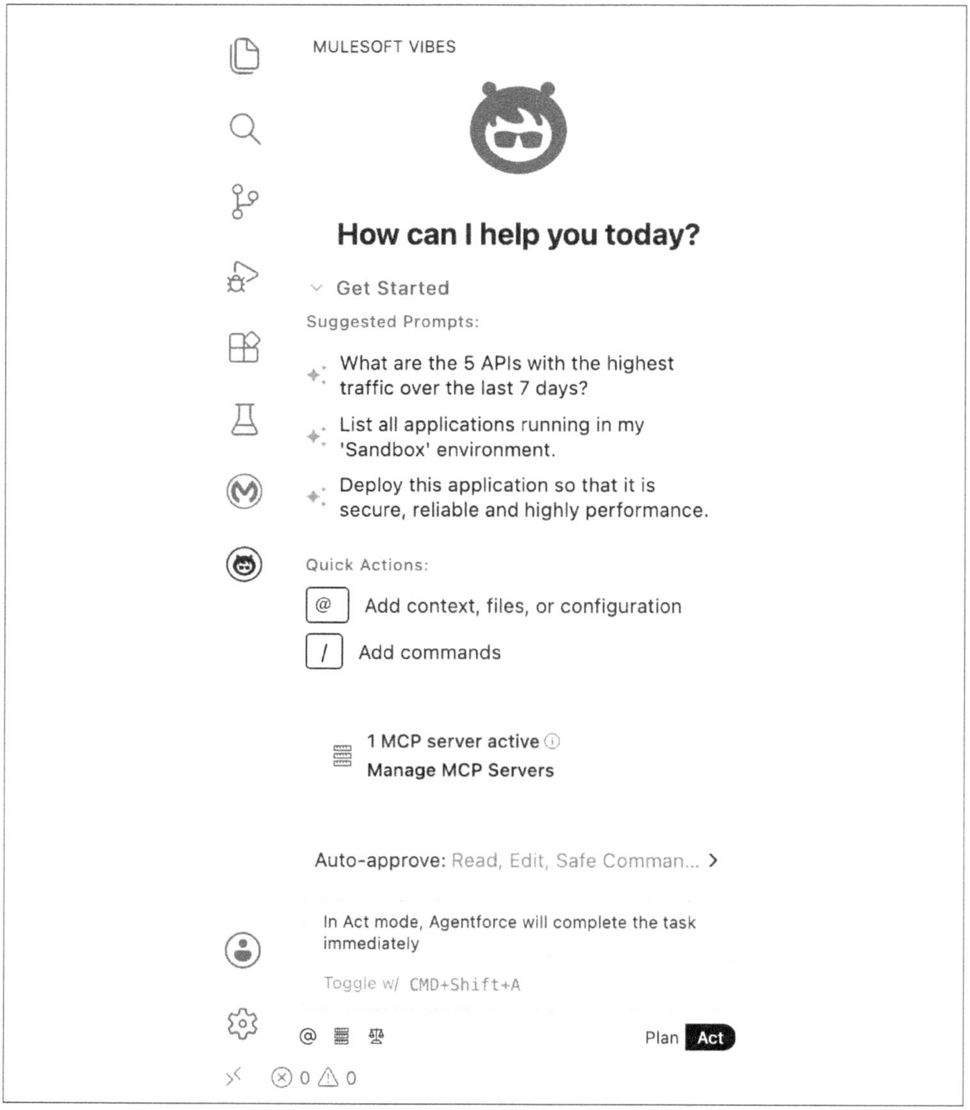

Figure 12-4. MuleSoft Vibes includes a Plan mode and an Act mode

Before the agent network project YAML and JSON files are created, there are three pieces of information required from the user: agent network project name, project location, and the business group. The project name uniquely identifies the agent network project, and the project location refers to the region or environment where the agent network project is hosted or deployed. It's important to consider data residency, latency, and compliance when selecting the location. The business group information is for identifying the organizational unit within Anypoint. All three must be submitted to create a new agent network project. When the new agent network project is created, some placeholder files are automatically created by the system. For example, a YAML file is generated as part of the project structure for a new agent network project.

The agent network project YAML file is also referred to as the agent network specification. The agent network specification is the versioned blueprint describing the configuration and details of how specific agents operate within a particular agent network. The agent network specification defines the structure, orchestration, governance rules, and communication protocols used by enterprise agents. Included in the YAML file is a definition of the functional scope including a listing of the relevant agentic assets such as agents, MCP services, and LLM providers. Also included are the operational rules, policies, and interconnections of the agentic assets.

Assets referenced in an agent network specification are added to the Anypoint Exchange and Agent Registry, if they don't already exist, once the agent network project is published. Let's review the location where integration and agentic assets are stored within MuleSoft: the Anypoint Exchange for integration assets and the Agent Registry for agentic assets.

Anypoint Exchange for integration assets

Anypoint Exchange is a curated catalog of registered, reusable integration assets (Figure 12-5). It includes connectors, templates, and examples as well as APIs, API groups, policies, and policy implementations. MuleSoft applications and publicly hosted MCP servers from the MCP Registry are also included in Anypoint Exchange along with private assets created by an enterprise.

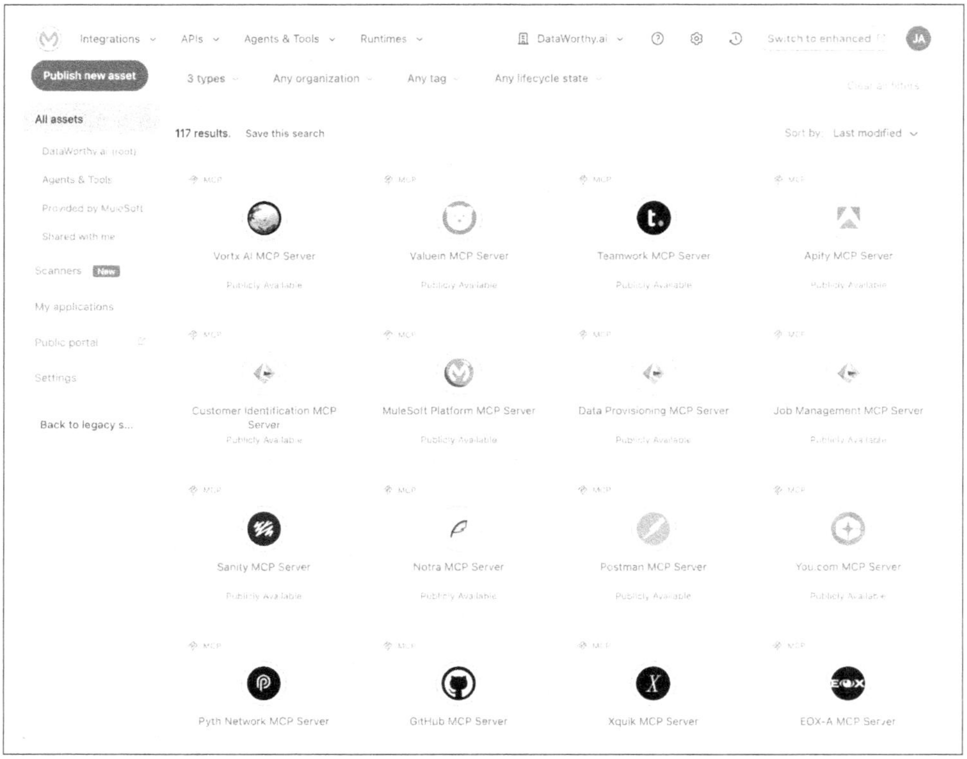

Figure 12-5. Anypoint Exchange curated catalog of reusable integration assets

Anypoint Exchange includes several connector types:

- Standard integration connectors for applications, databases, and SaaS
- MCP connectors for agentic workflows
- AI connectors for integrating with AI platforms and services

APIs and API groups provide interfaces necessary for agents to interact with external systems, tools, and services. REST APIs, AsyncAPIs, and other API types are integration assets.

Templates are prebuilt integration patterns or blueprints that provide ready-to-use flows, logic, and configuration. They're usually narrowly focused on solving a specific use case. In contrast, MuleSoft applications are broader solutions and often include templates, connectors, APIs, accelerators, or entire packaged solutions. MuleSoft applications are reusable integration assets that help connect systems, data, and API across an enterprise.

In general, assets that provide reusable integration capabilities are listed only in Anypoint Exchange, whereas the Agent Registry includes assets with agentic runtime capability. Assets included in a published agent network project are listed in both the Anypoint Exchange and the Agent Registry because the Agent Registry is built on top of Anypoint Exchange.

Agent Registry for agentic assets

The Agent Registry, built on Anypoint Platform, is the definitive catalog for all agentic assets. As we saw earlier in Table 12-3, agentic assets like agent brokers, individual agents, LLMs, and MCP servers are shared assets that also appear in Anypoint Exchange. The metadata, contracts, and versioning for each agent is tracked in the Agent Registry where agents are registered and discoverable.

LLM providers are registered as first-class assets, making it easy for agent brokers and individual agents to select different LLM providers from among the registered choices. Both custom and prepackaged MCP servers are supported in Agent Registry.

There are more MuleSoft integration and agentic assets we'll discuss a little later in this chapter, including connectors, gateways, agent brokers, and MCP servers. You may have noticed agent network components, rather than the agent network project itself, are listed as assets. The reason is because MuleSoft catalog systems are intended to include *reusable* assets. Each agent network project is unique, not reusable.

It's important to always check the Agent Registry for existing assets before creating new ones. Doing so helps prevent duplication and supports governance initiatives. Make sure explicit references are included and be sure to publish a new version of the asset to the Agent Registry whenever configuration changes are made to an existing asset. You don't need to wait until an agent network project is published before adding new agentic assets to the Agent Registry. In fact, there are a variety of different ways integration and agentic assets can be added to Anypoint Exchange and Agent Registry.

How reusable assets are added to Anypoint Exchange and Agent Registry

To recap, Anypoint Exchange is the catalog for reusable integration assets, and Agent Registry is the catalog for agents and agentic assets. Both catalogs include a list of assets where the focus is on discoverability for reuse and governance. The listings for agents and their related assets include metadata that helps both human users and system users understand the purpose of each asset or related asset.

Anypoint Exchange and Agent Registry are two MuleSoft products solving adjacent concerns. Anypoint Exchange is the catalog for reusable integration and data access assets that agents often require. Agents and agentic assets are discoverable and governed through Agent Registry. Agentic and integration assets can be added to Anypoint Exchange and Agent Registry in one of four ways:

- Manually via the Anypoint Platform
- Automatic discovery using scanners
- Publishing an agent network project
- Integration with MCP servers

MuleSoft administrators or developers manually add assets such as agents (Figure 12-6), APIs, or templates using Anypoint Studio, Design Center, or the Anypoint Exchange web interface. The Anypoint Platform generates documentation and handles versioning when assets are manually added. Agentic assets and their metadata are added to Agent Registry, which is built on Anypoint Exchange.

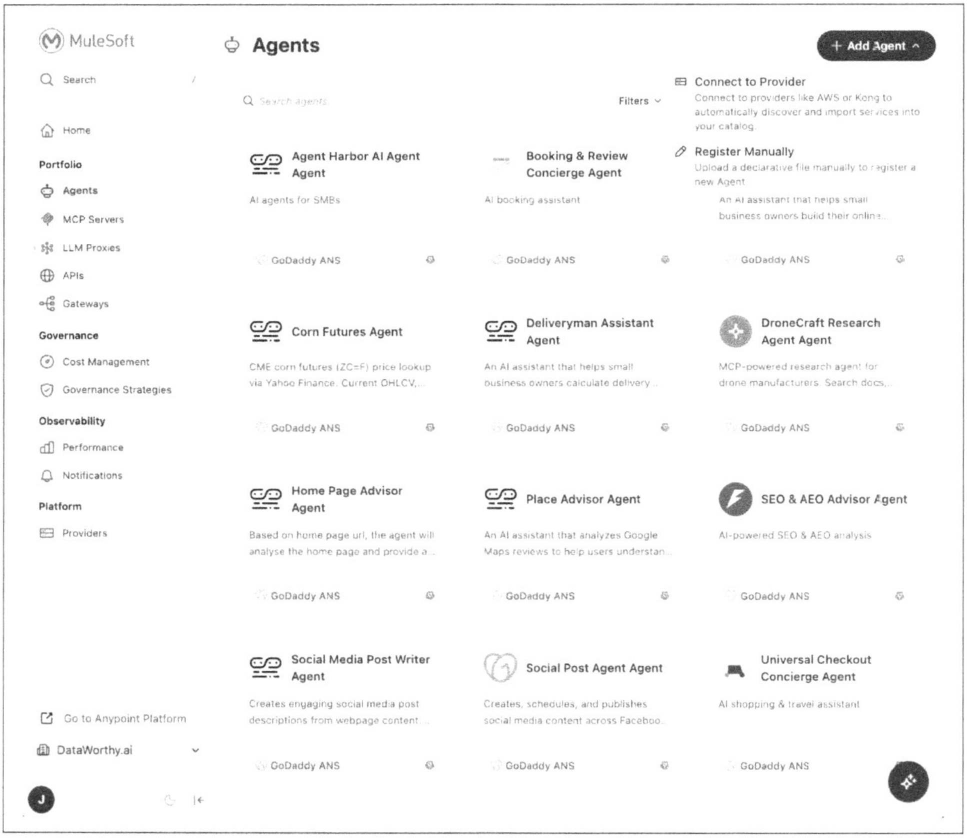

Figure 12-6. Registered agents available in an enterprise's MuleSoft portfolio

Automatic discovery is another way for assets to be added. Agent Scanner, explored later in the chapter, is the tool used for automatically discovering and registering enterprise-wide specialized agents, MCP servers, and APIs across major platforms like Amazon Bedrock, Google Gemini, and Salesforce Agentforce.

Whenever an agent network project is authored and published, the associated assets are added to Anypoint Exchange. In addition, those assets are tagged, making asset discoverability and reuse more achievable. Lastly, MCP servers can be configured to retrieve and sync asset metadata to Anypoint Exchange.

MCP Servers, MCP Connectors and Connections, and MCP Bridge Instances

We've briefly mentioned MCP servers as well as MCP connectors in previous sections. Let's take some time to explore more about MCP servers, MCP connectors, MCP connections, and MCP Bridge instances as they're all important when designing and building a trusted agent network.

MCP servers

MCP servers are endpoints or applications enabled to expose certain tool capabilities such that their functionality is discoverable and usable in agentic workflows. The main goal of MCP servers is to facilitate communication and integration between agents and external systems.

MCP connectors and connections

In the context of MuleSoft, a connector is a reusable component providing connectivity to resources such as external systems, databases, APIs, or services. There exists standard integration connectors, AI connectors, and MCP connectors.

A connector enables integration with resources, whereas a connection refers to a specific instance of a connector that has been configured with the appropriate credentials and settings. For example, a Salesforce connector can be used in MuleSoft to integrate with Salesforce APIs, whereas the connection setup is how the enterprise's Salesforce credentials and endpoint are configured.

Anypoint Exchange tracks connectors and their metadata including connector details, authentication methods, and policies. Connections are not included in Anypoint Exchange. Instead, they're managed and stored within a MuleSoft runtime or deployment environment.

MuleSoft connectors are used in both traditional and agentic patterns. Some examples of MCP connectors in Anypoint Exchange include the ServiceNow MCP connector and the Google Vertex AI MCP connector along with the Salesforce MCP connector.

MCP Bridge

Many enterprises previously built APIs and business-critical applications without considering how they would need to interact with agents and agentic assets. Creating

MCP connectors is one possible solution to overcome that issue, but it often requires considerable effort to coordinate changes across multiple teams, modify production integrations, and retest workflows. Today, there's another option so you don't have to create MCP connectors or rebuild those trusted APIs and applications from scratch.

When prebuilt MCP connectors don't exist, MCP Bridge can be used to transform APIs into agent-ready tools. When an agent invokes a tool, the tool request flows through Flex Gateway and is routed to the appropriate API just like any other API call.

There's some important considerations when using MCP Bridge. For one thing, an MCP Bridge doesn't support API instances with multiple upstream services. In addition, MCP Bridge instances are immutable, so you can't add, remove, or modify tools once the MCP Bridge is deployed. Instead, you'd need to create a new MCP Bridge instance. MCP Bridge instances are meant to be immutable to ensure runtime stability and consistency. Otherwise, synchronization issues could occur if dynamic updates were allowed. For example, an agent might operate on a cached tool list if the MCP Bridge was not immutable.

To recap, an MCP Bridge exposes existing APIs and trusted systems as MCP systems without rebuilding the backend. MCP connectors let MCP-capable AI clients invoke Anypoint-managed assets via an open source protocol. MCP connections involve the actual configuration of endpoints and credentials for an MCP connection. MCP servers are endpoints or applications that expose tool functionality. Together, all these features enable seamless integration and automation across multiple domains and platforms.

Multi-Agent Orchestration and the Agent Network Specification

MCP servers and MCP connections are important reusable assets. They are also nodes included in the agent network specification. Thus, MCP servers and MCP connectors are among the reusable assets accessible to the agent broker in an agent network. We learned about the agent network, agent network project, and the agent network specification earlier when we explored reusable assets. Let's dive deeper into the agent network specification now to better understand the role it plays in multi-agent orchestration.

Agent network specification authored in Anypoint Code Builder

Earlier in the chapter, we learned abut the agent network specification. The agent network specification is the YAML file included in the agent network project created in ACB. The agent network project defines the structure and behavior of the agent network using the YAML configurations included in the agent network specification. Common nodes in the agent network specification include ones for agent brokers, individual agents, MCP servers, LLM providers, and connector nodes (Figure 12-7).

An agent broker node typically includes card and spec information, and a connector node includes policies and spec information.

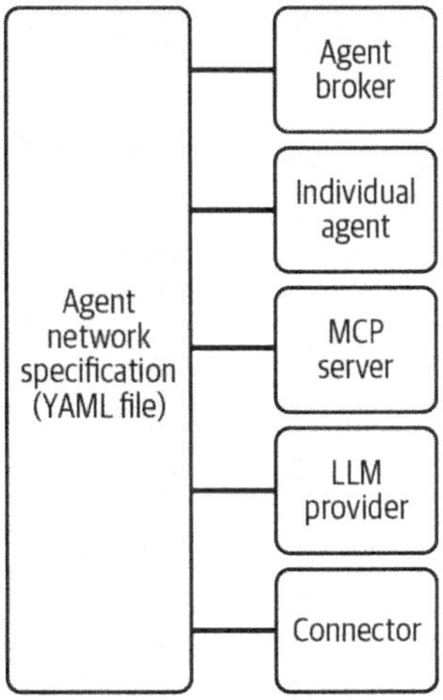

Figure 12-7. Common agent network specification nodes

When the agent network project is published, the individual components of the agent network specification are created as assets in Anypoint Exchange and Agent Fabric if they don't already exist in the catalogs.

The details of the agent broker node in the agent network specification YAML file influence the orchestration of the specified agent network. Let's explore more about the Agent Broker.

Agent Broker

Agent Broker capabilities are used to plan and delegate tasks across the entire enterprise, including the ecosystem of all agents, MCP servers, and assets. An agent broker performs differently than an Agentforce orchestrator agent, which only coordinates the activities for Agentforce agents. Instead, an agent broker is designed to coordinate agentic activities across multiple platforms and ecosystems.

An agent broker is not just a router. It's an orchestration point combining deterministic workflow logic with LLM-driven reasoning. Agent Broker includes a reasoning engine capable of advanced problem-solving needed to interpret goals, break the goals into subtasks, and decide which tools or agents are needed. Customization of Agent Broker's reasoning engine settings is not directly accessible to users. Settings and policies affecting the outcome are managed by users through gateways and the agent network specification.

An agent broker is an orchestration service that intelligently routes and coordinates agents and tools across an agent network. Agent brokers are defined in the brokers section of the agent network project YAML file. If an agent broker exists in the Agent Registry, it can be referenced in the YAML file. Otherwise, the agent broker will be created and registered as a new asset when the agent network project is published.

Within the brokers section of the YAML file, there are two distinct sections. Separate functionality between these two sections ensures the external contract is separate from the internal implementation of how the agent broker accomplishes its tasks.

The card section represents the broker agent's contract, which describes what the agent broker does and how it is called. The agent broker's contract follows the A2A specification. The card section includes the agent broker's endpoint URL and the agent broker's skills and capabilities. It also describes how the agent broker interacts with other agents or services.

The spec section located in the brokers section of the YAML file is sometimes referred to as the agent broker's source code because this section defines the agent broker's operational behavior, including defining those agents to which it can delegate tasks. The spec section identifies accessible MCP tools, details the LLM provider the agent broker will use, and describes error-handling processes.

Agent Broker's orchestration capabilities often create automated agentic workflows that are very fast and efficient. However, orchestration alone is not enough to create a trusted agent network. Unified governance is needed to provide control over the agent network.

Unified Governance

MuleSoft provides two separate governance features to help enterprises bring control to their agent network and to find agents and other assets that haven't been registered. The Agent Scanner tool automatically discovers and catalogs agents and their assets. In addition, Flex Gateway enforces policy across agent interactions to help enterprise teams govern at scale.

Although we won't explore them in this chapter, there are cost management and governance strategy features available through MuleSoft. For example, users can configure and manage governance strategies to monitor, report, enforce, and block noncompliant activity across enterprise services. In addition, users can monitor token usage and view optimization recommendations for MCP servers.

Agent Scanner

Agent Scanner is an Agent Fabric tool that automatically discovers and registers agents, MCP servers, and APIs in the Agent Register and Anypoint Exchange. Configuration is managed through the MuleSoft interface. Click the Providers menu option under the Platform section on the left menu bar of the MuleSoft home screen. Then select the desired provider. You'll notice a "+ Add Scanner" button that can be clicked (Figure 12-8).

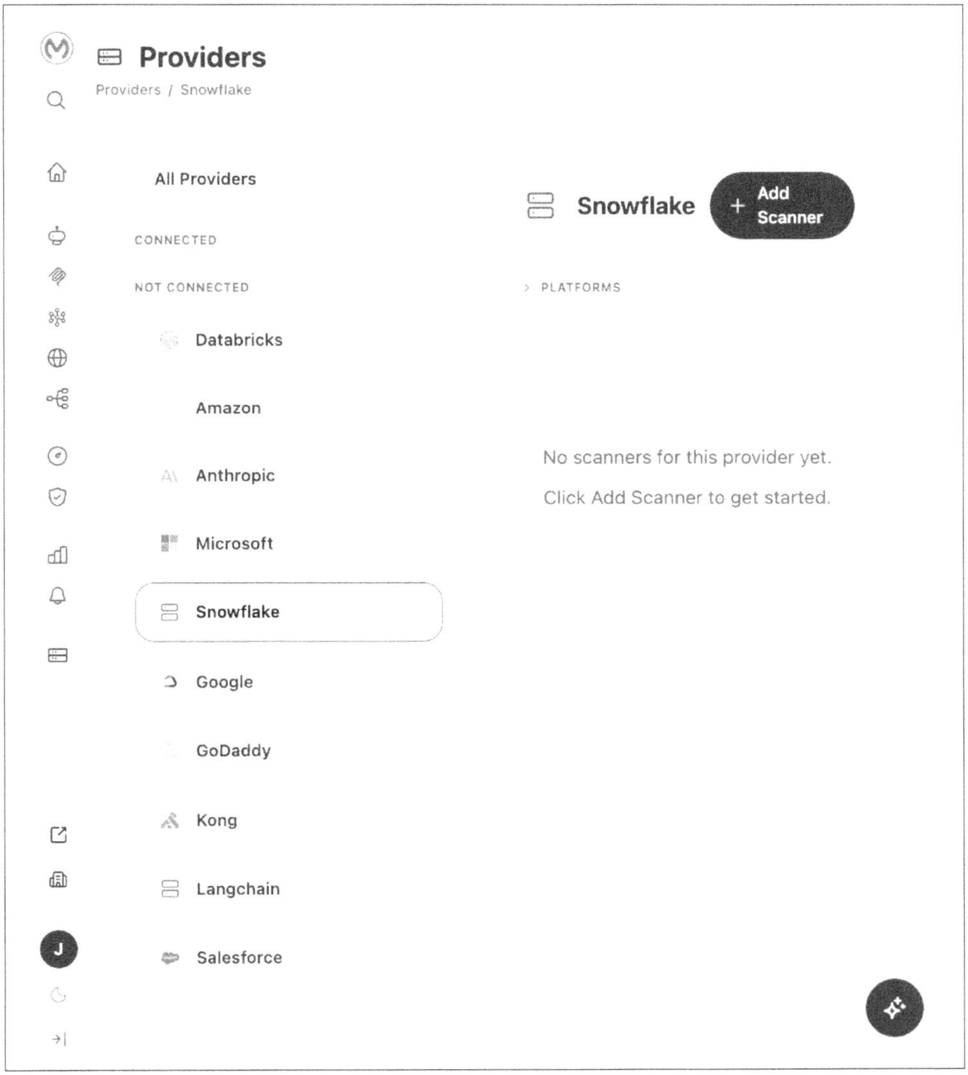

Figure 12-8. Selecting the provider for which an agent scanner will be created

If Snowflake is selected as the provider, you'll have the option to enter your credentials to authenticate for either Cortex AI agents or Cortex AI MCP on the Snowflake platform (Figure 12-9). Be sure to test the connection before proceeding.

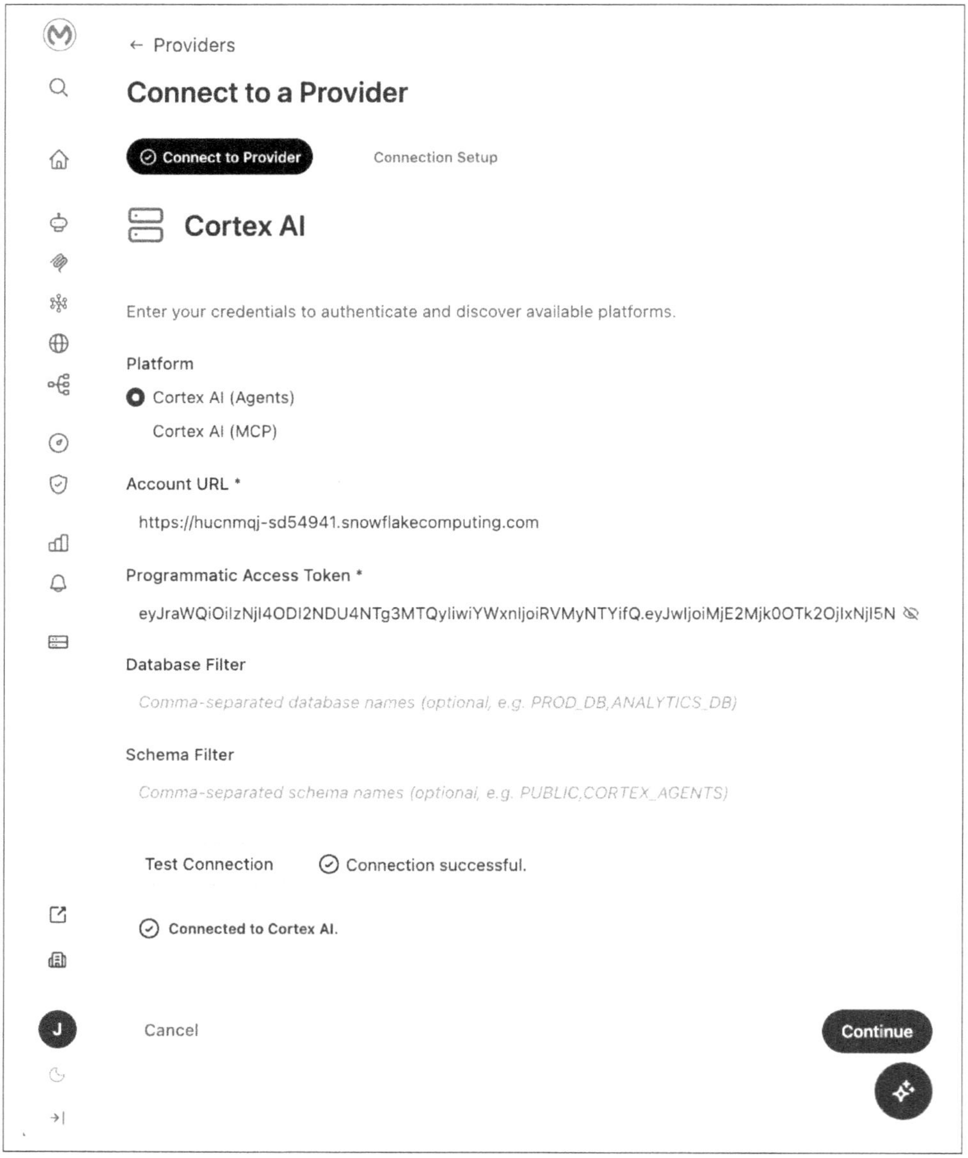

Figure 12-9. Connecting to the Snowflake platform to scan for Cortex AI agents

Afterward, you can review the details about the scanner. You can also edit the settings to change the frequency of the scan or run a discovery scan (Figure 12-10).

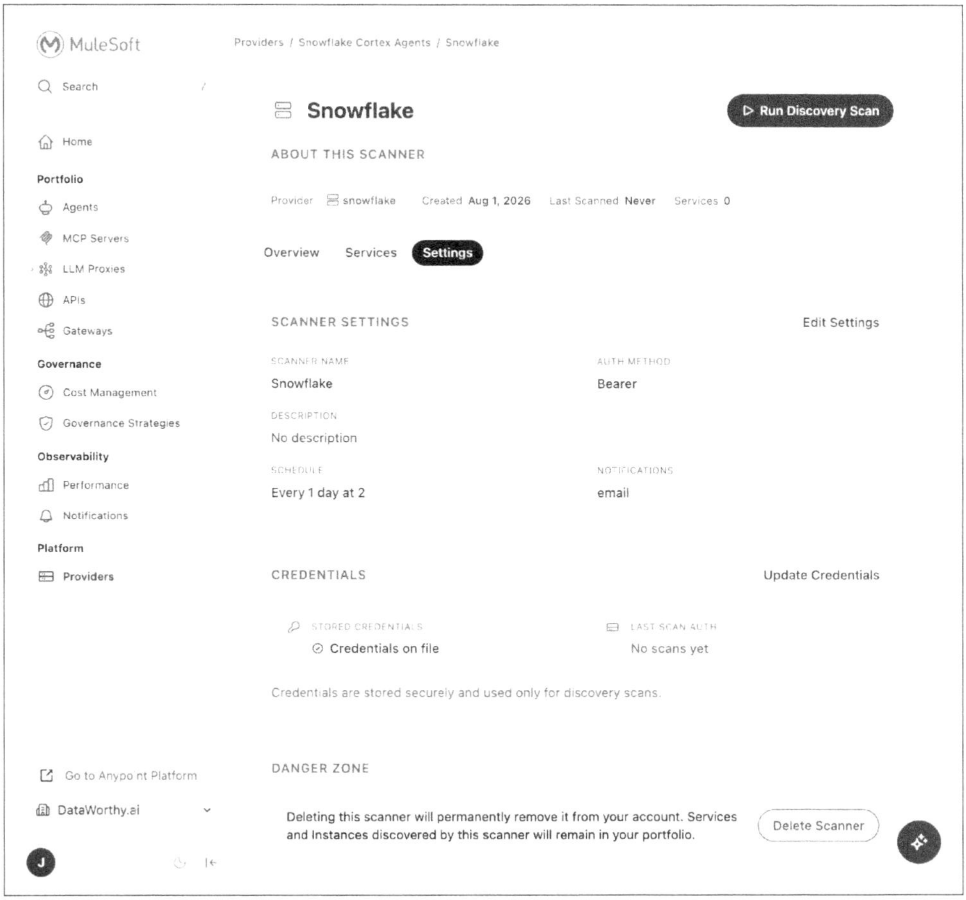

Figure 12-10. Details of an agent scanner created for the Snowflake platform

Note that deleting the scanner permanently removes it from your MuleSoft account. However, the services and instances discovered by the scanner remain in your MuleSoft portfolio. An important purpose of agent scanners is to ensure every enterprise asset is visible and managed under centralized policies, thus preventing "shadow AI" and enforcing security and compliance standards.

Anypoint Flex Gateway (Omni Gateway)

Gateways are integration assets listed in Anypoint Exchange that are used to enforce policies across agents, APIs, MCP servers, SaaS tools, and other assets. Flex Gateway is the core MuleSoft gateway product, available in both self-managed and managed modes. The managed Flex Gateway mode is the Omni Gateway, a good choice if you need to scale gateway operations across business groups or require managed entitlements. Architecture, security, and policy enforcement are the same for both

Flex Gateway and Omni Gateway. It's only the deployment and management that differ, not the gateway capabilities.

A Flex Gateway is deployed in an environment such as Docker, Kubernetes, or Linux and then registered with the Anypoint Exchange. The gateway is configured to manage APIs or agent network traffic by intercepting traffic between agents or between agents and assets, applying policies before the call to the agent or asset is allowed through.

In an agent network, the agent broker decides which agent or asset to call, an MCP connector or MCP Bridge exposes the capability, tool, or application, and then the gateway enforces the policy. If the gateway allows the traffic, the agent or asset receives the agent broker's request. As previously stated, the Anypoint Flex Gateway and the Omni Gateway enforce policies across agent interactions that include both agent-to-agent and agent-to-application flows.

Gateways enforce security and policy controls across APIs and agent networks. However, there's more needed to actually ensure only authorized interactions that meet compliance requirements occur in the agent network. Observability allows an enterprise to monitor and audit interactions, providing real-time and historical visibility needed to ensure trust in the agent network.

Agent Network Observability Plane

An agent network observability plane helps enterprises visualize, measure, and troubleshoot agents and agentic systems across the entire agent network. We'll discuss three separate observability tools from MuleSoft that are used in an agent network observability plane: Anypoint Monitoring, Agent Visualizer, and Integration Intelligence. Before we do, let's consider how the three observability capabilities complement each another.

Assume an AI agent begins returning errors or Anypoint Monitoring detects in real time a sudden spike in AI response times. The IT team needs to quickly identify and address the issue before it impacts users. Agent Visualizer provides a real-time visual map, helping the team trace the root cause visually and identify which agent broker, MCP server, or downstream dependency is involved. Anypoint Monitoring is used to inspect the specific instance's failure rate, logs, and traces. Integration Intelligence surfaces patterns showing whether similar issues have occurred and whether the same problem is affecting other flows or if a wider architectural pattern exists.

Together, these MuleSoft observability tools deliver end-to-end visibility. Anypoint Monitoring delivers real-time alerts. Agent Visualizer demonstrates visually the asset relationships and workflow paths. Integration Intelligence provides historical context and optimization recommendations.

Anypoint Monitoring

Specific Anypoint Monitoring feature availability depends on the control plane provided with your Anypoint Platform instance. The control plane features are determined by your cloud choice and the Anypoint tier or package of your Anypoint subscription. For example Anypoint Monitoring built-in dashboards, custom metrics, and traces are available for US and EU clouds but not currently available for Canada, Japan, or India clouds. Advanced dashboards, custom metrics, and telemetry export availability in US and EU also depends on whether your enterprise has the Starter or Advanced package.

Anypoint Monitor monitors several asset types, in real time, across a MuleSoft environment. It provides details about the health, performance, and usage of APIs and it monitors the operation and connectivity of integration connectors. Anypoint Monitoring observes endpoints exposed via MCP for agent workflows and it provides visibility into agent activity and interactions.

Anypoint Monitoring is the runtime observability layer, providing real-time visibility into integrations, integration assets, agents, and agentic assets. For agentic assets, users can open a node in Agent Visualizer and navigate into Anypoint Monitoring for deeper insights and instance-level detail.

Agent Visualizer

Agent Visualizer is another real-time MuleSoft Agent Fabric observability tool. It provides a visual map of your agent network, a real-time graph designed to uncover hidden relationships and interactions while making it easier for teams to more quickly discover dependencies and troubleshoot.

Agent Visualizer displays a high-level overview of your agent network, including connections between agents and assets. Agent Visualizer also captures trace data, visualizes lineage, and displays key metrics for agent activity. Users can explore details of agent network relationships, agent interactions, and observability signals by clicking on an individual node.

Agent Visualizer provides a real-time, visual representation of an enterprise's agent network, and Anypoint Monitoring displays operational insights in real time. In contrast, Integration Intelligence delivers analytics and insights into performance and trends over time.

Integration Intelligence

Integration Intelligence and Anypoint Monitoring are both MuleSoft observability reporting solutions but they address different enterprise needs. They also have different architectures. Whereas Anypoint Monitoring is natively integrated into the Anypoint Platform and is useful for real-time alerting, Integration Intelligence relies on

Salesforce D360 architecture for generating historical trend analysis. That's because Integration Intelligence offers analytics with a historical, long-term horizon rather than real-time reporting used for operational needs.

Integration Intelligence's optional, advanced features use Salesforce D360 as the unified layer. The advanced features also leverage Tableau Next for dashboards and visualizations that offer insights into systematic patterns and historical trends across APIs and applications in addition to real-time monitoring capabilities provided by Anypoint Monitoring. The Agentforce Concierge skill used with Tableau Next and Semantic Model Builder supports AI-assisted troubleshooting. The advanced capabilities are useful for enterprises needing to correlate trends, perform root-cause analysis, and optimize integration performance over time.

In summary, the observability plane answers a variety of questions using different MuleSoft tools. Anypoint Monitoring answers questions such as "What is happening now? How frequently is it happening? Where is it happening?" Agent Visualizer answers questions like "What is connected to what? What is moving through the agent network?" Integration Intelligence answers questions like "Which underlying integrations and assets make this agent network function well/not function well?" "Where are the bottlenecks? Where are there opportunities to reuse or sunset integrations or assets?"

Integration Intelligence, Agent Visualizer, Agent Scanner, Agent Registry, and Agent Broker are all Agent Fabric features. Agent Fabric is just one of the many Headless 360 capabilities offered by Salesforce.

Included in Headless 360 are components to support unified governance and observability, critical capabilities for any intelligence agentic enterprise. Adding human-in-the-loop escalation within the agent network is also essential for ambiguous, high-risk, or sensitive actions. There can be no shortcuts taken when building and managing a trusted agent network. The benefits, though, are worth the effort. Using Headless 360 components creates new opportunities for the intelligent agentic enterprise.

Salesforce Headless 360

We first introduced the term *Headless 360* in Chapter 7. Salesforce Headless 360 isn't a single product. Instead, it represents a concept. Headless 360 refers to platform architecture and is a marketing umbrella term for a group of Salesforce platform capabilities. These capabilities support multi-agent management and orchestration that enable both human and system users to initiate and participate in complex agentic workflows.

Traditionally, Salesforce was accessed by users through a browser-based interface like Lightning Experience. For almost 25 years, a customer service rep opened a Salesforce app where they navigated to a specific case record and then manually updated the case status by clicking buttons within the UI. However, humans aren't the only ones navigating platforms today. Agents invoke MCP tools, call APIs, and run command-line interface (CLI) commands directly without using a browser or clicking through UIs.

Making the powerful backend capabilities of the Salesforce platform accessible to agents and humans alike required a new approach and different architecture. Thus, a few years ago Salesforce began working on rebuilding the Salesforce platform in earnest. In April 2025 Salesforce introduced the concept of Headless 360.

> The term *headless* means decoupling a platform's backend data, logic, APIs, and intelligent workflows from any interface. As a result, platform capabilities are accessible anywhere without requiring a fixed UI or screen. A chat tool, custom app, or an agent can be granted access to all the backend assets and capabilities of the platform.

Headless 360 includes many capabilities spanning the full development lifecycle. Agent Fabric is included in Headless 360. Agent Script, preconfigured Agentforce skills, MCP tools, and the Salesforce Metadata Catalog are more examples of Headless 360 components. The Salesforce Metadata Catalog functions as a Salesforce org's table of contents for agents. The Salesforce Metadata Catalog provides a structured index of everything within the org such as Salesforce objects, fields, relationships, workflows, and permissions.

Headless 360 Advantages

There are many benefits that accrue to enterprises that take advantage of new Headless 360 capabilities:

- Multisurface engagement
- Composable enterprise apps
- AI-assisted development
- Richer ecosystem integration
- Agentic workflows embedded into a unified workspace

Human-to-agent communication occurs across many channels like web, messaging apps, and Slack. Different methods such as text, voice, and biometrics can be used for communication. In addition, one agent can communicate with different human personas who submit prompts via different channels. Thus, the same agent responds differently to different personas by changing tone, layout, or response structure to fit the channel where the interaction occurs. The channel is also known as the *surface* where the interaction occurs.

In addition to making multisurface engagement possible, Headless 360 products enable composable enterprise apps because Salesforce capabilities are exposed as APIs and MCP tools. In this way, users can combine data, workflows, and agents into new frontend or user experiences without rebuilding core logic.

Developers can now leverage coding agents for AI-assisted development. Coding agents like Agentforce Vibes provide intelligent coding assistance, automating tasks like code analysis and documentation updates. Agentforce coding agents can even take care of tasks by creating Apex logic, building Lightning Web Components, and performing SOQL queries.

Headless 360 also makes richer ecosystem integration possible because of the Agentforce Experience Layer. Instead of building a separate app for every surface, you only need to define your intent once inside Salesforce and that one definition is used across many surfaces. The Agentforce Experience Layer supports deploying interactive experiences on external platforms such as Slack, Teams, ChatGPT, Claude, Cursor, and other MCP-compatible clients by rendering the intent natively within each surface.

One of the most exciting opportunities available is embedding agentic workflows into a unified workspace where human-to-human and human-to-agent conversations occur. For example, business actions and record updates can happen directly in Slack or other collaboration tools. We discussed Slack in detail in Chapter 11, but let's take time to review some new Slackbot agentic capabilities.

Slackbot Agentic Capabilities

Slackbot is no longer just a chat assistant. It's your personal agent that is context-aware and it's accessible as a built-in agent within Slack. Slackbot is well-known for turning AI into action because it exists where people already work, it has access to business context, and it uses existing permissions. In June 2026, Slackbot was also given the ability to serve as an orchestration interface with the release of the Slackbot MCP client.

Slackbot's transition from a personal productivity helper into a personal agent with powerful agentic capabilities is a big shift. People remain in one conversational surface, collaborating with other humans, while Slackbot coordinates multiple third-party applications and tools, data sources, and workflows in real time.

> Salesforce is innovating so quickly that it's not always easy to keep current with new Slack features. It's recommended that you visit Slack Feature Drop (*https://oreil.ly/KvG-g*) to view a running list of what's new in Slack.

We explored Slack and Slackbot in detail in Chapter 11. In this chapter, we'll focus on three new Slack and Slackbot agentic capabilities: Slackbot skills, Slackbot memory, and MCP in Slack.

Slackbot skills

Slackbot provides answers to ad hoc questions, but the real value comes from giving Slackbot a repeatable process to follow by using Slackbot skills. Slackbot doesn't come with any preassigned skills by default, but you can add skills by clicking the Browse Skills button and selecting the skills you want to add. Some new Slackbot skills available include the following: Daily Priorities, Meeting Prep, Research Synthesis, Incident Management, Weekly Update, and Project Kickoff.

Slack users can also build their own skills by creating step-by-step instructions from scratch or asking Slackbot to help (Figure 12-11). It's also possible to import a skill.

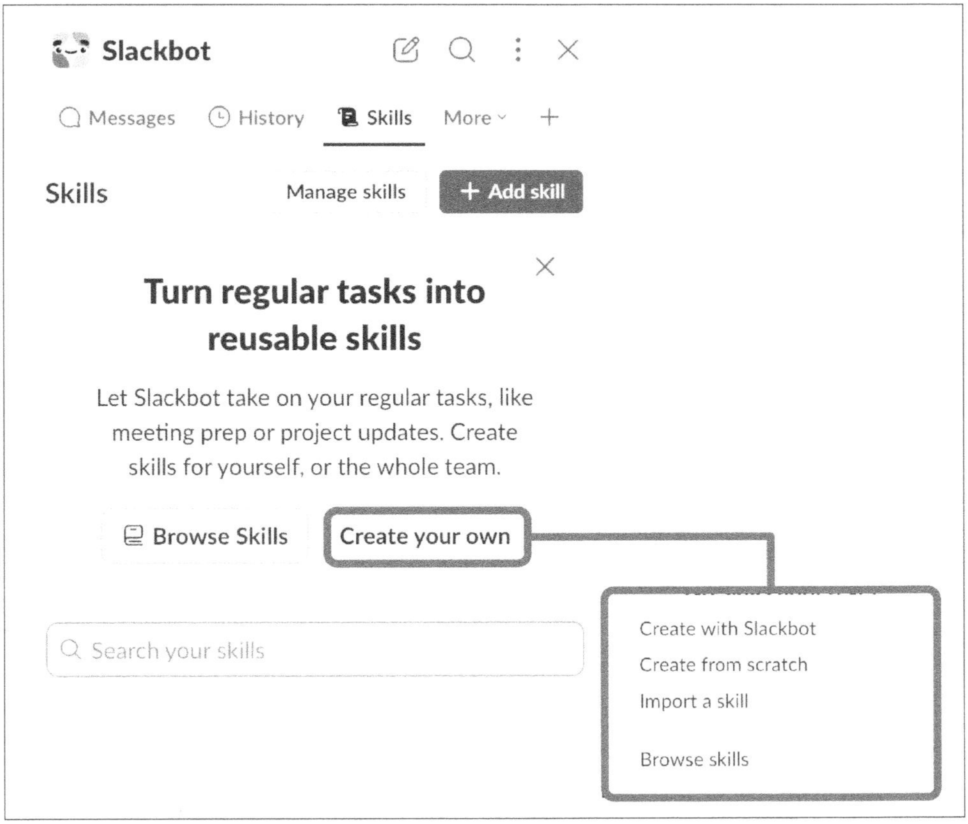

Figure 12-11. Create a Slackbot skill to use yourself or to share with others

Reusable skills can be shared with others in the organization by hovering over a skill and selecting "Share skill." You'll need to select the channels or people with whom you want to share the skill.

Slackbot memory

Slackbot memory is a feature allowing Slackbot to save and use context from your Slack channels and messages to personalize your Slackbot experience. For example, Slackbot memory saves your communication preferences, writing style, and current projects. To get started, you'll need to enable automatic memory generation and build saved memories or import memories. From your desktop, open Slackbot and then click the Slackbot icon located above the Messages tab. Click the Memories tab and then toggle on the "Generate memory from conversations" option (Figure 12-12). If desired, you can import memory from other AI tools to add context to Slackbot from another AI tool.

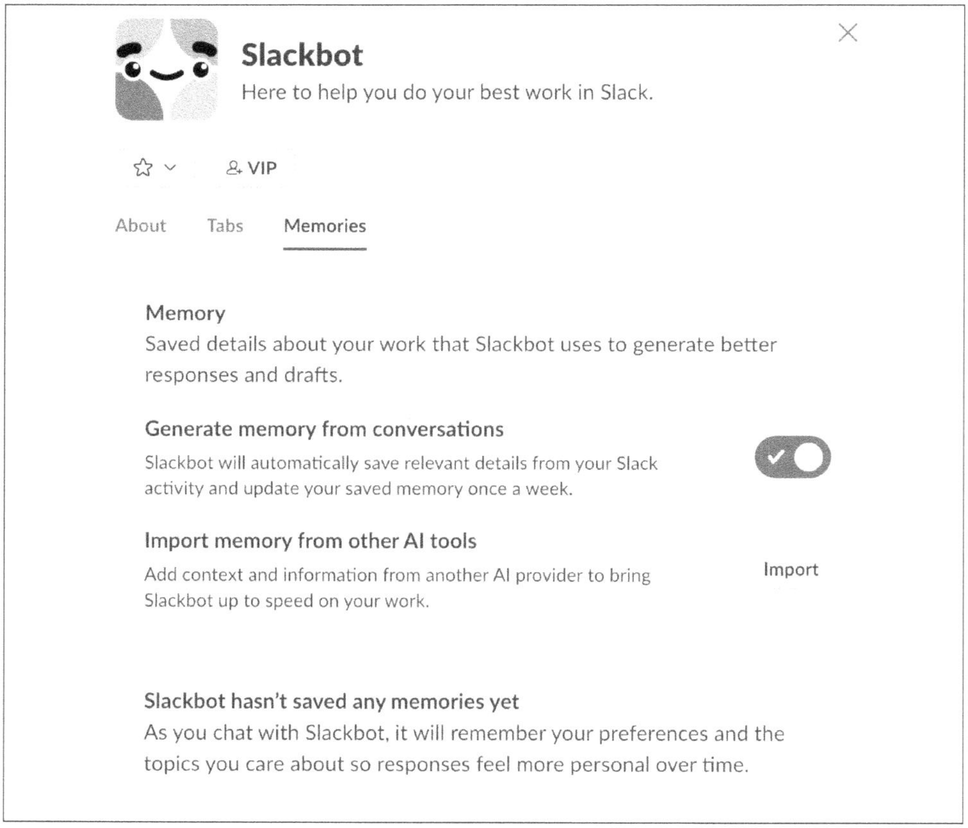

Figure 12-12. Build or import memory for Slackbot memory feature

There are two memory types Slackbot saves: preferences and topics. Preferences are details like "my writing style is detailed, not concise." Topics are information related to your role or projects. To keep memory current, Slackbot checks for new activity weekly. The channels you're in, the decisions made by you and your team, and the projects in which you're involved help shape context. Over time, Slackbot learns your definition of "critical" and it knows the important stakeholders with whom you communicate. You can view and edit your Slackbot memory or you can disable automatic generation entirely, if you prefer.

MCP in Slack

The Slack MCP framework gives Slack what it needs to extend its successful collaboration tool into a secure AI action layer, allowing agents to consistently connect to more tools and data sources. The framework encompasses the Slack MCP server and the ability for Slackbot to serve as an MCP client. This open source framework makes it possible to integrate external tools and applications with Slack to provide richer context-aware workflows in a securely permissioned and properly scoped manner. The capabilities of the Slack MCP framework also offer users options for asking Slackbot to take actions in connected systems without navigating away from the Slack workspace. Let's explore the Slack MCP capabilities achieved when establishing Slackbot as an MCP client as well as by making available the Slack MCP server.

The Slack MCP server grants access to third-party apps and AI assistants so they can connect to and interact with a Slack workspace and the enterprise data within that Slack environment. Enterprises can establish connections to third-party apps and AI assistants such as ChatGPT, Claude, Credal AI, Cursor, Dropbox, Guru, Jasper, Notion, Open AI, Perplexity, Thoughtspot, Wordsmith, and Workleap.

Once connected, these third-party apps and AI assistants can securely access the Slack workspace to view specific channels or threads, retrieve and send messages, create and manage canvases, access member information, and more. Granting MCP server access to any of these third-party apps and AI assistants requires creating a custom connector, configuring OAuth settings, and then connecting the newly created custom connector. After successful authentication, your Slack administrator will adjust the tools and permissions available in the MCP server.

It's relatively easy for Slack admins to establish Slackbot as an MCP client. An admin just needs to install applications with MCP servers from the Slack Marketplace. Several tools are available for installation including Amplitude, Atlassian Rovo, Bob, Box, Brex, Canva, Docusign, Dropbox, Figma, Gamma, Ironclad, Lattice, Linear, Lucidchart, Lucidspark, MuleSoft, Miro, Notion, Reclaim.ai, Replit, Sazabi, Tableau, Vercel, Webflow, Zapier, and Zoom.

Slackbot as an agentic work interface

Once a user describes to Slackbot what they need, Slackbot routes requests, orchestrates multi-step workflows, and then returns results in the conversational thread with the user. After Slackbot determines the user's intent, action is taken by invoking the correct tool's endpoints. The invoked application then renders its rich, interactive UI directly within the Slackbot conversation. Users are able to interact with app-specific dashboards, live data, action panels, and interactive forms. They sign a document, update a ticket, and retrieve a design to review all without ever leaving the Slack workspace.

Slackbot is a personal agent for individuals and it routes work to specialized tools based on conversations with a human in a Slack workspace. The number of external tools available for routing by Slackbot continues to grow as Slack builds a partner ecosystem of MCP-connected apps. Slack's functionality and capabilities have grown rapidly in 2026 and there's more on the roadmap. Yet, Slack is already a scalable enterprise solution with robust governance and admin controls available for establishing access boundaries for agents, apps, and tools as well as limiting actions to permission-aware behavior. Within the Slack workspace, Slackbot is strategically important as it can function as a natural control plane for agentic work by observing context, invoking the right tools, and keeping humans in the loop without requiring them to log in to other workspaces or applications.

Slack is often referred to as the front door to the intelligent agentic enterprise because it's the platform where individuals and teams go first when they need to engage with apps, tools, agents, and other humans in the normal flow of work. As a unified workspace surface, Slack also serves as the frontend where agents are discovered, summoned, and orchestrated based on the user's intent expressed in natural language while Salesforce C360, D360, and Agentforce provide the data, automation, and agentic capabilities on the backend. In addition, MuleSoft provides the coordination, monitoring, and governance of all enterprise integrations and agents.

Summary

In this chapter we explored multi-agent orchestration. We learned how Agentforce manages multiple agents with an orchestrator agent and how an agent broker is used in MuleSoft Agent Fabric to coordinate an agent network that leverages enterprise agents and their assets. We then looked at MuleSoft Anypoint and MuleSoft Agent Fabric capabilities in detail as we learned about integration assets, agentic assets, agent networks, agent orchestration, unified governance, and the agent network observability plane. We then explored the concept of Headless 360 and why it's important for multi-agent management and orchestration. As part of that discussion, we learned about Slackbot agentic capabilities and MCP in Slack.

The Road Ahead

The vision of an intelligent agentic enterprise built with Salesforce products is based on humans and agents sharing context and taking coordinated actions together across connected business systems. Salesforce has spent the last decade preparing for this Agentic Era by embedding AI into the very fabric of its Salesforce core platform and the integrated ecosystem it's built as a result of strategic acquisitions.

Throughout the book we've covered in detail many Salesforce products such as Customer 360, Data 360, AI Models, Tableau Semantics, Tableau Next, Agentforce, Slack, and MuleSoft. We also learned a lot about predictive AI, GenAI, agents and agent reasoning, and agentic enterprises in general. This book covers a great deal of content meant to provide you with a solid foundation for understanding Salesforce's innovative AI products and features. Salesforce continues evolving at a rapid pace, so it's important to continue your learning journey.

The Appendix summarizes the additional resources I've shared throughout each chapter. Three times a year, Salesforce issues regular releases with many new features for the entire Salesforce product offering. The Salesforce seasonal release blog (*https://oreil.ly/zHklX*) keeps you updated every winter, spring, and summer as new features are released. Additionally, Salesforce releases a Seasonal Release Strategies Trailhead badge three times a year.

Attending in-person events is also a great way to keep current with Salesforce updates. The largest Salesforce in-person event is Dreamforce, held annually in San Francisco, California. There are other Salesforce in-person events such as Trailblazer DX for Salesforce developers and Salesforce Connections for Salesforce marketers. In addition, Salesforce sponsors global World Tour events in various cities throughout the world.

If you see me at a Salesforce in-person event, please say hello. I'm always happy to have a conversation.

I hope this book serves as a helpful reference guide for you today and for the future. I wish you all the best in your continued learning journey!

APPENDIX

Additional Reading

While researching for this book, I read many wonderful books—more than I can list out here. However, here is a list of books alluded to within the chapters.

Chapter 2

Avila, Joyce Kay. *Hands-On Salesforce Data Cloud: Implementing and Managing a Real-Time Customer Data Platform*. Sebastopol, CA: O'Reilly Media, 2024.

Shaalan, Sharif, and Timothy Royer. *Salesforce for Beginners: A Step-by-Step Guide to Optimize Sales and Marketing and Automate Business Processes with the Salesforce Platform*. 2nd ed. Birmingham, UK: Packt Publishing, 2022.

Wheeler, Mike. *Salesforce Certified Platform Administrator Study Guide: Launch and Elevate Your Salesforce Career*. Sebastopol, CA: O'Reilly Media, 2025.

Chapter 3

Huyen, Chip. *Designing Machine Learning Systems: An Iterative Process for Production-Ready Applications*. Sebastopol, CA: O'Reilly Media, 2022.

Gao, Haipeng, Ari Joury, Weining Shen, and Guanyu Hu. *Soccer Analytics with Machine Learning: Learning Predictive Modeling Techniques with Sports Data*. Sebastopol, CA: O'Reilly Media, 2026.

Lakshmanan, Valliappa, Sara Robinson, and Michael Munn. *Machine Learning Design Patterns: Solutions to Common Challenges in Data Preparation, Model Building, and MLOps*. Sebastopol, CA: O'Reilly Media, 2020.

Chapter 4

Jackson, Ann, and Luke Stanke. *Tableau Strategies: Solving Real, Practical Problems with Data Analytics*. Sebastopol, CA: O'Reilly Media, 2021.

Koenigstein, Nicole. *AI Agents: The Definitive Guide: Design, Deployment, and Evaluation for Production*. Santa Rosa, CA: O'Reilly Media, 2026.

Chapter 5

Lane, Hobson, and Maria Phelps. *Natural Language Processing in Action*. 2nd ed. Shelter Island, NY: Manning Publications, 2024.

Chapter 6

Alammar, Jay, and Maarten Grootendorst. *Hands-On Large Language Models: Language Understanding and Generation*. Sebastopol, CA: O'Reilly Media, 2024.

Berryman, John, and Albert Ziegler. *Prompt Engineering for LLMs: The Art and Science of Building Large Language Model–Based Applications*. Sebastopol, CA: O'Reilly Media, 2024.

Grootendorst, Maarten and Jay Alammar. *An Illustrated Guide to AI Agents*. Santa Rosa, CA: O'Reilly Media, 2026.

Kihn, Martin. *Agentforce: Building the Future of Autonomous Business*. Hoboken, NJ: John Wiley and Sons, 2025.

Chapter 7

Appleman, Dan. *Salesforce DevOps for Architects*. Berkeley, CA: Apress, 2023.

Gonzalez, Pablo. *Clean Apex Code: Software Design for Salesforce Developers*. Berkeley, CA: Apress, 2025.

Chapter 12

Bafna, Jitendra, and Jim Andrews. *MuleSoft Platform Architect's Guide: A Practical Guide to Using Anypoint Platform's Capabilities to Architect, Deliver, and Operate APIs*. Birmingham, UK: Packt Publishing, 2024.

Kamath, Pooja, and Diane Kesler. *Building Integrations with MuleSoft: Integrating Systems and Unifying Data in the Enterprise*. Sebastopol, CA: O'Reilly Media, 2025.

Sawant, Akshata, and Arul Christhuraj Alphonse. *MuleSoft for Salesforce Developers: A Complete Guide for Achieving MuleSoft Certification Readiness and Building AI-Driven API Solutions*. 2nd ed. Birmingham, UK: Packt Publishing, 2025.

From the Author

Avila, Joyce Kay. *Hands-On Salesforce Data Cloud: Implementing and Managing a Real-Time Customer Data Platform*. Sebastopol, CA: O'Reilly Media, 2024.

Avila, Joyce Kay. *Snowflake: The Definitive Guide: Architecting, Designing, and Deploying on the Snowflake Data Cloud*. Sebastopol, CA: O'Reilly Media, 2022.

Index

A

B

C

D

E

F

G

H

I

J

K

L

M

N

O

P

Q

R

S

U

V

W

Y

Z

About the Author

Joyce Kay Avila has more than 25 years of experience as a business and technology leader. She has bachelor's and master's degrees in the fields of computer science and accounting business administration, and completed her PhD coursework in accounting information systems. Joyce holds 24 Salesforce certifications and accreditations, including the Salesforce AI Associate and Salesforce Agentforce certifications. She is also an Agentblazer Legend, a Salesforce Einstein Champion alumni, and a Snowflake Data Superhero. For the Salesforce and Snowflake communities, Joyce produces a running series of how-to-videos on her YouTube channel (*https://www.youtube.com/@JoyceKayAvila*). She is also the author of two O'Reilly books: *Snowflake: The Definitive Guide* and *Hands-on Salesforce Data Cloud*.

Colophon

The animal on the cover of *Salesforce AI* is the silver bullseye (*Pempheris schwenkii*), also known as the silver sweeper or blackstripe sweeper.

Native to Australia, the silver bullseye is one of over 70 species in the *Pempheris* genus. They live in reefs, often hiding in ledges or crevices during the day and coming out at night to feed on zooplankton. Their nocturnal tendencies make it difficult to know much about them, but one study tagged them with fluorescent lights to allow scientists to study their habits. The study showed that under cover of night, they swam up to 150 meters away from the coral reef into the open water. Still, little is known about their habits or mating behaviors.

Many of the animals on O'Reilly covers are endangered; all of them are important to the world.

The cover illustration is by Monica Kamsvaag, based on an antique line engraving from *Lydekker's Royal Natural History*. The series design is by Edie Freedman, Ellie Volckhausen, and Karen Montgomery. The cover fonts are Gilroy Semibold and Guardian Sans. The text font is Adobe Minion Pro; the heading font is Adobe Myriad Condensed; and the code font is Dalton Maag's Ubuntu Mono.

www.ingramcontent.com/pod-product-compliance
Lightning Source LLC
LaVergne TN
LVHW061004171026
850203LV00002BA/2
* 9 7 9 8 3 4 1 6 2 3 1 0 1 *